W9-ANR-343

Stay Connected
@Glencoe.com

GLENCOE
Sociology
& YOU

Access the Online Student Edition,
activities, homework help, and
self-check quizzes.

GLENCOE
Sociology & YOU

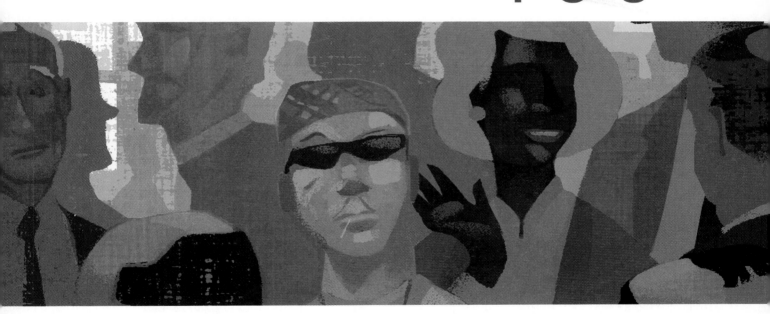

JON M. SHEPARD
ROBERT W. GREENE

McGraw Hill **Glencoe**

New York, New York   Columbus, Ohio   Chicago, Illinois   Woodland Hills, California

About the Authors

Jon M. Shepard

Jon M. Shepard earned a Ph.D. in sociology at Michigan State University before assuming a teaching position at the University of Kentucky. The ninth edition of his popular college sociology textbook is currently being revised. He also has written extensively for academic journals and professional sociology associations. Dr. Shepard has received teaching awards at both the University of Kentucky and Virginia Tech. His love of sociology and extensive experience with introductory sociology students have motivated and guided him in the creation of this unique text for high school students.

Robert W. Greene

Robert W. Greene taught high school sociology for sixteen years and in the past eight years has taught at several Wisconsin colleges. He currently teaches courses such as Introductory Sociology, Contemporary American Society, and Social Problems at Madison and Milwaukee area technical colleges. Mr. Greene is a former president of the Wisconsin Sociological Association, having served two nonconsecutive terms, and is the only high school teacher to have served in that capacity. He also has been involved in high school sociology on the national level, serving for seven years as Chair of the Sociology Special Interest Group of the National Council for the Social Studies and was a member of the American Sociological Association's task force to bring Advanced Placement Sociology to American high schools.

 Glencoe

The McGraw-Hill Companies

Send all inquiries to:
Glencoe/McGraw-Hill
8787 Orion Place
Columbus, OH 43240-4027

ISBN: 978-0-07-874519-5
MHID:0-07-874519-5
Printed in the United States of America.

3 4 5 6 7 8 9 10 058/043 10 09 08

Carolyn Andrews
Eisenhower High School
Houston, TX

Nancy Browning
Land O'Lakes High School
Land O'Lakes, FL

Dianne Brunt
Canyon Springs High School
Moreno Valley, CA

John D. Bush
Bedford No. Law High School
Bedford, IN

Candee Collins
Pine Tree High School
Longview, TX

Barb Damon
Merrimack High School
Merrimack, NH

Patricia Darnell
Killeen High School
Killeen, TX

Diane G. Dowler
Buena High School
Ventura, CA

Tom Dubay
Trinity High School
Louisville, KY

Frances D. Duncan
Hudson's Bay High School
Vancouver, WA

Richard B. DuRall
Evergreen High School
Seattle, WA

Beth Duron
Santa Clarita Christian School
Canyon Country, CA

Sandy Eichhorst
Centennial High School
Champaign, IL

Debbie Stuart Everett
Park Tudor High School
Indianapolis, IN

Matthew Ferren
Seminole High School
Sanford, FL

James E. Flora
New Holstein High School
New Holstein, WI

Glenn Gritzon
Preble High School
Green Bay, WI

Robin Heisig
South Grand Prairie High School
Grand Prairie, TX

Mark R. Henthorn
Shadyside High School
Shadyside, OH

Kim Ibach
Kelly Walsh High School
Casper, WY

Debra Ann Jones
Bloomington High School North
Bloomington, IN

Donna Juren
Denton High School
Denton, TX

B. Dale Kinney
Ralston High School
Omaha, NE

Kathleen M. Knoll
South Milwaukee High School
Milwaukee, WI

Jim Kraft
Wausau West High School
Wausau, WI

Kimberly Landers-George
McNeil High School
Austin, TX

Kathrine Leonard
Southern High School
Louisville, KY

Linda McDanal
Machebeaf High School
Denver, CO

Susan Mirra
West Genesee High School
Camillus, NY

Jeff Morgenstein
Land O'Lakes High School
Land O'Lakes, FL

Catherine Morris
Grapevine High School
Grapevine, TX

Ed Pottenger
Lakota West High School
West Chester, OH

Tom Ramos
Bay High School
Panama City, FL

Sally Raskoff
University of Southern California
Los Angeles, CA

Alison Record
A&M Consolidated High School
College Station, TX

Rebecca Reeves
Cullman High School
Cullman, AL

Tom Robertson
Carlsbad High School
Carlsbad, CA

Lianne K. Schneider
Msgr. Kelly Catholic High School
Beaumont, TX

Sandra Setter
Eagan High School
Eagan, MN

Dan Sheesley
North Platte High School
North Platte, NE

Toni C. Tropiak
Parkland High School
El Paso, TX

Bob Walls
Lakeview High School
Cortland, OH

Mary Beth Wilson
Gallatin County High School
Warsaw, KY

Table of Contents

Table of Contents

Features

Another Time Another Place

Focus on Research

Sociology Today

Tech Trends

Features

Enrichment Reading

World View

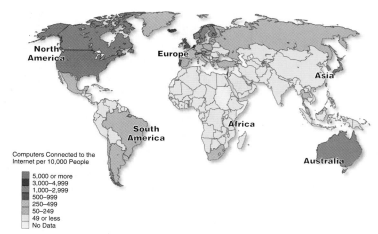

Computers Connected to the
Internet per 10,000 People

- 5,000 or more
- 3,000–4,999
- 1,000–2,999
- 500–999
- 250–499
- 50–249
- 49 or less
- No Data

**Percentage of Children Under
18 Who Are Uninsured**

- ■ 4.9% and below
- 5.0%–9.9%
- 10%–14.9%
- 15%–19.9%
- 20% and above

Charts and Graphs

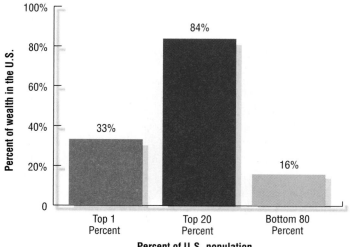

Charts and Graphs

Occupational category	Percent of total	Percent male	Percent female
Management, professional, and related occupations	34.9	49.7	50.3
Service occupations	16.3	43.2	56.8
Sales and office occupations	25.4	36.1	63.9
Natural resources, construction, and maintenance occupations	10.5	95.6	4.4
Production, transportation, and material moving occupations	12.9	77.0	23.0

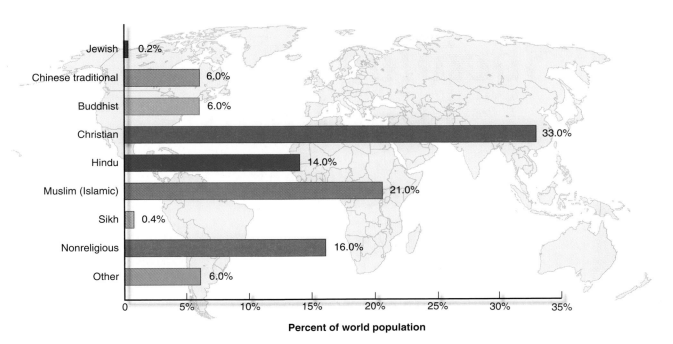

Percent of world population

Trade Tools Technology Goods Services Jobs Business Transportation Communications Food, Shelter, Clothing	Family Government Education Religion Economy	Art Literature Dance Theater Music Crafts Folk tales	Words Expressions Pronunciations Alphabet Symbols	Communities Geography Geology Habitat Wildlife Climates Resources	Games Toys Arts Media Holidays Festivals	Values Traditions Ethnicity Customs Religions Morals
ECONOMY	INSTITUTIONS	ARTS	LANGUAGE	ENVIRONMENT	RECREATION	BELIEFS

CULTURAL UNIVERSALS

Sociology Handbook

Contents

Thinking Like a Sociologist

Why Should You Study Sociology?

If someone in the United States is asked why he or she acted in a certain way, most of us would expect the person to provide an explanation that described the causes of the behavior in terms of his or her *individual* choices. Americans are generally taught to think that they totally determine their own thoughts, feelings, and actions. However, sociologists recognize that the groups, or social structures, that one belongs to have a profound influence over the way individuals think, feel, and act. Sociology provides tools to understand what these social structures are, how they affect our beliefs and behaviors, and how individuals relate to each other. Developing a sociological imagination—the mindset that enables individuals to see the relationship between events in their personal lives and events in their society—will help you to see how social forces affect your life in a way that a more individualistic perspective does not.

Sociologists recognize the influence that groups have on individuals.

What Should You Expect?

As you begin your study of sociology, you will probably find that it is very different from other classes you have taken. This is because sociology looks at groups rather than at individuals. It is this focus on groups, rather than on individuals, that distinguishes sociology from psychology, the study of individual behavior. Although sociology employs a distinct perspective, it does share some common features with other social sciences, including anthropology, psychology, economics, political science, and history. You will find elements of all of these disciplines in this sociology textbook. You will also find that you will begin to look at your life and your interactions with other people and with social institutions in a different way as you proceed through this course.

Sociologists as Scientists

In your study of sociology, you will learn to think like a social scientist. Scientists constantly question their own assumptions and look for alternative evidence and conclusions. All scientists—including sociologists—use the scientific method as a problem-solving tool. It teaches them to think critically by encouraging open-mindedness, intellectual curiosity, and evaluation of reasons. Using the scientific method will help you think critically and be objective when applying sociological principles to everyday events, issues, and problems.

Study and Writing Skills

Study Skills

To get the most out of any course you take, you must be active in learning the material. All fields of study have their own terminology, and sociology is no different in that respect. However, in sociology, understanding the central concepts is confounded by the fact that many of the terms used by sociologists are often also used in everyday language with different meanings. Because it is important for you to understand such definitional differences, sociological concepts are carefully defined throughout the textbook.

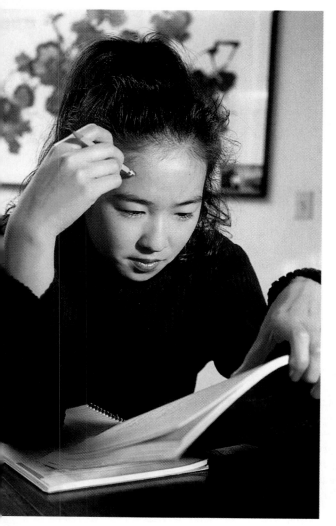

Studying sociology can open doors for you.

Learning the Skill

To understand the central concepts used in sociology:

- Identify the terms that sociologists use to represent specific scientific concepts. You must be careful at this point, because many of the words that sociologists use are also used in everyday language. You may mistakenly think that you already understand a word, when, in fact, its scientific meaning is different.

- Be sure that you understand the words that are used to define a sociological term.

- Try to put the definition in your own words. If you cannot do this at first, keep working at it until you can. But be careful not to lapse back into everyday usage of the term.

- Understand the context in which the term is used, not just its specific definition.

- Practice using sociological terms with their scientific meanings.

Practicing the Skill

Read the following paragraph and then answer the questions below.

Prejudice is a widely held preconception of a group and its individual members. These preconceptions are often based on strong emotions and unchallenged ideas. Consequently, they are difficult to change, even in the face of overwhelming evidence to the contrary. Prejudice involves an either/or type of logic: A group is either good or bad, and it is assumed that each of the members of that group possesses the characteristics attributed to the group. Prejudice, then, involves an overgeneralization based on biased or insufficient information. While prejudice refers to an attitude, discrimination describes unequal treatment of others. Prejudice does not always result in discrimination, but it often does.

1. Define *prejudice* in its sociological meaning. Do the same for *discrimination*.
2. Based on their sociological meanings, are prejudice and discrimination always negative?
3. Based on their sociological meanings, can discrimination occur without prejudice?

Applying the Skill

1. Look up the sociological definitions of culture and society. How are these meanings different from everyday usage?
2. How are these terms similar to each other?
3. How are they different?

The Writing Process

Researching and writing allow you to organize your ideas in a logical manner. Actually, writing a paper is only the final step in a process that involves using other skills you have already learned, such as identifying central issues, distinguishing fact from opinion, and making generalizations.

Learning the Skill

Use the following guidelines in the writing process:

- Select an interesting topic. As you identify possible topics, focus on resources that are available. Do preliminary research to determine whether your topic is too broad or too narrow.

- Write a thesis statement that defines what you want to prove, discover, or illustrate in your writing. This will be the focus of your entire paper.

- Research your topic. First, formulate a list of central questions. Prepare note cards on each question, listing the information sources.

- Organize your information by building an outline. Then follow your outline in writing a rough draft of your report.

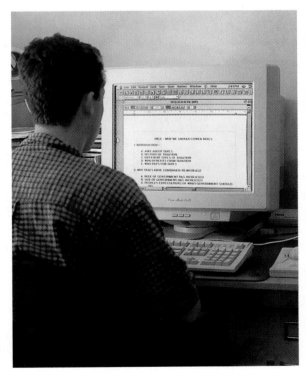

The Internet has made certain kinds of research much quicker and easier. But, the researcher must still use critical thinking skills to evaluate the information obtained from the Internet.

- A report should have three main parts: the introduction, the body, and the conclusion. The introduction briefly presents the topic and gives your topic statement. In the body, follow your outline to develop the important ideas in your argument. The conclusion summarizes and restates your findings.

- Each paragraph should express one main idea in a topic sentence. Additional sentences support or explain the main idea by using details and facts.

- Revise the draft into a final report. Wait for a day, then reread and revise it.

Practicing the Skill

Suppose you are writing a report on the role family income plays in the children's educational attainment. Answer the following questions about the writing process.

1. How could you narrow the topic?
2. Write a thesis statement.
3. What are the main ideas?
4. What are three possible sources of information?

Applying the Skill

Use research resources in your library to find information on the role of the family in society. Narrow the topic and write a short report on it.

Critical Thinking Skills

Identifying Central Issues

Identifying central issues will help you organize information and assess the most important concepts to remember.

Good debaters must identify the central issues in a topic and in their opponents' arguments. Do you think political candidates do this well?

Learning the Skill

To identify a central issue, follow these steps:

1. Understand the context in which the reading was written.
2. Skim the material to identify its general subject. Look at headings and subheadings.
3. Read the information carefully to pinpoint the ideas that the details support.
4. Identify the central issue. Ask what part of the reading conveys the main idea.

Read the following excerpt from a paper entitled "The Crisis of the Young African American Male and the Criminal Justice System."

> *In recent years policy attention regarding the crisis of the African American male has focused on a variety of areas in which African American males have suffered disproportionately from social ills. These have included*

education, housing, employment, and health care, among others. Perhaps in no other area, though, have these problems been displayed as prominently as in the rate of crime and the criminal justice system. African Americans have been affected in this area in two significant regards. First, African Americans are more likely to be victimized by crime than are other groups…. Second, the dramatic rates at which African American males have come under some form of criminal justice supervision has created a complex set of consequences which affect not only individual victims and offenders, but families and communities as well (Mauer, 1999).

A first step in identifying the central issue is to find out who wrote the piece and understand the author's purposes in writing it. Marc Mauer is the Assistant Director of The Sentencing Project, a non-profit organization engaged in research on criminal justice issues. In this paper, Mr. Mauer wanted to explore the current status of African American males in America's criminal justice system and recommend policies that would help change the system's destructive impacts on public safety.

Practicing the Skill

Read another paragraph from Mr. Mauer's paper and answer the questions that follow.

In assessing the extent to which racial bias within the criminal justice system has contributed to these disparities, there is mixed research evidence. Imposition of the death penalty provides the most compelling evidence for ongoing racial disparity. A series of studies has demonstrated that . . . the race of both victim and offender has a significant impact on the determination of a sentence of death as opposed to life in prison. [M]urder defendants charged with killing whites faced a 4.3 times greater chance of receiving death than those charged with killing blacks (Mauer, 1999).

1. According to Mauer, is it clear that African Americans receive harsher treatment from the courts?
2. Summarize the central issue of this paragraph in one sentence.

Applying the Skill

1. Bring to class three editorials from your local newspaper, national newspaper, or a newsmagazine. Try to find examples written by the publications' readers ("Letters to the Editor" are a good source for these) and professional writers.
2. Identify the central issue in each editorial.
3. Discuss how clearly each writer made his or her main point(s).

Determining Cause and Effect

Understanding cause and effect involves determining *why* an event occurred. A cause is the action or situation that produces an event. What happens as a result of a cause is an *effect*. Despite the seeming simplicity of this relationship, determining the true cause of an event is often very difficult. This is the case because there is seldom a single cause of any effect. Like other scientists, sociologists realize that almost all events occur as a result of several factors operating in combination. This viewpoint is known as the principle of multiple causation.

Calvin has obviously discovered the difficulties of determining cause-and-effect relationships.

Learning the Skill

Just because two things happen at nearly the same time, or they seem to occur regularly together, does not mean that they have a causal relationship. To identify cause-and-effect relationships, follow these steps:

- Identify two or more events.
- Decide whether one event caused the other. Look for clue words such as *because, led to, brought about, produced, as a result of, so that, since,* and *therefore.*
- Look for logical relationships between events, such as "She overslept, and then she missed her bus."
- Identify the outcomes of events. Remember that some effects have more than one cause, and some causes lead to more than one effect. Also, an effect can become the cause of yet another effect.

Practicing the Skill

Sociologists have studied the relationship between violence on television and violent behavior for many years. For decades, no one was willing to conclude that there was a cause-and-effect relationship between the two, but in 1999 the Milton S. Eisenhower Foundation issued a report that established a causal link between viewing violence on television and increased levels of violent behavior among viewers.

1. Why do you think that earlier researchers were reluctant to say that watching violence on television caused violent behavior?
2. Why did the Milton S. Eisenhower Foundation conclude that a cause-and-effect relationship does exist (see page 126 of the text)?

Applying the Skill

1. Do some research on the causes of criminal behavior. Prepare a short report that summarizes your findings.
2. Discuss how the principle of multiple causation applies to criminal behavior.
3. What other questions does your research raise?

Separating Fact from Opinion

Being able to distinguish fact from opinion can help you make reasonable judgments about what others say and write. Unfortunately, fact and opinion are often confused with each other, and separating them can be difficult. Facts must be verified by evidence. Opinions are simply based on people's differing values and beliefs.

Learning the Skill

The following steps will help you distinguish facts from opinions:

● Read or listen to the information carefully. Identify the facts by asking: Can these statements be proved? Where would I find information to verify them?

● If a statement can be verified, it is factual. Check the sources for the facts. Often statistics sound impressive, but they may come from an unreliable source.

● Identify opinions by looking for statements of feelings or beliefs. If the statement refers to situations that are desirable or undesirable, important or unimportant, or likely or unlikely, then the statement is an opinion. Opinions may also contain words like *should, would, could, best, greatest, all, every,* or *always.*

Separating fact from opinion can be very important to you in everyday life.

Practicing the Skill

Read the following paragraph, then answer the questions below it.

According to data collected by the Census Bureau, African Americans who have received a high school diploma earned a median income in 1999 of $23,990, and their white counterparts earned $29,261, nearly 22 percent more. The gap between blacks and whites with bachelor's degrees is even greater—median earnings of $36,930 for African Americans and $45,737 for whites, or 24 percent more (U.S. Bureau of the Census, 2000). Does this discrepancy between blacks and whites extend to other areas of life as well? Almost seven out of ten whites say that blacks are treated the same as whites in their communities, but only 41 percent of African Americans agree with that statement. Less than half of African Americans believe they *receive equal housing opportunities, while 83 percent of whites responded that their communities provide equal housing opportunities for everyone (Ludwig, 2001).*

1. Which of the statements in the preceding paragraph are facts? How did you identify the facts?
2. Which of the statements in the preceding paragraph are opinions? How did you identify them?

Applying the Skill

1. Watch a television interview. List three facts and three opinions that were stated.
2. Can you verify the facts?
3. How did you identify the opinions?
4. What statements, if any, seemed to contain both fact and opinion?

Making Generalizations

Generalizations are statements assumed to represent the truth by those who make them. If you say, "People who work hard make more money," you are making a generalization. If you also say that every hardworking person you know makes more money, you are attempting to support your generalization. Keep in mind that making a generalization from a small number of observations does not provide strong evidence that your generalization is actually true.

Sociologists study processes of socialization and make generalizations about how these processes shape individuals' ways of thinking, feeling, and acting.

Learning the Skill

To make a valid generalization, you must first collect factual information relevant to the topic. Follow these steps:

- Identify the subject matter.
- Gather related facts and examples.
- Identify similarities among these facts.
- Use these similarities to form some general conclusions about the subject.

Practicing the Skill

Read this paragraph, and then answer the questions below:

Many people in America believe that people at the bottom of the economic scale belong there because they don't have the motivation to succeed in a competitive marketplace. In a series of surveys, Americans were asked to account for poverty in the U.S. The most popular reasons blamed the poverty on the poor themselves. However, in studies of the poor and those receiving welfare, researchers have consistently found that a majority want to work, to support themselves, and to get off the welfare rolls.

1. Based on the preceding paragraph, what generalizations are made about the poor?
2. Is the generalization about the poor based on facts?
3. Is the generalization accurate? If so, how does that influence our policies regarding the poor? If not, why does the generalization persist?

Applying the Skill

Read the editorials in your local or a national newspaper for one week. Then write a list of generalizations about the newspaper's position on issues such as political ideology, economic policy, or the environment.

Analyzing Graphics

Line Graphs and Bar Graphs

A graph, like a picture, may present information in a more concise way than words. Line graphs and bar graphs are drawings that compare numerical values. They often are used to compare changes over time or differences between places, groups of items, or other related events. Both types of graphs can be used to display the same information, and the choice between the two is often at the discretion of the author. In general, however, line graphs are used to show trends over time related to one type of data (e.g. percentage of the population that believes in God, average age at first marriage, or number of households headed by a single woman). Bar graphs may be used to show trends over time or to compare different types of information, such as median income for men and women or age groups of a population.

Learning the Skill

Follow these steps to learn how to understand and use line and bar graphs.

- Read the title of the graph. This should tell you what to expect or look for.
- Note the information on the left side of the graph—the vertical axis. The information being compared usually appears on this axis.
- Note the information along the bottom of the graph—the horizontal axis. Time often appears along this axis.
- Determine what the line(s) or bar(s) symbolizes.
- Select a point on the line or bar, then note the date below this point on the horizontal axis and the quantity measured on the vertical axis.
- Analyze the movement of the line (whether increasing or decreasing over time), or compare bars to determine the point being made.

Practicing the Skill

Review the graphs, then answer the questions. Note that both graphs present the same information.

1. About what percentage of families with children under 18 were headed by single parents in 1985? In 1996?
2. How would you describe the general trend shown by these graphs?
3. Based on the data for the last four years shown, can you state what the current trend is for families headed by single parents?
4. Which graph represents this data in a more meaningful way?

**Percent of Families with Children
Under 18 Headed by a Single Parent, 1975-2004**

Source: 2005 Kids Count Data Sheet. Baltimore, MD: The Annie E. Casey Foundation, 2005.

**Percent of Families with Children Under 18
Headed by a Single Parent, 1975–2004**

Source: 2005 Kids Count Data Sheet. Baltimore, MD: The Annie E. Casey Foundation, 2005.

Applying the Skill

1. Create line and bar graphs that show the number and percent of children living in poverty in the United States from 1975 through 2004.
2. Pose two questions that the graphs you created raise in your mind.
3. Answer the questions you pose.
4. Which graph do you think is easier to understand and presents the information more meaningfully?

Circle Graphs and Tables

Circle graphs (also called pie charts) are often used to present information that shows the proportions of a whole. The particular data being presented can vary widely, but the common element in circle graphs is to show how the entire population is divided into subgroups. The same information can be presented in tables, but in numerical, rather than graphic, form. Tables have the advantage of being able to present multiple categories of data in one location, whereas circle graphs are limited to one type of data.

Learning the Skill

Follow these steps to learn how to understand and use circle graphs and tables.

- Read the graph or table title to determine the content being presented.
- Read the labels (on circle graphs) or row headings (in tables). These will tell you what information is to be compared.
- For tables, examine the labels in the left-hand column. They describe ranges or subgroups and are often organized chronologically or alphabetically.
- Note the source of the data. It may tell you about the reliability of the data or where to go for further information.
- Compare the data presented to discover the relationships among categories.

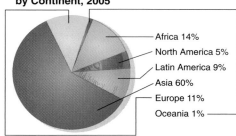

Percentage of World Population by Continent, 2005

Africa 14%
North America 5%
Latin America 9%
Asia 60%
Europe 11%
Oceania 1%

Source: 2005 World Population Data Sheet. Washington, DC: Population Reference Bureau, 2005.

Practicing the Skill

Study the table and circle graph, and then answer the following questions.

1. Which medium presents more information to the reader?
2. If you were concerned solely with the world's population, which graph/table would you prefer? Why?

Demographic Data for Regions of the World

Location	Population 2005 (in millions)	Crude Birth-rate	Crude Death Rate	Life Expectancy
World	6,477	21	9	67
Africa	906	38	15	52
North America	329	14	8	78
Latin America	559	22	6	72
Oceania	33	17	7	75
Asia	3,921	20	7	68
Europe	730	10	11	75

Source: 2005 World Population Data Sheet. Washington, D.C.: Population Reference Bureau, 2005.

Applying the Skill

1. Gather information on the demographics (for example, age, sex, parental income) of high school students in your state.
2. Present selected information in a table and in circle graphs.

Maps

Maps are visual tools that show the relative size and location of specific geographic areas. There are political maps, which show human-made boundaries; physical maps, which show physical features of an area; and special purpose maps that can show historical change, cultural features, population, climate, land use, resources, or any other information of interest. Regardless of type, all maps use symbols to convey information.

Learning the Skill

Follow these steps to learn how to understand and use maps.

- Read the title to determine the map's content.
- Examine the map's scale, which indicates the ratio between the map's size and the actual area being represented. However, for many special purpose maps, this information will not be provided, and is not relevant to the information being presented.
- Read the legend, or key, to interpret any shapes, colors, boundary lines, or symbols. This step is, in many ways, the most important for maps of interest to sociologists.
- Interpret the information being presented. Determine patterns or other interesting points of interest. What questions does the map raise in your mind?

Practicing the Skill

Study the map and answer the questions that follow.

1. What information does this map present to the reader?
2. Do you see any patterns in the information?
3. What questions does the map raise for you?
4. Where could you find the answers to the questions you posed?

Applying the Skill

1. Do research on participation of high school students in school-sponsored music programs, by state.
2. Summarize your findings by preparing a map of the United States that depicts the information you found.

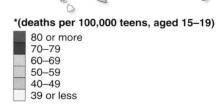

Rate of Teen Deaths by Accident, Homicide, and Suicide*

*(deaths per 100,000 teens, aged 15–19)

- 80 or more
- 70–79
- 60–69
- 50–59
- 40–49
- 39 or less

Source: 2005 Kids Count Data Sheet. Baltimore, MD: The Annie E. Casey Foundation, 2005.

Interpreting Data

Percentages

Sociologists use the concept of percentages quite often in their work on groups and social structures. Percent means "parts per hundred." So when a sociologist notes that, say, 18 percent of a group has a certain trait, she means that 18 out of 100 members of that group possess the trait in question. Changes in the size or number of a particular item (usually over time) can be expressed in percentages also. Stating the amount of change as a percentage allows you to analyze the relative size of the change. For example, if you knew that the populations of two states each increased by 250,000 people, you would have some information. But knowing that the percentage change in one state was 1 percent, while in the other state it was 15 percent, would provide you with substantially more information about the relative size of the increase, and would allow you to infer some of the possible consequences for the states.

The individuals in this group can be categorized in many different ways. What percentage of the group is male? Female? African American? Redheaded?

Learning the Skill

Follow these steps to learn how to calculate and use percentages.

- Calculate the percentage by dividing the number of the subgroup or change by the number of the original group population. Multiply your answer by 100 to express it as a percentage.

- Compare the percentage you calculated with other relevant measures.

- Remember that numbers or percentages by themselves tell you very little. This type of information is most useful when compared to other, similar types of information, so that you can put it into its proper context.

Practicing the Skill

Complete the table on page HB-16 by calculating the missing percentages. Then answer the questions below the table.

1. Look at the percentages of students studying sociology at each school. Do you see a pattern? Does sociology seem to be more popular at some schools than others?
2. Now look at the differences between the percentages studying sociology in 1990 and 2000 at each school. Do you see a pattern of change during the ten-year period?
3. What might account for the changes you noticed?

	1990			2000		
School	# Student Body	# Studying Sociology	% Studying Sociology	# Student Body	# Studying Sociology	% Studying Sociology
Cave Spring	928	83	8.9%	1008	164	
Glenvar	316	40		421	44	10.5%
Northside	745	52		763	79	
Patrick Henry	866	54	6.2%	940	30	
William Byrd	643	37		715	55	
Wm. Fleming	872	91		948	116	

Applying the Skill

1. Survey 50 students at your high school to determine their favorite style of music. Based on the results of your survey, determine the percentages of your sample that listed each kind of music as their favorite.
2. Do the results of your survey surprise you? Why or why not?
3. How did you categorize students who named more than one style of music as their favorite?

Mean, Median, and Mode

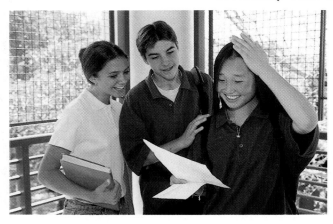

Suppose a group of your friends wanted to compare scores on a college entrance exam. How would you calculate the group's mean score? Its median score? Its mode score? Which measure would be most meaningful?

The most commonly used summary statistic is the average. Generally speaking, an average is a measure of central tendency, indicating where the middle of a series of number lies. There are three ways to compute the average: the mean, median, and mode. The mean is the arithmetic average of a series of items. However, using the mean to represent the average can sometimes be misleading. This generally occurs when a few of the numbers in the series are much higher or lower than the others, resulting in a skewed or biased mean. When this happens, using the median or mode to represent the average may be more meaningful. The median is the midpoint in a series of numbers when they are arranged in order from low to high. The mode is the number that appears most frequently in the series.

Learning the Skill

Follow the steps below to learn how to determine and use measures of central tendency.

- To find the mean, add all of the numbers in the series. Then divide the sum by the number of observations in the series.
- Locate the median by arranging all of the numbers in the series from low to high. Then find the number that is the midpoint in the series. When

an even number of figures is in the series, the median is the mean of the two middle numbers.

- The mode is the number in the series that appears most frequently. Simply look at the series and count which number appears the most.
- Compare the mean, median, and mode. Determine which one or combination is the most accurate in a particular case.

Practicing the Skill

Read the paragraph below and answer the questions.

An academic department at a major university conducts a survey each year of its recent graduates. One of the questions on the survey asks the respondents to report their annual income. Suppose this question drew the following responses from some graduates:

$23,500	$18,760	$43,000	$32,400
$26,750	$28,410	$1,466,980	$27,600
$26,750	$34,500	$24,580	

1. Determine the mean, median, and mode for these earnings figures.
2. Which measure of central tendency would you recommend using for this series? Why?

Applying the Skill

1. What are some of the data that you would want to know?
2. Which of the three measures of central tendency would you use for each type of data?
3. Explain your choices.

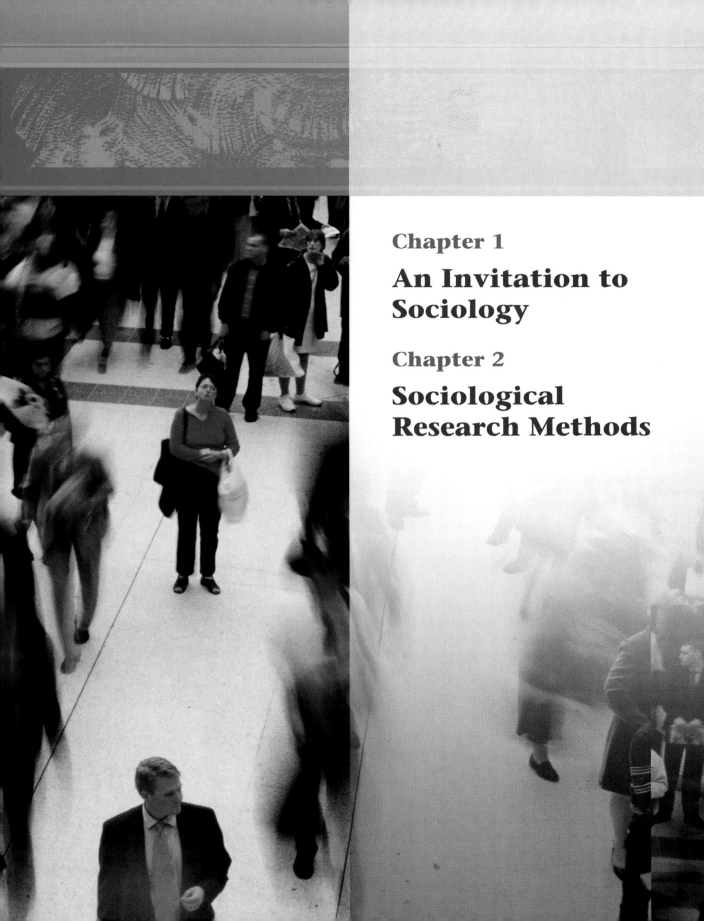

Chapter 1

An Invitation to Sociology

Chapter 2

Sociological Research Methods

An Invitation to Sociology

Sections

1. **The Sociological Perspective**
2. **The Origins of Sociology**
3. **Theoretical Perspectives**

Learning Objectives

After reading this chapter, you will be able to

- define *sociology*.
- describe two uses of the sociological perspective.
- distinguish sociology from other social sciences.
- outline the contributions of the major pioneers of sociology.
- summarize the development of sociology in the United States.
- identify the three major theoretical perspectives in sociology today.

Applying Sociology

Sociologists study how people behave in groups. Often sociologists look for the recurring patterns in human behavior. Many of us make assumptions about society every day. In the photo at left, for example, what characteristic assumptions about American society are portrayed? You might respond that the photo suggests that young Americans are positive, multicultural, fashion-conscious, value individualism, but also value equality. (After all, none of the students seems to be more important than any other.)

Questioning and researching assumptions is an important part of sociology. By learning to question conventional wisdom (what most people believe to be true), you will be in a better position to make decisions or judgments. Your decisions will be based on reality rather than on socially accepted false beliefs. This does not mean that all conventional wisdom is false, of course, but it is important to know that the facts are accurate when policies affecting people's lives are made.

Sociology is a relatively new field of study. It only became a well recognized discipline in the late 1800s. As you will see when you read this chapter, it is the "infant of the social sciences." This chapter will introduce you not only to the pioneers of the field but also to the basic ways that sociologists approach their subject.

Sociology nline

Chapter Overview
Visit the *Sociology and You* Web site at glencoe.com and click on **Chapter 1—Chapter Overviews** to preview chapter information.

1

The Sociological Perspective

Section Preview

Sociology studies human social behavior. It assumes a group, rather than an individual, perspective. Sociologists look for the patterns in social relationships. Individuals can benefit by using their sociological imaginations to look at events in their personal lives.

Key Terms

- perspective *(p. 6)*
- sociology *(p. 6)*
- sociological perspective *(p. 6)*
- social structure *(p. 9)*
- sociological imagination *(p. 11)*

- **perspective**
  a particular point of view

- **sociology**
  the scientific study of social structure (patterned social behavior)

- **sociological perspective**
  a view that looks at behavior of groups, not individuals

The Nature of Sociology

A **perspective** is a particular point of view. Babies are usually brighter and better looking to their parents than they are to others. Newlyweds nearly always find their spouses much more attractive than do their friends. We all see what is happening around us through our own perspectives—our own points of view.

We normally do not realize how much of our attitudes and beliefs are determined by our perspectives. Sometimes, though, when our outlook is challenged, we may be jarred into realizing how much we take it for granted. As you will see, sociology has its own perspective. To understand it, you must have an idea of just what sociology is.

What is sociology? As a newcomer to the field, you may at first view sociology as the study of human social behavior. As you go along, however, you will acquire a more precise understanding of **sociology** as the scientific study of *social structure*. (Social structure is discussed later in this section.)

What is unique about sociology? Sociology, as stated earlier, has its own perspective. The **sociological perspective** never focuses on the individual. Psychologists may study the individual, but not sociologists. The view through the lens of sociology always remains at the social, or group, level.

These elephant tusks were burned to discourage trade in ivory. Whether you support this action depends upon your beliefs about conservation and national sovereignty.

Social Science	Description	Example
Sociology	Sociology investigates human social behavior from a group rather than an individual perspective. It concentrates on patterns of social relationships, primarily in modern societies.	Relationship between the employment of women and family size
Anthropology	Anthropology investigates culture, the customary beliefs and material traits of groups. It is the social science most closely related to sociology. Anthropologists, however, concentrate on the study of preliterate societies (societies that do not use writing). Sociologists focus on modern, industrial societies.	Nature of the family in preliterate societies
Psychology	Psychology investigates human mental and emotional processes. While sociologists concentrate on the group, psychologists also study the development and functioning of the individual.	Effects of birth order on emotional development
Economics	Economics is the study of the production, distribution, and consumption of goods and services.	Annual income levels of American families
Political science	Political science investigates the organization, administration, history, and theory of government. Political scientists are concerned, for example, with voting patterns and participation in political parties.	Relationship between a family's social class and voting behavior
History	History examines past events in human societies. Historians generally rely on newspapers, historical documents, and oral histories as sources of information.	Nature of family life in colonial society

The Social Sciences

Social science is a branch of learning that deals with human society. It includes a number of disciplines, which we generally refer to as the social sciences. These disciplines differ, but they share enough in common to overlap. Descriptions of the major social sciences are presented in this table.

Industrial Revolution

American Revolution

George Washington
is president

French Revolution

Louisiana Purchase
1803

Francis Lowell builds nation's
largest textile factory
1813

Indian Removal Act
1830

Herbert Spencer publishes
Social Statics
1850

Charles Darwin publishes
On the Origin of Species
1859

Harriet Martineau publishes
Society in America
1837

Auguste Comte's book,
Positive Philosophy, identifies
science of sociology
1838

Karl Marx publishes
The Communist Manifesto,
promoting a classless society
1848

Time Line of Early Sociologists

Both landmark dates in sociology (blue dots)
and American history (red dots) are placed
on this time line. Can you suggest how the
development of the box camera in 1888 might
have influenced the growth of sociology as a
field of study?

| 1770 | 1780 | 1790 | 1800 | 1810 | 1820 | 1830 | 1840 | 1850 | 1860 |

Sociologists do not focus on the behavior of individuals but on the patterns of behavior shared by members of a group or society. The person on the street might explain human behavior in individualistic or personal terms—a young man joins a gang to prove his toughness; a woman divorces her husband to develop her potential; a teen commits suicide to escape depression.

Sociologists attempt to explain these same events *without* relying on personal factors. They look for social rather than personal explanations when they examine delinquency, divorce, or suicide. Sociologists might explain the events in the following ways:

• Young men join gangs because they have been taught by their society to be "masculine."

• More women divorce because of the social trend toward sexual equality.

• Teens commit suicide because of peer group expectations of performance, material possessions, and physical appearance.

Sociologists do not speak of *a* young man, *a* married woman, or *a* teenager. They concentrate on *categories* of people—young men, married women, and teenagers.

Joining a gang provides some young men—and women—with a sense of security and belonging they haven't found elsewhere.

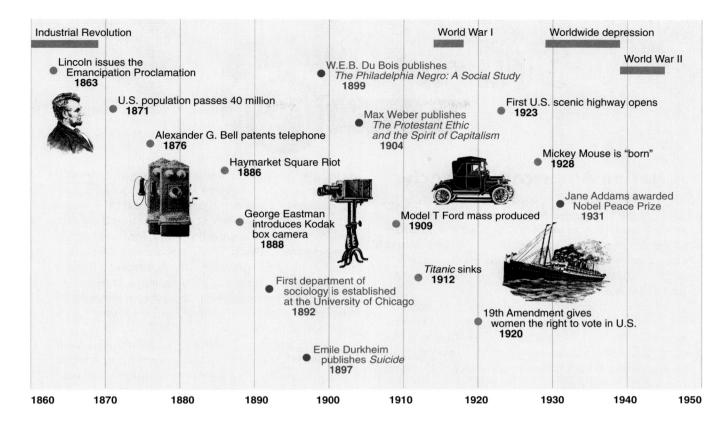

Industrial Revolution

World War I

Worldwide depression

World War II

Lincoln issues the
Emancipation Proclamation
1863

U.S. population passes 40 million
1871

Alexander G. Bell patents telephone
1876

Haymarket Square Riot
1886

George Eastman
introduces Kodak
box camera
1888

First department of
sociology is established
at the University of Chicago
1892

Emile Durkheim
publishes *Suicide*
1897

W.E.B. Du Bois publishes
The Philadelphia Negro: A Social Study
1899

Max Weber publishes
*The Protestant Ethic
and the Spirit of Capitalism*
1904

Model T Ford mass produced
1909

Titanic sinks
1912

19th Amendment gives
women the right to vote in U.S.
1920

First U.S. scenic highway opens
1923

Mickey Mouse is "born"
1928

Jane Addams awarded
Nobel Peace Prize
1931

1860　1870　1880　1890　1900　1910　1920　1930　1940　1950

The Importance of Patterns

As you well know, high school students in a classroom behave in different ways. Some students listen to everything their teacher says. Some tune in and out, and others spend much of the time daydreaming. Yet, if you visit almost any high school, you will find *patterned* relationships. Teachers walk around the room, work with students, lecture, and give tests. Students follow the teacher's lesson plan, make notes, and take tests. Although the personal characteristics of students and teachers may vary from school to school, students and teachers relate in similar patterned ways. It is the patterned interaction of people in social relationships—what sociologists call **social structure**—that captures the attention of sociologists.

How do group behavior and individual behavior differ?

Sociologists assume that social relationships are not determined only by the particular characteristics of the people involved. Emile Durkheim, a pioneering nineteenth-century sociologist, helped develop the sociological perspective. He argued, for example, that we do not attempt to explain bronze in terms of its separate parts (lead, copper, and tin). Instead, we consider bronze a totally new metal created by the combination of several other metals. We cannot even predict the characteristics of bronze from the traits of its parts. For example, bronze is hard, while lead, copper, and tin are soft and pliable. The mixing of the individual parts creates a new whole with new characteristics. Durkheim reasoned that a similar process happens with groups of people.

Indeed, people's behavior within a group setting cannot be predicted from their personal characteristics. Something new is created when individuals

● **social structure**
the patterned interaction of
people in social relationships

Student Web Activity
Visit the *Sociology and You* Web
site at glencoe.com and click
on **Chapter 1—Student Web
Activities** for an activity on
social patterns.

A Native American's Speech

Virginia colonists had offered to "properly edu-cate" some young Indian boys at the College of William and Mary in Williamsburg. To the surprise of the colonists, the benefits of a white gentleman's education were not highly valued by the tribal elders. Below is a Native American's reply to the white men's offer.

We know that you highly esteem the kind of learning taught in . . . [your] colleges. . . . But you, who are wise, must know that different nations have different conceptions of things; and you will not therefore take it amiss, if our ideas of this kind of education happen not to be the same with

yours. We have had some experience of it; several of our young people were formerly brought up at the colleges of the northern provinces; they were instructed in all your sciences; but, when they came back to us, they were bad runners, ignorant of every means of living in the woods, unable to bear either cold or hunger, knew neither how to build a cabin, take a deer, nor kill an enemy, spoke our language imperfectly, were therefore neither fit for hunters, warriors, nor councellors; they were totally good for nothing.

We are however not the less obligated by your kind offer, though we decline accepting it; and, to show our grateful sense of it, if the gentlemen of Virginia will send us a dozen of their sons, we will take care of their education, instruct them in all we know, and make men of them.

Thinking It Over

1. Describe your reaction to this passage. What does it tell you about the importance of per-spective in interpreting the social world?

2. Describe a social encounter where you person-ally experienced a "clash of perspectives" with someone from another culture.

3. Do you think your education is preparing you to succeed in the world outside school?

come together. For example, in 2005 the New England Patriots won the Super Bowl championship. Following the game, a few otherwise law-abiding foot-ball fans, as a group, disrupted the peace and challenged the police in ways they would not have done as individuals.

Tragedy, as well as joy, can change group behavior. In 2005, for example, the destructive forces of Hurricane Katrina devastated the city of New Orleans. Large portions of the city were underwater, and many families lost every-thing they had. In the days following the hurricane, when help was slow in coming, looting, violence, and other criminal activities became serious prob-lems for law-enforcement officials. Many of the looting incidents involved normally law-abiding residents gathering food, water, and other essential goods from unattended grocery stores.

Why do people conform? Groups range in size from a family to an entire society. Regardless of size, all groups encourage conformity. We will study conformity in more detail later. For now, you need to know only that members of a group think, feel, and behave in similar ways. For example, Americans, Russians, and Nigerians have eating habits, dress, religious beliefs, and attitudes toward family life that reflect their group.

Conformity within a group occurs, in part, because members have been taught to value the group's ways. Members generally tend to conform even when their personal preferences are not the same as the group's. Some teens, for example, start smoking only to gain group acceptance.

Behavior within a group cannot be predicted simply from knowledge about its individual members. This could be because members truly value their group's ways or because they give in to social pressures. Like bronze, the group is more than the sum of its parts.

Acquiring the Sociological Imagination

The sociological perspective enables us to develop a sociological imagination. That is, knowing how social forces affect our lives can prevent us from being prisoners of those forces. C. Wright Mills (2000), an American sociologist, called this personal use of sociology the **sociological imagination**—the ability of individuals to see the relationship between events in their personal lives and events in their society.

● **sociological imagination**
the ability to see the link between society and self

What is gained by using our sociological imagination?
People do not make decisions, big or small, in isolation. Historically, for example, American society has shown a strong bias against childless and one-child marriages. Couples without children have been considered selfish, and an only child has often been labeled "spoiled" (Benokraitis, 2004). These values date back to a time when large families were needed for survival. Most people lived on family farms, where children were needed to help with the work. Furthermore, many children died at birth or in infancy. People responded to society's needs by having large families. Now, as the need for large families is disappearing, we are beginning to read about benefits of one-child families— to the child, to the family, and to society. This change in attitude is reflected in the decrease in family size.

The sociological imagination helps us understand the effects of events, such as the social pressures just discussed, on our daily lives. With this understanding, we are in a better position to make our own decisions rather than merely conform (Erikson, 1997; Game and Metcalfe, 1996).

This social awareness permits us to read the newspaper with a fuller understanding of the events. Instead of interpreting a letter opposing welfare as an expression of someone with no compassion, we might instead see the writer as a person who places great importance on independence and self-help. The sociological imagination questions common interpretations of human social behavior. It challenges *conventional social wisdom*—ideas people assume are true.

To the outsider, these teenagers seem to be dressed alike. How does this photo show that a group is more than the sum of its parts?

Sociology Today

Job Opportunities in Sociology

In general, all employers are interested in four types of skills regardless of what specific career path you choose. These skills are:

- the ability to work with others
- the ability to write and speak well
- the ability to solve problems
- the ability to analyze information

Because computers have revolutionized the office, for example, information analysis skills are becoming much more important to managers in all types of organizations. The increasing complexity of work demands greater critical thinking and problem-solving skills. Knowledge is of limited use if you can't convey what you know to others.

The study of sociology helps students to develop these general skills, so it is a solid base for many career paths. For sociology majors, the following list of possibilities is only the beginning—many other paths are open to you.

- **Social services**—in rehabilitation, case management, group work with youth or the elderly, recreation, or administration
- **Community work**—in fund-raising for social service organizations, nonprofits, child-care or community development agencies, or environmental groups
- **Corrections**—in probation, parole, or other criminal justice work
- **Business**—in advertising, marketing and consumer research, insurance, real estate, personnel work, training, or sales
- **College settings**—in admissions, alumni relations, or placement offices
- **Health services**—in family planning, substance abuse, rehabilitation counseling, health planning, hospital admissions, and insurance companies
- **Publishing, journalism, and public relations**—in writing, research, and editing
- **Government services**—in federal, state, and local government jobs in such areas as transportation, housing, agriculture, and labor
- **Teaching**—in elementary and secondary schools, in conjunction with appropriate teacher certification; also in universities, with research opportunities.

Doing Sociology

1. Which of the above career paths is most interesting to you? What is it about this area that you find interesting?

2. Evaluate your current strengths and weaknesses in the four primary skill areas.

3. Look at the employment opportunities in the Sunday edition of your local paper. Clip out ads for jobs that you might qualify for with a sociology degree.

Adapted from *Careers in Sociology,* American Sociological Association, 2006.

Snapshot of America

Health Insurance

Americans tend to believe that all children have the right to receive good medical care. Research has shown, however, that American children do not have equal access to medical care. One reason for this is a lack of health insurance. This map shows, by state, the percentage of children under age eighteen who do not have health insurance.

Percentage of Children Under 18 Who Are Uninsured

- 4.9% and below
- 5.0%–9.9%
- 10%–14.9%
- 15%–19.9%
- 20% and above

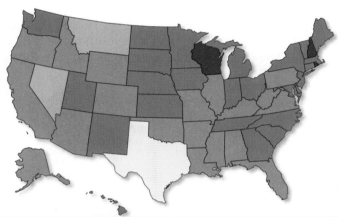

Interpreting the Map

1. Which states have the fewest uninsured children? Which state has the most?
2. How does your state rate on health insurance coverage for children?
3. How might using your sociological imagination help you to explain why children in the United States have unequal access to medical care?

Source: U.S. Census Bureau, *Statistical Abstract of the United States: 2004–2005.*

Section 1 Assessment

1. Define sociology.
2. Explain the significance of patterns for sociologists.
3. Give an example from your life that illustrates conformity within a group.
4. How does the sociological imagination help people to understand the effects of society on their personal lives?

Critical Thinking

5. **Making Comparisons** Examine the idea of perspectives by identifying an issue that you look at in one way and your parent(s) or other adults look at in a different way. Write about the issue from both perspectives.

2 The Origins of Sociology

Key Terms

- positivism *(p. 14)*
- social statics *(p. 14)*
- social dynamics *(p. 14)*
- bourgeoisie *(p. 16)*
- capitalist *(p. 16)*
- proletariat *(p. 16)*
- class conflict *(p. 16)*
- mechanical solidarity *(p. 17)*
- organic solidarity *(p. 17)*
- verstehen *(p. 18)*
- rationalization *(p. 18)*

Section Preview

Sociology is a young science. It started with the writings of European scholars like Auguste Comte, Harriet Martineau, Herbert Spencer, Karl Marx, Emile Durkheim, and Max Weber. Jane Addams and W.E.B. DuBois helped to focus America's attention on social issues. After World War II, America took the lead in developing the field of sociology.

European Origins

Sociology is a relatively new science. It began in late nineteenth-century Europe during a time of great social upheaval. The social and economic effects of the Industrial Revolution and the French Revolution were touching all aspects of life. People were moving from farms to factory life, losing a sense of community.

Some intellectuals were fascinated and troubled by the sudden changes. Auguste Comte, Harriet Martineau, and others began to grapple with ideas for bringing back a sense of community and for restoring order. These ideas led to the rise of the science of sociology. Examining the central ideas of the major pioneers of sociology will help you better understand what sociology is today.

What were Auguste Comte's major ideas? Auguste Comte (1798–1857), a Frenchman, is recognized as the father of sociology. As a child he was often ill, but he proved early to be an excellent student. He had difficulty balancing his genuine interest in school and his rebellious and stubborn nature. In fact, he was expelled for protesting against the examination procedures at the elite *Ecole Polytechnique.*

Auguste Comte is considered to be the founder of sociology. He was the first to advocate the scientific study of society.

- **positivism**
  the belief that knowledge should be derived from scientific observation

- **social statics**
  the study of social stability and order

- **social dynamics**
  the study of social change

As an adult, Comte's main concern was the improvement of society. If societies were to advance, Comte believed, social behavior had to be studied scientifically. Because no science of society existed, Comte attempted to create one himself. He coined the term *sociology* to describe this science.

Comte wanted to use scientific observation in the study of social behavior. He called this **positivism.** He meant that sociology should be a science based on knowledge of which we can be "positive," or sure. Comte also distinguished between **social statics,** the study of social stability and order, and **social dynamics,** the study of social change. This distinction between social stability and social change remains at the center of modern sociology.

Comte published his theories in a book titled *Positive Philosophy,* but he died before people generally came to appreciate his work. His belief that sociology could use scientific procedures and promote social progress, however, was widely adopted by other European scholars.

What were Harriet Martineau's contributions? Harriet Martineau (1802–1876), an Englishwoman, is another important figure in the founding of sociology. She was born into a solidly middle-class home. Never in good health, Martineau had lost her sense of taste, smell, and hearing before reaching adulthood. Her writing career, which included fiction as well as sociological work, began in 1825 after the Martineau's family textile mill was lost to a business depression. Without the family income, and following a broken engagement, Martineau was forced to seek a dependable source of income to support herself. She became a popular writer of celebrity status, whose work initially outsold Charles Dickens's.

Harriet Martineau emphasized sociology as a science and introduced feminism. Her profound deafness prevented her earning a living as a teacher so she became an author.

Martineau is best known today for her translation of Comte's great book. Her English translation remains even today the most readable one. Despite being severely hearing impaired, she also made original contributions in the areas of research methods, political economy, and feminist theory.

In *Society in America,* Martineau established herself as a pioneering feminist theorist. Because she saw a link between slavery and the oppression of women, she was a strong and outspoken supporter of the emancipation of both women and slaves. Martineau believed women's lack of economic power helped keep them dependent. By writing about the inferior position of women in society, she helped inspire future feminist theorists.

Why did Herbert Spencer oppose social reform? Herbert Spencer (1820–1903), the sole survivor of nine children, was born to an English schoolteacher. Spencer was taught exclusively by his father and uncle, mostly in mathematics and the natural sciences. He did not enjoy scholarly work or the study of Latin, Greek, English, or history, and therefore he decided not to apply to Cambridge University, his uncle's alma mater. As a result, his higher education was largely the result of his own reading. Spencer's career became a mixture of engineering, drafting, inventing, journalism, and writing.

Herbert Spencer was an early proponent of Social Darwinism and evolutionary social change.

To explain social stability, Herbert Spencer compared society to the human body. He explained that, like a body, a society is composed of parts working together to promote its well-being and survival. People have brains, stomachs, nervous systems, limbs. Societies have economies, religions, governments, families. Just as the eyes and the heart make essential contributions to the functioning of the human body, religious and educational institutions are crucial for a society's functioning.

Spencer also introduced a theory of social change called *Social Darwinism,* based on Charles Darwin's theory of evolution. Spencer thought that evolutionary social change led to progress—provided people did not interfere. If left alone, natural social selection would ensure the survival of the fittest society. On these grounds, Spencer opposed social reform because it interfered with the selection process. The poor, he wrote, deserve to be poor and the rich to be rich. Society profits from allowing individuals to find their own social-class level without outside help or hindrance. To interfere with the existence of poverty—or the result of any other natural process—is harmful to society.

When Spencer visited America in 1882, he was warmly greeted, particularly by corporate leaders. After all, his ideas provided moral justification for their competitive actions. Later, public support for government intervention increased, and Spencer's ideas began to slip out of fashion. He reportedly died with a sense of having failed. His contribution in sociology was a discussion of how societies should be structured.

Who was Karl Marx?

Karl Marx (1818–1883), a German scholar, did not consider himself a sociologist, but his ideas have had a major effect on the field. Marx felt great concern for the poverty and inequality suffered by the working class of his day. His life was guided by the principle that social scientists should try to change the world rather than merely study it. Marx's friend and coauthor Friedrich Engels helped put his ideas into writing.

Marx identified several social classes in nineteenth-century industrial society. Among them were farmers, servants, factory workers, craftspeople, owners of small businesses, and moneyed capitalists. He predicted that at some point all industrial societies would contain only two social classes: the *bourgeoisie* and the *proletariat*. The **bourgeoisie** (burzh-wa-zee) are those who own the means for producing wealth in industrial society (for example, factories and equipment). The means for producing wealth are called capital. Thus, those who own them are also called **capitalists.** The **proletariat** work for the bourgeoisie and are paid just enough to stay alive.

Karl Marx was the social scientist who underscored the importance of conflict in social change. Parts of his writings were later used as a basis for communism.

For Marx, the key to the unfolding of history was **class conflict**—a clash between the bourgeoisie, who controlled the means for producing wealth, and the proletariat, who labored for them. Just as slaves overthrew slave owners, wage workers would overtake capitalists. Out of this conflict would come a classless *(communistic)* society—one in which there would be no powerless proletariat.

- **bourgeoisie**
  class owning the means for producing wealth

- **capitalist**
  person who owns or controls the means for producing wealth

- **proletariat**
  working class; those who labor for the bourgeoisie

- **class conflict**
  the ongoing struggle between the bourgeoisie (owners) and the proletariat (working) classes

Planned revolution, Marx was convinced, could speed up the change from capitalism to communism. His political objective was to explain the workings of capitalism in order to hasten its fall through revolution. He believed, though, that capitalism would eventually self-destruct anyway.

What were Emile Durkheim's greatest contributions?

Emile Durkheim (1858–1917) was the son of a French rabbi. Durkheim was a brilliant student even during his early school years. In college, he was so intensely studious that his schoolmates nicknamed him "the metaphysician."

According to Durkheim, society exists because of broad *consensus*, or agreement, among members of a society. In preindustrial times, societies were based on what sociologists call **mechanical solidarity.** With these societies, there was widespread consensus of values and beliefs, strong social pressures for conformity, and dependence on tradition and family. In contrast, industrial societies are based on **organic solidarity**—social interdependency based on a web of highly specialized roles. These specialized roles make members of a society dependent on one another for goods and services. For example, instead of being self-sufficient, people need bankers and bankers need customers.

Although early sociologists emphasized the need to make sociology scientific, they did not have the research tools that are available today. Later sociologists developed the methods to replace speculation with observation, to collect and classify data, and to use data for testing social theories.

Durkheim was the most prominent of these later sociologists. He first introduced the use of statistical techniques in his groundbreaking research on suicide, which we will discuss in Chapter 2. In that study, Durkheim demonstrated that suicide involves more than individuals acting alone and that suicide rates vary according to group characteristics. Durkheim showed that human social behavior must be explained by social factors rather than just psychological ones.

Emile Durkheim was the first sociologist to use statistical methods in the study of human groups. He was also the first to teach a university sociology course.

- **mechanical solidarity**
  social dependency based on a widespread consensus of values and beliefs, enforced conformity, and dependence on tradition and family

- **organic solidarity**
  social interdependency based on a high degree of specialization in roles

Who was Max Weber? Max Weber (1864–1920) was the eldest son of a father who was a well-to-do German lawyer and politician. His mother, in stark contrast, was a strongly devout Calvinist who rejected the worldly lifestyle of her husband. Weber was affected psychologically by the conflicting values of his parents. Weber eventually suffered a complete mental breakdown from which he recovered to do some of his best work. As a university professor trained in law and economics, Weber wrote on a wide variety of topics, including the nature of power, the religions of the world, the nature of social classes, and the development and nature of bureaucracy. His most famous book is *The Protestant Ethic and the Spirit of Capitalism,* published in 1906.

Max Weber's model of a bureaucracy reflected greatly increased efficiency in business and government. Today, however, *bureaucratic* is often used as a synonym for unimaginative, plodding, or despotic.

Through the quality of his work and the diversity of his interests, Weber has had the single most important influence on the development of sociological theory. Human beings act on the basis of their own understanding of a situation, Weber said. Thus, sociologists must discover the personal meanings, values, beliefs, and attitudes underlying human social behavior. Weber believed that an understanding of the personal intentions of people in groups can be best accomplished through the method of **verstehen**—understanding the social behavior of others by putting yourself mentally in their places. Putting yourself in someone else's "shoes" allows you to temporarily shed your values and see things from a different point of view.

Weber also identified *rationalization* as a key influence in the change from a preindustrial to an industrial society. **Rationalization** is the mind-set that emphasizes the use of knowledge, reason, and planning. It marked a change from the tradition, emotion, and superstition of preindustrial society. For example, agriculture became grounded in science rather than belief in luck, fate, or magic. In stressing rationality and objectivity, Weber pioneered research techniques that helped prevent personal biases from unduly affecting the results of sociological investigations.

Sociology in America

Although the early development of sociology occurred in Europe, the greatest development of sociology has taken place in the United States. Because sociology has become a science largely through the efforts of American sociologists, it is not surprising that the majority of all sociologists are from the United States. Sociological writings in English are used by sociologists throughout the world, reflecting the global influence of American sociologists.

In 1892, the first department of sociology was established at the University of Chicago. From its founding up to World War II, the sociology department at the University of Chicago stood at the forefront of American sociology. After World War II, sociology departments at eastern universities such as Harvard and Columbia, midwestern universities such as Wisconsin and Michigan, and western universities such as Stanford and the University of California at Berkeley emerged as leaders.

In later chapters we will be studying the works of major American sociologists. Two early contributors, however, who are often left out of the history of American sociology are Jane Addams and W.E.B. DuBois. Although neither of these remarkable people were researchers or scientists, both were greatly concerned with social problems in America.

"Hmmm...what shall I wear today...?"

Everyone manages his or her behavior to create a desired impression. What face have you put on today?

Why should we remember Jane Addams?

The best known of the early women social reformers in the United States was Jane Addams (1860–1935). Although her mother died when she was two years old, Addams's wealthy father provided a loving and comfortable home for her and her eight brothers and sisters. Addams was an excellent student. Her early education emphasized practical knowledge and the improvement of "the organizations of human society." She attended the Women's Medical College of Philadelphia but was compelled to drop out of the school because of illness.

Jane Addams was a social reformer who spent her life working on the social problems created by the imbalance of power among social classes.

When she was a child, Addams saw many examples of government corruption and business practices that harmed workers. She never forgot their suffering. While on one of her European trips, she saw the work being done to help the poor in London. With this example of social action, Addams began her life's work seeking social justice. She co-founded Hull House in Chicago's slums. Here, people who needed refuge—immigrants, the sick, the poor, the aged—could find help.

Addams focused on the problems caused by the imbalance of power among the social classes. She invited sociologists from the University of Chicago to Hull House to witness firsthand the effects of industrialism on the lower class. In addition to her work with the underclass, Addams was active in the woman suffrage and peace movements. As a result of her tireless work for social reform, Addams was awarded the Nobel Peace Prize in 1931—the first sociologist to receive this honor. The irony is that Addams herself suffered a sort of class discrimination. She was not considered a sociologist during her lifetime because she did not teach at a university. She was considered a social worker (then considered a less prestigious career) because she was a woman and because she worked directly with the poor.

Secondary Analysis: The McDonaldization of Higher Education

Research is to sociology what lab experiments are to chemists. Through the research process sociologists gather information, or data, to help them understand how people behave in social settings. (In the next chapter, you will learn more about how sociologists do research.) The research project described below will give you some idea of how sociologists use already-collected data to study human social behavior.

In this study, George Ritzer investigated how Max Weber's process of *rationalization* (see page 18) is being used by a popular fast-food company. Like Weber, Ritzer was interested in the movement of organizations toward ever-increasing efficiency, predictability, calculability, and control. After explaining each of these characteristics, Ritzer applies rationalization to the field of education in what he calls the "McDonaldization" of higher education.

Efficiency refers to the relationship between effort and result. An organization is most efficient when the maximum results are achieved with minimum effort. For example, fast-food restaurants are efficient in part because they transfer work usually done by employees to customers. For example, self-service drink centers allow customers to get refills on drinks while disguising the fact they are waiting on themselves. *Calculability* involves estimation based on probabilities. High calculability exists when the output, cost, and effort associated with products can be predicted. A McDonald's manager trains employees to make *each* Big Mac within a rigid time limit. *Predictabilty* pertains to consistency of results. Predictability exists when products turn out as planned. Big Macs are the same everywhere. *Control* is increased by replacing human activity with technology. McDonald's drink machines stop after a cup has been filled to its prescribed limit.

Because Ritzer believes that McDonald's restaurants reflect the rationalization process, he refers to the "McDonaldization" of society (1998). His sources of information include newspapers, books, magazines, and industry

According to George Ritzer, universities share some of the organizational characteristics of popular fast-food restaurants.

publications. Since many of you are now thinking about attending college, Ritzer's findings on the "McUniversity" should be of interest.

Increasingly, students and parents view a college degree as a necessity to compete successfully in the job market. "Shopping" for the right college requires many of the consumer skills used in making any major purchase. This consumer orientation, Ritzer asserts, can be seen on most college campuses in the United States. For example, students want education to be conveniently located and they want it open as long as possible each day. They seek inexpensive parking, efficient service, and short waiting lines. Students want high-quality service at the lowest cost. A "best buy" label in national academic rankings catches the attention of parents and students.

Public colleges and universities, Ritzer contends, are responding to this consumer orientation. They are doing so in part because government funding for higher education is becoming more scarce. To meet reduced funding, colleges and universities are cutting costs and paying more attention to "customers." For example, Ritzer points to student unions. Many of them are being transformed into mini-malls with fast-food restaurants, video games, and ATMs.

Ritzer predicts that a far-reaching, customer-oriented tactic will be to "McDonaldize" through new technology. The "McUniversity" will still have a central campus, but it will also have convenient satellite locations in community colleges, high schools, businesses, and malls. "Students will 'drop by' for a course or two. Parking lots will be adjacent to McUniversity's satellites (as they are to fast-food restaurants) to make access easy" (Ritzer, 1998: 156).

McDonaldization, Ritzer contends, will dehumanize the process of education. Most instructors at satellites will be part-timers hired to teach one or more courses. They will come and go quickly, so students will not have the opportunity to form relationships as with more permanent faculty members. In order to make the courses alike from satellite to satellite, course content, requirements, and materials will be highly standardized, losing the flavor individual professors bring to their classes. Students will not be able to choose a particular instructor for a course because there will be only one per satellite. Often, there may be no teacher physically present at all. More courses will be delivered by professors televised from distant places.

In spite of these predictions, colleges and universities will not be a chain of fast-food restaurants or a shopping mall, Ritzer concludes. Institutions of higher education will retain many traditional aspects, but there will undoubtedly be a significant degree of McDonaldization.

Working with the Research

1. Do you think the benefits of the "McUniversity" outweigh the disadvantages? Why or why not?

2. In what ways have American high schools been affected by McDonaldization? Give examples.

Du Bois used science and sociology to disprove racist assumptions about African Americans.

W.E.B. Du Bois focused on the question of race inside and outside the United States.

What were the contributions of W.E.B. Du Bois?

W.E.B. Du Bois (1868–1963), an African American educator and social activist, also influenced the early development of sociology in the United States. Du Bois attended an integrated high school in Great Barrington, Massachusetts, and was the first African American to receive a diploma there. He earned a doctorate degree from Harvard University in 1895 and taught at a number of predominantly black universities during his career.

Du Bois learned firsthand about racial discrimination and segregation when he attended Fisk University in Nashville, Tennessee, as an undergraduate student. Partly from this experience, and from teaching in rural, all-black schools around Nashville, Du Bois decided to attack the "Negro problem." This racist policy was based on the assumption that African Americans were an inferior race. Du Bois analyzed the sophisticated social structure of African American communities, first in Philadelphia and later in other places.

Du Bois's concern for his race did not stop at the borders of the United States—he was also active in the Pan African movement, which was concerned with the rights of all African descendants, no matter where they lived. While documenting the experience and contributions of African people throughout the world, Du Bois died in the African country of Ghana, at the age of ninety-five.

Section 2 Assessment

1. Define the term *positivism*.
2. Name and explain the theory of social change proposed by Herbert Spencer.
3. Give an example to illustrate Emile Durkheim's idea of organic solidarity.

Critical Thinking

4. **Evaluating Information** Max Weber introduced the concept of *verstehen*. How would you use this approach to social research if you wanted to investigate the importance of money to your peers? Explain.

Theoretical Perspectives

Section Preview

Sociology includes three major theoretical perspectives. Functionalism views society as an integrated whole. Conflict theory looks at class, race, and gender struggles. Symbolic interactionism examines how group members use shared symbols as they interact.

The Role of Theoretical Perspectives

Perception is the way the brain interprets an image or event. Similarly, perspective is the way you interpret the meaning of an image or event. Your perspective is influenced by beliefs or values you hold. It draws your attention to some things and blinds you to others. This is demonstrated in two drawings psychologists often use to illustrate the concept of perception. (See Figure 1.1.) If you stare at the old woman long enough, she becomes a beautiful young woman with a feather boa around her neck. If you stare at Figure 1.1b, it alternates between two facing profiles and a vase. You cannot, however, see the old woman and the young woman or the faces and the vase at the same time.

Which image is real depends on your focus—your perspective influences what you see. One perspective emphasizes certain aspects of an event, while another perspective accents different aspects of the same event. When a perspective highlights certain parts of something, it necessarily places other parts in the background.

What is a theoretical perspective?

A **theoretical perspective** is a set of assumptions about an area of study—in this case, about the workings of society. A theoretical perspective is viewed as true by its supporters and it helps them organize their research.

Competing, even conflicting, theories in science usually exist at the same time. Perhaps not enough evidence exists to determine which theory

Key Terms

- **theoretical perspective** *(p. 23)*
- **functionalism** *(p. 25)*
- **manifest functions** *(p. 26)*
- **latent functions** *(p. 26)*
- **dysfunction** *(p. 26)*
- **conflict perspective** *(p. 26)*
- **power** *(p. 27)*
- **symbol** *(p. 30)*
- **symbolic interactionism** *(p. 30)*
- **dramaturgy** *(p. 31)*

- **theoretical perspective**
  a set of assumptions accepted as true

a.   b.

Figure 1.1

These two famous images are used by psychologists to illustrate perception and perspective. What did you see first in Figure 1.1a—an old woman or a beautiful young lady? What did you see first in Figure 1.1b—a vase or two human faces?

A World Turned Upside Down

Without turning this book upside down, try to locate the United States. If you find this view of the world disorienting because you are used to conventional maps, you may reject this new worldview. So it is with any perspective. In this book you will be asked to abandon the conventional or psychological perspective in favor of the sociological perspective.

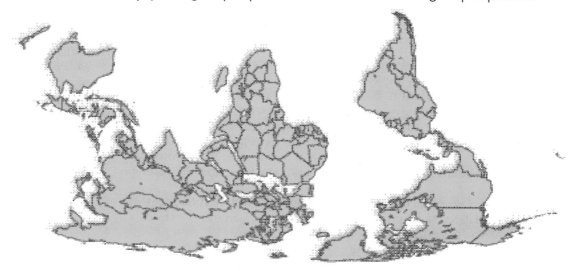

Interpreting the Map

1. What does your reaction to this map tell you about the power of the perspective you bring to a situation?

2. Look at world maps in your various social studies classes as you progress through the day. Where are North America and Europe located on these maps? What does that tell you about the perspective of these map publishers and their customers?

is accurate, or different theories may explain different aspects of the problem. This is even true in the so-called hard sciences like modern physics. Einstein's theory of general relativity, for example, contradicts the widely accepted Big Bang theory of the origin of the physical universe. Einstein himself never accepted the quantum theory. Nonetheless, this theory has become the foundation of modern developments in such fields as chemistry and molecular biology (Hawking, 2005). Today theories are being put forth that hold promise for combining relativity and quantum theory. If theories still compete in physics, it should not be surprising that several major theoretical perspectives exist in sociology.

Sociology has three overarching theoretical perspectives: *functionalism*, *conflict theory*, and *symbolic interactionism*. Each of these perspectives provides a different slant on human social behavior. The exclusive use of any one of them prevents our seeing other aspects of social behavior, just as one cannot see the old woman and the young woman at the same time. All three perspectives together, however, allow us to see most of the important dimensions of human social behavior.

Functionalism

Functionalism emphasizes the contributions (functions) of each part of a society. For example, family, economy, and religion are "parts" of a society. The family contributes to society by providing for the reproduction and care of its new members. The economy contributes by dealing with production, distribution, and consumption of goods and services. Religion contributes by emphasizing beliefs and practices related to sacred things.

● **functionalism**
approach that emphasizes the contributions made by each part of society

How does functionalism explain social change? Function-
alists see the parts of a society as an integrated whole. A change in one part of a society leads to changes in other parts. A major change in the economy, for example, may change the family—which is precisely what happened as a result of the Industrial Revolution. Before the Industrial Revolution, when most people made their living by farming, a large farm labor force was needed. Families fulfilled this need by having many children. The need disappeared as industrialization proceeded, and smaller families became the norm.

Functionalism assumes that societies tend to return to a state of stability after some upheaval has occurred. A society may change over time, but functionalists believe that it will return to a stable state. It will do this by changing in such a way that society will be similar to what it was before. Student unrest and other protests during the late 1960s illustrate this. The activities of protesters helped bring about some changes:

- Many Americans became suspicious of the federal government's foreign policy.
- Schools and universities became more responsive to students' needs and goals.
- Environmental protection became an important political issue to many Americans.

These changes, however, have not revolutionized American society. They have been absorbed into it. As a result, our society is only somewhat different from the way it was before the student unrest. In fact, most of the student radicals are now part of the middle-class society they once rejected.

Because of social and economic changes, norms that dictate women's roles have changed greatly over the years. Functionalists study how a change in one part of a society affects other parts.

manifest functions
intended and recognized consequences of an aspect of society

latent functions
unintended and unrecognized consequences of an aspect of society

dysfunction
negative consequence of an aspect of society

conflict perspective
approach emphasizing the role of conflict, competition, and constraint within a society

Do all functions have a positive effect? Most aspects of a society exist to promote a society's survival and welfare. It is for this reason that all complex societies have economies, families, governments, and religions. If these elements did not contribute to a society's well-being and survival, they would disappear.

Recall that a function is a contribution made by some part of a society. According to Robert Merton (1996), there are two kinds of functions. **Manifest functions** are intended and recognized. **Latent functions** are unintended and unrecognized. One of the manifest functions of school, for example, is to teach math skills. A latent (and positive) function of schools is the development of close friendships.

Not all elements of a society make a positive contribution. Elements that have negative consequences result in **dysfunction.** Dysfunctions of bureaucracies, for example, include rigidity, inefficiency, and impersonality. When you go to the division of motor vehicles to register your car or get your driver's license, the clerk may treat you like a "number" rather than as an individual. You don't like his bureaucratic inflexibility and impersonality.

How does functionalism view values? Finally, according to functionalism, there is a consensus on values. Most Americans, for example, agree on the desirability of democracy, success, and equal opportunity. This consensus of values, say the functionalists, accounts for the high degree of cooperation found in any society.

Conflict Perspective

The **conflict perspective** emphasizes conflict, competition, change, and constraint within a society (Giddens, 1987, 2005). Understanding the conflict perspective is easier when you understand functionalism, because the assumptions behind these two perspectives are the reverse of each other. This is shown in Figure 1.2 on the next page.

How does this photo emphasize the approach to studying society that is taken by the conflict perspective?

Figure 1.2 **Assumptions of the Major Theoretical Perspectives**

This table compares the most important assumptions of the functionalist, conflict, and symbolic interactionist perspectives. Do you believe, as the functionalists do, that society is relatively well integrated? Or do you support the conflict theorists' assumption that society experiences conflict on all levels?

Functionalism	Conflict Perspective	Symbolic Interactionism
1. A society is a relatively integrated whole. 2. A society tends to seek relative stability. 3. Most aspects of a society contribute to the society's well-being and survival. 4. A society rests on the consensus of its members.	1. A society experiences inconsistency and conflict everywhere. 2. A society is continually subjected to change. 3. A society involves the constraint and coercion of some members by others.	1. People's interpretations of symbols are based on the meanings they learn from others. 2. People base their interaction on their interpretations of symbols. 3. Symbols permit people to have internal conversations. Thus, they can gear their interaction to the behavior that they think others expect of them and the behavior they expect of others.

What is the role of conflict and constraint? Functionalists see a basic agreement on values within a society. This leads them to emphasize the ways people cooperate to reach common goals. The conflict perspective, in contrast, focuses on the disagreements among various groups in a society or between societies. Groups and societies compete as they attempt to preserve and promote their own special values and interests.

Supporters of the conflict perspective, then, see social living as a contest. Their central question is "Who gets what?" It is those with the most **power**—the ability to control the behavior of others—who get the largest share of whatever is considered valuable. Those with the most power have the most wealth, prestige, and privileges. Because some groups have more power than others, they are able to constrain, or limit, the less powerful.

● **power**
the ability to control the behavior of others

Sociology Looks at the Internet

The number of Americans paying for an on-line Internet service is skyrocketing. The Internet began as a way for military and scientific users to share information after a nuclear war. ARPAnet (the Internet's forerunner) was formed in 1969 with only four connected computers. By the end of 2004, more than 185 million Americans had access to the Internet. According to some estimates, the year 2005 will witness more than 1 billion Internet users worldwide.

Because of its rapid spread through American society, cyberspace technology is a timely example for showcasing the usefulness of the three theoretical perspectives. The viewpoints of functionalism, conflict theory, and symbolic interactionism contribute to an understanding of the social implications of this new technology in very different ways.

Functionalism. Functionalists see cyberspace technology as having both positive and negative consequences. On the one hand, computer links bring advantages. Parents can work at home and spend more time with their children. Individuals with disabilities can do jobs at home that would be denied them otherwise, thus becoming more fully integrated into society. On the other hand, there are dysfunctions. Young people may have easy access to pornographic material, which can distort their view of the opposite sex. Hate groups can be formed by strangers who live hundreds or thousands of miles apart. Their anonymity may encourage them to engage in antisocial or violent behavior that they would otherwise avoid.

Conflict Theory. The Internet is clearly changing American society. The Internet, conflict theorists point out, is contributing to the increasing speed of technological change. An advocate of conflict theory might investigate the social instability created by this rapid change. Workers may be let go by corporations in increasing numbers as more tasks are performed by computers.

Conflict theory could guide an investigation comparing the numbers of computers used in school districts of varying socioeconomic levels.

How does the conflict perspective explain social change?
Many conflicting groups exist in a society. As the balance of power among these groups shifts, change occurs. For example, the women's movement is attempting to change the balance of power between men and women. As this movement progresses, we see larger numbers of women in occupations once limited to men. More women are either making or influencing decisions in business, politics, medicine, and law. Gender relations are changing in other ways as well. More women are choosing to remain single, to marry later in life, to have fewer children, and to divide household tasks with their

Computer literacy is becoming an essential skill for obtaining a well-paying job. Thus, students who attend wealthy schools with access to computers have an advantage over students in poorer schools.

Symbolic Interactionism. Symbolic interactionists are interested in how the Internet can affect a child's social development. The popularity of cartoon characters on television is reinforced by Web pages that allow children to join fan clubs, interact with other fans, and view video clips of their favorite cartoon characters whenever they want. The popular cartoons *The Simpsons* and *South Park* feature children behaving in ways unacceptable in nearly all American homes. Television provides limited exposure to these characters, but the Internet allows them to become an important part of a child's daily life. What children come to accept as desirable behavior is being based increasingly on their interpretations of the symbols and behaviors represented by these characters. Symbolic interactionists might conclude that to the extent this occurs, the Internet lessens adult influence on children.

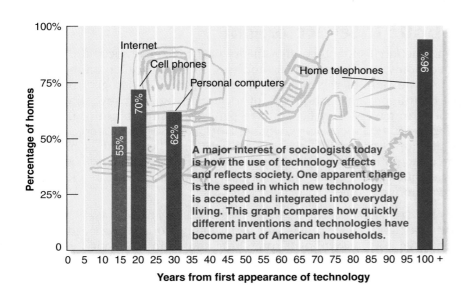

A major interest of sociologists today is how the use of technology affects and reflects society. One apparent change is the speed in which new technology is accepted and integrated into everyday living. This graph compares how quickly different inventions and technologies have become part of American households.

Analyzing the Trends

1. Which perspective would you choose to conduct an in-depth study of the Internet's effect on society? Explain why you chose this perspective.
2. Do you think that the Internet has some dysfunctions that Americans should consider? Consider the advantages and disadvantages of the Internet on society.

husbands. According to the conflict perspective, these changes are the result of increasing power among women.

Which perspective is better? There is no "better" theoretical perspective. Each perspective highlights certain areas of social life. The advantages of one perspective are the disadvantages of the other. Functionalism explains much of the consensus, stability, and cooperation within a society. The conflict perspective explains much of the constraint, conflict, and change. Each chapter, throughout the text, will illustrate both perspectives, as well as the perspective discussed next—*symbolic interactionism.*

According to conflict theory, the interests of groups will clash at times. If questioned, the men around the water cooler may offer a functionalist interpretation of their pastime—talking sports brings them together. Women who are not "sports savvy" may see their exclusion from such office talk more from a conflict perspective.

● **symbol**
anything that stands for something else and has an agreed-upon meaning attached to it

● **symbolic interactionism**
approach that focuses on the interactions among people based on mutually understood symbols

Symbolic Interactionism

Both functionalism and conflict theory deal with large social units, such as the economy, and broad social processes, such as conflict among social classes. At the close of the nineteenth century, some sociologists began to change their approach to the study of society. Instead of concentrating on large social structures, they began to recognize the importance of the ways people interact. Two sociologists, Charles Horton Cooley and George Herbert Mead, developed the insight that groups exist only because their members influence each other's behavior. These early American sociologists, in short, created symbolic interactionism, a perspective that focuses on the actual *interaction* among people.

What is the significance of symbols in symbolic interactionism?
To understand social interactionism, we need to talk first about symbols. A **symbol** is something chosen to represent something else. It may be an object, a word, a gesture, a facial expression, a sound. A symbol is something observable that often represents something not observable, something that is abstract. For example, your school's team mascot is often used as a symbol of school loyalty. The American flag is used as a symbol of the United States.

The meaning of a symbol is not determined by its own physical characteristics. Those who create and use the symbols assign the meanings to them. If people in a group do not share the same meanings for a given symbol, confusion results. For example, if some people interpreted the red light of a traffic signal to mean go, while others interpreted it to mean stop, chaos would result.

The importance of shared symbols is reflected in the formal definition of **symbolic interactionism.** It is the theoretical perspective that focuses on interaction among people—interaction based on mutually understood symbols.

What are the basic assumptions of symbolic interactionism?
Herbert Blumer (1969, 1986), who coined the term *symbolic interactionism,* outlined three assumptions central to this perspective. (Refer to Figure 1.2 on page 27.)

First, according to symbolic interactionism, we learn the meaning of a symbol from the way we see others reacting to it. For example, American musicians in Latin America soon learn that when audience members whistle at the end of a performance, they are expressing disapproval. In other words, their whistling is a symbol of disapproval, as booing is in the United States.

Second, once we learn the meanings of symbols, we base our behavior (interaction) on them. Now that the musicians have learned that whistling symbolizes a negative response, they will definitely avoid an encore if the crowd begins whistling. (They would likely have the opposite response in the United States, where the symbol of whistling has a very different meaning.)

Finally, we use the meanings of symbols to imagine how others will respond to our behavior. Through this capability, we can have "internal conversations" with ourselves. These conversations enable us to visualize how others will respond to us *before* we act. This is crucial because we guide our interactions with people according to the behavior we think others expect of us and we expect of others. Meanwhile, these others are also having internal conversations. The interaction (acting on each other) that follows is therefore *symbolic interaction*.

In an attempt to better understand human interaction, Erving Goffman introduced **dramaturgy**, which depicts human interaction as theatrical performance (Goffman, 1961a, 1963, 1974, 1979, 1983; Lemert and Branaman, 1997). Like actors on a stage, people present themselves through dress, gestures, tone of voice. Teenagers sometimes act in a particular way in order to attract the attention of someone they want to like them. Goffman calls this *presentation of self* or *impression management*.

● **dramaturgy**
approach that depicts human interaction as theatrical performances

According to symbolic interactionism, social life can be likened to a theatrical performance. Don't we convey as much about ourselves in the way we dress as do the actors above?

Section 3 Assessment

1. What is a theoretical perspective?

2. Indicate whether the following statements represent functionalism (F), the conflict perspective (C), or symbolic interactionism (S).

   a. Societies are in relative balance.

   b. Power is one of the most important elements in social life.

   c. Religion helps hold a society together morally.

   d. Symbols are crucial to social life.

   e. Many elements of a society exist to benefit the powerful.

   f. Different segments of a society compete to achieve their own self-interest rather than cooperate to benefit others.

   g. Social life should be understood from the viewpoint of the individuals involved.

   h. Social change is constantly occurring.

   i. Conflict is harmful and disruptive to society.

3. Does dramaturgy explain human interaction in a way that is meaningful to you? Why or why not?

Critical Thinking

4. **Analyzing Information** Analyze the causes of the looting incidents in New Orleans following Hurricane Katrina. Which of the three theoretical perspectives would you use to help you understand this behavior? Explain your choice.

Summary

Section 1: The Sociological Perspective

Main Idea: Sociology studies human social behavior. It assumes a group, rather than an individual, perspective. Sociologists look for the patterns in social relationships. Individuals can benefit by using their sociological imaginations to look at events in their personal lives.

Section 2: The Origins of Sociology

Main Idea: Sociology is a young science. It started with the writings of European scholars like Auguste Comte, Harriet Martineau, Herbert Spencer, Karl Marx, Emile Durkheim, and Max Weber. Jane Addams and W.E.B. Du Bois helped to focus America's attention on social issues. After World War II, America took the lead in developing the field of sociology.

Section 3: Theoretical Perspectives

Main Idea: Sociology includes three major theoretical perspectives. Functionalism views society as an integrated whole. Conflict theory looks at class, race, and gender struggles. Symbolic interactionism examines how group members use shared symbols as they interact.

Sociology Online

Self-Check Quiz
Visit the *Sociology and You* Web site at glencoe.com and click on **Chapter 1—Self-Check Quizzes** to prepare for the chapter test.

Reviewing Vocabulary

Complete each sentence using each term once.

a. mechanical solidarity
b. positivism
c. social structure
d. bourgeoisie
e. sociology
f. symbol
g. latent function
h. conflict perspective
i. presentation of self
j. theoretical perspective

1. _____ is a set of assumptions accepted as true by supporters.
2. The perspective that emphasizes conflict is called _____ .
3. _____ is an unintended and unrecognized consequence of some element of a society.
4. _____ is the way that people attempt to make a favorable impression of themselves in the minds of others.
5. The patterned interaction of people in social relationships is called _____ .
6. _____ is the study of social structure from a scientific perspective.
7. The use of observation, experimentation and other methods to study social life is known as _____ .
8. A _____ is something that stands for or represents something else.
9. _____ is social unity based on a consensus of values and norms, strong social pressure to conform and a dependence on family and tradition.
10. The _____ are members of an industrial society who own the means for producing wealth.

Reviewing the Facts

11. According to C. Wright Mills, what is the sociological imagination?
12. Explain "sociology" as defined in this chapter.

13. What did Herbert Spencer believe about the relationship between people, progress, and social change?

14. List and explain the three sociological perspectives.

15. What are manifest functions and latent functions? Provide an example of each.

16. Using the chart below, give a major idea expressed by each of the sociologists listed. Briefly explain each idea. The first one has been completed. Use this as your model and complete the chart.

Sociologist	Major Idea	Brief Explanation
Marx	class conflict	Struggle between bourgeoise class and the proletariat class
Weber		
Comte		
Durkheim		

"*Religion is the opium of the people, Fred.*" "*Just say no, Karl.*"

Thinking Critically

17. Applying Concepts

Give three examples of how the sociological perspective can be applied to your life.

18. Analyzing Information

Using your own words, define the term sociological imagination. What is the relationship to the sociological perspective?

19. Making Inferences

Select two early sociologists discussed in your text and construct a dialogue between them about the current social issue of homelessness.

20. Making Comparisons

Both a sociologist and a psychologist would be interested in the ACT (achievement) and SAT (assessment) test scores of high school students. Consider how the scientific interest of the sociologist would differ from that of the psychologist. Compare the similarities and contrast the differences.

21. Analyzing Information

In this chapter you read about Karl Marx. In the cartoon above, Marx is shown making a comment to "Fred" (Frederick Engels, his collaborator). Research this quote on the Web and then explain what Marx meant by it—and how the cartoonist is twisting its meaning.

Sociology Projects

22. Theoretical Perspectives

Based on what you read about the Internet from the functionalist, conflict, and symbolic interactionist perspectives, how is each perspective useful in understanding the popularity of the Internet? Write a brief statement describing how each perspective would approach this issue. You might see positive or negative effects, depending upon your interpretation. (For instance, the conflict perspective may focus on the fact that the underprivileged classes would not have full access because of the cost.)

23. Developing a Commercial

Develop a commercial for sociology using a video camera. Think of the field of sociology as a product to sell. Market it as "a way to improve your understanding of the world around you."

24. Observations

Go to a public place (such as a mass, school cafeteria, or restaurant) and discreetly observe people for 15 minutes. Write down your observations, noting such details as the type of dress, general interactions, and level of activity. Do not make value judgments, but restrict your notes to factual observations.

When you return home, rewrite your observations applying the sociological concepts in this chapter. Consider and list the ways your second analysis is different from the first. Compare and contrast them. How does sociology help to describe what you observed? What might you want to study from your observation?

25. Sociology and Careers

Research one of the career options for sociology majors that interest you. Look for such important information as the education requirements, income expectations, and management opportunities. Write a short report on the advantages and disadvantages of that particular career in sociology.

Technology Activities

26. In this chapter, you learned about several of the founders of sociology and their contributions to the field. To learn more about these sociologists and others, go to the Dead Sociologists Society Web page at www2.pfeiffer.edu/~Iridener/DSS/DEADSOC.HTML. Select three sociologists named on the Web site who were not included in the textbook and create a database including their year of birth, place of birth, and primary contributions they made to sociology.

27. Use the Internet to do further research on the pioneers of sociology. Design a poster representing the pioneers in sociology. Describe each one's basic ideas, including their theories and information attained through research. You may want to start your research at the Dead Sociologists Web page listed above.

28. In this chapter, the Tech Trends feature on pages 28–29 discusses the increasing use of the Internet from various sociology perspectives. If you were analyzing conflict theory on this issue, you might research data such as that presented in the table below.

As a technology activity, research additional measures for differences in the population in Internet access and how that has changed in recent years (for example, different age groups, or people in other countries around the world). Then create this table on a computer available to you and expand it, according to the categories you have researched.

How Internet Access Has Changed			
	2000	2002	2004
Access by Gender			
Male	51%	60%	66%
Female	46%	56%	61%
Access by Education Level			
No high school degree	17%	23%	32%
Some college	63%	72%	75%
College plus	75%	82%	88%
Access by Race/Ethnicity			
White	50%	60%	67%
Black	34%	45%	43%
Hispanic	43%	54%	59%

Source: *Time Almanac*, 2006

29. Use the Internet to contact the American Sociological Association and request the booklet "Majoring in Sociology." Using standard grammar, spelling, sentence structure, and punctuation, prepare a report for your class from the information. The URL is www.asanet.org.

Invitation to Sociology
by Peter L. Berger

- **demarcation**
  setting apart, separation

- **degradation**
  low esteem, corruption

- **conceptual construction**
  personal idea of reality

Read and React

How is this excerpt different in style from most articles by scientists? Why do you think the author chose this style to describe his field of study?

The sociologist . . . is a person intensively, endlessly, shamelessly interested in the doings of men. His natural habitat is all the human gathering places of the world, wherever men come together. The sociologist may be interested in many other things. But his consuming interest remains in the world of men, their institutions, their history, their passions. And since he is interested in men, nothing that men do can be altogether tedious for him. He will naturally be interested in the events that engage men's ultimate beliefs, their moments of tragedy and grandeur and ecstasy. But he will also be fascinated by the commonplace, the everyday. He will know reverence, but this reverence will not prevent him from wanting to see and to understand. He may sometimes feel revulsion or contempt. But this also will not deter him from wanting to have his questions answered. The sociologist, in his quest for understanding, moves through the world of men without respect for the usual lines of **demarcation.** Nobility and **degradation,** power and obscurity, intelligence and folly—these are equally interesting to him, however unequal they may be in his personal values or tastes. Thus his questions may lead him to all possible levels of society, the best and the least known places, the most respected and the most despised. And, if he is a good sociologist, he will find himself in all these places because his own questions have so taken possession of him that he has little choice but to seek for answers. . . .

The sociologist moves in the common world of men, close to what most of them would call real. As a result, there is a deceptive simplicity and obviousness about some sociological investigations. One reads them, nods at the familiar scene, remarks that one has heard all this before and concludes that people have better things to do than to waste their time on truisms—until one is suddenly brought up against an insight that radically questions everything one had previously assumed about this familiar scene. This is the point at which one begins to sense the excitement of sociology.

It can be said that the first wisdom of sociology is this—things are not what they seem. This . . . is a deceptively simple statement. It ceases to be simple after a while. Social reality turns out to have many layers of meaning. The discovery of each new layer changes the perception of the whole.

People who feel no temptation before closed doors, who have no curiosity about human beings, who are content to admire scenery without wondering about the people who live in those houses on the other side of that river, should probably . . . stay away from sociology. And people whose interest is mainly in their own **conceptual constructions** will do just as well to turn to the study of little white mice. Sociology will be satisfying, in the long run, only to those who can think of nothing more entrancing than to watch men and to understand things human.

Source: Excerpted from *Invitation to Sociology.* New York: Doubleday & Company, Inc., 1963.

Sociological Research Methods

Sections

1. **Research Methods**
2. **Causation in Science**
3. **Procedures and Ethics in Research**

Learning Objectives

After reading this chapter, you will be able to

- describe the basic quantitative and qualitative research methods used by sociologists.
- discuss basic research concepts, including variables and correlations.
- list the standards for proving cause-and-effect relationships.
- explain the steps sociologists use to guide their research.
- discuss ethics in sociological research.

Applying Sociology

People who know what questions to ask about a topic can protect themselves from acting on wrong information. In this chapter you will examine the basic ways that sociologists carry out the research to answer their questions. The chapter also discusses ethical issues that sometimes arise in doing research.

In the photo at left, a focus group is being conducted. A focus group represents one type of interviewing sociologists use to learn about social attitudes, ideas, and values. In a typical focus group, a small number of people who share a certain characteristic have an organized discussion on a topic. A facilitator or trained interviewer leads the discussion by asking predetermined questions.

For example, a group of Republicans might be gathered for questions about the direction of the Republican Party leadership. Or a group of farmers might be guided in a discussion of free trade. The group interaction can help sociologists gain many insights on a topic fairly quickly.

In this chapter you will read about several research methods sociologists use, including survey research, secondary analysis, the experiment, and the case study.

Sociology Online

Chapter Overview
Visit the *Sociology and You* Web site at glencoe.com and click on **Chapter 2—Chapter Overviews** to preview chapter information.

1

Research Methods

Key Terms

- survey *(p. 38)*
- population *(p. 39)*
- sample *(p. 39)*
- representative sample *(p. 39)*
- questionnaire *(p. 40)*
- interview *(p. 40)*
- closed-ended questions *(p. 40)*
- open-ended questions *(p. 41)*
- secondary analysis *(p. 42)*
- field research *(p. 42)*
- case study *(p. 42)*
- participant observation *(p. 42)*

Section Preview

When sociologists do quantitative research, they generally use either surveys or precollected data. Each has its own advantages and disadvantages. Qualitative research uses descriptive rather than numerical data. Field studies are best used when interaction needs to be observed in a natural setting, and when in-depth analysis is needed. The case study is the most popular approach to field research.

Doing Research in the Social Sciences

Like all scientists, sociologists gain their knowledge by doing research. The goal of sociological research is to test common sense assumptions and replace false ideas with facts and evidence. Part of the sociological perspective is to ask "why" and "how" questions and then to form hypotheses to arrive at accurate understandings.

Social scientists differ from other scientists, however, in how they conduct much of their research. Unlike chemists, biologists, or physicists, sociologists (and often psychologists) are very limited in their ability to set up laboratory experiments to replicate real-life conditions. Even if they reproduce conditions as they are in the outside world, the ethical issues involved in manipulating people and controlling events would prevent most sociologists from pursuing this kind of research. For sociologists, the world is their laboratory.

How then do sociologists do research? The methods that sociologists rely on are described below. These methods are classified as either *quantitative* or *qualitative*. Quantitative research uses numerical data, while qualitative research rests on narrative and descriptive data. Quantitative research tools include *surveys* and *precollected data*. About 90 percent of the research published in major sociological journals is based on surveys, so this approach is discussed first.

Survey Research

The **survey**, in which people are asked to answer a series of questions, is the most widely used research method among sociologists. It is ideal for studying large numbers of people.

- **survey**
  research method in which people respond to questions

The survey is the most widely used research method for collecting data in sociology.

OKAY, ONE FINAL QUESTION. "WHAT DO YOU GENERALLY THINK ABOUT POLLS?"

WELL, FRANKLY, I THINK THERE ARE TOO MANY OF THEM. ALSO, I THINK THEY OFTEN BECOME SELF-FULFILLING PROPHECIES. PEOPLE CAN'T HELP BUT BE INFLUENCED BY THEM.

ACTUALLY, MIKE, THAT'S SOMETHING OF A MISCONCEPTION. IN A RECENT POLL, 93% OF THE RESPONDENTS INDICATED THAT POLLS HAD NO EFFECT ON THEIR OPINIONS.

OH. WELL, I SUPPOSE I COULD BE WRONG..

WHY DON'T I JUST PUT YOU DOWN AS UNDECIDED?

Survey researchers must guard against affecting a respondent's answer.

How are effective surveys conducted?
In survey research, care must be taken that surveys are sent to the right number and type of people (Black, 1998; Wysocki, 2003). Researchers describe the people surveyed in terms of *populations* and *samples*.

A **population** is all those people with the characteristics a researcher wants to study. A population could be all high school seniors in the United States, all retired postal workers living in Connecticut, or the number of freshmen who buy school yearbooks.

Sociologists would like to collect information on all members of a population, but most populations are too large. Surveys including the entire population would cost too much and take too long for most research projects. Instead, a sample is drawn. A **sample** is a limited number of cases drawn from the larger population. A sample must be selected carefully if it is to have the same basic characteristics as the general population—that is, if it is to be a **representative sample.** If a sample is not representative of the population from which it is drawn, the survey findings cannot be used to make generalizations about the entire population. For example, if you were to conduct a survey using ten students from an advanced biology class, this sample would not be representative of your school. On the other hand, if you randomly selected ten students who walked into the school cafeteria for your survey, these students would probably be more representative of the student body. The sample would probably be too small, however, to give accurate results. The United States Census Bureau regularly uses sample surveys in its highly accurate work. The Gallup Poll and Harris Poll are recognized all over the country as reliable indicators of national trends and public opinion because they use representative samples in their surveys.

How are representative samples selected?
The standard way of getting a representative sample is by random, or chance, selection. A random sample can be selected by assigning each member of the population a number and then drawing numbers from a container after they have been thoroughly scrambled. An easier and more practical method uses a table of random numbers. After each member of the population has been assigned a number, the researcher begins with any number in the table and goes down the list until enough subjects have been selected.

population
a group of people with certain specified characteristics

sample
a group of people that represents a larger population

representative sample
a sample that accurately reflects the characteristics of the population as a whole

Sociology Online

Student Web Activity
Visit the So*ciology and You* Web site at glencoe.com and click on **Chapter 2—Student Web Activities** for an activity on survey research.

- **questionnaire**
  a written set of questions to be answered by a research participant

- **interview**
  a survey method in which a trained researcher asks questions and records the answers

- **closed-ended questions**
  questions a person must answer by choosing from a limited, predetermined set of responses

How is survey information gathered? In surveys, information is obtained through either a questionnaire or an interview. A **questionnaire** is a written set of questions that survey participants answer by themselves. In an **interview,** a trained interviewer asks questions and records the answers. Questionnaires and interviews may contain *closed-ended* or *open-ended* questions.

Closed-ended questions are those that a person answers by choosing from a limited, predetermined set of responses. Multiple choice questions are closed ended, for example. Because participants are limited to certain responses, closed-ended questions sometimes fail to uncover underlying attitudes and opinions. On the positive side, closed-ended questions make answers easier to tabulate and compare.

Please indicate whether you strongly agree, agree, disagree, or strongly disagree with each of the following statements.

Figure 2.1	Closed-ended and Open-ended Questions			
Examples of Closed-Ended Questions	Strongly Agree	Agree	Disagree	Strongly Disagree
a. Most schoolteachers really don't know what they are talking about.	1	2	3	4
b. To get ahead in life, you have to get a good education.	1	2	3	4
c. My parents encouraged me to get a good education.	1	2	3	4
d. School is a lonely place.	1	2	3	4
e. Too much emphasis is put on education these days.	1	2	3	4
f. Most students cheat on tests.	1	2	3	4

Examples of Open-Ended Questions

1. In your own words, please describe your view on the education you have received so far.

2. Do you think school adequately prepares you for employment? Why or why not?

In your own words, please describe the importance of education to you.

Figure 2.2 Closed-ended Survey Research

Advantages	Disadvantages
• Closed-ended answers can be more precisely measured.	• Surveys are expensive to produce and distribute.
• Responses can be easily compared.	• Responses are limited to preset answers.
• Statistical techniques can be used to make sense of the data.	• Many people don't respond to surveys, resulting in low cost effectiveness.
• A large number of responses can be collected.	• The way a question is stated may influence the answer given. (Negatively phrased questions are more likely to get a negative answer.)

Open-ended questions ask the person to answer in his or her own words. Answers to open-ended questions can reveal many attitudes. However, these answers are not easy to quantify or compare. Another problem may arise if an interviewer changes the meaning of questions by rephrasing them. The same question phrased in different ways can place the emphasis on different issues and evoke different responses.

● **open-ended questions**
questions a person is to answer in his or her own words

Secondary Analysis (Precollected Data)

Using precollected information—that is, information someone else has already gathered—is known as **secondary analysis.** It is a well-respected method of collecting data in sociology. In fact, the first sociologist to use statistics in a sociological study—Emile Durkheim—relied on precollected data. (See Focus on Research on page 56.)

● **secondary analysis**
using precollected information for data collection and research purposes

What are some sources for secondary analysis? Types of precollected data include government reports, company records, voting lists, prison records, and reports of research done by other social scientists.

The United States Census Bureau is one of the most important sources of precollected data for American sociologists. The Census Bureau collects information on the total population every ten years and conducts countless specific surveys every year. The census contains detailed information on such topics as income, education, race, sex, age, marital status, occupation, and death and birth rates.

Other government agencies also collect information that is of great value to sociologists. The U.S. Department of Labor regularly collects information on the nation's income and unemployment levels across a variety of jobs. The U.S. Department of Commerce issues monthly reports on various aspects of the economy.

Figure 2.3	Secondary Analysis	
Advantages		**Disadvantages**
• Precollected data provide sociologists with inexpensive, high-quality information.		• The existing information may not exactly suit the researcher's needs because it was gathered for a different reason.
• Existing sources of information permit the study of a topic over a long period of time. (With census data, for example, we can trace the changes in the relative income levels of African Americans and whites.)		• Sometimes precollected data are outdated.
• The researcher cannot influence answers because the data have been collected by others.		• Little may be known about collection methods. The people who first collected the data or the collection methods may have been biased.

Field Research

Qualitative research uses narrative or descriptive data rather than quantitative, numerical data. Some aspects of society can best be revealed by qualitative methods. Most of these methods fall under the heading of *field research*. **Field research** looks closely at aspects of social life that cannot be measured quantitatively and that are best understood within a natural setting. High school cliques and "jock" culture are examples of topics best studied by field research.

What is the most popular approach to field research? The most often used approach to field research is the **case study**—a thorough investigation of a single group, incident, or community. This method assumes that the findings in one case can be generalized to similar situations. The conclusions of a study on drug use in Chicago, for example, should apply to other large cities as well. It is the researcher's responsibility to point out the factors in the study that are unique and that would not apply to other situations.

When do case studies involve participant observation? In **participant observation,** a researcher becomes a member of the group being studied. A researcher may join a group with or without informing its members that he or she is a sociologist.

A compelling account of undercover participant observation appears in *Black Like Me,* a book written by John Howard Griffin (2003). Griffin, a white journalist, dyed his skin to study the life of African Americans in the South. Although he had previously visited the South as a white man, his experiences while posing as an African American were quite different.

Participant researchers sometimes do not keep their identities secret. Elliot Liebow studied disadvantaged African American males. Even though he was a white outsider, Liebow was allowed to participate in the daily activities of the men. He said, "The people I was observing knew that I was observing them, yet they allowed me to participate in their activities and take part in their lives to a degree that continues to surprise me" (Liebow, 1967:253).

• **field research**
research that takes place in a natural (nonlaboratory) setting

• **case study**
intensive study of a single group, incident, or community

• **participant observation**
a case study where the researcher becomes a member of the group being studied

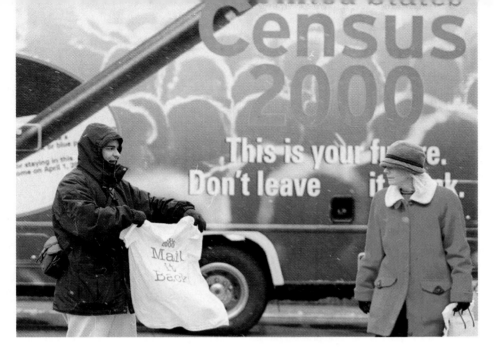

Every ten years the Constitution of the United States requires a count of the nation's population. The Census Bureau uses survey research techniques to create this statistical picture. Why do you think the Census Bureau asked Congress to authorize the use of sampling techniques?

Figure 2.4 **Investigating School Violence and School Funding**

This table illustrates the research method a sociologist of a particular theoretical persuasion would most likely choose to investigate school violence and school funding. Any of the three sociologists, of course, could use any of the three research methods.

Theoretical Perspective	Research Method	Approach to the Research Questions
Functionalism	Survey	A questionnaire on violence in high schools is sent to a national, random sample of principals. The survey examines a possible relationship between incidence of school violence and level of school funding.
Conflict Theory	Case Study	A particular high school with low funding is studied with respect to a relationship between school violence and school funding. Researchers interview administrators, teachers, and students. Findings are then generalized.
Symbolic Interactionism	Participant Observation	Concealing her identity, a researcher takes a temporary job at a high school with low funding. She attempts to observe covertly a possible link between school violence and school funding.

Scientists who conduct field research have a responsibility to follow a code of ethics that protects all of their subjects, animal or human.

Section 1 Assessment

Match terms a–e with statements 1–5.

    a. population
    b. representative sample
    c. random sample
    d. sample
    e. survey

1. selected on the basis of chance, so that each member of a population has an equal opportunity of being selected

2. all those people with the characteristics the researcher wants to study within the context of a particular research question

3. a limited number of cases drawn from the larger population

4. a sample that has basically the same relevant characteristics as the population

5. the research method in which people are asked to answer a series of questions

6. Provide an example of using precollected data.

7. For what reasons would you use participant observation instead of a survey?

Critical Thinking

8. Analyzing Information Would you consider the looters in New Orleans following Hurricane Katrina to be a representative sample of the disaster victims? If so, why? If not, why were some news reports presenting them as such?

9. Drawing Conclusions You are a sociologist who wants to see if receiving welfare benefits affects long-term job commitment. Describe the research method you would use. Why is the method you chose the best for this topic?

10. Synthesizing Information Suggest several areas in your school or community where field research could be used for a research project.

Figure 2.5 Summary of Research Methods

Research Method	Definition	Advantages	Disadvantages
Quantitative Methods			
Survey Research	People answer a series of questions, usually predetermined.	• Precision and comparability of answers • Use of statistical techniques • Information on large numbers of people • Detailed analysis	• Expensive due to large numbers • Low response rate • Phrasing of questions introduces bias in favor of certain answers • Researcher's behavior can affect answers given
Secondary Analysis	Information gathered by one researcher is used by another researcher for a different purpose.	• Inexpensive • Can study a topic over a long period of time • Researcher's influence on subjects avoided	• Information collected for a different reason may not suit another researcher's needs • Original researcher may have already introduced biases • Information may be outdated
Experiment	Research occurs in a laboratory setting with a minimum of contaminating influences (not often used in social research).	• Can be replicated with precision • Variables can be manipulated • Can be relatively inexpensive • Permits the establishment of causation (rather than just correlation)	• Laboratory environment is artificial • Not suited to most sociological research • Number of variables studied is limited
Qualitative Methods			
Case Study	Thorough investigation is done of a small group, incident, or community.	• Provides depth of understanding from group members' viewpoint • Unexpected discoveries and new insights can be incorporated into the research • Permits the study of social behavior not feasible with quantitative methods	• Difficult to generalize findings from one group to another group • Presence of researcher can influence results • Hard to duplicate • Takes lots of time • Difficult to be accepted as a group member (in case of participant observation)

Skills at a Glance

Using Basic Statistical Measures

Statistics are methods used for tabulating, analyzing, and presenting quantitative data. Sociologists, like all scientists, use statistical measures. You will encounter certain statistical measures in this textbook and in periodicals such as *Time, Newsweek,* or *The Economist*. Among the basic statistical measures are averages—including modes, means, and medians.

An *average* is a single number representing the distribution of several figures. For example, suppose the following figures are the salaries of the nine highest-paid major league baseball players:

$3,300,000 (catcher)
$3,600,000 (second base)
$3,600,000 (third base)
$4,200,000 (center field)
$4,300,000 (shortstop)
$4,500,000 (first base)
$4,900,000 (starting pitcher)
$5,300,000 (left field)
$6,100,000 (right field)

There are three kinds of averages that will make these numerical values more meaningful. Each gives a slightly different picture.

- The *mode* is the number that occurs most frequently. In this case, it is $3,600,000, which occurs twice. The mode is appropriate only when the objective is to indicate the most popular number. Suppose a researcher investigating these major league baseball salaries reported the mode alone. Readers would be misled, because the mode would give them no hint of the wide range of salaries ($3,300,000 to $6,100,000).

- The *mean* is the measure closest to the everyday meaning of the term *average*. It lies somewhere in the middle of a range. The mean of the salary figures above—$4,422,222—is calculated by adding all of the salaries together ($39,800,000) and dividing by the number of salaries (9). The mean, unlike the mode, takes all of the figures into account. It is distorted, however, by the highest figure, $6,100,000. Although one player earns $6,100,000, most players make considerably less—the highest-paid player earns nearly twice as much as the lowest-paid player. The mean is distorted when there are extreme values at either the high or the low end of a scale. The mean is more accurate when the high and low values are not widely separated.

The World Champion Boston Red Sox celebrate after winning the World Series. This win might result in salary increases for next year.

• The *median* is the number that divides a series of values in half. Half of the values lie above the median, half below. In this example, the median is $4,300,000. Half of the salaries are above $4,300,000, and half are below it. The advantage here is that the median is not distorted by extremes at either end. If the median falls between two numbers, the average of those two numbers becomes the median.

Working with Statistics

1. Cassie collected newspapers for a recycling plant at the rate of $2.30 per pound of paper. On consecutive days she turned in the following weights: 12 lbs., 13 lbs., 8 lbs., 22 lbs., 8.5 lbs., 13 lbs., and 19 lbs. What was her average pay per day? What was the median pay?

2. The grades on a student's sociology quizzes for a six-week period were 99 percent, 99 percent, 68 percent, 99 percent, 75 percent, and 80 percent. Determine the mean score, the mode, and the median score for that student.

Evaluating Internet Resources

The Internet is one of the most exciting research tools developed in the last century. It can put a library of the most current information at your fingertips. Like every tool, however, it is only as good as its operator. Reading the "instruction manual" and following a few basic "safely rules" will ensure that you get the best results from your online research efforts.

To determine if the site is a valid one, consider the source material. The questions on the following page will help you evaluate the reliability of the information. They will also let you deselect those sources (or articles) that are not particularly relevant to your needs.

WHO

- Who maintains the site? An established authority? An organization? A government?
- Who produced the information? Is he or she qualified, a noted authority? Are you sure?
- Has the site been reviewed, recommended, or given an award? By whom?
- Are there standards or selection criteria that must be met for information to be on this site?
- Can the webmaster be contacted by e-mail?

WHAT

- Is the information reliable?
- Is the information original?
- Is the information scholarly, professional, popular? Is there documentation?
- Is the site comprehensive? Are other sites more comprehensive?
- Does the site contain information, links to other sites, or both?

WHEN

- Is the information up-to-date? Are other sites more current?
- When was the site last updated? How often is the site updated?
- Do the links work?

WHERE

- From where was the information derived?
- Is the information based on personal opinion, experience, interviews, library research, questionnaires, or laboratory experiments?
- How did you access the information on the Internet (for example, web, ftp, telnet, listserv, newsgroup, e-mail)?

HOW

- How is the information presented? Is it presented clearly, accurately, and objectively?
- Is there distortion or bias in meaning?
- Is more than one viewpoint represented?
- Is the information modified in any way?

WHY

- Why is the information being presented?
- What is the purpose/motive? Is it easy to determine the purpose?
- Who is the intended audience?
- Does a sponsoring organization influence what is published here? Is there an e-mail or "snail mail" address to contact the organization?
- Does the information suit your purpose?

Applying Skills

Select a sociology-related Internet site. Evaluate it based on the criteria above.

Reading Tables and Graphs

Tables and graphs present information concisely. Figures 2.6 and 2.7 on the following page show the same information in two different formats. Use these figures to complete these steps for decoding tables and graphs.

1. Begin by reading the title of the table or graph carefully. It will tell you what information is being presented. What information is being presented in Figure 2.6?

2. Find out the source of information. You will want to know whether the source is reliable and whether its techniques for gathering and presenting data are sound. What is the source of the information in these figures? Is it a reliable source?

3. Read any notes accompanying the table or graph. Not all tables and graphs have notes, but if notes are present, they offer further information about the data. The notes in Figure 2.6 and in Figure 2.7 explain that the data refer to the total money earnings of full-time and part-time workers, aged 18 and over, in a March 2003 survey. Why is the note in this table important?

4. Examine any footnotes (marked with a superscript a). Footnotes in Figure 2.6 and Figure 2.7 indicate that the data are categorized by the highest degree actually completed. What other interpretation could be made from the term *educational attainment*?

5. Look at the headings across the top and down the left-hand side of the table or graph. To observe any pattern in the data, it is usually necessary to keep both types of headings in mind. Figure 2.6 and Figure 2.7 show the median annual earnings of African American and white males and females for several levels of education.

6. Find out what units are being used. Data can be expressed in percentages, hundreds, thousands, millions, billions, means, and so forth. Figure 2.6 and Figure 2.7 use two different units. What are they? When making comparison, it is important that you compare like units.

7. Check for trends in the data. For tables, look down the columns (vertically) and across the rows (horizontally) for the highest figures, lowest figures, repeat numbers, irregularities, and sudden shifts. If you read Figure 2.6 vertically, you can see how earnings vary by race and sex within each level of education. If you read the table horizontally, you can see how earnings vary with educational attainment for white males, African American males, white females, and African American females. What is the advantage of presenting this information as a graph, as in Figure 2.7? What is the disadvantage of using a graph?

8. Draw conclusions from your own observations. Looking carefully at these figures, write a narrative paragraph that summarizes your conclusions based on the data presented in these figures.

Figure 2.6
Median Earnings in Dollars

Demographic group	Overall median earnings	Median earnings in dollars as compared with education attainment[a]				
		<HS degree	HS or GED	Associate's degree	Bachelor's degree	Master's degree
White males	34,176	18,447	30,174	39,239	51,160	62,460
African American males	26,807	15,727	25,095	35,945	41,664	51,146
White females	22,639	11,508	19,483	26,313	32,003	42,447
African American females	21,548	12,268	18,036	25,068	35,107	41,553

Note: These figures include the total money earnings of full-time and part-time workers, ages 18 and over, surveyed as of March 2003.

[a] In terms of highest degree completed.

Figure 2.7
Median Annual Earnings by Gender, Race, and Education

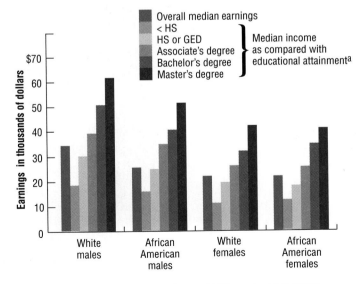

Note: These figures include the total money income of full-time and part-time workers, ages 18 and over, surveyed as of March 2003.

[a] In terms of highest degree completed.

Source: U.S. Bureau of the Census.

2

Causation in Science

Key Terms

- causation *(p. 50)*
- multiple
  causation *(p.50)*
- variable *(p. 51)*
- quantitative
  variable *(p. 51)*
- qualitative
  variable *(p. 51)*
- independent
  variable *(p. 52)*
- dependent
  variable *(p. 52)*
- intervening
  variable *(p. 52)*
- correlation *(p. 52)*
- spurious
  correlation *(p. 53)*

- **causation**
  the belief that events
  occur in predictable ways
  and that one event leads
  to another

- **multiple causation**
  the belief that an event
  occurs as a result of
  several factors working
  in combination

Section Preview

Causation in science is the idea that one event leads to another event. Scientists assume that all events have causes, or determinants. Social events are so complex, however, that many factors may be identified as causes. Three standards must be met before causation can be proved.

The Nature of Causation

Scientists assume that an event occurs for a reason. According to the concept of **causation,** events occur in predictable, nonrandom ways. One event leads to another. Why does this book remain sitting on your desk rather than rising slowly, going past your eyes, and resting against the ceiling? Why does a ball thrown into the air return to the ground? Why do the planets stay in orbit around the sun? Today, the main goal of scientists is to discover the factors that cause events to happen. Social scientists look for the factors that cause social events to happen.

Why do sociologists look for multiple causes? Leo Rosten, a twentieth-century novelist, once wrote, "If an explanation relies on a single cause, it is surely wrong." Social events are generally too complex to be explained by any single factor. The concept of **multiple causation** states that an event occurs as a result of several factors working in combination. What, for example, causes crime? Cesare Lombroso, a nineteenth-century Italian criminologist, mistakenly believed that the tendency to commit crimes was inherited. Criminals, he thought, could be identified by certain physical traits such as large jaws or receding foreheads. Modern criminologists have shown that many factors contribute to crime, including peer pressure, the use of drugs, hopeless poverty, and poor parenting. Each of these single factors is called a *variable.*

What is the cause and effect in this interaction?

World View

The Wired World

This map shows the number of telephone mainlines per thousand people for 2002. This data is an example of a quantitative variable.

Projected Number of Telephone Mainlines per 1,000 People

- 600 and above
- 450–599
- 300–449
- 150–299
- 1–149
- No data

North America

Europe

Asia

Africa

South America

Australia

Source: United Nations Development Programme, 2004.

Interpreting the Map

1. Explain why the data in this map constitutes a quantitative variable.
2. What would need to be done with the data to make it a qualitative variable?
3. If you were using telephone mainlines per 1,000 people in research, would it likely be a dependent or independent variable?

Variables and Correlations

A **variable** is a characteristic—such as age, education, or occupation—that is subject to change. Variables can be *quantitative* or *qualitative, independent* or *dependent.*

How do variables differ? Some materials have greater density than others. Some people have higher incomes than others. The literacy rate is higher in developed countries than in developing countries. Each of these characteristics is a **quantitative variable,** a variable that can be measured and given a numerical value.

In contrast, a **qualitative variable** is identified by membership in a category. It is an "either/or" or a "yes/no" variable. Sex, marital status, and group membership are three qualitative variables often used by sociologists. People are either male or female; they are married or unmarried; they are band members, football players, sophomores—or they are not.

● **variable**
a characteristic that is subject to change

● **quantitative variable**
a characteristic that can be measured numerically

● **qualitative variable**
a characteristic that is defined by its presence or absence in a category

- **independent variable**
  a characteristic that causes something to occur

- **dependent variable**
  a characteristic that reflects a change

- **intervening variable**
  a variable that changes the relationship between an independent and a dependent variable

- **correlation**
  a measure of the relationship between two variables

When they conduct studies, sociologists and other scientists identify the qualitative and quantitative variables to investigate. They then define these variables as either independent or dependent. The **independent variable** in a study is the variable that causes something to occur. The researcher changes, or looks for changes, in this variable. The **dependent variable** is what results from the change in the independent variable. For example, you might look at the time spent studying for a test as an independent variable that could cause a change in a grade—a dependent variable. The independent variable of poverty is one of several independent variables that can produce a change in the dependent variable of hunger. Whether a variable is dependent or independent can change depending on the situation. The extent of hunger may be a dependent variable in a study of poverty; it may be an independent variable in a study of crime.

An **intervening variable** influences the relationship between an independent and a dependent variable. The existence of a government support program, for example, may intervene between poverty and hunger. If a strong safety net exists, for instance, very poor parents and their children may experience no more hunger than those in the working class. Poverty is the cause of hunger but does not have to be if government intervention in the form of income and food exists. The poor *without* a safety net will experience more hunger. The poor *with* a safety net will not.

What is a correlation? A **correlation** is simply a measure of how things are related to one another. When a change in a trait, behavior, or an event (independent variable) is tied to a change in another trait, behavior, or event (dependent variable), a correlation exists. The correlation may be positive or negative.

A *positive correlation* exists if both the independent variable and the dependent variable change in the same direction. A positive correlation exists if we find that grades (dependent variable) improve as study time increases (independent variable). (See Figure 2.8.)

Figure 2.8 Positive and Negative Correlations

In a positive correlation, increases in the independent variable are associated with increases in the dependent variable. Grades improve with time spent studying.

In a negative correlation, increases in the independent variable are associated with decreases in the dependent variable. Grades decrease as time spent watching television increases.

Positive Correlation

Time spent studying (independent variable)

Grades (dependent variable)

Negative Correlation

Time spent watching television (independent variable)

Grades (dependent variable)

"In the social sciences we hardly use numbers, but we can write long, complicated sentences."

The man in this cartoon believes social science research is not very scientific. What do you think?

In a *negative correlation,* the variables change in opposite directions. An increase in the independent variable is linked to a decrease in the dependent variable. A negative correlation exists if we find that grades (dependent variable) go down as time spent watching television (independent variable) increases.

It is very important to remember that the existence of a correlation does not necessarily mean a cause-and-effect relationship exists. People with long arms often have long legs. However, the length of a person's arms does not cause the legs to grow longer. Both of these variables are controlled by other factors. It is much easier to show a correlation between two variables than it is to show causation.

Standards for Showing Causation

In a causal relationship, one variable actually causes the other to occur. Three standards are commonly used to determine causal relationships. Let's look at the example of church attendance and juvenile delinquency.

- **Standard 1:** *Two variables must be correlated.* Some researchers found that juvenile delinquency increases as church attendance declines—a negative correlation. Does this negative correlation mean that not attending church causes higher delinquency? To answer this question, the second standard of causality must be met.

- **Standard 2:** *All other possible factors must be taken into account.* The fact that two events are correlated does not mean that one causes the other. The negative correlation between church attendance and delinquency occurs because age is related to both church attendance (older adolescents attend church less frequently) and delinquency (older adolescents are more likely to be delinquents). In fact, the correlation between lower church attendance and delinquency is known as a **spurious correlation**—an apparent relationship between two variables that is actually caused by a third variable affecting both of the other variables. Thus, before we can predict that a causal relationship exists between church attendance and delinquency, we need to take other factors into consideration. In this instance, the age variable reveals that the relationship between church attendance and

- **spurious correlation**
  a relationship between two variables that is actually caused by a third factor

Reason and Science

Seventeenth-century Europe was an exciting place for those interested in using scientific methods in the search for truth. Copernicus was an astronomer who held that the sun was at the center of the solar system. Traditional belief at the time placed the earth at the center. Galileo sought to replace traditional myths with new knowledge based on reason and observation. This is one essential aspect of the scientific method.

In 1609, . . . Galileo turned his recently constructed telescope to the heavens, and through his

startling observations made available to astronomy the first qualitatively new evidence it had known since the ancients. And each of his observations— the craters and mountains on the surface of the Moon, the moving spots on the Sun, the four moons revolving around Jupiter, the phases of Venus, the "unbelievably" numerous individual stars of the Milky Way— was interpreted by Galileo as powerful evidence in favor of the Copernican heliocentric [sun-centered] theory.

. . . Many individuals not previously involved in scientific studies now took up the telescope and saw for themselves the nature of the new Copernican universe. Astronomy, by virtue of the telescope and Galileo's compelling writings, became of vital interest to more than specialists. Successive generations of late Renaissance and post-Renaissance Europeans, increasingly willing to doubt the absolute authority of traditional doctrines both ancient and ecclesiastical, were finding the Copernican theory not only plausible but liberating. A new celestial world was opening up to the Western mind, just as a new terrestrial world was being opened by the global explorers.

Source: Excerpted from *The Passion of the Western Mind.* Copyright, © 1993 by Richard Tarnas. Reprinted by permission of Ballantine Books, a Division of Random House, Inc.

Thinking It Over

1. Can you analyze two important effects that the scientific revolution fueled by Galileo has had on individual behavior in the West?

2. How did Galileo employ the sociological imagination in his work?

delinquency is not a causal one. Finding hidden causes and exposing spurious correlations is one of the greatest challenges in scientific research.

- **Standard 3:** *A change in the independent variable must occur before a change in the dependent variable can occur.* This means that the cause must occur before the effect. Do people stop attending church before they become delinquents? Or does delinquent behavior occur before people stop attending church? Or do these variables appear at the same time? Even if age were not a factor in this correlation and no other factor could be found, causality between these two variables still could not be established since it cannot be determined which occurs first.

Figure 2.9
A Spurious Correlation
As you read on page 53, the correlation between juvenile delinquency and not attending church is a spurious correlation.

Section 2 Assessment

Match terms a–i with the numbered statements below.

a. causation
b. multiple causation
c. variable
d. quantitative variable
e. qualitative variable
f. independent variable
g. dependent variable
h. correlation
i. spurious correlation

1. something that occurs in varying degrees
2. the variable in which a change or effect is observed
3. a change in one variable associated with a change in another variable
4. the idea that an event occurs as a result of several factors operating in combination
5. a factor that causes something to happen
6. the idea that the occurrence of one event leads to the occurrence of another event
7. a factor consisting of categories
8. when a relationship between two variables is actually the result of a third variable
9. a variable measured in numerical units

Critical Thinking

10. **Making Comparisons** In your own words, explain the difference between correlations and causation. Illustrate each with an example not found in the text.

Focus on Research

Secondary Analysis: A Model for Research

Emile Durkheim was the first person to be formally recognized as a sociologist. (See p. 17 for more on this pioneer.) He was also the most scientific of the pioneers. Durkheim conducted a study that stands as a classic research model for sociologists today. His investigation of suicide was, in fact, the first sociological study to use statistics. In Suicide (1964, originally published in 1897), Durkheim argued that some aspects of human behavior—even something as personal as suicide—can be explained on the societal level, without reference to individuals.

To carry out his secondary analysis, Durkheim used precollected data from the government population reports of several countries. Much of it was from the French government statistical office. He collected data for approximately 26,000 suicides and classified them by age, sex, marital status, whether there were children in the family, religion, location, time of year, method of suicide, and other factors. (And all this before there were computers!) As he gathered his data, he continually refined and adjusted his hypotheses.

Durkheim wanted to see if suicide rates were related to how socially involved individuals felt. He identified three suicide types in his study: egoistic, altruistic, and anomic.

He hypothesized that *egoistic* suicide increases when individuals do not have sufficient social ties. For example, he proposed that adults who never married and were not heavily involved with family life were more likely to commit suicide than married adults.

He also predicted that *altruistic* suicide was more likely to occur when social ties are too strong. The mass suicides of cult members is one example. Military personnel trained to lay down their lives for their countries (such as Japanese kamikaze pilots) is another illustration.

Durkheim also thought that *anomic* suicide increased when existing social ties were broken. For example, suicide rates spike during economic depressions. People suddenly without jobs are more prone to kill themselves. Suicide may also increase during periods of prosperity. People may loosen their social ties by taking

Map A
Suicide Rates for the Year 2002

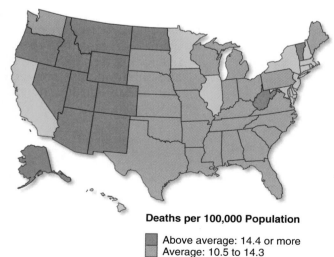

Deaths per 100,000 Population

- Above average: 14.4 or more
- Average: 10.5 to 14.3
- Below average: 10.4 or fewer

Source: *National Vital Statistics Reports,* from the Centers for Disease Control and Prevention, 2005.

Map B
People Per Square Mile

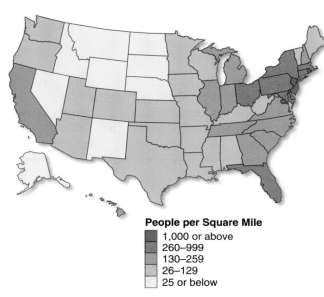

People per Square Mile
- 1,000 or above
- 260–999
- 130–259
- 26–129
- 25 or below

Source: U.S. Census Bureau, *Statistical Abstract of the United States: 2004–2005.*

new jobs, moving to new communities, or finding new mates.

Durkheim found strong support for his predictions. Suicide rates were higher among unmarried than married people and among military personnel than civilians. They were also higher among people involved in nationwide economic crises.

As a result of his study, Durkheim drew several important conclusions. First, social behavior can be explained by social rather than psychological factors. Second, suicide is affected by the closeness of social ties. Finally, society can be studied scientifically, and sociology is worthy of academic recognition (Ritzer, 1996).

Working with the Research

1. Emile Durkheim's study of suicide suggested that one factor in the suicide rate is the degree to which the individual has group ties. One indication of social ties is population density. Based on Map B, where would you expect to find the highest suicide rates in the United States? Does Map A agree with your predictions?

2. Durkheim noted that "psychological explanations are insufficient when analyzing social behavior." In your own words, tell what this statement means.

3. Which perspective do you think Durkheim followed in his study of suicide: the functionalist, the conflict, or the symbolic interactionist? Give reasons for your answer.

4. Using what you have learned from Durkheim's research, formulate a hypothesis about mass suicide.

Procedures and Ethics in Research

Key Terms

- scientific method *(p. 58)*
- hypothesis *(p. 58)*

● **scientific method**
the recognition and formulation of a problem, the collection of data through observation and experiment, and the formulation and testing of hypotheses

● **hypothesis**
testable statement of relationships among variables

Section Preview

The research process is made up of several distinct steps. These steps represent an ideal. It is not always necessary or even possible that they be strictly followed. Researchers have an ethical obligation to protect participants' privacy and to avoid deceiving or harming them. Preserving the rights of subjects must be weighed against the value of the knowledge to be gained.

Steps for Doing Research

Scientists use a research model known as the **scientific method.** It involves the pursuit of knowledge in a systematic way. As shown in Figure 2.10 on the following page, the steps in the scientific method include identifying a problem, reviewing the literature, formulating hypotheses, developing a research design, collecting data, analyzing data, and stating findings and conclusions.

1. **Identify the Problem.** Researchers begin by choosing an object or topic for study. Most topics are chosen because they interest the researcher, address a social problem, test a major theory, or respond to a government agency's or organization's needs.

2. **Review the Literature.** Once the object or topic of study has been identified, the researcher must find out all he or she can about any earlier research. This process is called a *literature search.* For example, a sociologist investigating suicide will probably develop an approach related to the classic study of suicide by Emile Durkheim, as well as to the work of other sociologists who have since researched the topic.

3. **Formulate Hypotheses.** The next step is to develop a *hypothesis* based on what is known. A **hypothesis** is a testable statement of relationships among well-defined variables. One hypothesis might be, "The longer couples are married, the less likely they are to divorce." The independent variable is length of marriage, and the dependent variable is divorce.

4. **Develop a Research Design.** A research design states the procedures the researcher will follow for collecting and analyzing data. Will the study be a survey or a case study? If it is a survey, will data be collected from a cross-section of an entire population, such as the Harris and Gallup polls, or will a sample be selected from only one city? Will simple percentages or more sophisticated statistical methods be used? These and many other questions must be answered so the researcher will have a sound plan to follow.

5. **Collect Data.** There are three basic ways of gathering data in sociological research—asking people questions, observing behavior, and analyzing existing materials and records. Sociologists studying interracial marriages could question couples about ways they communicate. They could locate an organization with many interracially married couples and observe couples'

behavior. Or they could compare the divorce rate among interracially married couples with the divorce rate of the population as a whole.

6. **Analyze Data.** Once the data have been collected and classified, they can be analyzed to determine whether the hypotheses are supported. It is not unlike putting together pieces of a jigsaw puzzle. This is not as easy or automatic as it sounds, because results are not always obvious. Because the same data can be interpreted in several ways, judgments have to be made. Guarding against personal preferences for particular outcomes is especially important in this phase of research.

7. **State Findings and Conclusions.** After analyzing the data, a researcher is ready to state the conclusions of the study. It is during this phase that the methods are described (for example, survey, case study) and hypotheses are formally accepted, rejected, or modified. By making the research procedures public, scientists make it possible for others to duplicate the research, conduct a slightly modified study, or go in a very different direction.

Realistically, do sociologists follow these steps? Some sociologists believe that this research model is too rigid to be used in studying human society. Even though most sociologists do follow the model, they do not necessarily follow it mechanically. They may conduct exploratory studies prior to stating hypotheses and developing research designs. Or they may change their hypotheses and research designs as their investigations proceed.

THE RESEARCH PROCESS

STEP 7: Stating findings and conclusions
STEP 6: Analyzing data
STEP 5: Collecting data
STEP 4: Developing a research design
STEP 3: Formulating hypotheses
STEP 2: Reviewing the literature
STEP 1: Identifying a problem

Figure 2.10
Steps in the Research Process

Ethics in Social Research

Research is a distinctly human activity. Although there are principles for conducting research, such as objectivity and verifiability, scientists sometimes fail to live up to these principles. At times, even the ethics of research is not honored by researchers.

Unfortunately, there is a long list of examples of ethical lapses in medical research. During the Nuremberg trials, 16 Nazi doctors were convicted of conducting sadistic experiments on concentration camp inmates. From 1932 to 1972, the Public Health Service of the U.S. government deliberately did not treat 399 syphilitic African American agricultural workers and day laborers so that biomedical researchers could study the full evolution of the disease (Jones, 1993). For twenty years, researchers at Germany's University of Heidelberg used human corpses, those of adults and children, in high-speed automobile crash tests (Fedarko, 1993). Federal investigators in the United States have documented over ten years of fraud in some of the most important breast cancer research ever done (Crewdson, 1994).

Several social scientists, also, have been criticized for conducting research considered unethical. In each case, subjects were placed in stressful situations without being informed of the true nature of the experiments (See pages 144 and 188 for a discussion of two of these studies).

More often, however, sociologists routinely protect the rights of research subjects and avoid deceiving or harming them. For example, Mario Brajuha, a graduate student at a major American university, kept detailed field notes while doing a participant observation study of restaurant work (Brajuha and Hallowell, 1986).

It is generally thought that using human corpses in automobile crash tests is unethical. Do you agree?

TECH TRENDS

Has Technology Made Privacy Obsolete?

A recent episode of NBC's *Today* show featured a segment about a Louisiana woman whose male neighbor had secretly installed video cameras in her bedroom and bathroom. Because of the cameras, the neighbor was able to secretly observe this woman in her most private moments. While researchers have been observing subjects for many years, it is alarming that this immoral and extremely illegal use of technology is now within the financial range and technical ability of many people.

Some sociologists and psychologists are concerned about the ethics of videotaping research subjects. One of the requirements of the Code of Ethics of the American Sociological Association (see Appendix) is to protect the privacy of research subjects. Imagine, then, that a sociologist came to your school to conduct research and asked permission to place video cameras in the hallways, classrooms, and cafeteria. Do you think that permission from school administrators would meet this requirement? What if every student in the school gave permission for the cameras? How would you feel if you gave your permission, but then did something really silly or wrong in front of one of the cameras?

Lawsuits have been filed in some states by workers after discovering that their employers had installed hidden cameras in rest rooms or changing

rooms to reduce high levels of employee theft. Managers claim that dishonest employees often use these areas to hide company products in their purses or bags. Workers argue that they are entitled to expect a minimum level of privacy and that hidden cameras violate that expectation. But, objects management, if workers know the cameras are there, they won't be caught. Similarly, if researchers begin videotaping with the consent of their subjects, will they get a true record of behavior? If they do not advise their subjects of the taping, what happens if a criminal act is recorded? Do the researchers have an obligation to release the tape to the authorities? Ethical issues will continue to arise as technology allows investigators to invade new areas.

Analyzing the Trends

Develop an argument for or against the use of video equipment in a sociological research project. Be sure to use logical arguments and evaluate the issues of maximizing benefits to society while minimizing the harms sociological work might create.

Because of suspected arson at a restaurant where Brajuha was employed as a waiter, his field notes became an object of interest to the police, the district attorney, the courts, and some suspects. For two years, he refused to reveal the contents of his field notes to the police. He did so in the face of a subpoena, the threat of imprisonment, and possible harm to himself, his wife, and his children. Brajuha was protecting the privacy rights of those individuals described in his notes.

What is sociology's code of ethics? Conducting ethical research means showing objectivity; using superior research standards; reporting findings and methods truthfully; and protecting the rights, privacy, integrity, dignity, and freedom of research subjects. The American Sociological Association has published guidelines for conducting research. (This code has been reproduced in full in the Appendix of this text.) Briefly put, the Code of Ethics is concerned with getting the greatest possible benefit with the least possible harm.

Can researchers act ethically and still get the information they need? Sometimes acting ethically is difficult. The researcher must sometimes make hard decisions about morally questionable issues, such as the situation in which Mario Brajuha found himself. Moreover, the researcher must balance the interests of those being studied against the need for accurate, timely data. Balance is the key to the issue of ethics. At the least, the people involved in sociological research should be protected from social, financial, or psychological damage or legal prosecution.

Section 3 Assessment

1. The steps below describe a research project on children without brothers or sisters ("only" children). Put steps a–g in order of how they would occur according to the steps in the research process.

   a. A researcher reads many articles about theory and research on the intelligence level of only children.

   b. From previous research and existing theory, a researcher states that only children appear to be more intelligent than children with siblings.

   c. A researcher collects data on only children from a high school in a large city.

   d. A researcher writes a report giving evidence that only children are more intelligent than children with brothers or sisters.

   e. A researcher decides to study the intelligence level of only children.

   f. A researcher classifies and processes the data collected in order to test a hypothesis.

   g. A researcher decides on the data needed to test a hypothesis, the methods for data collection, and the techniques for data analysis.

Critical Thinking

2. **Drawing Conclusions** What issues in studying society might interfere with following the scientific method precisely?

3. **Analyzing Information** Can secret observation of people ever be considered ethical? Why or why not?

Sociology Today

Should You Believe Everything You Read?

It is sometimes said that we are living in the "age of instant information." One unfortunate side effect is the tendency for studies and research results to be reported in the media without background or explanation. There are, however, some easy steps you can follow that will make you a savvy consumer in the information marketplace.

Be Skeptical. Be suspicious of what you read. The media sound-bite treatment tends to sensationalize and distort information. For example, the media may report that $500,000 was spent to find out that love keeps families together. In fact, this may have been only one small part of a larger research project. Moreover, chances are the media have oversimplified even this part of the researcher's conclusions.

Consider the Source of Information. The credibility of a study may be affected by who paid for the results. For example, you should know whether a study on the relationship between cancer and

tobacco has been sponsored by the tobacco industry or by the American Cancer Society. Suppose that representatives of tobacco companies denied the existence of any research linking throat and mouth cancer with snuff dipping. Further suppose that an independent medical researcher concluded that putting a "pinch between your cheek and gum" has led to cancer in humans. The self-interest of the tobacco companies taints their objectivity.

At the very least, you want to know the source of information before making a judgment. This caution is especially relevant to Internet research. Because Internet information varies widely in its accuracy and reliability, sources must be evaluated with great care.

Do Not Mistake Correlation for Causation. Remember that a correlation between two variables does not mean that one caused the other. At one time, the percentage of Americans who smoked was increasing at the same time that life expectancy was increasing. Did this mean that smoking caused people to live longer? Actually, a third factor—improved health care—accounted for the change. Do not assume that two events are related causally just because they occur together.

Doing Sociology

Bring to class an article reporting on a study. These can often be found in news magazines. Be prepared to explain how these three safeguards apply to the article's report.

Summary

Section 1: Research Methods

Main Idea: When sociologists do quantitative research, they generally use either surveys or precollected data. Each has its own advantages and disadvantages. Qualitative research uses descriptive rather than numerical data. Field studies are best used when interaction needs to be observed in a natural setting and when in-depth analysis is needed. The case study is the most popular approach to field research.

Section 2: Causation In Science

Main Idea: Causation in science is the idea that one event leads to another event. Scientists assume that all events have causes, or determinants. Sociologists work to discover these causes. Three standards must be met before causation can be proved.

Section 3: Procedures and Ethics In Research

Main Idea: The research process is made up of several distinct steps. These steps represent an ideal. It is not always necessary or even possible that they be strictly followed. Researchers have an ethical obligation to protect participants' privacy and to avoid deceiving or harming them. Preserving the rights of subjects must be weighed against the value of the knowledge to be gained.

Chapter Overview
Visit the *Sociology and You* Web site at glencoe.com and click on **Chapter 2—Self-Check Quizzes** to prepare for the chapter test.

Reviewing Vocabulary

Complete each sentence using each term once.

a. causation
b. code of ethics
c. correlation
d. dependent variable
e. field research
f. independent variable
g. multiple causation
h. qualitative variable
i. quantitative variable
j. representative sample
k. scientific method
l. secondary analysis

1. A variable that can be measured and given a numerical value is called a _____ .
2. _____ states that an event occurs as a result of several factors working in combination.
3. The use of existing information as a method of collecting data best describes _____ .
4. A random sample that accurately reflects the whole population is called a _____ .
5. The _____ is a research principle that is concerned with achieving the greatest possible benefit with the least possible harm.
6. The idea that events occur in predictable ways, with one event leading to another, is called _____ .
7. _____ is a measure of how things are related to one another.
8. _____ is a variable identified by membership in a category.
9. The steps that include identifying a problem, reviewing the literature, and collecting data are part of the _____ .
10. _____ is used to investigate aspects of social life that cannot be measured quantitatively and are best understood in a natural setting.
11. _____ is a variable in which change has occurred.
12. A variable that causes something to occur is called _____ .

Reviewing the Facts

13. If a sociologist wanted to study high school cliques, what would be the best method for collecting data? Support your choice by giving two benefits of using this method.

14. Examine Figures 2.6 and 2.7 on page 49 showing median annual earnings by sex, race, and education. What is the scientific name given for this type of information?

15. Sociologist Elijah Anderson studied gangs in Philadelphia. In order to do that, he had to take off his shirt and tie and dress like the young men he was going to study. What is the name of the method of research that Anderson used here?

16. What are the seven steps in the scientific method?

17. Survey research is obtained through the use of questionnaires and interviews containing closed-ended questions and/or open-ended questions. Using a table like the one below, list the advantages and disadvantages of open-ended survey research.

Advantages	Disadvantages

Thinking Critically

18. Applying Concepts

In this chapter you read about positive and negative correlations. Give two examples each of relationships that you suspect may be positive and negative correlations. For example, you may propose that an increase in income is positively correlated to increased dining out.

"I FIND IT HARDER AND HARDER TO GET ANY WORK DONE WITH ALL THE ETHICISTS HANGING AROUND."

ScienceCartoonsPlus.com

19. Analyzing Visuals

In this chapter you read about the problems sociologists face when they conduct research with human subjects. In the cartoon above, what position does the cartoonist take on this issue? Can you suggest who might be the employer of the figures in the background?

20. Identifying Alternatives

Identify the methods of research you would use if you wanted to study the effects of alcoholism on the work force. Explain why you would use this method. Briefly describe how you might conduct the research.

21. Drawing Conclusions

Figure 2.6 on page 49 indicates that males make more money on average than females. Some sociologists would tell you that pregnancy contributes to the variations in male vs. female earnings. What variables might explain this conclusion?

22. Interpreting Graphs

Use the graph below to answer the following questions.

a. According to the graph, in 2004, Hispanics represented about 14 percent of the American population. What percent are Hispanics expected to represent in 2010? In 2020?

b. Based on a visual or "eyeball" estimate of the graph, what percentage of the American population will be non-white in 2020?

U.S. Population Growth by Race and Hispanic Origin, 1990–2020

* Projected

Sociology Projects

23. Qualitative Research

In order to strengthen your skills in qualitative research, perform the following activity. Look around your classroom and select an object such as a blackboard eraser. Imagine that you have never seen this object before and have no idea what it is or what it is used for. Write a brief description of the object in terms of its physical nature, but do not try to determine its function. Compare your description with those of your classmates.

24. Conducting a Research Study

Write a proposal for a study that you would like to see conducted at your school. Will it be a survey, interview, or observation? Follow the standards set out in the textbook on pages 58–59, indicating variables, research design, hypothesis, and a review of the literature if possible. Include information on how you will identify your sample population. Also include sample questions (open or closed). Be prepared to present this study to your class "ethics board" for approval.

25. Quantitative Research

Try this quantitative research project at home. Over the next few days or nights, watch three television shows, each at least thirty minutes long. The programs you select should be prime-time dramas for mature audiences. Record the number of times a person or animal is subjected to physical violence. Remember that physical violence is everything from shoving to shooting. Then create a graph that illustrates the number of violent acts for the shows. You have just done quantitative research and you will probably be amazed at the results.

26. Filtering

Some high schools are concerned about Internet use by high school students and are considering *filtering*, a process that blocks access to Web sites that have certain words or phrases in their text. Some teachers are concerned that this imposed censorship will hamper student research, since the filtering process looks for words only and generally does not evaluate the context in which the word is used. Choose a partner to debate this issue and develop arguments that support your position. Support your arguments with research.

Technology Activity

27. Visit an Internet site on a current events topic that interests you. Using the criteria for determining a valid Web site on pages 47–48, determine if your site qualifies. If not, keep searching until you find one that does. Bring your recommended URL to class to create a database of great current events sites.

School Talk
by Donna Eder

This excerpt describes research methods and ethical issues in a well-known study of middle school culture.

- **extracurricular**
  after school; beyond the normal school courses

- **transcribed**
  made a written copy; put into written form

Collecting data on students' experiences. We used a variety of means to collect data on students' experiences with peers in school. All four researchers observed lunchtime interaction at least twice weekly for periods of time ranging from five months to twelve months. We never took notes openly during the lunch period, but sometimes recorded brief notes in the bathroom or hallway between lunch sessions. These notes were expanded upon and all notes were recorded fully immediately after leaving the setting.

Donna Eder and Steve Parker also attended male and female **extracurricular** activities twice weekly for an entire academic year. Given the importance of athletic activities and cheerleading, we focused primarily on them, going to athletic games and practices, pep rallies, and cheerleading practices and tryouts. In addition, we observed choir and band practices and concerts, talent shows, and the one school play that was performed during the three-year period of the study. We were able to take some notes during these events, since our roles were more those of observers than participants. Afterward, we expanded on these notes and recorded them fully.

Once we had been in the setting for several months, we began doing informal interviews with individuals or groups of students on issues that arose from our observations. They included questions about the meaning of popularity, attitudes toward other students in the school, and views on male-female relationships. While some were so informal they were simply recorded as *field notes*, ten of the more extensive interviews were tape-recorded and **transcribed** in full.

Finally, we tape-recorded conversations in most of the lunch groups which we observed. Typically, we sat with the group members for three to seven months prior to taping them, so they were already used to our presence. We got written permission from both the students and their parents before we made a recording. On the permission forms we assured them that no one who knew them would be able to listen to or watch the tapes. We also told them that their real names would not be used in any written report. To further insure the participants' privacy, we have also changed all names of identifying locations and modified discussions about particular people or events. Only one parent requested that her daughter not participate in the study. Since she could not be asked to separate from her group, we decided to omit the entire group from the study. . . .

Ethical issues. When we first began the study, we openly informed all of the students that we were from Indiana University and were doing a study of middle school students. We assured students of our concern with protecting their privacy by not using their actual names or revealing private information to others who might know them. The only concern expressed by a few students was that they not get in trouble for swearing. Since we were not aware of a no-swearing rule and had not been asked to enforce it, they soon lost this concern. Several students again expressed a similar concern when they were first tape-recorded, asking us who would be allowed to hear the tapes. We assured them that the tapes would not be seen or heard by anyone who could identify them and that we would not use their names in papers or books about the study.

We were prepared in advance for these particular ethical issues and had ready responses that relieved people's concerns. Other ethical dilemmas arose during the course of the study for which we did not have clear solutions. [Two of the researchers] . . . witnessed several incidents of verbal harassment, and Steve witnessed one incident that included physical harassment. Since we had tried from the start to minimize our roles as authority figures in the school, neither of them intervened as adults to stop these incidents. Instead they relied on non-intrusive strategies such as not participating themselves, or drawing the attention of others away from the target of ridicule to some other activity.

These incidents raise challenging questions about the role of researchers as observers of naturally occurring behavior, as opposed to interventionists who try to change the behavior of others, especially if it appears to be cruel or abusive. Had we decided to intervene more directly, we would have been seen as authority figures, and it is likely that students would no longer have acted as naturally in our presence, thus limiting the extent to which we could gain information about peer interactions. On the other hand, it was deeply disturbing to the researchers to witness these events without intervening. We struggled with the question of whether nonintervention might convey an implicit message that such behavior is acceptable to adults.

Source: Donna Eder, *School Talk,* New Brunswick, N.J.: Rutgers University Press, 1995, pp. 172–175.

- **non-intrusive**
  not obviously noticeable; non-threatening

- **interventionist**
  someone who gets involved to make a change

Read and React

1. In the first paragraph, the author writes that the observers did not openly take notes. Wouldn't it make more sense to take notes while the events were happening? Why would the observers wait to record their observations?

2. What do you think the author means by the term *field notes* in the third paragraph?

3. What steps did the research team take to ensure that the students' privacy rights were not abused?

4. What ethical problems did the researchers face in the course of their observations? Would you have taken the same steps as the researchers? What other action could have been taken?

Chapter

3

Culture

Sections

1. **The Basis of Culture**
2. **Language and Culture**
3. **Norms and Values**
4. **Beliefs and Material Culture**
5. **Cultural Diversity and Similarity**

Learning Objectives

After reading this chapter, you will be able to

- explain how culture and heredity affect social behavior.
- describe how language and culture are related.
- name the essential components of culture.
- discuss how cultural diversity is promoted within a society.
- understand the role of ethnocentrism in society.
- identify similarities in cultures around the world.

Applying Sociology

The crowing rooster wakes Jabu very early. Already her mother has carried a bucket of water from the village tap and put it on the fire to heat. Bread is laid out on a newspaper on the ground, ready to be cut and spread with jam. Meanwhile, Jabu wraps her baby brother in a blanket and ties him on her back, soothing him with a melody as she begins her chores. The goats must be milked and the cattle need to be watered.

After her chores, Jabu dresses for the two-mile walk to school. On the way, she stops to greet a village elder who asks about her father who works in the distant diamond mines. By the time she arrives at school, Jabu sees that school assembly has already begun. The headmistress decides to set an example of Jabu and calls her up front to slap her hand with a ruler. After singing hymns and the national anthem, Jabu goes outside for her first class, held under a large acacia tree in the courtyard.

Jabu's life seems very different from yours, but if you use your sociological imagination, you will see that both you and she attend school, obey authority figures, and have strong family ties. When sociologists look at societies, they discover there are common patterns in all cultures. This chapter will look at the common elements that make up culture.

Sociology Online

Chapter Overview
Visit the *Sociology and You* Web site at glencoe.com and click on **Chapter 3— Chapter Overviews** to preview chapter information.

The Basis Of Culture

Key Terms

- culture *(p. 72)*
- society *(p. 73)*
- instincts *(p. 73)*
- reflexes *(p. 73)*
- drives *(p. 73)*
- sociobiology *(p. 74)*

- **culture**
  knowledge, values, customs, and physical objects that are shared by members of a society

Section Preview

Culture defines how people in a society behave in relation to others and to physical objects. Although most behavior among animals is instinctual, human behavior is learned. Even reflexes and drives do not completely determine how humans will behave, because people are heavily influenced by culture.

Culture and Society

The term **culture** refers to the knowledge, language, values, customs, and physical objects that are passed from generation to generation among members of a group. It is a human creation. On the *material* side, the culture of the United States includes such physical objects as skyscrapers, computers, cell phones, and cars. On the *nonmaterial* side, American culture includes beliefs, rules, customs, family systems, and a capitalist economy.

Culture helps to explain human social behavior. What people do and don't do, what they like and dislike, what they believe and don't believe, and what they value and discount are all based on culture. Culture provides the blueprint that people in a society use to guide their relationships with others. It is because of culture that teenage girls are encouraged to compete for a position on the women's basketball team. It is from culture that teenage boys come to believe that "pumping iron" is a gateway to masculinity.

Coming from a different culture than that of the other sunbathers doesn't prevent this Amish family from enjoying a day at the beach.

Culture and society are tightly interwoven. One cannot exist without the other, but they are not identical. A **society** is a group of people who live in a defined territory and participate in a common culture. Culture is that society's total way of life.

Human behavior, then, is based on culture. Since people are not born knowing their culture, human cultural behavior must be learned. In this section we will examine the relative importance of biology in influencing behavior.

Culture and Heredity

Instincts are genetically inherited patterns of behavior. Nonhuman animals, especially insects, are highly dependent on instincts for survival. Human infants, in contrast, cannot go very far on instincts alone. Instincts are not enough to solve the problems that humans face.

Why is culture more important than instinct in determining human behavior? If humans were controlled by instincts alone, they would all behave in the same way with respect to those instincts. If, for example, women had an instinct for mothering, then *all* women would want children, and all women would love and protect their children. In fact, some women do not want to have children, and some women who give birth abuse or abandon their children.

Without instincts to dictate the type of shelter to build, the kind of food to eat, the time of year to have children, or when to mate, humans are forced to create and learn their own ways of thinking, feeling, and behaving. Even for meeting basic needs such as those involving reproduction, food, and survival, humans rely on the culture they have created.

How does heredity affect behavior? Of course, culture is not the only influence on human behavior. Genetic inheritance plays a role. For example, you may have heard people argue about how much of personality is a result of heredity and how much is the product of the environment. (This is sometimes called the "nature versus nurture" argument.) Using studies of identical twins, researchers have determined that about half of your personality traits are determined by your genetic makeup and about half by environmental factors (Tellegen et al., 1993).

In addition, humans have **reflexes**—simple, biologically inherited, automatic reactions to physical stimuli. A human baby, for example, cries when pinched; the pupils of the eyes contract in bright light. We also have biologically inherited **drives**, or impulses, to reduce discomfort. We want to eat, drink, sleep, and associate with others.

You should realize, however, that genetically inherited personality traits, reflexes, and drives do not control human social behavior. Culture *channels* the expression of these biological characteristics. Boys in some Native American cultures, for example, are taught not to cry in response to pain. This is very different from boys in Jewish and Italian cultures, who are taught to pay more attention to physical discomfort and express it more openly (Zborowski, 1952, 1969).

- **society**
  a specific territory inhabited by people who share a common culture

- **instincts**
  innate (unlearned) patterns of behavior

- **reflex**
  automatic reaction to physical stimulus

Studies of identical twins show that about half of your personality traits are inherited.

- **drive**
  impulse to reduce discomfort

Sociobiology

● **sociobiology**
the study of the biological basis of human behavior

Sociobiology is the study of the biological basis of human behavior. It combines Darwin's theory of natural selection with modern genetics.

How do sociobiologists view human behavior? According to Darwin's theory of evolution, organisms evolve through natural selection. The plants and animals best suited to an environment survive and reproduce, while the rest perish. Sociobiologists assume that the behaviors that best help people are biologically based and transmitted in the genetic code (Degler, 1991; Wright, 1996). Behaviors that would contribute to the survival of the human species include parental affection and care, friendship, sexual reproduction, and the education of children.

Sociobiologists do not draw a sharp line between human and nonhuman animals. They claim that nonhuman animals also act on knowledge—as when baboons use long sticks to pull ants from an anthill for a meal. Many nonhuman animals, claim sociobiologists, show intelligence of a kind formerly thought to be unique to humans, such as the ability to use language (Begley, 1993; Linden, 1993a).

Folds of skin around the eyelids of this Inuit fisherman protect his eyes from the sun's glare off the ice and snow.

What are some criticisms of sociobiology? The major criticism of sociobiology is that the importance placed on genetics could be used as a justification to label specific races as superior or inferior. Critics of sociobiology also point out that there is too much variation in societies around the world for human behavior to be explained on strictly biological grounds. They believe that the capacity for using language is uniquely human and that humans have created a social life that goes far beyond what heredity alone could accomplish.

Is there a middle ground? Some common ground has emerged in this debate. A growing body of sociologists believe that genes work with culture in a complex way to shape and limit human nature and social life. They would like this relationship to be further examined (Lopreato, 1990; Weingart, 1997; Konner, 1999).

A 1998 study found that women look for one set of characteristics in men they marry while men value different characteristics in women (Buss, Malamuth, and Windstad, 1998). The researchers believe this behavior is programmed into the genetic code. Studies have also determined that

DNA, the genetic material in all cells, is the molecular basis of heredity. Sociobiology focuses on the relationship between heredity and human behavior.

stepfathers are more likely than biological fathers to abuse their children (Daly and Wilson, 1997). Is this because men are more protective of their own biological offspring? Because of the speed of discoveries in the field of biology, the relationships between heredity, culture, and behavior are of growing interest to sociobiologists.

Section 1 Assessment

1. How is society different from culture?

2. About what percentage of personality is determined by genetics?

3. What are two arguments against the theory of sociobiology?

4. Predict which of the following are drives (D), which are reflexes (R), which are instincts (I), and which are creations of culture (C).
   a. eye blinking in dust storm
   b. need for sleep
   c. reaction to a loud noise
   d. socialism
   e. reproduction
   f. racial inequality

Critical Thinking

5. **Synthesizing Information** Name three nonmaterial and three material elements that represent American culture to you.

6. **Making Generalizations** Do you think human behavior is more a result of culture or of heredity? Give reasons to support your answer.

The Mysterious Fall of Nacirema

The following reading is excerpted from a review of a little-known North American culture.

Although the Nacirema left a large number of documents, our linguists have been unable to decipher any more than a few scattered fragments of the Nacirema language. Eventually, with the complete translation of these documents, we will undoubtedly learn a great deal about the reasons for the sudden disappearance of what . . . must have been an explosive and expansive culture. . . .

When we examine the area occupied by these people . . . it is immediately apparent that the Nacirema considered it of primary importance to completely remake the environment. . . . Trees . . . were removed. . . . Most of the land . . . was sowed each year with a limited variety of plants. . . .

For a period of about 300 solar cycles . . . the Nacirema devoted a major part of their effort to the special environmental problem of changing the appearance of air and water. Until the last fifty solar

cycles of the culture's existence, they seemed to have had only indifferent success. But during the short period before the fall of the culture, they mastered their art magnificently. They changed the color of the waters from the cool end of the spectrum (blues and greens) toward the warm ends (reds and browns). . . .

Early research has disclosed the importance of . . . the presence of the . . . Elibomotua [RAC] Cult, which sought to

create an intense sense of individual involvement in the community effort to completely control the environment. . . .

There seems to be little doubt that the Cult of the Elibomotua was so fervently embraced by the general population, and that the daily rituals of the RAC's care and use were so faithfully performed, that the minute quantities of [chemicals] thus distributed may have had a decisive effect on the chemical characteristics of the air. The Elibomotua, therefore, may have contributed in a major way toward the prized objective of a totally man-made environment.

In summary, our evaluation of . . . the Nacirema's man-made environmental alterations . . . lead us to advance the hypothesis that they may have been responsible for their own extinction. The Nacirema culture may have been so successful in achieving its objectives that . . . its people were unable to cope with its manufactured environment.

If the Nacirema seem vaguely familiar, it's because *Nacirema* is *American* spelled backward. Neil Thompson's description strikes us as strange. This is because Americans are not used to looking at their culture as others from the outside might see it. Like fish in water, Americans are so close to their own customs and rituals that they are in a sense unaware of them. Looking at culture from the sociological perspective will heighten your awareness of your own culture as well as the cultures of others.

Source: Neil B. Thompson, "The Mysterious Fall of Nacirema." *Natural History* (December, 1972). Copyright the American Museum of Natural History (1972). Reprinted with permission.

Thinking It Over

1. Describe how your feeling toward the Nacirema changed when you knew their true identity.

2. What other items in today's American culture might be misinterpreted by future anthropologists?

Language and Culture

Section Preview

Humans can create and transmit culture. The symbols of language play a role in determining people's views of reality.

Key Terms

- symbols *(p. 77)*
- hypothesis of linguistic relativity *(p. 78)*

Symbols, Language, and Culture

If culture is to be transmitted, it must be learned anew by each generation. Both the creation and the transmission of culture, known as *cultural transmission,* depend heavily on the use of symbols. The most powerful symbols are those that make up language.

What are symbols? In Lewis Carroll's *Through the Looking Glass,* Humpty Dumpty says to Alice, "When I use a word, it means just what I choose it to mean—neither more nor less." So it is with **symbols**—things that stand for or represent something else.

- **symbol**
  a thing that stands for or represents something else

Symbols range from physical objects to sounds, smells, and tastes. As you read in Chapter 1, the meaning of a symbol is not based on physical characteristics. For example, there is nothing naturally pleasing about the sound created by hands loudly clapping together. Applause warms the heart of an entertainer, a politician, or a high school athlete in the United States, but in Latin America the same sound means disapproval. In the sports world, the Nike "swoosh" has become a symbol for golfer Tiger Woods. The Confederate flag that represents oppression for many African Americans and a proud cultural heritage for many white Southerners is a symbol with different meanings attached.

How are language and culture related? Language frees humans from the limits of time and place. It allows us to create culture. The Wright brothers' successful flight did not come just from their own personal efforts. They built their airplane according to principles of flight already existing in American culture. Through language they could read, discuss, and recombine existing ideas and technology.

Equipped with language, humans can pass their experiences, ideas, and knowledge to others. Although it may take time and repetition, children can be taught the dangers of fire and heights without being burned or toppling down stairs. This process of social learning, of course, applies to other cultural patterns as well, such as eating, showing patriotism, or staying awake in class.

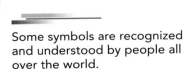

Some symbols are recognized and understood by people all over the world.

How to Speak with Your Hands

Figure 3.1 Sign Language.
Hand movements in sign language are symbols.

The Sapir-Whorf Hypothesis

According to Edward Sapir (1929) and Benjamin Whorf (1956), language is our guide to reality. How we think about a thing relates to the number and complexity of words available to describe that thing. In effect, our perceptions of the world depend in part on the particular language we have learned. Since languages differ, perceptions differ as well. This theory is known as the Sapir-Whorf Hypothesis, or the **hypothesis of linguistic relativity.**

● **hypothesis of linguistic relativity**
theory stating that our idea of reality depends largely upon language

What can vocabulary tell you about a culture? When something is important to a society, its language will have many words to describe it. The importance of time in American culture is reflected in the many words that describe time intervals—*nanosecond, moment, minute, hour, era, interim, recurrence, century, light-year,* and *afternoon,* to name a few. When something is unimportant to people, they may not have even one word for it. When Christian missionaries first went to Asia, they were dismayed because the Chinese language contained no word for sin. Other missionaries were no less distressed to learn that Africans and Polynesians had no word to express the idea of a single, all-powerful God. While English has only a few words that describe snow, the Inuit (Eskimo) language has over twenty. The Pirahã of Brazil lack words to express numbers greater than two.

Does the hypothesis of linguistic relativity mean we are prisoners of our language? Even if our view of the world is shaped largely by language, we are not forever trapped by our own language. Exposure to another language or to new words can alter a person's perception. (This is one reason why it is important to avoid stereotypical labels.) People can begin to view the world differently as they learn a new language. Most people do confine themselves to the language and vocabulary they learned from birth, but you can either expand or limit your outlook, depending upon how you use language.

What other factors help shape our perception of reality? How we perceive the world around us is influenced by more than vocabulary. Cultures may differ in many ways, and these differences influence how their members experience the world. The Japanese use paper walls to create the sense of privacy and are not bothered by noise in adjacent rooms. Americans staying at hotels in Japan complain they are being bombarded with noise because Westerners have not been *conditioned* (mentally trained) to screen out sound.

Privacy is so important to most Germans that German executives generally have a "closed-door policy." Problems arise, as you might imagine, in American firms located in Germany because American executives leave their doors open.

In Japanese culture an emphasis on politeness has helped people learn to live harmoniously in close quarters.

Sociology Online

Student Web Activity
Visit the *Sociology and You* Web site at glencoe.com and click on **Chapter 3—Student Web Activities** for an activity on language.

Section 2 Assessment

1. What are symbols?
2. How does language affect culture?

Critical Thinking

3. **Understanding Cause and Effect** Describe some specific ways you see language affecting social behavior among students in your school.

4. **Drawing Conclusions** Some experts believe that without language there is no thought. Do you agree? Why or why not?

Cultural Relativism

Doing Sociology

1. What assumptions did the volunteer make about the needs of the villagers? What were the actual needs? Who was more right about what the villagers needed? Why?

2. Describe a time when you made assumptions that turned out to be culturally based.

Different behaviors, traditions, and expectations can often result in mis-understandings between people of different cultures. Learning to look at things from a point of view different from your own, and not making value judgments based on your beliefs and norms, is called *cultural relativism.* Having mutual respect and understanding for other cultures is sometimes more effective than modern technology and money in producing change and goodwill between nations.

Cultural relativism is illustrated in the true story of a young Peace Corps volunteer who was sent to a remote village to help build a well. The stream that was near the village was used for everything from water-ing goats to bathing to washing clothes to cooking and drinking. It was obvious that clean drinking water would benefit the village and improve health. Armed with plans, equipment, and budget and schedule, the hopeful volunteer arrived ready to begin.

At first, the village people were not very willing to help. After sev-eral weeks of lonely effort the volunteer met with the council to ask why nobody was helping her with this urgent project. "A well would be nice," the people agreed, "but what we really need is a good soccer field where we can play without getting hurt on the stones and uneven ground." So the volunteer agreed that some of the money and equipment could be used to build a good soccer field first.

After several weeks of effort, the soccer field was complete and a vil-lage soccer team was formed. Now work was able to start on the well, but once again the villagers seemed reluctant to help. Another council meet-ing was held, and the volunteer was told, "Ah yes, the well would be nice, but what we really need is a bridge across the stream so other villages can easily come to play soccer on our field." Since she couldn't dig the well alone, the volunteer agreed that some more time and money would be used to build a bridge. Unfortunately, the bridge proved to be more difficult than expected, and by the time it was complete, the budget and schedule were both used up.

The volunteer went back to the capital, disappointed and resentful that she had not been able to improve the village. Some weeks later, she was invited back by the villagers for a festival to celebrate the success of the soccer tournament they had arranged. When she arrived she was astonished to find a new well in the very center of the village. She asked the village elders for an explanation.

"The soccer tournament is important to us," she was told, "because it gives us pride and importance and gives us a reason to meet with the people of the other villages. We really never wanted a well."

"Then why did you build it?" she asked.

"We didn't build it because we wanted it," was the answer. "We built it because YOU wanted it."

Norms and Values

Section Preview

Two essential components of culture are norms and values. There are several types of norms—folkways, mores, and laws. Sanctions are used to encourage conformity to norms. Values, the broadest cultural ideas, form the basis for norms.

Norms: The Rules We Live By

If you wanted to describe your culture, what would you look for? How could you begin to classify the elements of the American way of life? Sociologists begin with the defining components of a culture: its norms, its values and beliefs, and its use of material objects.

Norms are rules defining appropriate and inappropriate behavior. A Hindu peasant in India can be found lying dead of starvation beside perfectly healthy cattle. In order to strengthen bonds between clans, a young Basarwa girl in Africa might become engaged to a man she has not met. Roman emperors routinely exiled relatives to small isolated islands for "disgracing" the family. Each of these instances reflects cultural norms—ways of behaving in specific situations. Norms help to explain why people in a society or group behave similarly in similar circumstances.

William Graham Sumner (1906) was an early sociologist who wrote about norms. Anything, he stated, can be considered appropriate when norms approve of it. This is because once norms are learned, members of a society

- **norms**
  rules defining appropriate and inappropriate behavior

All cultures have norms relating to marriage and family life; weddings are always important occasions. This Hindu couple is celebrating their marriage with a garland ritual.

Figure 3.2   Cultural Etiquette

It might prevent some embarrassing moments if you were aware of norms and customs before traveling to foreign places.

Country	Custom
England, Scotland, and Wales	Appointments are essential. You may be ten minutes late but not ten minutes early.
Greece	Be careful not to praise a specific object too enthusiastically or the host may insist on giving it to you.
Libya	If you are invited to a Libyan home for dinner, only men will be present. Take a gift for the host but not for his wife.
Senegal	Never eat food with the left hand, as this is considered offensive.
Zambia	Avoid direct eye contact with members of the opposite sex—it may suggest romantic overtures.
Saudia Arabia	It is an insult to sit in such a way as to face your host with the soles of your shoes showing. Do not place your feet on a desk, table, or chair.
Oman	If an Arab businessman takes your hand and holds it as you walk, do not be alarmed. He means it only as a sign of friendship.
China	A visit to a Chinese home is rare—unless the government has given prior approval.
Japan	If you are offered a gift, thank the person and wait for one or two more offers before accepting it. Receive the gift with both hands.
South Korea	Men go through doors first. Women help men with their coats.

Source: Roger E. Axtell, *Do's and Taboos Around the World*, 3rd ed. (New York: John Wiley & Sons, 1993).

Norms help define a culture's perception of beauty for both males and females. What are some norms that shape the American ideal of beauty?

use them to guide their social behavior. Norms are so ingrained they guide behavior without our awareness. In fact, we may not be consciously aware of a norm until it has been broken. For instance, you may not think about standing in line for concert tickets as a norm until someone attempts to step in front of you. Then it immediately registers that waiting your turn in line is expected behavior. Cutting in front of someone violates that norm. Norms range from relatively minor rules, such as the idea that we should applaud after a performance, to extremely important ones, such as laws against stealing.

Folkways, Mores, and Laws

Sumner identified three basic types of norms: *folkways, mores,* and *laws.* These three types of norms vary in their importance within a society. Accordingly, their violation is tolerated to different degrees.

What are folkways? Rules that cover customary ways of thinking, feeling, and behaving but lack moral overtones are called **folkways.** For example, sleeping in a bed versus sleeping on the floor is not a moral issue; it qualifies as a folkway. Folkways in the United States include supporting school activities, speaking to other students in the hall, and, if you are male, removing your hat in church.

Because folkways are not considered vital to group welfare, disapproval of those who break them is not very great. Those who consistently violate folkways—say, by talking loudly in quiet places, wearing shorts with a suit coat and tie, or wearing a different-colored sock on each foot—may appear odd. We may avoid these people, but we do not consider them wicked or immoral.

Some folkways are more important than others, and the social reaction to their violation is more intense. Failure to offer a woman a seat on a crowded bus draws little notice today. In contrast, obnoxious behavior at a party after excessive drinking may bring a strong negative reaction from others.

● **folkways**
norms that lack moral significance

mores
norms that have moral dimensions and that should be followed by members of the society

taboo
a rule of behavior, the violation of which calls for strong punishment

law
a norm that is formally defined and enforced by officials

What are mores? The term **mores** (pronounced "MOR-ays") is based on the word *moral*. Morality deals with conduct related to right and wrong. Mores are norms of great moral significance. They are vital to the well-being of a society. Conformity to mores draws strong social approval; violation of this type of norm brings strong disapproval. For example, Americans believe that able-bodied men should work for a living. Able-bodied men who do not work are scorned.

Although following folkways is generally a matter of personal choice, conformity to mores is a social requirement. Still, some mores are more vital to a society than others. Failure to stand at attention while the national anthem is being played is not as serious a violation of American mores as using loud profanity during a religious service.

The most serious mores are taboos. A **taboo** is a norm so strong that its violation demands punishment by the group (or, some people think even the supernatural). In India, followers of Hinduism have a taboo forbidding the killing of cows. Other taboos are related to sexual behaviors. Although definitions of incest vary from society to society, the incest taboo (forbidding sexual contact with close relatives) is generally regarded as the only taboo that is present in all societies. The "mother-in-law" taboo existing in some societies prohibits or severely restricts social contact between a husband and his wife's mother.

How do laws differ from mores? The third type of norm is **law.** Laws are norms that are formally defined and enforced by officials. Folkways and mores emerge slowly and are often unconsciously created, while laws are consciously created and enforced.

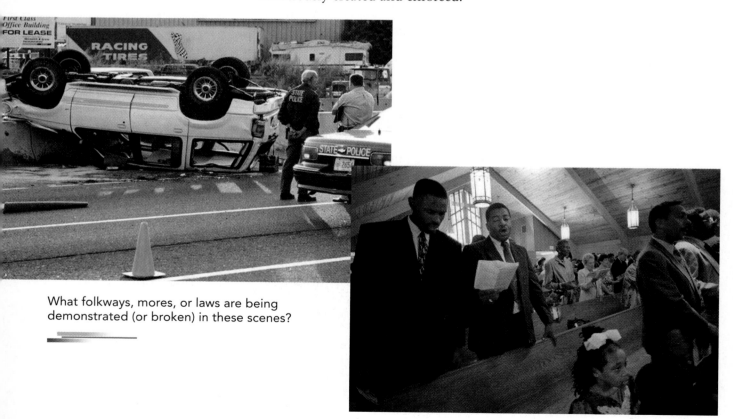

What folkways, mores, or laws are being demonstrated (or broken) in these scenes?

World View

Patterns of Tourism

Although people often want to observe and experience cultures different from their own, exposure to cultural diversity can be uncomfortable. Most international tourist travel occurs among countries sharing common cultural traditions and languages.

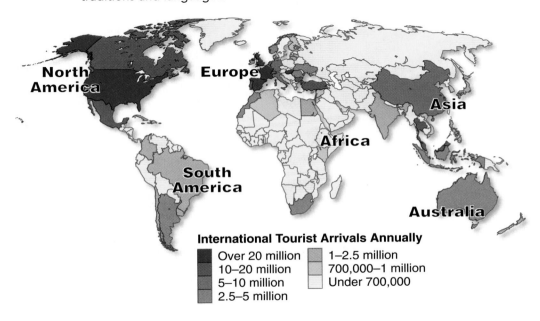

International Tourist Arrivals Annually

- Over 20 million
- 10–20 million
- 5–10 million
- 2.5–5 million
- 1–2.5 million
- 700,000–1 million
- Under 700,000

Interpreting the Map

1. Identify the world regions that receive the highest and lowest number of tourists.

2. Are there any reasons to believe that these travel patterns might change in the near future? If so, what factors might bring about this change?

Adapted from the *Student Atlas:* DK Publishing, Inc.

Mores are an important source for laws. At one time, the norm against murder was not written down. But as civilization advanced, the norm against murder became formally defined and enforced by public officials.

Folkways can become mores or laws. Smoking, for example, was an acceptable behavior to most Americans until the late 1970s, when mounting health concerns convinced many that smoking should be limited or banned in public places. Today, many states have laws against smoking in airports, government buildings, restaurants, and other places open to the general public.

Figure 3.3 Silly Laws Still on the Books

There are many laws throughout the country whose purposes and existence have long been forgotten. At the time, they may have been perfectly logical. As society changed, the need for them disappeared.

State	Law
Alabama	It is illegal for a driver to be blindfolded while operating a vehicle.
Arizona	Hunting camels is prohibited.
Florida	If an elephant is left tied to a parking meter, the fee has to be paid just as it would be for a vehicle.
Illinois	You must contact the police before entering the city in an automobile.
Iowa	Kisses may last for as much as, but no more than, five minutes.
Maine	You must not step out of a plane in flight.
Massachusetts	No gorilla is allowed in the back seat of any car.
Minnesota	A person may not cross state lines with a duck atop his or her head.
Vermont	Whistling underwater is illegal.
Washington	It is illegal to pretend that one's parents are rich.

Not all mores become laws. For example, it is not against the law to cheat on an exam (although you may be suspended or punished by the teacher). Furthermore, not all laws started out as mores. Fines for overtime parking and laws against littering have never been mores.

Laws often remain on the books for a long time after the mores of a society have changed. It is illegal in Minnesota to hang male and female undergarments on the same clothesline. New York prohibits card playing on trains; elephants in Natchez, Mississippi, cannot legally drink beer; and it is against the law to wear roller skates in public bathrooms in Portland, Oregon. (For additional laws that seem strange to us today, see Figure 3.3.)

Enforcing the Rules

People do not automatically conform to norms. Norms must be learned and accepted. Groups teach norms, in part, through the use of *sanctions*. **Sanctions** are rewards and punishments used to encourage conformity to norms. They can be formal or informal.

What are formal sanctions?
Formal sanctions are sanctions that may be applied only by officially designated persons, such as judges and teachers. Formal sanctions can take the form of positive as well as negative rewards. A soldier earns a Congressional Medal of Honor as a positive sanction for heroism. Teachers reward outstanding students with A's. Of course, formal sanctions can also take the form of punishments.

Formal punishments range widely in their severity. From the Middle Ages to the Protestant Reformation, it was an unpardonable sin for lenders to charge interest on money. (This practice was called *usury* and was condemned in the Bible.) This crime was punishable on the third offense

- **sanctions**
  rewards and punishments used to encourage people to follow norms

- **formal sanctions**
  sanctions imposed by persons given special authority

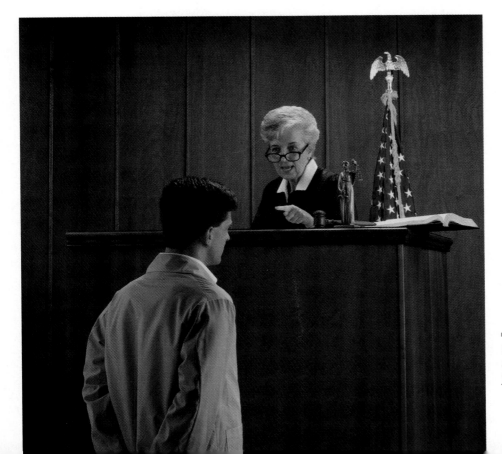

Formal sanctions often involve action in the criminal or civil judicial systems.

by public humiliation and social and economic ruin. More recently, a few courts across the United States have handed down sentences involving public shaming. For example, some courts have required child molesters to display, in front of their homes, signs describing their crimes (El Nasser, 1996). In 2004, an American Hockey League player lost eligibility for the remainder of the season after slamming his hockey stick into the face of an opponent. The victim of this attack subsequently required twenty stitches to close the injury to his face.

● informal sanctions
rewards or punishments that can be applied by most members of a group

What are informal sanctions? Informal sanctions are sanctions that can be applied by most members of a group. They, too, can be positive or negative. Informal sanctions include thanking someone for pushing a car out of a snowbank (positive) or staring at someone who is talking loudly during a movie (negative).

Sanctions are not used randomly or without reason. Specific sanctions are associated with specific norms. A high school student who violates his parents' curfew is not supposed to be locked in a closet, for example.

After we reach a certain age, most of us conform without the threat of sanctions. We may conform to norms because we believe that the behavior expected of us is appropriate, because we wish to avoid guilt feelings, or because we fear social disapproval. In other words, we sanction ourselves mentally.

THE FAR SIDE   By GARY LARSON

"Frank. ... Don't do that."

Frank seems to have forgotten that "real men" don't cross their legs. This informal sanction will probably bring him into line.

Values—The Basis for Norms

Norms and sanctions are relatively specific. The next major component of culture—*values*—is much more general.

What are values? **Values** are broad ideas about what most people in a society consider to be desirable. Values are so general that they do not dictate precise ways of thinking, feeling, and behaving. Thus, different societies or different groups within the same society can have quite different norms based on the same value.

For instance, consider the norms used to express the value of freedom in America and in the former Soviet Union. Soviet leaders said their people were free because the leaders claimed to provide full employment, medical care, and education. Americans have different norms based on the value of freedom. These norms include the right to free speech and assembly, the right to engage in private enterprise, and the right to a representative government. Identical values do not result in identical norms.

Why are values important? Values have a tremendous influence on human social behavior because they form the basis for norms. A society that values democracy will have norms ensuring personal freedom. A society that values human welfare will have norms providing for its most unfortunate members. A society that values hard work will have norms against laziness.

Values are also important because they are so general that they are involved in most aspects of daily life. In America, for example, the influence of the value of freedom goes beyond political life. The value of freedom affects how family relationships are conducted, how people are treated within the legal system, how organizations are run, and how people worship.

● **values**
broad ideas about what is good or desirable shared by people in a society

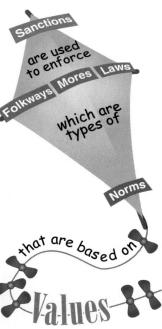

Figure 3.4 The Norm Kite.
If a society is to fly, it must have these basic elements of social structure. Sanctions (rewards and punishments) are needed to enforce norms (folkways, mores, laws). Guiding the Norm Kite are a society's values, the basis for norms.

After winning a gold medal in the 2004 Olympics, members of the U.S. women's soccer team became role models for many girls. What cultural values do these women demonstrate?

Basic Values in the United States

The United States is home to many different groups. No single set of values is likely to hold across the entire country. Despite this problem, sociologist Robin Williams (1970) identified important values that guide the daily lives of most people in the U.S. A partial list includes:

- *Achievement and success.* People emphasize achievement, especially in the world of work. Success is supposed to be based on effort and competition and is viewed as a reward for performance. Wealth is viewed as a symbol of success and personal worth.

  - *Activity and work.* People tend to prefer action over inaction in almost every case. For most Americans, continuous and regular work is a goal in itself. Promotion should be for merit rather than favoritism. Finally, all citizens should have the opportunity to perform at their best.

  - *Efficiency and practicality.* People pride themselves on getting things done by the most rational means. We search for better (faster) ways of doing things, praise good workmanship, and judge performance by the results. We love to rely on science and technology.

  - *Equality.* From the very beginning of our history as a nation, we have declared a belief in equality for all citizens. As minority groups and women achieved citizenship, our concept of equality grew. We tend to treat one another as equals, defend everyone's legal rights, and favor equal opportunity—if not equal results—for everyone.

  - *Democracy.* People emphasize that all citizens are entitled to equal rights and equal opportunity under the law. In a democracy, the people elect their government officials. Power is not in the hands of an elite few.

  - *Group superiority.* Despite their concern for equality of opportunity, people in the U.S. tend to place a greater value on people of their own race, ethnic group, social class, or religious group.

These values are clearly interrelated. Achievement and success affect and are affected by efficiency and practicality, for example. But we can also see conflicts among some values. For instance, people in the U.S. value group superiority while at the same time stressing equality and democracy.

How fluid are America's basic values?
Williams identified these major values more than thirty-five years ago—about the time many of your parents were teenagers or young adults. Although these values have remained remarkably stable over the years, some have changed. Today there is less emphasis on group superiority in America than in the past. This can be seen in the decline of openly racist attitudes and behaviors (Farley, 1998; Rochen, 2000). In reality, however, it is usually norms and behavior rather than underlying values that change radically. It is probably because of the passage of civil rights laws that many Americans are now less likely to make overt racist statements. Racism, based on a belief in the superiority of one group over another, remains part of the fabric of American culture.

What cultural values are represented in these photos?

Calvin and Hobbes

by Bill Watterson

Calvin's father is trying to transmit the cultural value of competition. As usual, Calvin has his own view. What is yours?

The norms related to hard work and activity have also changed in recent years. Many Americans now work as hard at their leisure activities (for example, long-distance running and mountain climbing) as they do at their jobs.

Although Williams's analysis of major American values remains basically sound today, some sociologists believe that his list is incomplete. They would add, for example, optimism, honesty, and friendliness to the list of major values in the United States.

Section 3 Assessment

1. Indicate whether these statements best reflect a folkway (F), a more (M), a law (L), or a value (V).
   a. norm against cursing aloud in church
   b. norm encouraging eating three meals daily
   c. idea of progress
   d. norm against burning a national flag
   e. norm encouraging sleeping in a bed
   f. norm prohibiting murder
   g. norm against overtime parking
   h. idea of freedom

2. Sociologists make a distinction between norms and values. How are these concepts different? Support your answer with examples.

Critical Thinking

3. **Analyzing Information** You have been thinking about Americal values, norms, and sanctions. What Iraqi values, norms, and sanctions do you think influence the conflict in Iraq?

Beliefs and Material Culture

Key Terms

- nonmaterial culture *(p. 92)*
- beliefs *(p. 92)*
- material culture *(p. 92)*
- ideal culture *(p. 94)*
- real culture *(p. 94)*

- **nonmaterial culture**
  ideas, knowledge, and beliefs that influence people's behavior

- **beliefs**
  ideas about the nature of reality

- **material culture**
  the concrete, tangible objects of a culture

Section Preview

Besides norms and values, beliefs and physical objects make up culture. Ideal culture includes the guidelines we claim to accept, while real culture describes how we actually behave.

Beliefs and Physical Objects

The **nonmaterial culture** involves beliefs, ideas, and knowledge. The *material culture* is about how we relate to physical objects. Values, norms, knowledge, ideas (nonmaterial), and physical objects (material) make up a culture.

Why do beliefs matter?   **Beliefs** are ideas about the nature of reality. Beliefs can be true or false. The Romans believed Caesar Augustus to be a god; the Tanala, a hill tribe of Madagascar, believed that the souls of their kings passed into snakes; and many Germans believed that pictures of Hitler on their walls would prevent the walls from crumbling during bombing raids. We would certainly consider these beliefs to be false. In contrast, other beliefs—such as the belief that the human eye can distinguish over seven million colors and the belief that no intelligent life exists on Mars—are supported by factual evidence. We consider these to be true. Beliefs are important because people base their behavior on what they believe, regardless of how true or false the beliefs are.

What is material culture?   **Material culture** consists of the concrete, tangible objects within a culture—automobiles, Harry Potter books, chairs, highways, art. These physical objects have no meaning or use apart from the meanings people give them.

Acres of discarded cars in a junkyard plainly show that the automobile is one of the most common objects of America's material culture.

Consider newspaper and pepper as physical objects. Each has some meaning for you, but can you think of a use for them in combination? Some Americans have used pepper and newspaper in a process known as "nettling." An elderly medical doctor tells the story of his first encounter with nettling:

> The ink of my medical license was hardly dry, and as I was soon to find out, my ears would not be dry for some time. I had never delivered a baby on my own and faced my maiden voyage with some fear.
>
> Upon entering Mrs. Williamson's house, I found a local midwife and several neighbors busily at work preparing for the delivery. My fear caused me to move rather slowly and my happiness over my reprieve prompted me to tell the women that they were doing just fine and to proceed without my services.
>
> Having gotten myself off the hook, I watched the ladies with a fascination that soon turned to horror.
>
> At the height of Mrs. Williamson's labor pains, one of the neighbors rolled a piece of newspaper into a funnel shape. Holding the bottom end of the cone, she poured a liberal amount of pepper into it. Her next move was to insert the sharp end of the cone, into Mrs. Williamson's nose. With the cone in its "proper" place, the neighbor inhaled deeply and blew the pepper from the cone into the inner recesses of Mrs. Williamson's nose—if not her mind.
>
> Suddenly alert, Mrs. Williamson's eyes widened as her senses rebelled against the pepper. With a mighty sneeze, I was introduced to nettling. The violence of that sneeze reverberated through her body to force the baby from her womb in a skittering flight across the bed. An appropriately positioned assistant fielded the baby in midflight and only minor details of Orville's rite of birth remained.

For this country doctor, the physical objects of newspaper and pepper took on new meaning.

Before this doctor was introduced to nettling, this particular combination of newspaper and pepper had no meaning for him. And until nettling was devised, the combination was without meaning for anyone, even though the separate physical objects existed as part of the culture.

How is material culture related to nonmaterial culture?

The uses and meanings of physical objects can vary among societies. Although it is conventional to use a 787 jet for traveling, it is possible that a 787 downed in a remote jungle region of the world could be used as a place of worship, a storage bin, or a home. In the United States, out-of-service buses, trains, and trolley cars have been converted to restaurants.

Clearly, the cultural meaning of physical objects is not determined by the physical characteristics of the objects. The meanings of physical objects are based on the beliefs, norms, and values people hold with regard to them. This is obvious when new meanings of a physical object are considered. At one time, only pianos and organs were used in church services. Guitars, drums, and trumpets were not "holy" enough to accompany a choir. Yet many churches today use these "worldly" instruments regularly in their worship activities. The instruments have not changed, but the cultural meanings placed on them have.

Though American ideal culture values natural athletic ability, in reality, some professional and amateur athletes use drugs or steroids to improve their performances.

Ideal and Real Culture

A gap sometimes exists between cultural guidelines and actual behavior. This gap is captured in the concepts of ideal and real culture. **Ideal culture** refers to cultural guidelines publicly embraced by members of a society. **Real culture** refers to actual behavior patterns, which often conflict with these guidelines.

One value of America's ideal culture is honesty. Yet in real culture, honesty is not always practiced. Some taxpayers annually violate both the letter and spirit of existing tax laws. Some businesspeople engage in dishonest business practices. Some students cheat on exams. Some college athletes do the "high $500" handshake, during which a team booster leaves illegal money in their palms. These are not isolated instances. They are real cultural patterns passed on from generation to generation.

It is important to remember that we are not referring here to individuals whose violations of norms include murder, rape, and robbery. These types of antisocial behavior violate even real culture.

Does the fact that we sometimes ignore cultural guidelines make ideal culture meaningless? Absolutely not. In an imperfect world, ideal culture provides high standards. These ideals are targets that most people attempt to reach most of the time. Ideal culture also permits the detection of deviant behavior. Individuals who deviate too far from the ideal pattern are sanctioned. This helps to preserve the ideal culture.

- **ideal culture**
  cultural guidelines that group members claim to accept

- **real culture**
  actual behavior patterns of members of a group

Section 4 Assessment

1. How is the material culture influenced by the nonmaterial culture?
2. How is real culture different from ideal culture?

Critical Thinking

3. **Drawing Conclusions** Think of an example of real and ideal culture in your school. Should the aspect of ideal culture be abandoned? Why or why not?

Cultural Diversity and Similarity

Section Preview

Cultures change according to three major processes. Cultures contain groups within them called *subcultures* and *countercultures* that differ in important ways from the main culture. People tend to make judgments based on the values of their own cultures. While apparently very different on the surface, all cultures have common traits or elements that sociologists call *cultural universals*.

Key Terms

- **social categories** (p. 98)
- **subculture** (p. 98)
- **counterculture** (p. 98)
- **ethnocentrism** (p. 98)
- **cultural universals** (p. 100)
- **cultural particulars** (p. 100)

Cultural Change

So far we have talked about culture as if it did not change. Actually the processes that govern cultural change are so important they are discussed in Chapter 17 on social movements and collective behavior. Briefly, however, you should realize that all cultures experience change. Norms, values, and beliefs are relatively stable, but they do change over time. For example, many of your grandparents never went to college; as teenagers, your parents never e-mailed friends or made last-minute dates on their cell phones. It was not that long ago that middle-class women with young children were discouraged from working outside the home. Interracial dating, while still relatively uncommon, is becoming more acceptable in the United States. These are aspects of culture that are changing in response to certain processes.

Why does culture change? Culture changes for three reasons. One cause is *discovery*, the process of finding something that already exists. The United States is currently discovering the generally unrecognized athletic abilities of females. This is changing the perception of women and the relationship between males and females.

Culture also changes through *invention*, the creation of something new. Science has led to inventions that have changed the world since the fifteenth century, from the creation of the steam engine to the cellular phone and the iPod. Such inventions have greatly altered our way of life.

A third cause of cultural change is *diffusion*, the borrowing of aspects of culture from other cultures. One aspect of culture that diffuses rapidly is food. Tacos, pizza, and hamburgers can be found on menus all over the world. Christmas trees and piñatas are part of celebrations in many countries. Ideas are also diffused. Japanese society has been fundamentally transformed as a result of the adoption of democracy and capitalism after World War II. As stated earlier, these three processes will be examined more closely in a later chapter.

Modern technology can bring new and different ideas to people in remote parts of the world.

Focus on Research

Survey Research: How Do Schools and Parents Fail Teens?

Adolescence is often marked with drama and difficulty. Jacquelynne Eccles (1993) investigated the experience of American teenagers entering a midwestern junior high school and discovered that some teenage troubles are more than hormonal—they are cultural as well.

Eccles studied 1,500 early adolescents moving from sixth-grade elementary schools to seventh-grade junior high schools. The junior high schools were located in twelve school districts in middle-class Michigan communities. Students filled out questionnaires at school for two consecutive years—the sixth and seventh grades. This procedure permitted Eccles to document changes the teenagers experienced after the first year of their transition.

The findings were not encouraging. The relationships between students and teachers tended to worsen over the year. At the very time when the young adolescents especially needed supportive relationships outside of their homes, personal and positive relationships with teachers were strained by cultural and organizational changes in junior high school.

There was more grouping based on academic achievement and more comparing of students with one another. This increased emphasis on student ranking comes just when young adolescents are most insecure about their status relative to their peers. In addition, in the junior high culture, the students experienced less opportunity to participate in classroom decision making.

As a result, student motivation and self-confidence declined. Eccles concluded that junior high school culture denies adolescents the emotionally supportive environment they need for proper social development.

Junior high students who are in supportive environments are more likely to have higher motivation and self-esteem than students in less supportive schools and families.

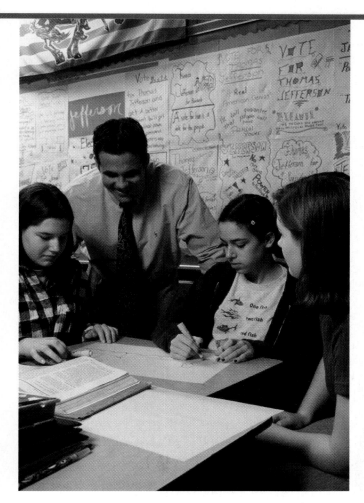

Eccles's news was no better on the home front. Changes in family paralleled those of the school system. Parental control over teenagers went up during the year, often to excessive levels. At the same time, school motivation and self-esteem of the junior high students went down.

As a check on these general findings, Eccles compared students in more supportive schools and families with those in less supportive ones. In both the school and the family settings, she found more positive results in supportive environments. Students who were able to participate in school and family decision making showed higher levels of academic motivation and self-esteem than their peers with less opportunity to participate.

The solution to this problem, Eccles concludes, lies in a change in the norms and values of the schools and families. Schools and families need to develop balanced cultural expectations of young adolescents based on their developmental needs. Adolescents, Eccles points out, have a growing need for independence that is rarely encouraged in the culture of the public school system. Neither cracking down on them nor giving up control strikes the proper balance. The task is for the family and school to provide "an environment that changes in the right way and at the right pace" (Eccles, 1993:99).

Working with the Research

1. Do you recall your junior high experience? Was your situation similar to the one described by Eccles? Did you feel the same pressures?

2. Which of the three theoretical perspectives do you think is most helpful in understanding the social relationships Eccles describes? Apply this perspective to explain her findings.

Cultural Diversity

Cultural diversity exists in all societies. Some diversity is a result of **social categories**—groups that share a social characteristic such as age, gender, or religion. Certain behaviors are associated with particular ages, genders, or religions. For example, devout Catholics are expected to attend Mass regularly.

What are subcultures and countercultures? Cultural diversity also comes from groups that differ in particular ways from the larger culture. These groups participate in the larger culture. They may speak the language, work regular jobs, eat and dress like most others, and attend recognized houses of worship. But despite sharing in the broader culture, these groups have some ways of thinking, feeling, and behaving that set them apart. Such groups—known as *subcultures* and *countercultures*—are usually found in large, complex societies.

Subculture is part of the dominant culture but differs from it in some important respects. The subculture of San Francisco's Chinatown is a good example. Early Chinese immigrants brought much of their native culture with them to America and have attempted to retain it by passing it from generation to generation. Although Chinese residents of Chinatown have been greatly affected by American culture, they have kept many cultural patterns of their own, such as language, diet, and family structure. Other examples of subcultures are those formed by youth, circus people, musicians, and mental patients (Fine, 1996; Redhead, 1997; Kephart and Zellner, 2000).

Counterculture is a subculture deliberately and consciously opposed to certain central beliefs or attitudes of the dominant culture. A counterculture can be understood only within the context of this opposition.

Examples of primarily teenage countercultures include the "goth" and the "punk" scenes. Goth is a shortening of the term *gothic*, meaning dark, strangely mysterious, and remote. Punk is a philosophy of rebellion and sexual revolution popularized by the lyrics and music of punk-rock bands.

Prison counterculture surfaced at the trial of John King, a man convicted of the gruesome truck-dragging murder of James Byrd, Jr. During an earlier prison stretch, King had become a member of a white supremacist gang that promoted many forms of violence. The gang's motto was "blood in, blood out," meaning that entry into the gang demanded a violent act, and leaving the gang would result in violence as well (Galloway, 1999). Delinquent gangs, motorcycle gangs, certain types of drug groups, and revolutionary or religious groups may also form countercultures (Zellner, 1999).

- ● **social categories**
  groupings of persons who share a social characteristic

- ● **subculture**
  a group that is part of the dominant culture but that differs from it in some important respects

- ● **counterculture**
  a subculture deliberately and consciously opposed to certain central beliefs or attitudes of the dominant culture

- ● **ethnocentrism**
  judging others in terms of one's own cultural standards

The punk movement began in Britain and quickly developed into an American counterculture.

Ethnocentrism

Once people learn their culture, they tend to become strongly committed to it. In fact, they often cannot imagine any other way of life. They may judge others in terms of their own cultural standards—a practice referred to as **ethnocentrism.**

TECH TRENDS

Star Wars and the Internet

When *Star Wars* first appeared in theaters in the late 1970s, director George Lucas probably did not realize that he had almost single-handedly created a full-fledged cultural phenomenon. Virtually everyone in the United States now recognizes Luke Skywalker, Darth Vader, and Yoda. Most Americans know what "May the Force be with you" means.

The movies in the *Star Wars* series have certainly been extremely popular in their own right, but the Internet has also been important in their penetration into popular culture. In 1999, *Star Wars* fans kept in touch over the Internet as they eagerly awaited *The Phantom Menace,* the first new *Star Wars* film in sixteen years. Anticipation of the first "prequel" was incredibly intense, and pirated footage spread to more than sixty Web sites within

hours of first being posted. In response, Lucasfilm's official Web site posted the film's trailer and was promptly overwhelmed with 340 "hits" per second. The impact of the Internet on this bit of American culture is undeniable.

"Everyone said this was the most top-secret movie ever made, that it was tighter than Fort Knox, no leaks whatsoever," says Scott Chitwood, age twenty-five, who's the emperor of TheForce.net. "Well, most web site operators knew the plot a year ago. That's all because of the Internet."

Of course, the cultural effects of *Star Wars* are not limited to the box office. Over the years, *Star Wars* has become much more than a movie to people worldwide. It has its own icons, symbols, and language. It has become a mini-culture, or subculture unto itself.

It is commerce over the Internet, or e-commerce, that has allowed many elements of this subculture to enter the larger culture. By 2005, the now six-film *Star Wars* franchise had earned nearly $20 billion, much of it through merchandising over the Internet. Among the many items sold are toys, soundtracks, costumes, licensing fees, and DVDs.

Analyzing the Trends

1. What other recent events are now part of popular culture in the United States? Tell what aspects of these events have made their way into our thinking, feeling, and behaving.

2. Predict ways in which the increasing popularity of the Internet may alter our understanding of culture.

What are some examples of ethnocentrism? Examples of ethnocentrism are plentiful. The Olympic Games are much more than an arena of competition for young men and women. In addition to competition, the games are an expression of ethnocentrism. Political and nationalistic undercurrents run through the Olympics. A country's final ranking in this athletic competition for gold, silver, and bronze medals is frequently taken as a reflection of the country's worth and status on the world stage.

Ethnocentrism also exists within societies. Regional rivalries in the United States are a source of many humorous stories, but these jokes reflect an underlying ethnocentrism. Boston is said by some (mostly Bostonians) to be the hub of the universe. Texans often claim to have the biggest and best of everything. New Yorkers bemoan the lack of culture in Los Angeles. Finally, members of churches, schools, and political parties all over America feel that their particular ways of living should be adopted by others.

Does ethnocentrism help or hurt society? Ethnocentrism has two faces—it offers both advantages and disadvantages. People feel good about themselves and about others in their group when they believe that what they are doing is right and superior to what other groups do. Stability is promoted because traditions and behaviors are highly valued. If a society is too rigid, however, it becomes inflexible. Extreme ethnocentrism can prevent change for the better. Societies whose members are firmly convinced of their superiority tend not to create anything new. The ancient Chinese built a wall to keep both invaders and new ideas out. The civil rights movement was born to combat racial ethnocentrism. Hitler's Final Solution was ethnocentrism at its worst. Today many states are passing laws that increase the penalties against people who commit violent acts against others based on their race, origin, or religion. (Civil rights and hate crimes are discussed in more detail in Chapter 9.)

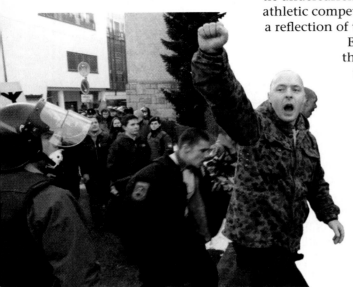

Ethnocentrism is still a divisive force in Germany. A riot erupts when members of the ultraright National Democratic Party march in support of their racist policies.

Cultural Universals

Although it may seem that different cultures have little in common, researchers have identified more than seventy common cultural traits. These **cultural universals** are traits that exist in all cultures. They include such things as sports, cooking, courtship, division of labor, education, etiquette, funeral rites, family, government, hospitality, housing, inheritance rules, joking, language, medicine, marriage, mourning, music, property rights, religious rituals, sexual restrictions, status differences, and tool making (Murdock, 1945). Because all societies have these cultural universals, they are more similar than you think. (See Figure 3.5 on page 102 for a more detailed list of cultural universals.)

How are cultural universals expressed? Cultural universals are not always carried out in the same way. In fact, different cultures have developed quite different ways to express universals. These are called **cultural particulars.** One cultural universal is caring for children. In the United States, women have traditionally worked within the home caring for children, and men have worked outside the home. (Although this is changing,

● **cultural universals**
general cultural traits that exist in all cultures

● **cultural particulars**
the ways in which a culture expresses universal traits

Immigration to the United States

The United States has long been the destination of immigrants from around the world. These immigrants have contributed to the nation's rich cultural diversity in a wide variety of ways. This map shows the number of immigrants who came to the United States in 2004 and the states in which they settled.

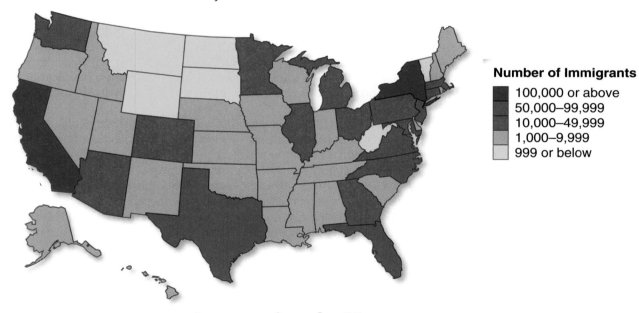

Number of Immigrants

- 100,000 or above
- 50,000–99,999
- 10,000–49,999
- 1,000–9,999
- 999 or below

Interpreting the Map

1. Which states had the most immigrants in 2004? Which states had the fewest?
2. About how many immigrants settled in your state in 2004?
3. Why would it be correct to say that the United States is a nation of immigrants?

Source: Bureau of U.S. Citizenship and Immigration Services: *2004 Yearbook of Immigration Statistics.*

women in this country are still largely responsible for child care.) Among the Manus of New Guinea, in contrast, the man is completely in charge of child rearing. Among the Mbuti pygmies, the Lovedu of Africa, and the Navajo and Iroquois Indians, men and women share equally in domestic and economic tasks (Little, 1975).

ECONOMY	INSTITUTIONS	ARTS	LANGUAGE	ENVIRONMENT	RECREATION	BELIEFS
Trade Tools Technology Goods Services Jobs Business Transportation Communications Food, Shelter, Clothing	Family Government Education Religion Economy	Art Literature Dance Theater Music Crafts Folk tales	Words Expressions Pronunciations Alphabet Symbols	Communities Geography Geology Habitat Wildlife Climates Resources	Games Toys Arts Media Holidays Festivals	Values Traditions Ethnicity Customs Religions Morals

CULTURAL UNIVERSALS

Figure 3.5 **Cultural Universals** Researchers have identified more than seventy traits that appear to one degree or another in all cultures.

Why do cultural universals exist? The biological similarity shared by all human beings helps to account for many cultural universals. If a society is to survive, children must be born and cared for, and some type of family structure must exist. (Groups that deliberately eliminate the family—such as the Shakers religious sect of New England—disappear.) Because people become ill, there must be some sort of medical care. Because people die, there must be funeral rites, mourning, and inheritance rules. Because food is necessary, cooking must be done.

The physical environment provides another reason why cultural universals exist. Because humans cannot survive without protection from the environment, some form of shelter must be created. Armies were formed to settle disputes over boundaries and important waterways.

Finally, cultural universals exist because societies face many of the same social problems. If a society is to survive, new members must be taught the culture. Goods and services must be produced and distributed. Tasks must be assigned, and work must be accomplished. Cultures develop similar methods of solving these problems.

Section 5 Assessment

1. Identify each of the following as a social category (SC), subculture (S), or counterculture (C).
   a. Chinatown in New York City
   b. motorcycle gang
   c. Catholics
   d. females
   e. revolutionary political group
   f. the super rich

2. Define ethnocentrism.

3. What are cultural universals? Why do they exist?

Critical Thinking

4. **Analyzing Information** Are you and your friends members of a subculture? If so, describe some specific elements of that subculture.

5. **Making Comparisons** From the chart above, choose a cultural universal. Compare or contrast how this cultural universal is addressed by two different cultures. For example, how do the United States and Mexico differ in recreational activities?

Summary

Section 1: The Basis Of Culture

Main Idea: Culture defines how people in a society behave in relation to others and to physical objects. Although most behavior among animals is instinctual, human behavior is learned.

Section 2: Language and Culture

Main Idea: Humans can create and transmit culture. The symbols of language play a role in determining people's view of reality.

Section 3: Norms and Values

Main Idea: Two essential components of culture are norms and values. Norms include folkways, mores, and laws. Sanctions are used to encourage conformity to norms. Values, the broadest cultural ideas, form the basis for norms.

Section 4: Beliefs and Material Culture

Main Idea: Besides norms and values, beliefs and physical objects make up culture. Ideal culture includes the guidelines we claim to accept, while real culture describes how we actually behave.

Section 5: Cultural Diversity and Similarity

Main Idea: Cultures, which contain subcultures and countercultures, change through three major processes.

Sociology Online

Self-Check Quiz
Visit the *Sociology and You* Web site at glencoe.com and click on **Chapter 3—Self-Check Quizzes** to prepare for the chapter test.

Reviewing Vocabulary

Complete each sentence using each term once.

a. sociobiology
b. sanctions
c. real culture
d. beliefs
e. society
f. laws
g. mores
h. subculture
i. ethnocentrism
j. informal sanctions

1. _____ are the ideas about the nature of reality.
2. A group that belongs to the larger culture but differs from it in some significant way is called _____ .
3. _____ is the study of the biological basis of human behavior.
4. Formally defined norms enforced by officials are called _____ .
5. _____ are rewards and punishments that can be applied by most members of a group.
6. Actual behavior patterns of the members of a group are called _____ .
7. _____ are rewards and punishments used to encourage desired behaviors.
8. Norms with moral dimensions are called ____ .
9. A specific territory composed of people who share a common culture is called a _____ .
10. Judging others in terms of one's own cultural standards is called _____ .

Reviewing the Facts

11. According to sociobiology, how is human behavior influenced?
12. What are the differences between reflexes and drives?
13. What are folkways? Give three examples of folkways in the United States.

14. Explain the Sapir-Whorf hypothesis.

15. What are the three basic types of norms?

16. Describe the relationship between norms and sanctions.

17. How does a social category differ from a subculture?

18. What are cultural universals?

Thinking Critically

19. Making Inferences

More than any other symbol of our country, the American flag provokes emotional responses. Some people are willing to give their lives for it, while others have burned it in protest. In groups, discuss why this symbol is so powerful.

20. Applying Concepts

All societies have cultural universals, as discussed in this chapter. Why, then, are so many groups in conflict? Think of examples of groups in this country that seem to be in conflict (such as animal rights activists and fur shop owners), and examine the reasons for these conflicts.

21. Making Comparisons

Discuss how you think a functionalist would look at the topic of culture. How do you think a conflict theorist would view it?

22. Evaluating Information

Some Amish parents have gone to jail rather than enroll their children in public schools. What does this say about Amish cultural values?

23. Categorizing Information

We have created a whole new language as a result of computers—a mouse is no longer necessarily an animal. Make a list of the words in your school that are unique to your community and that would need to be learned.

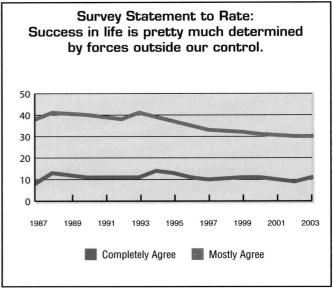

Survey Statement to Rate:
Success in life is pretty much determined by forces outside our control.

Pew Research Center, *The 2004 Political Landscape*

24. Interpreting Graphs

The Pew Research Center has conducted surveys of basic politiical, economic and social values over a number of years. One question and the responses to it is traced in the graph above.

a. Expain how this question relates to American values about the nation's economic system?

b. In 1987 what percentage of Americans believed that people did control their chances of success? How did that percent change in 2003?

Sociology Projects

25. Culture

You are an archaeologist and you have just uncovered a civilization called "America." Find at least one item from each of these aspects of culture: economy, religion, sports, science/ technology, education, families, and politics/ government. For example, you might uncover a checkbook as an example of the economy. As you find these items, try to imagine what they might mean to this American culture by answering the following questions.

a. Is this item culturally universal? Can it be found in other cultures?

b. What uses might someone from another culture find for this item? Be creative.

c. What does this item tell us about this culture?

26. Handshakes in U.S. Cultures

Handshakes are also symbolic representations of cultures. List some situations in which people shake hands in U.S. culture. For example, do boyfriends and girlfriends shake hands in the hallway when they meet? Do some students use special handshakes when they greet other students? As a class, determine all the ways in which handshakes are used in U.S. culture, and explain how the social situation can change the meaning of a handshake.

27. Cultural Lag

Material tools of a culture, such as computers, change faster than nonmaterial tools, such as norms and values. This difference creates what has been called *cultural lag*. (You will learn more about this topic in Chapter 17.) Computers have been around for some time. Still, many Americans lag behind in their proficiency with the technology. Interview people you know of varying ages: someone under age twelve, some fellow teens, some young adults, and some elderly adults. Ask them how computer literate they are. Do they know how to use Windows? The Internet? Does cultural lag exist in your sample? If so, try to find reasons or explanations for the lag.

28. Cultural Norms

Create a chart comparing cultural norms among U.S. subculture groups such as ethnic, socioeconomic strata, and gender groups.

"IT'S NOT THAT I REJECT YOUR VALUES, MOM AND DAD. IT'S JUST THAT I'VE EVOLVED AND YOU HAVEN'T."

www.cartoonstock.com

29. Cultural Change

The cartoon above touches on the subject of cultural change discussed in this chapter. Write a paragraph that describes the cartoonist's point of view on: 1) how parents and children view each other; and, 2) how values change. Conclude this activity by finding one other cartoon in a magazine or newspaper that addresses cultural change in some way.

Technology Activities

30. Compare the use of language between two social categories within your culture (e.g., teenagers and parents). Make a list of ten examples of words or phrases that differ in meaning between the members of each social category. Using the Internet and your school or local library, find the original derivation of the word or phrase. Record your information in a database.

Cultural Explanations for Teen Violence

from an article by James Gilbert

● **annihilation**
total destruction

● **scourge**
a cause of widespread distress

● **malevolent**
vicious or harmful

Every social crisis generates its share of easy explanations, but adolescent crime wins the contest for pat answers. Not only is everyone an expert, but out-of-control children are often already the focus of uneasiness about social change, general anxiety, and just plain undisguised dislike. The tragic shootings at Columbine High School in Littleton, Colorado, have generated more than the usual number of theories. Few of these are original, and, in fact, many of them repeat a formula tried out almost 45 years ago, during the national panic over juvenile delinquency. True, the supposed cultural influences have changed, with blame pointed now at the dark lyrics of Marilyn Manson or virtual-reality, murder-and-mayhem computer games, but the ultimate message is pretty much the same: our children's behavior is out of control because our culture is out of control. The only solution is to find a form of censorship that can block adolescents' access to the violent images that impel them to behave violently.

One problem with the cultural explanation for teen violence is that, notwithstanding numerous scientific attempts to do so, it is impossible to prove—there are simply too many other possible causes.... Not that this should necessarily deter critics of our current teen culture. But it is one thing to regard what young people listen to, play, or consume as strange or vulgar or even mildly threatening, and another to argue that it incites specific behavior. Teenagers might be persuaded by advertising to buy a Big Mac or smoke a Camel, but that doesn't mean that song lyrics can make them commit mass murder.

Another problem with the cultural explanation is that we have been there before and ought to recognize from our experience some of the outcomes and implications of the argument. In the mid-'50s, especially between 1954 and 1956, Americans worried as deeply about juvenile delinquency as they did about the cold war, atomic **annihilation,** unemployment, and other social ills. The reason for this is not hard to figure out. Government commissions, the FBI . . . , and a number of leading psychologists and social critics were all warning of a terrible **scourge** of juvenile crime. Cities and towns rushed to pass new ordinances. . . . The favorites of these were local curfews, naming the hour when children under 18 had to be home. Quite naturally, this led to some increased incidence of lawbreaking by youths. But, overall, during the '50s juvenile crime was no higher than the decade that preceded it. Yet fears of juvenile delinquency continued to soar.

While there were many explanations offered for delinquency, the one most printed in the pages of popular magazines and voiced during congressional hearings convened to examine the problem was the malevolent **malevolent** transcribed influence of crime and horror comic books. . . . Comic books, on the other hand,

concerted
organized; mutually arranged

particularly violent and horror comics, . . . became the focus of a **concerted** effort to censor youth culture. The effort was founded on the psychological theories of Fredric Wertham, whose 1954 best-seller, *Seduction of the Innocent,* inspired a vast outcry against the comics. Wertham's theory was based on asking teenage criminals if they read comic books—not much different from the logic behind today's blaming of computer games or music. . . .

If the anti–comic-book agitation did nothing much to end juvenile crime . . . what explains this panic? Clearly, something was happening in the '50s. . . . The postwar era was a revolutionary time, the first generation in American history wherein children had substantial amounts of spending money. The result was the explosion of a youth culture designed to appeal specifically and exclusively to young people. The teenage market expanded rapidly. . . . Children were growing up faster; they acted more like adults or at least demanded adult privileges. All of this looked immensely threatening. . . . Parents and parenting experts in our age are also confronting a major new development. In this case, it's the advent of the Internet—which has exponentially increased the amount and scope of influences to which American kids are exposed.

So what can we learn from the experience of the '50s . . . ? First, we should be wary of the attempt to link behavior directly and precisely to culture. There is no clear evidence to support this, and, besides, we can probably never develop a form of acceptable censorship anyway. It is also important to separate things that we don't like (or understand) from those social problems that might, in fact, cause teenage alienation and criminal behavior. Banning Marilyn Manson, hip-hop clothes, and rap music will certainly have an effect, but not the desired one. And, finally, we need to remind ourselves that youth culture is something that modern society has invented and celebrated. By extending affluence to children, by giving them computers and spending money, by making them consumers and therefore members of the marketplace, we have given them access to an adult world and an adult culture. We will have to learn to live with the consequences of that.

Source: Excerpted from James Gilbert, "Juvenilia," *The New Republic* (June 14, 1999), 54. Reprinted by permission of *The New Republic,* © 1999, *The New Republic,* Inc.

Read and React

1. Why does Gilbert think it is not possible to scientifically prove how culture affects a particular behavior?

2. In two or three sentences, state the main point that the author makes. Do you agree or disagree with him and why?

Chapter 4

Socialization

Sections

Learning Objectives

After reading this chapter, you will be able to

- define the term *socialization*.
- discuss the role socialization plays in human development.
- describe the effects of extreme isolation on children.
- explain key concepts of socialization from the symbolic interactionist perspective.
- analyze the role of the family, school, peer group, and media in socializing young people.
- discuss processes for socialization in adulthood.

Applying Sociology

Many of us assume that the love we feel for family and friends comes naturally. Actually, we learn these feelings from the people around us. In the photo at left, for example, the girls are learning how to share common feelings about the show they're watching.

When sociologists talk about learning how to express feelings, they use the word socialization. How have sociologists researched this process? One way is through cases of children who were isolated. Take the case of Genie. From the time she was nearly two, Genie's father kept her in a locked room. When she was discovered at the age of thirteen, much of her behavior was subhuman. Because Genie's father severely punished her for making any sounds, she never sobbed when she cried or spoke when angry. Because her father never gave her solid food, she could not chew. Her social behavior was primitive. If another person had something she liked, she would take it without asking.

Attempts to socialize Genie failed. After four years, she still could not read and spoke only in short phrases. In this chapter you will see how socialization occurs and dramatic examples of what happens when it does not.

Sociology nline

Chapter Overview
Visit the *Sociology and You* Web site at glencoe.com and click on **Chapter 4—Chapter Overviews** to preview chapter information.

The Importance of Socialization

Key Term

● **socialization** *(p. 110)*

Section Preview

Socialization is the cultural process of learning to participate in group life. Without it, we would not develop many of the characteristics we associate with being human. Studies have shown that animals and human infants who are deprived of intensive and prolonged social contact with others are stunted in their emotional and social growth.

Socialization and Personality

Nearly all the human social behavior we consider natural and normal is learned. It is natural to us in the United States for husbands and wives to walk along side-by-side. In many places in India, however, it seems natural for wives to walk slightly behind their husbands. In fact, nearly all aspects of social life (including walking patterns) are not natural but learned through the process of socialization. Human beings at birth are helpless and without knowledge of their society's ways of thinking, feeling, and behaving. If a human infant is to participate in cultural life, much learning has to take place. **Socialization** is the cultural process of learning to participate in group life. Such learning takes place through cultural transmission.

● **socialization**
the process of learning to participate in a group

Monkeys fail to develop psychologically and socially when deprived of their mothers. Can we generalize from monkeys to human children?

Orphanages, such as this one in Havana, Cuba, are of interest to sociologists. They worry what effect growing up without prolonged social contact with parents will have on children.

Socialization begins at birth and continues throughout life. Successful socialization enables people to fit into all kinds of social groups. Socialization must occur if high school freshmen are to adjust to a new situation, if graduating seniors are to look for employment, and if presidents of the United States are to govern successfully.

The most important learning occurs early in life. Psychological case studies reveal that without prolonged and intensive social contact, children do not learn such basics as walking, talking, and loving. Without socialization, a human infant cannot develop the set of attitudes, beliefs, values, and behaviors associated with being an individual.

How do we know socialization is important? Suppose you wanted to design an experiment to see how socialization affects infants. You would have to set up an experiment that compared a group of normally socialized infants (the *control* group) with a group of isolated infants—infants with little or no human contact (the *experimental* group). For obvious reasons, such experiments are not conducted with human infants. We do, however, have some nonexperimental evidence from studies of socially isolated children. Experiments have been done with monkeys.

How do monkeys react to social isolation? A psychologist, Harry Harlow, devised a famous experiment that showed the negative effects of social isolation on rhesus monkeys (Harlow and Zimmerman, 1959; Harlow and Harlow, 1962; Harlow, 1967). In one experiment, infant monkeys, separated from their mothers at birth, were exposed to two artificial mothers—wire dummies of the same approximate size and shape as real adult monkeys. One of the substitute mothers had an exposed wire body. The other was covered with soft terry cloth. Free to choose between them, the infant monkeys consistently spent more time with the soft, warm mother. Even when the exposed wire dummy became the only source of food, the terry cloth mother remained the favorite. Apparently, closeness and comfort were more important to these monkeys than food. When frightened by a mechanical toy bear or a rubber snake, these infant monkeys consistently ran to their cloth mothers for security and protection.

TECH TRENDS

Can the Internet Stunt Your Social Growth?

You will read in this section about the effects of extreme social isolation in Anna, Isabelle, and Genie. Although no one expects the results to be nearly as harmful, many sociologists today are concerned about how the increased use of computers and the Internet might affect young people. They wonder if this will be the first generation of children to grow up lacking adequate social skills.

Traditional games—sandlot ball games, for example—are socially oriented. These games require interaction and negotiation with other people, encourage sensitivity to others' viewpoints, help establish mutual understanding, and increase cooperative behavior (Casbergue and Kieff, 1998). These social skills are not developed by children who spend a great deal of time in isolated computer activities.

One researcher, Sherry Turkle, claims that the social isolation brought about by heavy use of the Internet leads to the destruction of meaningful social contact (Katz and Aspden, 1997). Similarly, Cliff Stoll (1995) says that excessive Internet activity lowers people's commitment to real friendships.

According to an important nationwide study, the Internet is promoting social isolation (Nie and Erbring, 2000). As people spend more time on the Internet, they experience less meaningful social contact. Impersonal electronic relationships are replacing face-to-face interaction with family and friends. According to the author of this study, political scientist Norman Nie, "When you spend time on the Internet, you don't hear a human voice and you never get a hug."

A more recent nationwide study (Nie et al., 2004) found that the average Internet user spends nearly three hours a day online. This translates into a daily reduction of one hour and ten minutes in face-to-face interaction with family. It also reduces sleep time each night by about 25 minutes.

Defenders of computers and the Internet point to a survey (based on 2,500 Americans) that showed Internet users were just as likely as non–Internet users to join religious, leisure, or community groups (Katz and Aspden, 1997). The survey results, according to these observers, indicate that Internet users are just as socially active as other people.

Critics of this survey point out that the researchers failed to ask some important questions. They did not distinguish between heavy users of the Internet and more moderate users. Also, those surveyed were adults who had already gone through the early years of socialization. There will have to be more research before we understand the effects of new technologies on children's social growth.

Analyzing the Trends

What is your position in the debate about whether heavy Internet use stunts social skills? Give reasons for your answers.

Harlow showed that infant monkeys need intimacy, warmth, physical contact, and comfort. Infant monkeys raised in isolation became distressed, apathetic, withdrawn, hostile adult animals. They never exhibited normal sexual patterns. As mothers, they either rejected or ignored their babies. Sometimes, they even physically abused them.

Can we generalize from monkeys to humans?

It is risky to assume that knowledge gained about non-humans also applies to humans. Nevertheless, many experts on human development believe that for human infants—as for Harlow's monkeys—emotional needs for affection, intimacy, and warmth are as important as physiological needs for food, water, and protection. Human babies denied close contact usually have difficulty forming emotional ties with others. Touching, holding, stroking, and communicating appear to be essential to normal human development. According to a classic study by Lawrence Casler (1965), the developmental growth rate of institutionalized children—who receive less physical contact than normal—can be improved with only twenty minutes of extra touching a day.

Studies have shown that children raised under extremely isolated conditions have little or no chance of ever being socialized.

Case Studies on Isolated Children: Anna and Isabelle

To understand more about how socialization affects development, we will look at the case histories of two children—Anna and Isabelle—who were socially and emotionally abused. You already know the story of Genie from the Applying Sociology feature on page 109. Anna and Isabelle also had traumatic childhoods. Although these three children were born many years ago, similar situations still occur today, unfortunately.

Who was Anna?

Anna was the second child born to her unmarried mother. At first, Anna's strict grandfather had forced her mother to take Anna and leave home, but desperation drove them back again. Anna's mother so feared that the sight of the child would anger her father that she kept Anna confined to a small room on the second floor of their farmhouse. For five years, Anna received only milk to drink. When finally found, she was barely alive. Her legs were skeleton-like and her stomach bloated from malnutrition. Apparently, Anna had seldom been moved from one position to another, and her clothes and bedding were filthy. She did not know what it was like to be held or comforted. At the time of her discovery, Anna could not walk or talk and showed few signs of intelligence.

During the first year and a half after being found, Anna lived in a county home for children. Here, she learned to walk, to understand simple commands, and to feed herself. She could recall people she had seen. But her speech was that of a one-year-old.

Anna was then transferred to a school for learning disabled children, where she made some further progress. Still, at the age of seven, her mental age was only nineteen months, and her social maturity was that of a two-year-old. A year later, she could bounce and catch a ball, participate as a follower in group activities, eat normally (although with a spoon only), attend to her toilet needs, and dress herself (except for handling buttons and snaps). At this point, she had acquired the speech level of a two-year-old. By the time of her death at age ten, she had made some additional progress. She could carry out instructions, identify a few colors, build with blocks, wash her hands, brush her teeth, and try to help other children. Her developing capacity for emotional attachment was reflected in the love she had developed for a doll.

Who was Isabelle? Nine months after Anna was found, Isabelle was discovered. She, too, had been hidden away because her mother was unmarried. Isabelle's mother had been deaf since the age of two and did not speak. She stayed with her child in a dark room, secluded from the rest of the family. When found at the age of six and a half, Isabelle was physically ill from an inadequate diet and lack of sunshine. Her legs were so bowed that when she stood the soles of her shoes rested against each other, and her walk was a skittering movement. Some of her actions were like those of a six-month-old infant. Unable to talk except for a strange croaking sound, Isabelle communicated with her mother by means of gestures. Like an animal in the wild, she reacted with fear and hostility to strangers, especially men.

At first, Isabelle was thought to be severely learning disabled. (Her initial IQ score was near the zero point.) Nevertheless, an intensive program of rehabilitation was begun. After a slow start, Isabelle progressed through the usual stages of learning and development at a faster pace than normal. It took her only two years to acquire the skills mastered by a normal six-year-old. By the time she was eight and a half, Isabelle was on an educational par with children her age. By outward appearances, she was an intelligent, happy, energetic child. At age fourteen, she participated in all the school activities normal for other children in her grade.

To Isabelle's good fortune, she, unlike Anna, benefited from intensive instruction at the hands of trained professionals. Her ability to progress may also have been because she was confined with her mother for company and comforting.

What can we learn from these case studies? The implication of the cases of Anna, Isabelle, and Genie is unmistakable. The personal and social development associated with being human is acquired through intensive and prolonged social contact with others.

Section 1 Assessment

1. Define the term *socialization.*
2. What did Harlow's research on rhesus monkeys reveal?

3. Did the case studies on Anna, Isabelle, and Genie support Harlow's conclusions? Why or why not?

Critical Thinking

4. **Analyzing Information** Do you think sociologists have overemphasized the importance of social contact in learning? What are some legal and moral implications for the government in this kind of child abuse? Should the state protect children from their parents?

Socialization and the Self

Section Preview

All three theoretical perspectives agree that socialization is needed if cultural and societal values are to be learned. Symbolic interactionism offers the most fully developed perspective for studying socialization. In this approach, the self-concept is developed by using other people as mirrors for learning about ourselves.

The Functionalist and Conflict Perspectives on Socialization

Each of the three major theoretical perspectives provides insights into socialization. However, the symbolic interactionist perspective allows a more complete understanding than the other two.

How does the functionalist perspective explain socialization? Functionalism stresses the ways in which groups work together to create a stable society. Schools and families, for example, socialize children by teaching the same basic norms, beliefs, and values. If it were otherwise, society could not exist as a whole. It would be fragmented and chaotic.

How does the conflict perspective explain socialization? The conflict perspective views socialization as a way of perpetuating the status quo. When people are socialized to accept their family's social class, for example, they help preserve the current class system. People learn to accept

According to the conflict theory, these young boys are being socialized to accept their social class.

their social status before they have enough self-awareness to realize what is happening. Because they do not challenge their position in life, they do not upset the existing class structure. Consequently, socialization maintains the social, political, and economic advantages of the higher social classes.

Symbolic Interactionism and Socialization

In the early part of the twentieth century, Charles Horton Cooley and George Herbert Mead developed the symbolic interactionist perspective. They challenged the once widely held belief that human nature is biologically determined (that you are a certain way because you were born that way). For them, human nature is a product of society.

How does symbolic interactionism help us understand socialization? Symbolic interactionism uses a number of key concepts to explain socialization. These concepts include

- the self-concept
- the looking-glass self
- significant others
- role taking (the imitation stage, the play stage, the game stage)
- the generalized other.

Where does the self-concept come from? Charles Horton Cooley developed the idea of the **self-concept** from watching his own children at play. Your self-concept is your image of yourself as having an identity separate from other people.

Cooley (1902) realized that children interpreted how others reacted to them in many ways. For example, young children learn quickly that causing some disturbance when adult visitors are present turns attention from the guests to themselves. From such insights, children learn to judge themselves in terms of how they imagine others *will* react to them. Thus, other people serve as mirrors for the development of the self. Cooley called this way of learning the **looking-glass self**—a self-concept based on our idea of others' judgments of us.

How does the looking-glass process work? According to Cooley, we use other people as mirrors to reflect back what we imagine they think of us. In this view, the looking-glass self is the product of a three-stage process that is constantly taking place.

1. First, we imagine how we appear to others. (What is our perception of how others see us?)

2. Next, we imagine the reaction of others to our (imagined) appearance.

3. Finally, we evaluate ourselves according to how we imagine others have judged us.

This is not a conscious process, and the three stages can occur in very rapid succession. The result of the process is a positive or negative self-evaluation.

Consider this example of the looking-glass process. Suppose you have a new teacher you want to impress. You prepare hard for the next day's class.

● **self-concept**
an image of yourself as having an identity separate from other people

● **looking-glass self**
an image of yourself based on what you believe others think of you

Figure 4.1	Socialization and Mass Media

Each theoretical perspective has a unique view of the socialization process. This table identifies these views and illustrates the unique interpretation of each view with respect to the influence of the mass media on the socialization process.

Theoretical Perspective	View of Socialization	How the Media Influence Socialization
Functionalism	Stresses how socialization contributes to a stable society	Network television programs encourage social integration by exposing the entire society to shared beliefs, values, and norms.
Conflict Theory	Views socialization as a way for the powerful to keep things the same	Newspaper owners and editors exercise power by setting the political agenda for a community.
Symbolic Interactionism	Holds that socialization is the major determinant of human nature	Through words and pictures, children's books expose the young to the meaning of love, manners, and motherhood.

In class, as you are making a comment on the assignment, you have an image of your performance (stage 1). After finishing your comments, you think your teacher is disappointed (stage 2). Because you wanted your teacher to be impressed, you feel bad about yourself (stage 3).

Can the looking glass be distorted? Because the looking glass we use comes from our imaginations, it may be distorted. The mirror may not accurately reflect others' opinions of us. The teacher in the above example may not have been disappointed at all.

Unfortunately, the looking-glass process works even if we are mistaken about others' perceptions of us. If we incorrectly believe that a teacher, or a date, or our parents dislike us, the consequences to us are just as real as if it were true.

Do we use some people as mirrors more than others? George Herbert Mead pointed out that some people are more important to us than others (Mead, 1934). The people whose judgments are most important to our self-concepts are called **significant others.** For a child, significant others are likely to include mother, father, grandparent, teachers, and playmates. Teenagers place heavy reliance on their peers. The variety of significant others is greater for adults, ranging from spouses, parents, and friends to ministers and employers.

● **significant others**
those people whose reactions are most important to your self-concept

What is role taking? As humans, we carry on silent conversations. That is, we think something to ourselves and respond internally to it. All of us do this when we predict the behavior of others. Through internal conversation, we can imagine the thoughts, emotions, and behavior of others in any social situation. **Role taking** allows us to see ourselves through the eyes of someone else. It allows us to take the viewpoint of another person and then respond to ourselves from that imagined viewpoint.

With role taking we can play out scenes in our minds and anticipate what others will say or do. For example, you might want to ask your teacher for an "A." If you could not mentally put yourself in your teacher's place, you would have no idea of the objections that she might raise. But by role-playing her reaction mentally, you can prepare for those objections and be ready to justify your "A."

How does the ability for role taking develop? According to Mead, the ability for role taking is the product of a three-stage process. He called these the imitation stage, the play stage, and the game stage.

In the **imitation stage,** which begins at around one and a half to two years, the child imitates (without understanding) the physical and verbal behavior of a significant other. This is the first step in developing the capacity for role taking.

At the age of three or four, a young child can be seen playing at being mother, father, police officer, teacher, or astronaut. This play involves acting and thinking as a child imagines another person would. This is what Mead called the **play stage**—the stage during which children take on roles of others one at a time.

The third phase in the development of role taking Mead labeled the **game stage.** In this stage, children learn to engage in more sophisticated role taking as they become able to consider the roles of several people simultaneously. Games they play involve several participants, and there are specific rules designed to ensure that the behaviors of the participants fit together. All participants in a game must know what they are supposed to do and what is expected of others in the game. Imagine the confusion in a baseball game if young first-base players have not yet mastered the idea that the ball hit to a teammate will usually be thrown to them. In the second stage of role taking (the play stage) a child may pretend to be a first-base player one moment and pretend to be a base runner the next. In the game stage, however, first-base players who drop their gloves and run to second base when the other team hits the ball will not remain in the game for very long. It is during the game stage that children learn to gear their behavior to the norms of the group.

When do we start acting out of principle? During the game stage, a child's self-concept, attitudes, beliefs, and values gradually come to depend less on individuals and more on general concepts. For example, being an honest person is no longer merely a matter of pleasing significant others such as one's mother, father, or minister. Rather, it begins to seem wrong *in principle* to be dishonest. As this change takes place, a **generalized other** —an integrated conception of the norms, values, and beliefs of one's community or society—emerges.

● **role taking**
assuming the viewpoint of another person and using that viewpoint to shape the self-concept

● **imitation stage**
Mead's first stage in the development of role taking; children begin to imitate behaviors without understanding why

● **play stage**
Mead's second stage in the development of role taking; children act in ways they imagine other people would

● **game stage**
Mead's third stage in the development of role taking; children anticipate the actions of others based on social rules

● **generalized other**
integrated conception of the norms, values, and beliefs of one's community or society

What is the self? According to Mead, we can think of the self as being composed of two parts: the "me" and the "I." The **"me"** is the part of the self created through socialization. The "me" accounts for predictability and conformity. Yet much human behavior is spontaneous and unpredictable. An angry child may, for example, unexpectedly yell hurtful words at the parent whom he loves. To account for this spontaneous, unpredictable, often creative part of the self, Mead proposed the **"I."**

The "I" does not operate only in extreme situations of rage or excitement. It interacts constantly with the "me" as we conduct ourselves in social situations. According to Mead, the first reaction of the self comes from the "I." Before we act, however, this reaction is directed into socially acceptable channels by the socialized "me." When the "I" wants a piece of a friend's candy bar, the "me" reflects on the consequences of taking the candy without permission. Thus, the "I" normally takes the "me" into account before acting. However, the unpredictability of much human behavior demonstrates that the "me" is not always in control!

What do you think is the developmental level of the "generalized other" in each of these two shoplifters?

- **"me"**
  the part of the self formed through socialization

- **"I"**
  the part of the self that accounts for unlearned, spontaneous acts

Section 2 Assessment

1. What is the looking-glass self?

2. What are the consequences of having a distorted looking glass?

3. Which "self" is the first to react to a situation, the "me" or the "I"?

Critical Thinking

4. **Applying Concepts** Describe an experience you have had with the looking-glass process. How did this experience touch or change your self-concept?

Surviving a Prisoner-of-War Camp

By learning the culture around them—whatever that culture is—human beings can and do adapt to almost any situation. This learning process is a type of socialization. The following description of adaptation in a German prison camp during World War II was written by Bruno Bettelheim, a noted American scholar who survived imprisonment.

When a prisoner had reached the final stage of adjustment to the camp situation, he had changed his personality so as to accept various values of the SS [Hitler's elite troops] as his own. A few examples may illustrate how this acceptance expressed itself.

Slowly prisoners accepted, as the expression of their verbal aggressions, terms which definitely did not originate in their previous vocabularies, but were taken over from the very different vocabulary of the SS. From copying the verbal aggressions of the SS to copying its form of bodily aggressions was one more step, but it took several years to make this step. It was not unusual to find old prisoners, when in charge of others, behaving worse than the SS.

Old prisoners who identified themselves with the SS did so not only in respect to aggressive behavior. They would try to acquire old pieces of SS uniforms. If that was not possible, they tried to sew and mend their uniforms so that they would resemble those of the guards. The length to which prisoners would go in these efforts seemed unbelievable, particularly since the SS punished them for their efforts to copy SS uniforms. When asked why they did it, the old prisoners admitted that they loved to look like the guards.

The old prisoners' identification with the SS did not stop with the copying of their outer appearance and behavior. Old prisoners accepted Nazi goals and values, too, even when these seemed opposed to their own interests. It was appalling to see how far even politically well-educated prisoners would go with this identification. At one time American and English newspapers were full of stories about the cruelties committed in these camps. The SS punished prisoners for the appearance of these stories, true to its policy of punishing the group for whatever a member or a former member did, since the stories must have originated in reports from former prisoners. In discussions of this event, old prisoners would insist that it was not the business of foreign correspondents or newspapers to bother with German institutions, expressing their hatred of the journalists who tried to help them.

After so much has been said about the old prisoners' tendency to conform and to identify with the SS, it ought to be stressed that this was only part of the picture. The author has tried to concentrate on interesting psychological mechanisms in group behavior rather than on reporting types of behavior which are either well known or could reasonably be expected. These same old prisoners who identified with the SS defied it at other moments, demonstrating extraordinary courage in doing so.

Source: From *Surviving and Other Essays,* by Bruno Bettelheim. © 1979 by Bruno Bettelheim and Trude Bettelheim as Trustees.

Thinking It Over

1. Describe an experience you have had in which you or someone you know, as a new member of a group, imitated the ways of the group.

2. How does gang affiliation (such as wearing gang colors or using their slogans) demonstrate the tendency to conform?

Agents of Socialization

Section Preview

During childhood and adolescence, the major agents of socialization are the family, school, peer group, and mass media. The family's role is critical in forming basic values. Schools introduce children to life beyond the family. In peer groups, young people learn to relate as equals. The mass media provide role models for full integration into society.

Key Terms

- hidden curriculum *(p. 122)*
- peer group *(p. 123)*
- mass media *(p. 124)*

The Family and Socialization

The child's first exposure to the world occurs within the family, which is the primary agent of socialization. Some essential developments occur through close interaction with a small number of people—none of whom the child has selected. Within the family the child learns to

- think and speak
- internalize norms, beliefs, and values
- form some basic attitudes
- develop a capacity for intimate and personal relationships
- acquire a self-image (Handel, 1990).

The impact of the family reaches far beyond its direct effects on the child. Our family's social class shapes what we think of ourselves and how others treat us, even far into adulthood. Author Jean Evans offers an illustration of this in the case of Johnny Rocco, a twenty-year-old living in a city slum.

Johnny hadn't been running the streets long when the knowledge was borne in on him that being a Rocco made him "something special"; the reputation of the notorious Roccos, known to neighbors, schools, police, and welfare agencies as "chiselers, thieves, and trouble-makers," preceded him. The cop on the beat, Johnny says, always had some cynical smart crack to make. . . . Certain children were not permitted to play with him. Wherever he went—on the streets, in the neighborhood, settlement house, at the welfare agency's penny milk station, at school, where other Roccos had been before him—he recognized himself by a gesture, an oblique remark, a wrong laugh. (Evans, 1954:11)

The infant in the photo on the left is likely to be socialized in a very different way from the two children above. What are some differences in attitudes that will probably be formed by these children because of their different family life?

And then when I was talking to him he took the clicker and tried to turn me off.

machlis   11·23

Parents are no longer the only significant socializing force in their children's lives, as the cartoon suggests.

Socialization in Schools

In school, children are under the care and supervision of adults who are not relatives. For the first time, many of the child's relationships with other people are impersonal. Rewards and punishments are based on performance rather than affection. Although a mother may cherish any picture that her child creates, a teacher evaluates her students by more objective standards. Slowly, children are taught to be less dependent emotionally on their parents. The school also creates feelings of loyalty and allegiance to something beyond the family.

How do schools socialize students? The socialization process in school involves more than reading, writing, and arithmetic. Underlying the formal goals of the school is the **hidden curriculum** —the informal and unofficial aspects of culture that children are taught in preparation for life. The hidden curriculum teaches children discipline, order, cooperation, and conformity—characteristics required for success in the adult world of work. (You will learn more about the hidden curriculum in Chapter 12.)

School also teaches children how we experience time in the real world. According to education critic John Holt (1995), life in schools is run by the clock, as it is in the working world. A bell signals when children must move to the next scheduled event, whether or not they understand what they have been working on and whether or not they are ready to switch to a different subject. Getting through a preset number of activities within a given time period often becomes more important than learning.

● **hidden curriculum**
the informal and unofficial aspects of culture that children are taught in school

Schools have rules and regulations to cover almost all activities—how to dress, how to wear one's hair, which side of the hall to walk on, when to speak in class. Teachers reward children with praise and acceptance when they recite the "right" answers, behave "properly," or exhibit "desirable" attitudes.

Children are isolated from the working adult society by being set apart in school for most of their preadult lives. Because they are separated from the adult world for such a long time, young people must depend on one another for much of their social life.

Peer Group Socialization

The family and the school are both agencies of socialization organized and operated by adults. The child's **peer group**—composed of individuals of roughly the same age and interests—is the only agency of socialization that is not controlled primarily by adults. Children usually belong to several peer groups. A child may belong to a play group in the neighborhood, a clique at school, an after-school club, or a sports team.

How do peer groups contribute to socialization? In the family and at school, children are subordinated to adults. In the peer group, young people have an opportunity to engage in give-and-take relationships. Children experience conflict, competition, and cooperation in such groups. The peer group also gives children experience in self-direction. They can begin to make their own decisions; experiment with new ways of thinking, feeling, and behaving; and engage in activities that involve self-expression.

● **peer group**
set of individuals of roughly the same age and interests

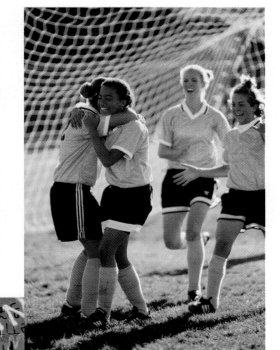

Socialization is occurring in each of the peer groups pictured here, perhaps with far different consequences for the larger society.

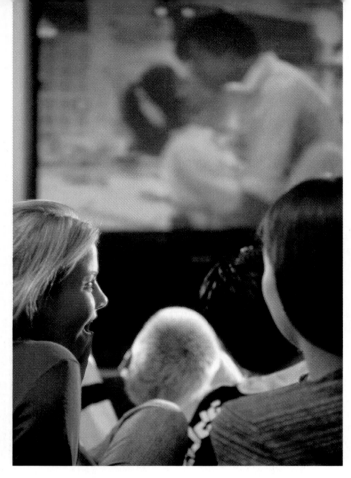

Independence from adults is also promoted by the peer group, because often the norms of the peer group conflict with those of the adult world. Children learn to be different from their parents in ways that help to develop self-sufficiency.

The peer group also provides an opportunity for children to develop close ties with friends outside the family, including members of the opposite sex. At the same time, they are learning to get along with large numbers of people, many of whom are quite different from themselves. This helps develop the social flexibility needed in a mobile, rapidly changing society.

Do friends or family have more influence on young people? The majority of Americans now live in either urban or suburban areas. In both two-income families and single-parent families, parents may commute many miles to work and spend much of their time away from home. Consequently, once children reach the upper levels of grade school, they may spend more time with their peers than they do with their parents.

According to psychologist Judith Harris (1998), peers are more important than parents in socializing children. Even though most sociologists do not agree with this extreme conclusion, many do believe that the peer group is having a growing effect on social development.

The mass media are a relatively new source of socialization. How does television advertising influence the dating behavior of teenagers?

● **mass media**
means of communication designed to reach the general population

The Mass Media and Socialization

Mass media are means of communication designed to reach the general population. They include such things as television, radio, newspapers, magazines, movies, books, the Internet, tapes, and discs. Many popular images presented in the mass media are highly distorted. For example, detective and police work are not as exciting and glamorous as depicted in books, in movies, and on television. Nevertheless, it is often through the mass media that children are first introduced to numerous aspects of their culture (Fishman and Cavender, 1998).

What role do the mass media play in socialization? The mass media display role models for children to imitate. Learning these role models helps to integrate the young into society.

The mass media, by their content alone, teach many of the ways of the society. This is evident in the behavior we take for granted—the duties of the detective, waitress, or sheriff; the functions of the hospital, advertising agency, and police court; behavior in hotel, airplane, or cruise ship; the language of the prison, army, or courtroom; the relationship between nurses and doctors or secretaries and their bosses. Such settings and relationships are portrayed time and again in films, television shows, and comic strips; and all "teach"—however misleadingly—norms, status positions, and institutional functions (Elkin and Handel, 1991:189).

World View

Availability of Television

The mass media play a key role in the socialization process. Since nearly every U.S. home has at least one television (the majority have more), this medium is one of the most influential in the United States. This map shows that ownership of televisions varies widely around the world.

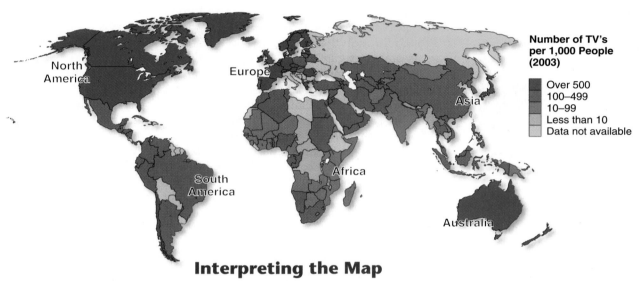

Number of TV's per 1,000 People (2003)

- Over 500
- 100–499
- 10–99
- Less than 10
- Data not available

Interpreting the Map

1. What geographical factor(s) might contribute to the density of TV households in South America?

2. Do you think the attitudes of members of societies with more televisions are influenced more by government advertising than members of societies with fewer televisions? Why or why not?

Source: The World Bank, *2005 World Development Indicators.*

The mass media also offer children ideas about the values in their society. They provide children with images of achievement and success, activity and work, equality and democracy.

What about violence in the mass media?   On the negative side, consider the relationship between violence on television and real-life violence. By age sixteen, the average American child will have seen twenty thousand homicides on television (Leonard, 1998). Social scientists have been reluctant in the past to recognize a causal connection between television violence and real-life violence. However, based on hundreds of studies involving over ten thousand children, most now conclude that watching aggressive behavior on television significantly increases aggression in society (Dudley, 1999; U.S.Department of Health and Human Services, 2001; Donnerstein, 2004).

Sociology Online

Student Web Activity
Visit the *Sociology and You* Web site at glencoe.com and click on **Chapter 4—Student Web Activities** for an activity on mass media and socialization.

Sociology Today

Struggling Through the Teen Years

Adolescents do not get good press. They are often portrayed by the media as awkward, unreasonable, strong-willed, and overconfident. Some parents, taking their cue from comedian Bill Cosby, jokingly attribute teen behavior to temporary "brain damage." Researcher David Elkind (1981) offers another explanation for much troublesome adolescent behavior. Teens' problem, he concludes, is not brain damage. They are simply struggling through the emotional and physiological changes of the teen years as best they can.

Teenagers may appear to behave irrationally (by adult standards) because of new thinking capabilities not yet under their control. Contrary to the long-accepted belief that the human brain is fully developed by the age of 8 or 12, startling new research reveals that the brain remains a construction site even into the 20s (Begley, 2000). And the part of the brain that undergoes the greatest change between puberty and young adulthood is responsible for such activities as judgment, emotional control, and organization and planning.

Whereas adults are accustomed to looking at situations from several different viewpoints, teens are not. Confusion can result when inexperienced young people attempt to move from making simple, one-factor decisions to consideration of several factors simultaneously. For example, a teen who wants to join friends in a ride from a night football game may consider that the driver has a license, but may fail to consider the driver's experience, driving habits, or drinking behavior.

Teens assume that other people have as much interest in them as they have in themselves. Consequently, they surround themselves with an "imaginary audience." Since teenagers believe that everyone is watching

Consider a few examples. A two-year-old girl died when her older brother, age five, set the house on fire with matches while imitating behavior he had seen on the cartoon program *Beavis and Butt-Head*. Just on the basis of televised reports of violence, a rash of would-be copycat crimes followed the shooting massacre of thirteen students and one teacher at Columbine High School by two students who then shot themselves. Television's effects, of course, are usually more hidden, subtle, and long term:

> . . . [N]ot every child who watched a lot of violence or plays a lot of violent games will grow up to be violent. Other forces must converge, as they did [at Columbine]. . . . But just as every cigarette increases the chance that someday you will get lung cancer, every exposure to violence increases the chances that some day a child will behave more violently than they would otherwise (To Establish Justice, 1999:vi).

and evaluating them, they are extremely self-conscious. In groups, adolescents often play to this imaginary audience by engaging in loud and provocative behavior. Yet they fail to understand why adults become annoyed with them. Gradually, they begin to realize that others have their own preoccupations, and the imaginary-audience behavior lessens.

Teenagers frequently have the feeling of invulnerability. For example, they may think that drug addiction, cancer from smoking, pregnancy, and death happen only to others. Their reckless behavior must be seen within this context.

Young people tend to assume that fairly common adolescent experiences are unique. Common complaints include "Mom, you just don't know how much it hurt for Carlos to take out Maria," and "Dad, you don't know what it's like not to have my own bike." At the other extreme, adolescents may feel that their own perceptions are shared by everyone. A young boy, for example, may believe that others find him unattractive because of what he thinks is a large nose. No amount of talking can convince him that he is exaggerating the size of his nose or that others pay little attention to it. This self-centered view of reality begins to decrease as teens discover that others are having similar feelings and experiences.

Doing Sociology

Identify three ways in which adults and adolescents could use this developmental awareness to ease the struggle of the teen years.

Section 3 Assessment

1. Why does the family have such strong influence on a child's socialization?

2. What aspect of socialization does the child first encounter in school that he or she does not meet in the family?

3. What is the hidden curriculum?

4. Besides family and school, identify two other socializing agents.

Critical Thinking

5. **Evaluating Information** Some pyschologists believe that peer groups have more influence on later socialization than the family group. Give reasons why you agree or disagree with that premise.

Processes of Socialization

Key Terms

- **total institutions** *(p. 128)*
- **desocialization** *(p. 128)*
- **resocialization** *(p. 128)*
- **anticipatory socialization** *(p. 129)*
- **reference group** *(p. 132)*

Section Preview

Symbolic interactionism views socialization as a lifelong process. Desocialization is the process of having to give up old norms. Resocialization begins as people adopt new norms and values. Anticipatory socialization and reference groups are concerned with voluntary change as when moving from one life stage to another.

Desocialization and Resocialization

Whenever change occurs over the course of your life, you will learn new behaviors and skills. This learning is important to socialization. Symbolic interactionism describes four processes associated with socialization after childhood: *desocialization, resocialization, anticipatory socialization,* and *reference groups.*

How does desocialization prepare people for new learning? Mental hospitals, cults, and prisons are **total institutions**—places where residents are separated from the rest of society. These residents are not free to manage their own lives, but are controlled and manipulated by those in charge. The end purpose of this control and manipulation is to permanently change the residents. The first step is **desocialization**—the process by which people give up old norms, values, attitudes, and behaviors. For those in total institutions, desocialization often means the destruction of old self-concepts of personal identity.

Desocialization in institutions is accomplished in many ways. Replacing personal possessions with standard-issue items promotes sameness among the residents. It deprives them of the personal items (long hair, hair brushes, ball caps) they have used to present themselves as unique individuals. The use of serial numbers to identify people and the loss of privacy also contribute to the breakdown of past identity. Cult members, for example, may be denied use of their given names.

How does resocialization begin? Once the self-concept has been broken down, **resocialization**—the process in which people adopt new norms, values, attitudes, and behaviors—can begin. Those in

- **total institutions**
  places in which people are separated from the rest of society and controlled by officials in charge

- **desocialization**
  the process of giving up old norms, values, attitudes, and behaviors

- **resocialization**
  the process of adopting new norms, values, attitudes, and behaviors

The military, a total institution, resocializes soldiers by first forcing them to give up many aspects of their individuality.

Rates of Imprisonment

The U.S. has one of the highest rates of imprisonment in the industrialized world—over four times that of any Western European country. Justice officials worry that some prisons function as "schools for crime." If prisons do first desocialize and then resocialize inmates toward a criminal identity, then the U.S. prison system is unintentionally increasing the criminal portion of the population. This map shows the number of prisoners with sentences of more than one year per 100,000 U.S. residents.

Rates of Imprisonment

- 600 or more
- 500–599
- 400–499
- 300–399
- 200–299
- 200 or less

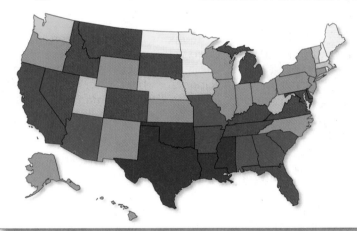

Interpreting the Map

1. Where does your state rank in terms of imprisonment rate? Can you relate the extent of imprisonment in your state to the nature of the socialization that occurs in your state?

2. Do the states adjoining your state have imprisonment rates that are similar or dissimilar to your state?

Source: U.S. Department of Justice, Bureau of Justice Statistics, 2005.

control of total institutions, using an elaborate system of rewards and punishments, attempt to give residents new self-concepts. Rewards for taking on a new "identity" can include extra food, special responsibilities, or periods of privacy. Punishments for nonconformity involve shaming, loss of special privileges, physical punishment, and physical isolation.

The concepts of desocialization and resocialization were developed to analyze social processes in extreme situations. They still apply to other social settings, including basic training in the U.S. Marine Corps and plebe (freshman) year at the United States Military Academy. In much less extreme form, these concepts illuminate changes in our normal life course. Desocialization and resocialization occur as a child becomes a teenager, when young adults begin careers, and as the elderly move into retirement or widowhood.

Anticipatory Socialization

Anticipatory socialization is the process of preparing (in advance) for new norms, values, attitudes, and behaviors. It does not generally occur in prisons or mental hospitals because it involves *voluntary change*.

- **anticipatory socialization**
the voluntary process of preparing to accept new norms, values, attitudes, and behaviors

Case Study: High School Reunions

Socialization occurs throughout life. Even high school reunions play a part. If you asked most Americans to talk about their experiences at a recent high school reunion, what would they say?

"It was great seeing old friends."

"I was curious about how things turned out for people I loved and hated as a teenager."

"I plan to get together with some old friends in the near future."

High school reunions are generally thought to be a time to recapture fond memories of youth.

One researcher wished to investigate the meaning of high school reunions. Keiko Ikeda (1998) studied eight reunions in the American Midwest. He observed these reunions armed with a camera, a tape recorder, and a notebook. After each reunion, he also conducted in-depth, life-story interviews with samples of participants.

Ikeda's results are too complex and varied to easily summarize. (This is typical of in-depth observational studies.) One aspect of the study, however, reveals the socializing aspect of high school reunions. Ikeda compared several reunions of one high school—tenth, fifteenth, twentieth, thirtieth, fortieth, and fiftieth. He focused on the relative emphasis on the past and the present. As you can see from the passage below, the past becomes more important as age increases.

> In the earlier reunions (the tenth and fifteenth years), a concern with relative status and a sense of competitiveness is expressed, often blatantly, through award-giving ceremonies. . . . The hall was decorated in the school colors, and images of the high school mascot were present, but beyond this no high school memorabilia were displayed. The music, too, was current, and not the rock 'n' roll of the late sixties and early seventies.

> The twentieth-year reunion of the Class of '62 is typical of a transitional phase in which elements from the past begin to assume an important role. The past is expressed in high school memorabilia . . . in . . . films and slides taken during high school, and in . . . high school anecdotes that are playfully interwoven throughout the ceremonial events.

> In the thirtieth-year reunion of the Class of '52, the past firmly occupied center stage. A carefully crafted, chronological narrative of the senior year, entitled "The Way We Were," was read, in which major class activities were recalled month by month. . . .

Cathy, © 1990, Cathy Guisewite,
Universal Press Syndicate.
(Reprinted with permission.
All rights reserved.)

In the fiftieth-year reunion, we find a dramatic disappearance of all ritual activities. According to the president of the Class of '32, his class had held reunions every ten years since graduation, and in earlier ceremonies they had given awards, but this time, "none of the folks in the reunion committee felt like doing that kind of thing." It seemed that attendees at the fiftieth-year reunion, for the most part, had risen above concerns of past and present and were content to celebrate together the simple fact that they all still had the vigor to attend a reunion.

Source: Keiko Ikeda, *A Room Full of Mirrors.* Stanford, CA: Stanford University Press, 1998, pp. 143–145.

Working with the Research

1. Ask an adult to describe the activities at one or more high school reunions that he or she has attended. Compare the description with Ikeda's findings.
2. Suppose you had a class assignment to study an upcoming reunion at your school. Select a research question you would want to ask. Identify the research methods you would use.

The dress on these young people indicates they are preparing for entry into the adult world of work or higher education. How does a peer group act as a tool for anticipatory socialization?

Anticipatory socialization may occur in people who are moving from one stage in their lives to another. Consider teenagers, for example. Because they want to resemble those their own age, they may willingly abandon many of the norms, values, attitudes, and behaviors learned previously. This process generally begins in the preteen years. Preteens begin early to observe the ways of teenagers. Teens become their new **reference group**—the group they use to evaluate themselves and from which they acquire attitudes, values, beliefs, and norms. In this situation, the new reference group is a tool for anticipatory socialization.

● **reference group**
group whose norms and values are used to guide behavior; group with whom you identify

Seniors in college, normally seen on campus only in jeans and oversized sweatshirts, suddenly, as graduation nears, are wearing tailored suits and much more serious expressions. In preparing for entry into the business world, they are talking with friends who have graduated as well as company recruiters. In effect, they are preparing themselves for the resocialization they know awaits them (Atchley, 2003).

Section 4 Assessment

1. Identify the following actions as desocialization (D), resocialization (R), or anticipatory socialization (A).
   a. First-year students acquire a new identity during their freshman year at a military academy.
   b. Prison personnel deliberately attempt to destroy the self-concepts of inmates.
   c. High school students identify with college students.

2. Which of the following is *not* an example of a reference group?
   a. Rock-star subculture
   b. United States Military Academy
   c. Terrorists
   d. Mass media

Critical Thinking

3. **Applying Concepts** Which group do you feel is the most influential in the present stage of your socialization—family, peers, school, or the media? Why?

Summary

Section 1: The Importance of Socialization

Main Idea: Socialization is the cultural process of learning to participate in groups. Studies have shown that animals and human infants who are deprived of intensive and prolonged social contact are stunted in their emotional and social growth.

Section 2: Socialization and the Self

Main Idea: Symbolic interactionism offers the most fully developed perspective for studying socialization. In this approach, the self-concept is developed by using other people as mirrors for learning about ourselves.

Section 3: Agents of Socialization

Main Idea: During childhood and adolescence, the major agents of socialization are the family, school, peer group, and mass media.

Section 4: Processes of Socialization

Main Idea: Symbolic interactionism views socialization as a lifelong process. Desocialization is the process of having to give up old norms. Resocialization begins as people adopt new norms and values. Anticipatory socialization and reference groups are concerned with voluntary change as when moving from one life stage to another.

Self-Check Quiz
Visit the *Sociology and You* Web site at glencoe.com and click on **Chapter 4—Self-Check Quizzes** to prepare for the chapter test.

Reviewing Vocabulary

Complete each sentence using each term once.

a. socialization
b. personality
c. anticipatory socialization
d. looking-glass self
e. role taking
f. generalized other
g. total institutions
h. resocialization

1. _____ is the attitudes, beliefs, values, and behaviors associated with an individual.
2. The cultural process of learning to participate in group life is called _____ .
3. _____ allows us to assume the viewpoint of another person and use that viewpoint to shape our self-concept.
4. _____ are places in which people are separated from the rest of society and controlled by officials in charge.
5. The process of adopting new norms, values, attitudes, and behaviors is known as _____ .
6. An image of yourself based on what you believe others think of you is called _____ .
7. _____ is the voluntary process of preparing to accept new norms, values, attitudes, and behaviors.
8. The integrated conception of the norms, values, and beliefs of one's society is called the _____ .

Reviewing the Facts

9. What does the study involving rhesus monkeys suggest about the choices that human infants would make in the same situation?
10. What is socialization from the viewpoint of symbolic interactionism?
11. Which agent of socialization has been the most powerful force in your life? Explain.
12. What concept discussed in this chapter relates to the song lyric: "Walk a Mile in My Shoes"?

13. What is a distinguishing characteristic of total institutions?

14. How does resocialization differ from anticipatory socialization?

Thinking Critically

15. Making Predictions

A growing concern about computers is that some people and groups of people are being "left behind" because they don't have equal access to technology. How might this become a problem for your generation?

16. Analyzing Visuals

Look at the cartoon below and review what you have read in Section 1 and Section 2 of the chapter.

a. How do you think a sociologist would diagnose the problem of the man in the shrubbery?

b. What does the cartoon imply about bureacratic workplaces and their ability to utilize them?

"Bill, have you ever tried plugging your solitary genius into a team setting?"

www.cartoonstock.com

17. Evaluating Information

This chapter discusses the socializing influences of mass media. Our perceptions of the ideal body types seem to be largely a product of media socialization. In a later chapter, you will have an opportunity to look at how the media idealizes body types. Girls feel the need to be thin and boys tend to measure how muscular they are. Discuss how television, magazines, CDs, and video games reinforce these images. Give examples from your experience of how the media has socialized Americans to admire certain figure and body types.

18. Analyzing Information

Your daily life includes many social networks, or groups that regularly contribute to your socialization. They include family, friends, teachers, people at work, teammates, and so forth. Identify one of these groups, and imagine your day if you suddenly lost contact with those people. What support would you be missing? What key elements are provided by this particular social network?

19. Interpreting Information

Sociologists claim the average American watches television seven hours a day, yet some students say they never watch TV. How could you account for this fact? Remember to refer to what you learned from the chapter in discussing this question.

20. Making Generalizations

Total institutions, such as prisons, presume that desocialization and resocialization occur, since one of their goals is to make prisoners law abiding. Yet more than half of the inmates released in the United States return to prison. If desocialization and resocialization really do take place, why is the recidivism rate (the number of prisoners who return to prison) so high? Propose a theory for what might be happening, using the concept of resocialization.

Sociology Projects

21. Socialization and the Media

In this chapter, you read that television plays a key role in the socialization process. Television presents powerful role models to children, even though parents and other adults play an important role interpreting what young viewers see. Based on the table below, frame a hypothesis to test the relationship between socialization and the increase in TV and cable viewing options.

Characteristics of TV/VCR Ownership in U.S. Households (As percentage of TV households)					
	1975	1985	1995	2000	2003
Multi-set	43	57	71	76	79
Color	74	91	99	99	99
VCR	—	14	79	86	95
Remote Control	—	29	91	95	95
Cable and/or satellite	—	26	28	32	85*

* 2003 is the first year for which satellite information was given.
Source: *Time Almanac*, 2006.

22. TV and Real Life

This activity asks you to assess how "real" TV is compared with what we see and do every day. You are to watch two hours of TV. Watch shows that fictionally portray real life (sporting events, the news, and documentaries are not appropriate for this activity). Take detailed notes on the characters, body types, occupations, social class, race, ethnic group, and age. Then venture out into the real world, to a public place such as a park, laundromat, mall, or airport, and observe for two hours. Concentrate on several people, and note the same features that you did for the TV characters. Write a paragraph comparing the characters on television with those you observed in real life.

23. Major Agents of Socialization

Some children without parents or close family find themselves being moved from one foster home to another for the greater part of their childhood. Write an essay of at least one page in length, using standard grammar, proper spelling, and good sentence structure, in which you examine the role of each major agent of socialization in the development of an individual growing up in this environment.
HINT: Family is a major agent of socialization. Family exists in the traditional sense and in variations of all kinds.

Technology Activities

24. As indicated in this chapter, the process of socialization occurs throughout a person's life. The Internet has assumed a significant role in the socialization of Americans. It actually aids television in the process.
   1. What are the most popular television shows among your friends?
   2. Use a search engine to see if these shows have a Web site and what kind of information they present.
   3. What benefits do the Web sites provide to the viewers? To the television show?

25. Using the Internet and your school or local library, research the role the following technological inventions of their time played in the socialization of Americans: the popularity of the radio during 1940–1950; the growing popularity of color television from 1960 to the present; and the popularity of the Internet over the last five years. Consider the positive and negative effects, analyzing how norms and behaviors were changed by the available programming and/or advertising.

National Television Violence

Key Findings

Today, violence is not only seen on the streets but also in the schools. During the last five years of the twentieth century, there were over 120 people shot in schools. We now hear stories in the news about young people participating in violent shootings on school grounds and killing innocent bystanders. In a Michigan school in 2000, one six-year-old shot and killed a classmate at school. These violent acts raise questions: Why is there an increase in violence, especially among today's youth? Does television have a negative effect on individuals? Does television encourage violent behaviors?

In 1994, the National Television Violence Study initiated the first part of its three-year project to assess violence on television. This study, which is the largest study of media content ever undertaken, was funded by the National Cable Television Association. The project examined approximately 2,500 hours of television programming that included 2,693 programs.

The first of the three studies analyzes violent content in television programming. The second study examines children's reactions to ratings and viewer advisories. The final study analyzes the content of antiviolence public service announcements (PSAs).

Following is a summary of the first study conducted in 1994–1995. Collectively, these findings establish the norms that exist in the overall television environment. Many of the patterns observed cause some concern.

Overall Conclusions about Violence on Television

- **Violence predominates on television, often including large numbers of violent interactions per program.**

  The majority (57 percent) of programs on television contain violence, and roughly one third of violent programs contain nine or more violent interactions. The frequency of violence on television can contribute to desensitization and fear, as well as provide ample opportunities to learn violent attitudes and behaviors.

- **In the majority of the episodes of violence, the perpetrator engages in repeated violent acts.**

  The perpetrator engages in repeated acts of violence in more than half (58 percent) of all violent interactions. This increases the amount of violence to which viewers are exposed.

- **predominate**
  to exert control over; to hold an advantage in numbers

- **desensitization**
  the process of preventing an emotional response; make less sensitive

- **perpetrator**
  someone who carries out or brings about an action; in law, one who commits a crime

On a daily basis, children are exposed to countless episodes of violence on their televisions.

● **contextual**
  meaning that is derived from the setting or the environment; not stated, but implied

● **trivialize**
  to make something less important or serious than it is

● **In one-quarter of the violent interactions, a gun is used.**

Certain visual cues, such as weapons, tend to activate aggressive thoughts in viewers. Later, these thoughts cause individuals to interpret neutral events as possibly threatening or aggressive.

● **In about three-quarters of all violent scenes, perpetrators go unpunished.**

The portrayal of rewards and punishments is probably the most important of all **contextual** factors for viewers as they interpret the meaning of what they see on television. Viewers who would otherwise think of a class of behaviors such as violence as bad may eventually learn that those behaviors are good (useful, successful, or desirable) if they are repeatedly and consistently portrayed as rewarded or unpunished. Across all channel types, this study discovered a common pattern that the majority of violent scenes lack any form of punishment for the perpetrators.

● **In a high proportion of violent episodes, the consequences are not realistically portrayed.**

Less than half of violent interactions show the victims experiencing any signs of pain. Furthermore, only about one in six programs depict any long-term negative consequences, such as physical suffering or financial or emotional harm. All of these patterns increase the risk that viewers will believe that violence is not a particularly painful or harmful behavior.

● **Violence is often presented as humorous.**

More than one third of all violent scenes involve a humorous context. Humor tends to **trivialize** or undermine the seriousness with which violence is regarded. Humorous violence can serve to desensitize viewers to the serious or harmful effects of violence.

● **Violent programs rarely employ a strong antiviolence theme.**

Only 4 percent of all television programs emphasize a strong antiviolence theme. *Touched by an Angel, Little House on the Prairie,* and *Mr. Rogers* are among the exceptions.

Source: Adapted from "National Television Violence Study: Executive Summary." Studio City, CA: Mediascope, Inc., 1998.

Read and React

1. What was the stated purpose of the first study?
2. Why does the report state that the contextual factors for viewing violence are the most important?
3. Do you think the report reaches its stated purpose (see Question #1)? Why or why not?

Chapter 5

Social Structure and Society

Learning Objectives

After reading this chapter, you will be able to

- explain what sociologists mean by *social structure*.
- discuss how statuses and roles are related to social structure.
- identify and illustrate the concepts of social structure.
- explain how culture and social structures are related.
- describe the means of subsistence in preindustrial societies.
- discuss the characteristics of industrial society.
- compare and contrast preindustrial, industrial, and postindustrial societies.

Applying Sociology

Because we are deeply involved in our own world, we forget that our ability to participate in daily life is based on decades of being socialized into a specific social structure.

What do we mean by social structure? If we look at other or older societies, the concept may be easier to see. In the photo at left, for example, the British monarch, Queen Elizabeth II, arrives for the opening of Parliament. Because the British still have a monarch, many of their outward traditions recall an earlier social structure, a time when nobles bowed before the monarch, and peasants did the bidding of the nobles.

Even in modern American society, all members of a group have roles they are expected to play. Students are expected to attend class and listen to the teacher. Teachers are expected to be in the classroom when students arrive, hold class, and give tests. If you found yourself in a class where the teacher raised his hand to talk and students napped on the classroom floor, you would wonder what planet you were on. You would not know how to act. To fit in, you would need an awareness of the underlying social structure. In this chapter, we will look at the concepts behind social structure.

Chapter Overview
Visit the *Sociology and You* Web site at glencoe.com and click on **Chapter 5—Chapter Overviews** to preview chapter information.

1

Social Structure and Status

Key Terms

- social structure (p. 140)
- status (p. 140)
- ascribed status (p. 141)
- achieved status (p. 141)
- status set (p. 142)
- master status (p. 142)

- **social structure**
  the underlying patterns of relationships in a group

- **status**
  a position a person occupies within a social structure

Section Preview

The underlying pattern of social relationships in a group is called social structure. Status is one very important element of social structure. Ascribed statuses are assigned at birth; achieved statuses are earned or chosen.

Social Structure Is All Around You

You learned in Chapter 4 that culture shapes human social behavior. In the absence of biological pre-programming, culture guides us in our thinking, feeling, and behaving. Without culture, humans would have no blueprint for social living. This chapter helps explain the relationship between culture and social structure.

So, what is social structure? The chapter opening described a situation in which unexpected classroom behavior resulted in confusion for a newcomer. We are usually spared such confusion when entering a new group because we bring some knowledge of how people will normally relate to one another. In our minds, we carry a "social map" for various group situations. We have mental images of the new group with its patterns of social relationships. This underlying pattern is called **social structure.**

Everyone Has Status

We are not born with mental maps of social structure; we must learn them from others. In the process, we learn about *statuses* and *roles*—major elements of social structure.

What do sociologists mean by status? People may refer to themselves as students, doctors, welders, secretaries, mothers, or sons. Each of these labels refers to a **status**—a position a person occupies within a social structure. Status helps us define who and what we are in relation to others within the same social structure. Some social statuses are acquired at birth. For example, a newborn female instantly becomes a child and a daughter. From then on, she assumes an increasingly larger number and variety of statuses.

Sociologists are interested in the relationships among social statuses. A sociologist investigating delinquency, for example, may focus on the status of the social worker in relation to the statuses of the police officer, judge, and teacher. Figure 5.1 illustrates the status of a high school

The two different status people in this photograph are behaving exactly as most people would expect.

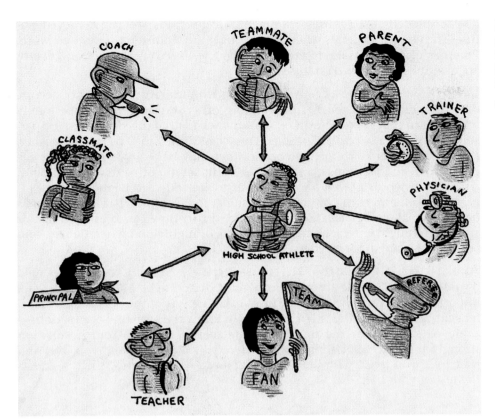

athlete related to various other statuses. There are two basic types of social statuses—*ascribed* and *achieved*.

What is an ascribed status? An **ascribed status** is neither earned nor chosen; it is assigned to us. At birth, an infant is either a male or a female. We do not choose our gender. Age is another example of an ascribed social status. In some societies, religion and social class are ascribed by the family of birth. If you were born into a lower-class home in India, for example, you would not be permitted to rise to a higher social class.

How is status achieved? An **achieved status** is earned or chosen. Achieving statuses is possible where people have some degree of control and choice. In most modern societies, for example, an individual can

● **ascribed status**
a position that is neither earned nor chosen but assigned

● **achieved status**
a position that is earned or chosen

Pictured is an African Masai man in traditional clothes. Do you think that his clothing reflects an ascribed or an achieved status?

decide to become a spouse or a parent. Occupations are also achieved statuses in modern societies where people have freedom to choose their work. Plumber, electrician, sales representative, nurse, executive, lawyer, and doctor are examples of achieved statuses.

What is a status set?

A person who is a social worker does not occupy only one status. This person holds various other statuses that may be totally unrelated to that of social worker. A **status set** is all of the statuses that a person occupies at any particular time. One social worker may be a wife, mother, author, and church choir director. Another may be a single parent, service club leader, and jazz musician. Another status set might be that of a student, a brother, a tennis player, a tutor, and a store clerk. Each of these statuses is part of another network of statuses. Assume, for example, that in addition to being a social worker, an individual is also a part-time jazz musician. In this status, she might interact with the statuses of nightclub owner, dancer, and fellow musician, among others.

Are all of a person's statuses equal?

Among the statuses held by an individual, some are more important than others. **Master statuses** are important because they influence most other aspects of the person's life. Master statuses may be achieved or ascribed. In industrial societies, occupations—achieved statuses for the most part—are master statuses. Your occupation strongly influences such matters as where you live, how well you live, and how long you live. "Criminal" is an achieved master status, since it affects the rest of your life.

● **status set**
all of the statuses that a person occupies at any particular time

● **master status**
a position that strongly affects most other aspects of a person's life

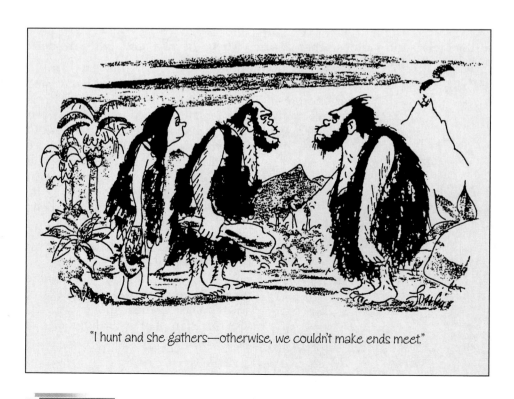

"I hunt and she gathers—otherwise, we couldn't make ends meet."

Expected behavior is often based on master statuses such as gender.

Eileen M. Collins, commander of the 2005 space shuttle *Discovery*, was the first woman to command a U.S. space shuttle. Her master status of astronaut is achieved; her master status of woman is ascribed.

Age, gender, race, and ethnicity are examples of ascribed master statuses. These statuses are master statuses because they significantly affect the likelihood of achieving other social statuses. When will the United States have a female president? Would you let a nineteen-year-old or a ninety-year-old handle your case in court? Or remove your appendix?

Sociology Online

Student Web Activity
Visit the *Sociology and You* Web site at glencoe.com and click on **Chapter 5—Student Web Activities** for an activity on social status.

Section 1 Assessment

1. Briefly define the term *social structure*.

Match the definition with the type of status (a–d) it best describes.

2. wife, mother, author, church choir director

3. electrician, spouse

4. the president of the United States, professional athlete

5. sex, gender, race

6. daughter, son

7. quarterback, coach, fan, trainer

a. ascribed status

b. achieved status

c. master status

d. status set

Critical Thinking

8. Categorizing Information On a separate piece of paper, make a diagram of your life—the statuses you possess and the responsibilities or role expectations for each. Examples of statuses include son/daughter, student, band member, etc.

9. Applying Concepts What is the most important master status you have held? Has the master status helped or hindered you? What master status would you like to achieve? Why?

Focus on Research

Experiment: Adopting Statuses in a Simulated Prison

Social psychologist Philip Zimbardo and his colleagues designed an experiment to observe the behavior of people without criminal records in a mock "prison." They were amazed at the rapidity with which statuses were adopted and roles fulfilled by the college students playing "prisoners" and "guards." This experiment reveals the ease with which people can be socialized to statuses and roles. Zimbardo's own words describe the design and results of this experiment.

In an attempt to understand just what it means . . . to be a prisoner or a prison guard, Craig Haney, Curt Banks, Dave Jaffe and I created our own prison. We carefully screened over 70 volunteers who answered an ad in a Palo Alto city newspaper and ended up with about two dozen young men who were selected to be part of this study. They were mature, emotionally stable, normal, intelligent college students from middle-class homes. . . . They appeared to represent the cream of the crop of this generation. None had any criminal record. . . .

Half were arbitrarily designated as prisoners by a flip of a coin, the others as guards. These were the roles they were to play in our simulated prison. The guards . . . made up their own formal rules for maintaining law, order and respect, and were generally free to improvise new ones during their eight-hour, three-man shifts. The prisoners were unexpectedly picked up at their homes by a city policeman in a squad car, searched, handcuffed, fingerprinted, booked at the Palo Alto station house and taken blindfolded to our jail. There they were stripped, deloused, put into a uniform, given a number and put into a cell with two other prisoners where they expected to live for the next two weeks. . . .

At the end of only six days we had to close down our mock prison because what we saw was frightening. It was no longer apparent to most of the subjects (or to us) where real-

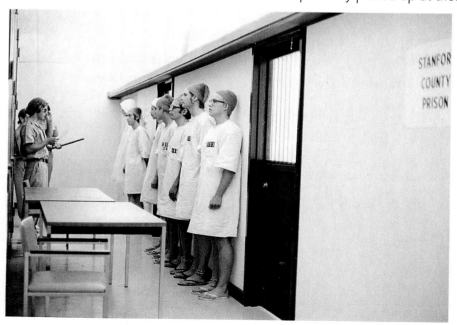

Students on the right in Zimbardo's mock prison experiment held very low statuses.

ity ended and their roles began. The majority had indeed become prisoners or guards, no longer able to clearly differentiate between role playing and self. There were dramatic changes in virtually every aspect of their behavior, thinking and feeling. . . . We were horrified because we saw some boys (guards) treat others as if they were despicable animals, taking pleasure in cruelty, while other boys (prisoners) became servile, dehumanized robots who thought only of escape, of their own individual survival and of their mounting hatred for the guards. We had to release three prisoners in the first four days because they had such acute situational traumatic reactions as hysterical crying, confusion in thinking, and severe depression. Others begged to be paroled, and all but three were willing to forfeit all the money they had earned [$15 per day] if they could be paroled. By then (the fifth day) they had been so programmed to think of themselves as prisoners that when their request for parole was denied they returned docilely to their cells. . . .

About a third of the guards became tyrannical in their arbitrary use of power, in enjoying their control over other people. They were corrupted by the power of their roles and became quite inventive in their techniques of breaking the spirit of the prisoners and making them feel they were worthless. . . . By the end of the week the experiment had become a reality. . . .

Excerpted with permission of Transaction, Inc., from **Society,** Vol. 9, No. 6. Copyright © 1972 by Transaction, Inc.

Working with the Research

1. If you were asked to discuss Zimbardo's experiment in light of one of the three major theoretical perspectives, which would you choose? Why?

2. One of Zimbardo's conclusions, not stated in the above account, is that the brutal behavior found in real-life prisons is not due to the antisocial characteristics or personality defects of guards and prisoners. Can you argue, sociologically, that he is right in this conclusion? How?

3. There was some controversy over the ethics of this experiment. Do you think this experiment could be carried out today under the ASA Code of Ethics? Why or why not?

Social Structure and Roles

Section Preview

People interact according to prescribed roles. These roles carry certain rights and obligations. Sometimes conflict or strain occurs when an individual has too many roles to play.

Key Terms

- role *(p. 146)*
- rights *(p. 146)*
- obligations *(p. 146)*
- role performance *(p. 147)*
- social interaction *(p. 147)*
- role conflict *(p. 149)*
- role strain *(p. 150)*

● **role**
an expected behavior associated with a particular status

● **right**
a behavior that individuals can expect from others

● **obligation**
a behavior that individuals are expected to perform toward others

Rights and Obligations

An expected behavior associated with a particular status is a **role.** Any status carries with it a variety of roles. The roles of a modern doctor, for example, include keeping informed about new medical developments, scheduling office appointments, diagnosing illnesses, and prescribing treatments.

Roles can be thought of as statuses "in action." Whereas statuses describe positions, roles describe behaviors. These behaviors are based on the rights and obligations attached to various statuses. **Rights** are behaviors that individuals expect from others. **Obligations** are behaviors that individuals are expected to perform toward others. The rights of one status correspond to the obligations of another. Doctors, for example, are obligated to diagnose their patients' illnesses. Correspondingly, patients have the right to expect their doctors to diagnose to the best of their ability. Teachers have an obligation to be prepared to teach the daily lesson. Students have a right to expect that

"No, Hoskins, you're not going to do it just because I'm telling you to do it. You're going to do it because you believe in it."

Hoskins is being forced to follow roles whether he wants to or not. Are such cues ever sent your way?

teachers will be adequately prepared to explain the material. Correspondingly, teachers have a right to expect that students will make the attempt to learn. Students have the obligation to make that effort.

In his play, *As You Like It,* Shakespeare wrote "All the world's a stage, and all the men and women merely players." In a play, roles are the part of the script that tells the actors (status holders) what beliefs, feelings, and actions are expected of them. A playwright specifies the content of a performer's part. In the same way, culture underlies the parts played in real life. Mothers, for instance, have different maternal "scripts" in different cultures. Most American mothers emphasize independence more than most Iranian mothers.

Role Performance and Social Interaction

Statuses and roles provide the basis for group life. It is primarily when people interact with each other socially that they "perform" in the roles attached to their statuses.

Role performance is the actual conduct, or behavior, involved in carrying out (or performing) a role. Role performance can occur without an audience (as when a student studies alone for a test). Most role performance, though, involves social interaction.

Social interaction is the process of influencing each other as people relate. For example, before two people begin to fight, they have probably gone through a process of insulting and challenging each other. Fortunately, most social interaction is not as negative and violent, but the same process of influence and reaction to others is involved.

Think again of the analogy of the play. If statuses are like the parts in a play and roles are like the script, then social interaction represents the way actors respond to cues given by other actors. Role performance is the performance itself.

● **role performance**
the actual behavior of an individual in a role

● **social interaction**
the process of influencing each other as people relate

These students each have particular roles and statuses within their group.

How does play-acting differ from social interactions?

The play analogy is a valid one, but it is dangerous to take it too far. For one thing, "delivery of the lines" in real life is not the conscious process used by actors. Unlike stage performances, most real-life role performance occurs without planning.

Second, although actors may sometimes ad-lib, change lines to suit themselves, and so forth, overall they stick pretty closely to the script. Departures are fairly easy to detect and control. This is not the case with differences between a role and a role performance.

Third, on the stage, there is a programmed and predictable relationship between cues and responses. One performer's line is a cue for a specific response from another actor. In life, we can choose our own cues and responses. A student may decide to tell a teacher that her tests are the worst he has ever encountered. On hearing this, the teacher may tell the student that it is not his place to judge, or the teacher may ask for further explanation so that improvement may be made. In effect, the teacher can choose from several roles to play at that time. Likewise, the student can choose from a variety of responses to the teacher's behavior. If the teacher tells the student he is out of line, the student may report the matter to a counselor, or he may decide to forget it altogether. The process of choosing the role and then acting it out occurs in nearly all instances of social interaction.

Keep in mind, however, that the range of responses is not limitless. Only certain responses are culturally acceptable. It is not an appropriate response for the teacher to bodily eject the student from her classroom, and the student would be very foolish to pound the teacher's desk in protest.

Figure 5.2 outlines the connection between culture and social structure. As you can see at the top of the figure, the first link between culture and social structure is the concept of role (behavior associated with a status). Roles are in turn attached to statuses (a position a person occupies within a group). Yet people do not always follow roles exactly. The manner in which roles are actually carried out is role performance, the third link in the conceptual chain. Role performance occurs through social interaction. This is the fourth link between culture and social structure. Social interaction based on roles

This illustration draws an analogy between rehearsed behavior on the stage and real social behavior. How do community cultural standards affect the role behavior of students and teachers?

Figure 5.2 The Links Between Culture and Social Structure Sociologists concentrate on the study of social structure. They have developed a set of concepts and an understanding of their relationships in order to examine the basic nature of social structure.

Unemployment Rates

For many Americans, occupation serves as their primary master status. Americans tend to define themselves and be defined by what they do for a living. Sometimes, however, that master status is disrupted by unemployment. Unemployment is the situation that occurs when a person does not have a job but is actively seeking one. Unemployment prevents people from fulfilling their role expectations as earner, which can also affect the performance of spousal and parental roles. This map shows the percentage of each state's civilian labor force, aged 16 and older, that was unemployed in 2004.

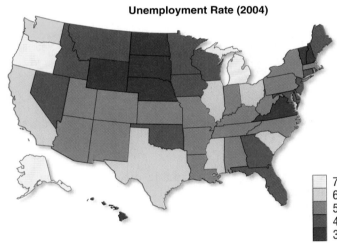

Unemployment Rate (2004)

7% or above
6.0%–6.9%
5.0%–5.9%
4.0%–4.9%
3.9% or below

Source: U.S. Department of Labor, Bureau of Labor Statistics, 2005.

Interpreting the Map

1. Which states had the highest unemployment rates in 2004? Which states had the lowest rates?

2. About what percentage of the civilian labor force in your state was unemployed in 2004?

3. How can unemployment affect the performance of spousal and parental roles?

is observable as patterned relationships, which make up social structure. In turn, existing social structure affects the creation of and changes in culture.

Role Conflict and Role Strain

The existence of statuses and roles permits social life to be predictable and orderly. At the same time, each status involves many roles, and each individual holds many statuses.

How does role diversity invite conflict and strain?

Role conflict exists when the performance of a role in one status clashes with the performance of a role in another. Many teenagers, for example, hold the statuses of student and employee. Those who do often find it difficult to balance study and work demands.

● **role conflict**
condition in which the performance of a role in one status interferes with the performance of a role in another status

Figure 5.3 Illustrating Social Structure Concepts

This table illustrates how each theoretical perspective might approach the study of social structures. The concepts could be switched to any other theoretical perspective and illustrated from that perspective. Associate each concept with a different theoretical perspective and provide your own example.

Theoretical Perspective	Social Structure Concept	Example
Functionalism	Role	Social integration is promoted by culturally defined rights and obligations honored by group members.
Conflict Theory	Ascribed Master Status	Ascribed master statuses such as gender and race empower some to subjugate others.
Symbolic Interactionism	Social Interaction	Roles are carried out by individuals on the basis of the symbols and meanings they share.

role strain
condition in which the roles of a single status are inconsistent or conflicting

Role strain occurs when a person has trouble meeting the many roles connected with a single status. College basketball coaches, for example, have to recruit for next year's season while trying to win games in the current season. Besides preparing daily lessons, high school teachers often are required to sponsor social clubs. Each of these roles (coach and recruiter or teacher and advisor) is time consuming, and the fulfillment of one role may interfere with the performance of the others. If your expectations as a high school student require you to perform well academically, join a social organization, pursue a sport, date, and participate in other school activities, you will probably experience some degree of role strain as a result of these expectations.

How do we manage role conflict and strain? Role conflict and strain may lead to discomfort and confusion. To feel better and to have smoother relationships with others, we often solve role dilemmas by setting priorities. When roles clash, we decide which role is most important to us and act accordingly. For example, a student who frequently misses school-related activities because of work demands will have to assess her priorities. She can eliminate the role conflict completely by quitting work and putting a priority on school activities. If she remains in both statuses, she can reduce work hours or cut down on extracurricular school activities.

We also segregate roles. That is, we separate our behavior in one role from our behavior in another. This is especially effective for reducing the negative effects of conflicting roles. A college coach experiencing the role strain associated with coaching and recruiting simultaneously can decide to give priority to one over the other. He may, for example, let his assistant coach do most of the recruiting until the season ends. Ranking incompatible roles in terms of their importance is a good way to reduce role conflict and strain. An organized-crime member may reduce role conflict by segregating his criminal activities from his role as a loving father.

Because of role conflict and role strain, meeting the goals and expectations of all our roles is impossible. This poses no problem as long as role performance occurs within accepted limits. Professors at research-oriented universities may be permitted to emphasize teaching over research. Coaches may accent fair play, character building, and scholarship rather than a winning record. Professors at research universities who do too little publishing or coaches who win too few games, however, usually will not be rewarded for very long. At some point they will be judged as failing to meet expected role performance. (For more on handling role conflict, see Sociology Today on the next page.)

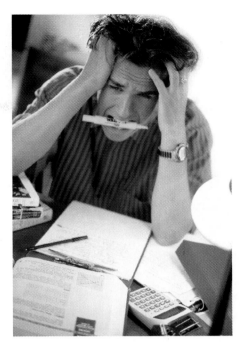

Do you think this young man is suffering from role conflict or role strain?

Section 2 Assessment

Match each situation below with the key term (a–e) it illustrates.

1. A husband and wife discuss the disciplining of one of their children.
2. A mother is expected to take care of her children.
3. A businessperson has no time for his children.

   a. role
   b. role conflict
   c. role performance
   d. role strain
   e. social interaction

4. A school principal hands out diplomas at a graduation ceremony.
5. A corporate chief executive officer is economically forced to terminate employees who are her friends.
6. Which of the following is *not* one of the differences between a play and social life?
   a. There is considerably more difference between roles and role performance in social life than between a script and a stage performance.
   b. Unlike the stage, there are no cues and responses in real life.
   c. Role performance in real life is not the conscious process that actors go through on the stage.
   d. In social life, the cues and responses are not as programmed and predictable as on the stage.

Critical Thinking

7. **Applying Concepts** Are you presently experiencing role conflict or role strain? If you are, analyze the source. If not, explain why at this time you are free from role conflict and role strain, making clear the meaning of the concepts.

Sociology Today

Reducing Conflict in Two-Career Families

Families with two working adults have special strains. While in 1960, less than 20 percent of married women with young children worked outside of the home, by 2004, the figure was about 65 percent (U.S. Bureau of Labor Statistics). This increase has resulted in added role conflict for women. In a two-career family, the woman is more likely to suffer from conflict because she is still generally expected to balance her traditional homemaker roles with her career roles. The women are not the only ones who suffer, however. The effects of this conflict are felt by husbands and children as well. Since you will likely be faced with the stress associated with dual-career families, you would be wise to learn now some techniques for reducing role conflict.

1. **Focus on the Positive**
   Conflict can be reduced when couples define their situation positively. If both partners are working from choice rather than necessity, it can be helpful to remember some of the reasons why they first made the choice for both to work. These reasons might include additional income or personal satisfaction.

2. **Put Family Needs First**
   Role conflict can be most effectively managed when family roles are placed ahead of working roles. When a baby-sitter fails to show up, when a child is sick, or when a parent-teacher conference is called, one of the parents can place these demands above work-related demands. Placing a higher priority on family needs will help keep the family support structure intact.

3. **Assume One Role at a Time**
   Conflict can be reduced if a person focuses on only one role at a time. Leaving job-related problems at work and family issues at home is often difficult but is very effective in reducing role conflict.

4. **Find the Compromise Balance**
   Although many men take active roles in child care today in order to meet family obligations, women still make the most compromises in their careers. With the increasing number of women in better-paying professional careers, we should expect more equality in career compromises between husbands and wives.

Doing Sociology

Identify three ways that you believe would help reduce role conflict in dual-career families. Provide specific examples not given in the text.

Preindustrial Societies

Section Preview

The way a society provides for basic needs greatly affects its culture and social structure. Preindustrial, industrial, and postindustrial societies meet basic needs in different ways. Preindustrial societies include hunting and gathering, horticultural, pastoral, and agricultural societies.

Key Terms

- society *(p. 153)*
- hunting and gathering society *(p. 154)*
- horticultural society *(p. 155)*
- pastoral societies *(p. 156)*
- agricultural society *(p. 156)*

- **society**
  people living within defined territorial borders and sharing a common culture

Types of Society

The culture and social structure of a society are greatly affected by the way the society provides for basic needs. A **society,** as you may remember from Chapter 3, is composed of people living within defined territorial borders who share a common culture. Societies meet their members' basic needs, such as the needs for food and shelter, in diffferent ways. These differences form the basis of a system anthropologists often use to classify societies. In this system, societies are classified as preindustrial, industrial, or postindustrial. We will look at preindustrial societies in this section and examine industrial and postindustrial societies in the following sections.

In theory, a society is independent of outsiders. It contains enough smaller social structures—family, economy, and so forth—to meet the needs of its members. As you will see, preindustrial societies actually could be independent and self-sufficient. Modern societies, although capable of caring for most members' needs, must have political, military, economic, cultural, and technological ties with other societies. In fact, modern societies are rapidly moving toward the creation of a global society.

In the next few pages, several basic types of societies will be distinguished. Each type of society is unique in important ways. All societies, however, are comprised of social structures. Members in each type of society know what is expected of them and what they can expect from others. Members of a particular type of society engage in the same basic social patterns time after time because they share patterned and predictable social relationships that are passed from generation to generation.

Even the earliest societies had patterned and predictable social relationships.

Through mostly grunts and exaggerated gestures, two fishermen/gatherers attempt to communicate.

Preindustrial

| Hunting and gathering
2 million to 10,000 years ago | Horticultural gardening
12,000 to 10,000 years ago | Pastoral herding
12,000 to 10,000 years ago |

Hunting and Gathering Societies

The **hunting and gathering society** survives by hunting animals and gathering edible foods such as wild fruits and vegetables. This is the oldest solution to the problem of providing for the basic need for food, or subsistence. In fact, it was only about nine thousand years ago that other methods of solving the subsistence problem emerged.

Hunting and gathering societies are usually nomadic—they move from place to place as the food supply and seasons change. Because nomads must carry all their possessions with them, they have few material goods. Hunting and gathering societies also tend to be very small—usually fewer than fifty people—with members scattered over a wide area. Because the family is the only institution in hunting and gathering societies, it tends to all the needs of its members. Most members are related by blood or marriage, although marriage is usually limited to those outside the family or band.

Economic relationships within hunting and gathering societies are based on cooperation—members share what they have with other members. Members of hunting and gathering societies seem simply to give things to one another without worrying about how "payment" will be made. In fact, the more scarce something is, the more freely it is shared. Generosity and hospitality are valued. Thrift is considered a reflection of selfishness. Because the obligation to share goods is one of the most binding aspects of their culture, members of hunting and gathering societies have little or no conception of private property or ownership.

Without a sense of private ownership and with few possessions for anyone to own, hunting and gathering societies have no social classes, no rich or poor. These societies lack status differences based on political authority because they have no political institutions; there is no one to organize and control activities. When the traditional Inuit in Canada and Alaska, for example, want to settle disputes, they use dueling songs. The people involved in the dispute prepare and sing songs to express their sides of the issue. Their families, as choruses, accompany them. Those listening to the duel applaud their choice for the victor (Hoebel, 1983).

Preindustrial (continued) →	Industrial →	Postindustrial →
Agricultural farming 6,000 years ago	Industrial England 240 years ago	Mid-1950s to present. More than half of employed are in the service sector

The division of labor in hunting and gathering societies is limited to the sex and age distinctions found in most families, since the family is the only institution. Men and women are assigned separate tasks, and certain tasks are given to the old, the young, and young adults. There is more leisure time in hunting and gathering societies than in any other. Today, few true hunting and gathering societies remain other than the Khoi-San (Bushmen) in Southern Africa, the Kaska Indians in Canada, and the Yanomamö of Brazil. (See Another Place on page 158.)

Horticultural Societies

A **horticultural society** solves the subsistence problem primarily through the growing of plants. This type of society came into being about ten to twelve thousand years ago, when people learned they could grow and harvest certain plants instead of simply gathering them. The gradual change from hunting and gathering to horticultural societies occurred over several centuries (Nolan and Lenski, 2005).

The shift from hunting and gathering to horticulture, or gardening, led to more permanent settlements. People no longer needed to move frequently to find food. Even without plows and animals to pull them, they could work a piece of land for extended periods of time before moving on to more fertile soil. This relative stability permitted the growth of multicommunity societies averaging one thousand to two thousand people each.

The family is even more basic to social life in horticultural societies than in hunting and gathering societies. In hunting and gathering societies, the survival of the group usually has top priority. In horticultural societies, primary emphasis is on providing for household members. This is because producing food in horticultural societies can be handled through the labor of family members. With the labor necessary for survival, households depend more on themselves and less on others outside the family unit for their subsistence.

> ● **horticultural society**
> a society that survives primarily through the growing of plants

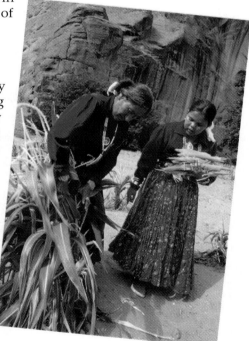

Judging from this photograph, to what type of society do these Navajo women belong?

Pastoral Societies

pastoral society
a society in which food is obtained primarily by raising and taking care of animals

Most horticultural societies keep domesticated animals such as pigs and chickens. They do not, however, depend economically on the products of these animals the way *pastoralists*, or herders, do. In **pastoral societies,** food is obtained primarily by raising and taking care of animals. For the most part, these are herd animals such as cattle, camels, goats, and sheep, all of which provide both milk and meat. Since grains are needed to feed the animals, pastoralists must also either farm or trade with people who do (Nanda and Warms, 2003; Peoples and Bailey, 2005).

There is more migration in pastoral societies than in those based more fully on cultivation of land. However, permanent (or at least long-term) villages can be maintained if, as seasons change, herd animals are simply moved to different pastures within a given area. In such societies, the women remain at home while the men take the herds to different pastures. With men being responsible for providing food, the status of women in pastoral societies is low. These societies are male dominated.

Because both horticultural and pastoral societies can produce a surplus of food, they usher in important social changes unknown in hunting and gathering societies. With a surplus food supply, some members of the community are free to create a more complex division of labor. People can become political and religious leaders or make goods such as pottery, spears, and clothing. Because nonedible goods are produced, an incentive to trade with other peoples emerges.

The creation of a surplus also permits the development of social inequality (class or caste), although it is limited. Even a relatively small surplus, however, means that some families, villages, or clans have more wealth than others.

agricultural society
a society that uses plows and draft animals in growing food

Agricultural Societies

An **agricultural society,** like a horticultural society, subsists by growing food. The difference is that agricultural societies use plows and animals. In fact, the transition from horticultural to agricultural society was made possible largely through the invention of the plow (Nolan and Lenski, 2005).

The plow not only allows the farmer to control weeds but also turns the weeds into fertilizer by burying them under the soil. By digging more deeply into the ground than was possible with sticks, hoes, and spades, the plow is able to reach nutrient-rich dirt that had sunk below root level. The result is more productivity—more food per unit of land.

This Bali farmer lives in an agricultural society. How does his society differ technologically from a horticultural society?

This medieval manuscript shows a noble instructing peasants on crop harvesting. Why would this type of superior-subordinate behavior first appear in an agricultural society?

Using animals also increases productivity, because larger areas can be cultivated with fewer people. As a result, more people are free to engage in noneconomic activities such as formal education, concerts, and political rallies. Cities can be built, and occupations appear that are not directly tied to farming, such as politician, blacksmith, and hat maker. New political, economic, and religious institutions emerge. Although family ties remain important, government replaces the family group as the guiding force for agricultural societies.

In the past, agricultural societies were headed by a king or an emperor. Distinct social classes appeared for the first time. Wealth and power were based on land ownership, which was controlled by the governing upper class. These elites enjoyed the benefits of the work done by the peasants. Urban merchants were better off than peasants, but they, too, worked hard for their livings. An economy based on trade began to emerge as an identifiable institution during this time. Monetary systems, which use money rather than goods for payment, began to be used as well. Increasingly, religion and government became separate as institutions. Rulers were believed to be divinely chosen, but few of them were also religious leaders.

Section 3 Assessment

1. Briefly restate the chief traits of each type of society: hunting and gathering, horticultural, pastoral, and agricultural.

2. In which type of society did a marked class system first appear? Explain why.

Critical Thinking

3. **Synthesizing Information** Using information from this section, develop a theory that would explain why conflict increases as society becomes more complex.

Another Place

The Chest-Pounding Duel

A description of the "chest-pounding" ritual that takes place among the Yanomamö tribe in Southern Venezuela was recorded by anthropologist Napoleon Chagnon. It provides a good example of social structure in a preindustrial society. All of the participants in this activity—even those merely observing—knew exactly what was expected of them and what to expect of the others. This is what sociologists mean by social structure.

. . . There were about sixty adult men on each side in the fight divided into two arenas, each comprised of hosts and guests. Two men, one from each side, would step into the center of the milling, belligerent crowd of weapon-wielding partisans, urged on by their comrades. One would step up, spread his legs apart, bare his chest, and hold his arms behind his back, daring the other to hit him. The opponent would size him up, adjust the man's chest or arms so as to give himself the greatest advantage when he struck and then step back to deliver his close-fisted blow. The striker would painstakingly adjust his own distance from his victim by measuring his arm length to the man's chest, taking several dry runs before delivering his blow. He would then wind up like a baseball pitcher, but keeping both feet on the ground, and deliver a tremendous wallop with his fist to the man's left pectoral muscle, putting all of his weight into the blow. The victim's knees would often buckle and he would stagger around a few moments, shaking his head to clear the stars, but remain silent. The blow invariably raised a "frog" on the recipient's pectoral muscle where the striker's knuckles bit into his flesh. After each blow, the comrades of the deliverer would cheer and bounce up and down from the knees, waving and clacking their weapons over their heads. The victim's supporters, meanwhile, would urge their champion on frantically, insisting that he take another blow. If the delivery were made with sufficient force to knock the recipient to the ground, the man who delivered it would throw his arms above his head, roll his eyes back, and prance victoriously in a circle around his victim, growling and screaming, his feet almost a blur from his excited dance. The recipient would stand poised and take as many as four blows before demanding to hit his adversary. He would be permitted to strike his opponent as many times as the latter struck him, provided that the opponent could take it. If not, he would be forced to retire, much to the dismay of his comrades and the delirious joy of their opponents. No fighter could retire after delivering a blow. If he attempted to do so, his adversary would plunge into the crowd and roughly haul him back out, sometimes being aided by the man's own supporters. Only after having received his just dues could he retire. If he had delivered three blows, he had to receive three or else be proven a poor fighter. He could retire with less than three only if he were injured. Then, one of his comrades would replace him and demand to hit the victorious opponent. The injured man's two remaining blows would be canceled and the man who delivered the victorious blow would have to receive more blows than he delivered. Thus, good fighters are at a disadvantage, since they receive disproportionately more punishment than they deliver. Their only reward is . . . [prestige]: they earn the reputation of being fierce.

Source: Excerpted from Napoleon A. Chagnon, *Yanomamö: The Fierce People* (New York: Holt, Rinehart and Winston, 1977), pp. 113–115.

Thinking It Over

Describe an activity in your culture that illustrates patterned social relationships. Explain the statuses and roles involved.

Industrial and Postindustrial Societies

Section Preview

The Industrial Revolution created a new type of society, called industrial society. Characteristics that distinguish this society from all earlier ones include the growth of large cities and a wide-spread dependence on machines and technology. Postindustrial society has a predominately white-collar labor force that is concentrated in service industries. Social instability has been linked to the transition from an industrial to a postindustrial society.

Basic Features of Industrial Societies

The Industrial Revolution created a society that is dependent upon science and technology to produce its basic goods and services. Sociologists call this an **industrial society.**

What happens when agricultural societies become industrial societies? Smelser and Swedberg (2005) have identified some basic structural changes that occur in societies shifting from an agricultural to an industrial base. Industrialism brings with it a change—*away* from simple,

Key Terms

- industrial society *(p. 159)*
- mechanization *(p. 160)*
- urbanization *(p. 160)*
- gemeinschaft *(p. 160)*
- gesellschaft *(p. 160)*
- social solidarity *(p. 160)*
- mechanical solidarity *(p. 161)*
- organic solidarity *(p. 161)*
- postindustrial society *(p. 162)*

- **industrial society**
  a society that depends on science and technology to produce its basic goods and services

Ford Motor Company employees work on the Model T assembly line. What technology underlies industrial society?

mechanization
the process of replacing animal and human power with machine power

urbanization
the shifting of population from farms and villages to large cities

Job skills in an industrial society, like those needed here, cannot be learned in the home. What does this mean for education in an industrial society?

gemeinschaft
preindustrial society based on tradition, kinship, and close social ties

gesellschaft
industrial society characterized by weak family ties, competition, and impersonal social relationships

social solidarity
the degree to which a society is unified

traditional technology (plows, hammers, harnesses) *toward* the application of scientific knowledge to create more complex technological devices. Early examples of industrial technology include the steam engine and the use of electrical power in manufacturing. More recent technological developments include nuclear energy, aerospace-related inventions, and the computer.

In industrial societies, intensive animal and human labor is replaced by power-driven machines, a process known as **mechanization.** These machines are operated by wage earners who produce goods for sale on the market. With the help of machinery, farmers are able to produce enough food to support themselves and many others. This surplus allows people to move away from farms and villages, adding to the growing population in large cities. **Urbanization,** then, is also a basic feature of industrial societies.

How does the role of the family change? With industrialization, family functions change in many ways. Economic activities, once carried out in the home, move to the factory. Similarly, the education of the young, which in agricultural societies centered on teaching farming, moves from the home to the formal school. An industrial society requires a more broadly educated and trained labor force, so young people can no longer be prepared for the work force by their families. Blood relationships decline in importance as families begin to separate socially and physically due to urbanization and the necessity of taking jobs in distant locations where factories have been built. Personal choice and love replace arranged marriages. Women, through their entrance into the work force, become less subordinate to their husbands. Individual mobility increases dramatically, and social class is based more on occupational achievement than the social class of one's parents. Because the United States has been an industrial society for so long, its characteristics are taken as a given. The effects of industrialization are easier to observe in societies currently moving from an agricultural to an industrial economic base. For example, Vietnam and Malaysia are experiencing mechanization and urbanization at the beginning of the twenty-first century (Singh, 1998; Phu, 1998).

A Conversation with Two Sociologists

Ferdinand Tönnies and Emile Durkheim were two early sociologists who wrote about preindustrial and industrial societies. Sociologists today still study their writings.

What were Tönnies's views? Ferdinand Tönnies (1957, originally published in 1887), was an early German sociologist. In his writing, he distinguished between *gemeinschaft* (ga MINE shoft) and *gesellschaft* (ga ZELL shoft). **Gemeinschaft** is German for "community." It describes a society based on tradition, kinship, and intimate social relationships. These are the types of communities found in preindustrial societies. **Gesellschaft** is German for "society." This concept represents industrial society and is characterized by weak family ties, competition, and less personal social relationships.

What were Durkheim's views? Shortly after Tönnies published his theory, Emile Durkheim (1964a, originally published in 1893) made a similar observation. He distinguished the two types of societies by the nature of their social *solidarity*. **Social solidarity** is the degree to which a society is unified or can hold itself together in the face of obstacles.

Social solidarity, Durkheim contended, is a result of society's division of labor. In societies in which the division of labor is simple—in which most

World View

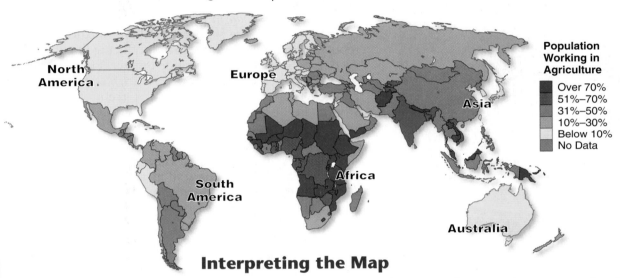

Agricultural Employment

As societies move from the preindustrial to the postindustrial stage, fewer people are required to raise food to feed the population. This map shows the percentage of each country's population involved in the production of agricultural products.

North America

Europe

Asia

Africa

South America

Australia

Population Working in Agriculture

- Over 70%
- 51%–70%
- 31%–50%
- 10%–30%
- Below 10%
- No Data

Interpreting the Map

1. After examining this map, what generalizations about types of societies around the world would you make? Explain.

2. Which countries do you think could be ready to move from one type of society to another? Be specific about countries and types of societies.

3. What parts of the world are least likely to change in the near future? Explain your answer.

Source: U.S. Central Intelligence Agency, *The World Factbook*, 2005.

people are doing the same type of work—**mechanical solidarity** is the foundation for social unity. A society based on mechanical solidarity achieves social unity through a consensus of beliefs, values, and norms; strong social pressures for conformity; and dependence on tradition and family. In this type of society, which is best observed in small, nonliterate societies, people tend to behave, think, and feel in much the same ways, to place the group above the individual, and to emphasize tradition and family.

In contrast, in an industrial society, members depend on a variety of people to fulfill their needs—barbers, bakers, manufacturers, and other suppliers of services. This modern industrial society is based on **organic solidarity.** It achieves social unity through a complex of specialized statuses that make members of the society interdependent.

- **mechanical solidarity**
  a type of social unity achieved by people doing the same type of work and holding similar values

- **organic solidarity**
  a type of social unity in which members' interdependence is based on specialized functions and statuses

The term *organic solidarity* is based on an analogy with biological organisms. If a biological organism composed of highly specialized parts is to survive, its parts must work together. Similarly, the parts of a society based on organic solidarity must cooperate if the society is to survive.

Major Features of Postindustrial Society

● **postindustrial society**
a society in which the economic emphasis is on providing services and information

Some societies, such as the United States, have passed beyond industrial society into **postindustrial society.** In this type of society, the economic emphasis is on providing services and information rather than on producing goods through basic manufacturing.

Sociologist Daniel Bell (1999) identifies five major features of a postindustrial society, a society based on a service economy.

1. *For the first time, the majority of the labor force are employed in services rather than in agriculture or manufacturing.* These industries emphasize services (banking, medical care, fast food, entertainment) rather than producing tangible goods, such as oil or steel. They include organizations in the areas of trade, finance, transportation, health, recreation, research, and government. In 2004, about 75 percent of all employed workers in the United States were in service jobs.

2. *White-collar employment replaces much blue-collar work.* White-collar workers outnumbered blue-collar workers in the United States for the first time in 1956, and the gap is still increasing. The most rapid growth has been in professional and technical employment.

3. *Technical knowledge is the key organizing feature in postindustrial society.* Knowledge is used for the creation of innovations as well as for making government policy. As technical knowledge becomes more important, so do educational and research institutions.

4. *Technological change is planned and assessed.* In an industrial society, the effects of a technology are not assessed before its introduction. When the automobile engine was invented, no one asked whether it would have an effect on the environment. In postindustrial societies, the effects—good and bad—of an innovation can be considered before it is introduced.

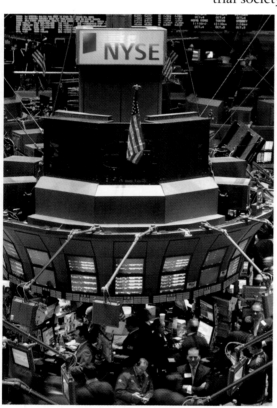

The New York Stock Exchange symbolizes the shift from production-based work to knowledge-based work in postindustrial society.

5. *Reliance on computer modeling in all areas.* With modern computers, it is possible to consider a large number of interacting variables simultaneously. For example, "intellectual technology" allows us to manage complex organizations—including government at national, state, and local levels.

Social Instability in Postindustrial Society

Historian Francis Fukuyama (1999) believes that the transition to a service economy has increased social instability in nations undergoing this change. He writes the following about deteriorating social conditions that began in the mid-1960s.

Crime and social disorder began to rise, making inner-city areas of the wealthiest societies on earth almost uninhabitable. The decline of kinship as a social institution, which has been going on for more than 200 years, accelerated sharply in the second half of the twentieth century. Marriages and births declined and divorce soared; and one out of every three children in the United States and more than half of all children in Scandinavia were born out of wedlock. Finally, trust and confidence in institutions went into a forty-year decline (Fukuyama, 1999:55).

Will social instability continue? According to Fukuyama, this social instability is now lessening. He sees current indications of a return to social stability. The establishment of new social norms, he believes, is reflected in the slowing down of increases in divorce, crime, distrust, and illegitimacy. In the 1990s, Fukuyama notes, many societies have even seen a reversal of these rates—crime, divorce, illegitimacy, and distrust have actually declined.

This is particularly true in the United States, where levels of crime are down a good 15 percent from their peaks in the early 1990s. Divorce rates peaked in the early 1980s, and births to single mothers appear to have stopped increasing. Welfare rolls have diminished almost as dramatically as crime rates, in response both to the 1996 welfare-reform measures and to opportunities provided by a nearly full-employment economy in the 1990s. Levels of trust in both institutions and individuals have also recovered significantly since the early 1990s (Fukuyama, 1999:80).

What has caused the return to social stability? Fukuyama believes that humans find it difficult to live without values and norms:

The situation of normlessness . . . is intensely uncomfortable for us, and we will seek to create new rules to replace the old ones that have been undercut (Fukuyama, 1999:76).

Because culture can be changed, it can be used to create new social structures better adapted to changing social and economic circumstances.

Section 4 Assessment

1. Explain why blood relationships are less important in an industrial society than in a preindustrial society.

2. State whether each of the following is or is not a major feature of a postindustrial society.

   a. emphasis on technical knowledge

   b. employment of the majority of the labor force in service industries

   c. reliance on advanced technology

   d. increased dependence on skilled blue-collar workers

   e. shift toward the employment of white-collar workers

Critical Thinking

3. **Analyzing Information** Explain from your own observation why family relationships would probably weaken in an industrial society.

4. **Making Predictions** As the United States becomes a more complete information society, how may life for you change?

TECH TRENDS

The Dark Side of Workplace Technology

A video camera has been implanted inside the smoke detector above. These tiny cameras are part of the technological revolution that is currently changing society. Would you want one of these in your school?

According to one business visionary, one of the most important changes that will occur in the postindustrial workplace is the "virtual organization"— a workplace of digital technologies, wireless transfer of information, computer networks, and telecommuting. In this picture, the worker will have more freedom, independence, and job satisfaction than ever before (Barner, 1996).

If this optimistic view is correct, workers in high-tech jobs should be much happier than employees doing low-tech work. However, in a survey of 1,509 workers in California's Silicon Valley, a center of high-tech industry, researchers found no differences in job satisfaction between employees in high-tech companies and those in more traditional firms. They also found that there are still large social class differences in the workplace. These findings challenge the belief that work in high-tech society will be more satisfying and equitable (Gamst and Otten, 1992).

Other researchers found that job security declines in high-tech jobs. Employees must learn new skills and then continually upgrade them to survive. Managers are also at risk since traditional management functions like decision making and training will now be performed by technology programs.

Another feature of the high-tech workplace is the use of technology to monitor employees. This practice can make employees feel helpless, manipulated, and exploited. Many workers feel that their managers are spying on them (Barner, 1996). In fact, there has been a dramatic rise in employer workplace surveillance. Over three-fourths of major U.S. companies now electronically monitor their employees: reviewing e-mail, examining computer files, and documenting Internet connections (Gertzen, 2003). Nearly 30 percent of companies with more than 1,000 employees actually employ staff whose job it is to read and track employee e-mail (Koprowski, 2005).

Digitally based technology offers many benefits. It has boosted productivity and created many new employment opportunities. Like any technology that has wide-ranging effects on society, there are some undesirable consequences. Postindustrial societies are just beginning to deal with the dark side of a very bright technology.

Analyzing the Trends

1. Which theoretical perspective do you think underlies this research and speculation?

2. Does the use of technology to monitor employees clash with any values in American society? Explain.

Summary

Section 1: Social Structure and Status

Main Idea: The underlying pattern of social relationships in a group is called social structure. Ascribed statuses are assigned at birth; achieved statuses are earned or chosen.

Section 2: Social Structures and Roles

Main Idea: People interact according to pre-scribed roles. These roles carry certain rights and obligations.

Section 3: Preindustrial Societies

Main Idea: The way a society provides for basic needs greatly affects its cultural and social structure. Preindustrial, industrial, and postin-dustrial societies meet basic needs in different ways. Preindustrial societies include hunting and gathering, horticultural, pastoral, and agricultural societies.

Section 4: Industrial and Post-industrial Societies

Main Idea: The Industrial Revolution created a new type of society marked by the growth of large cities and a dependence on machines and technology. Postindustrial society has a predominantly white-collar labor force that is concentrated in service industries.

Sociology Online

Self-Check Quiz
Visit the *Sociology and You* Web site at glencoe.com and click on **Chapter 5—Self-Check Quizzes** to prepare for the chapter test.

Reviewing Vocabulary

Complete each sentence using each term once.

a. social structure
b. achieved status
c. ascribed status
d. roles
e. role conflict
f. society
g. horticultural society
h. hunting and gathering society
i. agricultural society
j. industrial society
k. organic solidarity
l. mechanical solidarity

1. The underlying pattern of social relationships is called _____ .
2. _____ is the social unity achieved through interdependence based on specialized functions.
3. _____ is status that is assigned.
4. _____ is a society that solves the subsistence problem by learning to grow and harvest plants.
5. _____ is a nomadic society characterized by economic cooperation.
6. Status that can be earned is called _____ .
7. People living within defined territorial borders and sharing a common culture are called a _____ .
8. Culturally defined rights and obligations attached to statuses are known as _____ .
9. The society that releases some people from the land to engage in noneconomic activities is called _____ .
10. _____ occurs when the roles of a single status are inconsistent or conflicting.
11. Social unity accomplished through a consensus of values, beliefs, and norms is known as _____ .
12. _____ is a society characterized by the replacement of human labor with mechanical labor.

Chapter 5 Assessment

Reviewing the Facts

13. What is the sociological term for the dilemma of women who have careers and who also must run households?

14. What do sociologists mean by social structure?

15. What is the difference between role strain and role conflict?

16. In what ways do workers in the "virtual organization" differ from low-tech workers? In what ways are the workers the same?

17. As people move from agricultural to industrial societies, they also move from the personal to the impersonal. What sociological terminology did Emile Durkeim give to this shift? Use the diagram below to show the causes of this shift.

Thinking Critically

18. Making Inferences

The chapter suggests that society functions because social patterns are usually predictable. History records that John D. Rockefeller, the founder of Standard Oil Company, was so rich he would walk down the street and pass out dimes to children. Allegedly, he gave out three million dollars' worth of dimes before he died. Let's say you decided to go to the mall and hand out a dollar to all the children who passed by. How do you think people would react? Would they be suspicious? Do you think mall security would be concerned by your behavior? What has changed since the days of Rockefeller that would make your behavior suspect?

"Oh, yes, indeed. We all keep a sharp eye out for those little clues that seem to whisper 'law' or 'medicine.'"

Donald Reille/Cartoonbank.com

19. Analyzing Visuals

Section 1 of this chapter examines what sociologists mean by status and two categories of status—ascribed status and achieved status. In the cartoon above, the cartoonist is examining occupation, an achieved status in American society. How does the cartoonist challenge the idea that being a lawyer or doctor might have characteristics of an ascribed status in wealthy families?

20. Applying Concepts

What are some of the roles and statuses that you fill in the course of your day? List them, and describe the basic rights connected to each status.

21. Analyzing Information

In hunting and gathering societies, resources are distributed equally. If one person eats, everyone eats. Is that the case in industrial and postindustrial societies? Should Americans be concerned whether everyone eats every day? Why might they *not* be concerned?

22. Interpreting Graphs

The graph below compares selected countries on the basis of how great a percentage of their manufactured exports are high-tech products, an indicator that suggests the existence of a postindustrial society, or one moving in that direction. Examine the chart. Then answer these questions:

a. Since Japan has long been known for its technology exports, why isn't the bar representing these higher?

b. What does the high "mark" for Ireland tell you about the rest of its exports?

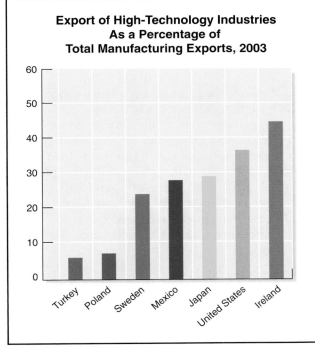

Export of High-Technology Industries As a Percentage of Total Manufacturing Exports, 2003

Source: Organisation for Economic Cooperation and Development Factbook 2006

Sociology Projects

23. Role Performance

George Herbert Mead said that humans are social beings because they can "take on the role of another person." Your task here is to create a one-minute improvisational skit in which you react to the statement *Teenagers today need to assume more responsibility* through the "persona" of another individual. This person might be the school principal, a favorite teacher, a school liaison police officer, or a parent.

24. Social Cues

TV watching is so common that we often do it without really paying attention. To prepare for this project, first watch the TV set for ten minutes without turning it on, but concentrate on everything else around you. Next, turn the TV on, but watch it for ten minutes with no sound. Try to figure out the program or ad through visuals only. Next try watching news for ten minutes with no sound. Then watch the news with sound, but focus on camera angles, facial expressions, graphics, music, and other non-content elements. In a paragraph, identify which non-content cues helped you correctly interpret a situation.

Technology Activities

28. This chapter describes rights as the behaviors individuals can expect from others and obligations as the behaviors others expect from them. Different societies place emphasis on rights and obligations, but there is a common understanding of some basic human rights. One organization that lists these basic rights is the European Commission of Human Rights. Visit its Web site at www.coe.int/commissioner. From its home page, select the Mandate link. Then go to the Reference document, Convention for the Protection of Human Rights and Fundamental Freedoms. Scroll down to Section I Article 2.

a. What basic human rights are listed?

b. Are any of these rights built into some of the roles you are expected to perform? Explain.

Social Functions of Malls

by Wayne S. Wooden

In *The Mall: An Attempted Escape from Everyday Life*, Jerry Jacobs presents an **ethnographic** account of a midsize, enclosed suburban shopping center. Karen Lansky's article, "Mall Rats," for *Los Angeles* magazine discusses what it means for teenagers when they "just hang out" at these "indoor shopping palaces."

- **ethnographic**
  the descriptive study of human cultures

- **social phenomenon**
  a fact or event of social interest subject to scientific interpretation or explanation

- **instant gratification**
  the immediate satisfaction of wishes or wants

In recent years several excellent books and magazine articles have been published on the **social phenomenon** of teenagers and suburban shopping malls.

The modern mall, Jacobs argues, provides three things for its participants. First, it offers people entertainment or just plain diversion. Second, it provides the public with convenient shopping. And, third, the mall offers public, social space—a place to meet and interact with others. In other words, the modern shopping center has become an "indoor street corner society."

Karen Lansky contends that kids spend so much time in the mall partly because parents encourage it, assuming it is safe and that there is adult supervision. The structured and controlling environment of the mall is ideal for them. According to Lansky,

> *True mall rats lack structure in their home lives, and adolescents about to make the big leap into growing up crave more structure than our modern society cares to acknowledge.*

Lansky also believes that the mall has become the focus of these young people's lives.

> *Malls are easy. Food, drink, bathrooms, shops, movie theaters—every part of the life-support system a modern kid needs is in the mall.* **Instant gratification** *for body and senses—and all of it close at hand, since malls are designed to make life more comfortable by eliminating parking problems, long walks, heavy doors, hot sun, depressing clouds. It is ironic, in fact, that the mall is becoming all that many kids know of the outside world, since the mall is a placeless space whose primary virtue is that it's all inside. Kids come in from the cold (or heat) for a variety of reasons, of course. But the main reason kids seek the mall, especially in the summer when school's out, seems to be because they can't think of anything better to do.*

Lansky sees mall rats as kids with nowhere else to go.

> *Their parents may drink or take drugs, be violent or just gone. Whatever, the mall becomes the home they don't have. For them, the mall is a rich, stimulating, warm, clean, organized, comfortable [social] structure—the only [social] structure in some of their lives.*

In gathering research for her article, Lansky interviewed several adolescents. Although teenagers in several high schools would be approached as well, the vast majority of the interviews and surveys gathered for the Youth Survey portion of this study were completed by over four hundred youths contacted in Southern California malls. The initial focus of this study, therefore, began with my meeting and talking with these so-called teenage mall rats.

One male expressed the belief that the mall "belongs to the mall rats." Arguing that the mall is *his* property, his mission in life, he said, is to become "top mall rat," adding, "Without the mall, we'd be street people."

Another female mall **habitué** interviewed by Lansky complained that the only place in the mall that is "theirs" is the arcade. She and her friends get kicked out of the other places. Security warns them to keep moving if they are not buying anything. It is these kids, according to Lansky, that the mall owners do not like. The managers resent having to set limits for these kids—limits that should be the responsibility of the community or the family. The owners discourage these kids because they often do not have much money to spend.

One of the first young men so contacted was Bob Bogan, or "Skidd Marx," as he preferred to be called, who allowed me to spend several afternoons with him as he wandered through the Brea Mall. Seventeen and 5'9" tall, Skidd struck a mean pose. With his black hair spiked all over with three separate 1-foot tails in back, Skidd also sported eye makeup, a leather jacket studded with spikes, a white T-shirt with a punk band logo on it, black Levis rolled up high, and black Converse high tops. Skidd also sported four hanging earrings in each ear and a loop pierced into his right nostril. Skidd, decked out in full punk regalia, cut the swaggering image of the "young man about the mall."

Skidd, like all of the teenagers studied in this book, resided in suburbia. He came from a middle-class background. Both of his parents worked. He defined himself as "a suburban punk bordering on the punk funk." Skidd, in true mall-rat fashion, spent much of his free time and social life in the Brea Mall.

Q: *When did you first define yourself as being into punk or punk funk? How did the process occur?*

A: *It was in my third year of high school. I really wasn't feeling that good about myself at the time. I felt very self-conscious at school. I always kind of dressed differently. Being tall, people usually looked at me physically, and I used to be very insecure about that. So I kind of had the attitude, if I do something a little bit different, then that would be the reason why they're staring at me. I can't do anything about the fact that I'm tall.*

Q: *So it gave you a rationalization?*

A: *Right. The punk thing is when I just didn't care what I looked like. My parents were always saying, "You're such a nice looking young man. Why do you want to do that?" That really used to bother me.*

Source: Adapted from an article by Wayne S. Wooden, *Renegade Kids, Suburban Outlaws: From Youth Culture to Delinquency,* Belmont: Wadsworth Publishing Company, 1994.

habitué
one who regularly visits a place

Read and React

1. According to this reading, what effect do malls have upon teenage values?
2. Given what you have learned in this chapter, what does it mean to say that people have no social structure in their lives except in the malls? Could this really be true? Explain.
3. Do you agree with the claims in this writing? Why or why not?

Chapter 6

Groups and Formal Organizations

Sections

1. **Primary and Secondary Groups**
2. **Other Groups and Networks**
3. **Types of Social Interaction**
4. **Formal Organizations**

Learning Objectives

After reading this chapter, you will be able to

- define the concepts of group, social category, and social aggregate.
- list the major characteristics of primary and secondary groups.
- describe five types of social interaction.
- discuss the advantages and disadvantages of bureaucracy.
- distinguish between formal and informal organizations.
- discuss the use of power within an organization and demonstrate its importance with examples.

170

Applying Sociology

Most people assume that conflict should be avoided because it disrupts a group. It is true that an organization's success depends on cooperation and conformity to group values and norms.

The photo here shows business people standing in line. It represents the conformity found in many organizations. People in businesses, universities, and many other organizations are expected to conform.

Conformity and cooperation bond a group together, but conflict has benefits, too. Willingness to tolerate disagreement can prevent what sociologists call *groupthink*. The space program provides an example groupthink leading to a catastrophic decision. On January 28, 1986, the *Challenger* space shuttle was launched from Kennedy Space Center. Just over a minute later, the shuttle exploded, killing seven astronauts.

Before the launch, engineers had recommended against takeoff because crucial parts had not been adequately tested. Victims of groupthink, the NASA leaders screened out the objections of the engineers because they were not making the expected decision. In this chapter, we will look closely at the behaviors of groups and organizations.

Sociology nline

Chapter Overview
Visit the *Sociology and You* Web site at glencoe.com and click on **Chapter 6—Chapter Overviews** to preview chapter information.

Primary and Secondary Groups

Key Terms

- group *(p. 172)*
- social category *(p. 173)*
- social aggregate *(p. 173)*
- primary group *(p. 173)*
- primary relationships *(p. 173)*
- secondary group *(p. 174)*
- secondary relationships *(p. 174)*

- **group**
  at least two people who have one or more goals in common and share common ways of thinking and behaving

Section Preview

Groups are classified by how they develop and function. Primary groups meet emotional and support needs, while secondary groups are task focused.

Groups, Categories, and Aggregates

A **group** is composed of people who share several features, including the following.

- They are in regular contact with one another.
- They share some ways of thinking, feeling, and behaving.
- They take one another's behavior into account.
- They have one or more interests or goals in common.

Groups play important roles in the lives of their members, as well as influence society around them. Groups range from the small and informal to the large and formal. They tend to draw lines around themselves, creating insiders and outsiders. Some groups have tighter, more definite boundaries than others. Boundaries between African Americans and whites in the South of the early 1960s were rigid. Members of the minority were unable to drink from the same water fountains, use the same rest rooms, or eat at the same restaurants as whites. Group boundaries may change over time, however. Since the 1960s, boundaries between African Americans and whites in the United States are much looser.

Compare these Korean choir members with the Denver concert goers. Explain why one is a group and the other is not.

A group is not the same as a **social category**—people who share a social characteristic. High school seniors are a social category, for example. Women belong to another social category. A group is also sometimes confused with a **social aggregate**—people who happen to be in the same place at the same time, such as students waiting in line for concert tickets.

Although neither categories nor aggregates are groups, some of their members may form groups. Witnesses of a disaster (an aggregate) may work together to cope with an emergency. Citizens of a state (a social category) may band together in an organized tax revolt. These people may form a group if they begin to interact regularly; share ways of thinking, feeling, and behaving; take one another's behavior into account; and have some common goals.

Primary Groups

Two principal types of groups are *primary* and *secondary*. At the extremes, the characteristics of these two types of groups—and the relationships that occur within them—are opposites. But most groups sit at different points along a continuum from primary to secondary.

What is a primary group? Charles Horton Cooley, one of the founders of symbolic interactionism, was the first to use the term *primary group*. A **primary group** is composed of people who are emotionally close, know one another well, and seek one another's company. The members of a primary group have a "we" feeling and enjoy being together. These groups are characterized by **primary relationships** that are intimate, personal, caring, and fulfilling.

Primary groups are the most important setting for socialization. Family and childhood play groups are the first primary groups a child experiences. People, of course, participate in primary groups throughout life. Close friends in high school and college, neighbors who keep an eye on one another's children, and friends who meet weekly for golf are all examples of primary groups.

How do primary groups develop? A number of conditions favor the development of primary groups and primary relationships.

- **Small size.** It is hard for members of large groups to develop close emotional ties. The chances of knowing everyone fairly well are far greater in small groups. The boys or girls who play for the school basketball team are more likely to develop primary relationships than the multitude of student spectators who cheer them on.

- **Face-to-face contact.** Primary relationships occur more easily when interaction is face to face. People who can see each other and who can experience nonverbal communication such as facial expressions, tone of voice, and touch are much more likely to develop close ties.

- **Continuous contact.** The closeness typical of a primary relationship rarely develops in a short period of time. In spite of reported love at first sight, most of us require repeated social contact for the development of a primary relationship.

- **Proper social environment.** Just seeing someone every day in a close setting is not enough to form a primary relationship. You may visit your

social category
people who share a social characteristic

social aggregate
people temporarily in the same place at the same time

primary group
people who are emotionally close, know one another well, and seek one another's company

primary relationships
interactions that are intimate, personal, caring, and fulfilling

What type of group do you think is pictured above?

local video store every day and never form a relationship with the video clerk. The social setting does not encourage personal relationships, and the statuses are unequal. This is why primary relationships do not usually develop between students and teachers, bosses and employees, or judges and lawyers.

What are the functions of primary groups? Primary groups provide three important functions in society.

- **Emotional support.** At the end of World War II, the German army refused to crumble despite years of being outnumbered, undersupplied, and outfought. These conditions should have led to desertion and surrender, but they did not. Strong emotional support ties within German combat units kept them fighting against overwhelming odds.

- **Socialization.** For children, the family is the primary group that teaches them how to participate in social life. In like manner, primary groups promote adult socialization—as adults enter college, take new jobs, change social classes, marry, and retire.

- **Encourage conformity.** Primary groups not only teach new members the appropriate norms and values, these groups provide pressure to conform. William F. Whyte's (1993) study of an Italian slum gang illustrates encouragement to conform within primary groups. Whyte reported that bowling scores corresponded with status in the gang—the higher the rank, the higher the score. If a lower-ranked member began to bowl better than those above him, verbal remarks—"You're bowling over your head" or "How lucky can you get?"—were used to remind him that he was stepping out of line.

Secondary Groups

● **secondary group**
people who share only part of their lives while focusing on a goal or task

● **secondary relationships**
impersonal interactions involving limited parts of personalities

Unlike a primary group, a **secondary group** is impersonal and goal oriented. It involves only a segment of its members' lives. Secondary groups exist to accomplish a specific purpose. Work groups, volunteers during disasters, and environmentalist organizations are examples of secondary groups. Members of secondary groups interact impersonally, in ways involving only limited parts of their personalities. These interactions are called **secondary relationships.** Interactions between clerks and customers, employers and workers, and dentists and patients are secondary relationships.

What are secondary relationships like? Members of secondary groups may be friends and identify with one another, but the purpose of the group is to accomplish a task, not to enrich friendships. In fact, if friendship becomes more important than the task, a secondary group may become ineffective. If the members of a Hurricane Katrina relief group became more interested in the emotional relationships among themselves than in meeting the needs of the victims, their performance could suffer.

Do secondary groups ever include primary relationships? Although primary relationships are more likely to occur in primary groups and secondary relationships in secondary groups, there are a number of exceptions. Many secondary groups include some primary relationships. Members of work groups may relate in personal terms, demonstrate genuine

Why are these young people probably not a primary group?

concern for one another, and have relationships that are fulfilling in themselves. Similarly, members of a primary group sometimes engage in secondary interaction. One family member may, for example, lend money to another member of the family with a set interest rate and repayment schedule.

Section 1 Assessment

1. Listed below are some examples of primary and secondary relationships. Indicate which examples are most likely to be primary relationships (P) and which are most likely to be secondary relationships (S).
   a. a marine recruit and his drill instructor at boot camp
   b. a married couple
   c. a coach and her soccer team
   d. a teacher and his students
   e. a car salesperson and her potential customer

2. Which of the following is not a condition that promotes the development of primary groups?
   a. small group size
   b. face-to-face contact
   c. continuous contact
   d. interaction on the basis of status or role

3. What are the three main functions of primary groups?

Critical Thinking

4. **Making Comparisons** Identify a primary group and a secondary group to which you belong. Describe three functions of each of these groups based on your personal experiences. Then compare and contrast your relationships in each group. (Note: It may help if you create a diagram.)

Work Life in China

Generally, Americans separate their work and nonwork life. When they don't, we say that they are "married" to their jobs. This means that most American work relationships are secondary relationships. They are impersonal and goal oriented. In China, however, work relationships are mostly primary because they are intimate, personal, caring, and fulfilling in themselves. This excerpt from **Streetlife China** *describes a typical work situation in present-day China.*

Everyone exists in China in terms of a work unit. When meeting for the first time, they will usually ask each other what work unit they are from. When ringing someone, the first question likely to be asked is, "What is your work unit?", which usually precedes the question of one's own name. When registering in a hotel, the registrar will list the guest in terms of "guest from such and such a work unit". . . .

The contemporary Chinese work unit, then, is really quite extraordinary. Apart from functioning as a department or organization, the work unit is also in charge of the management of the household register, the staple and non-staple food supply, all medical services, and all housing. It is also in charge of ideological remolding, political study, policing and security matters, marriages and divorce, entry into the Chinese Communist Youth League and into the Party, awarding merit and carrying out disciplinary action. If one wants to run for election as a deputy for either the National People's Congress or the Chinese People's Consultative Congress, one must firstly get the permission of one's work unit. When administrative sanctions are deployed to detain somebody, or they are to be sent for labor reform, then the authorities must consult with the work unit. "I am a person working in a work unit" is worn as a badge of pride in China; conversely, the expression "I don't have a work unit" basically identifies the speaker as little short of a swindler. . . .

Chinese have a love-hate relationship with the work unit. On the one hand, they cannot stand it, but on the other, they are unable to live without it. The work unit is like their family: they must love their commune as they love their family, love their factory as they love their home, and love their shop as they would their kin. In work units with a very rigid system, one's rank within the unit is a symbol of one's status; the individual's worth is realized in the rank attributed to them. Whether one's name is first or last, the order of arrival at the unit, their address, their living conditions, what transport is available to them, their access to documents of varying levels of classification are all things of great concern and are fought over at great length.

Source: Excerpted from Michael Dutton, *Streetlife China*, Cambridge: Cambridge University Press, 1998, pp. 43–44, 46–47.

Thinking It Over

Can you analyze the effects of the work unit in China in terms of its relationship to other groups to which workers belong?

Other Groups and Networks

Section Preview

Reference groups help us evaluate ourselves and form identities. In-groups and out-groups divide people into "we" and "they." Social networks extend our contacts and let us form links to many other people.

Key Terms

● reference
  group (p. 177)
● in-group (p. 178)
● out-group (p. 178)
● social
  network (p. 178)

Reference Groups

We use certain groups to evaluate ourselves and to acquire attitudes, values, beliefs, and norms. Groups used in this way are called **reference groups.**

Reference groups may include our families, teachers, classmates, student government leaders, social organizations, rock groups, or professional football teams. We may consider a group to be a reference group without being a member; we may only aspire to be a member. For example, junior high school girls may imitate high school girls' leadership style or athletic interests. Junior high school boys may copy high school boys' taste in clothing and music. Similarly, you need not be a member of a rock band to view musicians as a reference group. You need only evaluate yourself in terms of their standards and subscribe to their beliefs, values, and norms.

Reference groups do not have to be positive. Observing the behavior of some group you dislike may reinforce a preference for other ways of acting, feeling, and behaving. For example, a violent gang can provide a blueprint of behavior for people to avoid.

● **reference group**
  group used for self-evaluation and the formation of attitudes, values, beliefs, and norms

This choir commemorating the Emancipation Proclamation constitutes a positive reference group. Gangs are a negative reference group for neighborhood children.

In-Groups and Out-Groups

● **in-group**
exclusive group demanding intense loyalty

● **out-group**
group targeted by an in-group for opposition, antagonism, or competition

● **social network**
a web of social relationships that join a person to other people and groups

Busy people have social networks that interconnect like this old telephone switchboard.

In-groups and out-groups are like two sides of a coin—you can't have one without the other. An **in-group** requires extreme loyalty from its members. Its norms compel members to exclude others. The in-group competes with and is opposed to the **out-group.** An out-group is a group toward which in-group members feel opposition, antagonism, or competition. Based on membership in these groups, people divide into "we" and "they."

Where are these groups found? In-groups and out-groups may form around schools, athletic teams, cheerleading squads, racially or ethnically divided neighborhoods, or countries at war. High school students can easily identify the many "in" and "out" groups in their schools. Jocks, cheerleaders, geeks, and nerds are in-groups for some and out-groups for others.

What are group boundaries? In-groups must have ways of telling who is and is not "in." If nothing distinguishes "us" from "them," then there can be no "ins" and "outs." A boundary is often a symbol (badges, clothes, or a particular slang); it may be an action (handshake, high five); or it may be an actual place. New in-group members are often taught the boundaries at initiation ceremonies. To outsiders, group boundaries form an entrance barrier.

How are group boundaries maintained? Maintaining group boundaries requires intense loyalty and commitment from the group members. Unfortunately, this may involve clashes with outsiders. Urban gang members may injure or kill an enemy gang member who has entered their "territory."

Social Networks

As individuals and as members of primary and secondary groups, we interact with many people. All of a person's social relationships make up his or her **social network**—the web of social relationships that join a person to other people and groups. This social network includes family members, work colleagues, classmates, church members, close friends, car mechanics, and store clerks. Social networks tie us to hundreds of people within our communities, throughout the country, and even around the world (Doreian and Stokman, 1997).

Your broader social network can be thought of as containing smaller webs within the larger web of social relationships, depending on how finely you wish to break it down. All of your friends are only one part of your total social network. Another part might be composed of all the people at your school with whom you have social relationships of various kinds.

The Internet is expanding the amount of interaction and the flow of information within networks. Before the Internet, for example, humanitarian relief organizations in the United States had to solicit donations using slower, more cumbersome means of communication, such as the print media, the telephone, and letter writing. With the Internet, however, members of relief organizations can supply almost unlimited information to as many people as they can reach. In 2005, for example, many sites on the Internet instructed Americans and people around the world how to donate funds and provide help for the victims of Hurricane Katrina. Such relief efforts can now be organized very quickly. Feedback among network members can be instantaneous.

This increased ease, speed, and frequency of social contact can promote a sense of membership in a particular network. Whereas in the past, opponents to gun control were largely unaware of each other, they may now feel part of a nationwide social network.

Are social networks groups? Although a person's social network includes groups, it is not a group itself. A social network lacks the boundaries of a group and it does not involve close or continuous interaction among all members. Thus, all members of a social network do not necessarily experience a feeling of membership because many of the relationships are too temporary for a sense of belonging to develop.

How strong are the ties in a social network? Social networks include both primary and secondary groups. Thus, the social relationships within a network involve both strong and weak ties (Granovetter, 1973; Freeman, 1992). Strong ties exist in primary relationships. Weak ties are most often found in secondary relationships.

What are the functions of social networks? Social networks can serve several important functions. They can provide a sense of belonging and purpose. They can furnish support in the form of help and advice. Finally, networks can be a useful tool for those individuals who are entering the labor market. Getting to know people who can help you in your career is very important.

Section 2 Assessment

1. Provide an example, not given in the text, of each of the following:
   a. out-group
   b. in-group
   c. social aggregate
   d. social category
   e. reference group

2. How are social networks different from social aggregates?

Critical Thinking

3. **Making Comparisons** Your high school has in-groups and out-groups. Concentrate on two of these groups and analyze sociologically the differences in the roles of group membership in one in-group and one out-group.

Sociology Today

School Violence and Social Networks

The 1999 murders of twelve students and one teacher at Columbine High in Littleton, Colorado, captured the attention of the American public. There had been many earlier incidents of violence in schools, but the Columbine tragedy forced Americans to finally recognize that violence was not confined to troubled inner-city schools.

Explanations for the attack, which was carried out by two students, came rapidly. Some blamed the lack of gun control. Others looked to violent video games and movies. For others, it was the parents' fault. A fourth reason, suggested by many sociologists, involved failure of the community's social networks.

Social networks reduce violence in at least three ways.

1. Strong social bonds reinforce acceptable and unacceptable behavior.
2. Social networks allow community or neighborhood members to share information about other members.
3. Social networks provide help and social support.

According to Laub and Lauritsen (1998), when many people are involved in their community networks, "social capital" is amassed. Social capital is the degree to which a person can depend on others in the community for help and support. For young people, community support can help compensate for a lack of closeness in families.

The social capital of the community can to a considerable extent off-set its absence in particular families in the community. For example, children from single-parent families are more like their two-parent counterparts in both achievement and in continuation in school when the schools are in communities with extensive social capital (Coleman, 1987:10).

In the Littleton case, social capital seemed in short supply. The parents of Eric Harris, one of the students who carried out the attack, were out of touch with the bomb-making activity occurring in their own home. More important, the rest of the community seemed unaware of any problem with these students. The only exception was a family that alerted authorities to threats Harris had posted on the Internet. But upon receiving this information, the sheriff's office apparently did not seek additional information from other members of the community (Gegax and Bai, 1999).

School violence can be diminished through the building of community networks. Both parents and young people must be willing to build social ties with other people in their neighborhoods and communities.

Doing Sociology

Examine some of the social networks in your neighborhood and community. How strong are they? What could be done to strengthen them?

Types of Social Interaction

Section Preview

Five types of social interaction are basic to group life: cooperation, conflict, social exchange, coercion, and conformity.

Key Terms

- cooperation *(p. 181)*
- conflict *(p. 181)*
- social
  exchange *(p. 183)*
- coercion *(p. 184)*
- conformity *(p. 184)*
- groupthink *(p. 185)*

Five Types of Group Social Interaction

Social interaction is crucial to groups. In group settings, people take on roles and adopt appropriate norms and behaviors. These may be very different from the norms and behaviors that the individual holds in other settings. For example, you may behave one way as a member of a choir or a basketball team, but act quite differently when you are at home or out with your friends. In this section, we will look closely at those processes or forces that determine how individuals behave in a group setting. Robert Nisbet (1988) describes five types of social interaction basic to group life: *cooperation, conflict, social exchange, coercion, and conformity.* Some of these interactions keep the group stable and ongoing, while others encourage change.

Cooperation

Cooperation is a form of interaction in which individuals or groups combine their efforts to reach some goal. Cooperation usually occurs when reaching a goal demands the best use of limited resources and efforts. The survivors of a plane crash in a snow-covered mountain range must cooperate to survive. Victims of floods, mudslides, tornadoes, droughts, or famines must help one another to get through their crisis.

Cooperation exists outside of emergencies as well: Children agree to a set of rules for a game, couples agree to share household duties, and students organize to march in support of a community project. Indeed, without some degree of cooperation, social life could not exist.

- **cooperation**
  interaction in which individuals or groups combine their efforts to reach a goal

- **conflict**
  interaction aimed at defeating an opponent

Conflict

Groups or individuals that work together to obtain certain benefits are cooperating. Groups or individuals that work against one another for a larger share of the rewards are in **conflict.** In conflict, defeating the opponent is considered essential. In fact, defeating the opponent may become more important than achieving the goal and may bring more satisfaction than winning the prize.

These Habitat for Humanity volunteers are cooperating in an effort to provide shelter for a family in need.

A group of demonstrators protest continuing poverty in Africa and elsewhere during the Group of Eight (G-8) summit in Edinburgh, Scotland, during the summer of 2005. The G-8, made up of the United States, the United Kingdom, Canada, France, Germany, Italy, Japan, and Russia, meets annually to discuss economic and other issues.

Sociology Online

Student Web Activity
Visit the *Sociology and You* Web site at glencoe.com and click on **Chapter 6—Student Web Activities** for an activity on conflict resolution.

What are the societal benefits of conflict? As you read in the Applying Sociology feature at the beginning of the chapter, conflict is usually considered a disruptive form of interaction. A cooperative, peaceful society is assumed to be better than one in conflict. Conflict can be socially beneficial, however.

According to sociologist Georg Simmel (1858–1918), one of the major benefits of conflict is the promotion of cooperation and unity *within* opposing groups. The Revolutionary War drew many American colonists together, even though it brought them into conflict with the British. Similarly, a labor union often becomes more united during the process of collective bargaining. A neighborhood bully can unite (at least temporarily) even the most argumentative of brothers.

Another positive effect of conflict is the attention it draws to social inequities. Norms and values are reexamined when crises and conflicts erupt. Civil rights activists in the early 1960s, for instance, jarred the American Congress into passing laws that ensure basic rights and freedoms to all people.

Conflict may also be beneficial when it changes norms, beliefs, and values. Student protests in the late 1960s and early '70s (many of which were violent) resulted in changes to previously accepted norms and behaviors within universities. University administrations became more sensitive to diverse student needs, and more emphasis was placed on teaching.

Social Exchange

All men, or most men, wish what is noble but choose what is profitable; and while it is noble to render a service not with an eye to receiving one in return, it is profitable to receive one. One ought, therefore, if one can, to return the equivalent of services received, and to do so willingly.

In this passage from *The Nicomachean Ethics*, Aristotle touches on **social exchange,** a type of social interaction in which one person voluntarily does something for another, expecting a reward in return. If you help a friend wash her car, expecting that she will help you study for a test, the relationship is one of exchange.

In an exchange relationship, it is the benefit to be earned rather than the relationship itself that is key. When you do something for someone else, he or she becomes obligated to return the favor. Thus, the basis of an exchange relationship is *reciprocity*, the idea that you should do for others as they have done for you.

What is the difference between cooperation and social exchange?
While both cooperation and social exchange involve working together, there is a significant difference between these two types of interaction. In cooperation, individuals or groups work together to achieve a shared goal. Reaching this goal, however, may or may not benefit those who are cooperating. And although individuals or groups may profit from cooperating, that is not their main objective.

For example, group members may work to build and maintain an adequate supply of blood for a local blood bank without thought of benefit to themselves. This is an example of cooperation. Suppose, though, that the group is working to ensure availability of blood for its own members. In this case, it has an exchange relationship with the blood bank. In cooperation, the question is, "How can we reach our goal?" In exchange relationships, the implied question is, "What is in it for me?"

● **social exchange**
a voluntary action performed in the expectation of getting a reward in return

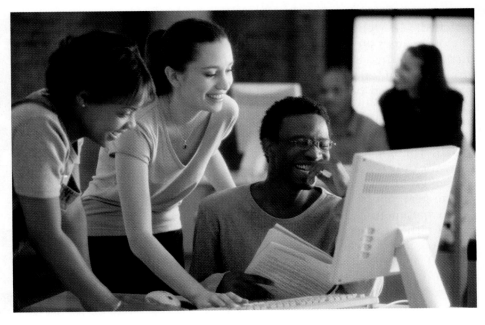

These high school students are working together in a computer lab. Explain why this could be a social exchange relationship.

Coercion

Coercion is social interaction in which individuals or groups are forced to give in to the will of other individuals or groups. Prisoners of war can be forced to reveal information to enemies, governments can enforce laws through legalized punishment, and parents can control the behavior of young children by threatening to withdraw privileges.

Coercion is the opposite of social exchange. Whereas social exchange involves voluntary conformity for mutual benefit, coercion is a one-way street. The central element in coercion, then, is domination. This domination may occur through physical force, such as imprisonment, torture, or death. More often, however, coercion is expressed more subtly through social pressure—ridicule, rejection, withdrawal of affection, or denial of recognition.

Conflict theory best describes this type of social interaction. When parents coerce children with a curfew, guards coerce prisoners with force, and governments coerce drivers with fines, obvious power differentials are at work.

Conformity

Conformity is behavior that matches group expectations. When we conform, we adapt our behavior to fit the behavior of those around us. Conformity is an expectation of socialization. Social life—with its uniformity, predictability, and orderliness—could not exist without this type of social interaction. Without conformity, there could be no churches, families, or governments. Without conformity, there could be no culture or social structure.

Do most people conform to group pressures? The tendency to conform to group pressure has been dramatically illustrated in a classic experiment by Solomon Asch (1955). In this experiment, many participants publicly denied their own senses because they wanted to avoid disagreeing with majority opinion.

Asch asked groups of male college students to compare lines printed on two cards. (See Figure 6.1.) The students were asked to identify the line on the second card that matched, in length, one of the lines on the first card. In each group, all but one of the subjects had been instructed by Asch to choose a line that obviously did not match. The *naive* subject—the only member of each group unaware of the real nature of the experiment—was forced either to select the line he actually thought matched the standard line or to yield to the unanimous opinion of the group.

- **coercion**
  interaction in which individuals or groups are forced to behave in a particular way

What type of social interaction is involved in city curfews?

- **conformity**
  behavior that matches group expectations

Card A   Card B

Figure 6.1
Cards for Asch's Experiments
Which of the lines on Card A matches the line on Card B? You may be surprised to learn that in a group setting many people associated the first and the third lines with the longer line on Card B. Read about Asch's experiment in the text.

In earlier tests of individuals in isolation, Asch had found that the error rate in matching the lines was only 1 percent. Under group pressure, however, the naive subjects went along with the majority's wrong opinion over one-third of the time. If this large a proportion of naive subjects yielded to group pressure in a group of strangers, it is not difficult to imagine the conformity rate in groups where people are emotionally committed to the welfare of the group (Myers, 2006).

What is groupthink? Because of the difficulty of going against decisions made by the group, Irving Janis (1982) has argued that many decisions are likely to be the product of groupthink. **Groupthink** exists when thinking in a group is self-deceptive, based on conformity to group beliefs, and created by group pressure. In groupthink, pressures toward uniformity discourage members from expressing their concerns about group decisions.

During the administration of President John F. Kennedy in the early 1960s, for example, the president and his advisers decided to launch an invasion of Cuba at the Bay of Pigs. The invasion failed. Analysis by Janis revealed that during the decision process, because of group pressure, several top advisers failed to admit that they thought the plan would probably not succeed.

Research indicates that groupthink can be avoided when leaders or group members make a conscious effort to see that all group members participate actively in a multisided discussion. In addition, members must know that points of disagreement and conflict will be tolerated (Moorhead, Neck, and West, 1998; Myers, 2006).

● **groupthink**
self-deceptive thinking that is based on conformity to group beliefs, and created by group pressure to conform

How is groupthink promoted?

"All those in favor say 'Aye.'"
"Aye."
"Aye."
"Aye."
"Aye."
"Aye."

Figure 6.2	Illustrating Types of Social Interaction

This table illustrates how each theoretical perspective might approach the study of social structures. The concepts could be switched to any other theoretical perspective and illustrated from that perspective. Associate each concept with a different theoretical perspective and provide your own example.

Theoretical Perspective	Type of Social Interaction	Example	
Functionalism	Conformity	Team integration is promoted when basketball players accept their roles on the floor.	
Conflict Theory	Coercion	Conflict in prisons is kept in check by the superior power of the guards.	
Symbolic Interactionism	Social Exchange	Two neighbors share recipes and ideas so each benefits.	

Section 3 Assessment

Match terms a–e with the numbered example.

1. Blood donors expect payment.
2. Students read what a teacher assigns.
3. The United States invades Iraq.
4. Flood victims help each other.
5. Employees are forced to work overtime or be fired.
6. Solomon Asch's experiment demonstrates the positive consequences of group pressure. *T* or *F*?
7. Why is conformity essential for the development of social structures?

a. cooperation
b. conflict
c. social exchange
d. coercion
e. conformity

Critical Thinking

8. **Analyzing Information**
   Describe an example of groupthink in your school. Analyze this situation in terms of its positive or negative consequences.

TECH TRENDS

Working in the Virtual Office

Vanishing are the traditional offices [in formal organizations] that occupy a common, fixed space, and employ a totally permanent workforce. Numerous companies are now utilizing what have come to be called "virtual offices." For the most part, these offices are staffed by at-home employees who telecommute, use Internet resources, and are frequently temporary employees.

Virtual offices offer many benefits in today's climate of global competition. For those workers who previously found it difficult to work outside the home (the elderly, [disabled], or parents with child-care responsibilities), telecommuting can be a vehicle into the workforce. What's more, corporate executives and managers enjoy advantages of the Internet: It provides rich resources of both people and information; it improves operations; it markets products. In fact, telecommuting has been shown to result in productivity gains of between 15–20%. Finally, virtual offices afford companies dramatic savings in the costs of employees and facilities.

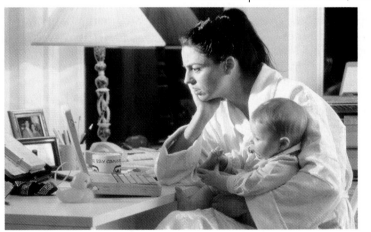

But what of the problems associated with telecommuting? Notable is the telecommuters' sense of alienation. They may feel isolated from fellow workers and the larger organization. This alienation can be minimized by bringing telecommuters together for periodic meetings. Ostensibly established to allow telecommuters to report to their supervisors, such get-togethers serve to reinforce the telecommuters' membership in, and loyalty to, the organization for which they work.

Two other difficulties confront the telecommuter. The first is low wages. In most instances, wages paid for work done by home telecommuters lag noticeably behind wages paid to office workers. This is unlikely to change given the difficulties that trade unions face in unionizing such workers. The second difficulty is the family tension stemming from the home/office merger. Until traditional views about appropriate work locations become more enlightened, home telecommuters are likely to be perceived by other family members as "not really working."

Source: William E. Snizek, "Virtual Offices: Some Neglected Considerations," *Communications of the ACM*, 38 (September 1995):15, 16. Reprinted by permission of the author.

Analyzing the Trends

Do you think the trend toward the virtual office is a good thing? Defend your answer from a functionalist viewpoint.

Experiment: Group Pressure and Obedience

Can a group cause a person to physically punish a victim with increasing severity despite the victim's pleas for mercy? Researcher Stanley Milgram (1963, 1974) has shown that this could happen.

As noted in the text, Solomon Asch demonstrated that group pressure can influence people to make false claims about what they see. Specifically, experimental subjects can be pressured to claim that two lines (drawn on a card) match in length even though they originally perceived these same two lines as different in length. Milgram wanted to know if group pressure can have the same effect on behavior. Can group pressure cause people to treat others in ways they otherwise would not?

To test this question, Milgram could have chosen a desired behavior relatively easy to induce, such as sharing food with a stranger or damaging someone else's property. Choosing a much harder case, Milgram asked research participants to administer increasingly stronger electric shocks to people who appeared to be in pain. And these research participants were people just like you and me!

Milgram placed eighty males in an experimental situation in which a team of three individuals (two "confederates" who knew the nature of the experiment and one "subject" who did not) tested a fourth person (who was also in on the experiment) on a learning task. Each mistake by the fourth party brought an apparent electric shock from the subject. The two confederates (participants cooperating with Milgram) on each team suggested increasingly higher shock levels for successive mistakes made by the "learner" (the third confederate in the electric chair). The researcher recorded the degree to which the "operator" (the subject of the experiment) resisted or went along with group pressure to increase the voltage levels.

After explaining to the subject that the purpose of the experiment was to determine the effects of punishment (electric shocks) on memory, the learner was strapped into an electric-chair apparatus in full view of the other three team members. These three were seated in front of a large shock generator whose switches were labeled from 15 to 450 volts in 15-volt increments. The lowest-level group of switches was labeled "Slight Shock"; the highest-level group of switches read "Danger: Severe Shock."

The "operator" controlled the maximum shock that could be administered. He could keep the shock level at 15 volts throughout or increase the shock level in line with the group's recommendation. It was his decision. (Remember—he was the only one not in on the real purpose.)

The learner was primed to always answer questions incorrectly. As the shocks became stronger, he grunted, protested, and finally demanded that the experiment stop. Each of these complaints was actually prerecorded and played in coordination with a given shock level. No discomfort

Photographs from Stanley Milgram's experiment show participants ordering higher and higher level shocks for the actor pretending to be shocked.

was indicated until a 75-volt shock was administered. At 120 volts, the learner shouted that the shocks were becoming painful. Groans followed a 135-volt shock, and at 150 volts the learner cried out to be released from the experiment, complaining of a heart condition. At 180 volts, the learner cried out, "I can't stand the pain," and 285 volts was followed by an agonized scream. From 300 to 450 volts, the learner continuously shouted desperately that he would no longer answer questions.

Milgram first needed to know how far the operator would go in administering shocks *without* group influence. To accomplish this, an identical experiment was run minus the two confederates in the punishing group. Response to group pressure was measured by the difference in the operator's behavior in the two situations.

Group pressure heavily affected the level of shock administered by the operator. That is, the average shock level in the three-person situation was significantly higher than in the one-person situation. Perhaps most interesting are the results on *maximum* shock levels. When alone, only two operators went beyond the point where the learner first vehemently protested. Under group pressure, twenty-seven of the operators went beyond this point. Nineteen of the operators went above 255 volts ("Intense Shock"), and ten went into the group of voltages labeled "Danger: Severe Shock." Seven even reached 450 volts (the highest shock level possible).

The research by Milgrim and Asch reveal the power of group pressure to create conformity in thought and behavior. Clearly, conformity must occur for social structure and society to exist. What worries many scholars is the extent to which social pressure can determine how humans think and act.

Working with the Research

1. Discuss the ethical implications of Milgram's experiment. (You may want to refer to Chapter 2, pp. 59–61, for a discussion about ethics in social research.)

2. If the researcher had not been present as an authority figure during the experiment to approve the use of all shock levels, do you think group pressure would have been as effective? Explain.

3. Discuss some implications of this experiment for democratic government. Can you relate it to George Orwell's novel *1984*?

4. Do you think society would be possible without this tendency to conform? Explain your position.

Formal Organizations

Key Terms

- formal organization
  (p. 190)
- bureaucracy (p. 190)
- power (p. 191)
- authority (p. 191)
- rationalization
  (p. 193)
- informal
  organization (p. 194)
- iron law of
  oligarchy (p. 196)

- formal organization
  a group deliberately
  created to achieve one
  or more long-term goals

- bureaucracy
  a formal organization based
  on rationality and efficiency

Section Preview

A formal organization is created to achieve some goal. Most are bureaucratic. The existence of primary groups and primary relationships within formal organizations can either help or hinder the achievement of goals.

The Nature of Formal Organizations

Until the 1920s, the majority of Americans lived on farms or in small towns and villages. Nearly all of their daily lives were spent in primary groups such as families, neighborhoods, and churches. As industrialization and urbanization have advanced, however, Americans have become more involved in secondary groups. Born in hospitals, educated in large schools, employed by huge corporations, regulated by government agencies, cared for in nursing homes, and buried by funeral establishments, Americans, like members of other industrialized societies, now often find themselves within *formal organizations* (Pfeffer, 1997).

How are formal organizations and bureaucracies related?

A **formal organization** is deliberately created to achieve one or more long-term goals. Examples of formal organizations are high schools, colleges, corporations, government agencies, and hospitals.

Most formal organizations today are also **bureaucracies**—formal organizations based on rationality and efficiency. Although bureaucracies are popularly thought of as "monuments to inefficiency," they have proven to be effective in industrial societies.

Both these bank customers in the U.S. and these Japanese workers feel the effects of the formal organization structure. Do you think most organizations are bureaucratic in nature?

Major Characteristics of Bureaucracies

All bureaucracies possess certain characteristics. The most important of these are listed below.

- **A division of labor based on the principle of specialization.** Each person in a bureaucracy is responsible for certain functions or tasks. (See Figure 6.3 for an organizational chart outlining the division of labor in a public school district.) This specialization allows an individual to become an expert in a limited area.

- **A hierarchy of authority.** Before discussing authority, it is necessary to define power. **Power** refers to the ability to control the behavior of others, even against their will. **Authority** is the exercise of legitimate power— power that derives from a recognized or approved source. People submit

power
the ability to control the behavior of others

authority
the legitimate or socially approved use of power

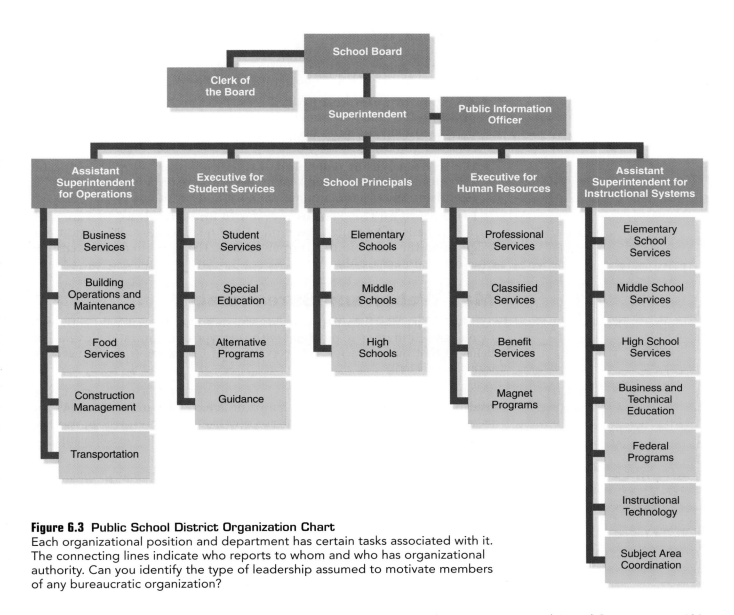

Figure 6.3 Public School District Organization Chart
Each organizational position and department has certain tasks associated with it. The connecting lines indicate who reports to whom and who has organizational authority. Can you identify the type of leadership assumed to motivate members of any bureaucratic organization?

Calvin doesn't think that bureaucratic rules should apply to him if they interfere with his wishes.

to authority because they believe it is the right thing to do. With respect to authority, bureaucratic organizations are like pyramids. The greatest amount of authority is concentrated in a few positions at the top, with decreasing amounts of authority in a larger number of lower positions. This is what is meant by "hierarchy of authority."

- **A system of rules and procedures.** Rules and procedures direct how work is to be done and provide a framework for decision making. They stabilize the organization because they coordinate activities and provide guidelines to follow in most situations.

- **Written records of work and activities.** Written records of work and activities are made and then kept in files. This organizational "memory" is essential to smooth functioning, stability, and continuity.

- **Promotion on the basis of merit and qualifications.** Jobs are filled on the basis of technical and professional qualifications. Promotions are given on the basis of merit, not favoritism. The norm in a bureaucracy is equal treatment for all.

Max Weber and Bureaucracy

Max Weber was the first to analyze the nature of bureaucracy. Although he recognized there were problems with this type of organization, overall he believed that bureaucracies were very efficient in dealing with the needs of industrial societies.

What are the advantages of bureaucracy? In Chapter 1, you read how Weber feared the dehumanizing effects of bureaucracies. As the values of preindustrial societies began to weaken, however, Weber also saw advantages to bureaucracy. On these advantages, he wrote the following:

The decisive reason for the advance of bureaucratic organization has always been its purely technical superiority over any other form of organization. The fully developed bureaucratic mechanism compares with other organizations exactly as does the machine with the nonmechanical modes of production (Gerth and Mills, 1958:214).

Earlier kinds of organizations, where the decision makers were chosen on the basis of family or wealth, were just not capable of dealing with an industrial economy. The fast-moving industrial economy required steadiness, precision, continuity, speed, efficiency, and minimum cost—advantages bureaucracy could offer. **Rationalization**—the mind-set emphasizing knowledge, reason, and planning rather than tradition and superstition—was on the rise. (See pages 17–18 for a review of this concept.)

Do bureaucracies undervalue people? As strange as it might sound, bureaucracy is designed to protect individuals. People often complain about the rules, procedures, and impersonal treatment that characterize bureaucracy. Without them, though, decision making would be arbitrary and without reason. It might sound great, for example, to abolish final exams, but then grading would not be objective. For example, a teacher might give higher grades to males. This is not to say that favoritism never occurs in bureaucratic organizations. Nevertheless, the presence of rules guarantees at least a measure of equal treatment.

● **rationalization**
the mind-set emphasizing knowledge, reason, and planning

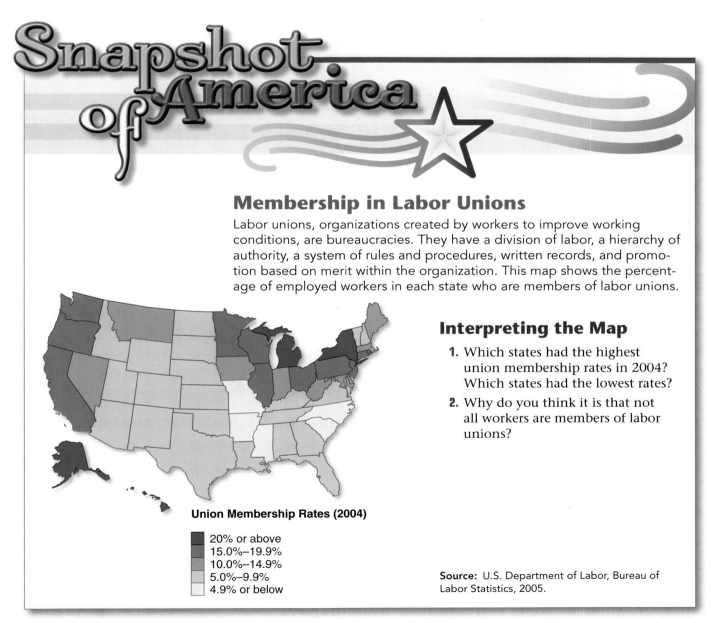

Snapshot of America

Membership in Labor Unions

Labor unions, organizations created by workers to improve working conditions, are bureaucracies. They have a division of labor, a hierarchy of authority, a system of rules and procedures, written records, and promotion based on merit within the organization. This map shows the percentage of employed workers in each state who are members of labor unions.

Interpreting the Map

1. Which states had the highest union membership rates in 2004? Which states had the lowest rates?

2. Why do you think it is that not all workers are members of labor unions?

Union Membership Rates (2004)

- 20% or above
- 15.0%–19.9%
- 10.0%–14.9%
- 5.0%–9.9%
- 4.9% or below

Source: U.S. Department of Labor, Bureau of Labor Statistics, 2005.

Human Development

Each year, the United Nations ranks the countries of the world in terms of their human development. The human development index (HDI) is based on each country's life expectancy, educational attainment, and adjusted real income. This map shows how the world's countries ranked on the HDI in 2004.

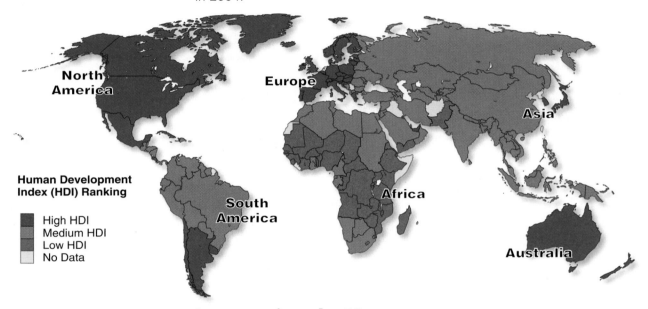

Human Development Index (HDI) Ranking

- High HDI
- Medium HDI
- Low HDI
- No Data

North America

Europe

Asia

South America

Africa

Australia

Source: United Nations Development Programme, *Human Development Report 2004.*

Interpreting the Map

Support or refute the following statement: "To achieve a high ranking on the HDI, a country must have well-established and stable bureaucracies in the areas of health care, education, and the economy."

Informal Structure Within Organizations

Bureaucracies are designed to act as secondary groups. As anyone who has worked in a bureaucratic organization knows, though, there are primary relationships as well. Primary relationships emerge as part of the **informal organization** —groups within a formal organization in which personal relationships are guided by norms, rituals, and sentiments that are not part of the formal organization. Based on common interests and personal relationships, informal groups are usually formed spontaneously.

When were informal organizations first studied? The existence of informal organizations within bureaucracies was first documented in the mid-1920s, when a group of Harvard researchers was studying the

● **informal organization**
groups within a formal organization in which personal relationships are guided by norms, rituals, and sentiments that are not part of the formal organization

Hawthorne plant of the Western Electric Company in Chicago. In a study of fourteen male machine operators in the Bank Wiring Observation Room, F. J. Roethlisberger and William Dickson (1964, originally published in 1939) observed that work activities and job relationships were based on norms and social sanctions of that particular group of male operators. Group norms prohibited "rate busting" (doing too much work), "chiseling" (doing too little work), and "squealing" (telling group secrets to supervisors). Conformity to these norms was maintained through ridicule, sarcasm, criticism, and hostility.

Why do informal organizations develop? Informal groups exist to meet needs ignored by the formal organization. Modern organizations tend to be impersonal, and informal groups offer personal affection, support, humor, and protection. The study of the Hawthorne plant mentioned above pointed out that informal organizations encourage conformity, but the resulting solidarity protects group members from mistreatment by those outside the group.

Despite working in a bureaucratic organization, these construction workers seem to be on very personal terms. How do sociologists explain this?

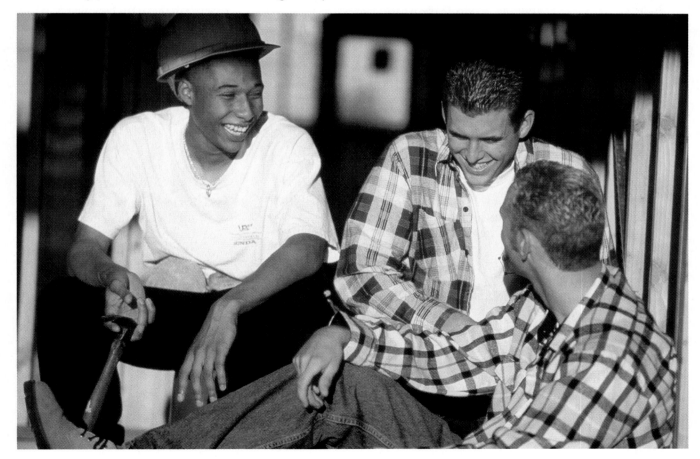

Iron Law of Oligarchy

If an organization's goals are to be achieved, power must be exercised. Sometimes this power may be grabbed by individuals for their own purposes. This process is described by the *iron law of oligarchy* (Michels, 1949; originally published in 1911).

What is the iron law of oligarchy? According to the **iron law of oligarchy,** formulated by German sociologist Robert Michels, power increasingly tends to become more and more concentrated in the hands of fewer members of any organization. Michels observed that, even in organizations intended to be democratic, a few leaders eventually gain control, and other members become virtually powerless. He concluded that this increased concentration of power occurs because those in power want to remain in power.

The government in communist China is a prime example of Michels's principle. Not subject to popular election, the aging individuals at the top have been able to consolidate, or strengthen, their power over a long period of time. Each of the leaders is able to build a loyal staff, control money, offer jobs, and give favors.

Why does organization lead to oligarchy? According to Michels, three organizational factors encourage oligarchy. First, organizations need a hierarchy of authority to delegate decision making. Second, the advantages held by those at the top allow them to consolidate their powers. They can create a staff that is loyal to them, control the channels of communication, and use organizational resources to increase their power. Finally, other members of the organization tend to defer to leaders—to give in to those who take charge.

● **iron law of oligarchy**
theory that power increasingly becomes concentrated in the hands of a few members of any organization

---

Section 4 Assessment

1. Define the term *formal organization.*
2. List the major characteristics of bureaucracy, according to Max Weber.
3. Identify whether the following are advantages (A) or disadvantages (D) of a bureaucracy:
   a. its use of appropriate criteria in hiring employees
   b. its use of rules to provide definite guidelines for behavior within the organization
   c. its ability to hide the true nature of authority relationships
   d. its encouragement of administrative competence in managers
4. Can you describe the form of leadership most suited to the operation of the iron law of oligarchy? Explain your answer.

Critical Thinking

5. **Synthesizing Information** Analyze your school as a bureaucracy. Give an example of the following characteristics of bureaucracy: (1) system of rules and procedures; (2) impersonality and impartiality (lack of favoritism). Discuss a positive and negative consequence of each characteristic.

Summary

Section 1: Primary and Secondary Groups

Main Idea: Groups are classified by how they develop and function. Primary groups meet emotional and support needs, while secondary groups are task focused.

Section 2: Other Groups and Networks

Main Idea: Reference groups help us evaluate ourselves and form identities. In-groups and out-groups divide people into "we" and "they." Social networks extend our contacts and let us form links to many other people.

Section 3: Types of Social Interaction

Main Idea: Five types of social interaction are basic to group life: cooperation, conflict, social exchange, coercion, and conformity.

Section 4: Formal Organizations

Main Idea: A formal organization is created to achieve some goal. Most are bureaucratic. The existence of primary groups and primary relationships within formal organizations can either help or hinder the achievement of goals.

Self-Check Quiz
Visit the *Sociology and You* Web site at glencoe.com and click on **Chapter 6—Self-Check Quizzes** to prepare for the chapter test.

Reviewing Vocabulary

Complete each sentence using each term once.

a. social category
b. social aggregate
c. primary group
d. secondary group
e. reference group
f. social network
g. social exchange
h. conformity
i. groupthink
j. formal organization
k. bureaucracy
l. rationalism

1. A _____ is an impersonal and goal-oriented group that involves only a segment of one's life.
2. A group of people who are in the same place at the same time is called a _____ .
3. A _____ is a web of social relationships that join a person to other people and groups.
4. A _____ is composed of people who are emotionally close, know one another well, and seek one another's company.
5. A situation in which pressures toward uniformity discourage members from expressing their reservations about group decisions is called _____ .
6. A type of social interaction in which one person voluntarily does something for another, expecting a reward in return, is called _____ .
7. _____ is behavior that goes according to group expectations.
8. A _____ is a group used for self-evaluation.
9. A _____ is deliberately created to achieve one or more long-term goals.
10. A _____ is a formal organization based on efficiency and rationality.
11. The solution of problems on the basis of logic, data, and planning is called _____ .
12. People who share a social characteristic are called a _____ .

Reviewing the Facts

13. Use the diagram below to list the basic societal functions of primary groups.

BASIC SOCIETAL FUNCTION OF PRIMARY GROUPS

14. List the major characteristics of primary and secondary groups.

15. What is the difference between a reference group and a social network?

16. What is the main difference between cooperation and social exchange?

17. Explain the relationship between in-groups and out-groups.

Thinking Critically

18. Applying Concepts
Your high school probably has diverse in-groups. Identify some of them with their own labels, and then list links common to the groups. For example, all groups might need to take two math classes. See how many items you can list that all the different groups share.

19. Making Generalizations
Social networks are an important component of group interactions. Are there people in your sociology class you would consider part of your social network? Are there classmates who are part of your family, work, church, or neighborhood groups? Are any of them among your best friends?

20. Evaluating Information
Some high school administrators and educators believe that school violence is an indication that many high school groups are in conflict. Do you believe conflicts exist between the in-groups in your school? How could your school work to lessen any potential group conflicts?

"The only solution I can see is to hold a series of long and costly hearings in order to put off finding a solution."

Jack Ziegler/Cartoonbank.com

21. Analyzing Visuals
In the Jack Ziegler cartoon above, what attitude does Ziegler convey about legislators? And which of the five characteristics of bureaucracies is most obviously at work when the legislator asks for hearings to be held?

22. Analyzing Information
You read about social exchange, the type of interaction in which someone does something for another and expects a reward in return. This might also be described as the "I'll scratch your back if you'll scratch mine" expectation. Do you think that this expectation is always present? Is it possible to perform truly random acts of kindness?

23. Making Inferences
The text discusses the issue of groupthink in the Kennedy administration. Have you ever been in a situation in which you disagreed with the majority opinion or felt that something that was about to happen was wrong? Did you speak up? If not, did the power of the group influence you? When might failing to speak up lead to harm?

Sociology Projects

24. Social Categories

In this activity, you will look at generations as social categories. Write down some of the things that you believe define your generation—for example, skateboarding, extreme sports, rap music, Gap clothes. Then find adults in their forties or early fifties and ask them to define their own generation. What were the things that identified their generation? What things define them now? Each list should include about ten cultural items of that generation. Share your findings with the class.

25. Qualitative Research

In this chapter you read about formal groups. Since people join such groups freely, volunteer groups may provide a strong measure of personal identity and cultural trends. For this project, study the statistics in the table below. Then write down at least two hypotheses about volunteering that could be tested by research, including survey research. For example, you might hypothesize that social service volunteering dips when people are in their mid-30s and 40s because people are building their careers and raising families.

Organization Type	16-24 years	25-34 years	35-44 years	45-54 years	55-64 years	65 and above
Civic & political	5.5	5.5	5.3	8.1	9.3	8.7
Educational & youth	32.4	34.1	39.8	26.0	13.2	6.4
Environment & Animal Care	1.5	2.4	1.4	1.5	2.0	1.4
Hospital & Health	8.6	6.4	5.5	6.9	8.9	10.9
Public Safety	1.7	2.2	1.4	1.4	1.5	1.1
Religious	28.5	30.4	30.5	35.3	39.6	45.2
Social Service	13.0	11.1	9.0	12.3	15.0	16.9
Sport/Hobby	3.4	2.8	3.4	4.2	4.3	3.6
Other*	4.9	5.2	3.8	4.2	6.1	5.9

* includes undetermined
Source: *Statistical Abstract of the United States, 2006*

26. Promotions According to Merit

The text discusses the major characteristics of a bureaucracy. One of these involves the principle of promoting people according to merit. Another principle, however, is that people are treated equally and not given special consideration. In many organizations, merit is sometimes synonymous with seniority so that the length of time on the job becomes just as important or more important than the skill exercised in the job. Do an informal interview of six people who work for relatively large corporations or businesses to determine what role they think seniority should play in promotion decisions. Should a satisfactory long-term employee be skipped over for a position in favor of an employee with much less time, but superior skills? Summarize the results of your interviews and share your ideas with the class.

Technology Activities

27. *Dilbert* is a popular cartoon strip that makes fun of the bureaucratic structures in American corporations. Go to the *Dilbert* web site at www.unitedmedia.com/comics/dilbert and read several of the comic strips.

   1. Find a few cartoons that illustrate some important ideas presented in this chapter. Explain the cartoons in terms of knowledge gained in this chapter.

   2. Discuss some of the strips with an adult who works in a corporation. What does that person think about the accuracy of the situations portrayed in *Dilbert*?

   3. Prepare a brief report describing what you learned about formal organizations and bureaucracies from your review of *Dilbert*.

Enrichment Reading

Bullies and Their Victims
by John Greenya

● **condone**
pardon or accept

● **impunity**
freedom from punishment

● **exacerbate**
make more severe

Today, bullying is widely regarded as a serious problem in the United States. Ron Stephens, executive director of the National School Safety Center, calls bullying "one of the most enduring problems" in schools. Up to 75 percent of American children have been victims of bullying, according to the National Crime Prevention Council.

During her first year of junior high school, a young woman recalls, "There were a bunch of them, and they were older than me. They took my backpack and kicked it along the ground like a soccer ball, and when I tried to stop them they kicked me. One boy pulled my hair so hard a big clump came out."

Bullying in high school has a different name, says Ralph Cantor, the Safe and Drug Free Schools Coordinator for the Office of Education in Alameda County, Calif. "It's called harassment," particularly when it has sexual overtones, he says, and a "hate crime" if it involves bullying based on sexual orientation. . . .

Some experts say American culture in some ways may **condone,** or even support, abusiveness as an acceptable way to get ahead—and not just on the playground. Television shows like "Scrubs," "House," and "ER," for instance, feature successful—albeit arrogant and rude—doctors frequently verbally humiliating and abusing underlings. Teen movies portray the most popular kids—cheerleaders and football players—as the most likely to bully. . . .

Others say the enormous size of today's public schools may contribute to the problem by providing long, unmonitored hallways or stairwells where vulnerable students can be victimized with **impunity.** And some teachers and parents may be reluctant to intervene—perhaps unintentionally encouraging the practice by their inaction—either because they see bullying as a natural part of childhood or because they fear adult intervention will **exacerbate** the situation. . . .

The National Education Association (NEA) says bullying can be direct—such as teasing, hitting or threatening—or indirect, involving exclusion, the spreading of untrue rumors or psychological manipulation. . . .

"When you and I were at school, mom or dad would say, 'Well, just ignore it and it will go away,' " recalls Rob Beaumont of Safe Schools, Safe Students. "Or, 'Stand up and fight for yourself.' Unfortunately, the level of violence has increased to the point where standing up and fighting back or ignoring it is not really an option," he said. . . .

Estimates of the prevalence of bullying vary widely. The U.S. Department of Education's Office of Safe and Drug Free Schools says 7 million school bullying incidents occur each year.

In April 2001, the first large-scale national survey of bullying in U.S. schools among students in grades six through 10 was published.

Conducted before Columbine, it found that bullying was a problem that needed immediate nationwide attention. . . . Victims of bullies are lonely and have trouble making friends; they are five times more likely than their peers to be depressed. Bullied boys are four times more likely than their peers to be suicidal, and girls eight times more likely, according to the study.

The bullies, meanwhile, were more likely to smoke, drink alcohol and get poor grades. Most troubled of all were those who had both been bullied and had bullied others: They not only reported being lonelier and having more trouble making friends but also did poorly in school, smoked cigarettes and used alcohol.

The negative effects of bullying can last a lifetime. . . . Indeed, society at large suffers from bullying. According to the NICHD, nearly 60 percent of boys who were bullies in middle school had at least one criminal conviction by age 24, and 40 percent had three or more convictions. . . .

While many schools have responded to bullying aggressively, experts say an anti-bullying program is only as good as a school administrator's resolve to implement it. . . .

"In fact, fewer than one in four schools has any real bullying-prevention programs," says [Sandford A.] Newman of Fight Crime: Invest in Kids. "It's clear that not enough is being done. There are still 3.2 million kids being bullied each year in America and 3.7 million who are bullying other children." . . .

Some experts blame bullying on the changes that have transformed society over the last few generations. For example, the anonymity provided by modern schools—often featuring large, unmonitored common areas—is frequently cited as a major reason bullies feel they can get away with abusive behavior. . . .

Others blame deeper cultural forces, specifically a society that seems to condone or reward rudeness and/or abusiveness by successful people. In some "reality" television shows, for instance, those who shout at their peers and are the most manipulative and backstabbing are often the ones who triumph. . . .

Other research has found that comprehensive, schoolwide, anti-bullying programs are most effective when they raise the awareness of how bystanders contribute to the bullying problem and aim to change peer dynamics that encourage the practice.

It is now thought—contrary to the beliefs of several decades ago—that bullies are made, not born.

Read and React

1. Why might some parents and teachers be reluctant to intervene in incidents of bullying?

2. Explain how bullying affects the victims.

3. How does society at large suffer from bullying?

4. What are some explanations for bullying?

Source: Excerpted from John Greenya, "Bullying," *CQ Researcher Online* (February 4, 2005), 101–124.

Deviance and Social Control

Learning Objectives

After reading this chapter, you will be able to

- define deviance.
- define social control and identify the major types of social control.
- discuss the positive and negative consequences of deviance.
- differentiate the major functional theories of deviance.
- discuss the conflict theory view of deviance.
- describe four approaches to crime control.

Applying Sociology

In any society, there are some people whose behavior stands out from the norm. In American society, deviance can be hard to define because there is so much cultural diversity. Senior citizens who live in a small town might define the tongue-piercing some teenagers practice as deviant. Most teenagers in New York or Los Angeles might not do so.

For sociologists, the term *deviance* refers to behavior that violates very important social norms. The most obvious example is crime. It is often possible to understand how deviant a crime is by the severity of the punishment.

The photo at left gives some clues to the way deviance is relative to the society in which it occurs. Here women prisoners in Arizona are being readied for a march to a chain gang site. First we are dealing with women who deviated from the norms of their society and imprisoned. Then these women violated prison norms. Their punishment was to be put in "lockdown" —four women are shut into a cell 8 x 12 feet wide for 23 hours a day. In this chapter, you will learn about how defiance is defined, controlled, and punished.

Sociology Online

Chapter Overview
Visit the *Sociology and You* Web site at glencoe.com and click on **Chapter 7—Chapter Overviews** to preview chapter information.

1 Deviance and Social Control

Key Terms

- deviance *(p. 204)*
- negative deviance *(p. 205)*
- positive deviance *(p. 205)*
- deviant *(p. 205)*
- social control *(p. 206)*
- social sanctions *(p. 207)*

● **deviance**
behavior that departs from societal or group norms

Section Preview

Deviance is the violation of social norms. It is difficult to define because not everyone agrees on what should be considered deviant behavior.

The Nature of Deviance

The term **deviance** refers to behavior that departs from societal or group norms. It can range from criminal behavior (recognized by almost all members of a society as deviant) to wearing heavy makeup (considered deviant by some religious groups). Some people violate norms by robbing banks or committing assault or murder. Incidents of deviance sometimes receive a great deal of attention because they involve prominent figures whose behavior is captured on national television. Former heavyweight boxing champion Mike Tyson, in a bout with a later champion, Evander Holyfield, actually bit off the tip of Holyfield's right ear and spat it onto the ring mat. Figure 7.1 illustrates the frequency of two types of juvenile deviance.

These examples appear clear-cut, but deviance is not always so easy to identify. Because deviance is subjective, or a matter of social definition, it can vary from group to group and society to society. In a diverse society like that of the United States, it is often difficult to agree on what is or is not deviant behavior. In a groundbreaking study, Simmons (1969) polled people on this issue:

The sheer range of responses [to the question "What constitutes deviant behavior?"] predictably included homosexuals, prostitutes, drug addicts, radicals, and criminals. But it also included liars, career women, Democrats, reckless drivers, atheists, Christians, suburbanites, the retired, young folks, card players, bearded men, artists, pacifists, priests, prudes, hippies, straights, girls who wear makeup, the President of the United States, conservatives, integrationists, executives, divorcees, perverts, motorcycle gangs, smart-alec students, know-it-all professors, modern people, and Americans.

To this list, one researcher would add obese people. For a week, she wore a "fat suit," adding 150 pounds to her normal body weight, in order to experience firsthand what it feels like to be an overweight woman in American society. She concluded that American

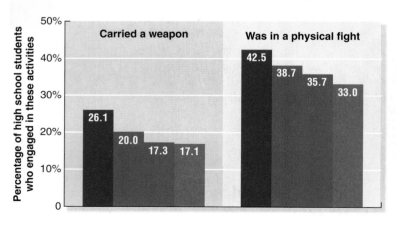

Figure 7.1 Two Types of Youth Deviance
What does the graph indicate about the trend in youth violence?

Source: Centers for Disease Control and Prevention, "Healthy Youth!" (2004).

"society not only hates fat people, it feels entitled to participate in a prejudice that at many levels parallels racism and religious bigotry" (Lampert, 1993:154).

Deviance may be either *positive* or *negative*. **Negative deviance** involves behavior that fails to meet accepted norms. People expressing negative deviance either reject the norms, misinterpret the norms, or are unaware of the norms. This is the kind of behavior popularly associated with the idea of deviance. There is, however, another type of deviance. **Positive deviance** involves overconformity to norms—leading to imbalance and extremes of perfectionism. Positive deviants idealize group norms. In its own way, positive deviance can be as disruptive and hard to manage as negative deviance. Think about the norms related to personal appearance in American society. The mass media are constantly telling young people that "lean is mean." Negative deviants will miss the mark on the obese side. Positive deviants may push themselves to the point of anorexia. Most young people will weigh somewhere between these two extremes.

Minor instances of behavior that some might consider deviant occur frequently in modern societies. For that reason, sociologists generally reserve the term *deviance* for violations of significant social norms. Significant norms are those that are highly important either to most members of a society or to the members with the most power. For a sociologist, a **deviant** is a person who has violated one or more of society's most highly valued norms. Reactions to deviants are usually negative and involve attempts to change or control the deviant behavior.

To maintain its clean and orderly streets, the government of Singapore strictly controls the behavior of its residents, imposing stiff fines on such negative deviance as littering and public spitting. A 12-year-long ban on chewing gum was recently lifted, but potential buyers must first register their names.

● **negative deviance**
involves behavior that underconforms to accepted norms

● **positive deviance**
involves behavior that overconforms to social expectations

● **deviant**
a person who breaks significant societal or group norms

This anorexic teenager in a made-for-television movie is displaying positive deviance. How would you explain to her mother that her child's behavior is "positive"?

Snapshot of America

Violent Crime

Although experiencing a recent decline, the U.S. has one of the highest violent crime rates of the major industrialized countries. In fact, the U.S. has the highest murder, rape, and robbery rates, and keeps pace in burglaries and auto thefts. This map indicates the number of violent crimes by state per 100,000 residents.

Interpreting the Map

1. Create a graph showing how the violent crime rate in your state compares with the rates in other states.

2. Pose a question that relates to the relative ranking of your state with other states.

3. What sociological conclusion can you draw from this map?

700 or above	**Number of Violent Crimes**
550–699	**Reported per 100,000**
400–549	**Population, 2003**
250–399	
150–249	
149 or below	

Source: Federal Bureau of Investigation, *Uniform Crime Reports*, 2003.

Social Control

All societies have ways to promote order, stability, and predictability in social life. We feel confident that drivers will stop for red lights, that waiters will not pour soup in our laps, and that store clerks will give us the correct change. Without **social control**—ways to promote conformity to norms— social life would be unpredictable, even chaotic. There are two broad types of social control: internal and external.

What is internal social control? Internal social control lies within the individual. It is developed during the socialization process. You are practicing internal social control when you do something because you know it is the right thing to do or when you don't do something because you know it would be wrong. For example, most people most of the time do not steal. They

* **social control**
  ways to encourage conformity to society's norms

act this way not just because they fear arrest or lack the opportunity to steal but because they consider theft to be wrong. The norm against stealing has become a part of them. This is known as the *internalization* of social norms.

What is external social control? Unfortunately for society, the process of socialization does not ensure that all people will conform all of the time. For this reason, external social control must also be present. External social control is based on **social sanctions**—rewards or punishments designed to encourage desired behavior. Positive sanctions, such as awards, increases in allowances, promotions, and smiles of approval, are used to encourage conformity. Negative sanctions, such as criticism, fines, and imprisonment, are intended to stop socially unacceptable behavior.

Sanctions may be formal or informal. Ridicule, gossip, and smiles are examples of informal sanctions. Imprisonment, low grades, and official awards are formal sanctions.

● **social sanctions**
rewards or punishments that encourage conformity to social norms

Because of its hurtful nature, gossip can be a very effective informal sanction.

Section 1 Assessment

1. What is the term sociologists use for behavior that significantly violates societal or group norms?

2. Explain why it is sometimes difficult to identify deviance.

3. What is the purpose of a social sanction?

Critical Thinking

4. **Applying Concepts** At some point in growing up, nearly everyone displays some minor deviant behaviors, such as cutting class or telling a lie. Getting "caught" in such behaviors generally results in attempts at social control. Recall such an instance for yourself. How successful were these controls in changing your behavior? (Be specific as to the types of social control and their precise application to you.)

Murder Among the Cheyenne

Historically, the Cheyenne believed that when a member of the tribe committed murder, the whole tribe suffered the consequences. The punishment for this terrible crime was banishment from the tribe. The Cheyenne way of dealing with murders illustrates both deviance and social control.

[The Cheyenne have] specific concepts related to the killing of a fellow tribesman and specific mechanisms for dealing with homicide when it does occur.

The first of these is purely mystical and relates to the major tribal fetish, the Four Sacred Arrows. A murderer becomes personally polluted, and specks of blood contaminate the feathers of the Arrows. The very word for murder is *he'joxones*, "putrid." A Cheyenne who kills a fellow Cheyenne rots internally. His body gives off a fetid odor, a symbolic stigma of personal disintegration, which contrition may stay, but for which there is no cure. The smell is offensive to other Cheyennes, who will never again take food from a bowl used by the killer. Nor will they smoke a pipe that has touched his lips. They fear personal contamination with his "leprous" affliction. This means that the person who has become so un-Cheyenne as to fly in the face of the greatest of Cheyenne injunctions is cut off from participation in the symbolic acts of mutuality—eating from a common bowl and smoking the ritual pipe. With this alienation goes the loss of many civil privileges and the cooperative assistance of one's fellows outside of one's own family. The basic penalty for murder is therefore a lifetime of partial social ostracism [forced isolation from society].

On the legal level, the ostracism takes the form of immediate exile imposed by the Tribal Council sitting as a judicial body. The sentence of exile is enforced, if need be, by the military societies. The rationalization of the banishment is that the murderer's stink is noisome to the buffalo. As long as an unatoned murderer is with the tribe, "game

shuns the territory; it makes the tribe lonesome." Therefore, the murderer must leave.

Banishment is not in itself enough, however. His act has disrupted the fabric of tribal life. Symbolically, this is expressed in the soiling of the Arrows, the allegorical identity of the tribe itself. As long as the Arrows remain polluted, bad luck is believed to dog the tribe. Not only does the spectre of starvation threaten, but there can be no success in war or any other enterprise. The earth is disjointed and the tribe out of harmony with it. The Arrow Renewal is the means of righting the situation. The oneness of the tribe is reasserted in the required presence at the ceremony of every family—save those of murderers. The renewed earth, effected by the rites in the Lone Tipi, is fresh and unsullied, once again free of the stain of killing.

Source: Excerpted from E. Adamson Hoebel, *The Cheyennes: Indians of the Great Plains* (New York: Holt, Rinehart and Winston, 1960), pp. 50–52. © 1960 by Holt, Rinehart and Winston, Inc. Reprinted by permission.

Thinking It Over

Many societies, both in the past and today, placed responsibility for the behavior of an individual on the family or tribe. Would you favor similar laws in the U.S., such as those making parents accountable for their children's actions? Why or why not?

Functionalism and Deviance

Section Preview

According to functionalists, deviance has both negative and positive consequences for society. Functionalism also forms the basis for two important theories of deviance: strain theory and control theory.

Costs and Benefits of Deviance

As you probably remember from earlier chapters, the functionalist perspective emphasizes social stability and the way the different parts of society contribute to the whole. It may surprise you to know that functionalists believe that some deviance can contribute to the smooth operation of society. Deviance, therefore, has both positive and negative consequences for society.

What are some of the negative effects of deviance?
Deviance erodes trust. If bus drivers do not follow planned routes, if television stations constantly change their schedules, if parents are not consistent in their discipline, trust will be undermined. A society with widespread suspicion and distrust cannot function smoothly.

If not punished or corrected, deviance can also cause nonconforming behavior in others. If bus drivers regularly pass students waiting for the bus, the students may begin to heave rocks at the bus. If television stations offer random programming, customers may picket the stations in protest. If parents neglect their children, more teenagers may turn to delinquency. Deviance stimulates more deviance in others.

Deviant behavior is also expensive. It diverts resources, both human and monetary. Police may have to spend their time dealing with wayward bus drivers and angry students rather than performing more serious duties.

How does deviance benefit society?
Society can sometimes benefit from deviance in spite of its negative effects. Emile Durkheim observed that deviance clarifies norms by exercising social control to defend its values; society defines, adjusts, and reaffirms norms. When parents are taken to court or lose their children because of neglect, for example, society shows other parents and children how it expects parents to act.

Deviance can be a temporary safety valve. Teens listen to music, watch television programs, and wear clothes that adults may view as deviating from expected behavior. This relatively minor deviance may act to relieve some of the pressure teens feel from the many authority figures in their lives, including parents, relatives, teachers, and clergy.

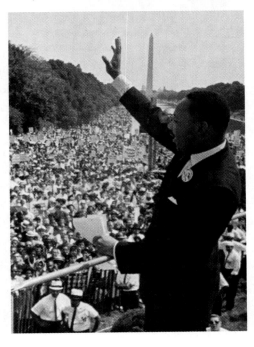

How did the Reverend King's philosophy of nonviolence benefit American society?

anomie
a social condition in which norms are weak, conflicting, or absent

Deviance increases unity within a society or group. When deviance reminds people of something they value, it strengthens their commitment to that value. Consider spies who sell government secrets to an enemy, for example. When they are discovered, citizens who read or hear about them experience stronger feelings of patriotism.

Deviance promotes needed social change. Suffragists who took to the streets in the early 1900s scandalized the nation but helped bring women the right to vote. Prison riots in the past have led to the reform of inhumane conditions.

Strain Theory

According to Emile Durkheim, **anomie** (*AN-uh-me*) is a social condition in which norms are weak, conflicting, or absent. Without shared norms, individuals are uncertain about how they should think and act. Societies become disorganized. In 1968, sociologist Robert Merton adapted Durkheim's concept of anomie to deviant behavior and called his hypothesis the **strain theory.** Deviance, said Merton, is most likely to occur when there is a gap between culturally desirable goals, such as money and prestige, and a legitimate way of obtaining them. Every society establishes some goals and socially approved ways of reaching them. In the United States, an important goal is success and the material possessions that go with it. Education and hard work are two of the approved means for being successful. This is when people accept the goal and the means to achieve it; Merton calls this *conformity*. Wealthy people conform, but so do poor people who continue to work hard in low-paying jobs in the hope of improving life for themselves or their children.

How do people respond to strain? By definition, conformity is not deviant behavior. Each of the remaining four responses to strain are considered deviant, however. (See Figure 7.2.)

- In *innovation*, the individual accepts the goal of success but uses illegal means to achieve it. People engaging in this response may use robbery, drug dealing, or other lucrative criminal behavior to be successful. Innovation is the most widespread and obvious type of deviant response.

- In *ritualism*, the individual rejects the goal (success) but continues to use the legitimate means. Here people go through the motions without really believing in the process. An example is the teacher who goes about the daily routines of work without any concern for students or the quality of his or her teaching.

- *Retreatism* is a deviant response in which both the legitimate means and the approved goals are rejected. Skid-row alcoholics, drug addicts, and the homeless are retreatists; they have dropped out. They are not successful by either legitimate or illegitimate means and they do not seek success.

- In *rebellion*, people reject both success and the approved means for achieving it. At the same time, they substitute a new set of goals and means. Some militia group members in the United States illustrate this response. They may live in near isolation as they pursue the goal of changing society through deviant means: creating their own currency, deliberately violating gun laws, and threatening (or engaging in) violent behavior against law enforcement officers.

According to strain theory, what kind of deviance is homelessness?

strain theory
theory that deviance is more likely to occur when a gap exists between cultural goals and the ability to achieve these goals by legitimate means

Figure 7.2 Merton's Strain Theory

Culturally Approved Goal: Success	Socially Accepted Way to Succeed: Hard Work	Conformity Response	Deviant Responses	Examples
Accepts goal of success (+)	Accepts hard work as the appropriate way to succeed (+)	**Conformity—** works hard to succeed		Business executive
Accepts goal of success (+)	Rejects hard work as the appropriate way to succeed (−)		**Innovation—** finds illegal ways to succeed	Criminal
Rejects goal of success (−)	Accepts hard work as the appropriate way to succeed (+)		**Ritualism—** acts as if he wants to succeed but does not exert much effort	Unmotivated teacher
Rejects goal of success (−)	Rejects hard work as the appropriate way to succeed (−)		**Retreatism—** drops out of the race for success	Skid row alcoholic
Rejects goal of success (−/+)	Rejects hard work as the appropriate way to succeed (−/+)		**Rebellion—** substitutes new way to achieve new goal	Militia group member

Adapted from Robert K. Merton, *Social Theory and Social Structure*, rev. ed. New York: Free Press.

Control Theory

Travis Hirschi's control theory (2001) is also based on Durkheim's views. According to **control theory,** conformity to social norms depends on the presence of strong bonds between individuals and society. If those bonds are weak—if anomie is present—deviance occurs.

In this theory, social bonds *control* the behavior of people, thus preventing deviant acts. People conform because they don't want to "lose face" with family members, friends, or classmates.

● **control theory**
theory that compliance with social norms requires strong bonds between individuals and society

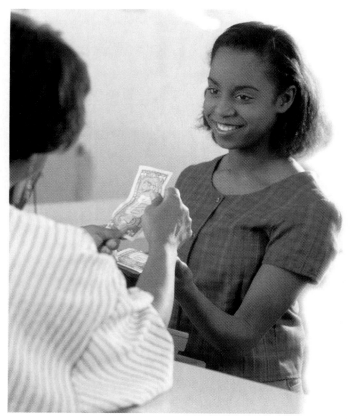

This young woman is completing her purchase in a clothing store. Relate this transaction to control theory and anomie.

What are the basic elements of social bonds? According to Hirschi, the social bond has four basic components:

1. *Attachment.* The stronger your attachment to groups or individuals, the more likely you are to conform. In other words, the likelihood of conformity varies with the strength of ties with parents, friends, and institutions such as schools and churches.

2. *Commitment.* The greater your commitment to social goals, the more likely you are to conform. The commitment of individuals who believe their hard work will be rewarded is greater than the commitment of people who do not believe they can compete within the system.

3. *Involvement.* Participation in approved social activities increases the probability of conformity. Besides positively focusing your time and energy, participation puts you in contact with people whose opinions you value.

4. *Belief.* Belief in the norms and values of society promotes conformity. A belief in the appropriateness of the rules of social life strengthens people's resolve not to deviate from those norms.

In short, when social bonds are weak, the chances for deviance increase. Individuals who lack attachment, commitment, involvement, and belief have little incentive to follow the rules of society.

Section 2 Assessment

1. Which of the following is *NOT* one of the benefits of deviance for society?
   a. It decreases suspicion and mistrust among members of a society.
   b. It promotes social change.
   c. It increases social unity.
   d. It provides a safety valve.
   e. It promotes clarification of norms.

2. Briefly describe the main idea of Merton's strain theory.

3. A high school teacher who simply goes through the motions of teaching classes without any thought of success is an example of which response in strain theory?

4. What are the four basic elements needed to create strong social bonds?

Critical Thinking

5. **Applying Concepts** Describe someone you know (anonymously, of course) who falls into one of the four deviant response categories identified by strain theory. Use specific characteristics of this person to show the influence of different aspirations on economic decisions.

Sociology Today

Is Teen Smoking a Deviant Behavior?

Sociologist Philip Hilts believes that tobacco companies target young people in their advertisements and that the strategy has a sociological basis.

> [C]hildren are just beginning to shape their image of themselves, elbowing out a niche in the world, and must somehow differentiate themselves from parents and other adults, and get out from under what the authorities in life want from them. They dress differently, sometimes shockingly. They listen to different, sometimes shocking, music. In this quest, the children are worried, insecure, seeking to make choices and have them supported by their friends or others they respect. Most obviously, their choices are supported by each other. They have learned to lean on each other for aid and assent. Sometimes older siblings lend support. But because the insecurity is great, as many supports as possible are needed (Hilts, 1997:33).

Cigarette advertising, claims Hilts, portrays smoking as another ally in teenagers' attempts to find their own identities. Smoking is portrayed as a pleasurable, cool way for them to declare their successful transition into adulthood. In other words, tobacco corporations assume correctly that teenagers are at a time in their lives when deviant behavior can serve a developmental need. To teens, smoking (like their choice of clothing, music, and slang) begins as simply a form of deviance.

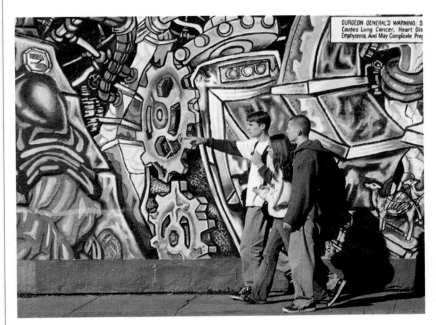

Doing Sociology

Do you agree with Hilts's analysis? State your arguments for or against it. Search magazines and newspapers for examples of advertising that emphasizes "young adult smokers" moving into adult activities. Or, see if you can find any advertisements that picture middle-aged or older people smoking. Why do you think these ads are virtually unknown?

This mural advertising a brand of cigarettes is designed to attract the attention and admiration of teenagers.

3

Symbolic Interactionism and Deviance

Key Terms

- differential association theory *(p. 214)*
- labeling theory *(p. 214)*
- primary deviance *(p. 215)*
- secondary deviance *(p. 216)*
- stigma *(p. 216)*

- **differential association theory**
  theory that individuals learn deviance in proportion to the number of deviant acts they are exposed to

- **labeling theory**
  theory that society creates deviance by identifying particular members as deviant

Section Preview

The symbolic interactionist perspective yields two theories of deviance. We read in Chapter 3 that culture is learned. Sociologists believe that deviance is a learned behavior that is culturally transmitted. Labeling theory holds that an act is deviant only if other people name it so.

Differential Association Theory

According to symbolic interactionism, deviance is transmitted through socialization in the same way that nondeviant behavior is learned. For example, an early study revealed that delinquent behavior can be transmitted through play groups and gangs. Even when new ethnic groups enter neighborhoods, they learn delinquent behavior from the current residents. *Differential association* and *labeling theory* are both based on symbolic interactionism.

How is deviance learned? **Differential association theory** emphasizes the role of primary groups in transmitting deviance. Just as we learn preferences in religion and politics from others we associate with closely, people can learn deviance by association, as well. The more that individuals are exposed to people who break the law, the more apt they are to become criminals. Three characteristics affect differential association:

- *the ratio of deviant to nondeviant individuals.* A person who knows mostly deviants is more likely to learn deviant behavior.
- *whether the deviant behavior is practiced by significant others.* A person is more likely to copy deviant behavior from a significant other than from people less important to him or her.
- *the age of exposure.* Younger children learn deviant behavior more quickly than older children.

Labeling Theory

Strain theory, control theory, and differential association theory help us understand why deviance occurs. **Labeling theory** explains why deviance is *relative*—that is, sometimes of two people breaking the norm only one may be labeled a deviant.

Is deviance defined by the act or by the individual? According to labeling theory, deviant behaviors are always a matter of social definition. In this view, deviance exists when some members of a group or society label others as deviants. Howard Becker, a pioneer of labeling theory, writes:

Social groups create deviance by making the rules whose infraction constitutes deviance, and by applying these rules to particular people and labeling them

Deviance is relative. Some members of a society, such as athletes and celebrities, are often treated more tolerantly.

as outsiders. *From this point of view, deviance is not a quality of the act the person commits, but rather a consequence of the application by others of rules and sanctions to an "offender." The deviant is one to whom that label has successfully been applied; deviant behavior is behavior that people so label (Becker, 1991:9).*

Labeling theory allows us to understand the relativity of deviance. It explains, for example, why unmarried pregnant teenage girls are more negatively sanctioned than the teenage biological fathers. An unsanctioned pregnancy requires two people, but usually only one of the pair is labeled deviant. Traditionally, society expects females to set the boundaries—to be the ones to say "no." When females become pregnant outside of marriage, they have violated this norm and are considered deviant. Even today, males are not considered as deviant, not because they do not literally bear the child, but because our ideas about their sexual responsibility are still different than for females. And, of course, it is easier to stigmatize women because advanced pregnancy is so visible. Teenage pregnancy illustrates the relativity of deviance in another way. That is, the extent to which something is considered deviant changes over time. While teenage pregnancy is still considered deviant, societal reaction to it has become less severe.

● **primary deviance**
deviance involving occasional breaking of norms that is not a part of a person's lifestyle or self-concept

Are there degrees of deviance?
Edwin Lemert's (1972) distinction between primary and secondary deviance helps clarify the labeling process. In cases of **primary deviance**, a person engages only in isolated acts of deviance. For example, when college students are asked to respond to a checklist of unlawful activities, most admit to having violated one or more norms. Yet the vast majority of college students have never been arrested, convicted, or labeled as criminals. Certainly, those who break the law for the first time do not consider themselves criminals. If their deviance stops at this

Student pranksters decorated the Massachusetts Institute of Technology dome to look like the *Star Wars* character, R2D2. Was this an example of primary or secondary deviance?

secondary deviance
deviance in which an individual's life and identity are organized around breaking society's norms

point, they have engaged in primary deviance; deviance is not a part of their lifestyles or self-concepts. Juveniles, likewise, may commit a few delinquent acts without becoming committed to a delinquent career or regarding themselves as juvenile delinquents.

Secondary deviance, on the other hand, refers to deviance as a lifestyle and as a personal identity. A secondary deviant is a person whose life and identity are organized around deviance. In this case, the deviant status has become the person's master status. Individuals identify themselves primarily as deviants and organize their behavior largely in terms of deviant roles. Other people label them as deviant as well and respond to them accordingly. When this occurs, these individuals usually begin to spend most of their time committing acts of deviance. Deviance becomes a way of life, a career (Kelly, 2002).

John Dillinger was at one time the FBI's "public enemy number 1." Explain why Dillinger is considered a secondary deviant.

Secondary deviance is reflected in the words of Carolyn Hamilton-Ballard—known as "Bubbles" to her fellow gang members in Los Angeles:

Because of my size, I was automatically labeled a bully-type person. . . . I mean, people saw that Bloods jacket and since everybody thought I was crazy, I started acting crazy. At first it was an act, but then it became me. After being the target for drive-bys and going through different things, that became my lifestyle. I started retaliating back and I got more involved (Johnson, 1994:209).

What are the consequences of labeling? Labeling people as deviants can cause them pain and suffering, as well as determine the direction of their lives. Erving Goffman examined some of the negative effects of labeling when he wrote about **stigma**—an undesirable characteristic or label used by others to deny the deviant full social acceptance. For example, an ex-convict is not accepted by many members of society. Why? Because a stigmatic label—*jailbird*—spoils the individual's entire social identity. One stigma, a

stigma
an undesirable trait or label that is used to characterize an individual

prison record, is used to discredit the individual's entire worth. The same may be true for a person with a disability or an unemployed person.

The words of a forty-three-year-old bricklayer, who was unemployed during the Depression, illustrate this point.

How hard and humiliating it is to bear the name of an unemployed man. When I go out, I cast down my eyes because I feel myself wholly inferior. When I go along the street, it seems to me that I can't be compared with an average citizen, that everybody is pointing at me with his finger. I instinctively avoid meeting anyone. Former acquaintances and friends of better times are no longer so cordial. They greet me indifferently when we meet. They no longer offer me a cigarette and their eyes seem to say, "You are not worth it, you don't work."

This young man in New York City in the 1940s probably felt the stigma of being unemployed. How does this stigma relate to the labeling of deviants?

Section 3 Assessment

1. Which of the following describes what is meant by differential association?
   a. Crime is more likely to occur among individuals who have been treated differently.
   b. People may become criminals through close association with criminals.
   c. Crime is not transmitted culturally.
   d. Crime comes from conflict between two cultures.

2. Name the sociological theory that takes into account the relativity of deviance.

3. What is secondary deviance?

4. What are the social consequences of labeling?

Critical Thinking

5. **Analyzing Information** Think of someone you know or know of who has been labeled as deviant by some members of society. Analyze the consequences of this labeling for the person identified as a deviant.

6. **Drawing Conclusions** What actions could be taken against students who are viewed as secondary deviants?

4

Conflict Theory and Deviance

Key Terms

- victim discounting *(p. 219)*
- white-collar crime *(p. 220)*

Section Preview

The conflict perspective looks at deviance in terms of social inequality and power. The most powerful members of a society determine who will be regarded as deviant. Conflict theorists point to some disproportional statistical relationships between minorities and crime.

Deviance in Industrial Society

From the conflict perspective, deviance in an industrial society is behavior that those in control see as threatening to their interests. Consequently, the rich and powerful use their positions to determine which acts are deviant and how deviants should be punished.

Sociologist Steven Spitzer (1980) proposed some basic ways in which the culture of an industrial society defends itself against deviants.

1. Critics of industrial society are considered deviants because their beliefs challenge its economic, political, and social basis.

2. Because industrial society requires a willing workforce, those who will not work are considered deviants.

3. Those who threaten private property, especially that belonging to the rich, are prime targets for punishment.

4. Because of society's need for respect of authority, people who show a lack of respect for authority—agitators on the job, people who stage nonviolent demonstrations against established practices—are treated as deviants.

5. Certain activities are encouraged depending on how well they fit within industrial society. For example, violent behavior in sports is accepted because it fosters competition, achievement, teamwork, and winning (Eder, 1995; Adler and Adler, 1999).

Race, Ethnicity, and Crime

The relationship between minorities and the judicial system is another way to view deviance from the conflict perspective.

What is the relationship between race, ethnicity, and crime? Supporters of the conflict perspective believe that minorities receive unequal treatment in the American criminal justice system. They cite statistics showing that African Americans and Latinos are dealt with more harshly than whites. This is true throughout the criminal justice

Conflict theorists predict that this suspect's race is likely to have a negative impact on his treatment in the criminal justice system.

process—from arrest through indictment, conviction, sentencing, and parole (Skolnick, 1998; Schaeffer, 2005).

Even when the criminal offense is the same, African Americans and Latinos are more likely than whites to be convicted, and they serve more time in prison than whites. Although African Americans account for only about 13 percent of the total population in the United States, approximately 42 percent of inmates under the death penalty are African American. In interracial murders, an African American is much more likely to be sentenced to death for the murder of a white person than a white person is for murdering an African American.

Nearly one-half of all homicide victims in the United States are African American (Federal Bureau of Investigation, 2003). Nevertheless, the overwhelming majority of prisoners on death row are there for murdering whites. Prosecutors are less likely to seek the death penalty when an African American has been killed, and juries and judges are less likely to impose the death penalty in cases involving African American victims.

Why are minorities and whites treated so differently?

The conflict theory suggests several reasons for differences in the way minorities and whites are treated in the criminal justice system. For one thing, conflict theorists point to the fact that minorities generally do not have the economic resources to buy good legal services. Thus, the outcomes of their trials are not likely to be as favorable to them.

Another source of difference involves the fact that crimes against whites tend to be punished more severely than crimes against minorities. Sociologists who follow the conflict perspective believe that this happens because society sees minority interests as less important than the interests of whites. **Victim discounting** reduces the seriousness of crimes directed at members of lower social classes (Gibbons, 1985). According to the logic behind victim discounting, if the victim is less valuable, the crime is less serious, and the penalty is less severe.

Even when they have committed the same crimes, African Americans and Latinos are more severely punished than whites.

● **victim discounting**
process of reducing the seriousness of the crimes that injure people of lower status

Figure 7.3	Deviance

This figure illustrates approaches to understanding deviance using concepts associated with a particular theoretical perspective. Construct some examples of your own.

Theoretical Perspective	Sociological Concept	Example of Deviance
Functionalism	Anomie	Delinquent gangs sell drugs because they want success without holding conventional jobs.
Conflict Theory	White-Collar Crime	A convicted Wall Street stock broker (a more powerful member of society) may spend less time in prison than a factory worker (a less powerful member of society) found guilty of a less serious crime.
Symbolic Interactionism	Labeling	Some high school students reject dating because they have been consistently treated and described as "not cool."

White-Collar Crime

• **white-collar crime**
job-related crimes committed by high-status people

White-collar crime is yet another way to view deviance. According to Edwin Sutherland (1940, 1983), **white-collar crime** is any crime committed by respectable and high-status people in the course of their occupations. As one researcher put it, lower-status people commit crimes of the streets; higher-status people engage in "crimes of the suites." Officially, the term *white-collar crime* is used for economic crimes such as price fixing, insider trading, fraud, embezzlement, bribery of a corporate customer, manufacture of hazardous products, toxic pollution, and tax evasion.

What are the costs of white-collar crime? According to the U.S. Department of Justice, it is impossible to know with any degree of certainty exactly what the annual costs of white-collar crime are. The following figures suggest, however, that such crime is a serious problem in the U.S. today.

For example, securities and commodities fraud alone totals $40 billion a year. U.S. businesses lose $10 billion a year to check fraud. Additionally, experts estimate annual losses from health care fraud to be $100 billion.

What kinds of punishment do the majority of white-collar criminals receive?

Despite the fact that white-collar crime costs taxpayers hundreds of billions of dollars every year, the people who commit these crimes often are treated more leniently than other criminals. In federal court, where most white-collar cases are tried, probation is granted to 40 percent of antitrust-law violators, 61 percent of fraud defendants, and 70 percent of embezzlers. In general, convicted white-collar criminals are less likely to be imprisoned. If they are imprisoned, they receive shorter average sentences and are more likely to be placed in prisons with extra amenities, such as tennis courts or private rooms. There are some recent exceptions, however. In 2005, for example, former WorldCom chief executive Bernard Ebbers was sentenced to 25 years in prison and forced to give up most of the millions he made from the $11 billion fraud he orchestrated. Adelphia Communications Corporation founder John J. Rigas received a 15-year sentence for his illegal behavior.

In 2004, nationally recognized celebrity and businessperson Martha Stewart was sentenced to five months in prison and five months home confinement for obstructing an investigation into illegal stock trading. Stewart served her prison sentence in a minimum-security prison in Alderson, West Virginia.

Section 4 Assessment

1. Which of the following is NOT one of the basic ways in which the culture of an industrial society defends itself in the face of deviance?
   a. People whose beliefs clash with those of industrial society are labeled deviants.
   b. Industrial society requires a willing workforce.
   c. Innovation is rewarded.
   d. People who fail to show respect for authority are likely to be considered deviant.

2. What is the term that describes reducing the seriousness of crimes against victims from lower social classes?

3. What is white-collar crime?

Critical Thinking

4. **Evaluating Information** How could the conflict theory be misused to rationalize deviant behavior?

5. **Summarizing Information** Using the concept of victim discounting, explain why lower-class criminals are usually punished more severely than white-collar criminals for the same crime.

Focus on Research

Case Study: Saints and Roughnecks

In this classic study, William Chambliss (1973) observed the behavior of two white teenage gangs at "Hanibal High School" over a two-year period. In addition to gang activity, Chambliss documented the responses of parents, teachers, and police to the delinquent behavior.

The Saints On weekends the automobile was even more critical than during the week, for on weekends the Saints [a delinquent high school gang] went to Big Town—a large city with a population of over a million. . . . Every Friday and Saturday night most of the Saints would meet between 8:00 and 8:30 and would go into Big Town. Big Town activities included drinking heavily in taverns or nightclubs, driving drunkenly through the streets, and committing acts of vandalism and playing pranks. . . .

Searching for "fair game" for a prank was the boys' principal activity after they left the tavern. The boys would drive alongside a foot patrolman and ask directions to some street. If the policeman leaned on the car in the course of answering the question, the driver would speed away, causing him to lose his balance. The Saints were careful to play this prank only in an area where they were not going to spend much time and where they could quickly disappear around a corner to avoid having their license plate number taken.

Construction sites and road repair areas were the special province of the Saints' mischief. A soon-to-be-repaired hole in the road inevitably invited the Saints to remove lanterns and wooden barricades and put them in the car, leaving the hole unprotected. The boys would find a safe vantage point and wait for an unsuspecting motorist to drive into the hole. Often, though not always, the boys would go up to the motorist and com-miserate [sympathize] with him about the dreadful way the city protected its citizenry.

Leaving the scene of the open hole and the motorist, the boys would then go searching for an appropriate place to erect the stolen barricade. An "appropriate place" was often a spot on a highway near a curve in the road where the barricade would not be seen by an oncoming motorist. The boys would wait to watch an unsuspecting motorist attempt to stop and (usually) crash into the wooden barricade.

A stolen lantern might well find its way onto the back of a police car or hang from a street lamp. Once a lantern served as a prop for a reenact-ment of the "midnight ride of Paul Revere" until the "play," which was taking place at 2:00 A.M. in the center of a main street of Big Town, was interrupted by a police car several blocks away. The boys ran, leaving the lanterns on the street. . . .

The Roughnecks [T]ownspeople never perceived the Saints' . . . delinquency. The Saints were good boys who just went in for an occasional prank. After all, they were well dressed, well mannered and had nice cars. The Roughnecks [a delinquent gang at the same high school] were a different story. Although the two gangs of boys were the same age, and both groups engaged in an equal amount of wild-oat sowing, everyone agreed that the not-so-well-dressed, not-so-well-mannered, not-so-rich boys were heading for trouble. . . .

From the community's viewpoint, the real indication that these kids were in for trouble was that they were constantly involved with the police. Some of them had been picked up for stealing, mostly small stuff, of course, "but still it's stealing small stuff that leads to big time crimes." "Too bad," people said. "Too bad that these boys couldn't behave like the other kids in town; stay out of trouble, be polite to adults, and look to their future." . . .

The fighting activities of the group were fairly readily and accurately perceived by almost everyone. At least once a month, the boys would get into some sort of fight, although most fights were scraps between members of the group or involved only one member of the group and some peripheral hanger-on. Only three times in the period of observation did the group fight together: once against a gang from across town, once against two [African Americans] and once against a group of boys from another school. For the first two fights the group went out "looking for trouble"— and they found it both times. The third fight followed a football game and began spontaneously with an argument on the football field between one of the Roughnecks and a member of the opposition's football team.

More serious than fighting, had the community been aware of it, was theft. Although almost everyone was aware that the boys occasionally stole things, they did not realize the extent of the activity. Petty stealing was a frequent event for the Roughnecks. Sometimes they stole as a group and coordinated their efforts; other times they stole in pairs. Rarely did they steal alone. . . . Types of thievery varied with the whim of the gang. Some forms of thievery were more profitable than others, but all thefts were for profit, not for thrills.

Roughnecks siphoned gasoline from cars as often as they had access to an automobile, which was not very often. Unlike the Saints, who owned their own cars, the Roughnecks would have to borrow their parents' cars, an event which occurred only eight or nine times a year. The boys claimed to have stolen cars for joy rides from time to time.

Source: Excerpted from William J. Chambliss, "The Saints and the Roughnecks," *Society* 11 (November/December, 1973):24–31.

Working with the Research

1. From your understanding of Chambliss's study, is deviance socially created? Explain.
2. Which of the three major theoretical perspectives best explains Chambliss's findings? Support your choice.

5

Crime and Punishment

Key Terms

- crime *(p. 224)*
- criminal justice system *(p. 227)*
- deterrence *(p. 227)*
- retribution *(p. 229)*
- incarceration *(p. 229)*
- rehabilitation *(p. 230)*
- recidivism *(p. 231)*

Section Preview

Crime statistics in the U.S. come from two major sources: the FBI and the Census Bureau. Differences in statistics between the two agencies are due to differences in methods of collecting data. Four approaches to crime control are deterrence, retribution, incarceration, and rehabilitation.

Measurement of Crime

Most Americans think of **crime**—acts in violation of statute law—as including a narrow range of behavior. On the contrary, more than 4,000 acts are classified as federal crimes. Many more acts violate state and local statutes.

How much crime is there in the United States today?

According to a national survey sponsored by the U.S. Department of Justice, approximately 15 percent of U.S. households, or 17 million households, experienced one or more crimes in 2003. Although this figure may seem high, it actually represents a decrease from 25 percent in 1994. These Department of Justice data include crimes both reported and unreported to the police. The majority of crimes included in the 2003 survey were property crimes, although more than 3 million households reported being the victims of violent crime. Households headed by African Americans were slightly more likely than those headed by whites to experience any type of crime.

- **crime**
  acts committed in violation of the law

The job of a forensic scientist is to examine evidence—fingerprints, DNA, handwriting, firearms—for indications that a crime has occurred.

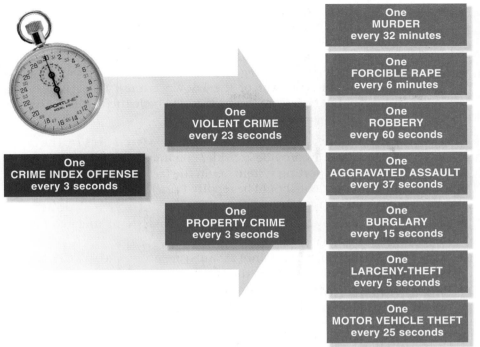

Figure 7.4
FBI's Crime Clock: 2003
How often do Americans commit crimes?
The number to the far left, of course, does not mean that one Crime Index offense actually occurs every three seconds. It does mean that when *all* Crime Index offenses for 2003 are divided by the total number of seconds in a year there are enough of them to be spaced out every three seconds.

Source: Federal Bureau of Investigation, *Uniform Crime Reports*, 2003.

How are crime statistics collected?

The major source of American crime statistics is the Federal Bureau of Investigation's *Uniform Crime Reports* (UCR). These official statistics are gathered from police departments across the country. Reports are submitted voluntarily by law enforcement agencies.

What do UCR statistics cover?

Nine types of crimes (called crime index offenses) are tracked: murder, forcible rape, robbery, aggravated assault, burglary, larceny–theft, motor vehicle theft, arson, and hate crimes.

Figure 7.4 shows UCR statistics on the frequency of seven of these crimes in the United States in 2003. Figure 7.5 presents another view of the 2003 statistics. Crimes known to the police totaled 11,816,782 (total violent crime plus total property crime). As the table shows, both violent crime and property crime have declined since 1994. Since murder receives the most publicity, it can be used to highlight this general, across-the-board reduction in crime. The murder rate in the United States has decreased nearly 37 percent

Types of crime	Number of crimes	Crime rate per 100,000 residents	1994–2003	
			Percent change in crime rate	Percent change in number of crimes
Violent crime	**1,381,259**	**475.0**	**-33.4**	**-25.6**
Murder	16,503	5.7	-36.7	-29.3
Forcible rape	93,433	32.1	-18.2	-8.6
Robbery	413,402	142.2	-40.2	-33.2
Aggravated assault	857,921	295.0	-31.0	-22.9
Property crime	**10,435,523**	**3,588.4**	**-23.0**	**-14.0**
Burglary	2,153,464	740.5	-28.9	-20.6
Larceny-theft	7,021,588	2,414.5	-20.2	-10.9
Motor vehicle theft	1,260,471	433.4	-26.7	-18.1

Figure 7.5 Crimes in the United States, 2003
If you were a law enforcement officer, would you be encouraged or discouraged by these data? Why?

Source: Federal Bureau of Investigation, *Uniform Crime Reports*, 2003.

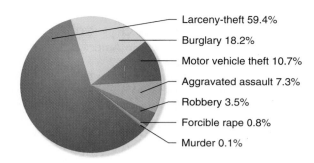

- Larceny-theft 59.4%
- Burglary 18.2%
- Motor vehicle theft 10.7%
- Aggravated assault 7.3%
- Robbery 3.5%
- Forcible rape 0.8%
- Murder 0.1%

Figure 7.6 Types of Crimes Americans Commit
This figure shows the contribution each major type of crime makes to the total of U.S. crime.

Source: Federal Bureau of Investigation, *Uniform Crime Reports*, 2003.

since 1994. One reason for this downward trend is a recent reduction in juvenile crime. In 2003, around 92 percent of murder offenders were over 18 years of age.

Figure 7.6 indicates that violent crime—murder, forcible rape, aggravated assault, and robbery—made up 11.7 percent of the known crimes. Property crime—burglary, larceny-theft, motor vehicle theft—accounted for 88.3 percent.

How reliable are UCR statistics? The UCR statistics provide considerable information about crime. A major strength of this reporting system lies in the fact that experienced police officers decide if an incident should be reported as a crime. The UCR statistics also have serious limitations, however:

- The UCR tends to overrepresent the lower classes and undercount the middle and upper classes.
- Some crimes (amateur thefts, minor assaults) are not as likely to be reported to the police as murder and auto thefts.
- Prostitutes and intoxicated persons are subject to arrest in public places, but are fairly safe in private settings where the police cannot enter without a warrant.
- About two-thirds of U.S. crimes are not reported at all.
- Crime reporting varies from place to place and crime to crime, and white-collar offenders are seldom included.

Are any other crime statistics available? In response to these criticisms, the *National Crime Victimization Survey* (NCVS) was launched in the early 1970s. This survey is conducted semiannually for the Bureau of Justice Statistics by the U.S. Census Bureau.

The NCVS has two advantages. First, it helps make up for the underreporting of crime. Second, its surveys are more scientifically sound than methods used in the UCR. At the very least, the NCVS is an increasingly important supplement to the FBI's official statistics. Together they provide a more complete account of the extent and nature of crime in the United States (Wright, 1987; U.S. Department of Justice, 2004).

Juvenile Crime

Juvenile crime refers to legal violations among those under 18 years of age. Juvenile offenders are the third largest category of criminals in the United States. Teenage criminal activity includes theft, murder, rape, robbery, assault, and the sale of illegal substances. Juvenile delinquent behavior includes deviance that only the young can commit, such as failing to attend school, fighting in school, and underage drinking and smoking.

What is the trend in juvenile crime? Violent juvenile crime reached its lowest level in a decade in 2003, a fall of 32 percent since 1994 (Office of Justice Programs, 2005). Between 1994 and 2003

- the juvenile murder arrest rate dropped by 68 percent.
- juvenile arrests for weapons violations declined by 41 percent.
- the juvenile rape arrest rate went down by 25 percent.

Sociology Online

Student Web Activity
Visit the *Sociology and You* Web site at glencoe.com for an activity on juvenile crime.

Types of crime	Number of juvenile arrests	Percent of total arrests	Percent change	
			1994–2003	1999–2003
Violent crime	**92,300**	**4.2**	**-32**	**-9**
Murder	1,130	.1	-68	-18
Forcible rape	4,240	.2	-25	-11
Robbery	25,440	1.1	-43	-8
Aggravated assault	61,490	2.8	-26	-9
Property crime	**463,300**	**20.9**	**-38**	**-15**
Burglary	85,100	3.8	-40	-15
Larceny-theft	325,600	14.7	-35	-15
Motor vehicle theft	44,500	2.0	-52	-15
Arson	8,200	.4	-36	-12

Figure 7.7 Juvenile Arrests in the United States, 2003
How would you describe the trend in juvenile arrests for property crimes? How does this trend compare with the trend in juvenile arrests for violent crimes?

Source: U.S. Department of Justice, Office of Justice Programs, 2005.

There were also fewer juvenile victims of murder—down from almost 3,000 to about 1,600. Juvenile crime, in short, returned to the rates typical of the years prior to the crack epidemic of the late 1980s.

Why has juvenile crime gone down? Several factors are said to account for this decline in juvenile crime. For one, there has been a decline in the demand for crack cocaine. Remaining crack gangs that provided guns to juveniles have reached truces. Repeat violent juvenile offenders have been given stiffer sentences. Finally, police are cracking down on illegal guns on the street.

Approaches to Crime Control

The **criminal justice system** is made up of the institutions and processes responsible for enforcing criminal statutes. It includes the police, courts, and correctional system. A criminal justice system may draw on four approaches to control and punish lawbreakers—*deterrence, retribution, incarceration,* and *rehabilitation.*

Does punishment discourage crime? The **deterrence** approach uses the threat of punishment to discourage criminal actions. A basic idea of this approach is that punishment of convicted criminals will serve as an example to keep other people from committing crimes. There is considerable debate on the effectiveness of deterrence (Dilulio and Piehl, 1991). Research indicates that the threat of punishment *does* deter crime if potential lawbreakers know two things: that they are likely to get caught and that the punishment will be severe. In the U.S., however, the punishment for crime is usually not certain, swift, or severe. Consequently, punishment does not have the deterrent effect that it could have (Pontell, 1984).

Capital punishment (the death penalty) is a special case. Nearly five thousand people have been executed in the United States since 1930, the year the federal government began gathering statistics on capital punishment. Unless it is premeditated, a murder is an extremely emotional and irrational act. Under such circumstances, you would not expect the threat of capital punishment to be a deterrent, and research shows that it is not. If the death penalty were a deterrent to murder, a decline in its use should be followed by an increase in the murder rate. Research indicates, however, that the murder rate remains constant, or even drops, following a decline

criminal justice system
system comprising institutions and processes responsible for enforcing criminal statutes

deterrence
discouraging criminal acts by threatening punishment

TECH TRENDS

Look Out for Identity Thieves!

One of the newest forms of deviance is "identity theft." An identity thief "steals" credit information belonging to another person, then commits fraud with it. The results for victims can be devastating.

In testimony before the Maryland legislature, one couple reported that a thief used their credit cards to purchase five automobiles. Graciela has been a victim of identity theft for more than ten years. A thief gained access to her Social Security number, birth certificate, and driver's license. With this information, the imposter has obtained credit cards, purchased furniture, bought cars, and obtained welfare. (All of these examples, and more, are available through the Privacy Rights Clearinghouse, http://www.privacyrights.org, a nonprofit group for consumers' privacy rights.)

Beth Givens of the Privacy Rights Clearinghouse explains that identity theft can occur in many ways. A thief can steal a wallet or purse, get copies of credit card slips from trash, or steal someone's mail. There are also high-tech methods of identity theft. The most common method is to illegally gain access to credit rating company computers. These companies maintain credit reports that provide valuable information about a consumer—Social Security number, birth date, credit card numbers, and address. Although credit rating companies try to prevent high-tech identity theft, the very nature of their service makes this information accessible through computer terminals. This access is an open invitation to criminals.

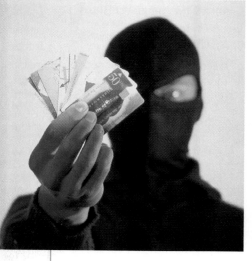

The victims of identity theft obviously suffer great damage. Unless the thief is caught in the act, there seems to be little the police can do to stop this kind of crime. Many victims also have to deal with abusive collection agencies. It has taken some people ten years or more to clean up the mess the thieves have created. Victims are often scarred emotionally and report feelings of violation, hopelessness, and great anger.

The goal of today's identity thieves is to get items at no cost, not to take over the victims' identities. But what if identity theft also involved losing one's identity? What would happen if a person's identity were actually "stolen"? This was the topic of a film called *The Net*. In this movie, a woman's entire identity is erased. The villains in the movie steal the documents that would prove her identity and destroy all of her existing computer records. Using her photograph and Social Security number, they create a whole new identity for her, including a new name, a bad credit report, and a criminal record. As the woman in the movie says, "They knew everything about me. It was all on the Internet."

Analyzing the Trends

Which theoretical perspective would be most useful in analyzing identity theft? Explain your choice, and apply that perspective to the issue of identity theft.

in the use of the death penalty (Sellin, 1991; Lester, 1998; Sarat, 2001).

Do Americans believe capital punishment deters criminals?

Only about 35 percent of Americans believe that the death penalty acts as a deterrent to murder. Nevertheless, attitudes regarding the ability of the death penalty to prevent crime do not seem to affect attitudes toward the death penalty itself. Of those Americans who favor the death penalty, approximately 69 percent indicate that they would continue to favor it even if new evidence showed that the death penalty does not deter murder and does not lower the murder rate. Feelings of revenge and a desire for retribution, then, appear to contribute more to the support of capital punishment than do its deterrent effects. When asked to choose, a significantly higher proportion of the American public supports the death penalty for murder (74 percent) than opposes it (23 percent; Gallup, 2005).

Why do attitudes toward the death penalty vary?

Attitudes toward the death penalty vary according to a number of factors. For example, a larger proportion of whites (73 percent) compared to nonwhites (58 percent) believe that the death penalty is a morally acceptable punishment. This may be due, in part, to the fact that nonwhites convicted of murder are more likely than whites to receive the death penalty. Although African Americans make up only about 13 percent of the U.S. population, they comprise about 42 percent of death row inmates. In addition to race, factors such as gender, education, political affiliation, and religiosity tend to affect attitudes toward the death penalty. Males, people with lower levels of education, Republicans, and people who attend religious services regularly are more likely to support the death penalty (Gallup, 2005).

What is retribution?

Retribution is a type of punishment intended to make criminals pay compensation for their acts. It comes from the idea of "an eye for an eye and a tooth for a tooth." The law allows designated officials to exact retribution. However, it does not allow individuals to take personal vengeance. If a mother "takes the law into her own hands" by shooting her son's killer, she must also answer to society for her action.

Why does society keep criminals in prisons?

The basic idea behind **incarceration**—keeping criminals in prisons—is that criminals who are not on the street cannot commit crimes. Recently, the United States has taken a tougher stance in favor of incarceration with such bills as the *Three Strikes Law.* As a result, the number of local, state, and federal prisoners increased from less than 1.6 million in 1995 to more than 2.1 million in 2004, an average annual increase of 3.5 percent. In more repressive societies, such as the former Soviet Union and present-day Nationalist China, people may spend their entire lives in prison for crimes ranging from political opposition to murder.

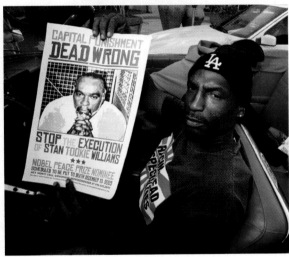

Capital punishment is one of the most controversial issues in American society today.

● **retribution**
punishment intended to make criminals pay compensation for their acts

● **incarceration**
a method of protecting society from criminals by keeping them in prisons

World View

Death Penalty Policy

Countries vary in their approach to the control of crime. The most extreme form of social control, the death penalty, is utilized in many countries, while some countries have abolished capital punishment completely. This map shows variations in national policy regarding the death penalty.

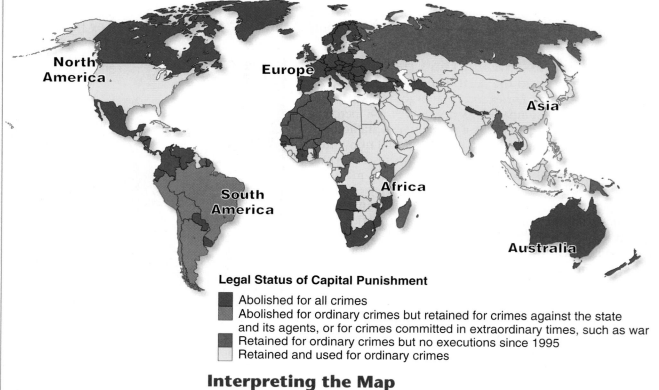

Legal Status of Capital Punishment

- Abolished for all crimes
- Abolished for ordinary crimes but retained for crimes against the state and its agents, or for crimes committed in extraordinary times, such as war
- Retained for ordinary crimes but no executions since 1995
- Retained and used for ordinary crimes

Interpreting the Map

1. Do you notice any pattern in the use of the death penalty? Describe it.

2. What additional information would you need to determine if capital punishment is an effective deterrent to crime? Explain.

Source: Amnesty International Online, 2005.

● **rehabilitation**
process of changing or reforming a criminal through socialization

Do prisons rehabilitate criminals? Rehabilitation is an approach to crime control that attempts to resocialize criminals. Most prisons have programs aimed at giving prisoners both social and work skills that will help them adjust to normal society after their release. Unfortunately, more than half of those released from penal institutions are sent back to prison in three to five years. This return to criminal behavior is called

recidivism. The relatively high rate of recidivism makes it seem unlikely that prison rehabilitation programs are working (Elikann, 1996; Zamble and Quinsey, 1997). Reasons for the high rate of recidivism include

● recidivism
a repetition of or return to criminal behavior

- the basic nature of the offenders
- influences of more hardened criminals
- the stigma of being an ex-convict.

It is difficult to change attitudes and behavior within the prison subculture. Conformity with the "inmate code" stresses loyalty among inmates as well as opposition to correctional authorities. Also, a released prisoner is likely to bring the toughness reinforced in prison life to the workplace. This transfer of prison norms does not work because most jobs in the service economy require interpersonal skills (Hagan, 1994b).

What are some alternatives to prisons? If prisons do not rehabilitate, what are some alternatives? Several are being considered.

1. *A combination of prison and probation.* A mixed or split sentence, known as *shock probation,* is designed to shock offenders into recognizing the realities of prison life. Prisoners serve part of their sentences in an institution and the rest on probation.

2. *Community-based programs.* These programs are designed to reintroduce criminals into society. By getting convicts out of prison for at least part of the day, community-based programs help break the inmate code. At the same time, prisoners have a chance to become part of society—participating in the community but under professional guidance and supervision.

3. *Diversion strategy.* Diversion is aimed at preventing, or greatly reducing, the offender's involvement in the criminal justice system. Diversion involves a referral to a community-based treatment program rather than a prison or a probationary program. Because offenders are handled outside the formal system of criminal law, authorities believe the offenders will not acquire stigmatizing labels and other liabilities (Morris and Tonry, 1991; Lanier and Henry, 2004).

Will any of these alternatives work? Most of the alternative programs have not been sufficiently evaluated to determine how well they work. Continued use of these alternatives will depend on what American voters believe are the appropriate functions of prisons. These programs can exist only so long as rehabilitation has a high priority. Recently, Americans have taken a harsher view toward criminals, so support for alternatives may be eroding.

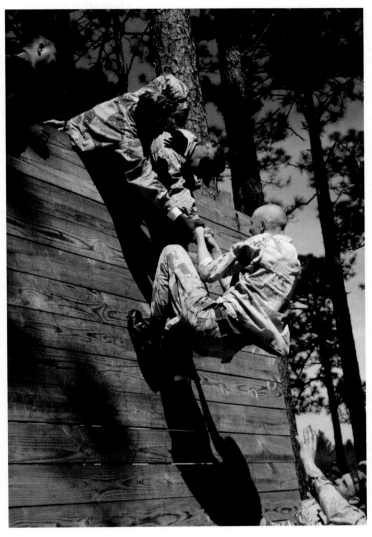

Juvenile boot camps are used as an alternative to confinement in juvenile corrections facilities. These boot camps focus on discipline and physical conditioning, and typically are restricted to nonviolent or first-time offenders.

Rank	Country	Prisoners*	Population (in millions)	Incarceration rate per 1,000
1	United States	2,033,331	290.0	7.01
2	China	1,512,194	1,294.4	1.17
3	Russia	864,590	142.7	6.06
4	India	304,893	1,041.1	0.29
5	Brazil	284,989	178.5	1.60
6	Thailand	258,076	64.3	4.01
7	Ukraine	198,858	47.9	4.15
8	South Africa	180,952	45.0	4.02
9	Iran	163,526	72.2	2.26
10	Mexico	154,765	98.9	1.56

*Approximate figures for latest year available.

Figure 7.8 Top Ten Countries in Number of Prisoners
What can you conclude from this table about a possible relationship between level of economic development and crime?

Source: British Home Office Online Research and Development Statistics, 2004.

Section 5 Assessment

1. Indicate whether the approaches to punishment listed below are rehabilitation (R), deterrence (D), retribution (Rb), or incarceration (I).
   a. imprisonment without parole
   b. longer prison sentences
   c. extremely harsh prison conditions
   d. psychological counseling in prison
   e. swift justice

2. According to the FBI's *Uniform Crime Reports,* has crime in the United States increased or decreased since 1994?

3. Do you believe that the cultural values of American society affect the policies of government regarding approaches to crime control? Why or why not?

4. Has research supported the position that the death penalty deters crime?

Critical Thinking

5. **Synthesizing Information** The text outlines several distinct approaches to crime control. Choose one approach, and explain why you believe it is or is not successful. Use functionalism, conflict theory, or symbolic interactionism as a reference point.

6. **Evaluating Information** What are your beliefs on capital punishment? Defend your viewpoint.

Summary

Section 1: Deviance and Social Control

Main Idea: Deviance is the violation of social norms. It is difficult to define because not everyone agrees on what is deviant behavior.

Section 2: Functionalism and Deviance

Main Idea: According to functionalists, deviance has both negative and positive consequences for society. Functionalism also shapes two theories of deviance: strain theory and control theory.

Section 3: Symbolic Interactionism and Deviance

Main Idea: According to symbolic interactionism, deviance is a learned behavior that is culturally transmitted, but an act is deviant only if other people label it as such (labeling theory).

Section 4: Conflict Theory and Deviance

Main Idea: Conflict theory looks at how social inequality affects deviance, pointing to crime statistics to support their theory.

Section 5: Crime and Punishment

Main Idea: Crime statistics in the U.S. come mainly from the FBI and the Census Bureau.

Self-Check Quiz
Visit the *Sociology and You* Web site at glencoe.com and click on **Chapter 7—Self-Check Quizzes** to prepare for the chapter test.

Reviewing Vocabulary

Complete each sentence using each term once.

a. deviance
b. stigma
c. social control
d. white-collar crimes
e. social sanctions
f. anomie
g. Uniform Crime Reports
h. strain theory
i. deterrence
j. control theory
k. recidivism
l. rehabilitation
m. differential association theory
n. retribution
o. labeling theory

1. The tactic that uses intimidation to prevent crime is called _____ .
2. _____ is the approach to crime control that attempts to resocialize criminals.
3. _____ is an undesirable characteristic or label used to deny the deviant acceptance.
4. A violation of social norms is called _____ .
5. _____ are crimes committed by high-status people in the course of their occupation.
6. _____ is a theory that states that people are defined by those in power as deviant.
7. The theory that states that deviance exists when there is a gap between culturally desirable goals and means is called _____ .
8. The theory that conformity to social norms depends on a strong bond between individuals and society is known as the _____ .
9. _____ are rewards or punishments designed to encourage desired behavior.
10. _____ states that deviance is learned in proportion to exposure to deviancy.
11. When past offenders return to prison, such an occurrence is called _____ .
12. _____ promotes social conformity.
13. _____ is the social condition in which norms are weak, conflicting, or absent.

14. The major source of American statistics on crime gathered from police departments is known as

_____.

15. _____ is the practice in which criminals pay compensation equal to their offenses.

Reviewing the Facts

16. In a famous study known as the Minneapolis Domestic Violence Study, sociologists discovered that arresting someone for hitting his wife did not necessarily stop him from hitting her again. What is the name of the theory upon which they based their hypothesis that arrest would stop the behavior?

17. A group of lower-class youths are accused of a crime for behavior that higher-status teens have engaged in without punishment. What sociological term describes this process?

18. When a high school student admits to cheating on a test, this behavior is labeled as primary deviance. Explain why.

19. Give two reasons why the crime statistics reported by the Uniform Crime Reports differ from those statistics reported by the National Crime Victimization Survey. Which report would you consider more reliable and why?

Thinking Critically

20. Interpreting Information

Use the information in this chapter to explain the following statement: "Deviance, like beauty, is in the eye of the beholder."

21. Applying Concepts

There is a chain of restaurants in this country known for the outrageous behavior of its servers. At these restaurants, servers might purposely spill drinks and food on the patrons. Despite this apparently deviant behavior, patrons seem to love the restaurants and recommend them to friends. How do these restaurants, which clearly violate concepts of social control, continue to attract customers?

"O.K.—let's review what you didn't know and when you didn't know it."

The New Yorker/Cartoonbank.com

22. Analyzing Visuals

In the Lee Lorenz cartoon above, the caption reads: "OK—let's review what you didn't know and when you didn't know it." What makes you understand that white-collar crime is the subject? How would you describe the cartoonist's view of white-collar crime?

23. Making Inferences

If a person is rarely deviant, people come to expect that behavior. If a person is often deviant, people expect *that* behavior. What do you think happens when people are deviant occasionally? How might unpredictability of behavior be more alarming or disturbing?

24. Drawing Conclusions

Some states are considering life imprisonment with no chance of parole as an alternative to the death penalty. The states argue that the capital punishment process is more costly than imprisonment over time. Proponents also claim that offenders given lifetime sentences are more likely to develop remorse for their crimes. Do you think this argument has merit? Why or why not?

Sociology Projects

25. Random Acts of Kindness and Positive Deviance

Go out of your way to help a stranger. You might give someone directions, help someone to carry parcels, or even say a friendly hello. *(Important note:* Remember to keep safety and sensitivity to others' feelings in mind as you do so.) Write answers to the questions below to help you evaluate the stranger's reactions to your act.

a. How do you think the stranger's race, age, and gender affected the situation?

b. How did you feel while performing the random act of kindness?

c. What surprised or impressed you the most about the individual's reaction?

26. Attitudes Toward Crime

Americans can have different attitudes about how big a problem crime represents compared to other problems, such as unemployment. The table below represents the results of a Pew Research Center survey and shows that attitudes varied according to where people lived. Study the table below. Then conduct your own mini-survey among friends, neighbors, and business-people. Did the results of your informal survey match the Pew Center survey results?

Most Important Community Problem				
Ranking	Large City	Suburb	Small City/ Town	Rural Area
1	Crime	Education	Education	Drugs
2	Drugs	Crime	Unemployment	Unemployment
3	Education	Sprawl	Crime	Education
4	Problems w/kids	Taxes	Drugs	Taxes
5	Infra-structure	Drugs	Sprawl	Infra-structure

Source: *Pew Research Center, March 2001 Report*

27. The Role of the Media

The text discussed how race is an important factor in understanding deviance. Another factor you might wish to consider is the role of the media in shaping our perceptions of crime and criminals. Your task is to collect one crime-related newspaper article per day for one week. Analyze the article for information such as the race, age, gender, and social status of the accused. Also consider the location of the crime. How does the newspaper describe the area where the crime took place? Do you detect any bias in the news report?

28. Preparing a News Broadcast

As an extension of project number 4, imagine yourself as a news anchor on the local news. Choose one of the stories that you have collected. Limiting yourself to one paragraph, prepare your news broadcast using the facts as reported in the newspaper. Now, evaluate your broadcast and write another version that is neutral (i.e., gives no indication of race, gender, or age). Which version do you feel the program producer would choose to put on the air? Why?

Technology Activity

29. Using the Internet or your school or local library, find a murder case from the year 1900. Find a similar type of murder case from the year 2005. Consider how each murder was reported and punished (i.e., the type of approach to crime control that was used). Design a database to illustrate similarities and differences between the two deviant acts. What can you conclude about society's view of deviance at the time the crime was committed?

The Police and the Black Male
by Elijah Anderson

- **anonymous**
  lacking individuality, distinction, or recognition

- **presuppositions**
  assumed knowledge

- **ambiguous**
  capable of being understood in two or more ways

The police, in the Village-Northton [neighborhood] as elsewhere, represent society's formal, legitimate means of social control. Their role includes protecting law-abiding citizens from those who are not law-abiding by preventing crime and by apprehending likely criminals. Precisely how the police fulfill the public's expectations is strongly related to how they view the neighborhood and the people who live there. On the streets, color-coding often works to confuse race, age, class, gender, incivility, and criminality, and it expresses itself most concretely in the person of the **anonymous** black male. In doing their job, the police often become willing parties to this general color-coding of the public environment, and related distinctions, particularly those of skin color and gender, come to convey definite meanings. Although such coding may make the work of the police more manageable, it may also fit well with their own **presuppositions** regarding race and class relations, thus shaping officers' perceptions of crime "in the city." Moreover, the anonymous black male is usually an **ambiguous** figure who arouses the utmost caution and is generally considered dangerous until he proves he is not. . . .

To be white is to be seen by the police—at least superficially—as an ally, eligible for consideration and for much more deferential treatment than that accorded to blacks in general. This attitude may be grounded in the backgrounds of the police themselves. Many have grown up in . . . "ethnic" neighborhoods. They may serve what they perceive as their own class and neighborhood interests, which often translates as keeping blacks "in their place"—away from neighborhoods that are socially defined as "white." In trying to do their job, the police appear to engage in an informal policy of monitoring young black men as a means of controlling crime, and often they seem to go beyond the bounds of duty. . . .

On the streets late at night, the average young black man is suspicious of others he encounters, and he is particularly wary of the police. If he is dressed in the uniform of the "gangster," such as a black leather jacket, sneakers, and a "gangster cap," if he is carrying a radio or a suspicious bag (which may be confiscated), or if he is moving too fast or too slow, the police may stop him. As part of the routine, they search him and make him sit in the police car while they run a check to see whether there is a "detainer" on him. If there is nothing, he is allowed to go on his way. After this ordeal the youth is often left afraid, sometimes shaking, and uncertain about the area he had previously taken for granted. He is upset in part because he is painfully aware of how close he has come to being in "big trouble." He knows of other youths who have gotten into a "world of trouble" simply by being on the streets at the wrong time or when the police were pursuing a criminal. In these circumstances, particularly at night, it is relatively easy for one black

extricate
to remove from an entanglement

arbitrarily
without meaning; resulting from the unrestrained exercise of power

circumscribe
to reduce the range or scope of action

Read and React

1. According to the article, what are some consequences to black youth of being arrested, innocent or not?

2. What presuppositions regarding race and class exist in your neighborhood?

3. Do you think color-coding exists in your town or city? Why or why not?

man to be mistaken for another. Over the years, while walking through the neighborhood I have on occasion been stopped and questioned by police chasing a mugger, but after explaining myself I was released.

Many youths, however, have reason to fear such mistaken identity or harassment, since they might be jailed, if only for a short time, and would have to post bail money and pay legal fees to **extricate** themselves from the mess. . . . When law-abiding blacks are ensnared by the criminal justice system, the scenario may proceed as follows. A young man is **arbitrarily** stopped by the police and questioned. If he cannot effectively negotiate with the officer(s), he may be accused of a crime and arrested. To resolve this situation he needs financial resources, which for him are in short supply. If he does not have money for any attorney, which often happens, he is left to a public defender who may be more interested in going along with the court system than in fighting for a poor black person. Without legal support, he may well wind up "doing time" even if he is innocent of the charges brought against him. The next time he is stopped for questioning he will have a record, which will make detention all the more likely.

Because the young black man is aware of many cases when an "innocent" black person was wrongly accused and detained, he develops an "attitude" toward the police. The street word for police is "the man," signifying a certain machismo, power, and authority. He becomes concerned when he notices "the man" in the community or when the police focus on him because he is outside his own neighborhood. The youth knows, or soon finds out, that he exists in a legally precarious state. Hence he is motivated to avoid the police, and his public life becomes severely **circumscribed** . . . .

To avoid encounters with the man, some streetwise young men camouflage themselves, giving up the urban uniform and emblems that identify them as "legitimate" objects of police attention. They may adopt a more conventional presentation of self, wearing chinos, sweat suits, and generally more conservative dress. Some youths have been known to "ditch" a favorite jacket if they see others wearing one like it, because wearing it increases their chances of being mistaken for someone else who may have committed a crime.

But such strategies do not always work over the long run and must be constantly modified. For instance, because so many young ghetto blacks have begun to wear Fila and Adidas sweat suits as status symbols, such dress has become incorporated into the public image generally associated with young black males. These athletic suits, particularly the more expensive and colorful ones, along with high-priced sneakers, have become the leisure dress of successful drug dealers. . . .

Ed. note: This article is based on the author's field research on two city neighborhoods he calls Village-Northton.

From: Elijah Anderson, *Streetwise* (Chicago: University of Chicago Press, 1990), pp. 190–206. © 1990 University of Chicago Press. Reprinted by permission of the publisher and author.

Sections

1. **Dimensions of Stratification**
2. **Explanations of Stratification**
3. **Social Classes in America**
4. **Poverty in America**
5. **Social Mobility**

Learning Objectives

After reading this chapter, you will be able to

- explain the relationship between stratification and social class.

- compare and contrast the three dimensions of stratification.

- state the differences among the three major perspectives on social stratification.

- identify the distinguishing characteristics of the major social classes in America.

- describe the measurement and extent of poverty in the United States.

- discuss social mobility in the United States.

Applying Sociology

On the streets of many American towns or cities, you will sometimes see someone who is asking for help. It might be a homeless person who has made a sort of makeshift "station" on the street corner of a big city. It might be a man or woman standing near a shopping mall entrance holding up a hand-made sign: "I Need a Job."

How do you react if you see someone like the man pictured in the photo at left? Do you feel sorry for him and want to help? Do you think he must be responsible for his situation? Do you think he might just be lazy and looking for "easy money?" Do you wonder if he is getting any benefits from a government program supported by taxes?

Your answer depends a lot on your social class and such characteristics as age, education, politics, and income. Sociologists know that most Americans seriously overestimate the number of people who rely on government programs or charity to survive.

At the same time, negative attitudes about people who do receive any kind of government payments have become part of the American culture. This chapter will look at social stratification and the attitudes and behaviors of different social classes.

Chapter Overview
Visit the *Sociology and You* Web site at glencoe.com and click on **Chapter 8—Chapter Overviews** to preview chapter information.

1

Dimensions of Stratification

Key Terms

- **social stratification** (p. 242)
- **social class** (p. 242)
- **bourgeoisie** (p. 243)
- **proletariat** (p. 243)
- **income** (p. 244)
- **wealth** (p. 244)
- **power** (p. 245)
- **prestige** (p. 246)

- **social stratification**
  ranking of people or groups according to their unequal access to scarce resources

- **social class**
  segment of society whose members hold similar amounts of resources and share values, norms, and an identifiable lifestyle

Section Preview

Stratification is the division of society into classes that have unequal amounts of wealth, power, and prestige. Karl Marx and Max Weber studied these dimensions of stratification in great detail.

Social Stratification and Social Class

In one of his best-known children's books, Dr. Seuss writes of the Sneetches, birds whose rank depends on whether or not they have a large star on their stomachs. Star-bellied Sneetches have high status, and plain-bellied Sneetches have low status. In the classic novel *Animal Farm,* George Orwell creates a barnyard society where the pigs ultimately take over the previously classless animal society. The animals' motto changes from "All animals are equal" to "All animals are equal—but some animals are more equal than others." Both books mock the tendency of humans to form ranks. **Social stratification** is the creation of layers (or strata)

In George Orwell's *Animal Farm,* the animals overthrow their human master to form their own soon-to-be stratified society.

of people who possess unequal shares of scarce resources. The most important of these resources are income, wealth, power, and prestige (Levine, 1998).

How is social stratification related to social class? Each of the layers in a stratification system is a **social class**—a segment of a population whose members hold similar amounts of scarce resources and share values, norms, and an identifiable lifestyle. The number of social classes in a society varies. Technologically developed countries generally have three broad classes—upper, middle, and lower—subdivided into smaller categories. In some developing countries, there might only be an upper class and a lower class.

Karl Marx and Max Weber made the most significant early contributions to the study of social stratification. (See Chapter 1, pages 16–18 for an introduction to these two pioneers of sociology.) Marx explained the importance of the economic foundations of social classes, while Weber emphasized the prestige and power aspects of stratification.

World View

Poverty and Death

Receiving basic nutrition and medical care is critical to survival in the early years of human life. Because wealth and income have a significant impact on a family's ability to provide these necessities of life, extreme poverty matters a great deal. This map shows the probable number of deaths of children less than five years old per 1,000 live births in each country.

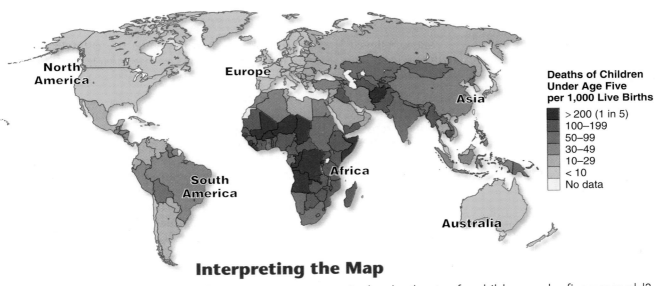

Deaths of Children Under Age Five per 1,000 Live Births

- > 200 (1 in 5)
- 100–199
- 50–99
- 30–49
- 10–29
- < 10
- No data

Interpreting the Map

1. Do you see a pattern in the death rates for children under five years old? Explain.
2. Why do you think the U.S. ranks low in early childhood deaths?
3. Imagine you have the job of reducing the world's death rate among children under age five. What programs would you introduce?

Source: World Health Organization, *World Health Statistics 2005.*

The Economic Dimension

Marx identified several social classes in nineteenth-century industrial society, including laborers, servants, factory workers, craftspeople, proprietors of small businesses, and moneyed capitalists. He predicted, however, that capitalist societies would ultimately be reduced to two social classes. He thought that those who owned the means of production—the **bourgeoisie**—would be the rulers. Those who worked for wages—the **proletariat**—would be the ruled. Marx predicted that because the capitalists owned the means of production (factories, land, and so forth), they would both rule and exploit the working class. The working class would have nothing to sell but its labor.

- **bourgeoisie**
  class that owns the means of production

- **proletariat**
  class that labors without owning the means of production

Figure 8.1

Percentage Change in After-Tax Income, 1977 to 2002
To what percentages do the labels Lowest, Middle, and Top Fifth refer?

Source: Washington, DC: Center on Budget and Policy Priorities, 2005.

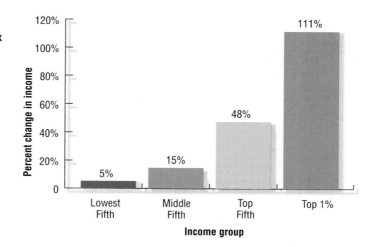

Marx believed that control of the economy gave the capitalists control over the legal, educational, and government systems as well. For Karl Marx, the economy determined the nature of society.

Are there extremes of income and poverty in the United States?

In his writings, Marx emphasized the unequal distribution of economic resources. How unequally are these resources distributed in the United States? When discussing this issue, economists often make a distinction between income and wealth. **Income** is the amount of money received within a given time period by an individual or group. **Wealth** refers to all the economic resources possessed by an individual or group. In brief, your income is your paycheck, and your wealth is what you own.

● **income**
amount of money received by an individual or group over a specific time period

● **wealth**
total economic resources held by a person or group

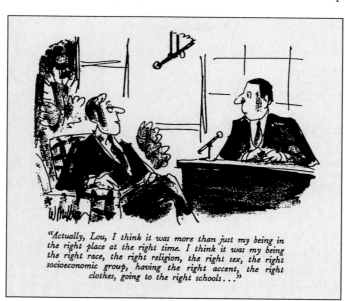

"Actually, Lou, I think it was more than just my being in the right place at the right time. I think it was my being the right race, the right religion, the right sex, the right socioeconomic group, having the right accent, the right clothes, going to the right schools . . ."

This cartoon is illustrating what sociologists have confirmed—usually, those who have, get.

In 2004, approximately 37 million Americans were living in poverty. (In 2004, the poverty threshold was set at $19,484 for a family of four.) At the other extreme, there were nearly 2.5 million millionaires and around 341 billionaires in the United States. The economist Paul Samuelson described income inequality in America in these words: "If we made an income pyramid out of a child's blocks, with each layer portraying $500 of income, the peak would be far higher than Mt. Everest, but most people would be within a few feet of the ground" (Samuelson and Nordhaus, 1995). The truth of this statement is supported by U.S. government figures on the distribution of income. In 2004, for example, the richest 20 percent of American households received over 50 percent of the nation's income. The poorest 20 percent received less than 4 percent (U.S. Bureau of the Census).

Income inequality exists and is growing. Figure 8.1 charts percentage changes in after-tax income in the United States over a twenty-five year period. During this period, the income of the top

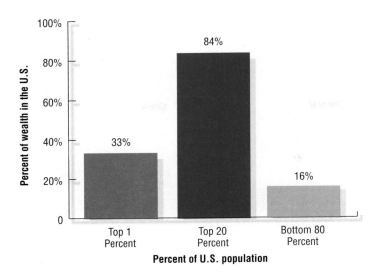

Figure 8.2 Shares of Wealth
Is this picture of the distribution of wealth different from what you would expect? Explain.

Source: Edward N. Wolff, "Changes in Household Wealth in the 1980s and 1990s in the U.S." (Working Paper No. 407). The Levy Economics Institute, May 2004.

1 percent of the population increased by 111 percent. Compare this to a 5 percent increase for the lowest fifth of the population. How much inequality in wealth exists in the United States?

Income distribution figures reveal economic inequality, but they do not show the full extent of inequality. For that, inequality in wealth (what you own) must be considered. In the United States, there is a high concentration of wealth. The richest 20 percent of the population holds 84 percent of the wealth. The top 1 percent alone has 33 percent of the total wealth in the United States. (See Figure 8.2.)

The Power Dimension

You will recall from Chapter 1 that **power** is the ability to control the behavior of others, even against their will. Individuals or groups who possess power are able to use it to enhance their own interests, often—but not necessarily—at the expense of society.

Can you exercise power without being wealthy?

According to Marx, those who own and control capital have the power in a society. Weber, on the other hand, argued that while having money certainly helps, economic success and power are not the same. Money and ownership of the means of production are not the only resources that can be used as a basis for power. Expert knowledge can be used to expand power, too. For example, many lawyers convert their expertise into substantial amounts of political power. Fame is another basis for power. In 1952, for example, Albert Einstein was offered the presidency of Israel. (He refused, saying, "I know a little about nature, and hardly anything about men.")

Power is also attached to the social positions we hold. Elected officers in organizations have more power than rank-and-file members. People in top executive positions in the mass media are powerful, even if they themselves do not have great wealth. People who are wealthy and powerful also are assumed to have characteristics they may not have. Not all of these people are as intelligent and wise as is usually assumed. Still, these attributed characteristics help them gain prestige.

● **power**
the ability to control the behavior of others, even against their will

Jesse Jackson has channeled his intense interest in civil rights into the exercise of power on behalf of the poor and disadvantaged.

Finally, we can overcome a lack of wealth if we have large numbers of people on our side or if we are skillful at organizing our resources. Hitler, for example, was able to turn the problem of limited resources into a mass political movement. He gained absolute power by promising to deliver Germany from economic hardship following World War I.

The Prestige Dimension

A third dimension of social stratification is **prestige**—recognition, respect, and admiration attached to social positions. Prestige is defined by your culture and society. Honor, admiration, respect, and deference are extended to

● **prestige**
recognition, respect, and admiration attached to social positions

Popular celebrities such as Johnny Depp and Jennifer Lopez have considerable wealth. Their prestige rating is stronger in some circles than others, however.

Occupations	Prestige Score	Occupations	Prestige Score	Occupations	Prestige Score
Surgeon	87	Police officer	61	Automobile dealer	43
Astronaut	80	Actor	60	Deep-sea diver	43
Lawyer	75	Journalist	60	Landlord	41
College professor	74	TV anchorman	60	Prison guard	40
Airline pilot	73	Businessperson	60	Auto mechanic	40
Dentist	72	Actress	59	Roofer	37
Priest	71	Nursery school teacher	55	Barber	36
Engineer	71	Fashion designer	55	Sales clerk in a store	36
TV anchorwoman	70	Firefighter	53	Bus driver	32
Secret Service agent	70	Airplane mechanic	53	Dry cleaner	32
School principal	69	Commercial artist	52	Waitress	29
Medical technician	68	Housewife	51	Taxicab driver	28
Optometrist	67	Funeral director	49	Used car salesperson	25
Registered nurse	66	Jazz musician	48	Bill collector	24
High school teacher	66	Mail carrier	47	Janitor	22
Air traffic controller	65	Insurance agent	46	Grocery bagger	18
Professional athlete	65	Mechanic	46	Street-corner drug dealer	13
Paramedic	64	Disc jockey	45	Fortune teller	13
Public grade school teacher	64	Photographer	45	Panhandler	11
Advertising executive	63	Plumber	45		
Veterinarian	62	Bank teller	43		

Figure 8.3 Prestige Rankings of Selected Occupations in the United States
Why do you think the highest listed prestige score is 87? What occupations might rate a higher score?

dons within the Mafia, for example; but outside their own circles Mafia chiefs do not have high prestige.

Prestige must be voluntarily given, not claimed. Scientists cannot proclaim themselves Nobel Prize winners; journalists cannot award themselves Pulitzer Prizes; and corporate executives cannot grant themselves honorary doctorates. Recognition must come from others; it is socially constructed.

People with similar levels of prestige share identifiable lifestyles. The offspring of upper-class families are more likely to attend private universities and Episcopalian churches. Children from lower-class homes are less likely to attend college at all and tend to belong to fundamentalist religious groups. In fact, some sociologists view social classes as subcultures because their members participate in distinctive ways of life.

How is prestige distributed? The social positions that are considered the most important, or are valued the most highly, have the most prestige. Because Americans value the acquisition of wealth and power, they tend to assign higher prestige to persons in positions of wealth and power.

In America, most people achieve prestige because of their occupations. (See Figure 8.3.) White-collar occupations (doctors, ministers, schoolteachers) have higher prestige than blue-collar jobs (carpenters, plumbers, mechanics). Even though wealth and power usually determine prestige, that is not always the case. You may find it somewhat surprising, for example, that priests and college professors have more prestige than bankers.

Associate each of these people with a prestige level. If an occupation is not obvious, choose a likely one for that person. Can the young girl even be ranked?

Section 1 Assessment

1. What is social stratification?
2. Match the dimensions of stratification with the examples below. Use (W) for wealth, (Po) for power, and (Pr) for prestige.
   a. the respect accorded doctors
   b. a politician considering the interests of a political lobby
   c. the Nobel Peace Prize
   d. stock market holdings
   e. a Supreme Court ruling
   f. real estate assets

3. The top 20 percent of U.S. households receive approximately what percentage of total U.S. income?
4. What are the most common sources of prestige in U.S. society?

Critical Thinking

5. **Analyzing Information** Social class level influences the likelihood of gaining political power. Can you analyze the relationship between social class level and political power?

You Are What You Wear

Social rank in Europe in the Middle Ages was reflected, as it is today, in clothing and accessories. The following excerpt describes some of the norms associated with dress and status.

Clothing [in medieval Europe] served as a kind of uniform, designating status. Lepers were required to wear gray coats and red hats, the skirts of prostitutes had to be scarlet, released heretics carried crosses sewn on both sides of their chests—you were expected to pray as you passed them—and the breast of every Jew, as [required] by law, bore a huge yellow circle.

The rest of society belonged to one of the three great classes: the nobility, the clergy, and the

commons. Establishing one's social identity was important. Each man knew his place, believed it had been [determined] in heaven, and was aware that what he wore must reflect it.

To be sure, certain fashions were shared by all. Styles had changed since Greece and Rome shimmered in their glory; then garments had been wrapped on; now all classes put them on and fastened them. Most clothing—except the leather gauntlets and leggings of hunters, and the crude animal skins worn by the very poor—was now woven of wool. (Since few Europeans possessed a change of clothes, the same [dress] was worn daily; as a consequence, skin diseases were astonishingly prevalent.) But there was no mistaking the distinctions between the parson in his vestments; the toiler in his dirty cloth tunic, loose trousers, and heavy boots; and the aristocrat with his jewelry, his hairdress, and his extravagant finery. Every knight wore a signet ring, and wearing fur was as much a sign of knighthood as wearing a sword or carrying a falcon. Indeed, in some European states it was illegal for anyone not nobly born to adorn himself with fur. "Many a petty noble," wrote historian W. S. Davis, "will cling to his frayed tippet of black lambskin, even in the hottest weather, merely to prove that he is not a villein [a type of serf]."

Source: Excerpted from *A World Lit Only by Fire*, © 1992 by William Manchester. By permission of Little, Brown and Company. Reprinted by permission of Don Congdon Associates, Inc. © 1993 by William Manchester.

Thinking It Over

Think about how you and your classmates dress. Identify some ways in which differences in dress reflect social status in your school.

Clothing in medieval society was strictly regulated.

Explanations of Stratification

Key Term

- **false consciousness**
  (p. 250)

Section Preview

Each of the three perspectives—functionalism, conflict theory, and symbolic interactionism—explains stratification in society in a different way.

Functionalist Theory of Stratification

According to the functionalists, stratification assures that the most qualified people fill the most important positions, that these qualified people perform their tasks competently, and that they are rewarded for their efforts. The functionalist theory recognizes that inequality exists because certain jobs are more important than others and that these jobs often involve special talent and training. To encourage people to make the sacrifices necessary to fill these jobs (such as acquiring the necessary education), society attaches special monetary rewards and prestige to the positions. That is why, for example, doctors make more money and have more prestige than bus drivers. A higher level of skill is required in the medical profession, and our society's need for highly qualified doctors is great.

- **false consciousness**
  adoption of the ideas of the dominant class by the less powerful class

How would functionalists explain the different places of these people on the stratification structure?

Conflict Theory of Stratification

According to the conflict theory of stratification, inequality exists because some people are willing to exploit others. Stratification, from this perspective, is based on force rather than on people voluntarily agreeing to it.

The conflict theory of stratification is based on Marx's ideas regarding class conflict. For Marx, all of history has been a class struggle between the powerful and the powerless, the exploiters and the exploited. Capitalist society is the final stage of the class struggle. Although the capitalists are outnumbered, they are able to control the workers. This is because the capitalists use a belief system that legitimizes the way things are. For example, the powerful contend that income and wealth are based on ability, hard work, and individual effort. Those who own the means of production are able to spread their ideas, beliefs, and values through the schools, the media, the churches, and the government. (More will be said about how this might happen in the next section.) Marx used the term **false consciousness** to refer to working-class acceptance of capitalist ideas and values.

Later conflict sociologists have proposed that stratification is based more on power than on property ownership. America's legal system, for example, is used by the wealthy for their benefit, and the political system is skewed toward the interests of the powerful. Conflict theorists would point to the unequal treatment experienced by the poorer residents of New Orleans after Hurricane Katrina. For conflict theorists, stratification occurs through the struggle for scarce resources.

Symbolic Interactionism and Stratification

Symbolic interactionism helps us understand how people are socialized to accept the existing stratification structure. According to this perspective, American children are taught that a person's social class is the result of talent and effort. Those "on top" have worked hard and used their abilities, whereas those "on the bottom" lack the talent or the motivation to succeed. Hence, it is not fair to challenge the system. In this way, people come to accept the existing system.

Conflict theorists believe that the various groups in society compete for scarce resources. Education is one means through which people gain access to these resources. Do conflict sociologists believe that everyone has equal access to education?

Understandably, people in the lower social classes or social strata tend to suffer from lower self-esteem. How could it be otherwise when messages from all sides tell them they are inferior? Remember that, in the symbolic interactionist view, self-esteem is based on how we think others see us. In other words, the looking-glass process is at work. Those at the top blame the victims; the victims blame themselves.

The reverse is true for the higher classes. Those profiting most from the stratification structure tend to have higher self-esteem. This, in turn, fuels their conviction that the present arrangement is just. In short, people's self-concepts also help preserve the status quo.

It isn't always easy being out of the "in–group."

Figure 8.4 Social Stratification

This table summarizes what issues of social stratification might be of interest to each of the major perspectives and predictions that they would make. Why would the symbolic interactionists be more likely than the functionalists to look at issues of self-esteem?

Theoretical Perspective	Research Topic	Expected Result	
Functionalism	Relationship between job performance and pay	Pay levels increase with job performance.	
Conflict Theory	Relationship between social class and the likelihood of punishment for a crime	The chances for prosecution decrease as the level of social class increases.	
Symbolic Interactionism	Link between social class and self-esteem	Self-esteem is higher among the upper class than the lower class.	

Section 2 Assessment

1. Identify which of the major perspectives describes the examples below.
   a. Corporate executives make more money because they decide who gets what in their organizations.
   b. Engineers make more money than butlers because of their education.
   c. Poor children tend to have low self-esteem.

2. How did Marx explain the stratification of society?

3. According to the symbolic interactionists, people are socialized to accept the existing stratification structure through _____ .
   a. the "I"
   b. evolution
   c. conflict
   d. the self-concept

Critical Thinking

4. **Making Comparisons** Compare and contrast the explanations given by functionalism, conflict theory, and symbolic interactionism for the existence of poor people in the United States.

Focus on Research

Field Research: Who's Popular, Who's Not?

In 1995, sociologist Donna Eder and her research team studied popularity among middle-schoolers. They observed lunchtime interactions and attended extracurricular activities. After several months of observation, informal interviews were conducted with individuals and groups. To capture interaction for closer study, the researchers received student and parental permission for audio and video recordings.

Eder and her colleagues found that in the sixth grade, there were no elite groups. Seventh and eighth graders, however, did not see each other as equals; popular seventh graders were divided along gender lines. By the eighth grade, the two groups intermingled. In both grades, popularity was based on how many others knew who you were and wanted to talk with you.

Status differences could arise in the seventh and eighth grades because cheerleading and team sports existed as a way to become highly visible. Realizing the source of their prestige, male athletes took every opportunity to display symbols of their team affiliation. Team uniforms, jerseys, and athletic shoes were among the most important items of dress. Bandages, casts, and crutches were worn with pride.

Girls could not use sports to gain visibility because female athletics were not as valued by faculty, administrators, or students. Girls, therefore, used cheerleading to make themselves widely known. In addition to performing at basketball and football games, cheerleaders appeared in front of the entire student body at pep rallies and other school events.

Boys made fun of this high-status female activity by mockingly imitating cheers. One male coach joined the mockery by telling football players that either they must practice harder or he would get them cheerleading skirts. He then pretended to cheer in a falsetto voice.

Girls, in contrast, regarded cheerleaders highly. Popular girls in the seventh and eighth grades were either cheerleaders or friends of cheerleaders. Flaunting their status (just as the male athletes did), cheerleaders put on their uniforms as far ahead of games as possible and wore their cheerleading skirts for extracurricular school activities.

Working with the Research

How is the stratification structure described in this feature similar to or different from the stratification structure found in your own school?

For adolescent males, playing sports is a way to become popular.

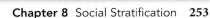

3

Social Classes in America

Key Terms

- class conscious-ness *(p. 254)*
- working poor *(p. 256)*
- underclass *(p. 256)*

class consciousness identification with the goals and interests of a social class

Section Preview

Sociologists have identified several social classes in the United States. They include the upper class, the middle class, the working class, the working poor, and the underclass.

Class Consciousness

Americans have always been aware of inequality, but they have never developed a sense of **class consciousness**—a sense of identification with the goals and interests of the members of a particular social class. In part because the American public has shown relatively little interest in class differences, sociologists began to investigate inequality rather late. It was not until the 1920s that sociologists in the United States began systematically to identify social classes. Since that time, however, research on this subject has been plentiful. Early efforts to study stratification were mostly case studies of specific communities. Only in relatively recent times have attempts been made to describe the stratification structure of America as a whole.

Since social classes are changeable and full of exceptions, any attempt to identify the social-class structure of American society is hazardous. Nevertheless, sociologists have described some of the major classifications. (See Figure 8.5.)

Figure 8.5
American Class Structure
What does this chart of the American class structure indicate about stratification in the U.S.?

Source: Adapted from Dennis Gilbert, *The American Class Structure in an Age of Growing Inequality* (6th ed.), 2003.

Typical Occupations

		Typical Incomes
Upper Class	Investors, heirs, chief executive officers	1% — $2 million
Upper Middle Class	Upper-level managers, professionals, owners of medium-sized businesses	14% — $120,000
Middle Class	Lower-level managers, semiprofessionals, non-retail salespeople	30% — $55,000
Working Class	Low-paid manual, clerical, craft, and retail sales workers	30% — $35,000
Working Poor	Lowest-paid manual, retail, and service workers	13% — $22,000
Underclass	Unemployed people, people in part-time menial jobs, people receiving public assistance	12% — $12,000

The Upper Class

The upper class includes only 1 percent of the population (Gilbert, 2003) and may be divided into the upper-upper class and the lower-upper class. At the top is the "aristocracy." Its members represent the old-money families whose names appear in high society—Ford, Rockefeller, Vanderbilt, and du Pont, among others. The basis for membership in this most elite of clubs is blood rather than sweat and tears. Parents in this class send their children to the best private schools and universities. People in this group seldom marry outside their class.

People are in the lower-upper class more often because of achievement and earned income than because of birth and inherited wealth. Some have made fortunes running large corporations or investing in the stock market. Members of this class may actually be better off financially than members of the upper-upper class. However, they often are not accepted into the most exclusive social circles.

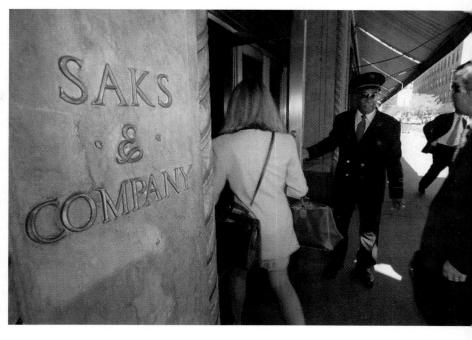

Upper-class people tend to shop at upscale stores such as Saks and Company.

The Middle Classes

Most Americans think of themselves as middle class. In reality, though, only about 40 to 50 percent of Americans fit this description. And most of these people are not in the upper-middle class.

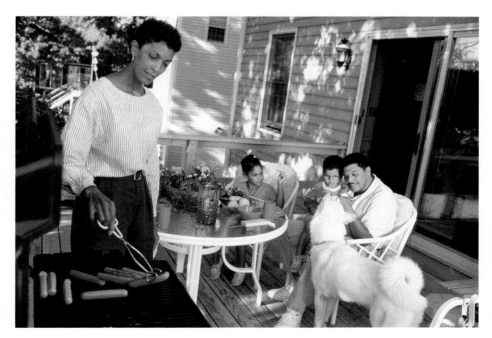

This family fulfills the American image of comfortable middle-class living.

Student Web Activity
Visit the *Sociology and You* Web site at glencoe.com and click on **Chapter 8—Student Web Activities** for an activity on social class.

The upper-middle class (14 percent of the population) is composed of those who have been successful in business, the professions, politics, and the military. Basically, this class is made up of individuals and families who benefited from the tremendous corporate and professional expansion following World War II. Members of this class earn enough to live well and to save money. They are typically college educated and have high educational and career goals for their children. They do not have national or international power, but they tend to be active in voluntary and political organizations in their communities.

The middle-middle class (30 percent of the population) is a very mixed bag. Its members include owners of small businesses and farms; independent professionals (small-town doctors and lawyers); other professionals (clergy, teachers, nurses, firefighters, social workers, police officers); lower-level managers; and some sales and clerical workers. Their household income level, which is above the national median income ($44,389 in 2004), does not permit them to live as well as the upper-middle class. Many have only a high school education, although many have some college, and some have college degrees. Members of this class are interested in civic affairs. They participate in political activities less than the classes above them but more than either the working class or the lower class.

The Working Class

The working class (often referred to as the lower-middle class) comprises almost one-third of the population. Working-class people include roofers, delivery truck drivers, machine operators, and salespeople and clerical workers (Rubin, 1994). Although some of these workers may earn more than some middle-class people, in general the economic resources of the working class are lower than those of the middle class.

Members of the working class have below-average income and unstable employment. They generally lack hospital insurance and retirement benefits. The threat of unemployment or illness is real and haunting. Outside of union activities, members of the working class have little opportunity to exercise power or participate in organizations. Members of the working class—even those with higher incomes—are not likely to enter the middle class.

The Working Poor

The working poor (13 percent of the population) consists of people employed in low-skill jobs with the lowest pay. Its members are typically the lowest-level clerical workers, manual workers (laborers), and service workers (fast-food servers). Lacking steady employment, the working poor do not earn enough to rise above the poverty line ($19,484 for a family of four in 2004). The working poor tend not to belong to organizations or to participate in the political process. (See also Enrichment Reading: No Shame in My Game on page 460 in Chapter 13.)

The Underclass

The underclass (12 percent of the population) is composed of people who are usually unemployed and who come from families with a history of unemployment for generations. They either work in part-time menial jobs (unloading trucks, picking up litter) or are on public assistance. In addition

● **working poor**
people employed in low-skill jobs with the lowest pay who do not earn enough to rise out of poverty

● **underclass**
people typically unemployed who came from families that have been poor for generations

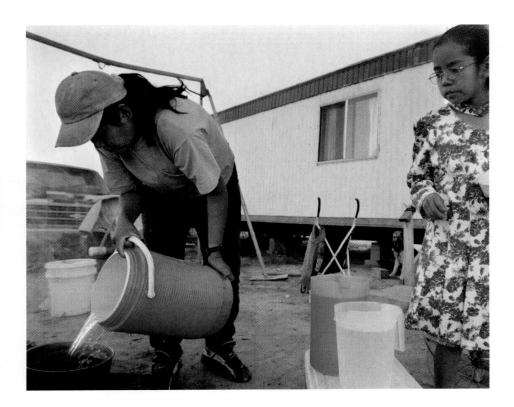

to a lack of education and skills, many members of the underclass have other problems. Physical or mental disabilities are common, and many are single mothers with little or no income.

The most common shared characteristic of the working poor and the underclass is a lack of skills to obtain jobs that pay enough to meet basic needs. There are many routes into these classes—birth, old age, loss of a marriage partner, lack of education or training, drug addiction or alcoholism, physical or mental disability. There are, however, very few paths out. Poverty in the United States, another way to discuss the working poor and the underclass, is the topic of the next section.

This Navajo single mother belongs to the underclass, America's poorest.

Section 3 Assessment

1. Statistically, out of 500 people, how many would belong to the upper class?
2. What is a major distinction between members of the upper-middle and the middle-middle classes?
3. Which class is the largest segment of society?

Critical Thinking

4. **Summarizing Information**
   Chapter 5 discussed the concept of status. How does ascribed status relate to social class? How does achieved status relate to social class?

Social Classes in World Perspective

The World Bank, whose business it is to dispense economic advice and loans to low- and middle-income countries, continuously monitors income levels around the world. The map below displays the World Bank's classification of countries in terms of per capita income. For example, the United States is one of the few nations with a "high-income" economy—one that has a gross national income (GNI) per capita of $10,066 or more.

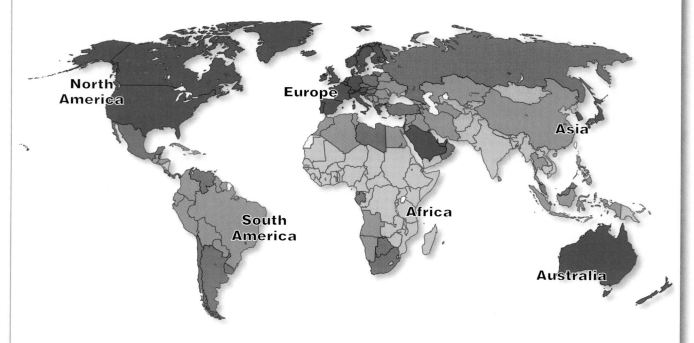

Low-income economies
($825 or less in 2004)

Lower middle-income economies
($826 to $3,255 in 2004)

Upper middle-income economies
($3,256 to $10,065 in 2004)

High-income economies
($10,066 or more in 2004)

No Data

Interpreting the Map

1. Explain the definitions of the four income groups.

2. Identify two countries within each of the four income categories.

3. Why do you think the U.S. is one of the few countries to fall within the high-income category?

4. Compare poverty in the United States to poverty in low-income economies.

Source: World Bank, 2005.

Poverty in America

Section Preview

Poverty can be measured in absolute or relative terms. The poor in the U.S. are disproportionately represented by African Americans, Latinos, women, and children.

Key Terms

● absolute
    poverty (p. 259)
● relative
    poverty (p. 259)
● feminization
    of poverty (p. 261)

Measuring Poverty

The term **absolute poverty** is the absence of enough money to secure life's necessities—enough food and a safe place to live. It is possible, however, to have the things required to remain alive and still be poor. We measure **relative poverty** by comparing the economic condition of those at the bottom of a society with that of other members of that society. According to this measure, the definition of poverty can vary. It would not, for example, be the same in India as in the United States.

How is poverty measured in the United States? Historically, the United States government has measured poverty by setting an annual income level and considering people poor if their income is below that level. As noted earlier, in 2004 that figure was $19,484 for a family of four.

How many Americans are poor? Poverty is widespread throughout the United States. According to 2004 U.S. Census Bureau reports, the poor comprise 12.7 percent of the American population, or about 37 million people. Great poverty existed when it became a national political and social issue in the 1960s. More than forty years later, poverty in America is still a problem (Newman, 1999). (See Figure 8.6 on page 260.)

● **absolute poverty**
the absence of enough money to secure life's necessities

● **relative poverty**
a measure of poverty based on the economic disparity between those at the bottom of a society and the rest of the society

From the slums of Calcutta to a project in the United States, what do these photos say about the relativity of poverty?

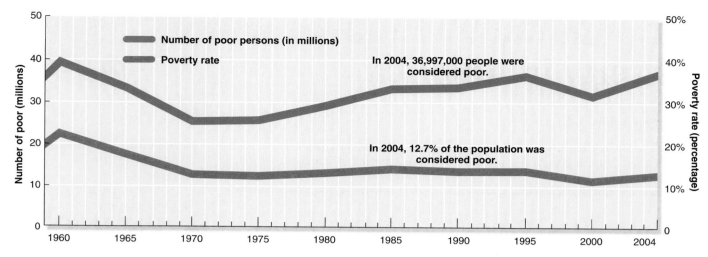

Source: U.S. Bureau of the Census, *Income, Poverty, and Health Insurance Coverage in the United States: 2004,* 2005.

Figure 8.6 Number of Poor and Poverty Rate: 1960–2004
This graph shows two types of information: (1) the number of poor in the total population and (2) the poverty rate as a percentage of the total population. Why is it often helpful to have related information plotted on the same graph?

Identifying the Poor

Minorities, people who live in female-headed households, children under eighteen years of age, elderly people, and people with disabilities make up the most disadvantaged groups living in the United States today.

How are race and ethnicity related to poverty? Nearly 46 percent of the poor in America today are non-Latino white. The poverty rate for African Americans and Latinos is much higher than that for whites, however. The poverty rate for whites is 8.6 percent; for African Americans and Latinos more than 20 percent. African Americans and Latinos together account for only about one-fourth of the total population, but they make up nearly half of the poor population. (See Figure 8.7.)

How are gender and age related to poverty? Another large segment of the poor population is made up of female-headed households. We can look at this issue in two different ways. We can look at all poor households as a group and determine what proportion of them are headed by females. When we do this, we find that about one-half of poor households are female headed. In contrast, when we look at nonpoor households, we find that only about 14 percent are headed by females. Another approach would be to look at all female-headed households as a group and determine what proportion of them are poor. We find that the poverty rate for these households is about 28 percent, compared with just over 10 percent for all families.

Figure 8.7 The Distribution of Poverty in the U.S.
What are the most important conclusions you would reach from this figure?

Source: U.S. Bureau of the Census, 2005.

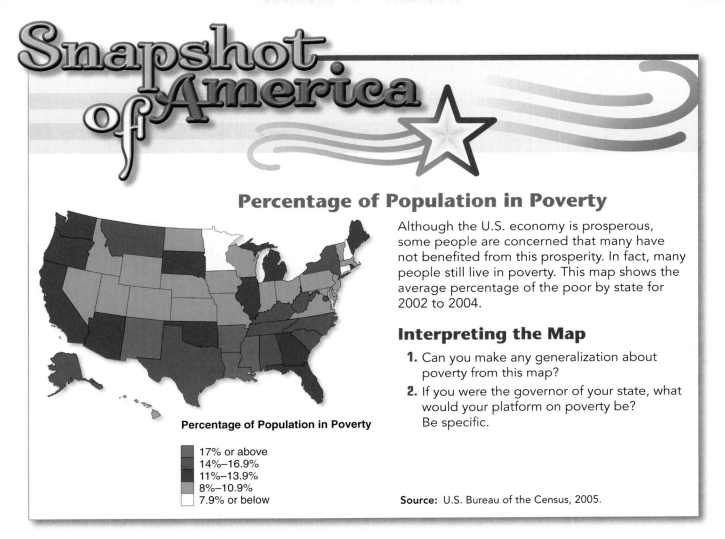

Snapshot of America

Percentage of Population in Poverty

Although the U.S. economy is prosperous, some people are concerned that many have not benefited from this prosperity. In fact, many people still live in poverty. This map shows the average percentage of the poor by state for 2002 to 2004.

Interpreting the Map

1. Can you make any generalization about poverty from this map?
2. If you were the governor of your state, what would your platform on poverty be? Be specific.

Percentage of Population in Poverty

- 17% or above
- 14%–16.9%
- 11%–13.9%
- 8%–10.9%
- 7.9% or below

Source: U.S. Bureau of the Census, 2005.

By either measure, then, households headed by females are poorer than those headed by males. A related factor is the poverty rate for children under eighteen years of age. The current rate for this group is about 18 percent—the highest rate for any age group in the United States (U.S. Bureau of the Census, 2005). The high poverty rates for women and children reflect a trend in U.S. society. Between 1960 and today, women and children make up a larger proportion of the poor. Sociologists refer to this trend as the **feminization of poverty.**

There are several reasons why women have a higher risk of being poor. As we discuss in more detail in Chapter 10 (see pages 323–324), women earn only about $.80 for every dollar earned by men. Women with children find it more difficult to find and keep regular, long-term employment. A lack of good child-care facilities adds to the likelihood that they will not be able to continue working.

Older Americans make up another large segment of the poor. Nearly 10 percent of people aged sixty-five or older live in poverty (U.S. Bureau of the Census, 2005). Another large segment of the poor are people who have disabilities. This group is three times as likely to live in poverty as people who are able-bodied. Also, people who have severe disabilities are more likely to live in poverty than are those who have less severe disabilities.

● **feminization of poverty**
a trend in U.S. society in which women and children make up an increasing proportion of the poor

Blaming the victim is easy. Accepting blame is harder.

Responses to the Problem of Poverty

Before the mid-1960s, fighting poverty was not a major goal of the federal government. Some programs, such as Social Security and Aid to Families with Dependent Children, had been enacted during the Great Depression. These measures did not usually reach the lowest levels of needy citizens, however. Finally in 1964, President Lyndon Johnson marshalled the forces of the federal government to begin a War on Poverty.

What were the goals of the War on Poverty? The philosophy behind the War on Poverty was to help poor people help themselves (Jacoby, 1997; Barry, 1999; Patterson, 2004). President Johnson's predecessor, President John F. Kennedy, believed that if the chains of poverty were to be broken, it had to be through self-improvement, not temporary relief. Accordingly, almost 60 percent of the first poverty budget was earmarked for youth opportunity programs and the work experience program (work and job training designed primarily for welfare recipients and unemployed fathers).

Hopes for positive results from the War on Poverty were high. However, not all of the programs were as successful as predicted. Indeed, some have come under severe criticism. These criticisms center around supposed widespread abuses and the fear that the system encourages people to become dependent upon the government longer than is necessary. "Fixing" the way social welfare should be provided and payments should be distributed has been the focus of many hot political debates.

Welfare Reform

Prior to 1996, the main source of welfare assistance for the needy was a program called Aid to Families with Dependent Children (AFDC). The most recent legislation on welfare reform, enacted in 1996, replaced AFDC with a program known as Temporary Assistance for Needy Families (TANF).

What is the nature of welfare reform? The Temporary Assistance for Needy Families (TANF) program limits the amount of time those able to work can receive welfare payments. The bill has three major elements: it reduces welfare spending, it increases state and local power to oversee welfare rules, and it adds new restrictions on welfare eligibility. For example, benefits to children of unwed teenage mothers are denied unless the mothers remain in school and live with an adult. Cash aid to able-bodied adults will be terminated if they fail to get a job after two years.

Has welfare reform worked? It is too early to make a final evaluation of this latest attempt at welfare reform. However, according to the Administration of Children and Families, the government agency that administers TANF, welfare rolls have decreased substantially since the new welfare-to-work program went into effect. In 1996, for example, more than 12 million people were receiving welfare. In 2003, the total number of TANF recipients was slightly less than 5 million. This number represents approximately 2 million families. Only a small percentage of recipients have been removed from the rolls because of the new time limits on benefits.

There is a darker side, however. Most of the people who left the welfare rolls in the late 1990s could find only low-wage jobs in industries such as food service, home health care, and retail sales. In the early 2000s, an economic downturn caused many of these types of jobs to disappear. At the same time, wages grew more slowly or actually fell (Boushey and Rosnick, 2003). As a result, many of those who left the welfare rolls continue to live in or near poverty. Research suggests that the current emphasis of welfare reform on reducing the welfare rolls rather than on reducing poverty hampers the long-term economic well-being of former recipients (McNamara, 2004).

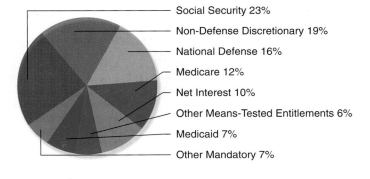

- Social Security 23%
- Non-Defense Discretionary 19%
- National Defense 16%
- Medicare 12%
- Net Interest 10%
- Other Means-Tested Entitlements 6%
- Medicaid 7%
- Other Mandatory 7%

Figure 8.8 The Federal Government Dollar—Where It Goes Where is the largest share of the federal dollar spent?

Source: "A Citizen's Guide to the Federal Budget," Washington, D.C., 2002.

Section 4 Assessment

1. Discuss the difference between absolute and relative measures of poverty.
2. Which of the following is *not* one of the major categories of poor people in the United States?
   a. children under age eighteen
   b. able-bodied men who refuse to work
   c. elderly people
   d. people with disabilities
   e. females who are single heads of households
3. How did the economic downturn of the early 2000s affect the jobs typically filled by former welfare recipients?

Critical Thinking

4. **Understanding Cause and Effect** Describe the feminization of poverty. How does this trend affect the motivation to have children?

TECH TRENDS

Street-Smart Technology

During the last century, when mass production changed the way goods were produced, a favorite adage of businesspeople was "Time is money." In today's service economy (where most people are not producing a tangible product), information is money. Children from disadvantaged families have far less access (both at school and at home) to information technology, such as computers and the Internet, than children in wealthier families. This puts them at a disadvantage in competition for grades and in the job market.

Because of this situation, educators are designing special school-based programs to provide computers in low-income schools and to train teachers in those schools to use them. Harlem-based "Playing 2 Win" is one of these programs. This computer center offers classes and workshops to both children and adults six days a week. It also provides assistance to other community groups that want to set up their own computer centers.

Another successful program is "Street-Level Youth Media" in Chicago's inner city. Street-Level's mission is to educate disadvantaged young people about new technologies. Street-Level began by asking inner-city youths to make videos about their everyday lives on the streets of Chicago. These videos helped residents to see the youths as real human beings trapped in desperate, life-threatening situations. Street-Level continues to work with youths who have been rejected by mainstream society, helping them find solutions to their problems, strengthen their communities, and achieve economic success. The program's staff members are both artists and mentors who provide Chicago's young people with formal training in the media arts (Street-Level, 2005).

Analyzing the Trends

Do you think the rise of computer technology is affecting the social stratification structure in America? Do you think these computer-training programs can seriously affect the cultural values and subsequent economic behavior of those who participate in them? Why or why not?

Computer training is the gateway to success in the information-based economy. Students in these classrooms will have an advantage in the job market because of their computer-based skills.

Social Mobility

Section Preview

Social mobility, the movement of individuals or groups within the stratification structure, is usually measured by changes in occupational status. Sociologists are most interested in upward or downward (vertical) mobility. Closed-class systems permit little vertical mobility; open-class systems, such as those in industrialized countries, allow considerable vertical mobility.

Types of Social Mobility

Mobility is the ability to move; **social mobility** is the movement of people between social classes.

What are the types of social mobility? Social mobility can be horizontal or vertical. **Horizontal mobility** involves changing from one occupation to another at the same social class level, as when an Army captain becomes a public school teacher, a minister becomes a psychologist, or a restaurant server becomes a taxi driver. Because horizontal mobility involves no real change in occupational status or social class, sociologists are not generally interested in investigating it. Vertical mobility, however, is another story.

With **vertical mobility,** a person's occupational status or social class moves upward or downward. When the change takes place over a generation, it is called **intergenerational mobility.** If a plumber's daughter becomes a physician, upward intergenerational mobility has occurred. If a lawyer's son becomes a carpenter, downward intergenerational mobility has occurred.

Key Terms

- **social mobility** (p. 265)
- **horizontal mobility** (p. 265)
- **vertical mobility** (p. 265)
- **intergenerational mobility** (p. 265)
- **caste (closed-class system)** (p. 266)
- **open-class system** (p. 267)

- **social mobility**
  the movement of individuals or groups between social classes

- **horizontal mobility**
  a change in occupation within the same social class

- **vertical mobility**
  a change upward or downward in occupational status or social class

- **intergenerational mobility**
  a change in status or class from one generation to the next

Night school is a popular way for adults to improve skills needed for upward social mobility.

These Indian women learning about computers belong to one of the upper castes, as indicated by their clothes and body ornamentation.

Caste and Open-Class Systems

The extent of vertical mobility varies from society to society. Some societies have considerable mobility; others have little or none. This is the major difference between *caste* (or closed-class) *systems* and *open-class systems*.

What is a caste system? In a **caste system**, there is no social mobility because social status is inherited and cannot be changed. In a caste system, statuses (including occupations) are ascribed or assigned at birth. Individuals cannot change their statuses through any efforts of their own. By reason of religious, biological, superstitious, or legal justification, those in one caste are allowed to marry only within their own caste and must limit relationships of all types with those below and above them in the stratification structure. Apartheid, as practiced in South Africa before the election of Nelson Mandela, was a caste system based on race.

The caste system in India is one based on occupation and the Hindu religion. It is as complex as it is rigid. In it are four primary caste categories, ranked according to their degree of religious purity. The Brahmin, the top caste, is composed of priests and scholars. Next comes the Kshatriyas, including professional, governing, and military occupations. Merchants and businessmen form the third caste, called the Vaisyas. Finally, there is the Sudra caste, containing farmers, menial workers, and craftsmen. Actually, there is a fifth category called the "untouchables." This group of Indians are thought to be so impure that any physical contact contaminates the religious purity of all other caste members. They are given the dirty, degrading tasks, such as collecting trash and handling dead bodies.

How is the caste system kept intact? People in urban India have become less rigid in their caste system than those in rural areas, but the system still plays a major role in daily life. Where traditional rules exist, these rules prevent movement into a higher caste. Members of different castes are not permitted to eat together, and higher-caste people will hardly accept

caste system
a stratification structure that does not allow for social mobility

anything to eat or drink from lower-caste persons. Untouchables, who must live apart from everyone else, cannot even drink water from the wells used by higher castes. Although the long-standing legal prohibition against dating or marrying someone in a higher caste no longer exists, such crossings are still extremely rare. Most important, the caste system is maintained as a result of the power, wealth, and prestige of the higher castes.

What is an open-class system? In an **open-class system,** an individual's social class is based on merit and individual effort. Individuals move up and down the stratification structure as their abilities, education, and resources permit. Most people in the United States believe they live in an open-class system. In reality, the opportunity for upward mobility is sometimes denied individuals or groups in America today. For example, because of race or ethnicity, some members of minority groups have been denied opportunities for social mobility. Therefore, because it imposes some limitations on upward mobility, U.S. society cannot be considered truly and completely open. It is, however, a relatively open-class system.

● **open-class system**
a system in which social class is based on merit and individual effort; movement is allowed between classes

Upward and Downward Mobility

Few places in the world provide the opportunities for advancement that are available in the United States. Nevertheless, countless Americans fail to be upwardly mobile, despite their talents and dedication to work. This is hard for many people to accept because American tradition—both historical and fictional—is filled with examples of upward mobility. Earlier generations have been raised on the "rags to riches" Horatio Alger stories. In these books, a young, down-on-his-luck boy "makes good" through honesty, pluck, and diligence. The lesson to be learned is that the only thing standing between any American citizen and success is talent, a willingness to work, and perseverance. Teachers point to political leaders such as Abraham Lincoln and to early business leaders such as Cornelius Vanderbilt, John D. Rockefeller, and Henry Ford to support the idea of unlimited mobility in American society. These men, in reality, are exceptions to the rule. While considerable upward mobility has occurred, great leaps in social-class level are rare (Gilbert, 2003). Upward mobility typically involves only a small improvement over the social class situation of one's parents.

Is upward mobility increasing? After World War II, an explosion in the availability of high-paying manufacturing jobs made it relatively easy for people to move upward. Americans came to expect that their children would have more than they had, but this may not be the case for future generations. This change is the result of new technology and the globalization of business. With computer-driven production, improved means of communication, and better transportation, it is possible for U.S. companies seeking to lower their costs to move their manufacturing operations overseas. And they are doing so often. As a result, high-paying U.S. manufacturing jobs are being transferred to lower-paid foreign workers. U.S. workers, then, who lack the education needed to perform the more technologically sophisticated jobs are being forced to take lower-paying jobs.

Why is Microsoft founder Bill Gates the exception to the rule in terms of social mobility?

The costs of downward mobility are already etched on this corporate executive's face.

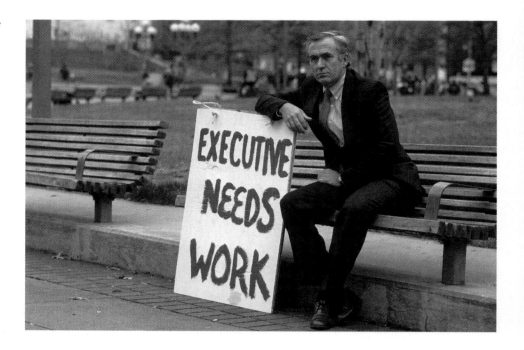

Compared to their parents, more U.S. workers are experiencing downward mobility (Newman, 1999).

What are the social and psychological costs of downward mobility? In *Falling from Grace*, sociologist Katherine Newman (1999) describes America's enduring belief in the rewards of hard work. This belief, she fears, prevents recognition of a major problem: downward mobility for many middle-class people. And, she argues, the consequences are enormous for people in a society that measures self-worth by occupational status. Downwardly mobile people experience lowered self-esteem, despair, depression, feelings of powerlessness, and a loss of a sense of honor.

Section 5 Assessment

1. What is social mobility?
2. Match the major types of social mobility with the examples. Use (IM) for intergenerational mobility, (VM) for vertical mobility, and (HM) for horizontal mobility.
   a. a restaurant waiter becomes a taxi driver
   b. an auto worker becomes a manager
   c. the daughter of a hairdresser becomes a college professor
3. How do you think that the cultural values associated with a caste and an openclass system differently affect economic behavior?
4. Why is the United States not a completely open-class system?

Critical Thinking

5. **Analyzing Information** Analyze the social mobility that has occurred in your family for the last two generations (or more, if you prefer). Use sociological concepts in your analysis.

Summary

Section 1: Dimensions of Stratification

Main Idea: Stratification is the division of society into classes that have unequal amounts of wealth, power, and prestige.

Section 2: Explanations of Stratification

Main Idea: Each of the three perspectives—functionalism, conflict theory, and symbolic interactionism—explains stratification in society.

Section 3: Social Classes in America

Main Idea: In the United States, sociologists see five classes: the upper class, the middle class, the working class, the working poor, and an underclass.

Section 4: Poverty in America

Main Idea: Poverty can be measured in absolute or relative terms.

Section 5: Social Mobility

Main Idea: Social mobility, the movement of individuals or groups within the stratification structure, is usually measured by changes in occupational status. Sociologists are most interested in upward or downward (vertical) mobility.

Sociology Online

Self-Check Quiz
Visit the *Sociology and You* Web site at glencoe.com and click on **Chapter 8—Self-Check Quizzes** to prepare for the chapter test.

Reviewing Vocabulary

Complete each sentence using each term once.

a. social stratification
b. feminization of poverty
c. social class
d. social mobility
e. bourgeoisie
f. vertical mobility
g. proletariat
h. intergenerational mobility
i. wealth
j. horizontal mobility
k. income
l. open-class system
m. prestige
n. absolute poverty
o. relative poverty
p. caste system

1. A class system with no social mobility is called _____ .

2. _____ is movement among social classes based on merit and individual effort.

3. _____ is upward or downward mobility based on occupational status.

4. Changing from one occupation to another at the same general status is called _____ .

5. _____ is the movement of individuals or groups within social classes.

6. The trend for more women and children to live in poverty is called _____ .

7. The recognition, respect, and admiration attached to social positions are known as ____ .

8. _____ is the amount of money received by an individual or group.

9. The economic resources possessed by an individual or group is called _____ .

10. _____ is the name given to those who are ruled; the worker class.

11. _____ is the name given to rulers; or those who own the means of production.

12. The measure defining poverty by reference to others' economic positions is called _____ .

13. The creation of layers, or strata, of people who possess unequal shares of scarce resources is called _____ .

14. _____ is the absence of enough money to secure life's necessities.

15. A segment of the population whose members hold similar amounts of resources and share values, norms, and an identifiable lifestyle is called _____ .

16. The mobility that occurs from one generation to the next is known as _____ .

Reviewing the Facts

17. Examine the graph in Figure 8.7 on page 260 of your text. The graph illustrates that just under 46 percent of all poor people in the United States are white, while only 12% of the population is poor. What can you conclude from the graph about the representation of white people in terms of the total population of poor people?

18. According to Figure 8.8 on page 263, where does the federal government spend the largest share of the federal budget?

19. Describe false consciousness.

20. Explain how a sociologist determines relative poverty.

21. Bill Gates has an estimated net worth of $51 billion. How would sociologists label Gates in terms of social class?

Thinking Critically

22. Analyzing Information

As suggested by the photo on page 241, Americans develop certain attitudes about the existence of poverty in our society and how important it is for government to alleviate it. Why do Americans seem to complain less about military expenditures than those for poverty programs?

"Let's see if you qualify for a handout. How many nuts do you have currently, and where are they buried?"

www.cartoonstock.com

23. Interpreting Visuals

In the image above, the cartoonist is making a statement about attitudes to poverty. What is the cartoonist suggesting about government programs for the poor? Is the cartoonist negative or positive toward poverty programs?

24. Analyzing Information

Herbert Gans, a noted sociologist, has written about the functions of poverty. He says that poverty serves many useful purposes in society. For example, the poor act as dishwashers, maids, and parking attendants. What are some other ways in which poverty might benefit society? What are some conflicts that poverty causes?

25. Summarizing Information

Can you describe the cultural values underlying the federal government's philosophy in the War on Poverty in the 1960s?

26. Making Inferences

The sinking of the luxury liner *Titanic* offers some insights into social class. Among first-class passengers, only 3 percent of the women died, and none of the children died. Among third-class passengers, 45 percent of the women died, and 70 percent of the children died. In all, 76 percent of the third-class passengers died, compared with 40 percent of the first-class passengers. What implications would you draw from these numbers? Is it important to know that the third-class passengers were restricted to the lower decks and thus farther away from the lifeboats?

Sociology Projects

27. Understanding Disadvantaged Groups

In the table below, data about expenditures of American households are presented. By studying the table, you can draw certain inferences about the income level and budgets of different groups. Based on this table, what research questions would you create to further study income and expenditure differences in American society?

Average Annual Household Expenditures by Race/Ethnicity, 2003 (in dollars)			
	All	**Black**	**Hispanic**
Food	5,340	4,007	5,717
Housing	13,432	10,622	12,300
Apparel and Services	1,640	1,601	1,756
Transportation	7,781	5,074	6,780
Healthcare	2,416	1,309	1,439
Education	783	442	477
Personal insurance and Pension	2,532	996	680

Source: U.S. Bureau of Labor Statistics

28. Perception and Reality

One of the themes of sociology is the difference between perception and reality. Write down five perceptions that you have heard people say about others based on their social class. Next to each, describe the reality based on information in this text or additional research. If not sure, write "unknown–needs further research." For example, a common perception of wealthy people is that they consider themselves superior to other people (snobbery). The reality is that no one has ever found a correlation between how much money you have and how nice you are.

Technology Activity

29. The National Center for Children in Poverty measures poverty rates for children in the United States. Visit its Web site at www.nccp.org

  a. From the home page, click on the Economic Security link, then on "Child Poverty in 21st Century America." When you go there, select "Who Are America's Poor Children."

  b. What is meant by the term *extreme child poverty?* What is the extreme poverty level for a family of four?

  c. Now examine the map entitled "Child poverty rates across the states, 2004." How does your state compare to the other states in the nation? How does your state compare to neighboring states?

  d. In which region of the United States are the highest rates of extreme child poverty concentrated?

  e. Now examine the bar graph entitled "Child poverty nationwide, by race, 2004." What groups are included in the bar graph? Which group of children had the highest poverty rate in 2004? Which group of children had the lowest poverty rate in 2004?

The Lives of Homeless Women
by Elliot Liebow

- **unremitting**
  constant; never ending

- **insurmountable hurdles**
  obstacles or barriers that
  cannot be overcome

- **catastrophic proportions**
  a size approaching disaster;
  too large to deal with
  individually

- **subsistence**
  meeting basic needs

On the street or in a shelter, homelessness is hard living. . . . How do they manage to slog through day after day, with no end in sight? How, in a world of **unremitting** grimness, do they manage to laugh, love, enjoy friends, even dance and play the fool? . . .

Simple physical survival is within the grasp of almost everyone willing and able to reach out for it. As the women thrash about, awash in a sea of need, emergency shelters, along with public assistance in the form of cash, food stamps, and medical assistance, make it just possible for many of the women to keep their heads above water. Through the use of shelters, soup kitchens, and hospital emergency rooms, it is even possible for most homeless people who do not get public assistance to survive at some minimal level without benefit of a structured assistance program.

At their very best, however, these bare-boned elements of a life-support system merely make life possible, not necessarily tolerable or livable. Serious problems remain. Homelessness can transform what for others are little things into **insurmountable hurdles.** Indeed, homelessness in general puts a premium on "little things." Just as some homeless women seem to have learned (more than most of us, perhaps) to value a small gesture of friendship, a nice day, a bus token, or a little courtesy that others might take for granted or not notice at all, so too can events or circumstances that would be trivial irritants to others approach **catastrophic proportions** for the homeless person.

For homeless women on the street, the struggle for **subsistence** begins at the animal level—for food, water, shelter, security, and safe sleep. In contrast, homeless women in shelters usually have these things; their struggle begins at the level of human rather than animal needs—protection of one's property, health care, and avoidance of boredom. The struggle then moves rapidly to the search for companionship, modest measures of independence, dignity, and self-respect, and some hope and faith in the future. . . .

For some of the women, day-by-day hardships begin with the problem of getting enough sleep. A few women complained they could never get any sleep in a shelter. Grace was one of them. "There's no getting sleep in a shelter," she said. "Only rest. . . ."

There was indeed much night noise and movement. There was snoring, coughing, sneezing, wheezing, retching, ... Grace was complaining about noise, and she found a partial remedy in ear plugs. But Kathleen [was] . . . kept awake not by noise but by questions: Is this for me? How did I end up here? How will I get out? . . .

Having to get up at 5:30 a.m. and be out of the shelter by 7:00 was a major hardship of shelter life. It was not simply the fact of having to get up and out, but rather that the women had to do this every day of the week, every day of the year (Thanksgiving and Christmas Day excepted), no matter

perennial
regularly repeated; enduring and persistent

what the weather or how they felt. On any given morning, as the women drifted onto the street, one might see two or three ailing women . . . pick up their bags and walk silently into the weather. . . .

Along with perennial fatigue, boredom was one of the great trials of homelessness. Killing time was not a major problem for everyone but it was high on most women's lists of hardships. Betty could have been speaking for most of them when she talked about the problem. On a social visit to the state psychiatric hospital where, four years earlier, she had been an inpatient in an alcoholic program, Betty sought out a nurse named Lou. They embraced and Lou asked Betty what she was doing these days. Betty said she was living in a shelter. Lou said that was a shame, and asked Betty how she spent her time.

"I walk the streets," said Betty. "Twelve hours and 15 minutes a day, every day, I walk the streets. Is that what I got sober for? To walk the streets?" Betty went on to say that she sits on a lot of park benches looking for someone to talk to. Many times there is no one, so she talks to the birds. She and the birds have done a lot of talking in her day, she said. . . .

. . . It is all too easy to think of homeless people as having few or no possessions . . . , but one of the major and most talked-about problems was storage—how to keep one's clothing, essential documents, and other belongings secure and accessible . . . . Stealing was believed to be common: "You've got to expect these things in shelters" was heard from staff and women alike. The end result was that many homeless women who would have left their belongings behind had they had a safe place to store them were forced to take most of their belongings with them. Some wore them in layers. Others carried them. They had become, in short, bag ladies.

During a discussion of Luther Place, one of the best-run shelters in downtown Washington, one of the women said Luther Place was OK but she didn't like the women there—they were all bag ladies. One of the other women objected that the women at Luther Place were no different from women in other shelters. They were bag ladies, she said, because Luther Place had no storage space. . . .

Past and future . . . and even one's self were embedded in one's belongings. When Louise could no longer pay for storage and lost her belongings to auction, she was surprised at her own reaction to the loss. Her belongings had been so much a part of her, she said, that now that she's lost them, she's not sure who she is.

Source: Excerpted from Elliot Liebow, *Tell Them Who I Am: The Lives of Homeless Women.* New York: Penguin Books, 1995.

accessible
available; easy to reach

embedded
made a part of; surrounded by

Read and React

1. What are the two major problems for the homeless discussed here?
2. Did this article change any of your ideas about the homeless? Explain.

Inequalities of Race and Ethnicity

Sections

Learning Objectives

After reading this chapter, you will be able to

- describe what sociologists mean by the terms *minority*, *race*, and *ethnicity*.

- discuss patterns of racial and ethnic relations.

- discuss the difference between prejudice and discrimination.

- explain how functionalists, conflict theorists, and symbolic interactionists view racial inequalities.

- compare the condition of American minorities with that of the white majority.

Applying Sociology

"The Four Americas" is a report published by a major think tank, a national newspaper, and a prestigious university (Brodie, 1995). These organizations used an extensive national survey to investigate race in the United States. The survey asked people to respond to such questions as "Do you think the average African American is better off, worse off, or as well off as the average white person in terms of jobs, education, housing, and health care?"

Most Asians and Latinos answered that African Americans are doing less well than whites. But most whites thought blacks were doing about equally well.

The evidence shows that the average income of African American households is considerably less than that of white households. Moreover, at each level of education, African American males earn less than white males. The report concluded that "whites stand alone in their misperceptions of the problems facing minorities in America today."

Whites, of course, are not the only group who would benefit from a better understanding of these issues. This chapter will take a close look at how race and ethnicity have affected the ability of people to achieve the American dream.

Chapter Overview
Visit the *Sociology and You* Web site at glencoe.com and click on **Chapter 9—Chapter Overviews** to preview chapter information.

Minority, Race, and Ethnicity

Key Terms

● minority *(p. 276)*
● race *(p. 277)*
● ethnic
    minority *(p. 278)*

Section Preview

Sociologists have specific definitions particular to their field of study for *minority, race,* and *ethnicity*. Ethnic minorities have historically been subjected to prejudice and discrimination.

Minorities

Imagine that one evening, you and eight friends are unable to decide whether to go bowling or to the movies. Being a democratic group, you decide to put the question to a vote. If only three of you vote for the show, the movie fans—being fewer in number—will make up a minority.

But numbers alone are not the basis of the sociological definition of minority. Women in the United States outnumber males, and yet they are still referred to as a minority. Blacks in South Africa and in many large cities in the United States are minority populations even though they outnumber the white population. For sociologists, then, a minority population is defined by something more than size or number.

What are the characteristics of a minority? In 1945, sociologist Louis Wirth offered the following definition of **minority:**

We may define a minority as a group of people who, because of their physical or cultural characteristics, are singled out from the others in the society in which they live for differential and unequal treatment, and who therefore regard themselves as objects of collective discrimination. The existence of a minority in a society implies the existence of a corresponding dominant group with higher social status and greater privileges. Minority carries with it the exclusion from full participation in the life of the society.

A minority, then, has several key features.

1. *A minority has distinctive physical or cultural characteristics that can be used to separate it from the majority.* Physical characteristics may include such things as skin color, facial features, and disabilities. Cultural characteristics may include accent, religion, language, and parentage. In the past, some people have been forced to carry papers or wear badges that marked them as members of a minority. For example, during the Nazi regime, Jews in German-occupied countries were forced to wear yellow stars to separate them from non-Jewish citizens.

2. *The minority is dominated by the majority.* Because the majority is the dominating group, it holds an unequal share of the desired goods, services, and privileges. Further, minority members have fewer opportunities to get these goods and services. The best jobs are hard for minorities to get because of a lack of education or unfair hiring practices.

● **minority**
a group of people with physical or cultural traits different from those of the dominant group in the society

Which of these teens are members of a minority group? Explain why.

3. *Minority traits are often believed by the dominant majority to be inferior.* This presumed inferiority can be used to justify unequal treatment. For example, a majority may justify job discrimination by depicting a minority as shiftless or lazy.

4. *Members of the minority have a common sense of identity, with strong group loyalty.* Efforts to keep the minority isolated create empathy among those suffering discrimination. Within the minority, there is a "consciousness of kind." Because of this sense of common identity, members of the minority accept a "we" and "they" vocabulary.

5. *The majority determines who belongs to the minority through ascribed status.* People become members of the minority at birth. Thus, membership is an ascribed status and is not easily changed. This is especially true when physical characteristics such as *race* are involved.

How many races are represented in this photo? On what basis did you make that determination?

Defining Race

Members of a **race** share certain biologically inherited physical characteristics that are considered equally important within a society. Biologists use characteristics such as skin color, hair color, hair texture, facial features, head form, eye color, and height to determine race. Traditionally scholars maintained there were three races—Negroid, Mongoloid, and Caucasoid—but today there is a much more complex understanding of race.

Is there a scientific basis for race? Although certain physical features have been associated with particular races, scientists have known for a long time that there is no such thing as a "pure" race. Features typical of one race often show up in other races. For example, some people born into African American families are assumed to be white because of their facial features and light skin color. Most scientists consider racial classifications arbitrary and misleading. For sociologists, social attitudes and characteristics that relate to race are more important than physical differences.

But aren't some physical characteristics superior? It has sometimes been argued that certain physical characteristics often associated with race are superior and others are inferior. In fact, physical characteristics are superior only in the sense that they provide advantages for living in particular environments. For example, a narrow opening between eyelids protects against bright light and driving cold such as found in Siberia or Alaska. A darker skin is better able to withstand a hot sun. But these physical differences are controlled by a very few genes. In fact, geneticists claim that there may be more genetic difference between a tall person and a short person than between two people of different races who are the same height. Only about six genes in the human cell control skin color, while a person's height is affected by dozens of genes. Thus a six-foot white male may be closer genetically to a black male of the same height than to a five-foot white male. What is important to remember is that there is no scientific evidence that connects any racial characteristic with innate superiority or inferiority (Hurley, 1998). There is, for example, no evidence of *innate* differences in athleticism or intelligence among the various races.

● **race**
people sharing certain inherited physical characteristics that are considered important within a society

Ethnicity

The term *ethnicity* comes from the Greek word *ethnos*, originally meaning "people" or "nation." Thus, the Greek word referred to cultural and national identity. Today, an **ethnic minority** is socially identified by unique characteristics related to culture or nationality. Just as physical characteristics define racial minorities, cultural differences define ethnic minorities.

- **ethnic minority**
  group identified by cultural, religious, or national characteristics

An ethnic minority is a subculture defined by its own language, religion, values, beliefs, norms, and customs. (See page 98 in Chapter 3 for an introduction to subcultures.) Like any subculture, it is part of the larger culture—its members work in the majority, or host, economy, send their children through the host educational system, and are subject to the laws of the land. Ethnic minorities are also separate from the larger culture. The separation may continue because the ethnic minority wishes to maintain its cultural and national origins or because the majority erects barriers that prevent the ethnic group from blending in with the larger culture. For example, Michael Novak (1996) makes a case that members of white ethnic minorities from southern and eastern Europe—Poles, Slavs, Italians, Greeks—have not been able to blend completely into American society. Compared with other white European immigrant groups, such as German immigrants, groups from southern and eastern Europe were more culturally different from the white Anglo-Saxon Protestant (WASP) majority and thus mixed less easily with the majority culture.

Why are ethnic minorities seen as inferior? Negative attitudes toward ethnic minorities exist in part because of *ethnocentrism*. As you read in Chapter 3, ethnocentrism involves judging others in terms of one's own cultural standards. Ethnocentrism creates the feeling of "us," the group one belongs to, versus "them," the other groups that are out there.

People in the majority, out of loyalty to and preference for their own values, beliefs, and norms, may consider other views to be inferior. Because members of ethnic minorities do not measure up to the majority's conception of appropriate ways of behaving, it may be assumed that something is wrong with them. Ethnocentric judgments are often expressed as prejudice and discrimination. Figure 9.1 shows American attitudes toward specific immigrant groups. In general, European immigrants are viewed more positively than non-European immigrants.

Figure 9.1
Attitudes of Americans Toward Immigrant Minorities
The results of a Gallup poll are displayed in this graph of attitudes toward various immigrant groups in the United States. What pattern is reflected in this graph among the groups that are most favored as helping the country?

Another Place

The Travelling People

The following excerpt describes the Irish "Travelling People," who are viewed by mainstream Irish as inferior.

They are Ireland's unrecognized minority—homeless and ostracized. Despite public disapproval, their family groups wander the Irish countryside. Other than a limited number of official halting sites they have no place to stop. Most live by the side of the road. They bathe, eat, and sleep in public. They live without electricity or permanent running water, bathing facilities, or toilets. Their child-mortality rate is similar to those in Third World countries, and there is a 98 percent illiteracy rate among adults. According to the Economic and Social Research Institute's 1985 report, "The circumstances of the Irish Travelling People are intolerable. No humane and decent society once made aware of such circumstances could permit them to persist."

But although local political groups and organizations have expressed the need to create permanent housing for the Travellers (most commonly described as "gypsies" or "tinkers"), the settled community prefers what Traveller Nell McDonaugh calls an "unspoken segregation." Travellers are evicted from areas not designated as official halting sites, and grassy lanes that Traveller groups have frequented for years are blocked and barred. Most official halting sites are located in undesirable, often industrial, areas.

Most settled people want nothing to do with Travellers. Popular belief has it that Travellers draw the dole [welfare] in more than one county at a time, are troublemakers, and leave piles of garbage in their wake. Many local people are opposed to having halting sites in their vicinity. Why should "respectable" people support itinerants?

But these "homeless" outcasts have filled a social niche in Ireland for centuries. Theirs may be a distinct lifestyle, and their traditions are unlike those of other Irish, but they are, nonetheless, Irish. In a traditionally rural society, Travellers served acceptable social purposes as itinerant farm workers, metal craftsmen, lace makers, and storytellers. But in today's settled urban society, this integrated group of nomads are a people displaced by and at odds with contemporary expectations. They are a community without a place in its own homeland and a cultural group in danger of losing its identity.

Source: Excerpted and reprinted with permission from *The World & I*, Amy Seidman, June 1993, *The Washington Times Corporation*, © 1993, pp. 250, 252.

Thinking It Over

Use either functionalism or conflict theory to explain this attitude toward the Travellers.

Section 1 Assessment

1. Summarize the five main characteristics of a minority.
2. What is the difference between race and ethnicity? Between race and nationality?

Critical Thinking

3. **Summarizing Information**
   Identify the main racial or ethnic minorities in your area. Are you a member of any minority groups? What are they?

2

Racial and Ethnic Relations

Key Terms

- assimilation *(p. 280)*
- cultural pluralism *(p. 281)*
- genocide *(p. 281)*
- subjugation *(p. 282)*
- de jure segregation *(p. 282)*
- de facto segregation *(p. 282)*

- **assimilation**
  the blending or fusing of minority groups into the dominant society

Section Preview

Patterns of racial and ethnic relations take two forms: assimilation and conflict. Patterns of assimilation include Anglo-conformity, melting pot, cultural pluralism, and accommodation. Conflict patterns include genocide, population transfer, and subjugation.

Patterns of Assimilation

Generally, minority groups are either accepted—which leads to *assimilation*—or rejected—which leads to *conflict*. Within these two broad approaches, however, is a wide range of outcomes.

Assimilation refers to the blending or fusing of minority groups into the dominant society. When a racial or ethnic minority is integrated into a society, its members are given full participation in all aspects of the society. Assimilation has taken several forms in the United States: *Anglo-conformity, melting pot, cultural pluralism, and accommodation.*

Anglo-conformity has been the most common form of assimilation in U.S. society.

What is the most common pattern of assimilation? Anglo-conformity has been the most prevalent pattern of assimilation in America. *Anglo* is a prefix used to indicate an American of English descent. In Anglo-conformity, traditional American institutions are maintained. Immigrants are accepted as long as they conform to the "accepted standards" of the society. Anglo-conformity is the least egalitarian pattern of assimilation because the immigrant minority is required to conform. By implication, it must either give up or suppress its own values.

Is America more like a melting pot or a tossed salad? A second pattern of assimilation is the *melting pot,* in which all ethnic and racial minorities

voluntarily blend together. Older history textbooks, in describing the immigrant experience in the United States, often referred to a melting pot of cultures. However, there is some question about how much fusing of cultures has really taken place. Instead of a melting pot, many sociologists are now using the idea of a "tossed salad," in which traditions and cultures exist side by side. The cultures of the Tejanos in Texas and the Creoles of New Orleans are examples. This pattern of assimilation is called **cultural pluralism.** It recognizes immigrants' desire to maintain at least a remnant of their "old" ways. In so doing, however, the immigrants have an impact on institutions in the United States. Because of the large numbers of Latino immigrants, for example, many states have instituted bilingual education programs in public schools. The government now routinely makes official forms available in both English and Spanish, many churches throughout the country conduct services in both languages, and cable television stations offer English and Spanish audio tracks.

Accommodation is an extreme form of cultural pluralism. It occurs when a minority maintains its own culturally unique way of life. The minority learns to deal with, or accommodate, the dominant culture when necessary but remains independent in language and culture. The Cubans in Miami and the Amish in Pennsylvania are examples of distinct groups within larger communities that have kept separate identities.

● **cultural pluralism**
desire of a group to maintain some sense of identity separate from the dominant group

Patterns of Conflict

In looking for broad patterns of conflict, sociologists examine historical records and analyze current events. Three basic patterns have emerged that describe approaches that dominant cultures take in their rejection of minority groups. These are *genocide, population transfer,* and *subjugation* (Mason, 1970).

What is the most extreme pattern of conflict? At the extreme, conflict takes the form of **genocide,** the systematic effort to destroy an entire population. One of the best-known examples is the Holocaust, Adolf Hitler's attempt to destroy all European Jews during the 1930s and 1940s. (See Figure 9.2 below.) Less well known is the "Rape of Nanking," begun in 1937, during which the Japanese massacred an estimated 260,000 to 350,000 Chinese men, women, and children (Chang, 1998).

● **genocide**
the systematic effort to destroy an entire population

Jewish Population in 1992 as a Percentage of Jewish Population in 1930

- 100% or more
- 75% to 99%
- 50% to 74%
- 25% to 49%
- 15% to 24%
- 10% to 14%
- 1% to 9%
- Less than 1%

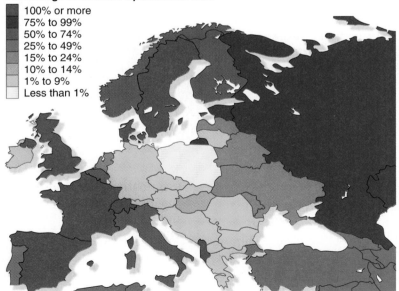

Figure 9.2 Impact of the Holocaust
One of the worst examples of genocide was the Nazis' attempt, in the 1930s and 1940s, to exterminate the European Jewish population. This map shows the decline in Jewish population in European countries as a result of the Holocaust.

Tragically, genocide campaigns are more common in world history than might be supposed. Recently, the Serbians have been accused of conducting campaigns of "ethnic cleansing" against the Muslims in Bosnia and Kosovo. In 1994, the Tutsi tribe of Rwanda slaughtered 500,000 to 800,000 of the minority Hutu tribe.

What is population transfer? In *population transfer,* a minority is forced either to move to a remote location or to leave entirely the territory controlled by the majority. This was the policy most often used against Native Americans. For example, in 1838, sixteen thousand Cherokee from the southeastern United States were set on a forced march along the "Trail of Tears" to Oklahoma reservations, where they became dependent on the U.S. government. An estimated four thousand Cherokee (nearly a fourth of the tribes) died because of harsh conditions along the Trail of Tears.

The Cherokee were not the only Native American population transferred from their homes. The Creek and the Seminole were also forcibly removed by U.S. troops.

What conflict pattern appears most often? Subjugation is the most common pattern of conflict. A subjugated minority is denied equal access to the culture and lifestyle of the larger society. Subjugation may be based on the law, or *de jure.* An example was the **de jure segregation** of public schools in the United States during the latter part of the nineteenth century and the first half of the twentieth century. In *Brown* v. *Board of Education of Topeka* (1954) the Supreme Court overturned previous case law that had made racial segregation legal in the U.S.

Subjugation may also arise from the everyday practices of people, even when specific laws do not exist to deny opportunities to minority groups. *De facto* is a term used in case law that describes the actual, or real, situation regardless of what the law is. **De facto segregation** is operating when, for example, neighboring homeowners agree among themselves not to sell to members of certain ethnic groups or races. De facto discrimination exists when people of certain backgrounds are not promoted to important positions in local government or in businesses because of widely held stereotypes. Although illegal, the difficulty of proving bias can make this type of subjugation a very effective tool for controlling a minority.

- **subjugation**
  process by which a minority group is denied equal access to the benefits of a society

- **de jure segregation**
  denial of equal access based on the law

- **de facto segregation**
  denial of equal access based on everyday practice

Section 2 Assessment

1. Identify and define four patterns of assimilation.
2. What is the difference between de jure and de facto segregation?

Critical Thinking

3. **Evaluating Information** Work with one or more of your classmates to research and evaluate the impact that the assimilation of Latinos is having on American institutions such as public schools, churches, and government agencies.

Sociology Today

Bridging the Digital Divide

In 2000, Delta Airlines and Ford Motor Company both publicly announced their multimillion-dollar (hundreds of millions, in fact) bet they are placing on their employees (Miller and Silverstein, 2000). Each intends to provide home computers and Internet access to all of their 422,000 workers. It is a new company benefit costing each employee as little as $5 per month.

The bet is that employees become more efficient and effective when they are proficient with computers. Expected payoffs for the companies is improved communication with their workforces, heightened employee morale, and increased employee loyalty. Employees at Ford and Delta enthusiastically welcomed the new benefit.

There is a possible downside for employees. When workers can be reached instantaneously at home day or night, the traditional boundaries between the home and the workplace could erode. And Ford and Delta do have plans to communicate with workers at home. According to sociologist Arlie Hochschild, this apparent gift could be a Trojan horse by extending the "long arm of the workplace." Even worse, some workers fear that companies might intrude on their private lives by monitoring their Internet activities. (See the *Tech Trends* feature entitled "The Dark Side of Workplace Technology" in Chapter 5.)

There could also be a social upside to wide-scale on-line access. Sociologists have recognized computer literacy as a key to social mobility in the twenty-first century. Since those nearer the bottom of the social class structure lack the resources necessary to be computer literate, sociologists fear they will be hopelessly left behind.

Given this situation, widespread exposure of less-skilled workers to computer technology could have benefits Ford and Delta employees may not have considered. Since both companies are encouraging workers' families to use the technology, the spouses and children of a significant number of individuals will have access to an indispensable tool for occupational advancement. While Ford and Delta may be concerned only about keeping their employees out of the digital divide, their action may unintentionally enable many more Americans to cross this divide. Company-provided computer technology at home may become a staple in most future corporate benefit packages.

Doing Sociology

1. Do you believe that computer literacy is a key element in today's job market? Tomorrow's?
2. Evaluate your own capabilities regarding computer technology.
3. Go to your library and examine the employment page of the Sunday edition of a major newspaper. Write a brief report on the extent to which computer literacy appears to be an important qualification in today's urban marketplace.

3

Theories of Prejudice and Discrimination

Key Terms

- prejudice *(p. 284)*
- racism *(p. 284)*
- discrimination *(p. 285)*
- hate crime *(p. 285)*
- stereotype *(p. 285)*
- self-fulfilling prophecy *(p. 288)*

- **prejudice**
  widely held negative attitudes toward a group (minority or majority) and its individual members

- **racism**
  an extreme form of prejudice that assumes superiority of one group over others

Section Preview

Prejudice involves attitudes, while discrimination is about behavior. Prejudice often leads to discrimination. Conversely, in some instances, discrimination creates prejudiced attitudes through stereotyping. Each of the three major perspectives looks at different aspects of prejudice.

Prejudice, Racism, and Discrimination

Individuals hold prejudices of many types. To a sociologist, though, **prejudice** has a very particular meaning. It refers to widely held preconceptions of a group (minority or majority) and its individual members. Prejudice involves a generalization based on biased or insufficient information. Prejudiced attitudes are based on strong emotions, so they are often difficult to change, even in the face of overwhelming evidence. It is easier to explain individuals who don't fit the stereotype as exceptions than it is to reexamine a whole set of established beliefs. For example, many people believe that Asian students have a particular "gift" for mathematics. Suppose that Susie is one of these people. In algebra class, she sits next to an Asian student who is not doing well. Will Susie change her idea about the mathematical abilities of Asian people as a result of this? Probably not. It will be less trouble for her to think that this one Asian student is the exception to the rule.

Racism is an extreme form of prejudice, because it not only involves judging people unfairly, but it assumes that a person's own race or ethnic group is superior. Racists believe that discrimination or exclusion is morally justified because of their own natural superiority.

Prejudice can lead to discrimination as simple as hostile looks or as serious as crimes against people and property.

How is discrimination different from prejudice? While prejudice involves holding biased opinions, **discrimination** involves acting upon those opinions by treating people unfairly. Prejudice does not always result in discrimination, but it often does.

Discrimination takes many forms, including avoiding social contact with members of minority groups, denying them positions that carry authority, and blocking their access to the more exclusive neighborhoods. It can also involve such extremes as attacking or killing minority members.

Hate Crimes

In 1998, James Byrd, Jr., an African American from Texas, was chained to a pickup truck, then dragged to death. That same year saw Matthew Shepard, a gay college student, tied to a fence and beaten to death. Both incidents fell under a special kind of crime called *hate crimes*.

These federal agency employees are searching through the ashes of an African American church in Mississippi. What would make this case of arson a hate crime?

How are hate crimes different? A **hate crime** is a criminal act that is motivated by extreme prejudice. Hate crimes involve bias related to race, religion, sexual orientation, ethnicity, or disability (Federal Bureau of Investigation, 2004). Victims include, but are not limited to, African Americans, Latinos, Asian Americans, Jews, gays and lesbians, and people with disabilities. Data on hate crimes were not formally collected until 1990, when Congress passed the Hate Crimes Statistics Act. Since then, these statistics have been a standard part of the FBI's Uniform Crime Report. Hate crimes occur in relatively small numbers, but the frequency is increasing. In 2003, more than 8,700 hate crime offenses were reported to the FBI.

How does sociology interpret hate crimes? Each of the theoretical perspectives discussed below can help us understand hate crimes. The functionalist might notice that members of a group are bolstering their sense of unity against a common enemy. Some hate crimes, consistent with conflict theory, are based on the belief that the victim is somehow threatening the person's livelihood or self-interest. This is the case when immigrants are attacked out of fear that they will take the jobs of the white majority. Finally, hate crimes always involve labeling. People who commit hate crimes have vocabularies filled with demeaning stereotypes that attempt to justify violence directed against the victims.

Stereotypes

A **stereotype** is a set of ideas—based on distortion, exaggeration, and oversimplification—that is applied to all members of a group. Stereotypes appear throughout any society. In the United States, examples of stereotypes include that athletes are "all brawn and no brain" and that politicians are corrupt.

Stereotypes are sometimes created to justify unethical behavior against minority groups. For example, very early relationships between the colonists and Native Americans in early colonial times were relatively peaceful and cooperative. As the population of the colonies grew, however, conflicts

● **discrimination**
treating people differently based on ethnicity, race, religion, or culture

● **hate crime**
a criminal act motivated by prejudice

● **stereotype**
a distorted, exaggerated, or oversimplified image applied to a category of people

Even marching band members suffer from stereotyping.

Student Web Activity
Visit the *Sociology and You* Web site at glencoe.com and click on **Chapter 9—Student Web Activities** for an activity on examples of stereotypes.

over land and resources became more frequent and intense. To justify expansion onto Indian territory, the colonists began perceiving Native Americans as "lying, thieving, un-Christian savages" who did not deserve the rights accorded to white settlers. This image helped the colonists defend their otherwise unjustifiable treatment of the Native American population.

The Functionalist Perspective

In studying prejudice and discrimination, functionalists focus on the dysfunctions caused by these practices. (We will look at this topic in greater detail in Section 4.) When minorities are exploited or oppressed, the social, political, educational, and economic costs to society are extremely high. Furthermore, the safety and stability of the larger society are at risk, because violence periodically erupts between the groups.

Functionalists recognize, however, that by fostering prejudice, a dominant group can create a feeling of superiority over minority groups. This feeling can strengthen its members' own self-concepts. Strangely, then, for the majority culture, functionalists can see a positive aspect to discrimination.

The Conflict Perspective

According to conflict theory, a majority uses prejudice and discrimination as weapons of power to control a minority. The majority does this to increase its control over property, goods, and other resources. The example about stereotypes used by colonists to portray Native Americans is based on the conflict perspective.

In the conflict perspective, despite being common targets, different minorities tend to view one another as competitors rather than as allies in their struggle against the majority (Olzak and Nagel, 1986). Conflict among minorities, particularly African Americans and Latinos, is increasing in the United States as whites leave cities and African Americans assume political power. To many urban blacks, Latinos appear to be benefiting from the civil rights movement waged by African Americans. Many Latinos, on the other hand, believe that African Americans are using their political clout to push an agenda that favors their own community at the expense of others. It remains to be seen if urban African Americans and Latinos will become allies for their mutual welfare or if they will engage in fierce conflict over the scarce resources available to them.

The Symbolic Interactionist Perspective

According to the symbolic interactionist perspective, members of a society learn to be prejudiced in much the same way they learn to be patriotic. Sociologist Gordon Allport (1979) described two stages in the learning of prejudice. In the *pregeneralized learning period,* children may overhear parents make racist or prejudiced statements, but they have not yet learned to separate people by race or ethnic group. By the time children reach the *total rejection stage,* however, they are able to use physical clues to sort people into groups. If children

Hate Groups in the United States

Hate groups are groups that have beliefs or practices that target an entire group of people. Each year, the Southern Poverty Law Center tracks the number of active hate groups operating in the United States. These groups include the Ku Klux Klan, Black Separatists, White Supremacists, and Neo-Nazis. In 2004, there were 762 such groups in the United States.

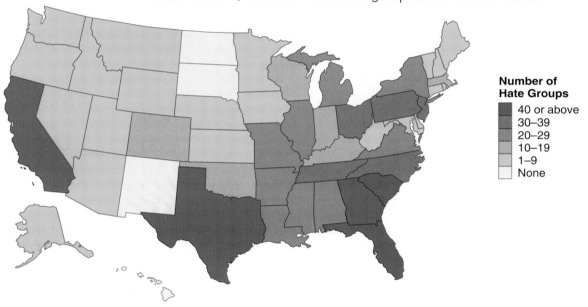

Number of Hate Groups

- 40 or above
- 30–39
- 20–29
- 10–19
- 1–9
- None

Source: Adapted from Southern Poverty Law Center Intelligence Project, "Active U.S. Hate Groups in 2004."

Interpreting the Map

1. Which states had the most hate groups in 2004? Which states had no active hate groups?
2. About how many hate groups are active in your state? Does this number surprise you? Explain.
3. Do you think it is important to track the number of hate groups in the United States? Why or why not?

repeatedly hear parents malign a minority, they will reject all members of the group, on all counts and in all situations.

Symbolic interactionists also point out that language itself can reflect prejudices. For example, in Anglo culture, many terms that include *black* are negative. Such terms as *blackball, blacklist, black mark,* and *black eye* illustrate the negative slant associated with the word *black*.

Figure 9.3 Prejudice and Discrimination

This table illustrates how a particular theoretical perspective views a central sociological concept. Switch the concepts around and illustrate how each theoretical perspective would view a different concept. For example, discuss some functions and dysfunctions of the self-fulfilling prophecy.

Theoretical Perspective	Concept	Example
Functionalism	Ethnocentrism	White colonists used negative stereotypes as a justification for taking Native American land.
Conflict Theory	Competition for power	African Americans accuse Latinos of using their political clout to win advantages for themselves.
Symbolic Interactionism	Self-fulfilling prophecy	Members of a minority fail because of the low expectations they have for their own success.

● **self-fulfilling prophecy**
an expectation that leads to behavior that causes the expectation to become reality

Symbolic interactionism underlies the concept of the **self-fulfilling prophecy**—an expectation that leads to behavior that then causes the expectation to become a reality. For example, if a student is continually encouraged and told that she is capable of succeeding at a task, she will likely act as if she can succeed. If, however, she is discouraged from trying and told she will probably fail, that same student will likely act in a manner that will cause her to fail. Similarly, if members of any minority are continually treated as if they are less intelligent or less competent than the majority, they may eventually accept this limitation. This acceptance, in turn, may lead them to place less emphasis on education as a way of succeeding. Given this negative interaction, and the lack of opportunity to develop their abilities, members of minorities may become locked in low-level jobs.

Section 3 Assessment

1. Can you hold a prejudice about a group without discriminating against that group? Why or why not?
2. Why do you think most stereotypes are negative? Can you think of any positive stereotypes?
3. Why does conflict exist between African Americans and Latinos?

Critical Thinking

4. **Evaluating Information** Discuss specific ways in which African Americans and Latinos have attempted to resolve their role conflicts.

Spinning a Web of Hate

White supremacists, neo-Nazis, and members of other hate groups have discovered the Internet as a channel to spread hatred of Jews, African Americans, and homosexuals, among others (Sandberg, 1999). From one hate site in 1995, the Anti-Defamation League estimates that there are now thousands of Web sites advocating racism, anti-Semitism, and violence. Aryan Nations identify Jews as the natural enemy of whites; White Pride World Wide targets African Americans and Jews; Posse Comitatus defends alleged abortion-clinic bomber Eric Robert Rudolph; World Church of the Creator is violently anti-Christian.

Organized racists use high technology to deliver their message to a mass audience. While members of hate groups used to be recognized by their white hoods or neo-Nazi swastikas, they can now just as easily be wearing business suits instead of brown shirts. The Southern Poverty Law Center is especially concerned about the repackaging of hate-based ideologies to make them appear more respectable to mainstream America. To reach the young, hate Web sites offer such child-friendly attractions as crossword puzzles, jokes, cartoons, coloring books, contests, games, and interactive comic strips.

Not all hate-group activity comes from white supremacists who target African Americans. The Southern Poverty Law Center also tracks the activities of Black Separatists and documents several recent hate crimes committed by blacks against whites. In addition, the continued immigration of Asians and Central and South Americans is drawing the angry attention of hate groups of all types. More information on hate group activities can be found at the Southern Poverty Law Center Web site, www.splcenter.org.

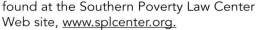

Analyzing the Trends

When the economy is not performing well, membership in hate groups rises, and membership declines when the economy is doing well. Relate this fluctuating membership pattern to scapegoating and conflict theory.

How is propaganda used by hate groups to deliver their message?

Young people today may grow up to be "Internet police officers." A number of software companies now design and market programs that prevent children from accessing Web sites their parents think unsuitable.

4

Minority Groups in the United States

Key Terms

- **institutionalized discrimination** *(p. 290)*
- **hidden unemployment** *(p. 293)*
- **underclass** *(p. 293)*

- **institutionalized discrimination**
  unfair practices that grow out of common behaviors and attitudes and that are a part of the structure of a society

Section Preview

Discrimination in the United States has caused some ethnic and racial groups to lag behind the white majority in jobs, income, and education. Progress is being made, but gains remain fragile. African American, Latino, Asian American, Native American, and white ethnics are the largest minority groups in this country.

Institutionalized Discrimination

Many people believe that discrimination in the United States ended when civil rights legislation was passed in the 1960s. These laws did stop many discriminatory practices. Nevertheless, minorities in this country still suffer from what sociologists call **institutionalized discrimination.** This type of discrimination results from unfair practices that are part of the structure of society and that have grown out of traditional, accepted behaviors.

Seniority systems, in which promotion and pay increase with years of service, for example, can discriminate against minority workers. Because they were shut out of jobs in the past, members of minorities are just now beginning to enter seniority systems. Having fewer years of service than majority members who have been in the system for years, minority members' chances

Institutionalized discrimination has contributed to the deterioration of some inner-city public schools.

for quick promotion are slight, even though the seniority systems may not have been intentionally designed to obstruct their progress.

Another example of institutionalized discrimination exists in public education. Schools with large numbers of minority students are more likely to be located in large urban areas than in wealthier suburbs. This is the case in part because of white flight to the suburbs. As a result, minority children in many states are more concentrated in school districts with a tax base too low to provide resources equal to those in the suburbs. This lack of funding means that teachers in minority schools receive fewer opportunities for training. Textbooks, when students have them, are outdated. Parental and community support is generally not as strong. There is little, if any, money for new technology, and buildings are badly in need of repair.

Institutionalized discrimination in the United States is reflected in the experiences of minorities—African Americans, Latinos, Native Americans, Asian Americans, white ethnics, and Jewish Americans. For each minority, the social and economic costs of discrimination have been enormous.

African Americans

African Americans make up the largest racial minority group in the United States, numbering over 37 million, or about 13 percent of the total population. They are also one of the oldest minorities, first brought to America as indentured servants and slaves in the early 1600s.

What are the barriers to African American assimilation?
There are many reasons for the lack of acceptance of African Americans into the mainstream of U.S. society. Skin color and physical features make it possible to identify at a glance people of African American lineage. This makes it easy for the dominant white ethnic group to create negative stereotypes based on physical characteristics.

A second reason for the continuing minority status of African Americans has its roots in early American history. Brought into the country to labor on plantations, African Americans were immediately assigned to the lowest class status. Even when freed, ex-slaves and their descendants in the United States

Minority group	Number (in thousands) 2000	Number (in thousands) 2003	Percent change 2000–2003
African American (non-Latino)	34,410	35,593	3.7
Latino	35,153	39,338	13.0
Asian (non-Latino)	10,457	11,673	12.7
Native American/Alaska Native (non-Latino)	2,104	2,180	4.0
Native Hawaiian/Other Pacific Islander (non-Latino)	369	391	6.4

Figure 9.4 U.S. Resident Minority Populations, 2000 and 2003
This table shows the percentage increase in the larger minority populations in the United States from 2000 to 2003. Are you surprised by the growth of any group?

Source: U.S. Bureau of the Census, *Statistical Abstract of the United States, 2004–2005.*

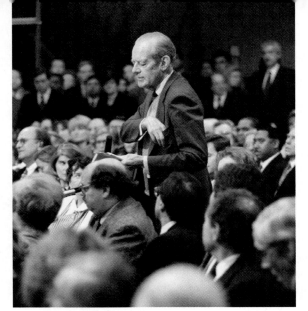

Could institutionalized discrimination help to account for the near absence of African Americans in this corporate merger meeting?

were rarely accepted as equal to free whites. Upward social mobility for freed slaves (or any African Americans) was virtually impossible.

Slavery was legally abolished by the Thirteenth Amendment (1865), but the legacy of prejudice and discrimination that grew out of slavery affects African Americans to this day. Practices and laws that segregated the races became institutionalized, especially in the South, but also throughout the country. Such practices continued until the late 1960s, when they were made illegal by the passage of civil rights legislation and by key Supreme Court decisions. In a very real sense, then, African Americans have experienced barely forty years of constitutional equality. The gap between African Americans and whites in education, income, and employment represents the legacy of centuries of prejudice and discrimination.

What are average income levels for African Americans? As noted in the Applying Sociology feature opening this chapter, average African American income in the United States is far from equal to the average income for whites. Specifically, African American income is approximately 62 percent that of whites. This means that for every $100 an average white family earns, an average African American family earns $62. Figure 9.5 shows differences in household income for various minority groups.

Not surprisingly, African Americans and whites also differ in wealth (home and car, business assets, and the like). The average African American household holds less than 20 percent of the wealth of the average white household (U.S. Bureau of the Census, 2005).

How do African Americans fare in the job market? Part of the reason for the economic differences can be traced to employment patterns. Compared with white men and women, a lower percentage of African American men and women are employed in professional, managerial, technical, and administrative occupations. African Americans are almost twice as likely as whites to work in low-level service jobs (U.S. Department of Labor, 2004).

Figure 9.5 Majority and Minority Median Household Incomes
Explain why sociologists consider Asian Americans a minority group despite their relatively high annual income.

Source: U.S. Bureau of the Census, 2005.

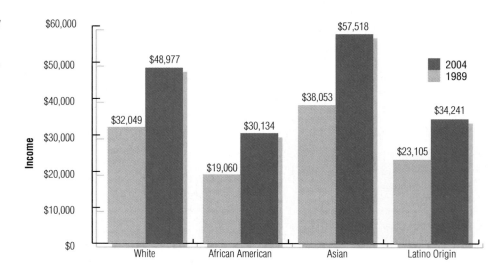

New long-term economic trends threaten to make matters even worse. These trends include a shift from higher-paying manufacturing jobs to lower-paying service jobs and replacement of workers because of the transfer of high-wage jobs to low-wage countries.

Patterns of unemployment also affect the economic status of African Americans. In 2005, for example, the jobless rate among African Americans was slightly more than double that of whites. Moreover, official jobless rates do not in reality account for all unemployed persons. Traditional unemployment rates are based on the number of unemployed people who are actively looking for work. They do not include so-called **hidden unemployment**—discouraged workers who have stopped looking or part-time workers who would prefer to have full-time jobs. When hidden unemployment is considered, the jobless rate for the nation is considerably higher than official numbers indicate. This is particularly true for African Americans (National Jobs for All Coalition, 2005).

● **hidden unemployment**
unemployment that includes people not counted in the traditional unemployment categories

Differences in unemployment rates between white and African American workers exist even for college-educated people. These differences, however, are not as large as for the nation as a whole (Hocker, 2004). The greatest unemployment problem exists among African American teenagers. According to official statistics, nearly 33 percent of African American teenagers were unemployed in 2005, compared to just over 13 percent of white teenagers.

To what degree are African Americans making advances?
Education is the traditional American path to economic gain and occupational prestige. The educational story for African Americans is mixed. As of 2003, 85 percent of whites had finished high school, compared with 80 percent of African Americans. Similarly, whereas nearly 28 percent of whites had completed college, only slightly more than 17 percent of African Americans had done so.

Moreover, higher educational attainment doesn't pay off for African Americans as it does for whites. Although income tends to rise with educational level for all races, it increases much less for African American men (and for women of both races) than for white men. White male high school graduates, on the average, earn nearly as much each year as African American men with college associate degrees. At each level of schooling, black men tend to gain less than their white peers.

While these figures may seem discouraging, real gains have been made. More than 25 percent of African Americans now work in professional and managerial occupations. These occupations include chief executives, lawyers, accountants, computer scientists, and teachers. Also, business ownership by African Americans has been increasing dramatically. Between 1997 and 2002, the number of black-owned businesses rose 45 percent, to 1.2 million. These businesses earned nearly $93 billion. As a result of the recent upward mobility of educated African Americans, some scholars see the emergence of two black Americas—a growing black middle class and a black **underclass** composed of unemployed people whose families have been poor for generations.

United States senator Barack Obama of Illinois has made helping working families a top priority.

● **underclass**
people typically unemployed who come from families that have been poor for generations

African Americans have also increased their political presence. Forty-three African Americans, a record number, now serve in Congress. More than 5,400 African Americans serve as city and county officials, up from 715 in 1970. In total, there are more than 9,000 black elected officials in the United States, a sixfold increase since 1970. The election of African Americans in predominantly white areas is a hopeful sign. African Americans, though still vastly underrepresented, have entered the "power elite" of America:

> Although the power elite is still composed primarily of Christian white men, there are now . . . blacks . . . on the boards of the country's largest corporations; presidential cabinets are far more diverse than was the case forty years ago; and the highest ranks of the military are no longer filled solely by white men (Zweigenhaft and Domhoff, 1999:176).

Latinos

Latino is a term that refers to ethnic minorities from Latin America, a region that includes Mexico, Central America, South America, and the islands of the Caribbean. High birth rates and immigration rates make Latinos (along with Asian Americans) one of the fastest-growing minorities in the United States. In fact, early in the twenty-first century, Latinos overtook African Americans as America's largest minority group (U.S. Bureau of the Census, 2000). By the time you are nearing retirement—about the year 2050—it is predicted that nearly one out of every four Americans will be Latino. (See Figure 9.6.)

What are the largest Latino groups in the United States?

Nearly 67 percent of Latinos today are of Mexican descent. Puerto Ricans make up a little less than 9 percent of the total Latino population. Most Puerto Ricans are concentrated in or near New York City, although the population is beginning to shift to the outlying areas. Cubans make up the third most populous group of Latinos, with nearly 1.4 million people. Most Cuban Americans are located in the Miami, Florida, area (U.S. Bureau of the Census, 2005).

Like Anglos, Native Americans, and African Americans, Latino peoples are diverse. Each group came to the United States under different circumstances

Figure 9.6 The U.S. Population by Race and Ethnicity, 2000 and 2050
The racial and ethnic composition in the U.S. is expected to look very different by 2050. Discuss some social consequences of this changing composition.

Source: U.S. Bureau of the Census, 2004.

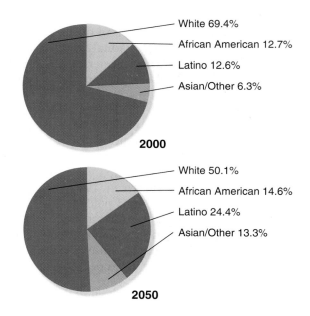

White 69.4%
African American 12.7%
Latino 12.6%
Asian/Other 6.3%

2000

White 50.1%
African American 14.6%
Latino 24.4%
Asian/Other 13.3%

2050

Percentages do not total 100% due to rounding.
Note: The White, African American, and Asian/Other categories exclude Latinos, who may be of any race.

and retains a sense of its own identity and separateness. In addition, there are significant internal differences within individual Latino minorities. For example, the first large group of Cuban immigrants to enter the United States were successful middle- and upper-class people who fled from Cuba when Fidel Castro instituted a communist government there in the late 1950s. These Cuban Americans differ substantially from later Cuban immigrants, who were relatively uneducated members of the lower class.

What is the general level of education among Latinos? Latinos fall behind white Americans in formal education. Just about 57 percent of adult Latinos have completed high school, compared with 85 percent of non-Latinos. Mexican Americans have the lowest levels of educational attainment. Cubans have the highest, owing to the fact that many Cuban immigrants to the United States were middle- and upper-class people, as explained earlier (Stefancic and Delgado, 1998).

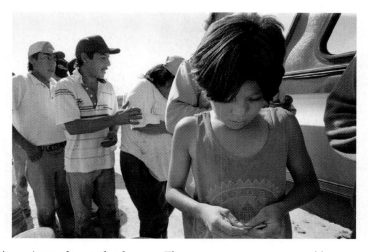

The meager wages earned by migrant farm laborers still keep many Latino children in the fields and out of schools where they could receive an education.

What is the income level for Latinos? Average income for Latinos ($34,241) is higher than that of African Americans but significantly lower than that of non-Latino whites ($48,977). Cubans are the most affluent Latinos, but their median income is only about 75 percent that of whites. The poorest among the large Latino groups are the Puerto Ricans, whose income is only half that of whites. Almost 22 percent of Latino families live below the poverty level, compared with slightly less than 9 percent of white non-Latinos (U.S. Bureau of the Census, 2005).

From the data above, it should come as no surprise that many Latinos work in low-paying and low-status jobs as semiskilled workers and unskilled laborers. Mexican Americans make up the majority of migrant workers in the country. Cuban men belong to the only Latino minority with occupations similar to those of the white Anglo majority (Moore and Pachon, 1985). The numbers of Latino-owned homes and businesses are increasing rapidly, but they still fall far behind the national averages.

How do Latinos stand politically? Politically, Latinos are becoming a force in shaping American politics. As of 2005, a record number of 29 Latinos are serving in the U.S. Congress—27 in the House of Representatives and 2 in the Senate. In total, there are more than 4,400 Latino elected officials in the United States, a 10-percent increase since 1990. Issues of education and immigration, as well as employment, income, and the quality of life, promise to keep Latinos politically active in the years to come.

Native Americans

Today, Native Americans number just over 4 million. More than 500 separate tribes and bands have been identified in the United States. This great diversity is generally unrecognized because of stereotyped images of Native Americans based on dated Hollywood films and paperback adventures of the Old West. In fact, however, tribal groups such as the Navajo and Sioux are as different from one another as Anglo Americans are from Italians or Brazilians.

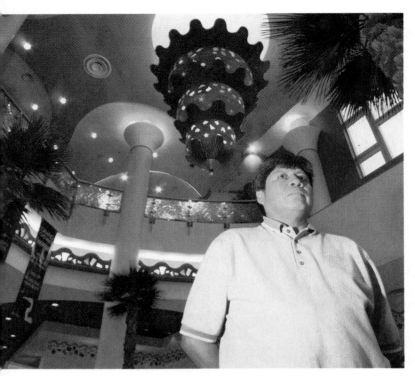

Some Native American tribes are becoming more economically independent through the gaming industry. Not everyone agrees that this will result in long-term gains.

What is the current situation of Native Americans? Native Americans, perhaps more than any other minority, are suffering today from the effects of hundreds of years of discrimination. Abject poverty remains a major fact of life among Native Americans, especially on reservations. Just over 24 percent of the Native American population live below the poverty line. Fewer Native Americans graduate from high school than any other major minority group.

Native Americans have the second-lowest annual income of any minority group in the United States ($33,132). Slightly more than 24 percent of all employed Native American people work in professional, managerial, and related occupations. Another 24 percent hold sales and office positions, and about 13 percent are in blue-collar jobs such as construction and maintenance. In 2005, only one Native American served in Congress, as a member of the U.S. House of Representatives.

How has Native American gaming affected life on reservations? A relatively recent development on Native American reservations is the introduction of casino-type gaming establishments. Native American gaming both on and off reservations has grown unexpectedly into an enormous, rapidly expanding industry. In 2004, for example, approximately 200 tribes were operating 367 gaming facilities in the United States. Gaming revenues for that year exceeded $19 billion. Not surprisingly, many Native Americans have embraced the gaming industry as a source of money. Most tribal governments use the proceeds from gaming to provide services and to promote economic and community development.

A recently completed study by Harvard University evaluated the extent to which gaming has affected the lives of Native Americans living on reservations (Taylor and Kalt, 2005). According to this study, between 1990 and 2000, the growth in median household income for Native American-held areas was six times that of the overall U.S. growth rate. Moreover, during that same time period, unemployment decreased about 5 percent on reservations with gaming and about 2.5 percent on reservations without gaming. While these findings are promising, life on Native American reservations still presents many challenges that need to be met. These challenges include improving the lives of Native Americans in the areas of health care, education, income, and housing.

Asian Americans

Nearly 12 million Asians live in the United States, comprising approximately 4 percent of the total population. Like Latinos, Asians come from many different national and ethnic backgrounds. The largest groups are from China, the Phillipines, Japan, India, Korea, and Vietnam.

If a success story can be told for any minority group in America, those groups are Chinese and Japanese Americans. Even for them, however, the road has not been smooth.

How have Chinese Americans fared over the years?

Attracted at first by the California gold rush, Chinese immigrants arrived in large numbers during the 1850s. They worked as agricultural laborers, on railroad crews, and in low-paying industrial jobs. When hard times hit in the 1870s, unemployed European Americans began to compete for jobs that the Chinese had held. Race riots erupted, and the children of Chinese immigrants were barred from attending schools in San Francisco. Chinese Americans were driven into large urban ghettos known as Chinatowns, where they are still concentrated today. Pressure by congressmen from California led to the Chinese Exclusion Act of 1882, which virtually ended Chinese immigration to the United States for nearly a hundred years.

Although Chinese Americans, in many ways, remain isolated from American life, their situation began to improve after 1940. American-born Chinese college graduates began to enter professional occupations, and Chinese American scholars and scientists began to make publicly recognized contributions to science and the arts. Most Americans today recognize Chinese Americans' willingness to work hard, their dedication to education, and their contributions to American society.

What has been the history of Japanese Americans in the United States?

Early diplomatic relations between the United States and Japan were warm and cordial. But beginning in 1885, large numbers of Japanese men immigrated to the West Coast of the United States. Their arrival coincided with the attempt described above to exclude Chinese immigrants. The Japanese suffered prejudice and discrimination during these early years. Nevertheless, they moved from being laborers in certain industries (railroads, canning, logging, mining, meat packing) to being successful farmers.

When the Japanese began to compete with white farmers, however, anti-Japanese legislation was passed. The California Alien Land Bill of 1913, for example, permitted Japanese to lease farmland for a maximum of three years; it did not allow land they owned to be inherited by their families. In 1924, the U.S. Congress halted all Japanese immigration, and the 126,000 Japanese already in the United States became targets for still more prejudice, discrimination, stereotyping, and scapegoating.

In 1941, Japan attacked the Pearl Harbor naval base in Hawaii, an act that brought the United States into World War II. Wartime hysteria generated a fear of a possible Japanese invasion that led President Franklin Roosevelt to issue Executive Order 9066. This emergency law moved more than 110,000 Japanese people into internment camps away from the West Coast. Historians later agreed that the Japanese Americans had posed no security threat during World War II. (Immigrants from Germany and Italy were not relocated, even though their countries were also at war with the United States.) Eventually, in the 1980s, the U.S. government formally apologized to Japanese American internees and paid them $20,000 each in compensation.

Over 100,000 Japanese residents in America were sent to internment camps during World War II. Many lost homes and businesses as a result.

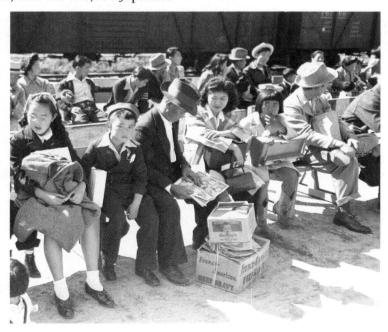

Focus on Research

Survey Research: The Legacy of Racism

According to many scholars, African Americans today suffer more from low economic class than from racism. In a well-known study of the early 1990s, one sociologist, Joe Feagin, challenged this line of argument. Feagin set up a study that looked at African Americans' access to public accommodations, including restaurants, hotels, and motels.

Feagin interviewed middle-class African Americans in several cities. He wished to study African Americans in the middle class because they would have the economic resources needed to take advantage of public accommodations. His research was guided by several questions:

Do middle-class African Americans still experience racism in public accommodations?

If so, how is it manifested?

What means do middle-class African Americans use to handle discrimination?

What are the effects of discrimination on its victims?

Feagin conducted 37 in-depth interviews. Those interviewed were drawn from a larger group of 135 middle-class African Americans in several large cities.

The interviewees were representative of the larger sample based on such characteristics as occupation, age, income, education, sex, and location. The initial participants in the study were identified as middle class by city-based consultants. Names of additional participants were suggested by the first people interviewed. (This is known as "snowball" sampling.) Middle class was defined as "those

Because of decades of racism and discrimination, this obviously successful African American couple may still have trouble getting a cab driver to stop for them.

holding a white-collar job (including those in professional, managerial, and clerical jobs), college students preparing for white-collar jobs, and owners of successful businesses."

Middle-class African Americans, Feagin concluded, still experience discrimination based on race. Several types of discrimination were reported by the respondents, including avoidance, verbal attack, physical abuse, and subtle slights. Rejection and poor service were the most common forms of discrimination, however.

According to Feagin, the most tragic cost of this continuing discrimination is the ongoing physical and psychological drain felt by the victims. Isolated discriminatory acts may appear insignificant to whites, but years of being the target of discriminatory actions have a cumulative effect. Many African Americans report having developed a "second eye" to analyze interracial situations. As one respondent said:

I think that it causes you to have to look at things from two different perspectives. You have to decide whether things that are done or slights that are made are made because you are black or they are made because the person is just rude, or unconcerned and uncaring. So it's kind of a situation where you're always kind of looking to see with a second eye or a second antenna just what's going on (Feagin, 1991:115).

Feagin concluded that what may appear to American whites as "black paranoia," then, is actually a developed sensitivity to continuous discriminatory encounters. Despite decades of legal protection, Feagin says, African Americans have not attained the full promise of the American dream. Although middle-class African Americans work hard for their success, it is too often overshadowed by the legacy of past racist actions.

Working with the Research

1. Do you agree that disadvantages related to economic class are currently more harmful to African Americans than racism and discrimination? Why or why not?

2. Do you believe that Feagin adequately tested his hypothesis? Explain your conclusion.

3. Which of the three major theoretical perspectives best fits Feagin's research study? Defend your choice.

Figure 9.7 Socioeconomic Characteristics of Minorities

This figure presents some important social and economic characteristics of the majority and larger minorities in the U.S. Can you make sociological generalizations about income level and education based on these data?

	Whites	African Americans	Latinos	Native Americans	Asian Americans
Percent of Families in Poverty	8.6%	24.7%	21.9%	24.0%	9.8%
Median Income	$48,977	$30,134	$34,241	$33,132	$57,518
Percent with High School Diploma	85.1%	80.0%	57%	76.0%	87.6%
Percent with College Degree	27.6%	17.3%	4.4%	14.0%	49.8%

Source: U.S. Bureau of the Census, 2005.

Japanese Americans have not had to deal with the centuries of prejudice and discrimination endured by African Americans and Native Americans. Nevertheless, they have overcome great hardship and have become one of the most successful racial minorities in the United States (Zwiegenhaft and Domhoff, 1998).

Why have so many Asian Americans been successful? In large part, Asian Americans have been successful because they have used the educational system for upward mobility. This is reflected in the academic achievement of school-aged Asian Americans, whose average SAT scores are more than 60 points higher than the general high school population. Furthermore, nearly 50 percent of Asian Americans have completed four years of college, compared with approximately 28 percent of whites and 17 percent of African Americans (U.S. Bureau of the Census, 2005).

White Ethnics

White ethnics are the descendants of immigrants from Eastern and Southern European nations, particularly Italy and Poland. They also include Greek, Irish, and Slavic peoples. The majority are blue-collar workers living in small communities surrounding large cities in the eastern half of the United States.

During the 1960s, white ethnics gained the undeserved reputation of being conservative, racist, pro-war "hardhats." In fact, surveys conducted during the 1960s showed white ethnics to be more against the Vietnam War than white Anglo-Saxon Protestants. Catholic blue-collar workers were found to be more liberal than either Protestant blue-collar workers or the country as a whole. They were more likely to favor a guaranteed annual wage, more likely to vote for an African American presidential candidate, and more concerned about the environment. Finally, white ethnics tended to be more sympathetic to government help for the poor and more in favor of integration.

Why do many of these descendants of European immigrants wish to be identified as a minority group?

White ethnics have not traditionally been the victims of occupational or income discrimination. Despite their relative success, many white ethnics have in recent years become very conscious of their cultural and national origins. There is, in fact, a white ethnic "roots" movement. The new trend toward white ethnic identity began with the black power movement of the 1960s. Just as many African Americans decided that they wanted to preserve their cultural and racial identities, many white ethnics now believe that "white ethnicity is beautiful." Many think that the price of completely abandoning one's cultural and national roots is simply too high.

Lillian Rubin (1994) links the continuing accent on white ethnicity to the rising demands of ethnic minorities. White ethnics, she believes, are attempting to establish a public identity that enables them to take a seat at the "multicultural table."

Section 4 Assessment

1. How are general discrimination and institutionalized discrimination different?

2. In what ways have white ethnics influenced American culture?

3. What does the level of Latino participation at the top of the American political structure suggest about the relationship between cultural group membership and political power in the United States?

4. Does the involvement of Native Americans in gaming operations today help or hurt the economy?

Critical Thinking

5. **Drawing Conclusions** Do you think that affirmative action has affected American culture positively or negatively? Explain.

Summary

Section 1: Minority, Race, and Ethnicity

Main Idea: Sociologists have specific definitions particular to their field of study for minority, race, and ethnicity. Ethnic minorities have historically been subjected to prejudice and discrimination.

Section 2: Racial and Ethnic Relations

Main Idea: Patterns of racial and ethnic relations take two forms: assimilation and conflict. Patterns of assimilation include Anglo-conformity, melting pot, cultural pluralism, and accommodation. Conflict patterns include genocide, population transfer, and subjugation.

Section 3: Theories of Prejudice and Discrimination

Main Idea: Prejudice involves attitudes, while discrimination is about behavior. Prejudice usually leads to discrimination.

Section 4: Minority Groups in the United States

Main Idea: Discrimination in the United States has caused some ethnic and racial groups to lag behind the white majority in jobs, income, and education.

Sociology Online

Self-Check Quiz
Visit the *Sociology and You* Web site at glencoe.com and click on **Chapter 9—Self-Check Quizzes** to prepare for the chapter test.

Reviewing Vocabulary

Complete each sentence, using each term once.

a. minority
b. stereotype
c. hate crime
d. self-fulfilling prophecy
e. race
f. institutionalized discrimination
g. ethnic minority
h. underclass
i. subjugation
j. assimilation
k. de jure segregation
l. de facto segregation
m. prejudice
n. discrimination
o. cultural pluralism
p. racism
q. genocide
r. hidden unemployment

1. An expectation that leads to behavior that causes the expectation to become a reality is called _____ .
2. _____ is a group identified by cultural, religious, or national characteristics.
3. A set of ideas based on distortion, exaggeration, and oversimplification is called _____ .
4. _____ is a group of people with physical or cultural characteristics different from the dominant group.
5. People living in poverty and either continuously unemployed or underemployed are known as _____ .
6. The denial of equal access based on law is called _____ .
7. A criminal act that is motivated by prejudice is called _____ .
8. _____ is a type of subjugation that takes place regardless of the law.
9. People who share certain inherited physical characteristics are known as _____ .
10. _____ refers to unfair practices that are part of the structure of a society.
11. Treating people differently because of their ethnicity, race, religion, or culture is called _____ .

12. _____ is the denial of equal access based on the law or everyday practice.

13. _____ is best described as negative attitudes toward some minority and its individual members.

14. _____ is the blending or fusing of minority groups into the dominant society.

15. Extreme prejudice is called .

16. _____ is assimilation that maintains elements of ethnic roots.

17. _____ is unemployment that includes people not counted in traditional work categories.

18. The systematic effort to destroy a population is known as _____ .

Reviewing the Facts

19. What is the name given to people who have some distinctive characteristic, are dominated by the majority, and are denied equal treatment?

20. What is a feature that is characteristic of a minority group?

21. Name the three patterns of assimilation.

22. How do we refer to the American historical phenomenon whereby immigrants eventually become part of the dominant class?

23. What does the lyric of the following song suggest about prejudice? "You've got to be taught to hate and fear, it's got to be drummed in your dear little ear."

24. How would sociologists explain the fact that on average, African Americans earn $62 for every $100 earned by whites?

25. What sociological perspective focuses on the majority's subjugation of minorities as a weapon of power and domination?

26 Examine Figure 9.7 on page 300. Which racial minority has come the closest to achieving mainstream white status?

27. How have white ethnics affected business in American society?

Thinking Critically

"Sticks and stones may break your bones, but hate speech is actionable."

Lee Lorenz/Cartoonbank.com

28 Analyzing Visuals

In the cartoon above, the father is advising a young son about hate speech. Like *hate crime*, this term is relatively new, but it is usually taken to mean speech which encourages violence or fear in victims. What is the father's message to his son and is it a good one for a multicultural society? (If you do not understand *actionable* in the caption, use your dictionary.)

29. Applying Concepts

Recently, the students and administration at a largely Latino high school wanted to change the name of the school to honor a deceased Latino community leader. When the school had been built, the neighborhood had been primarily Anglo. Many of the old graduates protested the name change, and the original name was kept. Can you use what you have learned in this chapter about the relationship between cultural group membership and political power to explain why the decision was made to keep the school's old name?

30. Interpreting Graphs

Recent studies have shown that many high school students have dated someone of another race, but interracial marriages are much less common. Attitudes toward interracial marriages have changed in recent years, however, as the graph below indicates.

a. What percentage of the public accepted interracial dating in the late 1980s?

b. By 2003, how much had that percentage increased by 2003?

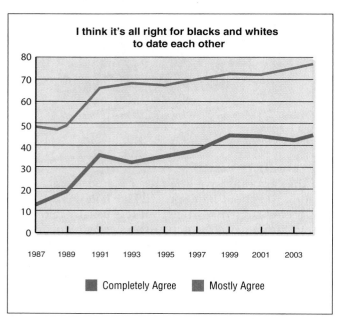

I think it's all right for blacks and whites to date each other

Completely Agree   Mostly Agree

Source: Pew Research Center, *The 2004 Political Landscape*

31. Drawing Conclusions

A recent documentary examined a suburb in the Midwest where the racial balance had gradually changed from mostly white to mostly African American. Even though statistics proved that school scores had not dropped and government services remained the same, the perception was that property values had declined. What do you think was responsible for this perception?

32. Implementing Solutions

Read the following scenario, and then answer the questions: Two people are in a twenty-mile race. The winner will receive a prize of $100,000. Two of the competitors—Lynn and Tony—are very good runners, and both are in good physical condition. At the beginning of the race Tony is told to put a set of ten-pound ankle weights on each leg, but Lynn is not. In fact, Lynn does not even know about the weights. When Lynn reaches the thirteen-mile marker, Tony is two miles behind. He is not only exhausted but is also experiencing a shortened running stride and is off-rhythm because of the weights. The judges decide to remove the ankle weights.

a. Is it fair to continue the race with each runner finishing from his or her present position, or should Tony be moved forward in the race?

b. What is fair to both parties?

c. Assume that the race cannot be restarted. How do we compensate the runner who had to carry extra weights for over half of the race?

d. Are there solutions to the problem?

e. Since the problem is difficult to solve, would it be fair simply to ignore it and conclude that things will eventually work out?

33. Evaluating Information

Explain how the experiences of various Native American tribes have been different from other racial and ethnic minority groups. Discuss whether you think allowing gaming on Indian reservations is a long-term benefit or disadvantage for Native Americans.

34. Making Comparisons

How has the African American experience in the United States been different from that of other racial and ethnic minority groups in thye United States?

35. Understanding Cause and Effect

Use the diagram below to show the cause-and-effect relationship between discrimination and poverty. Incorporate the elements of unequal educational opportunity, unfair hiring practices, and low-level jobs to complete your diagram.

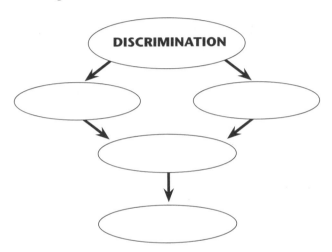

Sociology Projects

36. Ethnic and Racial Heritage

This project will give you an opportunity to create a family tree. Ask parents and other relatives about your ethnic/racial heritage, going back as far as you can. Chances are you have relatives who have old photos with dates and other pieces of information. As you trace your family tree, note when new cultures, races, or ethnicities join the family. If this has happened several times in your family, consider how it complicates assigning yourself to a specific racial and ethnic category. You might want to turn this project into an album that your whole family can enjoy and pass on.

37. Native Americans and Immigrant Cultures

This chapter deals extensively with the effects of American culture on various racial and ethnic groups. Minorities, of course, also affect American culture. For example, Mexican Americans play a pivotal role throughout the Southwest, including in Texas, where Mexican restaurants serving enchiladas and fajitas compete with those serving traditional Texas barbecue. In many parts of the nation, Native Americans have opened tourist-based businesses. Asian Americans have a significant presence in California, where sushi bars serve fresh fish and Chinese groceries cater to a large clientele. Businesses often tailor their print, radio, and television advertising to cater to immigrant tastes. To do so, advertising companies often employ ethnic Americans as models and consultants. Work with one or two of your classmates to find information about immigrant and Native American cultures in your community. Analyze changes such as those in advertising, food, and business in your local culture that have resulted from adaptations to various immigrant or Native American cultures.

Technology Activity

38. The textbook describes a stereotype as a set of ideas based on distortion, exaggeration, and oversimplification that is applied to all members of a social category. Popular media often use stereotypes to convey assumed meanings about characters and situations. The Movies Cliché List at www.moviecliches.com/ provides an abundant list of stereotypes used in films.

a. Select "Women" from the Cliché Topics. Name some of the stereotypes about women suggested by the list.

b. Do the same for "Men" and "Minorities."

c. Based on what you have read in the text and on these lists, do you think stereotypes are helpful in understanding social categories?

The Skin Color Tax
by Patricia J. Williams

- **criteria**
  standards on which
  judgments or decisions
  are made

- **compliance**
  agreement with;
  following the terms of

- **unbeknownst**
  not knowing; unaware

- **creative variability
  of all illegality**
  cleverness of wrongdoers
  to get what they want

- **procured**
  obtained

- **recalcitrance**
  reluctance; unwillingness

Several years ago, at a moment when I was particularly tired of the unstable lifestyle that academic careers sometimes require, I surprised myself and bought a real house. Because the house was in a state other than the one where I was living at the time, I obtained my mortgage by telephone. I am a prudent little squirrel when it comes to things financial, always tucking away stores of nuts for the winter, and so I meet the **criteria** of a quite good credit risk. My loan was approved almost immediately.

A little while later, the contract came in the mail. Among the papers the bank forwarded were forms documenting **compliance** with the Fair Housing Act, which outlaws racial discrimination in the housing market. The act monitors lending practices to prevent banks from redlining—redlining being the phenomenon whereby banks circle certain neighborhoods on the map and refuse to lend in those areas. It is a practice for which the bank with which I was dealing, **unbeknownst** to me, had been cited previously—as well as since. In any event, the act tracks the race of all banking customers to prevent such discrimination. Unfortunately, and with the **creative variability of all illegality,** some banks also use the racial information disclosed on the fair housing forms to engage in precisely the discrimination the law seeks to prevent.

I should repeat that to this point my entire mortgage transaction had been conducted by telephone. I should also note that I speak a Received Standard English, regionally marked as Northeastern perhaps, but not easily identifiable as black. With my credit history, my job as a law professor and, no doubt, with my accent, I am not only middle class but apparently match the cultural stereotype of a good white person. It is thus, perhaps, that the loan officer of the bank, whom I had never met, had checked off the box on the fair housing form indicating that I *was* white.

Race shouldn't matter, I suppose, but it seemed to in this case, so I took a deep breath, crossed out "white" and sent the contract back. That will teach them to presume too much, I thought. A done deal, I assumed. But suddenly the transaction came to a screeching halt. The bank wanted more money, more points, a higher rate of interest. Suddenly I found myself facing great resistance and much more debt. To make a long story short, I threatened to sue under the act in question, the bank quickly backed down and I **procured** the loan on the original terms.

What was interesting about all this was that the reason the bank gave for its new-found **recalcitrance** was not race, heaven forbid. No, it was all about economics and increased risk: The reason they gave was that property values in that neighborhood were suddenly falling. They wanted more money to buffer themselves against the snappy winds of projected misfortune.

The bank's response was driven by demographic data that show that any time black people move into a neighborhood, whites are overwhelmingly likely to move out. In droves. In panic. In concert. Pulling every imaginable resource with them, from school funding to garbage collection to social workers who don't want to work in black neighborhoods. The imagery is awfully catchy, you had to admit: the neighborhood just tipping on over like a terrible accident, whoops! Like a pitcher, I suppose. All that fresh wholesome milk spilling out running away . . . leaving the dark echoing, upended urn of the inner city.

In retrospect, what has remained so fascinating to me about this experience was the way it so exemplified the problems of the new rhetoric of racism. For starters, the new rhetoric of race never mentions race. It wasn't race but risk with which the bank was so concerned.

Second, since financial risk is all about economics, my exclusion got reclassified as just a consideration of class. There's no law against class discrimination, goes the argument, because that would represent a restraint on that basic American freedom, the ability to contract or not. If schools, trains, buses, swimming pools and neighborhoods remain segregated, it's no longer a racial problem if someone who just happens to be white keeps hiking up the price for someone who accidentally and purely by the way happens to be black. Black people end up paying higher prices for the attempt to integrate, even as the integration of oneself threatens to lower the value of one's investment.

By this measure of mortgage-worthiness, the ingredient of blackness is cast not just as a social toll but as an actual tax. A fee, an extra contribution at the door, an admission charge for the high costs of handling my dangerous propensities, my inherently unsavory properties. I was not judged based on my independent attributes or financial worth; not even was I judged by statistical profiles of what my group actually does. (For in fact, anxiety-stricken, middle-class black people make grovelingly good cake-baking neighbors when not made to feel defensive by the unfortunate historical strategies of bombs, burnings or abandonment.) Rather, I was being evaluated based on what an abstraction of White Society writ large thinks we—or I—do, and that imagined "doing" was treated and thus established as a self-fulfilling prophecy. It is a dispiriting message: that some in society apparently not only devalue black people but devalue *themselves* and their homes just for having us as part of their landscape.

"I bet you'll keep your mouth shut the next time they plug you into the computer as white," laughed a friend when he heard my story. It took me aback, this postmodern pressure to "pass," even as it highlighted the intolerable logic of it all. For by "rational" economic measures, an investment in my property suggests the selling of myself.

Source: Patricia J. Williams, "Of Race and Risk," *The Nation* (December 29, 1997):10.

Read and React

1. What does the author mean when she writes "All that fresh wholesome milk spilling out running away . . . leaving the dark echoing, upended urn of the inner city"?
2. What are the main issues of what the author calls the "problems of the new rhetoric of racism"?
3. Why has the author titled this article "The Skin Color Tax"?

"Let's just forget for a moment that you're black."

© 1996 *The New Yorker Collection*, Mick Stevens. (Reprinted with permission.)

Chapter 9 Inequalities of Race and Ethnicity **307**

Inequalities of Gender and Age

Sections

1. **Sex and Gender Identity**
2. **Theoretical Perspectives on Gender**
3. **Gender Inequality**
4. **Ageism**
5. **Inequality in America's Elderly Population**

Learning Objectives

After reading this chapter, you will be able to

- distinguish the concepts of sex, gender, and gender identity.

- summarize the perspectives on gender taken by functionalists, conflict theorists, and symbolic interactionists.

- describe the status of women in the United States.

- compare and contrast the ways in which functionalism, conflict theory, and symbolic interactionism approach ageism.

- discuss the inequality experienced by America's elderly.

Applying Sociology

Throughout history, men have dominated the social, political, and economic spheres while women have assumed responsibility for children and home. These domestic tasks are generally undervalued in industrial societies where value is pegged to monetary rewards. Women have been seen as dependent, passive, and deferential, while men have been seen as independent and strong. This division of labor based on sex has almost always led to gender inequality.

In the twentieth century, the feminist movement made enormous strides in gaining rights and opportunities previously available only to men. Many more women have college educations and professional jobs—and young girls believe they have more choices in life. Despite these gains, women have still not achieved equal rights. Women earn less than men even when they perform the same work, they hold the vast majority of low-paying jobs, and they make up a higher percentage of the poor.

Gender, race, and ethnicity are not the only factors that affect a person's place in the society. Inequality based on age also exists. This chapter examines the roles played by both gender and age in the stratification system.

Sociology Online

Chapter Overview
Visit the *Sociology and You* Web site at glencoe.com and click on **Chapter 10— Chapter Overviews** to preview chapter information.

1

Sex and Gender Identity

Key Terms

- sex *(p. 310)*
- biological determinism *(p. 311)*
- gender identity *(p. 311)*

Section Preview

All societies expect people to behave in certain ways based on their sex. Through socialization, members of a society acquire an awareness of themselves as masculine or feminine. Behavioral differences between men and women are culturally conditioned.

Defining Male and Female

What are little girls made of?
Sugar and spice
And everything nice
That's what little girls are made of.

What are little boys made of?
Snips and snails
And puppy dog tails
That's what little boys are made of.

- **sex**
  classification of people as male or female based on biological characteristics

As the above well-known nursery rhyme indicates, when it comes to males and females, most Americans believe that anatomy is destiny. If men and women behave differently, it is assumed to be because of their **sex**— the biological distinction between male and female. Males are assumed to be naturally more aggressive than females and to be built for providing and protecting. Females are believed to be naturally more passive than males and in greater need of protection. If this popular conception were true, men and

Many Americans believe that infant boys are just naturally more active than infant girls. Would you agree or not?

women in all societies would behave uniformly in their unique ways because of inborn biological forces beyond their control. This way of thinking is called **biological determinism**—the belief that behavioral differences are the result of inherited physical characteristics.

The theory of biological determinism lacks scientific proof. Significant behavioral differences between men and women have not been causally linked to biological characteristics. Although biology may create some behavioral tendencies in the sexes, such tendencies are so weak that they are easily overridden by cultural and social influences (Sapolsky, 1997; Ridley, 2003).

From the moment of birth—on the basis of obvious external biological characteristics—males and females are treated differently. Few parents in American society point with pride to the muscular legs and broad shoulders of their baby girls or to the long eyelashes, rosebud mouth, and delicate curly hair of their baby boys. Rather, parents stress the characteristics and behaviors that fit the society's image of the ideal male or female, including modes of dress, ways of walking, manner of talking, play activities, and life aspirations.

Girls and boys gradually learn to behave as their parents expect. From this process comes **gender identity**—an awareness of being masculine or feminine, based on culture. Sociologist Margaret Andersen succinctly captured the difference between sex and gender.

> *The terms sex and gender have particular definitions in sociological work. Sex refers to the biological identity of the person and is meant to signify the fact that one is either male or female. . . . Gender refers to the socially learned behaviors and expectations that are associated with the two sexes. Thus, whereas "maleness" and "femaleness" are biological facts, becoming a woman or becoming a man is a cultural process. Like race and class, gender is a social category that establishes, in large measure, our life chances and directs our social relations with others. Sociologists distinguish sex and gender to emphasize that gender is a cultural, not a biological, phenomenon (Andersen, 2005).*

Sociologists are part of an ongoing debate concerning the reasons for gender differences. At the heart of the debate is the so-called nature versus nurture issue: Does biology or socialization play a greater role in gender differences? Today, research by sociologists

- **biological determinism**
  principle that behavioral differences are the result of inherited physical characteristics

- **gender identity**
  a sense of being male or female based on learned cultural values

Gender identities go way back.

and other investigators is aimed at answering these questions scientifically. Definitions of masculinity and femininity are now based on research rather than just on tradition and "common knowledge."

Biology, Culture, and Behavior

As noted earlier, there are obvious biological differences between males and females. Biological differences between the sexes include distinctive muscle-to-bone ratios and how fat is stored. The differences in reproductive organs, however, are much more important, because they result in certain facts of life. Only men can impregnate; only women are able to produce eggs, give birth, and nurse infants. Throughout life reproductive hormones influence development in both males and females.

Are male and female brains different? Recent research indicates that the brains of men and women are slightly different in structure (Baron-Cohen, 2003). For example, men show more activity in a region of the brain thought to be tied to adaptive evolutionary responses such as fighting. Women have more activity in a newer, more highly developed region of the brain thought to be linked to emotional expression. The female brain is less specialized than the male brain. Women tend to use both sides of the brain simultaneously when performing a task. Whereas men tend to process verbal tasks on the left side of the brain, women are more likely to use both sides. Women tend to use both ears when listening and men tend to use the right ear.

Do such biological differences lead to differences in social behavior? This is precisely the question overlooked by biological determinists who, without evidence, assume that physical differences result in

Although gender stereotypes keep some people from pursuing certain activities, there are actually very few behaviors that cannot be performed by either sex.

biologically programmed differences in social behavior. It is true that female babies are more sensitive to sound, probably because they listen with both ears rather than one. And male infants and children are more active in play—shouting, yelling, hitting—than females.

Biological determinists point to research that indicates men and women in dozens of different cultures (at varying stages of economic development) are associated with some distinctly different ways of behaving. For example, men and women differ in what they look for in romantic and sexual partners. Men value physical appearance more than women do. Women place more emphasis on social class and income. Men tend to prefer slightly younger mates, while women favor slightly older ones. In addition, males in general tend more toward physical aggressiveness in conflict situations (Buss, Malamuth, and Winstead, 1998; Tremblay, 2005).

The fact that such differences appear in many cultures suggests to some people that they have a biological cause. However, we don't yet know for sure to what extent these differences result from biology or culture, and the debate on this issue can be furious.

How do sociologists view behavior?
The majority of sociologists argue that gender-related behavior is not primarily the result of biology. They look to culture for clues. In her classic study of three primitive New Guinean peoples, anthropologist Margaret Mead (1950) demonstrated the influence of culture and socialization on gender role behavior.

Among the Arapesh, Mead found that both males and females were conditioned to be cooperative, unaggressive, and empathetic. Both men and women in this tribe behaved in a way that is consistent with the more traditional concept of the female gender role. Among the Mundugumor, in contrast, both men and women were trained to be "masculine"—they were aggressive, ruthless, and unresponsive to the needs of others. In the Tchambuli tribe,

Anthropologist Margaret Mead's research on primitive cultures added greatly to our knowledge of gender and human nature.

Males have proven that they can also function successfully in careers that require a high degree of nurturing and communication skills.

the gender roles were the opposite of those found in Western society. Women were dominant, impersonal, and aggressive, and men were dependent and submissive.

On the basis of this evidence, Mead concluded that human nature is sufficiently flexible to rule out biological determination of gender roles. Cross-cultural research since Mead's landmark work has clearly supported her findings: gender roles are not fixed at birth (Janssen-Jurreit, 1982; Montagu, 1998).

Case studies have also been examined on infants whose parents intentionally treated their children as if they belonged to the opposite sex. Apparently, individuals can fairly easily be socialized into the gender of the opposite sex. What's more, after a few years, these children resist switching back. In general, research on gender identity indicates that biological tendencies can be greatly influenced by culture and society (Schwartz, 1987; Shapiro, 1990; Sapolsky, 1997; Ridley, 2003).

What can we conclude from studies about male and female behaviors? In general, researchers investigating behavioral differences between the sexes have not been able to prove that any particular behavior has a biological cause. One researcher's findings tend to contradict another's.

Any conclusions we reach should also take into account several difficulties with the research. Many studies seek to find differences but ignore the overriding similarities between males and females. To make matters worse, researchers often fail to note the variation that exists *within* each sex. Some men, for example, tend to be submissive and noncompetitive, and some women are aggressive and competitive.

While biological characteristics exist, they can be modified through social influences. In other words, men and women can learn to be submissive or aggressive by mirroring the behaviors of influential role models, such as parents or siblings. Also, this is a good time to remind ourselves that human behavior is the result of multiple causes.

Section 1 Assessment

1. How is gender different from sex?

2. How are gender traits acquired?

3. Researchers investigating behavioral differences between the sexes have now proven that several significant behaviors have a biological cause. *T* or *F*?

Critical Thinking

4. **Summarizing Information** Suppose that, after your graduation, one of your teachers invites you back to speak to the class on the biological determinism versus socialization debate as it relates to gender. How would you summarize the effects that scientific research on gender has had on males and females of your generation?

Manly Hearted Women

In the northern [Native American] Plains cultures, certain women adopted elements of male social behavior, acting aggressive and domineering. The Blackfoot called them *ninauposkitzipxe*, which means literally "the manly hearted women." Women ordinarily were passive and docile, but manly hearted women were aggressive and outspoken in public affairs. At the same time they were wives and mothers and were involved in female tasks.

Manly hearted women were invariably wealthy, due in large part to their own industry. They could tan more buffalo robes and produce better quality and greater amounts of quill and beadwork than other women. Many were also medicine women, which not only enhanced their status but also brought them additional wealth. Their wealth was a key factor in their relations with men, because among the Blackfoot wealth and generosity were more highly regarded than bravery and war deeds in determining social status.

Because of their wealth and industry, manly hearted women were major economic assets to their husbands, and thus desirable wives. These same characteristics also made them independent. Within the family a manly hearted woman had an equal say, if not the dominant voice. As a Blackfoot once commented . . . , "It's easy to spot a manly hearted woman; the husband simply has nothing to say." Not only did they retain control of their own wealth, but they frequently controlled the property of their husbands as well. Because they were economically more self-sufficient than other women, many manly hearted women chose to divorce their husbands and support their children by their own industry.

Their public behavior also distinguished them. Their wealth made it possible for them always to dress in the finest clothes. Whereas other women modestly covered themselves with shawls and blankets, manly hearted women usually did not. Whereas most women were retiring and quiet in public discussions, manly hearted women joined

The Blackfoot Indians thought manly hearted women made good wives.

in and even argued with others, "just as though they were men." Whereas other women were shy at dances, manly hearted women aggressively chose their own partners. They were known for their sharp and cutting remarks, and it was said that a manly hearted woman would "take no lip" from either a man or another woman.

Source: Excerpted from James Peoples and Garrick Bailey, *Humanity* (Belmont, CA: Wadsworth, 2000), pp. 164–165.

Thinking It Over

How would you use this manly hearted women story to argue that gender identity of American women is not biologically determined?

2

Theoretical Perspectives on Gender

Key Term

- gender socialization (p. 317)

Section Preview

The functionalist perspective focuses on the origins of gender differences. Conflict theory looks at the reasons gender differences continue to exist. Symbolic interactionism attempts to explain the ways in which gender is acquired.

Functionalism and Gender

Functionalists argue that any pattern of behavior that does not benefit society will become unimportant. According to functionalism, the division of responsibilities between males and females survived because it benefited human living. Early humans found that the division of labor based on sex was efficient. In part because of their size and muscular strength, men hunted and protected. In addition, men were assigned these dangerous tasks because they were more expendable than women. One male was enough to ensure the group's chances of surviving through reproduction; one woman was not. Thus, it hurt the group's chances of survival less to lose a man.

Today, functionalists recognize that the traditional division of labor has created problems, or dysfunctions, for modern society. These dysfunctions are examined later, in the discussion on gender inequality.

Conflict Theory and Gender

According to conflict theory, it is to men's advantage to prevent women from gaining access to political, economic, and social resources.

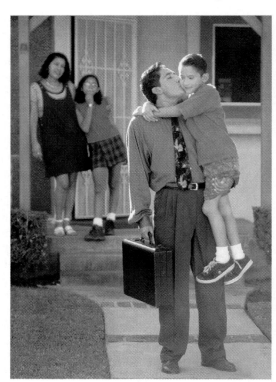

This family is structured along traditional gender roles. How would the functionalist interpret this arrangement?

If men can prevent women from developing their potential, they can maintain the status quo. By keeping the traditional division of labor intact, men can preserve the privileges they enjoy.

Perhaps the most recent example of maintaining the gender status quo was found in Afghanistan, when the ruling Taliban militia practiced "gender apartheid." This gender war trapped women in a way of life unknown elsewhere in the modern world (O'Dwyer, 1999). The Taliban prohibited girls from attending school and banned women from all work outside the home. Women who left home without the protection of a male relative were punished, and the windows of houses were painted black to prevent anyone from catching a glimpse of the women. In public, women remained mute; even the soles of their shoes were soft to prevent wearers from making noise and drawing attention to themselves.

Conflict theorists see traditional gender roles as outdated. Although these conventional roles may have been appropriate in hunting and gathering, horticultural, and agricultural societies, they are inappropriate for the industrial and postindustrial era.

Male physical strength may have been important when hunting was the major means of subsistence, but work in modern society does not place men at an advantage over women in that regard. In addition, demographic characteristics make women today more available for work outside the home. Women are marrying later, are having fewer children, are younger when their last child leaves home, are remaining single in greater numbers, and are increasingly choosing to be single parents. (See Chapter 11 for more information on women and the family.) According to conflict theorists, women who prefer careers in fields formerly reserved for men have every right to make that choice, whether or not it is "functional" for society.

Women are moving into traditional male roles in business in greater numbers. Not everyone appears to be ready for this.

Symbolic Interactionism and Gender

Symbolic interactionists focus on how boys and girls learn to act the way they are "supposed to act." This process is called **gender socialization**. Gender is acquired in large part from interaction with parents, teachers, and peers. In addition, gender concepts are taught through the mass media. Indeed, the effect of the media is very powerful.

gender socialization
the social process of learning how to act as a boy or girl

How do parents contribute to gender socialization? Parents are vitally important in gender socialization because they transfer values and attitudes regarding how boys and girls should behave. The learning of gender begins at birth and is well established by the time the child is two and a half

World View

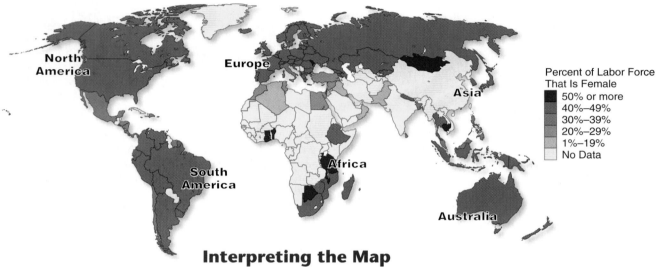

Women in the Workplace

In most countries of the world, fewer women than men are employed in the labor force. In addition, the higher-paying jobs and better opportunities mostly still go to men. This map shows the percentage of women in various national labor forces.

North America

Europe

Asia

Africa

South America

Australia

Percent of Labor Force That Is Female
- 50% or more
- 40%–49%
- 30%–39%
- 20%–29%
- 1%–19%
- No Data

Interpreting the Map

1. The countries with the highest percentage of women in the workplace include both highly developed countries such as the United States, Germany, and France and relatively undeveloped countries such as Mongolia, Tanzania, and Ghana. Can you think of some reasons for this?

2. Create a graph representing any other patterns you may find in this map.

Source: United Nations Statistics Division, *Statistics and Indicators on Women and Men*, 2005.

years old (Davies, 2003). Immediately after birth, friends and relatives give gifts "appropriate" to the child's sex, such as blue or pink blankets, baseball playsuits or frilly dresses, and trucks or dolls. (In fact, when boys do play with dolls, they are called action figures to distinguish the boys' toys from "girl" toys.) Studies of infant care have found that girls are cuddled more, talked to more, and handled more gently than are boys. Parents expect boys to be more assertive than girls are, and they discourage them from clinging.

Gender is also taught and reinforced in the assignment of family chores. In an investigation of almost seven hundred children between the ages of two and seventeen, Lynn White and David Brinkerhoff (1981) found that boys were often given "masculine" jobs, such as cutting grass and shoveling snow. Girls were more often assigned "feminine" chores, such as washing dishes and cleaning up the house.

In what ways do schools reinforce gender socialization?

Although the most critical period of gender socialization occurs during early childhood, gender socialization occurs through the schools as well (Martin, 1998). Observation of preschool teachers reveals that many teachers encourage different behaviors from boys and girls. This pattern continues in the elementary school years.

Myra and David Sadker, in an extensive study of fourth-, sixth-, and eighth-grade students, found boys to be more assertive in class. Boys were eight times more likely than girls to call out answers, whereas girls sat patiently with their hands raised. The researchers linked this classroom behavior to the differential treatment given boys and girls by teachers. Teachers were more likely to accept the answers given by boys who called out answers. Girls who called out in class were given such messages as, "In this class we don't shout out answers; we raise our hands." According to Sadker and Sadker, the message is subtle and powerful: "Boys should be academically assertive and grab teacher attention; girls should act like ladies and keep quiet" (Sadker and Sadker, 1995).

There are other areas in junior high school and high school where gender socialization is concentrated. These include clothing styles, school elections, social functions, and after-school activities.

In their book *Failing at Fairness,* the Sadkers examined sexism from elementary school through college. They concluded that, through differential treatment, America's schools often shortchange females. Academically, girls typically outperform boys in the early years of school. Through the transmission of gender role values, well-intentioned teachers often dampen female competitiveness. Girls, the study concludes, are subtly but systematically taught to be passive, to dislike math and science, and to defer to boys. Females tend to carry these attitudes into adult life and into the working world.

Sociology Online

Student Web Activity
Visit the *Sociology and You* Web site at glencoe.com and click on **Chapter 10—Student Web Activities** for an activity on gender socialization in schools.

Focus on Theoretical Perspectives

Figure 10.1 Gender Inequality

Each of the major theoretical perspectives can focus on gender inequality in its own unique way. Explain why the examples given fit each theoretical perspective. How would each of the other theories approach the same social arrangement differently?

Theoretical Perspective	Social Arrangement	Example
Functionalism	Gender-based division of labor	Women are expected to perform household tasks for the benefit of society.
Conflict Theory	Patriarchy (male domination)	Women are denied high status occupations for the benefit of men.
Symbolic Interactionism	Favoring males over females in the classroom	Few females believe they can become scientists.

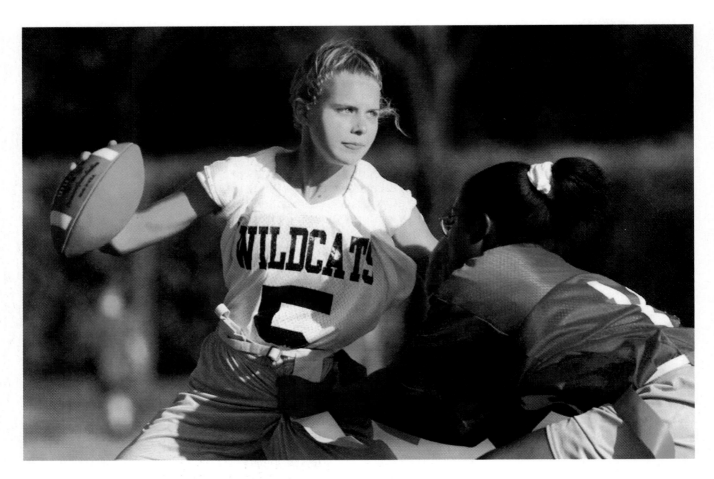

These active girls do not fit the stereotypical image of male football player/female cheerleader.

How do peers contribute to gender socialization?

Adolescents want to be liked, so acceptance or rejection by peers greatly influences their self-concepts. Teens who most closely mirror traditional gender roles, such as male football players and female cheerleaders, are generally given the greatest respect, whereas "feminine" boys and "masculine" girls are assigned low status. This peer group pressure encourages teenagers to try to conform to idealized role models. To do otherwise is to risk rejection and a significant loss of self-esteem (Erikson, 1964, 1982; Adler and Adler, 1998).

Section 2 Assessment

1. Why do functionalists believe that gender differences have survived?

2. How do symbolic interactionists explain gender roles?

3. How do teachers and peers influence the development of gender concepts?

Critical Thinking

4. **Analyzing Information** Of the major factors influencing gender identity, which do you think has had the most effect on your development? Explain.

Sociology Today

Gender-Based Hierarchy

In the not-too-distant past, most doctors were men, who worked closely on a daily basis with female nurses and receptionists who were clearly subordinate to them. This pattern has not disappeared despite the influx of women into the ranks of physicians. In many occupational settings today, most of the executives, supervisors, or higher-level professionals are men, assisted by female secretaries, clerks, aides, or lower-level managers. . . .

When women enter a workplace they frequently find a male hierarchy already established. Whether a woman's entry creates tensions for herself or others in the workplace presumably depends on the level of the job she takes and the source of any authority inherent in the job. She may come in at a subordinate level as a clerk or receptionist. But if she comes in at the same level as male co-workers, she will be faced with the unaccustomed process of jockeying for position among them, and competing with them for the attention and approval of the people higher up in the hierarchy. If she comes in as a manager or supervisor who has male subordinates, she must learn how to deal with people who may want her job, or who may find it difficult to adjust to being supervised by a woman. Some men believe so strongly in male superiority that they resist women's advancement up the workplace hierarchy. Such men sometimes say quite explicitly that it would be "an insult to their intelligence" to be supervised by a woman. . . . And there are fairly widespread male beliefs concerning the "natural" (male-dominant) relation between the sexes. In adulthood there is a strong stereotype associating power with masculinity . . . just as there was in childhood, so that women in supervisory positions generate ambivalent reactions in men: are they to treat this woman as a powerful person or a feminine person? If she is seen as feminine, then a man with traditional attitudes might feel it is appropriate to be protective and chivalrous, or at least courteous, while at the same time failing to take her seriously where work-related matters are concerned; clearly, he would expect to be the person who "takes charge" when they interact. Can he forget that a female supervisor is female, and adapt himself to a situation where she is the one who takes charge? It is much easier for men—and perhaps for many women too—to slip into a traditional male boss/female secretary or male doctor/female nurse kind of work relationship in which the "appropriate" power relationships between the sexes are maintained in the workplace hierarchy. Such traditional attitudes may be weakening, but they are still prevalent enough to impede the promotion of women in many situations.

Doing Sociology

Talk to several men and women with work experience. Ask them a few open-ended questions that you make up to test Maccoby's contention. In your verbal or written report, be specific about similarities or differences in male and female answers.

Excerpted from Eleanor E. Maccoby, *The Two Sexes: Growing Up Apart, Coming Together.* Cambridge, MA: Harvard University Press, 1998, pp. 247–248.

3

Gender Inequality

Key Terms

- sexism *(p. 322)*
- occupational sex segregation *(p. 323)*

- **sexism**
  a set of beliefs, attitudes, norms, and values used to justify sexual inequality

Section Preview

Although great progress has been made, women today are still subject to prejudice and discrimination. This imbalance of power is seen most clearly in the areas of economics, law, and politics.

Women as a Minority Group

Most scientists consider biological determinism to be a moral threat because historically it has been used to rationalize the treatment of some people as inferior. This view, in short, has led to racism and *sexism*. **Sexism** is defined as a set of beliefs, attitudes, norms, and values used to justify gender inequality. Just as minorities suffer from the effects of racism, women are hurt by sexism. Sexist ideology—the belief that men are naturally superior to women—has been used and is still being used to justify men's leadership and power positions in the economic, social, and political spheres of society.

Isn't sex discrimination disappearing? The answer is yes and no. Some segments of American society now have more positive attitudes about women. And a few women now hold key positions traditionally reserved for men. In 1999, for example, Carleton Fiorina became the first female CEO (chief executive officer) of one of the thirty companies that make up the Dow Jones Industrial Average. In that same year, Eileen Collins became the first female NASA shuttle commander.

Still, a careful examination reveals many gaps in social rights, privileges, and rewards for women in the United States (Valian, 1999). These gaps, although they have closed somewhat in recent years, are reflected in the continuing inequality experienced by American women (Riley, 1997; Lorber, 2005).

Under the leadership of CEO Patricia Russo, Lucent Technologies stock rose 198 percent between 2002 and 2004.

Occupational and Economic Inequality

By far the most important labor development in the United States over the past thirty years has been the dramatic increase in the number and proportion of women in the workforce. In 2004, 59 percent of women worked outside the home, compared with 73 percent of men. That same year, women represented just over 46 percent of the U.S. labor force. (See Figure 10.2 on the next page.)

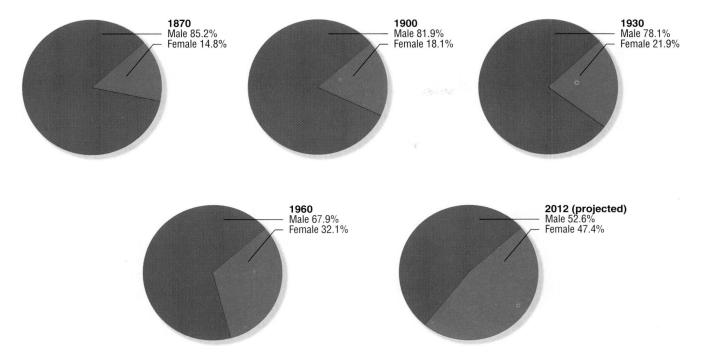

Figure 10.2 Composition of the U.S. Labor Force, by Sex: 1870–2012
As this figure demonstrates, the male-female composition of the U.S. labor force has steadily moved toward parity. The female percentage of the labor force has moved from less than 15 percent in 1870 to more than 46 percent today. What do you think is the most important social consequence of this change?

Source: U.S. Department of Labor, Bureau of Labor Statistics, 2005.

The greatest change in patterns of work involves married women with children under six years of age. The proportion of women in this group who work outside the home rocketed from 19 percent in 1960 to 37 percent in 1975 to 59.3 percent in 2004 (U.S. Bureau of Labor Statistics, 2005). (A discussion of working women's effects on the family appears in Chapter 11.)

What kinds of jobs are women doing?

Although women are participating in the labor force at increasing levels, they are concentrated in lower-status occupations. This is known as **occupational sex segregation.** Only about 12 percent of civil engineer positions are held by women, and about 29 percent of attorney jobs. By contrast, women occupy nearly all of the "pink-collar" jobs—secretaries, clerks, stenographers—whose purpose is to support those higher up the occupational ladder (U.S. Bureau of Labor Statistics, 2005). Moreover, when women are in high-status occupational groups, they are concentrated in lower-prestige, lower-paid jobs. Female lawyers in firms seldom occupy the higher-level administrative positions. Even within female-dominated occupations, such as public school administration, a disproportionate share of higher positions are filled by men.

Do women earn less than men?

As you read in the Applying Sociology feature at the beginning of the chapter, there is a wide discrepancy

● **occupational sex segregation**
the concentration of women in lower-status positions

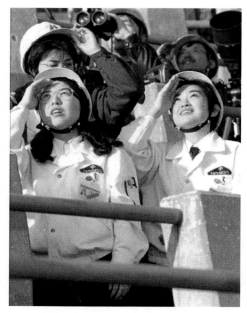

These Japanese women are almost certainly not earning as much as men in equivalent positions.

between the earnings of American women and men. In 2004, women who worked full-time earned only 80 cents for every dollar earned by men. To put it another way, women now work about seven days to earn as much as men earn in five days. The good news is that this salary gap has decreased since 1980, when women were earning 64 percent as much as men. (See Figure 10.3 below.)

Are all occupations affected? In virtually every occupational category, men's earning power outstrips that of women. The earnings gap persists, regardless of educational attainment. Women in the same professional occupations as men earn less than their male counterparts, as illustrated in Figure 10.4 on the opposite page. This is true even for women who have pursued careers on a full-time basis for all of their adult lives. Furthermore, males in female-dominated occupations typically earn more than women.

How do race and ethnicity affect women's earnings compared to men's? As mentioned earlier, women in the United States earn about 80 percent of what American men earn. Comparing groups of women by race and ethnicity, however, presents another picture. White women, for example, earn about 82 percent of what men earn, while the earnings for African American women are only about 71 percent of the earnings for men. Asian women have the highest female-to-male earnings ratio—nearly 86 percent. Latino women, on the other hand, have the largest earnings gap; they earn only about 59 cents for every dollar earned by men. (See Figure 10.5.)

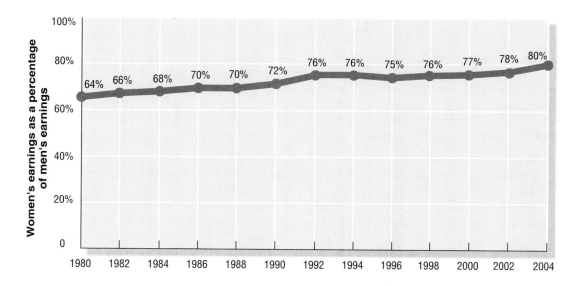

Figure 10.3 What Women Earn Compared to Men
This figure traces the ratio of women's to men's earnings since 1980. Discuss two important conclusions you can make from these data. Use material in the text to help.

Source: U.S. Department of Labor, Bureau of Labor Statistics, 2005.

Figure 10.4 Female-to-Male Earnings: 2004

On average, women in the U.S. earn about 80 cents for every dollar a man earns. In what way do the data in this figure support the contention that gender inequality is real?

Source: U.S. Department of Labor, Bureau of Labor Statistics, 2005.

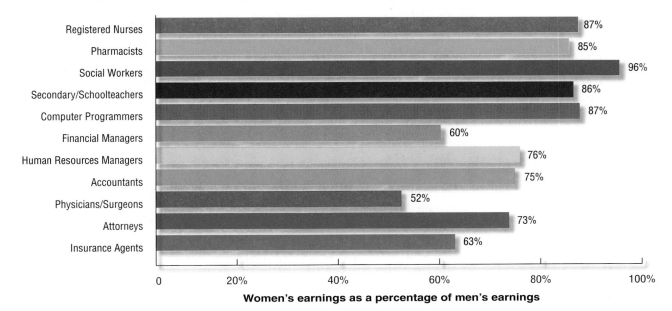

Registered Nurses 87%
Pharmacists 85%
Social Workers 96%
Secondary/Schoolteachers 86%
Computer Programmers 87%
Financial Managers 60%
Human Resources Managers 76%
Accountants 75%
Physicians/Surgeons 52%
Attorneys 73%
Insurance Agents 63%

Women's earnings as a percentage of men's earnings

Legal and Political Inequality

Supporters of women's rights point to laws that show a bias against women. National, state, and local legal codes, they claim, reflect a sexual bias that results in important differences between the levels of political power of women and men.

What are some biases in law? An example that women's groups point to is the U.S. Supreme Court decision that refused to grant women the legal guarantee of health insurance benefits for pregnancy-related medical costs. This was despite the fact that medical coverage for conditions unique to men—such as prostate problems and vasectomies—was routinely provided.

Some states have traditionally refused women the right to keep their own surnames after marriage. Other states have had protective legislation restricting women's rights. Such protective legislation limited the number of hours women could work. It also limited the conditions under which they could work, with actions such as barring women from toxic areas because of potential birth defects in their children. It even limited the kinds of work they could do by regulating such matters as the amount of weight a woman could be permitted to lift (thirty pounds). Supporters of

Figure 10.5 Women's Wages Compared with Men's Wages, by Race and Ethnicity

This figure compares what women of various races and ethnicities earn compared to men. Which group of women has the highest female-to-male earnings ratio?

Source: U.S. Department of Labor, Bureau of Labor Statistics, 2005.

All Women
White Women
African American Women
Asian Women
Latino Women

Women's earnings as a percentage of men's earnings

Chapter 10 Inequalities of Gender and Age **325**

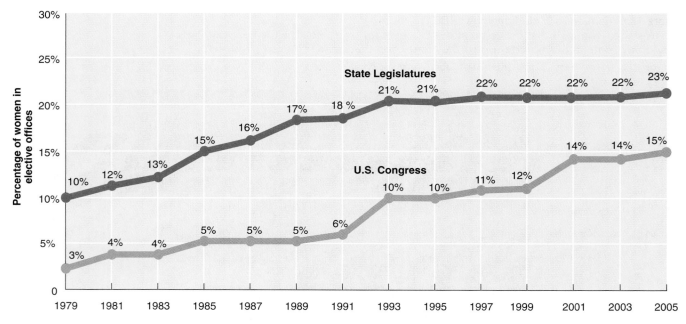

Figure 10.6 Percentages of Women in Elective Offices
This graph shows the degree of female success in elective politics from 1979 to today. Explain why the figures are still so low.

Source: Center for American Women and Politics, National Information Bank on Women in Public Office, Eagleton Institute of Politics, Rutgers University.

these laws viewed them as safeguards against abuse and exploitation of women. However, the end result was that women were denied certain jobs, many of which are better paid than more traditional occupations for women.

Passage of Title VII of the Civil Rights Act of 1964 nullified such laws, but their practice still lingers. Moreover, the Family and Medical Leave Act (1993), which requires that employees be given up to twelve weeks without pay for childbirth, adoption, personal illness, or caring for a family member with a serious illness, still negatively affects women. Because women are more likely to take maternity leave than men are to take paternity leave, this legislation gives employers another reason to give hiring preference to men.

There are differences by gender in criminal law as well. Certain crimes are typically associated with one gender or the other. For example, laws against prostitution are generally enforced against only the female prostitutes, while their male customers go free.

Are American women well represented in politics? Women appear to be participating in elective politics at an increasing rate. (See Figure 10.6 above.) Recently, the numbers of female governors, lieutenant governors, attorneys general, and mayors have been growing. Some increases have occurred at the national level as well. In 1984, Geraldine Ferraro became the first female vice-presidential candidate in U.S. history; Madeleine Albright was named the first female secretary of state in 1996; Elizabeth Dole campaigned for her party's nomination for president before the election of 2000. In 2005, Condoleezza Rice was named secretary of state.

Still, although women constitute more than half the population, they hold a relatively small proportion of important political positions. (See Figure 10.7.)

Figure 10.7

Women in National, State, and Local Political Positions, 2005

This table contains the number and percentage of women today in selected political positions. Identify the types of political offices in which women have been the most successful.

Position	Number of Women	Percentage Female
Federal legislative branch		
U.S. representative	67	15%
U.S. senator	14	14
House leadership post	7	2
Senate leadership post	7	7
Federal judicial branch		
Supreme Court justice	2	22
U.S. Court of Appeals, chief judge	1	8
U.S. District Court judge	7	8
Federal executive branch		
Cabinet member	4	27
Executive agency head	2	22
Principal advisor, office of the president	4	36
State executive branch		
Governor	8	16
Lt. governor	15	30
Attorney general	5	10
Secretary of state	12	24
State treasurer	8	16
State legislative branch		
State representative	1,262	23
State senator	406	21
Local executive branch		
Mayors of 100 largest cities	12	12
Mayors of cities over 30,000	187	16
Mayors of cities over 100,000	37	15

Source: Center for American Women and Politics, Rutgers University, "Fact Sheet," 2005.

Women are more likely than men to take extended leaves of absence for such things as maternity leave. How does this affect their lifetime earnings?

Women occupied only 15.4 percent of the seats in the U.S. House of Representatives in 2005. And although the number of female U.S. senators increased from two to thirteen over the 1990s, women still represented just 14 percent of the Senate in 2005 (Center for American Women and Politics, 2005). Women in Congress have seldom risen to positions of power. Only 14 women hold House or Senate leadership roles.

The record for women in appointed offices is also poor. Although there have been recent increases in the number of appointments, the total is extremely small. When President Jimmy Carter appointed two women to his cabinet in 1977, it was the first time two women had sat on the Cabinet at one time. President Bill Clinton, almost twenty years later, appointed three women to Cabinet posts. Still, the total number of women who have ever served as Cabinet officers is very small. President Ronald Reagan appointed the first woman Supreme Court justice, Sandra Day O'Connor, in 1981; and President Clinton elevated Ruth Bader Ginsburg to the high court in 1993. Only a small percentage of federal judges are women.

The number of women holding public office in the United States is among the lowest in the Western world. With some notable exceptions, Western European nations have much greater female political participation. In the Scandinavian countries, for example, up to 20 percent of members of parliament are women.

Sociologists Richard Zwiegenhaft and William Domhoff (1998) do point out that women are now part of the power elite. The power elite is no longer the exclusively male group it used to be. Still, women are seriously underrepresented, and most of those women who do join the power elite come from upper-class backgrounds.

Section 3 Assessment

1. Define *sexism*.
2. Give several examples of legal bias against women.

Critical Thinking

3. **Evaluating Information** Do you support or oppose affirmative action programs for women in the workplace? Give reasons for your answer.

Men, Women, and the Internet

Although women are still subject to discrimination in some technical careers, such as computer programming and information systems analysis, they are finding more and better opportunities in Internet business fields than in any other area of business. Women have founded and become chief executive officer (CEO) of many high-tech companies, including Marimba, Oxygen Media, iVillage, and Women.com. Kim Polese, CEO of Marimba, was featured on more business magazine covers in 1998 than Bill Gates, founder and CEO of Microsoft.

These unanticipated opportunities for women are due to several factors. First, whereas most American industries developed when women were expected to stay at home, the system that would become the Internet was started only about thirty years ago. The Internet itself did not become really popular until the mid-1990s. By that time, women had already entered the workforce in large numbers and had begun to occupy mid- and upper-level management positions.

Second, women are able to profit from the tremendous demand for experienced marketing managers created by the Internet. Because women are responsible for some 85 percent of purchasing decisions in non-Internet businesses, they have the experience to move into marketing management positions. Internet companies have turned to these women to fill important positions.

Third, the Internet has created an astronomical demand for skilled high-tech workers. American high-tech firms are desperate for workers, and they are turning to women as an underutilized resource.

Of course, not all women entering Internet businesses escape sexism. This trend, nonetheless, is a step toward greater workplace equality. Because the Internet has rapidly become such a large part of the U.S. economy, and because it will only continue to grow, the information age holds considerable promise for gender equality.

Meg Whitman is president and CEO of eBay, the world's largest online auction site. Under Whitman's leadership, eBay's revenue skyrocketed from about $5.7 million in 1998 to more than $4 billion in 2005.

Analyzing the Trends

Choose one of the three major theoretical perspectives, and analyze the rise of women in Internet businesses. Use information from this chapter to support your analysis. Predict whether or not the rise of women in Internet businesses will lead to improved gender equality in other workplace arenas.

Ageism

Key Terms

- age stratification *(p. 330)*
- ageism *(p. 330)*

age stratification
the unequal distribution of scarce resources based on age

ageism
a set of beliefs, attitudes, norms, and values used to justify age-based prejudice and discrimination

Section Preview

The relatively low social standing of older people is based on ageism. Each of the theoretical perspectives has a unique slant on ageism. Stereotypes are often used to justify prejudice and discrimination, which can harm the self-concepts of older people.

Defining Ageism

Chronological age is another basis for social ranking. For this reason, sociologists are interested in **age stratification**—when the unequal distribution of scarce resources (power, wealth, prestige) in a society is based on age. Like inequality based on race, ethnicity, or gender, age stratification must be socially justified. The rationale for age-base inequality comes in the form of **ageism**—a set of beliefs, attitudes, norms, and values used to justify prejudice and discrimination against a particular age group. Although age can be an advantage or disadvantage for any group, sociologists are especially interested in inequality among older people. As the median age of the U.S. population grows older, this form of ageism affects more and more people.

Functionalism and Ageism

According to functionalists, elderly people in a given society are treated according to the role the aged play in that society. In many societies, ageism is not an issue. In fact, elderly people in many cultures are treated with great respect and honor. (See the Focus on Research on page 334.)

In agricultural societies, elderly males usually play important roles, such as the role of priest or elder. Donald Cowgill and Lowell Holmes give examples of societies in which the elderly are highly valued.

> *In all of the African societies, growing old is equated with rising status and increased respect. Among the Igbo, the older person is assumed to be wise: this not only brings him respect, since he is consulted for his wisdom, it also provides him with a valued role in his society. The Bantu elder is "the Father of His People" and revered as such. In Samoa, too, old age is "the best time of life" and older persons are accorded great respect.*

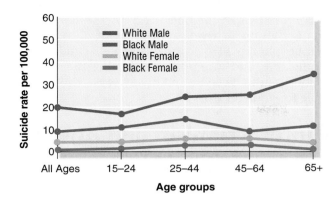

Figure 10.8

U.S. Suicide Rates by Age, Gender, and Racial Group, 2002

This figure charts U.S. suicide rates by age, gender, and racial category. Why do you think suicide rates climb for males at about age 65? Use material from the textbook in your answer.

Source: National Center for Health Statistics, *Health, United States, 2004.*

Likewise, in Thailand, older persons are honored and deferred to and Adams reports respect and affection for older people in rural Mexico (Cowgill and Holmes, 1972).

In early colonial America, no stigma was attached to age. In fact, to be elderly brought respect along with the opportunity to fill the most prestigious positions in the community. It was believed that God looked with favor on those who reached old age. The longer one lived, the more likely he or she was to have been chosen to go to heaven. The Bible linked age with living a moral life: "Keep my commandments, for length of days and long life and peace shall they add unto thee." During the 1600s and 1700s, Americans even tried to appear older than they actually were. Some people wore clothing that made them appear older and covered their hair with powdered wigs. During the 1700s, people often inflated their age when reporting to census takers.

Attitudes about aging changed greatly as industrialization changed the nature of work. In a technical society, an adult's value lessens when he or she no longer contributes fully to the common good. Thus, aging tends to lead to lower status. Because modern societies change rapidly, younger workers are more likely to possess the current skills needed in the workplace. As individuals get older, their skills are more likely to be out of date in the workplace. Thus, they lack the "wisdom" that is most highly valued.

This loss of status with older age might help explain the increase in the suicide rate for men beginning at about retirement age. (See Figure 10.8.) Men may have greater difficulty in older age than women because they have been socialized in a culture that encourages men to identify strongly with work while they are younger, but denies them a sense of value after retirement.

Conflict Theory and Ageism

Competition over scarce resources lies at the heart of ageism for the conflict perspective. Elderly people compete with other age groups for economic resources, power, and prestige. In preindustrial societies, older people often get a fair share of the scarce resources. This is because work in preindustrial society is labor intensive, and all available hands must be utilized. Also, the elderly are sources of valuable knowledge about practices and history.

Industrial society, in contrast, usually has more workers than it needs. In addition, industrial societies save scarce resources by replacing high-priced older workers with less costly younger ones. Forced retirement is one way the more powerful age groups remove elderly competitors.

According to conflict theory, prejudice and discrimination are used by the dominant group as weapons in the control of minority groups. If older people can be stereotyped as intellectually dull, closed-minded, inflexible, and unproductive, forcing their retirement from the labor market becomes relatively easy. This leaves more jobs available for younger workers.

Symbolic Interactionism and Ageism

Like racism, ageism involves creating negative stereotypes. According to symbolic interactionists, children learn negative images of older people just as they learn other aspects of culture. Through the process of socialization, stereotypes of elderly people are often firmly implanted into a child's view of the world. Negative images of older people have been observed in children as young as three years old (Hiller and Barrow, 1999).

What are some stereotypes of the elderly? By definition, stereotypes are inaccurate, because they do not apply to all members of a group. Stereotypes of older people are no exception, as much research has shown. Most elderly people are not senile, forgetful, or "daft." Old age is not a sexless period for the majority of those over sixty-five. There are few age differences on job-related factors. Most elderly people are able to learn new things and adapt to change (Atchley, 2003).

In summary, there is enough evidence to challenge the truth of popular stereotypes of elderly people. Of course, some older people do fit one or more of these stereotypes (as some young people fit societal stereotypes), and many individuals are likely to fit one or more of them as they reach age seventy. This fact, however, does not justify applying the stereotypes to all older people at any age or for mindlessly applying them to individuals in their fifties and sixties.

Many older Americans are realizing that learning computer skills will help them keep in touch with friends, keep updated on financial and health issues, and allow them to find part-time work, if desired.

Section 4 Assessment

1. How are sexism and ageism "two sides of the same coin"?

2. Below are several statements about older people. Identify each statement with one major theoretical perspective: functionalism (F), conflict theory (C), or symbolic interactionism (S).

   a. Ageism results in part from an oversupply of labor.

   b. Young people are uncomfortable around older people.

   c. The stigma attached to aging promotes a low self-concept among older people.

   d. Ageism is associated with industrialization.

   e. Older people are stereotyped.

   f. Ageism exists in part because older workers are inefficient.

Critical Thinking

3. **Evaluating Information** Do you think ageism is a problem in American society? Support your case with information.

Inequality in America's Elderly Population

Section Preview

The poverty rate for America's elderly population stands at 9.8 percent. Members of racial and ethnic minorities are in the poorest ranks. The political process offers the major source of power for elderly Americans. Older people exert political influence through their high voting rate and their support of special interest groups.

Key Term

● **interest group** *(p. 338)*

Elderly People as a Minority Group

Because early research tended to study older people in institutions, studies focused on people with diminished mental and physical capacities. This perspective coincided with the American public's negative view of elderly people. Sociologists believe that the best way to expose this blaming of older people for their situation is to view them as a minority (Hiller and Barrow, 1999).

Racial, ethnic, and religious groups have long been considered as minorities. As you have seen, women have recently been recognized as a minority group. Not until recently have researchers viewed older people as a distinct segment of society subject to the same discrimination and stereotyping as other minority groups.

Economics of the Elderly

The economic situation among America's older people has improved since 1960, but as a group older Americans are far from being well off. Several factors make it hard to determine exactly how elderly people compare economically with other groups, however. For one thing, the way poverty among older people is measured distorts the real picture.

Why is poverty measured differently for older people? Despite the fact that elderly people spend proportionately more on health care and housing than younger people, the federal government assumes that older people require less money to live. If the standard used for younger age categories were applied to elderly people, their poverty rate would increase from 9.8 percent to 15 percent. Poverty rates also fail to take into account the older people who are officially considered to be "near poor." These people make up nearly 7 percent of the elderly population. Counting these at-risk elderly people, about 16 percent of those over age sixty-five are poor (U.S. Bureau of the Census, 2005).

Nor do official statistics include the "hidden poor" among the elderly population. These older people live either in institutions or with relatives because they cannot afford to live independently. Inclusion of these people would substantially raise the poverty rate for elderly Americans.

Unfortunately, life is not this comfortable for a large segment of America's elderly population.

Case Study: A Town without Pity

In the mountains of Western Ireland lies the old agricultural town of Ballybran. Power in this town traditionally lay in the hands of the "old ones," particularly the senior males. Here, sociologist Nancy Scheper-Hughes spent a year doing fieldwork, studying the effects of modernization on the society. She identifies the basic demographic shift that has led to the death of the rural Irish gerontocracy [rule by elders], describes the negative consequences of this change for the elderly, and discusses several areas in which the loss of social standing among the elderly is reflected.

Scheper-Hughes found that with modernization and with dependence on imported food came a lessening of respect for the skills and knowledge of the old farmers.

Underlying this picture, of course, is the devaluating of the agricultural way of life among these people. At an earlier time, the patriarchal father delayed retirement and sparked intense competition among his sons for rights to the family lands. Now heir selection is determined more by the process of elimination than the choice of the father—"the last one to escape (usually the youngest son) gets stuck by default with an unproductive farm and saddled with a life of celibacy and greatly resented service to the 'old people'" (Scheper-Hughes, 1983:134).

As "progress" comes to both city and country, many of the local elderly population find their skills are not needed and that they have no role to play in the life of the community.

The result of all this for the aged parents is fairly clear: They no longer have the economic power base they once used to control the younger generation and to maintain their superior status in the family and community. Because young people prefer to be "liberated" from the land, the "old ones" control little that the youth want. The awe and respect for the elderly that once characterized the community has, in many cases, been replaced by not only pity but also contempt. The demise of the traditional family farming–based culture leaves the elderly father, in Scheper-Hughes's words, a "broken figure." Toleration from his adult children is the most he can expect, open ridicule the worst. With the erosion of their economic power, the elderly have also lost their cherished role as preservers of the ancient Celtic traditions—the myths, stories, songs, prayers, and proverbs. In fact, the young tend to reject these traditions. Worse, the majority of high school students resent having to study the Irish language, a "dead" language that they believe will be of no use to them in the commercial and professional world outside the rural community.

Ageism has had many negative effects on these older people. Without a meaningful work identity, the once-proud leaders have no sense of place in the community. Alcoholism, diminished self-esteem, and depression are widely seen among those over age fifty. Many are single, widows or widowers, without family or friends to take care of them. Scheper-Hughes writes, "The Irish village of the west coast today embodies a broken culture; a state of affairs most detrimental to the aged who are unable to flee or accept new values, and who, consequently, are left to contemplate the wreckage" (Scheper-Hughes, 1983:145).

Working with the Research

1. Which research methods are best suited to a study like this? Explain.

2. Which theoretical perspective do you think contributes most to how we can understand what happened in this village?

Figure 10.9 Poverty Rates Among Americans Aged 65 and Over: 1959–2004
This figure documents the changing poverty rate among Americans aged 65 and over since 1959. Explain why it would be misleading to cite the current poverty rate as evidence that America's aged population is economically well off.

Source: U.S. Census Bureau, *Historical Poverty Tables*, 2005.

This elderly woman is part of America's "hidden poor." What does that mean?

The income gap among elderly people also distorts the economic picture. Some older people have moderate to high incomes based on dividends from assets, cash savings, and private retirement programs. Most elderly Americans, however, do not have sources of income beyond Social Security benefits. The existence of a small percentage of high-income older people gives the false impression that most older people are economically well off. Figure 10.9 shows the poverty rate for elderly people since 1959.

What other factors affect elderly Americans? Older people who are members of racial or ethnic minority groups are generally in worse condition than older white Americans. The poverty rate among older African Americans is three times that for whites. For older Latinos, the poverty rate is more than two and one-half times that of non-Latino white Americans. Problems that racial and ethnic minorities face because of discrimination become magnified in old age.

Elderly women constitute one of the poorest segments of American society. Women over age sixty-five are nearly twice as likely to live in poverty as their male counterparts (CRS Report for Congress, 2005). Elderly women most likely to be poor are single women who either have never married or are divorced, separated, or widowed. This is not surprising, because the roots of poverty among older women lie in their work-related experiences. Because older women were discouraged or blocked from better jobs throughout their work lives, they are unable to support themselves in their later years (Sidel, 1998).

Overall, what is the economic position of older people in the United States? In summary, then, elderly people are economically better off than they were four decades ago. Despite this improvement, large segments of Americans over sixty-five years of age live either in poverty or near poverty. This is especially true for elderly members of racial and ethnic minorities and for elderly women.

Snapshot of America

Percentage of Population Aged Sixty-five and Over

The "graying of America" refers to the growing elderly population. Improved medical care, better nutrition, and healthier lifestyles have all contributed to longer life expectancies in the United States. This map shows the percentage of the population that is aged sixty-five years old and over in each state.

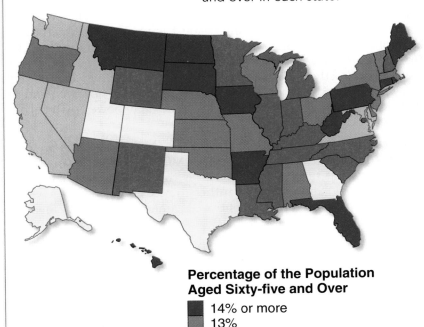

Percentage of the Population Aged Sixty-five and Over

- 14% or more
- 13%
- 12%
- 11%
- 1–10%

Interpreting the Map

1. Describe the distribution pattern of elderly people across the United States. Create a chart representing the distribution pattern.

2. Where is your state in this distribution?

3. Research the voting rate for elderly people in your state. Is it higher or lower than the national average?

Source: U.S. Bureau of the Census, *Statistical Abstract of the United States, 2004–2005.*

Political Power and the Elderly

Given the limited economic resources of older people, it is clear that any power they hold is gained through the political process. Especially important are the voting booth and political interest groups.

What is the voting turnout among elderly Americans?

Voting turnout in the United States increases with age. Since the mid-1980s, Americans aged sixty-five and over have been the most active voters in

Figure 10.10 Selected Socioeconomic Characteristics of Elderly Americans

From this figure, some comparative statements can be made about the economic situation of elderly Americans. What are two important statements that can be supported by these data?

Source: CRS Report for Congress, 2005.

	Whites	African Americans	Latinos	Women	Men
Median Income	$16,200	$11,500	$10,400	$12,100	$21,200
Percent in Poverty	8%	24%	19%	12%	7%

presidential and congressional elections. In 2004, for example, 71 percent of this group voted in the presidential election, compared with just under 47 percent of eighteen- to twenty-four-year-olds and just under 60 percent of twenty-five to forty-four-year-olds (U.S. Bureau of the Census, 2005).

Does voting lead to political power? Most analysts believe that the potential political power of elderly Americans as a group is not fully realized because of the diversity of the older population. Because older people cut across many important divisions in American society—social class, ethnicity, race, geographic area, religion—they do not speak with a unified political voice. In fact, they do not vote as a bloc on any political question, even on issues related directly to their interests. This lack of unity weakens their political clout. As the population of the United States ages, however, and the number of elderly voters increases, it is likely that "gray power" will become a significant political force.

● **interest group**
a group organized to influence political decision making

What is the role of interest groups? Interest groups are organized to influence political decision making. Millions of Americans belong to interest groups that target ageism, such as the American Association of Retired Persons (AARP) and the Gray Panthers. These groups have been effective in protecting programs that benefit older Americans, such as Medicare and Social Security.

Section 5 Assessment

1. Of the following, which is an accurate statement?

   a. Since 1960, the economic situation for elderly people in the United States has deteriorated.

   b. The poverty rate for Americans over age sixty-five is lower than the official count indicates.

   c. Problems of older Americans who are members of racial or ethnic minorities are generally more severe than problems of elderly whites.

   d. Older Americans are politically vulnerable.

2. What can older Americans do to increase their impact on government policy and legislation?

Critical Thinking

3. **Drawing Conclusions** Drawing on Hurricane Katrina or any other recent American crisis, identify three incidents of institutionalized discrimination against the elderly. What conclusions can you draw from these reports?

Summary

Section 1: Sex and Gender Identity

Main Idea: All societies expect people to behave in certain ways based on their sex.

Section 2: Theoretical Perspectives on Gender

Main Idea: The functionalist perspective focuses on the origins of gender differences. Conflict theory looks at the reasons gender differences continue to exist. Symbolic interactionism explains how gender is acquired.

Section 3: Gender Inequality

Main Idea: Despite many gains, women still face discrimination.

Section 4: Ageism

Main Idea: Each of the theoretical perspectives has a unique slant on ageism, bias based on a person's age.

Section 5: Inequality In America's Elderly Population

Main Idea: The poverty rate for America's elderly population stands at around 10 percent, with minority elderly in the poorest ranks. Because the elderly tend to go to the polls more than other groups, they have significant political power.

Self-Check Quiz
Visit the *Sociology and You* Web site at glencoe.com and click on **Chapter 10—Self-Check Quizzes** to prepare for the chapter test.

Reviewing Vocabulary

Complete each sentence using each term once.

a. gender identity
b. sex
c. gender socialization
d. sexism
e. occupational sex segregation
f. ageism
g. biological determinism
h. age stratification
i. interest group

1. An organization that attempts to influence political decision making is called _____ .
2. _____ is the unequal distribution of scarce resources based on age.
3. The classification of people as male or female based on biological characteristics is called _____ .
4. _____ is the concentration of one gender in certain occupations.
5. _____ is a set of beliefs, attitudes, norms, and values used to justify sexual inequality.
6. The belief that behavioral differences are due to inherited physical characteristics is called _____ .
7. _____ is a set of beliefs, attitudes, norms, and values used to justify age-based prejudice and discrimination.
8. _____ is an awareness of being masculine or feminine.
9. The social process of learning how to act as a boy or girl is called _____ .

Reviewing the Facts

10. According to the functionalist perspective, what was the main result of the division of labor?
11. Which sociological perspective emphasizes the effects of parents, teachers, and peers on gender socialization?
12. How would you explain the increase in women's participation in the labor force?

13. Give one reason why the gap between men's and women's salaries persists.

14. What segment of the poor population is often not included in the statistics on elderly poor people?

15. According to the text, what is the best way that the elderly can effect social change on their own behalf?

Thinking Critically

16. Analyzing Information

A common phrase in sociology is "you inherit your sex and learn your gender." What do you think this phrase means?

17. Applying Concepts

Physical strength is not as important for males today as it was in past times. The nature of work has changed so that not as many jobs require stamina or physical strength. What impact do you think this devaluing of muscle strength has on society? List five attitudes or values that could be affected.

18. Evaluating Information

Certain jobs, such as firefighting, still require great physical strength and stamina. Often, these positions have minimum requirements to ensure that employees can fulfill all the necessary duties. Because of biology, men generally find it easier to meet many of these physical requirements. Some cities have responded by changing the standards to ensure that women are represented in these vocations. Other cities have refused and have been subjected to discrimination lawsuits. What are some arguments for and against the policy of changing standards to ensure representation of women in certain jobs? Are there situations in which you would allow different standards? Are there situations in which you would not? Discuss your views.

Bernard Schoenbaum/Cartoonbank.com

19. Analyzing Visuals

The Bernard Schoenbaum cartoon above appeared in the *New Yorker* magazine in 1993. What social trend did it reflect? What "twist" is the cartoonist taking on that trend? How does the cartoon relate to what you read in the chapter about generational stereotypes?

20. Drawing Conclusions

U.S. society has definite expectations about female and male roles. What are the gender norms concerning personal appearance? Do these norms work against women? Do they work against males?

21. Making Inferences

The text discusses some of the stereotypes associated with older people. Using recent research on these stereotypes, do you think the norms underlying ageism will diminish? Check your thoughts against the opinions of a few elderly people.

Sociology Projects

22. Gender

This activity is a thought problem and requires a great deal of imagination. What would your day be like if you awoke one morning and suddenly found that you had changed gender? As you go about your day, think of everything that would be different. Write down several things that stand out as you go through the day. For example, if you are on a sports team, would you likely be on that team if you changed gender?

23. Observation

Observe people of all ages in a variety of settings, such as restaurants, malls, and offices. Do their clothing and actions fit age-appropriate norms of our culture? What exceptions do you note?

24. Global Wages for Men and Women

In this chapter, you read about global inequity in pay for men and women in most jobs. In the United Nations table below, differential pay is presented for different regions of the world. As a sociology project, study the table below. Then write down three different hypotheses suggested by the data. The hypotheses could make statements comparing regions or countries. A hypothesis might also be based on further research on the nature

Women's Wages in Manufacturing As a Percent of Men's		
	Year	Percent
Egypt	2002	68
Kenya	1997	123
Turkey	1997	97
Mexico	2001	70
Peru	1995	55
Japan	2003	60
United Kingdom	2003	79
Switzerland	2002	133

Source: UN Statistics Division, *The World's Women 2005*

25. Lifestyles for the Elderly

Create a poster or other visual aid that depicts how life has changed for elderly people during the twentieth century. You may want to talk to grandparents or others about what life was like for older people in the past.

26. The Elderly and Advertising

Analyze television commercials for the way older people are portrayed. How frequently are older people represented in advertising? What types of products do they normally market? Is a pattern or stereotype being perpetuated?

Technology Activity

27. The Center for the American Woman and Politics is a useful web site to learn about women in public office in the United States. Go to www. cawp. rutgers.edu/Facts4.html. Select "State by State Information" and click on your state in the map that appears.

a. How many women are serving in your state's legislature?

b. Where does your state rank in comparison to other states?

c. When was a woman first elected to a statewide office or to the U.S. Congress?

d. Now return to the Home or Main Page and click on Facts and Findings. Either scroll down to Women in Congress or click on that heading at the top. What percent of Senators are women? What percent of the House of Representatives are women?

e. Finally, click on the Women Officeholders: Historical link at the top of the Facts and Findings page. Survey some of the information at this link, and write two or three paragraphs summarizing the history of American women in politics.

The Story of Baby X
by Lois Gould

"Once upon a time, a baby named X was born. This baby was named X so that nobody could tell whether it was a boy or a girl." So begins a children's story by Lois Gould about gender stereotypes.

X was given to Mr. and Ms. Jones, a couple carefully screened from thousands of applicants, as an experiment. The Joneses were to follow only one rule: X was not to be socialized as masculine or feminine, but was to learn everything a child could. Assisted by a heavy *Official Instruction Manual*, the Joneses promised to follow this rule as closely as possible. They agreed to take equal turns feeding and caring for X, to spend as much time bouncing as cuddling the baby, and to praise X for being strong just as often as for being sweet. But trouble began almost right away when the Joneses' friends and relatives asked whether X was a boy or a girl.

When the Joneses smiled and said "It's an X!" nobody knew what to say. They couldn't say, "Look at her cute little dimples." And they couldn't say "Look at his husky little biceps!' And they couldn't even say just plain "kitchy-coo." In fact, they all thought that the Joneses were playing some kind of rude joke.

The Joneses were, of course, being quite serious, but all the same, other people became irritated and embarrassed:

"People will think there's something wrong with it!" some of them whispered.
"There *is* something wrong with it!" others whispered back.

And what did baby X think about all the fuss? It simply finished its bottle with a loud and satisfied burp.

Finding toys for X was another problem. The first trip to the toy store brought this immediate question from the store clerk: "Well, now, is it a boy or a girl?" In the storekeeper's mind, footballs and fire engine sets were for boys and dolls and housekeeping sets were for girls. But the Joneses knew that they had to be sure baby X had *all* kinds of toys to play with, including:

a boy doll that made pee-pee and cried "Pa-Pa." And a girl doll that talked. They also bought a storybook about a brave princess who rescued a handsome prince from his ivory tower, and another one about a sister and brother who grew up to be a baseball star and a ballet star, and you had to guess which was which.

But the biggest problem came when X was old enough to begin school, where the children were treated according to their sex. Boys and girls lined up separately, played games separately, and, of course, used different bathrooms. The other children had never met an X before, and just *had* to know what its sex really was. But the Joneses had raised X very carefully so that there was no easy answer:

> You couldn't tell what X was by studying its clothes; overalls don't button right-to-left, like girl's clothes, or left-to-right, like boy's clothes. And you couldn't tell whether X had a girl's short haircut or a boy's long haircut. And it was very hard to tell by the games X liked to play. Either X played ball very well for a girl, or else X played house very well for a boy.

The other children found X a very strange playmate: one day it would ask boys to weave some baskets in the arts and crafts room, and the next day it would ask some girls to go shoot baskets in the gym. But X tried very hard to be friendly to everyone and to do well in school. And X did very well in school, winning spelling bees, athletic events and coming in second in a baking contest (even X's aren't perfect). As other children noticed what a good time X was having in school, they began to wonder if maybe X wasn't having twice as much fun as they were!

> From then on, some really funny things began to happen. Susie who sat next to X in class, suddenly refused to wear pink dresses to school any more. She insisted on wearing red-and-white checked overalls—just like X's. Overalls, she told her parents, were much better for climbing monkey bars. Then Jim, the class football nut, started wheeling his little sister's doll carriage around the football field. He'd put on his entire football uniform, except for the helmet. Then he'd put the helmet *in* the carriage, lovingly tucked under an old set of shoulder pads. Then he'd start jogging around the field. He told his family that X did the same thing, so it must be okay. After all, X was now the team's star quarterback.

But this kind of behavior in the children horrified their parents. And when Peggy started using Joe's hockey skates while Joe enjoyed using Peggy's needlepoint kit, matters went from bad to worse. X was to blame for all this! So the Parents' Association at school demanded that X be identified as a boy or a girl and be forced to act accordingly. A psychiatrist was asked to conduct a full examination and report back to the

parents. If, as most suspected, X was found to be a very confused child, it should be expelled from school altogether.

The teachers were puzzled by this; after all, X was one of their very best students. But the school—as well as the Joneses—finally agreed to let X be examined.

The next day the psychiatrist arrived at the school and began a long examination of X while everyone waited anxiously outside. When the psychiatrist finally emerged from the examination room, the results were not what most people expected. "In my opinion," the psychiatrist told them, "young X here is just about the *least* mixed up child I've ever examined!" The doctor explained that by the time the X's sex really mattered, everyone would know what it was.

This, of course, made the Joneses very happy and delighted the scientists who had begun the experiment in the first place. And later that day, X's friends (dressed in red-and-white checked overalls) came over to X's house to play. They found X in the backyard playing with a new tiny baby.

> "How do you like our new baby?" X asked the other children proudly.
> "It's got cute dimples," said Jim.
> "It's got husky biceps, too," said Susie.
> "What kind of baby is it?" asked Joe and Peggy. X frowned at them. Can't you tell?" Then X broke into a big mischievous grin. "It's a Y!"

Source: Adapted from Lois Gould, "X: A Fabulous Child's Story," *Ms.*, Vol. 1 (December, 1972):74–76, 105–106.

Read and React

1. What was your first reaction to this story?
2. Summarize the underlying hypothesis in the Baby X story.
3. Could a scientific experiment be constructed to test this hypothesis? If so, describe it. If not, explain why.
4. Discuss the ethical implications of such an experiment if one were conducted.
5. How does propaganda regarding childrearing affect differences in the socialization of males and females?

Chapter

11

The Family

Sections

1. **Family and Marriage Across Cultures**
2. **Theoretical Perspectives and the Family**
3. **Family and Marriage in the United States**
4. **Changes in Marriage and Family**

Learning Objectives

After reading this chapter, you will be able to

- describe types of family structure and norms for marriage arrangements.
- compare and contrast views of the family proposed by the three major perspectives.
- outline the extent and cause of divorce in America.
- give an overview of family violence in the United States.
- discuss the future of the family in the United States.

Applying Sociology

Test your knowledge about the American family by identifying the following as true or false:

1. About half of the American couples who marry will divorce.
2. A new family structure develops after a divorce.
3. In more than half of all marriages, both husband and wife work outside the home.
4. The divorce rate has been steadily climbing since 1960.

If you thought the first three questions were true and the last question was false, you probably have a good sense of what is happening in American marriages and families today. While the divorce rate rose dramatically from 1960 to 1985, there has actually been a decline in the last twenty years.

The next five chapters will look at family, education, economics, politics, religion, and sports. Sociologists refer to each of these as social institution—a system of roles, norms and social structure that satisfy basic needs of society. Chapter 11 focuses on the most important—family.

Sociology Online

Chapter Overview
Visit the *Sociology and You* Web site at **glencoe.com** and click on **Chapter 11—Chapter Overviews** to preview chapter information.

1

Family and Marriage Across Cultures

Key Terms

- family *(p. 349)*
- marriage *(p. 349)*
- nuclear family *(p. 349)*
- extended family *(p. 349)*
- patrilineal *(p. 350)*
- matrilineal *(p. 350)*
- bilateral *(p. 350)*
- patriarchy *(p. 350)*
- matriarchy *(p. 350)*
- equalitarian *(p. 350)*
- patrilocal *(p. 351)*
- matrilocal *(p. 351)*
- neolocal *(p. 351)*
- monogamy *(p. 351)*
- polygamy *(p. 352)*
- polygyny *(p. 352)*
- polyandry *(p. 352)*
- exogamy *(p. 354)*
- incest taboo *(p. 354)*
- endogamy *(p. 354)*
- homogamy *(p. 354*
- heterogamy *(p. 355)*

Section Preview

In all societies, the family has been the most important of all social institutions. It produces new generations, socializes the young, provides care and affection, regulates sexual behavior, transmits social status, and provides economic support.

Defining the Family

If asked to identify a family, most of us would say we know one when we see one. We are surrounded by families wherever we go, and most of us live in family settings. However, families come in all shapes and sizes, and defining the term *family* is sometimes difficult. Legally, the word *family* is used to describe many relationships: parents and children; people related by blood, marriage, or adoption; a group of people living together in a single household, sharing living space and housekeeping. Since the word *family* does not have a precise meaning, many laws define the term when they use it. For example,

If asked to describe this image, the first thought of most people would be that of a happy family.

zoning laws that set aside certain areas for single-family homes define family one way. Laws involving insurance, social security programs, or inheritance may define family in other ways. For sociologists, however, **family** is defined as a group of people related by marriage, blood, or adoption. While the concept of family may appear simple on the surface, the family is a complex social unit with many facets. Of all the social institutions, the family has the greatest impact on individual behavior.

The family we are born into, or the family of birth, is called the *family of orientation.* It provides children with a name, an identity, and a heritage. In other words, it gives the child an ascribed status in the community. The family of orientation "orients" (or directs) children to their neighborhood, community, and society and locates them in the world.

The *family of procreation* is established upon marriage. **Marriage** is a legal union between a man and a woman based on mutual rights and obligations. (Marriages between two persons of the same sex have been ruled invalid by U.S. courts, with the exception of Massachusetts, although legal challenges are ongoing.) The marriage ceremony signifies that it is legal for a couple to have offspring and to give the children a family name. The family of procreation becomes the family of orientation for the children created from the marriage.

Two Basic Types of Families

There are two basic types of families. The **nuclear family**, the smallest group of individuals that can be called a family, is composed of a parent or parents and any children. The **extended family** consists of two or more adult generations of the same family whose members share economic resources and live in the same household. Extended families may also contain close relatives, such as grandparents, children, grandchildren, aunts, uncles, and cousins.

● **family**
a group of people related by marriage, blood, or adoption

● **marriage**
a legal union based on mutual rights and obligations

● **nuclear family**
family structure composed of one or both parents and children

● **extended family**
two or more adult generations of the same family whose members share economic resources and a common household

Why would sociologists not call these relatives an extended family?

How did family structures develop? As discussed in Chapter 5, the development of agriculture and industry shaped society. These developments also shaped family structure.

In the earliest societies, hunting and gathering were the primary family activities. Small bands of nuclear families followed herds of animals and changing seasons, moving around constantly, never staying long in any one place.

When humans domesticated animals to help with tilling the soil and cultivating crops (about ten thousand years ago), they no longer needed to be mobile to maintain a food supply. Families began to farm, settle down, and establish roots. Large families were needed to plow and harvest. The growth of family farms encouraged the development of the extended family and changed the division of labor. Agriculture became the basis of the economy, and the extended family was essential for successful farming.

As societies moved from agricultural economies to industrialized ones, the extended family was slowly replaced by the nuclear family. Large families were no longer needed to work on the farm. Industrial and postindustrial economies favor the nuclear family that has fewer mouths to feed and that is easier to move (Goode, 1970; Skolnick and Skolnick, 2004).

Patterns of Family Structure

Whether nuclear or extended, families behave in similar ways across cultures. These patterns of behavior relate to inheritance, authority, and place of residence.

Who inherits? Determining who becomes head of the family—for purpose of descent—and who owns the family property—for inheritance—are extremely important to families. Three arrangements are used.

- In a **patrilineal** arrangement, descent and inheritance are passed from the father to his male descendants. The people of Iran and Iraq and the Tikopia in the western Pacific live in patrilineal societies.
- In a **matrilineal** arrangement, descent and inheritance are transmitted from the mother to her female descendants. Some Native American tribes, such as the Pueblo peoples of the Southwest, are matrilineal.
- In some societies, descent and inheritance are **bilateral**—they are passed equally through both parents. Thus both the father's and mother's relatives are accepted equally as part of the kinship structure. Most families in the United States today are bilateral.

Who is in authority? Similar patterns govern authority in a family.

- In a **patriarchy,** the oldest man living in the household has authority over the rest of the family members. We see this in many countries around the world, such as Iraq and China. In its purest form, the father is the absolute ruler.
- In a **matriarchy,** the oldest woman living in the household holds the authority. So rare is matriarchal control that controversy exists over whether any society has ever had a genuinely matriarchal family structure.
- With **equalitarian** control, authority is split evenly between husband and wife. Many families in the Scandinavian countries and in the United States follow the equalitarian model.

Sidebar (glossary terms)

- **patrilineal**
  descent and inheritance are passed through the male line

- **matrilineal**
  descent and inheritance are passed through the female line

- **bilateral**
  descent and inheritance are passed equally through both parents

- **patriarchy**
  the pattern in which the oldest man living in the household has authority over the rest of the family members

- **matriarchy**
  the pattern in which the oldest woman living in the household has authority over all other family members

- **equalitarian**
  family structure in which authority is evenly shared between the husband and wife

Where do couples live? Where newly married couples set up their households also varies from culture to culture.

- The **patrilocal** pattern, such as in premodern China, calls for living with or near the husband's parents.

- Residing with or near the wife's parents is expected under a **matrilocal** pattern. The Nayar caste of Kerala in southern India is an illustration of this type of arrangement.

- In the **neolocal** pattern (if finances allow) married couples establish residences of their own. This is the Euro-American model. Extended families, of course, have different norms.

Marriage Arrangements

Mention a wedding and Americans commonly think of a bride walking down the aisle in a long white gown. She and the groom make vows that involve some form of loving, honoring, and (until recently, in some cases) obeying. In other cultures, the wedding ceremony looks very different. This is part of the ceremony among the Reindeer Tungus of Siberia:

> *After the groom's gifts have been presented, the bride's dowry is loaded onto the reindeer and carried to the groom's lodge. There, the rest of the ceremony takes place. The bride takes the wife's place—that is, at the right side of the entrance of the lodge—and members of both families sit around in a circle. The groom enters and follows the bride around the circle, greeting each guest, while the guests, in their turn, kiss the bride on the mouth and hands. Finally, the go-betweens spit three times on the bride's hands, and the couple is formally "husband and wife." More feasting and revelry bring the day to a close (Ember and Ember, 1999:310–311).*

Whatever form it takes, the marriage ceremony is an important ritual announcing that a man and woman have become husband and wife, that a new family has been formed, and that any children born to the couple can legitimately inherit the family name and property.

What forms do marriage take? **Monogamy**—the marriage of one man to one woman—is the most widely practiced form of marriage in the world today. In fact, it is the only form of marriage that is legally acceptable in the United States and in most Western societies. Some often-married

- **patrilocal**
  refers to the pattern in which married couples live with or near the husbands' parents

- **matrilocal**
  refers to the pattern in which married couples live with or near the wives' parents

- **neolocal**
  refers to the pattern in which newly married couples set up their own households

- **monogamy**
  a marriage consisting of one man and one woman

Although wedding ceremonies may vary, the basic social structures of marriage are common to all societies.

polygamy
the marriage of a male or female to more than one person at a time

polygyny
the marriage of one man to two or more women at the same time

polyandry
the marriage of one woman to two or more men at the same time

people practice *serial* monogamy—having several husbands or wives, but being married to only one at a time.

In contrast to monogamy, **polygamy** involves the marriage of a male or female to more than one person at a time. It takes two forms: polygyny and polyandry.

Polygyny is the marriage of one man to two or more women at the same time. An obvious example of polygyny is found in the Old Testament. King Solomon is reported to have had seven hundred wives and three hundred concubines. Although common in earlier societies and still legal in India, parts of Africa, and much of Southwest Asia, polygyny is not practiced widely in any society today. However, in 1999 the Muslim Russian republic of Ingushetia legalized the practice of polygyny.

Polyandry—the marriage of one woman to two or more men at the same time—is an even rarer form of marriage. It is known to have been common in only three societies: in Tibet, in parts of Polynesia, and among the Todas and other hill peoples of India (Queen et al., 1985). Where polyandry has existed, it usually has consisted of several brothers sharing a wife.

You have been introduced to a lot of new terms that relate to family structure and marriage arrangements. Figure 11.1 illustrates several of the characteristics of these family and marriage forms to help you understand and remember them.

Figure 11.1	Families/Marriages

This chart summarizes possible variations in family and marriage forms. Describe the general nature of the American family using terms from this table.

Nuclear Family Composition	parents and children
Extended Family Composition	parents, children, and other relatives
Inheritance	patrilineal (inherit through the father) or matrilineal (inherit through the mother) or bilateral (inherit through both)
Authority	patriarchal (father rules the family) or matriarchal (mother rules the family) or equalitarian (parents share authority)
Residence	patrilocal (couple lives with or near husband's parents) or matrilocal (couple lives with or near wife's parents) or neolocal (couple lives apart from both sets of parents)
Marriage Composition	polygyny (one husband, many wives) or polyandry (one wife, many husbands) or monogamy (one husband, one wife)

World View

Percentage of Women Aged 15–19 Ever Married

The age at which Americans marry has been rising for decades. Consequently, only a very small percentage of American teenagers are married. This is not the case in all countries around the world, however. This map shows the percentage of teenage women in each country who have ever been married.

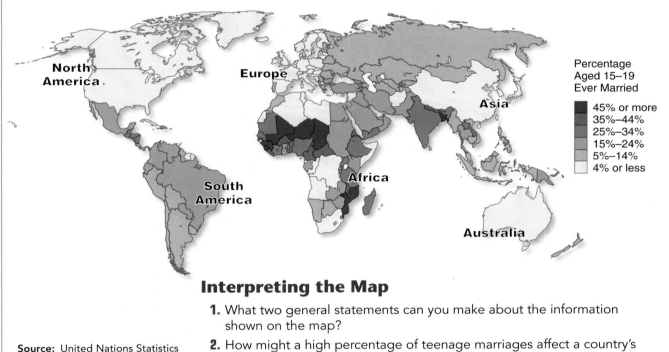

Percentage Aged 15–19 Ever Married

- 45% or more
- 35%–44%
- 25%–34%
- 15%–24%
- 5%–14%
- 4% or less

Interpreting the Map

1. What two general statements can you make about the information shown on the map?

2. How might a high percentage of teenage marriages affect a country's population size?

Source: United Nations Statistics Division, 2005.

Choosing a Mate

Suppose you came home from school one afternoon and your parents asked you to come into the living room to meet your future husband or wife. You might wonder if you had somehow been beamed to another planet. Similarly, you will probably never enroll in a college course entitled "Negotiating Dowries with Prospective In-laws," this being a skill not much in demand today. If, however, you assume that you have complete freedom of choice in the selection of a marriage partner, you are mistaken. All cultures and societies, including the United States, have norms and laws about who may marry whom.

exogamy
the practice of marrying outside one's group

incest taboo
a norm forbidding marriage between close relatives

endogamy
marriage within one's own group as required by social norms

homogamy
the tendency to marry someone similar to oneself

Exogamy refers to mate-selection norms requiring individuals to marry someone outside their kind or group. (*Exo* is a prefix meaning "outside.") The most important norms relating to exogamy are called **incest taboos,** which forbid marriage between certain kinds of relatives. In the traditional Chinese culture, for example, two people with identical family names could not marry unless their family lines were known to have diverged at least five generations previously (Queen et al., 1985). In the United States, you are not legally permitted to marry a son or daughter, a brother or sister, a mother or a father, a niece or nephew, or an aunt or uncle. In thirty-one states, marriage to a first cousin is prohibited. Furthermore, it is illegal to marry a former mother-in-law or father-in-law. Incest is almost universally prohibited, although exceptions were common among the royalty of ancient Europe, Hawaii, Egypt, and Peru. Even in these instances, most members of the royal families chose partners to whom they were not related by blood.

Endogamy involves mate-selection norms that require individuals to marry within their own kind. (*Endo* is a prefix that means "inside.") In the United States, for example, norms have required that marriage partners be of the same race. These norms are not as strong as they once were. Although they represent only five percent of all marriages in the United States, mixed marriages have quadrupled since 1980. Figure 11.2 shows the racial and ethnic breakdown of intergroup marriages today. Also, class lines are crossed with greater frequency because more Americans of all social classes are attending college together. Finally, norms separating age and religious groups have weakened.

Norms encouraging (rather than requiring) marriage within a group usually exist. And people are most likely to know and prefer to marry others like themselves. For these reasons, people tend to marry those with social characteristics similar to their own. This tendency, the result of the rather free exercise of personal choice, is known as **homogamy.**

Figure 11.2 Mixed Marriages and Intergroup Married Couples in the United States
Although only 5 percent of marriages in the U.S. are mixed, the number has quadrupled since 1980.

Sources: American Demographics, Population Reference Bureau, 1998; Miliken Institute, 2001.

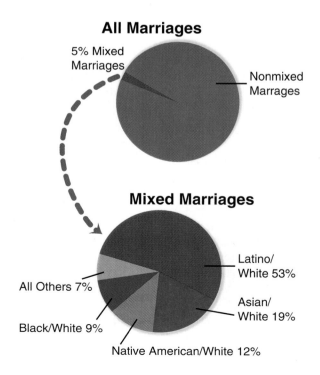

All Marriages

5% Mixed Marriages

Nonmixed Marrages

Mixed Marriages

Latino/White 53%

Asian/White 19%

Native American/White 12%

Black/White 9%

All Others 7%

For example, in spite of what fairy tales and movies often tell us, it is rare for the son or daughter of a multimillionaire to marry someone from a lower class. Furthermore, most marriages in the United States occur between individuals who are about the same age. Most people who are marrying for the first time marry someone who also has not been married before. Divorced people tend to marry others who have been previously married. Finally, people tend to choose marriage partners from their own communities or neighborhoods.

Although it is still the exception in the United States, **heterogamy** is rising. In heterogamous marriages, partners are dissimilar in some important characteristics. More American marriages, for instance, are crossing traditional barriers of age, race, social class, and ethnicity. This trend results from several factors. America has become more racially and ethnically integrated, so that people have an opportunity to mix more freely. The television and film industries help foster heterogamy by the sympathetic portrayal of couples and families from different racial and social backgrounds. In addition, class lines are crossed with greater frequency, and norms separating age and religious groups have weakened.

Are these two individuals in a homogenous or heterogamous relationship? Explain.

● **heterogamy**
marriage between people with differing social characteristics

Section 1 Assessment

1. What is the difference between a nuclear and an extended family? Which type represents your household?

2. Why are nuclear families more common in industrial societies?

3. What is another term for the family of birth?

4. Indicate whether exogamy (Ex), endogamy (En), or homogamy (H) is reflected in each of the following situations.
   a. Catholics are supposed to marry Catholics.
   b. A father is not permitted to marry his daughter.
   c. Members of the same social class marry.
   d. A brother and sister are legally prohibited from marrying.
   e. People tend to marry others of the same age.
   f. Rich people marry other wealthy people.

Critical Thinking

5. **Synthesizing Information** Write a paragraph based on personal knowledge or experience that supports or refutes the idea that homogamy dominates American society.

Courtship and Marriage Among the Hopi

Courtship and marriage customs among the Hopi Indians of the southwestern United States are quite different from those of the dominant U.S. culture.

Once the decision to marry is made by the young couple, the boy goes in the evening after supper to the girl's house and there states his intentions to her parents. If he is acceptable, he is told to go home and tell his parents about it. The girl then grinds cornmeal or makes bread, and carries it to the house of her prospective groom. At this time the mother of the boy may refuse the bread or meal, in which case the match is usually broken off. If, however, the food is accepted, it is given by the mother to her brothers and to her husband's clansmen, and the wedding plans go forward.

After this event the girl returns home to grind more meal with the help of her kinswomen, while the boy fetches water and chops wood for his mother. In the evening after these chores are completed, the bride dresses in her manta beads and her wedding blanket. Accompanied by the boy, who carries the meal she has ground, she walks barefoot to his house. There she presents the meal to her prospective mother-in-law and settles down for a temporary three-day stay before the wedding. During this period the young couple may see each other, but they [do not become intimate].

At some time during the three-day period the groom's house is visited, or "attacked," by his paternal aunts, who break in on the bride and shower her with [abusive language] and often with mud. They accuse her of laziness, inefficiency, and stupidity. The boy's mother and her clanswomen protect the girl and insist that the accusations are unfounded. In spite of appearances all this is carried off in a good-humored way, and finally the aunts leave, having stolen the wood their nephew had brought his mother. The wood is used to bake piki, which is given to the mother, and thus all damages are paid for.

On the morning of the fourth day the marriage is consummated. On this occasion the girl's relatives wash the boy's hair and bathe him, while the boy's relatives do the same for the girl. The couple may now sleep together as man and wife, but they remain at the boy's mother's house until the girl's wedding garments are complete. These garments are woven by the groom, his male relatives, and any men in the village who wish to participate.

Source: Stuart A. Queen and Robert W. Habenstein, *The Family in Various Cultures,* 4th ed. (Philadelphia: Lippincott, 1974, pp. 54–55, 56–58. Copyright 1952, © 1961, 1967, 1974 by J.B. Lippincott Company.) Reprinted by permission of Harper & Row, Publishers.

Thinking It Over

1. What do you think the staged "fight" with the groom's aunts signifies?

2. What are some of the advantages Hopi society gains by following these wedding customs?

Contemporary Hopi Indians play traditional roles during a formal ceremony.

Theoretical Perspectives and the Family

Section Preview

The family is the very core of human social life. It is not surprising that each of the major perspectives focuses on the family. Functionalism emphasizes the benefits of the family for society. The conflict perspective looks at the reasons males dominate in the family structure. Symbolic interactionism studies the way the family socializes children and promotes the development of self-concept.

Key Term

- **socioemotional maintenance** *(p. 357)*

Functionalism

For the functionalists, the family plays many roles, including socializing the young, providing social and emotional support, managing reproduction, regulating sexual activity, transmitting social status, and serving as an economic center. Let's look more closely at each of these functions.

How does the family socialize children? In addition to caring for an infant's physical needs, parents begin the vital process of teaching the child what he or she must learn to learn to participate in society. During the first year, the infant begins to mimic words and, later, sentences. During the second and third years, parents begin to teach the child values and norms of behavior. By being role models and through training and education, the family continues the process of socialization in each new stage of development.

What is the socioemotional function of the family? Another important function of the family is **socioemotional maintenance.** Generally, the family is the one place in society where an individual is unconditionally accepted and loved. Family members accept one another as they are; every member is special and unique. Without this care and affection, children will not develop normally. (See Chapter 4, pages 109–114, on children raised in isolation.) They may have low self-esteem, fear rejection, feel insecure, and eventually find it difficult to adjust to marriage or to express affection to their own children. Even individuals who are well integrated into society require support when adjusting to changing norms and in developing and continuing healthy relationships. Here again, the family can provide socioemotional maintenance.

- **socioemotional maintenance**
  provision of acceptance and support

What do functionalists believe about the roles associated with this father and daughter?

Figure 11.3 **American Youths Grade Their Parents**

In a national survey, Americans in the seventh through the twelfth grades were asked to "grade" their mothers and fathers. The results are shown below. The left-hand column lists various aspects of child rearing, and the remaining columns indicate the percentage of students who assigned each grade. For example, on the dimension "Raising me with good values," 69 percent gave their fathers an A, 17 percent a B, and so forth.

Grading Dad

Aspect of Child Rearing	Assigned Grade				
	A	B	C	D	F
Raising me with good values	69%	17%	8%	4%	2%
Appreciating me for who I am	58	21	11	8	2
Encouraging me to enjoy learning	58	24	12	4	2
Making me feel important and loved	57	22	13	6	2
Being able to go to important events	55	22	13	5	5
Being there for me when I am sick	52	20	16	8	4
Establishing traditions with me	41	26	15	11	7
Being involved in school life	38	24	19	12	7
Being someone to go to when upset	38	22	15	12	13
Controlling his temper	31	27	20	10	12
Knowing what goes on with me	31	30	17	12	10

Grading Mom

Aspect of Child Rearing	Assigned Grade				
	A	B	C	D	F
Being there for me when I am sick	81%	11%	5%	2%	1%
Raising me with good values	74	15	6	3	2
Making me feel important and loved	64	20	10	5	1
Being able to go to important events	64	20	10	3	3
Appreciating me for who I am	63	18	8	6	5
Encouraging me to enjoy learning	59	23	12	3	3
Being involved in school life	46	25	13	10	6
Being someone to go to when upset	46	22	13	8	9
Spending time talking with me	43	33	14	6	4
Establishing traditions with me	38	29	17	10	6
Knowing what goes on with me	35	31	15	10	9
Controlling her temper	29	28	19	12	11

1. Based on this data, what conclusions would you draw about the closeness of families in America?

2. Select the three aspects of child rearing you think are most important, and compare the grade you would give your parent or parents on these aspects with the grades in this national sample.

Source: Ellen Galinsky, *Ask the Children* (New York: HarperCollins, 2000).

What is the reproductive function of the family? Society cannot survive without new members. The family provides an orderly means for producing new members, generation after generation. So important is this function that for many cultures and religions, it is the primary purpose for sexual relations. In many societies in developing nations the failure of a wife to bear children can lead to divorce. Residents of places such as the Punjab region of North India, for example, view children as an economic necessity. The significance of having children is also seen in the hundreds of rituals, customs, and traditions that are associated with pregnancy and birth in virtually all cultures around the world. (Later in the chapter, we look at the rise of marriages without children in the United States.)

What important functions are being fulfilled by this family?

How does the family regulate sexual activity? In no known society are people given total sexual freedom. Even in sexually permissive societies, such as the Hopi Indians, there are rules about mating and marrying. Norms regarding sexual activities vary from place to place. Families in a few cultures, such as in the Trobriand Islands, encourage premarital sex. Other societies, like those in Iran and Afghanistan, go to great lengths to prevent any contact between nonrelated single males and females. The United States has traditionally fallen somewhere between these two extremes. In the ideal culture in the United States, adolescents would abstain from sexual activity. In real culture, however, the abundance of sexual references directed at teens by the advertising and entertainment industries make abstinence very difficult and even seem undesirable. Clearly, we are sending a mixed message to young people today. One of the consequences of this cultural confusion is the increase in teenage pregnancies and the number of teenagers having abortions. But whatever the norms, it is almost always up to the family to enforce them.

How does the family transmit social status? Families provide economic resources that open and close occupational doors. The sons and daughters of high-income professionals, for example, are more likely to attend college and graduate school than are the children of blue-collar workers. Consequently, the children of professionals are more likely as adults to enter professional occupations. The family also passes on values that affect social status. The children of professionals, for example, tend to feel a greater need to pursue a college degree than their counterparts from blue-collar families. In these and many other ways, the family affects the placement of children in the stratification structure.

What is the economic function of the family? At one time, families were self-sufficient economic units whose members all contributed to the production of needed goods. Every family member would join in such tasks as growing food, making cloth, and taking care of livestock. The modern American family is a unit of consumption rather than production. Adult members—increasingly including working mothers—are employed outside the home and pool their resources to buy what they need. But the end result is the same. The family provides what is needed to survive.

More than 25 percent of working wives now earn more money than their husbands. How do you think the fact that the wives out-earn their husbands changes the balance of power and responsibility in these marriages?

Conflict Theory

Conflict theorists focus on the way family members compete and cooperate. Most family structure throughout history has been patriarchal and patrilineal. Women have historically and traditionally been considered the property of men, and the control of family members and property has typically passed through male bloodlines. This male dominance has been considered "natural" and "legitimate." Thus, most family systems have had built-in gender inequality.

How does conflict theory explain gender relationships in the family? According to conflict theorists, males are dominant and in control; females have traditionally been expected to be submissive helpers. In the traditional division of labor, males work outside the home for finances to support the family. Women remain at home to prepare meals, keep house, and care for the children. Women are unpaid laborers who make it possible for men to earn wages. With men having control over the money, the wives and mothers are kept in a dependent and powerless role. According to the conflict perspective, families in the past, then, have fostered social inequality.

How do the ideas of feminist writers fit with conflict theory? Writers and activists who organize on behalf of women's rights and interests have come to be called feminists. Many feminists today view the family from the conflict perspective. They believe that family structure is the source of the inequality between men and women in society. They point out that men have had control over women since before private property and capitalism existed. Women's contributions in the home (mother and homemaker) are not paid and are therefore undervalued in a capitalist society. Attempts by women to gain more power within the family structure can result in conflict.

Symbolic Interactionism

According to symbolic interactionism, a key to understanding behavior within the family lies in the interactions among family members and the meanings that members assign to these interactions.

How does the family help develop a person's self-concept? Socialization begins within the family. As family members share meanings and feelings, children develop self-concepts and learn to put themselves mentally in the place of others. Interactions with adults help children acquire human personality and social characteristics. Children develop further as they meet others outside the home.

According to symbolic interactionists, relationships within the family are constantly changing. A newly married couple will spend many months (perhaps years) testing their new relationship. As time passes, the initial relationship changes, along with some aspects of the partners' personalities, including self-concepts. These changes occur as the partners struggle with such problem issues as chores and responsibilities, personality clashes, and in-laws.

Figure 11.4 **Perspectives on the Family**

Both functionalism and conflict theory are concerned with the ways social norms affect the nature of the family. Symbolic interactionism tends to examine the relationship of the self to the family. How might functionalism and conflict theory focus on the self?

Theory	Topic		Example
Functionalism	Sex norms		Children are taught that sexual activity should be reserved for married couples.
Conflict Theory	Male dominance		Husbands use their economic power to control the ways money is spent.
Symbolic Interactionism	Developing self-esteem		A child abused by her parents learns to dislike herself.

With the arrival of children comes a new set of adjustments. Parental views may differ on child-rearing practices, number of children desired, and education for the children. The situation is made even more complex by the new member of the family, who must also become part of the interaction patterns.

Section 2 Assessment

1. Match the following examples with the major theoretical perspectives: functionalism (F), conflict theory (C), symbolic interactionism (SI)
   a. fathers "giving away" brides
   b. having children
   c. development of self-concept
   d. newly married partners adjusting to each other
   e. child abuse
   f. social class being passed from one generation to another

Critical Thinking

2. **Finding the Main Idea**
   Select a memorable family experience (such as the Thanksgiving holiday) and interpret it from the viewpoint of one of the three major perspectives.

Looking for Mr. or Ms. Right

This activity will give you some ideas for evaluating whether a current boyfriend or girlfriend is a good candidate for a successful long-term relationship.

From the list on the right, (and on a separate sheet of paper), list the ten most important qualities to you. (Number 1 as the most important, number 2 the next most important, and so forth.) Then fold your paper in half. In the right-hand column, either have your partner fill out the questionnaire or rank the characteristics yourself according to how you think your partner would.

Evaluating Your Responses Which of the items listed on the right do you think are the most important in predicting marital success? According to research, the last seven items (17–23) are the most important. High compatibility between you and your partner on these seven characteristics would probably increase your chances of marital success. A low degree of matching does not, of course, ensure an unhappy marriage or a divorce, but it does suggest areas that may cause problems in the future.

Adapted from the Department of Human Development and Family Studies, Colorado State University.

Doing Sociology

Do you think that the qualities listed in the questionnaire are relevant to you in choosing a wife or a husband? Why or why not? Are there characteristics more important to you and your friends? Explain.

I am looking for a partner who . . .

	Partner	Self	
1.	_____	_____	is honest and truthful.
2.	_____	_____	is fun to be with.
3.	_____	_____	is of the same educational background.
4.	_____	_____	will take care of me.
5.	_____	_____	wants to have children.
6.	_____	_____	communicates well with me.
7.	_____	_____	will share household jobs and tasks.
8.	_____	_____	is a good friend with whom I can talk.
9.	_____	_____	is of the same religious background.
10.	_____	_____	makes decisions.
11.	_____	_____	earns good money.
12.	_____	_____	is physically attractive.
13.	_____	_____	is in love with me and I with him/her.
14.	_____	_____	encourages me to be my own person.
15.	_____	_____	has interests like mine in making money and having fun.
16.	_____	_____	makes me feel important.
17.	_____	_____	is faithful.
18.	_____	_____	shares mutual interests in home, children, romantic love, and religion.
19.	_____	_____	has had a happy childhood with happily married parents.
20.	_____	_____	is emotionally mature.
21.	_____	_____	is prepared to support a family.
22.	_____	_____	is interested in waiting to marry until age twenty-two or older.
23.	_____	_____	wants a six-month to two-year engagement period.

Family and Marriage in the United States

Section Preview

Modern marriages are based primarily on love, but there are many reasons for marrying—and as many reasons for divorce. Although the American family provides social and emotional support, violence in this setting is not uncommon. Child abuse and spousal abuse are serious problems in too many American families.

The Nature of the American Family

The United States is a large, diverse society. Describing the "typical" family might be impossible. There are, however, more similarities than differences among American families. As the various ethnic groups blend into life in the United States, their families tend to follow the American pattern described below.

- Families are nuclear (a household contains only a set of parents and their children).
- Families are bilateral (they trace lineage and pass inheritance equally through both parents).
- Families are democratic (partners share decision making equally).
- Families are neolocal (each family lives apart from other families).
- Families are monogamous (each includes only one husband and one wife at a time).

Romantic Love and Marriage

To Americans, it's like the old song—"Love and marriage go together like a horse and carriage." In a recent poll of the American public, 83 percent of both men and women rated "being in love" as the most vital reason to marry.

The relationship between love and marriage is not always viewed in this way. Among the British feudal aristocracy, romantic love was a game of pursuit played outside of marriage. Marriage was not thought to be compatible with deeply romantic feelings. In ancient Japan, love was considered a barrier to the arrangement of marriages by parents. Among Hindus in India today, parents or other relatives are expected to find suitable mates for the young. Criteria for mate selection include caste, wealth, family reputation, and appearance. Love is not absent in Hindu marriages, but love follows marriage rather than the other way around (Cox, 2005).

In the United States today, the norm is for love to precede the marriage vows. Not all societies share this norm.

Figure 11.5

Divorce and Marriage Rates: 1940–2005

Can you apply what you learned in history to interpret this chart? (a) What happened in the mid-1940s that caused the dramatic rise in marriage rates during this period? (b) Why do you think the marriage rate dropped so low in the 1950s? (c) What are some possible reasons that the divorce rate peaked in the early 1980s?

Sources: National Vital Statistics Reports; *Statistical Abstract of the United States.*

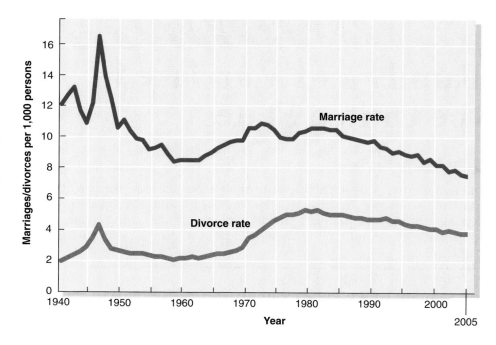

- **marriage rate**
  the number of marriages per year for every one thousand members of a population

- **divorce rate**
  the number of divorces per year for every one thousand members of the population

While romantic love is almost always stated as a condition for marriage in modern societies, it is seldom the only condition. People marry for many reasons, and romantic love may be only one of many reasons. A person may marry to enter a powerful family or to advance a career. One of the strongest motivations for marriage is conformity. Parents expect their children to marry after a certain age and worry about them—perhaps even pressure them—if their children remain single very long. Peers are another source of pressure. Since about 90 percent of all adults in the United States do marry, conformity must certainly be a motivating factor.

Americans typically believe that a marriage that is not based on romantic love cannot last. It is more accurate to say that a marriage based only on romantic love is almost sure to fail. While love may be a good start, it is only the beginning. For a marriage to last, a couple must build a relationship that goes beyond romantic love (Crosby, 1985).

The **marriage rate**—the number of marriages per year for every thousand members of the population—has fluctuated, in the United States, since 1940. As shown in Figure 11.5, the marriage rate peaked at over 16.0 immediately following World War II. Since then, the marriage rate, with ups and downs, has fallen more than fifty percent.

Divorce

The **divorce rate** is the number of divorces per year for every one thousand members of the population. Except for a peak and decline after World War II, the divorce rate in the United States increased slowly between 1860 and the early 1960s. A dramatic increase occurred over the next twenty years, when the divorce rate more than doubled (from 2.2 in 1960 to 5.3 in 1981). Since then, the divorce rate has been in a slow but steady decline, decreasing to 3.8 in 2005. (See Figure 11.5 above.)

Snapshot of America

Marriage Rates

As noted in the text, the U.S. marriage rate overall has declined dramatically since the mid-1940s. Variation in the marriage rate among individual states is interesting. The lowest marriage rate occurs in California. Nevada has far and away the highest marriage rate.

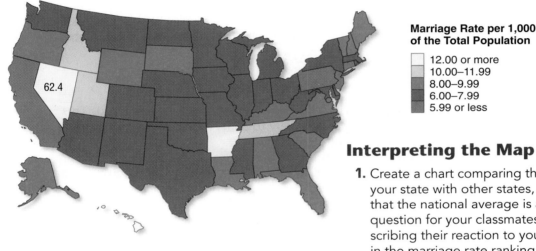

Marriage Rate per 1,000 Members of the Total Population

	12.00 or more
	10.00–11.99
	8.00–9.99
	6.00–7.99
	5.99 or less

Source: National Center for Health Statistics, Division of Vital Statistics, 2005.

Interpreting the Map

1. Create a chart comparing the marriage rate in your state with other states, keeping in mind that the national average is around 7.5. Pose a question for your classmates to answer describing their reaction to your state's position in the marriage rate ranking.

2. Would you expect the divorce rates of states to be correlated with their marriage rates? Make a prediction before looking up the divorce rates for comparison. Report your findings to the class.

What are the causes of divorce? Both personal and societal factors influence why people divorce. At the individual level, these factors include:

- the age of the people when they married. The later the age upon marriage, the lower the chance of divorce.
- how many years the partners have been married. The longer the marriage, the lower the chance of divorce.
- the nature and quality of the relationship. The more respect and flexibility exists between the partners, the lower the chance of divorce.

Sociologists are most concerned with how larger forces in society affect marriages. There are four main factors. First, the divorce rate rises during

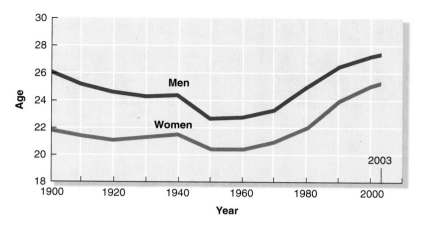

Figure 11.6 Median Age at First Marriage
This figure shows changes in the median age at first marriage in the U.S. since 1900. The marrying age for both men and women has been on the increase since the 1960s. How might this trend affect the future divorce rate?

Source: *The World Almanac and Book of Facts, 2005.*

economic prosperity and goes down when times are hard. This is probably because people are more likely to make changes and take chances when they are not worried about basic survival.

Second, the rise in the divorce rate after 1960 followed the growing up of the baby-boom generation. Baby boomers did not attach a stigma to divorce the way earlier generations did and so were more likely to leave unhappy marriages than to stay.

Third, the increasing financial independence of women means they are more willing to end bad marriages. They are not as dependent (especially if there are no children) upon the husband's willingness to support an ex.

Fourth, American values and attitudes about marriage and divorce are changing. Society is much more forgiving of divorce and remarriage. Women, especially, are no longer "punished," as they were in the past, for leaving a marriage.

What does the future for marriage look like? For several reasons, there is a good chance that the recent decline in the U.S. divorce rate may continue:

● The average age at first marriage in the United States is increasing. (See Figure 11.6.) We know that the later people marry, the less likely they are to divorce. (Mature individuals have more realistic expectations about their mates and have fewer economic and career problems.) This trend is likely to continue well into the twenty-first century.

● The average age of the population of the United States is increasing as baby boomers grow older. This exceptionally large generation set records for divorce in the late 1960s and 1970s. Baby boomers now range in age from the mid forties to the early sixties, which removes them from the age bracket that produces the highest divorce rates.

● American couples are having fewer children, and the children are spaced farther apart. This reduces pressure on marriages.

Tragically, violence has been a pattern of some family relationships throughout history.

Family Violence

Americans have traditionally denied the existence of widespread violence in the family setting. Violent behavior has in the past mistakenly been associated mostly with lower-class families. Part of the reason for this attitude was the fact that the first research in this area used law enforcement and public medical records. Because the police and hospitals dealt mostly with the lower classes (middle and upper classes had lawyers and private doctors), the statistics were skewed toward the lower class. We have since learned that domestic violence occurs at all social class levels.

Is violence in the family common? Although the family provides a safe and warm emotional haven, it can in some cases be a hostile environment. Family violence, or domestic violence, affects all members of the family—children, spouses, and older people. Celebrated trials during the 1990s brought increased public attention to the issue of domestic violence. For more than a year, media focus centered on the trial of football superstar O. J. Simpson, accused of the murder of his former wife Nicole Brown Simpson and Ronald Goldman. Trial evidence indicated that Simpson had abused her when they were married. In another high-profile case, the wealthy Menendez brothers were convicted of the murder of their parents. In 2005, Scott Peterson received the death penalty for the murder of his wife, Laci, and their unborn child.

According to a national survey, almost one-quarter of adults in the United States report having been physically abused as children. In most cases, physical violence involves a slap, a shove, or a severe spanking. However, kicking, biting, punching, beating, and threatening with a weapon are part of abusive violence as well. Furthermore, according to estimates, one of every four girls and one in ten boys are victims of sexual aggression, either within the home or outside (Helfer, Kempe, and Krugman, 1999; Pryor, 1999). Reported child

Country	Reported Abuse
Industrialized Countries	
Canada	**27%** of ever-married/common law–partnered women report being physically assaulted by a current or former partner since the age of sixteen.
Norway	**18%** of women report being hit or physically abused by a male partner.
Switzerland	**21%** of women report being physically assaulted.
United Kingdom	**30%** of women had been punched or slapped by a partner or ex-partner in their lifetimes.
United States	**22%** of women report at least one episode of physical violence from their partner.
Asia and the Pacific	
Korea	**38%** of wives report being physically abused by their spouses in the last year.
Thailand	**20%** of women report physical assault by a partner in their current relationship.
Middle East	
Egypt	**34%** of women report being beaten by their husbands at some point in their marriage.
Israel	**32%** of women report at least one episode of physical abuse by their partners during the last twelve months; 30% report sexual coercion by their husbands in the last year.
Africa	
Kenya	**42%** of women report ever being beaten by a partner; of those, 58% report that they were beaten often or sometimes.
Ethiopia	**45%** of women report ever being beaten by a partner; 10% report abuse within the last year.
Latin America and the Caribbean	
Chile	**26%** report at least one episode of violence by a partner, 11% report at least one episode of severe violence, and 15% of women report at least one episode of less severe violence.
Colombia	**19%** of women have been physically assaulted by their partners in their current relationships.
Mexico	**27%** report at least one episode of physical violence by a partner; 13% report physical violence within the last year.

Figure 11.7
Events of Domestic Violence Against Women in Selected Countries
Levels of domestic violence against women clearly vary from country to country.

Source: World Health Organization, 2002.

sexual abuse in the United States has skyrocketed in recent years. Between 1976 and 2003, the number of reported child abuse cases rose from 662,000 to more than 3.3 million. Statistics collected nationally indicate that 46 out of every 1,000 children are reported annually as victims of child maltreatment (Administration for Children & Families, 2003). Child sexual abuse goes beyond physical contact. Some children are forced into pornography or are made to view pornography in the presence of the abuser. What's worse, the abuser is usually someone the child trusts—a parent, friend of the family, child-care giver, brother.

At least four million women are battered by their husbands annually, probably many more. Over four thousand women each year are beaten to death. The extent of physical abuse is underestimated in part because three-fourths of spousal violence occurs during separation or after divorce, and most research is conducted among married couples.

Is abuse always directed against women?
Husband abuse is frequently overlooked in studies of physical abuse. Although marriages in the United States are generally male dominated, it seems there is equality in the

use of physical violence. One set of researchers found that almost one-third of the husbands in their survey had acted violently against their wives and that wives were almost as likely to have used physical violence against their husbands. Other studies also show that husbands and wives assault each other at about the same rate. Much of the violence committed by women, however, involves self-protection or retaliation, and as a category, females are not as violent as males (Gelles, 1997).

Is abuse always physical? Family violence is not limited to physical abuse. Verbal and psychological abuse are also a part of many families. Psychologists report that the feelings of self-hate and worthlessness that are often the effects of abuse can be as damaging as physical wounds. And approximately 8 million children in the United States suffer from neglect, a condition of being ignored rather than abused.

What is the most common form of family violence? Probably the most frequent and most tolerated violence in the family occurs between children. This *sibling violence* appears to be prevalent and on the rise. Abuse among siblings may be based on rivalry, jealousy, disagreements over personal possessions, or incest. Although it declines somewhat as children get older, it does not disappear.

Little is known about abuse of elderly people, because less research has been done in this area. Abuse of older people usually takes the form of physical violence, psychological mistreatment, economic manipulation, or neglect. Estimates of elder abuse range from 1 million to 2 million cases annually (National Center on Elder Abuse, 2005). Some observers fear that abuse of older people will increase as the population grows older.

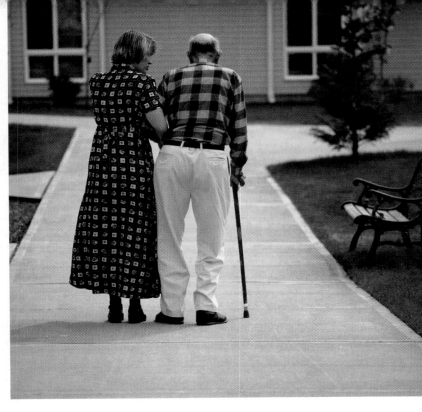

Abuse directed against the elderly in nursing homes has been a recent concern of social activists.

Section 3 Assessment

1. Choose the word from each pair that best describes the typical American family.
   a. nuclear or extended
   b. patrilineal or bilateral
   c. neolocal or matrilocal
   d. polygynous or monogamous

2. Identify three factors discussed in the text that are associated with divorce.

Critical Thinking

3. **Making Predictions** What is your prediction for the divorce trend in the United States in 2050? Use information in this section to support your answer.

TECH TRENDS

Technology and the Family

The computer, to an even greater degree than the television, is being credited with isolating family members.

According to many experts, the influence of technology is just as far-reaching in the home as in the office. Activities in the home are changing dramatically because of recent technological innovations.

Because more American families are living farther from relatives, more are using the Internet to stay in touch with each other. Birth announcements, reunion plans, gift registries for weddings, and funeral arrangements are now being shared with families and friends on-line (Turow and Kavanaugh, 2003). Although somewhat impersonal, these social connections may reduce social isolation and friction in families.

Many, however, see a darker side to new technology for the family. For example, one critic offers this concern: "If we wish to raise our children as androids who respond to Internet packets rather than parental guidance, I can't think of a better way to do that than to put computer networks in homes" (Wingfield, 1998:R23).

Another critic believes that high-tech home equipment like cable television, the Internet, and video games increasingly rules the lives of American families. Children who spend a great deal of time alone with these technological wonders are deprived of frequent and intense social contact with other children, their parents, and other adults in the neighborhood. Consequently, the current generation of children could very well be the first to grow up with highly deficient social skills. Offering indirect support for this conclusion is the fact that almost three-fourths of Americans say they do not know their neighbors. The number of Americans who admit they have spent no time with the people living next to them has doubled in the last twenty years (Quintanilla, 1996).

Technology can also separate, socially, those family members who use the new technology from those who do not. For example, some couples who depend on Web pages to inform their relatives of family news have found that some family members cannot share in this information. Older members of the family who do not have access to the Internet often feel cut off from the rest of the family (Turow and Kavanaugh, 2003).

Analyzing the Trends

A dark picture of the Internet has been presented in this feature. Think of some positive consequences of this technology for the family. Discuss two of them.

Changes in Marriage and Family

Section Preview

Many new patterns of marriage and family living have emerged in the United States. They include blended families, single-parent families, child-free families, cohabitation, same-sex domestic partners, and families with boomerang children. In spite of these new arrangements, the traditional nuclear family is not going to be replaced on any broad scale.

Blended Families

The relatively high divorce rate in the United States has created the **blended family**—a family formed when at least one of the partners in a marriage has been married before and has a child or children from the previous marriage. This type of family can become extremely complicated (Lebey, 2004; Lipman-Blumen and Gabe, 2005). Here's an example: A former husband (with two children in the custody of their biological mother) marries a new wife with two children in her custody. They have two children of their own. The former wife also remarries a man with two children, one in his custody and one in the custody of his former wife. That former wife has remarried and has had a child with her second husband, who has custody of one child from his previous marriage. The former husband's parents are divorced, and both have remarried. Thus, when he remarries, his children have two complete sets of grandparents on his side, plus one set on the mother's side, plus perhaps more on the stepfather's side (Cox, 2005).

Blended families create a new type of extended family, a family that is not based strictly on blood relationships. As the example above shows, it is possible for a child in a blended family to have eight grandparents. Of course, not

Key Terms

- **blended family** *(p. 371)*
- **adolescents** *(p. 373)*
- **dual-employed marriages** *(p. 374)*
- **cohabitation** *(p. 375)*
- **boomerang kids** *(p. 379)*

- **blended family**
  a family formed when at least one of the partners in a marriage has been married before and has a child or children from a previous marriage

Americans knew the "Brady Bunch" family long before the term blended families became common.

all blended families are this complicated. But about 32 percent of households in the United States contain biologically unrelated individuals.

Many blended families are successful, especially if they make adjustments during the first few years. Children from previous marriages, however, are one factor in the higher divorce rates among second marriages (Baca Zinn and Eitzen, 1998).

What major problems face blended families? Sociologists point to three major problems facing blended families—a lack of money, stepchildren's dislike of the new spouse, and uncertainty about the roles played by stepparents.

- **Money difficulties.** Financial demands from both the former and present families generally result in lower incomes in stepfamilies. Remarried husbands are often legally obligated to support children from their previous marriages. Second wives may resent losing the income spent on children from a previous marriage.

- **Stepchildren's antagonism.** Hoping for a reunion of their original parents, stepchildren may try to derail the new marriage. Even five years after divorce, about a third of stepchildren continue to strongly disapprove of their original parents' divorce. This is especially true for teenagers, who can be very critical of their stepparents' values and personalities.

- **Unclear roles.** The roles of stepparents in a blended family are often vague and ambiguous. A stepchild often doesn't consider a parent's new spouse as a "real" father or mother. It is also not clear to stepparents or stepchildren how much power the new spouse really has. Issues involving control and discipline reflect power struggles within the family, especially when there are teenagers involved.

Sociology Online

Student Web Activity
Visit the *Sociology and You* Web site at glencoe.com and click on **Chapter 11—Student Web Activities** for an activity on blended families.

Single-Parent Families

Nearly one out of four American families is a single-parent family. By far the greatest proportion of these households are headed by women. Only about 17 percent of children living with one parent are in a male-headed household.

Why do women head the vast majority of single-parent households? Although courts today are more sensitive to the fathers' claims, women in all social classes are still more likely to win custody of their children in cases of separation and divorce. Unwed mothers or women abandoned by their husbands and/or the fathers of their children make up a large part of poor single-parent households. Finally, poor women marry (or remarry) at a very low rate.

A debate exists over the appropriateness of celebrities choosing to be single mothers.

Though significantly fewer, there is an increasing number of well-educated, professional women who head single-parent households. With the stigma of unwed motherhood declining, more affluent unmarried women are *choosing* to have children and to care for them alone. These women have the economic resources to support an independent family. Finally, well-educated women are adopting higher standards for selecting husbands (Seligmann, 1999).

What are the effects of single-parent families on children?

Approximately 28 percent of America's children (defined as people under the age of eighteen) live in households with one parent. African American and Latino children are more likely than white children to live with only their mothers because of high divorce and out-of-wedlock birthrates, and lower rates of marriage and remarriage (U.S. Bureau of the Census, 2004–2005). Figure 11.8 shows how the number of never-married and single parents increased among African American, Latino, and white families from 1970 to 2003. In general, the chances are increasing that American children will live at least part of their youth in a fatherless home.

Adolescents (persons from the ages of twelve to seventeen) who live with one parent or with a stepparent have much higher rates of deviant behavior, including delinquency, drug and alcohol abuse, and teenage pregnancy, than adolescents living with both natural parents (Dornbush et al., 1985; Popenoe, 1999). A national sample of twelve- to seventeen-year-olds indicates that arrests, school discipline, truancy, running away, and smoking occur more often in single-parent and stepparent families, regardless of income, race, or ethnic background.

These figures do not point to a lack of concern in single parents as much as they show the built-in problems of single parenting. Single working parents must struggle to provide their children with the time, attention, and guidance that two parents can give. Because the single mother typically earns little money, she has added financial problems. Finding good child care and adequate housing in a suitable neighborhood is often very difficult.

● **adolescents**
youths from the ages of twelve to seventeen

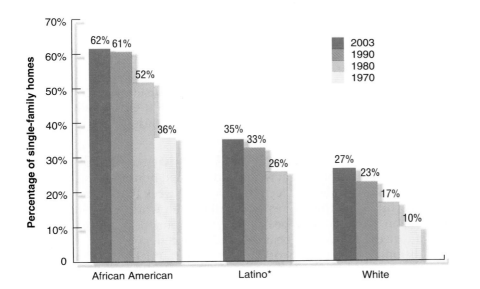

Figure 11.8
Percentage of Single-Parent Families: 1970–2003
This graph compares the percentage of African American, Latino, and white families that have never married or have one parent. What generalization can you make from this data?

*Note: Latino data not available for 1970.

Source: U.S. Bureau of the Census, *Statistical Abstract of the United States,* 2004–2005.

Childless Marriages

In the past, married women without children were seen as failing to fulfill their "duty" as wives. In fact, in many religions, the inability to have children is still one of the few allowed reasons for divorcing a woman. Historically, married childless women were pitied and looked down upon, and single women rarely achieved respectability outside the role of "spinster aunt."

Why are some married women now choosing not to have children? Around 19 percent of American women who have ever been married did not have children in 2002, compared with about 15 percent in 1970 (U.S. Bureau of the Census, 2003). It is unclear if this upward trend will continue. Today, the reasons married women give for choosing not to have children are varied. Social stigmas against childless married women are disappearing. It is no longer automatically accepted that having children is the primary reason for marriage. Some women have elected to pursue personal or career goals instead. Other people, both men and women, have basic moral issues about raising children in what they consider to be an immoral world. Sometimes, having children is put off so long that it becomes hard for couples to make the adjustment to raising a family. Finally, it is important to remember that not all couples without children have chosen to be that way. Physical or psychological problems keep some couples from having children.

Are marriages happier with or without children? The answer to this question generally depends upon the couple's decision about having children. Among childless couples who want children, marital happiness is generally lower than for married couples with children. However, research shows that couples who by choice have no children appear to be happier and more satisfied with their marriages and lives than couples with children (Cox, 2005).

Dual-Employed Marriages

In families where both parents are working outside the home, special strains are put on the marriage. Women in these **dual-employed marriages** are apparently expected to handle most of the household and child-care responsibilities in addition to their full-time jobs.

What are drawbacks to the dual-employed family? Because they must combine employment with child care and household tasks, married working women work about fifteen hours more a week than men. Sociologist Arlie Hochschild calls this home- and child-based work "the second shift." Although men spend an average of four to six hours per week in household and child-care duties, women bear the larger burden.

In addition to this greater workload, women in dual-employed marriages must cope with role conflict. They are torn between the time requirements

About one-fifth of couples today remain childless. Is this an upward or downward trend?

● **dual-employed marriages**
marriages in which both spouses work outside the home

of their jobs and their desire to spend more time with their children and husbands. Feelings of guilt may arise from not being able to meet all expectations of wife, mother, and breadwinner.

Men in dual-employed marriages are generally unwilling to assume household responsibilities equal to those of their wives. Even so, they feel the negative effects of role conflict and excessive demands on their time. In addition, having an employed wife, particularly if she earns more, may not fit with men's images of themselves as providers.

Is there a positive side to dual employment? Dual employment offers advantages as well as disadvantages. On balance, the effects of employment on the psychological well-being of women have been beneficial (Moen, 1992; Crosby, 1993; Cox, 2005). Working outside the home provides a wider set of social relationships and greater feelings of control, independence, and self-esteem. Employment also appears to provide a social and emotional cushion for women when their children leave home. Compared with women who do not work outside the home, employed women tend to have more outlets for self-expression (Adelmann et al., 1989; Wolfe, 1999). If a mother prefers working outside the home, other family members often benefit from her employment. With two incomes, there is more money to spend for purchases that raise the standard of living. Sons and daughters of working mothers also benefit in noneconomic ways. Daughters of working mothers are more likely to see themselves as working adults, as capable of being economically independent, and as benefiting from further education. Sons are more likely to choose wives with similar attitudes toward education and employment.

For men, benefits of a dual-employed marriage include freedom from the responsibility of being the sole provider, increased opportunity for job changes, and opportunities to continue education. Men with employed wives can share the triumphs and defeats of the day with someone who is in the same situation. If their wives are happier working outside the home, husbands enjoy a better marital relationship. Those husbands who take advantage of the opportunity can form a closer relationship with their children by being more active parents (Booth and Crouter, 1998).

A functionalist might suggest that this mother's economic function is clashing with her socioemotional function.

Cohabitation

Cohabitation—living with someone in a marriagelike arrangement without the legal obligations and responsibilities of formal marriage—has been a widely discussed alternative to traditional monogamy for some time. In fact, the number of American adults cohabiting increased from about one-half million to over nine million between 1970 and 2003. According to a nationwide survey, over one-fourth of adults in the United States have cohabited (U.S. Bureau of the Census, 2004).

● **cohabitation**
a marriagelike living arrangement without the legal obligations and responsibilities of formal marriage

Survey Research: Spanking and Antisocial Behavior

Like many children in the United States, you probably experienced spanking and other legal forms of physical corporal punishment from your parents. In the mid-1980s, research revealed that over 90 percent of parents used corporal punishment on young children, and more than half continued its use during the early teen years. Although high, this rate of corporal punishment was less than in the 1950s (99 percent) and the mid-1970s (97 percent). The rate has declined further since 1985, but nearly all American children still experience some form of corporal punishment.

The use of corporal punishment to correct or control the behavior of children is widely accepted in American culture. "Spare the rod and spoil the child" is a warning deep in our national consciousness. However, Straus and his colleagues (1997) present evidence contradicting the notion that corporal punishment improves children's behavior.

These researchers used data from interviews with a sample of over eight-hundred mothers of children aged six to nine years in a national study. (This was a longitudinal study, one that follows respondents over a period of time.) This study compared parents' use of corporal punishment with antisocial behavior in children. The study defined corporal punishment as "the use of physical force with the intention of causing a child to experience pain, but not injury, for the purpose of correction or control of the child's behavior" (Straus, Sugarman, and Giles-Sims, 1997:761). Slapping a child's hand or buttocks and squeezing a child's arm are examples. A measure of antisocial behavior was based on the mothers' reports of their children's behavior: "cheats or tells lies," "bullies or is cruel or mean to others," "does not feel sorry after misbehaving," "breaks things deliberately," "is disobedient at school," and "has trouble getting along with teachers."

Since this was a longitudinal study, information on the frequency of parents' use of corporal punishment was collected *before* reports on subsequent antisocial behavior. Contrary to common expectations, Straus found that the higher the use of corporal punishment, the higher the level of antisocial behavior two years later.

At the end of their report, the authors move from being strictly social scientists to making a practical child-rearing recommendation. Straus and his colleagues suggest that the reduction or elimination of corporal punishment could lower antisocial behavior in children. In addition, given research indicating a relationship between antisocial behavior in childhood and violence and other crime in adulthood, society at large could benefit from abandoning the use of corporal punishment in child rearing. They state it this way:

> Thus, because almost all American children experience [corporal punishment] in varying degrees, our findings suggest that almost all American children could benefit from a reduction or elimination of [corporal punishment]. Moreover, considering research showing that [antisocial behavior] in childhood is associated with violence and other crime as an adult, society as a whole, not just children, could benefit from ending the system of violent child-rearing that goes under the euphemism of spanking (Straus, Sugarman, and Giles-Sims, 1997).

"Don't spank!" cried George; "I'll
                    tell the truth,
   For still I'll honest be;
"'Twas I, dear father, took the ax
   And chopped the cherry tree."

"Oh, ho!" Said Mr Washington
   "Unless I punish thee
Thy truth will cost to me the loss
   Of every cherry tree!"

'Twas full a week before poor George
   Sat down with any ease,
His father sold the hatchet
   And saved his cherry-trees.

Spanking as a corrective for bad behavior was a norm in the past, as evidenced by this popular 1899 woodcut.

Working with the Research

1. Does a link between childhood corporal punishment and antisocial behavior surprise you? Explain.
2. Suppose that you are on a panel reporting on child rearing to the President of the United States. Using the Straus study as a model, describe the study you would conduct on a possible relationship between childhood corporal punishment and adult crime.
3. How do you anticipate these children will discipline their children later in life?
4. Describe what you think would be more effective means of discipline.
5. Do you think that social science evidence such as this has affected teacher disciplining behavior in schools? Will it? Should it? Explain.

Cohabitation has risen among people of all ages and marital statuses, particularly among the young and the divorced. By 2003, about 53 percent of all unmarried-couple households were maintained by someone under thirty-five years of age and about 41 percent involved at least one child under age eighteen.

Is cohabitation a workable alternative to marriage?

Research reports on cohabitation are not encouraging. Only about 25 percent of cohabiting couples stay together more than four years, reflecting a lower level of certainty about commitment than is true in married couples. This lack of commitment is probably an important reason for the lower satisfaction among cohabiting couples than among married couples. Another factor is the higher rate of abuse among cohabiting women than among married, divorced, or separated women (National Marriage Project, 2005).

Cohabitation has not fulfilled the promise of providing good experience for future marriage. Cohabitation does not appear to improve the quality of later marriage. Couples who cohabited have shown lower marital adjustment than couples who had not lived together. Finally, premarital cohabitation is associated with a higher risk of divorce (National Marriage Project, 2005).

Same-Sex Domestic Partners

Because of the social stigma that continues to surround homosexuality, it is impossible to know exactly how many Americans are gay. The Kinsey Institute, a leader in research on human sexuality, estimates that gays make up about 10 percent of the U.S. population. In 2000, the U.S. Census estimated that same-sex partners accounted for 6 percent of American households.

In recent years, gay activists and their supporters have fought to achieve the same rights for gay couples as married couples have—the tax benefits a married couple receives, for example, or the ability of a wife or husband to be covered by the spouse's health insurance policy. Except in Massachusetts, however, same-sex marriages are not legal. Several states do recognize "civil unions" for a gay couple, and these civil unions usually do qualify for the same benefits and burdens as a marriage. Same-sex unions are certain to remain controversial for some time.

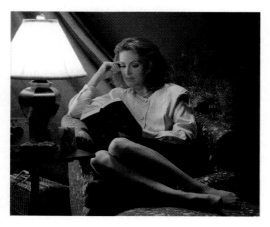

While marriage is still a thriving institution, more people today are embracing the single life.

Single Life

An increasing number of Americans are choosing to remain single rather than to marry. More than 29 million Americans over the age of fifteen now live alone, an increase of nearly 61 percent since 1980. Although many of these people will eventually marry, an increasing percentage will remain single all their lives (U.S. Bureau of the Census, 2005).

Why are more Americans choosing to live alone?

Remaining single has always been a choice that has carried a stigma in the United States. Historically, society frowned on men and women who did not marry. It was seen as a form of deviance. England started taxing bachelors at the end of the seventeenth century and Missouri followed suit in 1820. The stigma attached to remaining single has faded over the past several decades, however. More single Americans are choosing to remain unmarried, pursuing careers or raising children from a former marriage.

Will the current trend toward remaining single continue?

It is too early to predict whether the increase in singlehood will lead to a decline in marriage at all ages. Although singlehood is an increasingly popular alternative to traditional marriage, people are not necessarily rejecting marriage. The implication is that many young adults wish to expand the period of "freedom" after leaving home and are unwilling to rush into the responsibilities of early marriage and parenthood.

Boomerang Kids

The boomerang is a weapon that, when thrown, returns in a wide arc to its point of origin. The term **boomerang kids** is being applied to young adults who either leave home and return or stay at home and live with parents. American adults aged eighteen to thirty-four have a much higher probability of living in their parents' home than Americans of the same age thirty years ago. More than 26 percent of adults eighteen to thirty-four years old now live with one or both parents (U.S. Bureau of the Census, 2004).

● **boomerang kids**
adult children who return to the home of origin or who continue to live with parents

Why are more adult children returning home? Increasing numbers of adult children are living with their parents for several reasons. Because young adults are marrying later, more stay at home longer. In addition, more are continuing their education and find living at home the best solution to the problem of supporting themselves and paying school expenses. Many young adults return home even after completing their education because the high cost of living outstrips their earning capacity. Also, since parents tend to give their children a home after a failed marriage, the high divorce rate is increasing the proportion of young adults living at home.

What are some consequences of the boomerang effect? Costs associated with education, day-to-day living, and perhaps even a grandchild or two can create financial strain for older parents whose adult children live with them. Many parents complain that their adult children do not share in expenses or help around the house. The children's presence robs their parents of privacy and may prevent them from developing relationships with spouses and friends. It is not surprising that higher marital dissatisfaction among middle-aged parents is associated with adult children living at home.

Adult children who find themselves in this situation suffer as well. Adult children who have returned home have normally been forced by circumstances to do so. They are likely to be having difficulties balancing school and work, making their way economically, forming a family, or surviving the aftermath of a divorce. They know the burden they represent. In addition, returning home usually means giving up some freedom.

In spite of these problems, most families appear to adjust well to the return of older children (Mitchell and Gee, 1996; Ianzito, 2004). This is especially true when the returning older child is able to help with expenses and household duties.

"Can't I just stay here with you and Mom? I don't like what I've seen of the real world."

The thoughts of a boomerang kid.
Mom and Dad are not buying it, are they?

Belief that the family will continue is found even in the most futuristic views.

Looking Forward

In early 2000, Darva Conger and Rick Rockwell were big news. This couple, who had never met before, married as part of a television contest called "Who Wants to Marry a Multimillionaire?" Most Americans shook their heads, wondering if this event marked the final stages of deterioration of the family. While this was truly a bizarre media event, thankfully it is not representative of the state of the American family.

What is the future of the American family? If the frequency of marriage and remarriage is any indication, the nuclear family is not disappearing. Around 90 percent of men and women in the United States marry sometime during their lives. Although many Americans have been experimenting with alternative living arrangements, the nuclear family still remains the most popular choice (U.S. Bureau of the Census, 2005). Contrary to a long-standing fear, many Americans are not avoiding marriage permanently. They are simply postponing it or sampling it more often.

The American family is changing, however. So-called traditional households—those with a husband–wage earner, wife–homemaker, and two children—today account for less than one-fourth of all American households, compared with over 60 percent in 1950. This proportion is not expected to grow. Continued increases are expected for other family lifestyles, such as the dual-employed family and the single-parent family. The question, then, is not whether the family will survive. The question is what forms will the family take.

Whatever else happens, the trend toward more working parents is likely to continue. This trend promises increased strain for parents, children, and society. We have already discussed problems for parents associated with balancing work and home responsibilities. A reduction in close and continuous parental care for children during their early developmental years is another important consequence. Also, as more parents work, parental supervision of children and teenagers declines (Popenoe, 1999; Daniels, 2000; Casper and Smith, 2004).

Section 4 Assessment

1. How does a blended family differ from a nuclear family?

2. Which group is increasing more rapidly: the number of white single-parent families or the number of African American and Latino single-parent families? What reasons are offered for this?

3. Is your family a dual-employed family? How do the cultural values of your parents affect their economic behavior?

4. Is it true that Americans today are married for a smaller proportion of their lives than were Americans of previous generations?

Critical Thinking

5. **Making Predictions** Some people believe that in the future the nuclear family will be a reality for only a minority of Americans. Do you agree or disagree? Explain.

Summary

Section 1: Family and Marriage Across Cultures

Main Idea: In all societies, the family has been the most important social institutions, producing and socializing the next generation.

Section 2: Theoretical Perspectives and the Family

Main Idea: Each of the major perspectives focuses on the family. Functionalism emphasizes its social benefits. The conflict perspective looks at the reasons males dominate it. Symbolic interactionism studies the way the family socializes children.

Section 3: Family and Marriage in the United States

Main Idea: Modern marriages are based primarily on love, but there are many reasons for marrying. Although the American family provides support, it can also harm its members.

Section 4: Changes in Marriage and Family

Main Idea: Many new kinds of families have emerged, including blended families, single-parent families, and families headed by same-sex partners.

Sociology Online

Self-Check Quiz
Visit the *Sociology and You* Web site at glencoe.com and click on **Chapter 11—Self-Check Quizzes** to prepare for the chapter test.

Reviewing Vocabulary

Complete each sentence using each term once.

a. monogamy
b. polyandry
c. polygyny
d. exogamy
e. endogamy
f. homogamy
g. patrilineal
h. blended family
i. dual-employed marriage
j. boomerang kids

1. _____ is a family formed with children from a previous marriage.
2. The marriage of one woman to two or more men at the same time is called _____ .
3. The marriage of one man to two or more women at the same time is called _____ .
4. are young adults who live with their parents.
5. A marriage in which both partners work for pay is called _____ .
6. _____ is the marriage within one's own group as required by social norms.
7. The marriage of one man to one woman is called _____ .
8. The tendency to marry someone similar to oneself is called _____ .
9. _____ is the practice of marrying outside of one's group.
10. _____ is the arrangement in which descent is traced through the father.

Reviewing the Facts

11. Sociologists define three types of family structures. List and describe those structures.
12. In addition to providing an atmosphere that fulfills social and emotional needs, what are the other vital functions of the family?
13. How would conflict theorists describe the family?

14. What is the most widely practiced form of marriage around the world today?

15. Who are the victims of family violence?

Thinking Critically

16. Analyzing Information

According to Hochschild's *second shift* explanation, gender equity in the home does not exist. Why do men, on average, still do less housework than women? Do attitudes about masculinity have anything to do with this? Do women naturally feel inclined to do the housework, given their role as nurturers and caretakers? How might gender stereotypes contribute to inequality in the household?

17. Making Inferences

One characteristic of families is that they spend time together. As people grow busier and busier, however, spending time together becomes more difficult. Twenty years down the road, what do you think will be a typical amount of family time? Do you believe family time will disappear, or not? Explain your views.

18. Making Inferences

A prominent sociologist who studies marital relationships says that he can predict with 95 percent accuracy whether a newly married couple will fail or succeed in their marriage. He has newlyweds attend a retreat and perform a series of tasks, videotaping each couple's interactions as they work on projects together. At the end of the weekend, he tells the couples what he observed and what it could mean for the future of their marriages. Remember, his accuracy rating is 95 percent.

a. What do you think he looks for while he watches couples' interactions?

b. Do you believe his approach is ethical?

c. If you had the opportunity as a newlywed, would you attend this retreat?

Copyright 2006 Mike Lester/Cagle Cartoons

19. Analyzing Visuals

National debates about the schools—what should be taught, by whom, and when—have long been a part of American political life. Look at the cartoon above and then write a sentence that describes a) the cartoonist's belief about the relationship between family and schools; b) how much he thinks educational reforms matter.

20. Analyzing Information

Research on never-married individuals shows that they believe their marriages will be ideal. However, research suggests that their expectations don't last very long. Why do you think this is true?

21. Summarizing Information

Use a chart like the one below to summarize the view of the family as proposed by the three theoretical perspectives.

Sociological Perspective	View of the Family
Functionalism	
Conflict Theory	
Symbolic Interactionism	

Sociology Projects

22. Family Characteristics

On a piece of paper, rate your family members based on the following characteristics. Use a scale of 1 to 5, with 1 being the lowest (weakest) and 5 being the highest (strongest).

- spending time together
- expressing appreciation for each other
- dealing with conflict
- communicating with one another
- spiritual wellness
- commitment and follow-through

You can total your scores and divide by 6 to come up with a mean value for your family. After completing the activity, you may want to discuss your results with family members to see if they agree with your evaluation or share your perspectives. Are there other characteristics that are more important to your family than the ones on this list?

23. Divorce

The text listed several reasons why couples divorce. Working with a classmate, brainstorm several additional factors contributing to divorce (for example, no-fault divorce laws in some states). Give at least one reason why each of these factors has caused an increase in divorce over time. After you have come up with a list of at least five factors, discuss with your partner what would happen if the factors were eliminated (for example, if conditions allowing divorce were made stricter). Do you think these changes would improve society? Why or why not? Be prepared to present your findings to the class and to argue your position.

24. Conducting Interviews

The table below illustrates the changing role of husbands and wives in the labor force. What factors do you think might be contributing to the apparent trend? After listing your possible causes, interview two married couples you know, using your list as a basis for framing your questions to elicit their ideas. Then write a paragraph comparing the results you obtained from these interviews.

	Percent of Spouses in Labor Force, 1998–2004			
	Both Employed	Husband Only	Wife Only	Neither Employed
1998	56.3	21.3	5.7	16.7
1999	55.9	21.4	5.8	16.9
2000	56.2	21.4	6.0	16.4
2001	56.2	21.6	5.8	16.5
2002	55.8	21.7	6.0	16.6
2003	55.6	21.8	6.2	16.4
2004	54.5	22.6	6.4	16.5

Source: *Statistical Abstracts*, 2006

Technology Activity

25. Using your school or local library and the Internet, research family violence over the last 30 years—1970 to 1980; 1980 to 1990; 1990 to Present. Create a graph to show statistically the frequency of reported incidents of violence. In your own words, and terms learned in this chapter, write an essay that summarizes your graph. In the essay, consider reasons or changes in society that you believe influence the frequency of reported incidents of family violence. Consider the impact, if any, of hotlines and Public Service Announcements regarding family violence. Determine whether the information that you have found on reported incidents is correct and complete. Support your decision with at least two reasons.

Life Without Father

by David Popenoe

- **massive erosion of fatherhood**
  great numbers of fathers not present in the home

- **second shift**
  work to be done at home

- **ominous**
  dangerous; darkly threatening

- **pathological counterpart**
  diseased opposite

"Fathers should be neither seen nor heard," Oscar Wilde once wrote. "That is the only proper basis for family life." With each passing year, American society has increasingly become an immense social testing ground for this proposition. Unfortunately for Wilde's reputation as a social analyst, to say nothing about the health of our society, the results have proved highly unsupportive. American fathers are today more removed from family life than ever before in our history. And according to a growing body of evidence, this **massive erosion of fatherhood** contributes mightily to many of the major social problems of our time. . . .

The print pages and airwaves have been filled with discussions of fatherhood in recent decades. Yet most discussions have focused on just one issue—how to get fathers to share their traditional breadwinner role and take up a new (for them) child-care-provider role. The call from younger women has been loud and clear: We need a new conception of fatherhood, a "new father," one who will help equally in the home just as women now strive to help equally in the workplace; one who will share the **"second shift"** with his mate.

The father's role—what society expects of fathers—has indeed changed enormously in recent years. Fathers are expected to be more engaged with their children and involved with housework—if not nearly as much as most women would like, certainly far more than the past generation of fathers would have thought possible.

This role change has been highly positive in most respects. But with all the concentration on "role equality" in the home, the larger and more **ominous** trend of modern fatherhood has been mostly overlooked. We have been through many social revolutions in the past three decades—sex, women's liberation, divorce—but none more significant for society than the startling emergence of the absent father, a kind of **pathological counterpart** to the new father.

While the new father has been emerging gradually for most of this century, it is only in the past thirty years that we have witnessed the enormous increase in absent fathers. In times past, many children were left fatherless through his premature death. Today, the fathers are still alive and out there somewhere; the problem is that they seldom see much, if anything, of their children.

The main reason for contemporary father absence is the dramatic decline of marriage. . . . What this means, in human terms, is that about half of today's children will spend at least a portion of their growing-up years living apart from their fathers.

As a society, we can respond to this new fatherlessness in several ways. We can, as more and more of us seem to be doing, simply declare fathers to be unnecessary, superfluous. This is the response of "single parents by choice." It is the response of those who say that if daddies and mommies

indispensable
absolutely necessary

profound deterioration
very great decline

promulgates
teaches

Read and React

1. Briefly state the main point of Popenoe's reading. Is he correct? Is he too pessimistic? Explain.

2. Explain why Popenoe thinks that Oscar Wilde's statement that "fathers should be neither seen nor heard" is wrong. Do you think Wilde was wrong? Why or why not?

3. Discuss the reasons Popenoe gives for the decline of the father's presence in the contemporary American family.

4. According to Popenoe, nothing could be more serious for children than the trend he sees toward "life without father." Why do you agree or disagree?

Source: Excerpted from David Popenoe, *Life Without Father* (New York: The Free Press, 1996), pp. 1–2, 14.

are expected to do precisely the same things in the home, why do we need both? It is the response of those who declare that unwed motherhood is a woman's right, or that single-parent families are every bit as good as two-parent families, or that divorce is generally beneficial for children.

In my view, these responses represent a human tragedy—for children, for women, for men, and for our society as a whole. . . . Fathering is different from mothering; involved fathers are **indispensable** for the good of children and society; and our growing [trend in] national fatherlessness is a disaster in the making. . . .

No one predicted this trend, few researchers or government agencies have monitored it, and it is not widely discussed, even today. But its importance to society is second to none. Father absence is a major force lying behind many of the attention-grabbing issues that dominate the news: crime and delinquency; premature sexuality and out-of-wedlock teen births; deteriorating educational achievement; depression, substance abuse, and alienation among teenagers; and the growing number of women and children in poverty. These issues all point to a **profound deterioration** in the well-being of children. Some experts have suggested, in fact, that the current generation of children and youth is the first in our nation's history to be less well-off—psychologically, socially, economically, and morally—than their parents were at the same age. Or as Senator Daniel Patrick Moynihan has observed, "the United States . . . may be the first society in history in which children are distinctly worse off than adults."

Along with the growing father absence, our cultural view of fatherhood is changing. Few people have doubts about the fundamental importance of mothers. But fathers? More and more the question is being raised, are fathers really necessary? Many would answer no, or maybe not. And to the degree that fathers are still thought necessary, fatherhood is said by many to be merely a social role, as if men had no inherent biological predisposition whatsoever to acknowledge and to invest in their own offspring. If merely a social role, then perhaps anyone is capable of playing it. . . .

The decline of fatherhood and of marriage cuts at the heart of the kind of environment considered ideal for childrearing. Such an environment, according to a substantial body of knowledge, consists of an enduring two-parent family that engages regularly in activities together, has many of its own routines and traditions, and provides a great deal of quality contact with their parents' world of work. In addition, there is little concern on the part of children that their parents will break up. Finally, each of these ingredients comes together in the development of a rich family subculture that has lasting meaning and strongly **promulgates** such family values as responsibility, cooperation, and sharing. . . .

What the decline of fatherhood and marriage in America really means, then, is that slowly, insidiously, and relentlessly our society has been moving in an ominous direction—toward the devaluation of children. There has been an alarming weakening of the fundamental assumption, long at the center of our culture, that children are to be loved and valued at the highest level of priority. Nothing could be more serious for our children or our future.

Sections

1. **Development and Structure of Education**
2. **Functionalist Perspective**
3. **Conflict Perspective**
4. **Symbolic Interactionism**

Learning Objectives

After reading this chapter, you will be able to

- discuss schools as bureaucracies.
- outline the basic functions of education.
- evaluate the merit-based nature of public education.
- describe the ways in which schools socialize students.
- discuss educational inequality.

Applying Sociology

Columnist Ann Landers published this letter from a teacher about the hidden realities of teaching in America.

Let me see if I have this right . . . . I am also to instill a sense of pride in their ethnicity, modify disruptive behavior and observe them for signs of abuse.

I am to fight the war on drugs and sexually transmitted diseases, check their backpacks for guns and knives, and raise their self-esteem. I am to teach them patriotism, good citizenship... and fair play... . I am . . . to encourage respect for the cultural diversity of others, always making sure I give the girls in my class 50% of my attention.

I am required to work . . . toward additional certification and a master's degree... .

I am to be a paragon of virtue, such that my presence will awe my students into being obedient and respectful of authority. I am to do all of this with just a piece of chalk, a bulletin board and a few books (some of which I may have to purchase myself). . . .

Is that all?

(Excerpted from "A Lesson on the Realities of Teaching," *The Los Angeles Times*, January 28, 2000).

Sociology Online

Chapter Overview
Visit the *Sociology and You* Web site at glencoe.com and click on **Chapter 12— Chapter Overviews** to preview chapter information.

1

Development and Structure of Education

Key Terms

- **formal schooling** *(p. 390)*
- **open classroom** *(p. 390)*
- **cooperative learning** *(p. 391)*
- **integrative curriculum** *(p. 391)*
- **voucher system** *(p. 393)*
- **charter schools** *(p. 394)*
- **magnet schools** *(p. 394)*
- **for-profit schools** *(p. 395)*

Section Preview

Schools are becoming more bureaucratic. Advocates of open classrooms and cooperative learning contend that bureaucratically run schools fail to take into account the emotional and creative needs of individual children.

Bureaucracy in Education

School administration in the early 1900s was based on a factory model of education. Educators believed that children could be and should be educated in much the same way as cars were mass produced.

> *Schooling came to be seen as work or the preparation for work; schools were pictured as factories, educators as industrial managers, and students as the raw materials to be inducted into the production process. The ideology of school management was recast in the mold of the business corporation, and the character of education was shaped after the image of industrial production (Cohen and Lazerson, 1972:47).*

Although teachers and administrators work hard today to personalize the time you spend in school, public education in this country remains very much an impersonal bureaucratic process. Schools today are still based on specialization, rules and procedures, and impersonality.

The 1954 classroom on the left clearly reflects the traditional mass production approach to education. Recently, as seen in the photo at the right, there has been more of an attempt to personalize education.

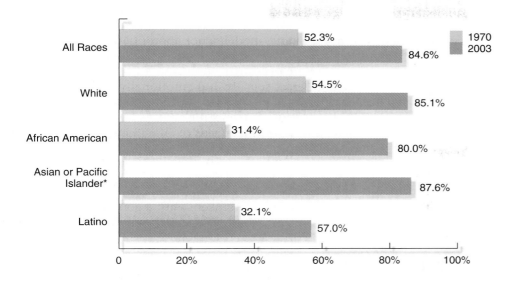

Figure 12.1 High School Graduates, 1970 and 2003
Displayed in this figure are the percentages, by racial and ethnic category, of persons 25 years old and older who have completed high school. Note that the proportion of high school graduates in each group has increased sharply between 1970 and 2003. As a result, each of these groups is placing more pressure on public schools to accommodate the needs of their members.

*Note: No data available for Asian or Pacific Islander for 1970.
Source: U.S. Census Bureau, *Statistical Abstract of the United States, 2004–2005.*

Why should schools be standardized? For administrators, there are many advantages to following a bureaucratic model. For instance, in the discussion of formal organizations in Chapter 6, you read that one of the characteristics of a bureaucracy is the tendency to specialize. Professional educators are specialists—administrators, classroom teachers, librarians, curriculum specialists who decide on courses and content, and so forth.

In the bureaucratic model, education can be accomplished most efficiently for large numbers of students when they are at similar stages in their ability and development. (There were, in fact, approximately 61 million students in the public school system in 2005. Figure 12.1 shows the increasing percentage of young people from all races and ethnic groups who are completing high school.) In this way, a teacher can develop one lesson plan for a number of students. Age-based classrooms, in which all students receive the same instruction, reflect the impersonal, bureaucratic nature of schools.

Efficiency, the ultimate goal of a bureaucracy, is also increased when teachers teach the same, or at least similar, content. Materials can be approved and purchased in bulk, and testing can be standardized. This practice also allows students to transfer from one school to another and continue studying approximately the same things. Rules and procedures exist to ensure that all of this happens.

Schools are also part of a much larger bureaucratic system. This system begins with the federal government and progresses layer by layer through state and local governments. (See page 191 in Chapter 6 for an organizational chart of a public school district.)

What do critics of the bureaucratic model say? Critics claim that the old factory, or bureaucratic, model is not appropriate for schooling. Children, they point out, are not inorganic materials to be processed on an assembly line. Children are human beings who come into school with previous knowledge and who interact socially and emotionally with other students. According to critics of **formal schooling,** education that is provided and regulated by society, the school's bureaucratic nature is unable to respond to the expressive, creative, and emotional needs of all children. These critics prefer several less rigid, more democratic alternatives.

● **formal schooling**
education that is provided and regulated by society

Democratic Reforms in the Classroom

Since colonial times, providing citizens with a good education has been an important value in the United States. The Puritans in Massachusetts in 1647 required towns with more than fifty families to hire a schoolmaster. The Land Ordinance of 1785 required that some of the income from land north of the Ohio River be used to support public schools. The first public schools were quite authoritarian, with firm rules and sharp lines drawn between students and teacher.

The American progressive education movement of the 1920s and 1930s was a reaction to the strict Victorian authoritarianism of early nineteenth-century schools. Educational philosopher John Dewey (1859–1952) led the progressive education movement, which emphasized knowledge related to work and to individual student interests. The progressive movement, with its child-centered focus, almost disappeared in the 1950s but reappeared in the 1960s as the humanistic movement. The humanistic movement supported the elimination of restrictive rules and codes and the involvement of students in the educational process. The aim of the humanistic movement was to create a more democratic, student-focused learning environment (Ballantine, 2001). It has proven to be an influential forerunner of classroom reform. Three ways to express the humanistic educational impulse are the *open classroom, cooperative learning,* and the *integrative curriculum.*

Working cooperatively in groups was one of the more democratic school reforms of the twentieth century.

● **open classroom**
a nonbureaucratic approach to education based on democracy, flexibility, and noncompetitiveness

What is the open classroom? The **open classroom** is a nonbureaucratic approach to education based on democratic relationships, flexibility, and noncompetitiveness. Here educators avoid the sharp authoritarian line traditionally drawn between teachers and students. The open classroom drops the idea that all children of a given age should follow a standardized curriculum. On the belief that competition is not a good motivator for children, the open classroom abandons the use of graded report cards based on comparison of student performance.

The open classroom, introduced in the 1960s, resurfaced in the 1990s. Cooperative learning and the integrative curriculum are two important extensions of the open-classroom approach.

What is cooperative learning? **Cooperative learning** takes place in a nonbureaucratic classroom structure in which students study in groups, with teachers as guides rather than as the controlling agents (the "guide on the side" versus the "sage on the stage" approach). According to the cooperative learning method, students learn more if they are actively involved with others in the classroom (Sizer, 2004). The traditional teacher-centered approach rewards students for being passive recipients of information and requires them to compete with others for grades and teacher recognition. Cooperative learning, with its accent on teamwork rather than individual performance, is designed to encourage students to concentrate more on the process of getting results than how their answers compare to those of other students. Cooperation replaces competition. Students typically work in small groups on specific tasks. Credit for completion of a task is given only if all group members do their parts.

Using this approach successfully requires some expertise on the part of the teacher and can initially discourage students who are motivated by letter grades based on individual work. Nevertheless, some benefits of the cooperative learning approach have been documented (Children's Defense Fund, 1991). For example,

- uncooperativeness and stress among students is reduced.
- academic performance increases.
- students have more positive attitudes toward school.
- racial and ethnic antagonism decreases.
- self-esteem increases.

What is the integrative curriculum? As you have seen, the curriculum is predetermined for students in the traditional classroom. In the **integrative curriculum**, however, the curriculum is created by students and teachers working together. Since students are asked to participate in curriculum design and content, the integrative curriculum is democratic in nature. Giving students such power obviously deviates from the traditional subject-centered curriculum. Students and teachers become collaborators (Bernt et al, 2005).

Subject matter is selected and organized around certain real-world themes or concepts. An example is a sixth-grade unit of study on water quality in Washington State.

The unit became a part of an actual water quality project that originated in the Great Lakes region of the United States but now spans the globe. Lessons were organized around the actual work of determining water quality in Puget Sound. These lessons culminated in students' reporting to community

- **cooperative learning**
  instructional method that relies on cooperation among students

- **integrative curriculum**
  an approach to education based on student-teacher collaboration

In an integrative curriculum, students apply teachings from many disciplines at the same time. Students shown here are on a field trip to explore mineral production in a local community.

Understanding Freedom and Education in America

One hundred years ago, Russian immigrant Marie Antin wrote about her first days at school in the United States. Reading about her reactions might make Americans more appreciative of the public school system they often criticize.

Education was free. That subject my father had written about repeatedly, as comprising his chief hope for us children, the essence of American oppor-

In the past, schools played an important role in transmitting American culture to many immigrant children. Are schools today still carrying on that function?

tunity, the treasure that no thief could touch, not even misfortune or poverty. It was the one thing that he was able to promise us when he sent for us; surer, safer, than bread or shelter.

On our second day I was thrilled with the realization of what this freedom of education meant. A little girl from across the alley came and offered to conduct us to school. My father was out, but we five between us had a few words of English by this time. We knew the word school. We understood. This child, who had never seen us till yesterday, who could not pronounce our names, who was not much better dressed than we, was able to offer us the freedom of the schools of Boston! No application made, no question asked, no examinations, rulings, exclusions; no machinations, no fees. The doors stood open for every one of us. The smallest child could show us the way.

This incident impressed me more than anything I had heard in advance of the freedom of education in America. It was a concrete proof—almost the thing itself. One had to experience it to understand it.

Source: Excerpted from Marie Antin, *The Promised Land* (New York: Houghton Mifflin Company, 1912).

Thinking It Over

1. Describe your thoughts and feelings about your school experiences as you think about Antin's perspective.

2. Do you agree with the author that education is the chief hope for children? Explain.

groups about the quality of the water. In this way learning was relevant to a real-world problem that the students contributed to solving (Simmons and El-Hindi, 1998:33).

Instruction in this unit emphasized hands-on experience and utilized the multiple intelligences of various students. The latter idea recognizes that not all students in a classroom learn in identical ways. Students bring to any unit of study a variety of learning styles, interests, and abilities. Different units of study will engage students in varying ways.

Back-to-Basics Movement

In the 1990s, the "back-to-basics" movement emerged alongside cooperative learning and the integrative curriculum. Worried by low scores on achievement tests, supporters of this movement pushed for a return to a traditional curriculum ("reading, writing, and arithmetic") based on more bureaucratic methods.

What started the back-to-basics movement? In 1983, America received an educational wake-up call. The National Commission on Excellence in Education issued a report dramatically entitled *A Nation at Risk*. Catching the attention of politicians and the general public, it warned of a "rising tide of mediocrity" in America's schools. Because of deficiencies in its educational system, the report claimed, America was at risk of being overtaken by some of its world economic competitors (Gardner, 1983).

Unlike the recommendations of the progressive and humanistic reform movements, most of the solutions offered by the commission were bureaucratic in nature. The report urged a return to more teaching of basic skills such as reading and mathematics. High school graduation requirements should be strengthened to include four years of English, three years of mathematics, three years of science, three years of social studies, and a half year of computer science. School days, the school year, or both should be lengthened. Standardized achievement tests should be administered as students move from one level of schooling to another. High school students should be given significantly more homework. Discipline should be tightened through the development and enforcement of codes for student conduct.

Alternatives to the Public School System

The debate over the most effective classroom methods continues. Meanwhile, educators and politicians are looking beyond the classroom to how schools are organized, funded, and administered. A new debate has arisen over school choice. The school choice movement promotes the idea that the best way to improve schools is by using the free enterprise model and creating some competition for the public school system. Supporters of school choice believe that parents and students should be able to select the school that best fits their needs and provides the greatest educational benefit. Methods used to accomplish this goal include the *voucher system, charter schools, magnet,* and *for-profit schools.*

What is a voucher system? People in favor of a **voucher system** say that the government should make the money spent per child on public education available to families to use for public, private, or religious schools. Families who chose a public school would pay nothing, just as in the current system. Parents who chose a religious or other private school would receive a government voucher to be used to pay a portion of the tuition equal to the amount the government spends per child in the public school system. Any additional tuition would be paid by the parents. A voucher plan in Cleveland, for example, provided publicly funded scholarships of about $2,000 annually to around four thousand city children in the 2001 school year. Most parents have chosen to spend the money at private schools rather than keep their children in public schools. The basic idea is that public schools would have

This charter school in Harlem is one alternative to the public school system.

● **voucher system**
system in which public school funds may be used to support public, private, or religious schools

to compete for the students and thus would improve their services. If parents were not happy with a school, they would have the freedom to remove their children and place them elsewhere.

Reaction to the school voucher approach has been mixed. So far, only six states and the District of Columbia have adopted school voucher programs (Peterson, 2005). Courts have generally treated voucher systems as unconstitutional because they may contradict the principle of separation of church and state. On the other hand, in 1998 the U.S. Supreme Court let stand a ruling by the Wisconsin Supreme Court that allowed state money to go to low-income students for either private or parochial education schools. In addition, the U.S. Supreme Court in 2002 upheld the constitutionality of Cleveland's voucher program, which allowed vouchers to be used in religious schools. The latest ruling by the Court, in the case of *Locke* v. *Davey*, permits the funding of education in religious schools but does not require it if a state's constitution prohibits it.

One reason for the slow spread of voucher programs among the states is that 36 state constitutions contain various restrictions on aid to private and religious institutions (Peterson, 2005). Amendments to an additional eleven state constitutions restrict the public funding of education to public schools only. Thus, the introduction of voucher systems in these states must first be tested in the courts. A number of state courts, including those in Florida, Vermont, Maine, and Pennsylvania, already have declared vouchers unconstitutional. However, legal challenges continue in some states.

School voucher programs have proved to be one of the most controversial issues of the twenty-first century. Supporters of school vouchers believe they will help children in failing schools achieve a better education and force public schools to improve in order to stay competitive. Opponents of voucher systems fear that they will drain needed funds from the public school system and result in racial and class segregation in American schools. Some states now are considering alternatives to vouchers that still provide parents with options, such as tax credits for private and religious school payments. The important role that education plays in the lives of Americans suggests that the issue of school vouchers will be debated for years to come.

What are charter schools and magnet schools? Charter schools are publicly funded schools operated like private schools by public school teachers and administrators. Freed of answering to local school boards, charter schools have the latitude to shape their own curriculum and to use nontraditional or traditional teaching methods.

The Mosaica Academy (now called School Lane), which opened in 1998 in Pennsylvania, is deliberately not organized along public school lines. The school day is about two hours longer than at public school and the school year is also longer. This school created its own curriculum with the goal of immersing students in the development of civilizations over 4,000 years (Symonds, 2000). In 2005 there were approximately 3,625 charter schools across the United States. The success of these schools is tied to the commitment of the teachers, principals, and parents.

Magnet schools are public schools that attempt to achieve high standards by specializing in a certain area. One school may emphasize the performing arts while another might stress science. Magnet schools are designed to enhance school quality and to promote desegregation. They have become a significant factor in improving urban education.

● **charter schools**
public schools that are operated like private schools by public school teachers and administrators

● **magnet schools**
public schools that focus on particular disciplines or areas, such as fine arts or science

What is the nature of for-profit schools? Some reformers do not believe local or federal government is capable of improving the educational system. Government, they say, is too wasteful and ineffective. Why not look to business and market forces to solve the problems facing schools today? **For-profit schools** would be supported by government funds but run by private companies. By borrowing from modern business practices, the argument goes, these schools could be efficient, productive, and cost effective. Marketplace forces would ensure that the best schools will survive.

The most comprehensive for-profit organization is Edison Schools, Inc., which launched a $40-million, three-year campaign in 1992 to develop its program. Edison schools feature challenging curriculums, along with a schedule that has children in school almost a third longer than the average public school. By 2005, Edison schools were serving more than 330,000 public school children in 25 states, the District of Columbia, and the United Kingdom.

Critics of this approach are bothered by the idea of mixing profit and public service. What would happen to the students when their needs were weighed against the profit margin? Would for-profit schools skimp on equipment, services, and training? Another problem involves oversight. That is, with a for-profit system, voters would lose the power to influence officials and educational policy.

Calvin expects to reap the rewards of education, but has a problem with the effort of getting educated.

● **for-profit schools**
schools run by private companies on government funds

Section 1 Assessment

1. State three ways in which schools in the United States follow the bureaucratic model.

2. Identify three specific types of reform in public education.

Critical Thinking

3. **Analyzing Information** Explain why such reforms as open classrooms and integrative learning are characterized as more democratic than the traditional or bureaucratic approach.

4. **Summarizing Information** First briefly summarize the ideas about school choice presented in this section. Then evaluate them. Do you favor one approach over another? Give reasons for your choice.

2

Functionalist Perspective

Key Terms

- manifest
  function *(p. 396)*
- latent
  function *(p. 396)*
- tracking *(p. 398)*

- **manifest function**
  an action that produces an
  intended and recognized
  result

- **latent function**
  an action that produces an
  unintended and unrecog-
  nized result

Section Preview

Functionalists see the emergence of the educational institution as a response to society's needs. The manifest functions of education include transmission of culture, creation of a common identity, selection and screening of talent, and promotion of personal growth and development. Schools also serve latent functions.

Manifest Functions of Education

According to the functionalists, social institutions develop because they meet one or more of society's basic needs. Functionalists distinguish between a **manifest function**, which is an intended and recognized result, and a **latent function**, which is an unintended and unrecognized result. (Refer to page 26 to review the meanings of these terms.) The educational institution performs several vital manifest functions in modern society. Schools teach obvious academic skills such as reading, writing, and mathematics. They also transmit culture, create a common identity for members of society, select and screen talent, and promote personal growth and development. Let's look more closely at each of these functions.

How do schools transmit culture? Schools transmit culture by instilling in students the basic values, norms, beliefs, and attitudes of the society. The value of competition, for example, is taught through emphasis on grades, sports, and school spirit. Teaching the culture is absolutely essential if a society is to survive from one generation to the next.

Is the teacher lecturing to these students fulfilling a manifest or latent function?

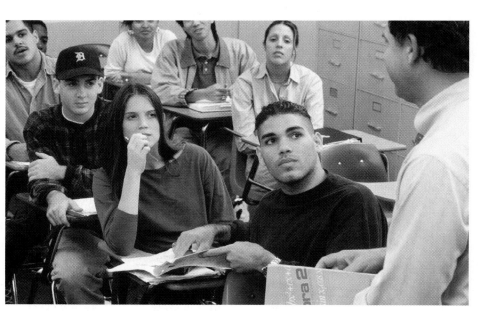

World View

Literacy Rates

One of the functions of education is to promote literacy—the key to continued learning, problem solving, and information analysis. This map shows rates of literacy among persons fifteen years of age and older in various countries of the world. Because of cultural norms and discrimination, more men than women are able to read and write.

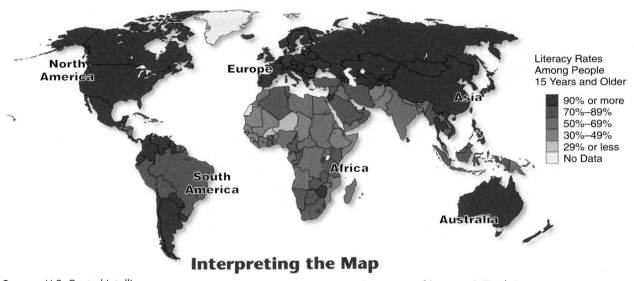

Literacy Rates Among People 15 Years and Older
- 90% or more
- 70%–89%
- 50%–69%
- 30%–49%
- 29% or less
- No Data

Source: U.S. Central Intelligence Agency, *The World Factbook,* 2005.

Interpreting the Map

1. Do you see a pattern in the rates of literacy? Explain.

2. How does the United States measure up?

How do schools help create a common identity? Although television is now a strong competitor, the educational system remains the major force in creating a common identity among a diverse population. Learning an official language, sharing in national history and patriotic themes, and being exposed to similar informational materials promote a shared identity. The result is a society with homogeneous values, norms, beliefs, and attitudes. Schools in the United States contribute to this process. By attending local schools, newly arrived immigrant children, without the ability to speak and write English, soon learn to participate in the American way of life.

The current debate in the United States over bilingual education touches on the role that schools play in creating a common identity. People who emphasize recognizing and honoring cultural diversity usually support teaching in the student's own language, at least for some period of time. Opponents of bilingual education argue that bilingual education hinders the development of a common American identity and has not been proven to help students succeed academically. Conservative political efforts have led 27 states to adopt English as their official language. The creation of a similar law for the nation is being discussed in Congress.

How do schools select and screen students? For over fifty years, scores on intelligence and achievement tests have been used for grouping children in school. The stated purpose of testing is to identify an individual's talents and aptitudes. Test scores have also been used for **tracking**—placing students in curricula consistent with expectations for the students' eventual occupations. (Tracking is discussed further in Section 3 when we look at inequalities in education.) Counselors use test scores and early performance records to predict careers for which individuals may be best suited.

How do schools promote personal growth and development? Schools expose students to a wide variety of perspectives and experiences that encourage them to develop creativity, verbal skills, artistic expression, intellectual accomplishment, and cultural tolerance. In this way, education provides an environment in which individuals can improve the quality of their lives. In addition, schools attempt to prepare students for the world of work.

● **tracking**
placement of students in programs according to academic ability levels

Do you consider the opportunity to flirt a positive or negative latent function of schools?

Latent Functions of Education

The educational institution has latent functions as well. Some are positive; others are not. Educators do not usually think of schools as day-care facilities for dual-employed couples or single parents. Nor do parents vote for additional school taxes so that their sons and daughters can find dates or marriage partners. Also, schools are not consciously designed to prevent delinquency by holding juveniles indoors during the daytime. Nor are schools intended as training grounds for athletes. Nonetheless, all of these activities are latent functions of the school system.

Each of the latent functions just mentioned is considered a positive contribution to society. But some consequences are negative, or dysfunctional. Tracking, for example, can perpetuate an unequal social-class structure from generation to generation. In addition, evidence suggests that tracking is harmful to those placed on "slower" tracks (Hurn, 1993; Bracey, 2003).

Section 2 Assessment

1. List the essential functions of education described in the text.

2. What is the difference between a manifest and a latent function in education?

3. What type of function do schools perform when they keep children for their working parents?

Critical Thinking

4. **Making Comparisons** What do you think is the most significant latent function schools perform? Consider the advantages and disadvantages.

Sociology Today

Educating Yourself for the Future

By the time you graduate from high school, the competition for well-paying entry-level jobs will be stiffer than ever before. Here are some tips to keep you in demand—whether you are college bound or going directly into the job market.

Career counselors urge job seekers to think in terms of *lifelong learning.* Never think of your education as coming to an end. The excerpt below is as true today as it was a generation ago.

> For education the lesson is clear: its prime objective must be to increase the individual's "cope-ability"—the speed and economy with which he can adapt to continual change. . . . It is not even enough for him to understand the present, for the here-and-now environment will soon vanish. Johnny must learn to anticipate the directions and rate of change. He must, to put it technically, learn to make repeated, probabilistic, increasingly long-range assumptions about the future (Toffler, 1970:403).

Preparation for the future involves attempting to predict the future demand for particular occupations. The *Occupational Outlook Handbook* and the *Occupational Outlook Handbook for College Graduates* can be very helpful in this regard. Each year in these volumes, the U.S. Department of Labor publishes detailed predictions for specific occupations.

Educating yourself for the future also means being prepared to enter an occupation for which you have no specific training. You must remain willing to retrain and to enter an entirely new occupation—for example, to move from bank teller to computer programmer.

In spite of the fact that you will probably change occupations over the course of your work life, you should try to determine your true job preference before you spend a great deal of time learning a job that turns out not to be the one you want. Over half of all young people entering a chosen field quit their jobs within one year. This fact has led some observers to argue that few young people really understand the nature of the work for which they are preparing. How do you find out what jobs you would really enjoy? Volunteering time in a specific work situation can help. For example, hospitals usually have volunteer programs in which medical practitioners can be observed. If you think you would like to be a physician, nurse, or other health-care worker, get involved in one of these programs. You will not only help others but will help yourself, as well.

Doing Sociology

Make an informal survey of as many working adults as possible. Ask them what additional training, if any, they have undergone since taking their first jobs. Then ask them what plans they have for future training. Summarize your results, and bring the report to class to share.

3

Conflict Perspective

Key Terms

- meritocracy (p. 400)
- competition (p. 400)
- educational equality (p. 403)
- cognitive ability (p. 404)
- cultural bias (p. 405)
- school desegregation (p. 406)
- multicultural education (p. 407)
- compensatory education (p. 407)

- **meritocracy**
  a society in which social status is based on ability and achievement

- **competition**
  system in which rewards are based on relative performance

Section Preview

In theory, America is a meritocracy in which social status is achieved. Proponents of the conflict perspective identify flaws in this model by pointing to inequality in our schools. Methods and programs aimed at promoting educational equality have been developed.

Meritocracy

Conflict theorists attempt to show that popular conceptions about the relationship between schools and society are not entirely accurate. Schools and society often touch each other in complicated and unobvious ways.

In a **meritocracy**, social status is based on ability and achievement rather than social-class background or parental status. In theory, all individuals in a meritocracy have an equal chance to develop their abilities for the benefit of themselves and their society. A meritocracy, then, gives everyone an equal chance to succeed. It is free of barriers that prevent individuals from developing their talents.

Meritocracy is based on competition. For this reason, sport is seen as the ultimate meritocracy. Although some sports have glaring shortcomings in this regard (see Chapter 15), sport does fit very closely with the definition of competition. For sociologists, **competition** is a social process that occurs when rewards are given to people on the basis of how their performance compares with the performance of others doing the same task or participating in the same event (Coakley, 2004).

Is America really a meritocracy? Although America claims to be a meritocracy, sociologists have identified barriers to true merit-based achievement, such as gender, race, and ethnicity. An example (greatly simplified) is how the education system favors the wealthy. Schools in wealthy neighborhoods are significantly better than schools in economically disadvantaged areas. It follows, then, that

Participating in academic contests, such as building robots, is one way teachers can find those students who merit special recognition.

students attending wealthier schools get a better education than students attending poorer schools. Furthermore, students attending poorer schools do not learn the values, manners, language, and dress of people in more affluent schools. Because the majority of students in poorer schools are members of racial and ethnic minorities, they find themselves at a disadvantage when applying for higher-level jobs that lead to higher incomes. (See Figure 12.2.)

How do minorities perform on college entrance exams?

There are related barriers to achievement faced by racial and ethnic minorities. An important one of these is lower performance on college entrance examinations. African Americans, Latinos, and Native Americans have lower average scores on the Scholastic Assessment Test (SAT) than whites. (See Figure 12.3 on page 402.) Sociologists attribute this fact, in part, to the differences in school quality noted above. And both school quality and SAT performance are related to social class. Children from upper-class and upper-middle-class families attend more affluent schools. These children also have higher SAT scores. Social class clearly affects SAT performance.

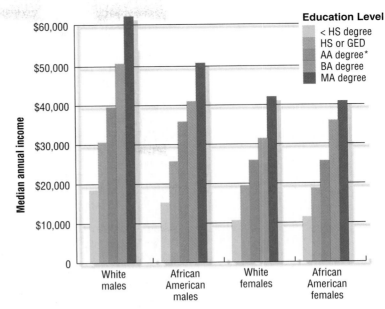

*An Associate Arts or AA degree is a two-year college program.

Figure 12.2 Median Annual Income by Gender, Race, and Education Clearly, this graph documents the income advantage that white males in the U.S. have over white females and African Americans of both sexes. Explain how this data challenges the existence of a true meritocracy.

Source: U.S. Bureau of the Census, 2004.

Social class is a strong predictor of success on the SATs. How is race related to social class?

Figure 12.3

SAT Scores by Race and Ethnicity

An examination of this table reveals the gap in average SAT scores for whites and Asian Americans versus African Americans, Latinos, and Native Americans. Interpret these data as a conflict theorist would in the context of the U.S. as a meritocracy.

Racial/Ethnic Category	SAT Verbal Mean Scores	SAT Math Mean Scores	Totals
Native American or Alaskan Native	489	488	977
Asian, Asian American, or Pacific Islander	511	577	1088
African American	433	427	860
Latino Background			
Mexican American	453	458	911
Puerto Rican	460	452	912
Latin American, South American, Central American, or Other Latino	463	465	928
White (excluding Latino origin)	532	531	1063

Source: The College Board, 2005.

Why are SAT scores considered vital to a meritocratic American society?

How do SAT scores influence economic achievement?
The SAT, created in 1926, was originally used to identify talented youth, regardless of social class background, so they could attend elite colleges and universities (Lemann, 1992). Ironically, as we have just seen, social class is a major factor in SAT performance. Consequently, social class (through SAT performance) still influences who will attend the institutions that are the gateway to America's higher social classes.

Don't the rewards tied to high SAT scores mean that America is a meritocracy?
On the surface it does seem that merit is being rewarded in the system just outlined. After all, it is those who do better academically who enjoy higher levels of success.

There are two problems with this conclusion. The first is the advantage some people have because their parents' social class creates an unlevel playing field. Talent in the lower social classes often does not get recognized and developed. Second is the assumption that SAT performance measures academic ability and the likelihood of success in both college and life. For example, African American students who attend the most prestigious schools—including those students with lower SAT scores (below 1000)—complete college at a higher rate than African American students attending less rigorous institutions. They are also more likely to go on to graduate or professional schools (Bowen and Bok, 2000). Apparently these students are succeeding because they attended better schools, even if they don't have high SAT scores.

At the least, these findings raise doubts about the ability of the SAT to achieve a level playing field. Recognizing this, an official at the Educational Testing Service (ETS)—developer and marketer of the SAT—announced in 1999 that ETS was creating a "strivers" score. The idea was to adjust a student's SAT score to factor in social class as well as racial and ethnic characteristics thought to place him or her at a competitive disadvantage. Any student whose original score exceeded by 200 points the score predicted for their social class, racial, or ethnic category would be considered a "striver." The strivers score would be made available to colleges and universities to use, if they desired, in their admissions decisions (Glazer, 1999; Wildavsky, 1999). The proposal was quickly withdrawn after a firestorm of criticism from both privileged and disadvantaged sources.

Equality and Inequality in Education

The situation for those disadvantaged by social class, racial, and ethnic background is actually even more complicated. As already implied, it is tied to the larger issue of educational equality and inequality. **Educational equality** exists when schooling produces the same results, in terms of achievement and attitudes, for lower-class and minority children as it does for less disadvantaged children. Results, not resources, are the test of educational equality (Coleman et al., 1966).

● **educational equality**
condition in which schooling produces the same results for lower-class and minority children as it does for other children

Do schools provide educational equality?
Research has shown that even the best teachers often evaluate students on the basis of their social class and their racial and ethnic characteristics. This tendency to judge students on nonacademic criteria is especially apparent in the practice of tracking. Researchers report that social class and race heavily influence student placement in college preparatory, vocational, or basic tracks regardless of their intelligence or past academic achievement (Oakes and Lipton, 1996; Taylor et al., 2005). Once students are placed, their grades and test scores are influenced

Would you expect to find educational equality in these two schools?

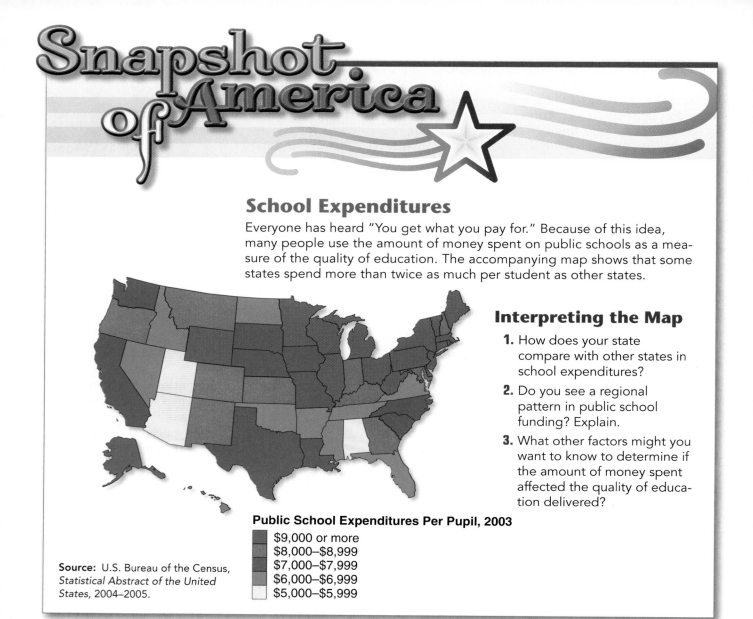

Snapshot of America

School Expenditures

Everyone has heard "You get what you pay for." Because of this idea, many people use the amount of money spent on public schools as a measure of the quality of education. The accompanying map shows that some states spend more than twice as much per student as other states.

Interpreting the Map

1. How does your state compare with other states in school expenditures?

2. Do you see a regional pattern in public school funding? Explain.

3. What other factors might you want to know to determine if the amount of money spent affected the quality of education delivered?

Public School Expenditures Per Pupil, 2003

- $9,000 or more
- $8,000–$8,999
- $7,000–$7,999
- $6,000–$6,999
- $5,000–$5,999

Source: U.S. Bureau of the Census, *Statistical Abstract of the United States, 2004–2005.*

more by the track they are on than by their current performance. Regardless of earlier school performance or intelligence, the academic performance of college-bound students increases, whereas the performance of those on a non-college track decreases. In other words, schools are not successfully providing educational equality for their students.

Cognitive Ability

● **cognitive ability**
capacity for thinking abstractly

The technical term for intelligence is **cognitive ability**—the capacity for thinking abstractly. Dating back to the turn of the twentieth century, there has been a tradition in schools to attempt to measure cognitive ability.

Because cognitive ability testing is an important element in sorting and tracking students, it contributes to educational inequality. Whenever cognitive ability tests are discussed, the question of inherited intelligence always arises.

Is intelligence inherited? In the past, some people assumed that individual and group differences in measured intellectual ability were due to genetic differences. This assumption, of course, underlies Social Darwinism. (See pages 15–16 for a brief explanation of these assumptions.)

A few researchers still take this viewpoint. More than thirty years ago Arthur Jensen (1969), an educational psychologist, contended that the lower average intelligence score among African American children may be due to heredity. A more recent book by Richard Herrnstein and Charles Murray (1994), entitled *The Bell Curve,* is also in the tradition of linking intelligence to heredity. According to these authors, humans inherit 60 to 70 percent of their intelligence level. Herrnstein and Murray further contend that the fact of inherited intelligence makes largely futile the efforts to help the disadvantaged through programs such as Head Start and affirmative action.

What are arguments against the inherited intelligence theory? Most social scientists oppose the genetic explanation of intelligence differences between races because it fails to consider the effects of the social, psychological, and economic environment on intelligence. Even those social scientists who believe that genetics plays an important role in intelligence criticize both the interpretations of the evidence and the public policy conclusions contained in *The Bell Curve.* They point to the body of research that runs counter to Herrnstein and Murray's thesis. More specifically, they see intelligence not as an issue of nature *versus* nurture but as a matter of genetics *and* environment (Morganthau, 1994; Wright, 1996). We know, for example, that city dwellers usually score higher on intelligence tests than do people in rural areas, that higher-status African Americans score higher than lower-status African Americans, and that middle-class African American children score about as high as middle-class white children. We also have discovered that as people get older, they usually score higher on intelligence tests. These findings, and others like them, have led researchers to conclude that environmental factors affect test performance at least as much as genetic factors (Samuda, 1998; Jencks and Phillips, 1998; Ross et al, 2003). One of these environmental factors is a cultural bias in the measurement of cognitive ability.

What are culturally biased intelligence tests? Many early social scientists have argued that intelligence tests have a **cultural bias**—that is, the wording used in questions may be more familiar to people of one social group than to those of another group. Tests with cultural bias unfairly measure the cognitive abilities of people in some social categories. Specifically, intelligence tests are said to be culturally biased because they are designed for middle-class children. The tests measure learning and environment as much as intellectual ability. Consider this intelligence test item cited by Daniel Levine and Rayna Levine:

A symphony is to a composer as a book is to what?

   a. paper
   b. a musician
   c. a sculptor
   d. a man
   e. an author

According to critics, higher-income children find this question easier to answer correctly than lower-income children because they are more likely to have been exposed to information about classical music. The same charge

In 2004, software engineer Ken Jennings won more than $2.5 million on *Jeopardy!*, a game show that tests knowledge in a broad variety of areas. Jennings's record-shattering winning streak lasted for 74 episodes before he was finally defeated.

● **cultural bias**
the unfair measurement of the cognitive abilities of people in some social categories

was made by critics of a recent SAT question that used a Bentley (a luxury-model automobile) as its illustration. Several studies have indicated that because most intelligence tests assume fluency in English, minorities cannot do as well on intelligence tests. Some researchers have suggested that many urban African American students are superior to their white classmates on several dimensions of verbal capacity, but this ability is not recognized, because intelligence tests do not measure those specific areas (Gould, 1996; Lee, 2002; Graham, 2005).

Some researchers have shown that the testing situation itself affects performance. Low-income and minority students, for example, score higher on intelligence tests when tested by adult members of their own race or income group. Apparently children can feel threatened when tested in a strange environment by someone dissimilar to them. Middle-class children are frequently eager to take the tests because they have been taught the importance both of test results and of academic competitiveness. Because low-income children do not recognize the importance of tests and have not been taught to be academically competitive, they ignore some of the questions or look for something more interesting to do. Other researchers report that nutrition seems to play a role in test performance. Low-income children with poor diets may do less than their best when they are hungry or when they lack particular types of food over long periods of time.

Promoting Educational Equality

Although it is difficult to completely overcome the barriers of economic and social class, policy makers and educators are exploring ways to promote educational equality. Two methods are *school desegregation* and *compensatory education*.

Does desegregation always promote equality?
In this discussion, **school desegregation** refers to the achievement of a racial balance in the classroom. Desegregated classrooms can have either positive or negative effects on the academic achievement of minority children. Mere physical desegregation without adequate support may actually harm both white and African American children. However, desegregated classrooms with an atmosphere of respect and acceptance improve academic performance (Orfield et al., 1992).

Minority students who attend desegregated public schools get better jobs and earn higher incomes than minority students who attend segregated schools. The formal education they receive is only part of the reason. Middle-class students become models for the behavior, dress, and language often required by employers in the middle-class hiring world.

● **school desegregation**
the achievement of a racial balance in the classroom

Many schools hold multicultural festivals to celebrate the wide variety of cultures that make up the United States.

In addition, exposure to people of different backgrounds can lead to better racial and ethnic relations (Hawley and Smylie, 1988). On this evidence rests the promise of **multicultural education**—an educational curriculum that accents the viewpoints, experiences, and contributions of minorities (women as well as ethnic and racial minorities).

What is the purpose of multicultural education?

Among minorities, school attendance and academic performance appear to increase with multicultural education. Multicultural education attempts to dispel stereotypes and to make the traditions of minorities valuable assets for the broader culture (McLaren, 1997; Ladson-Billings, 1998).

Multicultural education has its critics, however. According to some opponents, encouraging people to think of themselves as culturally separate and unique divides rather than unites American society. Some critics point to instances in which multicultural programs, such as African American studies programs, actually promote feelings of racial separation in schools.

Does compensatory education work?

The term **compensatory education** refers to specific curricular programs designed to overcome deficiency. Special compensatory programs provided during early childhood, it appears, can improve the school achievement of disadvantaged children (Campbell and Ramey, 1994; Oliver and Smith, 2000).

The best-known attempt at compensatory education is Head Start. This federally supported program prepares disadvantaged preschoolers for public school. Its goal is to provide disadvantaged children an equal opportunity to develop their potential. Follow-up studies report positive long-term results. Low-income youngsters between the ages of nine and nineteen who had been in preschool compensatory programs performed better in school. They had higher achievement test scores and were more motivated academically than low-income youths who had not been in compensatory education programs (Bruner, 1982; Etzioni, 1982). Later research also supports the benefits of Head Start (Mills, 1998; Zigler and Styfco, 2004). For example, compared to their peers, a group of children who scored lower on intelligence tests when they entered a Head Start program later had better school attendance, completed high school at a higher rate, and entered the workforce in greater proportion.

- **multicultural education**
  an educational curriculum that emphasizes differences among gender, ethnic, and racial categories

- **compensatory education**
  specific curricular programs designed to overcome a deficiency

Section 3 Assessment

1. Do you think the United States is a meritocracy, as stated in the text?
2. What is meant by the term *educational equality?*
3. What role conflicts does multicultural education pose for teachers?

Critical Thinking

4. **Finding the Main Idea** Students from higher social classes are more likely to go to college than students from the lower classes. How does this fit with the idea of meritocracy?

5. **Evaluating Information** If schools fail to provide educational quality, what do you think will be the consequences in terms of role conflict?

TECH TRENDS

School's Out . . . Forever?

In a recent book, *The Age of Spiritual Machines,* author Ray Kurzweil makes forecasts concerning life in the twenty-first century. He claims that, by the end of the century, computers will be the most intelligent "beings" on the planet. Specific predictions on education in 2009 include the following scenarios.

The majority of reading is done on displays, although the "installed base" of paper documents is still formidable. The generation of paper documents is dwindling, however, as the books and other papers of largely twentieth-century vintage are being rapidly scanned and stored. Documents circa 2009 routinely include embedded moving images and sounds.

Students of all ages typically have a computer of their own, which is a thin tabletlike device weighing under a pound with a very high resolution display suitable for reading. Students interact with their computers primarily by voice and by pointing with a device that looks like a pencil. Keyboards still exist, but most textual language is created by speaking. Learning materials are accessed through wireless communication.

Preschool and elementary school children routinely read at their intellectual level using print-to-speech reading software until their reading skill level catches up. These print-to-speech reading systems display the full image of documents, and can read the print aloud while highlighting what is being read. Synthetic voices sound fully human. Although some educators expressed concern in the early '00 years that students would rely unduly on reading software, such systems have been readily accepted by children and their parents. Studies have shown that students improve their reading skills by being exposed to synchronized visual and auditory presentations of text.

Learning at a distance (for example, lectures and seminars in which the participants are geographically scattered) is commonplace. This also helps to relieve congested campuses and cut back on the burning of gasoline in city limits.

Technology is changing the face of education in this country. Some futurists predict that distance learning technology may eventually replace the traditional school building.

Analyzing the Trends

1. If Kurzweil's predictions came true, how would education's role in the socialization of students change?

2. If Kurzweil's predictions came true, would social stratification play a more or less important role in education than it does now? Use information from the chapter to support your answer.

3. If the predictions in the article came to pass, would we still need schools? Why or why not?

Symbolic Interactionism

Section Preview

Symbolic interactionists emphasize the socialization that occurs in schools. Through the hidden curriculum, children are taught values, norms, beliefs, and attitudes. Much of this socialization helps young people make the transition from home to the larger society.

Key Terms
● hidden curriculum *(p. 409)*
● self-fulfilling prophecy *(p. 410)*

The Hidden Curriculum

Symbolic interactionists are very interested in how schools transmit culture through the socialization process. Besides teachers and textbooks, which we will discuss later, the most important agent of this socialization process is the *hidden curriculum*. Modern society places considerable emphasis on the verbal, mathematical, and writing skills an adult needs to obtain a job, read a newspaper, balance a checkbook, and compute income taxes. However, schools teach much more than these basic academic skills. They also transmit to children a variety of values, norms, beliefs, and attitudes.

What is the hidden curriculum? The **hidden curriculum** is the nonacademic agenda that teaches children norms and values such as discipline, order, cooperativeness, and conformity. These citizenship skills are thought to be necessary for success in modern bureaucratic society, whether one becomes a doctor, a college president, a computer programmer, or an assembly-line worker. Over the years, schools, for example, socialize children for the transition from their closely knit, cooperative families to the loosely knit, competitive adult occupational world. The school provides systematic practice for children to operate independently in the pursuit of personal and academic achievement. The values of conformity and achievement are emphasized through individual testing and grading. Because teachers evaluate young people as students, not as relatives, friends, or equals, students participate in a model for future secondary relationships—employer-employee; salesperson-customer; lawyer-client.

● **hidden curriculum**
the nonacademic agenda that teaches discipline, order, cooperativeness, and conformity

Requiring students to stand in line reinforces the importance of obedience and cooperation, part of the school system's hidden agenda.

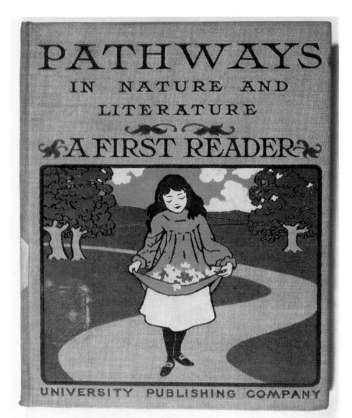

What, in addition to academic content, do textbooks teach students?

Textbooks

A critical part of the hidden curriculum is the development of patriotism and a sense of civic duty in future adults. For this reason, courses such as history and government generally present a view of history that favors the nation. Accounts of the American Revolution, for example, are not the same in British and American textbooks. Because few societies are willing to admit to their imperfections, schools tend to resist teaching critical accounts of history. For example, for many years U.S. history textbooks failed to portray the U.S. government's harsh treatment of Native American peoples.

Textbooks convey values and beliefs as much by what they omit as by what they include. While today's textbooks present a more balanced picture, surveys of primary school textbooks written before the 1980s found they almost always presented men in challenging and aggressive activities while portraying women as homemakers, mothers, nurses, and secretaries. Women were not only placed in traditional roles but also appeared far less frequently in the books than men did. When women did appear, they were not initiators of action, but played passive roles. Minority groups were rarely present in textbooks, and when they were it was often in a negative context.

Similarly, textbooks tended to portray all students as living in "little white houses with white picket fences." That image may have been part of the worldview of middle-class Americans, but parents of low-income or inner-city children complained that such pictures of middle-class life harmed their children. Poor children who compared their homes with middle-class homes felt out of place (Trimble, 1988; Gibson and Ogbu, 1991).

Today, active parent groups, minority special interest groups, and state boards of education work with textbook publishers to ensure that a more balanced picture of society is presented to students. Problems arise, however, when conflicts occur over whose view of society is the most accurate.

Teachers and Socialization

Classroom teachers have a unique and important role in socializing children. Teachers are usually a child's first authority figures outside the family, and children spend a lot of time in school. In addition, most parents urge their children to obey teachers, in part because their children's futures are affected by school performance.

How do teachers affect students' performance? All teachers set academic tasks for their students, but teachers affect children unintentionally as well. In a classic 1989 study, Robert Rosenthal and Lenore Jacobson explored the **self-fulfilling prophecy**—a prediction that results in behavior that makes the prediction come true. In their study, elementary school teachers were given a list of children in their classrooms who, according to the researchers, were soon to blossom intellectually. Actually, these children were picked at random from the school roster and were no different from other

● **self-fulfilling prophecy**
a prediction that results in behavior that makes the prediction come true

Figure 12.4   Investigating Education

This table illustrates differences in the ways the major theoretical perspectives investigate education as a social institution. It is, of course, possible for a theoretical perspective to study education using one of the concepts associated in this table with another perspective. Explain, for example, how conflict theory would interpret the hidden curriculum and tracking.

Theoretical Perspective	Concept		Example
Functionalism	Tracking		Schools shape the occupational future of children by placing them in educational programs based on test scores and early school performance.
Conflict Theory	Meritocracy		Students attending better schools have an occupational advantage over students from poorer schools.
Symbolic Interactionism	Hidden curriculum		Schools teach children the values of conformity and achievement.

children in the school. At the end of the year, this randomly selected group of children significantly improved their scores on intelligence tests, while their classmates as a group did not. According to Rosenthal and Jacobson, the teachers expected the "late bloomers" to spurt academically. Consequently, the teachers treated these students as if they were special. This behavior on the part of the teachers encouraged the students to become higher academic achievers. The term *Pygmalian effect* describes the situation in which some students perform better than others simply because they are expected to do so. (See Focus on Research on pages 414–415.)

Another early study by sociologist Eleanor Leacock (1969) found the self-fulfilling prophecy at work in a study of second and fifth graders in black and white low- and middle-income schools. And both studies demonstrate that self-fulfilling prophecies can transmit negative self-impressions as well as positive ones.

Do teachers foster sexism?

As described in Chapter 10, children are taught to adopt the "appropriate" gender identity in school (Martin, 1998). Following a long line of earlier researchers, Myra Sadker and David Sadker (1995) have contended that America's teachers are often unfair to girls because they treat girls differently than boys based on assumptions and stereotypes of what is appropriate behavior. Well-meaning teachers unconsciously transmit

Sociology Online

Student Web Activity
Visit the *Sociology and You* Web site at glencoe.com and click on **Chapter 12—Student Web Activities** for an activity on sexism in schools.

Snapshot of America

High School Dropouts

For many jobs, a high school diploma is a minimum requirement. People who do not complete high school earn only about three-fourths as much as high school graduates. This map shows the percentage of teenagers (aged sixteen to nineteen) in each state who are high school dropouts.

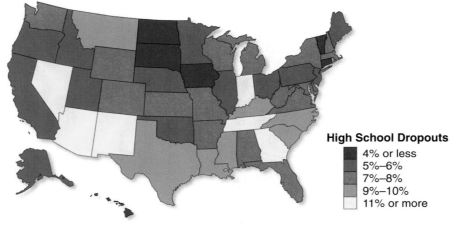

High School Dropouts
- 4% or less
- 5%–6%
- 7%–8%
- 9%–10%
- 11% or more

Source: Annie E. Casey Foundation, *2005 Kids Count Data Sheet.*

Interpreting the Map

1. Compare this map with the Snapshot on page 404. Do you see a relationship between the money spent per student and the percentage of high school dropouts?

2. Compare this map with the Snapshot on page 261. Do you see any relationship between the percentage of high school dropouts and the percentage of the population living below the poverty line?

sexist expectations of how male and female students should behave. Girls, for example, learn to talk softly, to avoid certain subjects (especially math and science), to defer to the alleged intellectual superiority of boys, and to emphasize appearance over intelligence. As a result, in a coeducational setting boys are

- five times more likely to receive the most attention from teachers.
- three times more likely to be praised.
- eight times more likely to call out in class.
- three times more talkative in class.
- twice as likely to demand help or attention.
- twice as likely to be called on in class.

The conclusions seem to be incontrovertible: in general boys talk more, move more, have their hands up more, do more, argue more, get more of the teachers' attention than do girls in a coeducational setting (Sadker and Sadker, 1995).

But, what about all the progress that has been made?

Contrary to the expectation of some, such inequalities are not gone from the educational scene. Writers who paint a rosier picture have so far failed to produce convincing evidence to support it (Deak, 1998).

There is objective evidence that girls are guided in school toward traditional female jobs and away from high-paying, powerful, and prestigious jobs in science, technology, and engineering (Bailey, 2002). True, significantly more high school girls want to go into engineering today than in the past. But four times more men than women receive bachelor's degrees in engineering.

These gender-based discrepancies cannot be explained by ability differences. Girls perform almost as well as boys on math and science tests (O'Sullivan, Reese, and Mazzeo, 1997). Girls score higher than boys at reading and writing at all grade levels and are more likely to attend college (Greenwald et al., 1999). Moreover, females fare better in single-gender schools and single-gender classes in coeducational schools (Deak, 1998; DeBare, 2004).

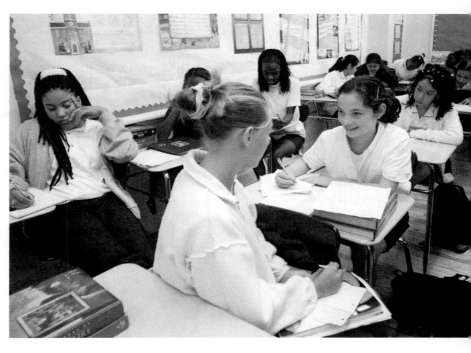

What evidence has been presented about the advantages of single-gender schools?

> *Girls in these situations, in general, get better grades, report that they learn more and are more positive about the learning situation, have higher self-esteem, and more often move on to advanced courses than do girls in regular coeducational situations (Deak, 1998:19–20).*

Section 4 Assessment

1. Cite an example from your earlier schooling that you believe presented a viewpoint of history that was incomplete or slanted toward one perspective.

Critical Thinking

2. **Making Generalizations** Besides parents and teachers, what authority figures do young children meet?

3. **Applying Concepts** Describe a time when you were the subject of a self-fulfilling prophecy.

4. **Applying Concepts** Provide examples from your own experience to support or contradict the existence of the hidden curriculum.

Focus on Research

Case Study: Pygmalion in the Classroom

Are your beliefs strong enough to affect your feelings or behavior? You have probably experienced how your feelings and behavior change upon receiving new information. A feeling of well-being usually follows learning that you did better on an important math exam than you thought you could. You may even be encouraged enough to study math more enthusiastically in the future. If your own perceptions can affect your feelings and behavior, is it possible that someone else's beliefs about you can also influence your feelings and behavior? The idea that this can happen is called the *self-fulfilling prophecy*. As noted earlier, two social scientists, Robert Rosenthal and Lenore Jacobson (1989), studied the self-fulfilling prophecy in a school setting.

For their case study, these researchers chose Oak School, a public elementary school located in a predominantly lower-class community. They hypothesized that children whose teacher expected their IQ scores to increase would in fact increase their scores more than comparable children whose teacher expected no IQ gains.

At the beginning of the study, a test was given to all of the Oak School students. Although it was falsely advertised as a predictor of academic "blooming" or "spurting," it was actually a non-verbal intelligence test. Rosenthal and Jacobson subsequently identified for the teachers 20 percent of the children who allegedly were ready for a dramatic increase in intellectual growth. In fact, the researchers had selected the names of these students by using a table of random numbers. The difference in potential for academic growth between the children said to be on the verge of "blooming" and the rest of the students existed only in the minds of the teachers.

Intellectual growth was measured by the difference between a child's IQ score at the end of the previous school year and that same child's IQ score eight months after the next school year began. As Rosenthal and Jacobson expected, the children in the "blooming" group gained more IQ points than the other children (a 12-point gain versus an 8-point

Students who are treated as if they are expected to perform at high levels often do.

gain). The IQ gain of the children in the "blooming" group over the other students was the most pronounced among first and second graders. First graders in the "blooming" group gained over 27 IQ points, compared with 12 points in the remainder of the class. Among second graders, the advantage was 16.5 IQ points to 7.

Low teacher expectations do not necessarily prevent good students from doing well in school. And high teacher expectations cannot spur poor learners to the highest levels of achievement; however, high teacher expectations can be a powerful motivator for low performers who are capable of doing much better (Madon, Jussim, and Eccles, 1997). This occurs because teachers with high expectations for students treat them in special ways—they tend to smile and look at them more often, set higher goals for them, praise them more frequently, coach them in their studies, and give them more time to study (Rendon and Hope, 1996).

Operation of the self-fulfilling prophecy has been confirmed by other researchers in many other social settings (Myers, 1999). Research subjects behave as they think researchers expect, and a client's progress in therapy is influenced by the therapist's expectation. People who are expected by others to be hostile will exhibit more hostile behavior.

Working with the Research

1. How do you think the self-fulfilling prophecy works? That is, how are expectations transmitted from one person to another, and how do these expectations produce behavior?

2. What are the implications of the self-fulfilling prophecy for students? For teachers?

3. Explain why the self-fulfilling prophecy supports the labeling process discussed on pages 214–217 in Chapter 7.

Chapter 12 Assessment

Summary

Section 1: Development and Structure of Education

Main Idea: Schools are becoming more bureaucratic. Advocates of open classrooms and cooperative learning contend that bureaucratically run schools fail to take into account the emotional and creative needs of individual children.

Section 2: Functionalist Perspective

Main Idea: The manifest functions of education include transmission of culture, creation of a common identity, and promotion of personal development. Schools also serve latent functions.

Section 3: Conflict Perspective

Main Idea: In theory, America is a meritocracy in which social status is achieved. Proponents of the conflict perspective, however, point to inequality in our schools. Programs for educational equality have been developed.

Section 4: Symbolic Interactionism

Main Idea: Symbolic interactionists emphasize the socialization that occurs in schools. Through the hidden curriculum, children are taught values, norms, beliefs, and attitudes that help young people make the transition from home to a larger society.

Self-Check Quiz
Visit the *Sociology and You* Web site at glencoe.com and click on **Chapter 12—Self-Check Quizzes** to prepare for the chapter test.

Reviewing Vocabulary

Complete each sentence using each term once.

a. open-classroom model
b. cooperative learning
c. tracking
d. meritocracy
e. educational equality
f. multiculturalism
g. hidden curriculum
h. self-fulfilling prophecy

1. _____ is a prediction that results in behavior that makes the prediction come true.
2. A nonbureaucratic classroom structure in which students study in groups is called _____ .
3. An educational curriculum that accents the viewpoints, experiences, and contributions of minorities is called _____ .
4. _____ is equality defined in terms of the effects or results of schooling.
5. Placing students in curricula consistent with expectations for their eventual occupations is called _____ .
6. _____ is social status based on achievement rather than social class or parental status.
7. _____ includes discipline, order, cooperation, and conformity.
8. _____ did away with the sharp authoritarian line between teacher and students.

Reviewing the Facts

9. Teachers tell a student he won't amount to anything; then he starts to fail subjects he used to pass. What does a sociologist call this?
10. Explain a manifest function of education and a latent function of education; give three examples of each.

FUNCTION	EXAMPLE 1	EXAMPLE 2	EXAMPLE 3
Manifest			
Latent			

11. What are the three agents that assist schools to transmit culture through the socialization process?
12. What is the hidden curriculum and what purpose does it serve?
13. What is compensatory education? Give an example.
14. What is the difference between a charter school and a magnet school?

Thinking Critically

15. **Understanding Cause and Effect**
An elementary school teacher was given a list of her students on the first day of class. Next to each student's name was a number. One was 132, another was 141, and so forth. The teacher saw these numbers and was tremendously excited to begin the school year. In fact, she went out and bought extra materials. At the end of the school year, her students had shown incredible progress. When the principal came up to the teacher and congratulated her, the teacher thanked the principal for giving her so many students with high IQs. The principal said, "What do you mean?" "Well," the teacher replied, "on the first day of class, you gave me that list of student names with their IQs." "Those weren't IQ numbers; they were locker numbers!" The principal responded. Whether this story is true or not, it is a good example of the self-fulfilling prophecy (or the Pygmalion effect). What might have happened if the numbers next to the students' names had been 94 or 97?

16. **Analyzing Information**
Do you think that our society benefits more from competitive situations or cooperative situations? Can both approaches be beneficial to society? In what instances might one approach be preferred?

Daryl Cagle/Cagle Cartoons

17. **Analyzing Visuals**
In this chapter, you read about a number of programs that have social goals, such as increasing educational equality or overcoming educational deficiencies among some students. Based on the cartoon, how do you think the cartoonist assesses these efforts. How would you characterize his political idealogy?

18. **Analyzing Information**
A recent study of high school advanced placement (AP) courses revealed that students who had taken numerous AP courses were admitted to the elite universities. Other students who had also taken AP courses, but had taken significantly fewer of them, were denied entrance to those schools. Does this finding support or weaken the claim that the United States is a meritocracy? Explain.

19. **Applying Concepts**
On pages 20–21 in Chapter 1, you read about the McDonaldization of higher education. Using the concepts of efficiency, calculability, predictability, and technology, discuss how high schools are becoming McDonaldized.

20. Drawing Conclusions

Most real-world work situations involve a high degree of cooperation. Still, much of our educational system remains competitive. ACT and SAT tests are not taken cooperatively, for example. As you read in the chapter, cooperative learning has been offered as an alternative to individual learning. Based on your experience with cooperative learning, do you agree that it is a better way of learning?

21 Analyzing Information

To ensure that all students have a minimum standard of knowledge before leaving school, several states now require high school students to pass a comprehensive exam. Passing the test would give employers and colleges some assurance that a certain standard of achievement was met. Some parents are challenging the exam, claiming that students with passing grades could fail to get into a good college if they failed the exam. Others contend that students who have failed to pass classes could pass the exam and get credit. They argue that many students are unmotivated learners but could pass such an exam. From a societal viewpoint, what position would you take? Could you propose a compromise solution?

Sociology Projects

22. School Board Meetings

Attend a school board meeting in your community. Obtain a copy of the agenda from the board of education several days before the meeting. Choose one controversial or proposed issue to research. After the meeting, approach one of the board members to interview on this issue and find out his or her position. Report back to your class about the issue, giving an objective view from various perspectives.

23. Mock School Board Meeting

Organize a mock school board meeting at your school. First, attend a regular school board meeting to become familiar with the procedures. (Many communities broadcast school board meetings on local cable channels.) Select an issue that is of interest to you or that will affect your high school. Work with classmates to fill these roles: school board president (to act as a neutral moderator), several school board members, several community members, and several students Each school board member will be allowed a few minutes for opening remarks. Community members must be allowed to express their views, and then a vote should be taken on the issue.

24. School Issues

Contact a student or students from another high school in your area. Compare how your schools function. Look at such issues as discipline and detention, attendance policy, and support for extracurricular activities. Identify two areas in which your schools differ. Discuss these differences with a counselor, your principal, or an assistant principal to see if you can explain them. (Are the differences a result of the bureaucracy, or do they have physical or geographical causes? Offer explanations for the differences, and arrange to present your findings to the class.

25. The Ideal School of the Future

You are an architect who has been hired by your school district to design the ideal school of the future. Money is no object, and property owners who pay taxes have stated that they will spare no expense to keep the project going. Your task is to create a draft of the floor plan for the building, outside space, ball fields, bathrooms, cafeteria, and so forth. Identify the purpose of all the rooms. Submit your plan to your class, which will act as the community. Be prepared to redo the plan based on class recommendations.

26. Quantitative Reserach

In this chapter, you read about the debate over whether the American school system provides an equal opportunity for every student. Based on the data in the table below, how would you rate the American school system for gender equality? Does the discussion on page 413 suggest that there are ways in which the data needs to be refined? For your project, conduct online or library research to create a similar table for educational achievement among racial and ethnic groups.

Educational Attainment by Gender, 1960–2004					
H.S. Grad or More	Male	Female	College Grad or More	Male	Female
1960	39.5%	42.5%	1960	9.7	5.8
1970	51.9	52.8	1970	13.5	8.1
1980	67.3	65.8	1980	20.1	12.8
1990	77.7	77.5	1990	24.4	18.4
2000	84.2	84.0	2000	27.8	23.6
2004	84.8	85.4	2004	29.4	26.1

Source: *Statistical Abstract of the United States, 2006*

27. Observing Classrooms

This mock experiment will you give some experience in recording data and formulating a conclusion. You should conduct the experiment for at least five days. As you sit in your classes throughout the day, discreetly keep track of what happens when students raise their hands. Can you determine a pattern for who is called upon? Do the teachers tend to call on boys more than girls? On noisy students more than quiet ones? On conservative dressers more than radical dressers? Summarize your findings. Remember to remain objective and to respect individuals' privacy at all times. (Don't feel bad if you can't seem to identify a pattern—it just means your teacher is sensitive to his or her students. This is still good research.)

28. School Culture

Do a study of your school culture, including norms, roles, statuses, groups and subcultures. Include information about where people gather, common symbols and traditions, educational rites of passage, etc.

29. Stakeholders

Stakeholders are people who have a vested interest in a process, or who are directly affected by a process. Identify the stakeholders of American education: the students, parents, colleges, technical schools, the military, employers, etc. What are their competing perceptions of the functions of education?

30. Schools in 2020

Design a school that will function in the year 2020, taking into account predicted advances in technology and presumed changes in social relationships and social roles.

Technology Activity

31. The Center for Education Reform maintains a Web site devoted to information about charter schools. Visit this site at www. edreform.com. Select Charter Schools that is colored blue. Then click on Quick Facts about Charter Schools.

a. Use the information in Quick Facts to write a short essay about charter schools.

b. Be prepared to discuss the advantages and disadvantages of charter schools.

c. Based on your review of this Web site, do you feel that the Center for Education Reform presents an unbiased picture of charter schools?

d. Now use your favorite search engine and see if there are any charter schools in your area with Web sites. If there are, visit the site and find out about them. Do any of them sound attractive to you?

Enrichment Reading

Home Schooling
by Brian D. Ray and Christopher Lubienski

One alternative to public-school education that has received a great deal of attention in recent years is home schooling. Although home-schooled students make up only slightly more than 2 percent of all school-aged children, their numbers have been rising. In 1999, for example, about 850,000 students were home-schooled. By 2003, this number had grown to nearly 1.1 million. Like all alternatives to public education, home schooling has its supporters and its opponents. Here, Brian D. Ray, president of the National Home Education Research Institute, and Christopher Lubienski, assistant professor at Iowa State University, debate the question, "Does home schooling promote the public good?"

Brian D. Ray

Research, experience and a philosophy of freedom show that home schooling promotes the public good because increasing the number of well-educated, socially stable and civically active individuals advances the public good.

Americans agree that several things benefit society. First, freedom of choice applies to directing the upbringing and education of one's own **progeny,** as the Supreme Court has affirmed. Second, having authentic educational choices is itself a democratic institution that protects citizens from government controlling knowledge and thought. Choice makes society richer and more diverse. Socially well-adjusted and educated citizens who are industrious and civically involved benefit society. Finally, particular values and principles, such as those listed above, as well as respectfulness and tolerance of others' beliefs and those embodied in the Constitution and Declaration of Independence, advance the common good. Research shows that home schooling promotes these things.

Research also shows home-schooled students score 15 to 30 percentile points above their peers in public schools on academic achievement tests, are above average in their social and psychological well-being and are involved in sports and community activities. Home-educated adults perform well in college and leadership activities and tend to be independent and critical thinkers who are gainfully employed. Home-school parents are more civically active than average.

Studies also show home schooling is accessible to a wide array of people. A rising tide of African-American and Hispanic families is flowing into home-based education and away from the public-good school experiment they **discern** can never make good on its promises. Many can afford the average $500 per student per year while saving taxpayers the burden of over $7,000 per public-school student.

Home-schooled young adults, regardless of their political, religious, economic or ethnic backgrounds, affirm values and behaviors that promote

- **progeny**
  children; offspring

- **discern**
  perceive

the common good. I have taught in public and private schools and in the home-school world and been a professor of education at the undergraduate and graduate levels. While 87 percent of Americans attend public schools, illiteracy, drug abuse, and incarceration rates climb and the battles over funding, power and defining "the common good" that riddle these schools continue. Meanwhile, an ever-increasing number of parents will successfully home school one child at a time, for his or her personal good and the furtherance of the public good.

Christopher Lubienski

The accelerated movement toward home schooling reflects a serious threat to the collective good—a threat encouraged by organized efforts to withdraw from common endeavors such as public education. Home schooling necessarily encourages individuals to focus on their own child, and diminishes concern for the education of other people's children. By emphasizing only personal benefits, the incentives inherent in home schooling essentially privatize the purpose of education. Home schooling fragments the public good into individual concerns that deny the public's interest in the education of all children.

Some argue that such individualization is not only appropriate but preferable in terms of the educational responsiveness home schooling can offer each child. In the **aggregate,** such a system better approximates the public good than does any bureaucracy, according to this logic.

Of course, home schooling is not an option available to all. While that is no reason to oppose home schooling, it raises questions about the factors that distinguish which child is home schooled and which are not. Home-schooling parents are by definition active and involved, having the means and initiative to guide their children's learning.

While home schooling may have beneficial effects on their own children's academic achievement, their withdrawal from the community's educational endeavors is a double loss for everyone else. Schools depend on such parents to demand accountability and results; if the channels for citizen participation in such institutions are not effectively exercised, **atrophy** occurs—making concerns about bureaucratic pre-eminence a self-fulfilling prophecy. Moreover, children from articulate and involved families would likely enhance the peer effect in the classroom, where children learn not just from a teacher, but from each other. Thus, while home schooling might produce a handful of academically elite individuals, it may also undermine the capacity to effectively educate the rest.

Home schooling advances from a thin conception of the public good premised on negative notions of liberty: freedom from others, rather than freedom—indeed, responsibility—to be involved with other members of the community. Such an orientation negates the public's legitimate interest in how children are educated. Families necessarily act to reproduce their values, while individual **autonomy** depends on free and informed choice within a broader social context. Such conditions are reflected more in a school attended by people from other families and backgrounds, than in a single family.

● **aggregate**
whole amount; sum total

● **atrophy**
a wasting away; progressive decline

● **autonomy**
state of being self-governing

Read and React

1. According to Ray, how do home-school students and public-school students compare on academic achievement tests?

2. According to Ray, how does the cost of educating a home-schooled student compare to that of a public-school student?

3. According to Lubienski, how is home schooling a "double loss" for society?

4. Lubienski states that Americans have a responsibility to be involved with others. Do you agree or disagree? Explain.

5. Do you think the number of home-schooled students will increase or decrease in the future? Explain.

Source: From Rachel S. Cox, "Home Schooling Debate," CQ Researcher Online (January 17, 2003), 25–48.

Chapter 13

Political and Economic Institutions

Sections

1. **Power and Authority**
2. **Political Power in American Society**
3. **Economic Systems**
4. **The Modern Corporation**
5. **Work in the Modern Economy**

Learning Objectives

After reading this chapter, you will be able to

- distinguish among power, coercion, and authority.
- identify three forms of authority.
- discuss differences among democracy, totalitarianism, and authoritarianism.
- explain how voting is an exercise of power.
- list characteristics of capitalism and socialism.
- describe America's changing workforce.
- discuss the consequences of corporate downsizing.

422

Applying Sociology

The American political system reflects the history of how our institutions were formed. It also reflects how that system has evolved over more than 200 years.

In the photo at left, groups of Americans—and no doubt, many tourists from other nations as well—are standing in line at the National Archives in Washington, D.C. Their quest? To view the U.S. Constitution. The Constitution embodies the political values that most Americans share. Those values include individual freedom, equality before the law, justice, opportunity, democracy, and tolerance. These values are mosts readily accessible in the Bill of Rights of the Constitution.

The American political system is pluralistic, that is, different groups organize to participate in decision-making. As people from other nations have often said, it is our shared values, however, that allows us to peacefully work through political differences.

In this chapter, we will examine not only political institutions, but the economic institutions that guide the division of economic resources.

Sociology Online

Chapter Overview
Visit the *Sociology and You* Web site at **glencoe.com** and click on **Chapter 13— Chapter Overviews** to preview chapter information.

1

Power and Authority

Key Terms

- economic institution *(p. 424)*
- political institution *(p. 424)*
- power *(p. 425)*
- coercion *(p. 425)*
- authority *(p.425)*
- charismatic authority *(p. 426)*
- traditional authority *(p. 427)*
- rational-legal authority *(p. 427)*
- representative democracy *(p. 428)*
- totalitarianism *(p. 430)*
- authoritarianism *(p. 431)*

- **economic institution**
  institution that determines how goods and services are produced and distributed

- **political institution**
  institution that determines how power is obtained and exercised

Section Preview

Authority is the sanctioned use of power. Political systems can be based on three types of authority: charismatic, traditional, and rational-legal. Democratic, totalitarian, and authoritarian are types of political systems. In democracies, power lies with elected officials. Totalitarian political systems have absolute rulers who control all aspects of political and social life. Authoritarian rulers possess absolute control but often permit some personal freedoms.

Definitions of Power and Authority

In 1997, the powerful Teamsters Union went on strike against United Parcel Service (UPS) to protest the company's cost-cutting policy of eliminating permanent positions and replacing them with part-time or temporary positions. When UPS asked then-president Bill Clinton to intervene in the dispute (on the grounds that the company provided an essential national service), it demonstrated the close connection between business and government in modern American society.

The set of functions that concern the production and distribution of goods and services for a society is called the **economic institution.** Because economic decisions affect how valuable resources are shared between organizations and the general public, conflicts inevitably arise. The responsibility for handling these conflicts lies with the institution through which power is obtained and exercised—the **political institution.** These two institutions are so closely interrelated that it is very hard to think of them as separate. For a

These prison inmates are subject to the power of the political institution that convicted them.

beginning study of sociology, however, we can think of economics as the distribution of resources and politics as the exercise of power. This chapter will look first at how politics affects group behaviors and then at the economic scene.

What is power? As stated in Chapter 1, Max Weber profoundly influenced sociological theory. You read about him again in Chapter 6, which examined formal organizations and bureaucracies. Weber's contribution to political sociology deals with his identification of different forms of power and authority. Weber defined **power** as the ability to control the behavior of others, even against their will. Power takes various forms. Some people, for example, wield great power through their personal appeal or magnetism. John F. Kennedy, Martin Luther King, Jr., and César Chávez were able to influence others through the force of their charismatic personalities.

Weber recognized another form of power that he called coercion. **Coercion** is the use of physical force or threats to exert control. A blackmailer might extort money from a politician. A government might take, without compensation, the property of one of its citizens. In such cases, the victims do not believe this use of power is right. In fact, they normally are resentful and want to fight back. Weber recognized that a political system based on coercive power is inherently unstable; that is, the abuses of the system itself cause people to rise against it.

What is authority? Weber also believed that a political institution must rest on a stable form of power if it is to function and survive. This more stable form of power is **authority**. Authority is power accepted as legitimate by those subject to it. For example, students take exams and accept the results they receive because they believe their teachers have the right (authority) to determine grades. Most citizens pay taxes because they believe their government has the right (authority) to collect money from them.

● **power**
the ability to control the behavior of others

● **coercion**
control through force

● **authority**
power accepted as legitimate by those subject to it

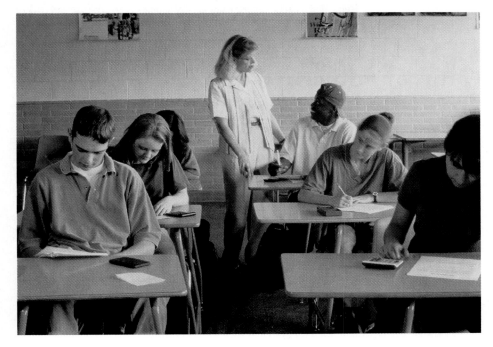

The authority that belongs to teachers is a stable form of power because most students accept a teacher's right to control certain processes.

César Chávez, John F. Kennedy, and Martin Luther King, Jr., were charismatic leaders. What does charismatic mean?

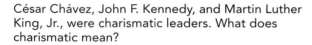

Forms of Authority

Weber identified three forms of authority—*charismatic, traditional,* and *rational-legal.* People who live under governments based on these forms recognize authority figures as holders of legitimate power.

● **charismatic authority**
authority that arises from the personality of an individual

What is charismatic authority? Charismatic authority arises from a leader's personal characteristics. Charismatic leaders lead through the power or strength of their personalities or the feelings of trust they inspire in a large number of people. In addition to Kennedy, King, and Chávez, Nelson Mandela and Fidel Castro have strong personalities that make them highly charismatic leaders.

For modern nation-states, however, charismatic authority alone is too unstable to provide a permanent basis of power. It is linked to an individual and is therefore difficult to transfer to another. When charismatic leaders die, the source of power is removed. Adolf Hitler, himself a charismatic leader, made an attempt at the end of World War II to name his successor. But as historian John Toland has noted:

Hitler's death brought an abrupt, absolute end to National Socialism. Without its only true leader, it burst like a bubble. . . . What had appeared to be the most powerful and fearsome political force of the twentieth century vanished overnight. No other leader's death since Napoleon had so completely obliterated a regime (Toland, 1976:892).

So even governments controlled by charismatic leaders must eventually come to rely on other types of authority. The two alternatives to charismatic authority identified by Weber are traditional authority and rational-legal authority.

What is traditional authority? In the past, most states relied on **traditional authority,** in which the legitimacy of a leader is rooted in custom. Early kings often claimed to rule by the will of God, or divine right. The peaceful transfer of power was possible because only a few individuals, such as offspring or other close relatives, were eligible to become the next ruler. The kings in eighteenth-century Europe, for example, counted on the custom of loyalty to provide a stable political foundation. Tradition provided more stability than charismatic authority could have provided.

What is rational-legal authority? Most modern governments are based on **rational-legal authority.** In this type of government, power resides in the offices rather than in the officials. Those people who hold government offices are expected to operate on the basis of specific rules and procedures that define and limit their rights and responsibilities. Power is assumed only when the individual occupies the office. Many leaders in religious organizations fall under this category of authority.

Since rational-legal authority is invested in positions rather than in individuals, persons lose their authority when they leave their formal positions of power. When a new president is elected, for example, the outgoing president becomes a private citizen again and gives up the privileges of the office. Furthermore, leaders are expected to stay within the boundaries of their legal authority. Even presidents (Richard Nixon, for example) can lose their power if their abuse of power is made public. Thus, legal authority also limits the power of government officials.

> ● **traditional authority**
> form of authority in which the legitimacy of a leader is rooted in custom

King Jigme Singye Wangchuck rules Bhutan through the exercise of traditional authority. The Bhutanese people believe that their king is the realization of a religious prophecy made more than three centuries ago.

> ● **rational-legal authority**
> form of authority in which the power of government officials is based on the offices they hold

Types of Political Systems

As societies have evolved through the centuries, so have different forms of political systems (Nolan and Lenski, 2005). In hunting and gathering societies, there was very little formal government. Political leaders were typically chosen on the basis of exceptional physical prowess or personal charisma. Formal governmental structures emerged with the development of agricultural economies and the rise of city-states. As societies became more diversified with the development of commerce, industry, and technology, government began to take the form of the national political state. The first strong nation-states, including France, Spain, and England, appeared in the late 1400s. Gradually, traditional authority was replaced by rational-legal authority. Contemporary nation-states can be classified into three basic types: *democratic, totalitarian,* and *authoritarian.*

Democracy

Democracy in its pure form, as practiced by the ancient Greeks, involves all citizens in self-government. This type of direct democracy is similar to that practiced in New England town meetings, where the citizens debated and voted directly on various issues. More familiar to us today is **representative democracy**, in which elected officials are responsible for fulfilling the wishes of the majority of citizens.

What assumptions are made in a representative democracy?
Representative democracy operates under two assumptions. The first is that realistically, not everyone in modern society can be actively involved in all political decision making. Thus, although citizens are expected to vote, most citizens are not expected to be deeply involved in politics. Second, political candidates who fail to satisfy the wishes of the majority are not expected to win reelections.

With the major two-party system of the United States, we have a "winner take all" form of representative democracy. Here, the party with the most votes wins the election. In other countries, as in Europe where third-party systems are common, political parties participate in the government to the extent that they win representation in general elections. For example, one party might win 40 percent of the vote and control 40 percent of the legislature. Three other parties might take 20 percent each and control a combined 60 percent of the legislature. This proportional representation system seems to be more democratic as it tends to encourage compromises and cooperation in forming governments. Governments formed under this system can be fragile, however, and shifting political alliances may be able to force new elections after short periods of time.

● **representative democracy**
a system of government that uses elected officials to fulfill majority wishes

Germany's parliamentary system is a representative democracy.

World View

Political Freedom

Democracy is unevenly distributed worldwide. The accompanying map classifies countries according to three degrees of political freedom: free, partly free, and not free.

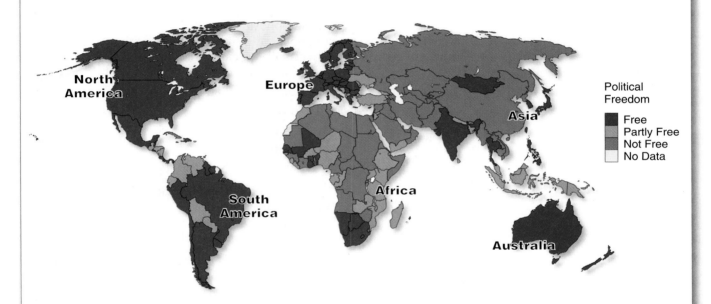

Political Freedom

- Free
- Partly Free
- Not Free
- No Data

Interpreting the Map

1. Do you see any pattern in the degree of political freedom around the world?

2. Predict how political freedom around the world will change in the next fifty years. Explain your predictions.

Source: Freedom House, Washington, D.C., 2005.

Is democracy spreading? The collapse of Soviet communism and the end of the Cold War created opportunities for more societies to adopt democratic forms of government. Current evidence does suggest that democratic societies are on the rise (Freedom House, 2005). For example, 46 percent of the world's countries were classified as "free" in 2004, up from 40 percent in 1994 (see World View above). Also in 2004, 44 percent of the world's people lived in free countries, up from 39 percent in 1999. This increase occurred even though Russia in 2004 was identified as "not free" for the first time since the breakup of the Soviet Union.

Figure 13.1
The Political Continuum
Political institutions offer varying degrees of freedom for their members.

Political Continuum

Pure Democracy	Representative Democracy	Authoritarianism	Totalitarianism
New England Town	United States	Fidel Castro (Cuba)	Adolf Hitler (Nazi Germany)

- **totalitarianism**
  a political system in which a ruler with absolute power attempts to control all aspects of a society

Totalitarianism

Totalitarianism lies at the opposite end of the political spectrum from democracy. In this type of political system, a ruler with absolute power attempts to control all aspects of a society. Characteristics of totalitarian states include

- a single political party, typically controlled by one person.
- a well-coordinated campaign of terror.
- total control of all means of communication.
- a monopoly over military resources.
- a planned economy directed by a state bureaucracy.

Examples of totalitarian states include Iraq under Saddam Hussein, the former Soviet Union, and Nazi Germany.

Hitler's National Socialist (Nazi) government, which came to power in Germany in the early 1930s, offers an example of the way a totalitarian system works. Despite presenting a false image of democracy to the world, Hitler and the National Socialist Party held all the power. The Nazis seized or shut down nearly all news media. Hitler's four-year economic plans included strategies for budgets, production, organization of factories, and forced labor. Hitler dominated the armed forces. His absolute control was strengthened by the Gestapo secret police and SS troops, who terrorized Hitler's political enemies and private citizens. The SS brutally and systematically put to death over six million European Jews and others—a mass killing now known as the Holocaust.

Why can we classify Adolf Hitler as a totalitarian leader?

What category of leader does Cuban president Fidel Castro represent?

Authoritarianism

For sociologists, authoritarianism is a middle category between democracy and totalitarianism, although it is closer to totalitarianism than to democracy. **Authoritarianism** refers to a political system controlled by elected or nonelected rulers who usually permit some degree of individual freedom but do not allow popular participation in government. Countless governments have leaned toward totalitarianism but have fallen short of all its defining characteristics. These governments are classified as authoritarian. Examples include certain monarchies (the dynasties of the shahs of Iran) and military seizures of power (Fidel Castro's takeover of Cuba).

● **authoritarianism**
a political system controlled by elected or nonelected rulers who usually permit some degree of individual freedom

Section 1 Assessment

1. What is the difference between authority and coercion?

2. Which type of authority places the strongest limits on government officials?

3. Explain how direct democracy differs from representative democracy.

4. Briefly describe the three major types of political systems.

Critical Thinking

5. **Sequencing Information** Like all organizations, high schools are based on some form of authority. Explain, with examples, which form

or forms of authority you believe are applicable to high schools.

6. **Synthesizing Information** In which form of government would you expect to find charismatic authority? Traditional authority? Rational-legal authority?

China's One-Child Policy

How much control a government has over the daily lives of its citizens varies greatly from one political system to another. The excerpt below describes one way in which a strict, authoritarian government exerts control.

China's communist government adopted the one-child policy in 1979 in response to the staggering doubling of the country's population during Mao Zedong's rule. Mao, who died in 1976, was convinced that the country's masses were a strategic asset and vigorously encouraged the Chinese to produce even-larger families.

China's family-planning officials wield awesome powers, enforcing the policy through a combination of incentives and deterrents. For those who comply, there are job promotions and small cash awards. For those who resist, they suffer stiff fines and loss of job and status within the country's tightly knit and heavily regulated communities. The State Family Planning Commission is the government ministry entrusted with the tough task of curbing the growth of the world's most populous country, where 28 children are born every minute. It employs about 200,000 full-time officials and uses more than a million volunteers to check the fertility of hundreds of millions of Chinese women.

When a couple wants to have a child—even their first, allotted one—they must apply to the family-planning office in their township or workplace, literally lining up to procreate. "If a woman gets pregnant without permission, she and her husband will get fined, even if it's their first," . . . "it is fair to fine her, because she creates a burden on the whole society by jumping her place in line."

The official Shanghai Legal Daily last year reported on a family-planning committee in central Sichuan province that ordered the flogging of the husbands of 10 pregnant women who refused to have abortions. According to the newspaper, the family-planning workers marched the husbands one by one into an empty room, ordered them to strip and lie on the floor and then beat them with a stick, once for every day their wives were pregnant.

Source: Excerpted from Daniela Deane, "The Little Emperors," *Los Angeles Times Magazine* (July 26, 1992): 138, 140. © Daniela Deane.

Thinking It Over

What implications does this governmental policy have for the future of the Chinese family and for the future of China in general.

China's authoritarian government gave it the power needed to institute strict population controls, often referred to as the "one-child policy.".

Political Power in American Society

Section Preview

The two major models of political power are elitism and pluralism. Advocates of the conflict perspective believe American society is controlled by elites. Pluralists, whose view is associated with functionalism, depict power as widely distributed among interest groups. Voting does not seem to be an effective means for nonelites to influence political decisions in the U.S.

Key Terms

- political socialization *(p. 434)*
- pluralism *(p. 435)*
- elitism *(p. 435)*
- interest group *(p. 437)*
- power elite *(p. 439)*

Influence of the Vote

Like all other democracies today, the United States emphasizes political participation through voting. Voting is an important source of power for citizens. It enables us to remove incompetent, corrupt, or insensitive officials from office. It also allows us to influence issues at the local, state, and national levels.

How much real choice do voters have?   In practice, the amount of real choice exercised through voting is limited. The range of candidates from which to choose is restricted because of the power of political parties. Usually, only a candidate endorsed by a major political party has a chance of winning a state or national office. To get party support, a candidate must appeal to the widest possible number of voters. As a result, candidates often resemble each other more than they differ. In addition, the cost of running a political campaign today limits the choice of candidates to those who have party backing or are independently wealthy. George W. Bush, for example, announced in August of 2000 that he had spent nearly $150 million to win the Republican Party nomination.

One way that candidates for the office of president of the United States make their views known to the American people is through the use of nationally televised debates.

Political socialization helps to determine what political battles we choose to fight.

• **political socialization**
informal and formal processes by which a person develops political opinions

Student Web Activity
Visit the *Sociology and You* Web site at glencoe.com and click on **Chapter 13—Student Web Activities** for an activity on political socialization.

On what do we base our votes? Most attitudes and beliefs that are expressed as political opinions are gained through a learning process called **political socialization.** This process can be formal, as in government class, or informal. The informal process interests sociologists because it involves such factors as the family, the media, economic status, and educational level. Studies have shown that most political socialization is informal.

A brief summary of the major agents of political socialization follows.

• **The family.** Children learn political attitudes the same way they learn values and norms, by listening to everyday conversations and by watching the actions of other family members. The influence of the family is strong. In one study, more high school students could identify their parents' political party affiliation than any other of their parents' attitudes or beliefs.

• **Education.** The level of education a person has influences his or her political knowledge and participation. For example, more highly educated men and women tend to show more knowledge about politics and policy. They also tend to vote and participate more often in politics.

• **Mass media.** Television is the leading source of political and public affairs information for most people. Television and other mass media can determine what issues, events, and personalities are in the public eye. By publicizing some issues and ignoring others, and by giving some stories high priority and others low priority, the media decide the relative importance of issues. The mass media obviously play an important role in shaping public opinion, but the extent of that role is unclear. Studies indicate that the media have the greatest effect on people who have not yet formed opinions.

- **Economic status and occupation.** Economic status clearly influences political views. Poor people are more likely to favor government-assistance programs than wealthy people, for example. Similarly, where you work affects how you vote. Corporate managers are more likely to favor tax shelters and aid to businesses than hourly workers in factories.

- **Age and gender.** Young adults tend to be more progressive than older persons on such issues as racial and gender equality. Women tend to be more liberal than men on such issues as abortion rights, women's rights, health care, and government-supported child care.

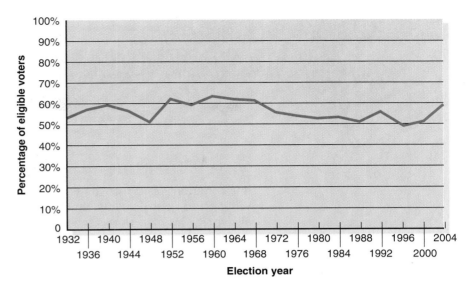

Figure 13.2
Voter Participation in Presidential Elections: 1932–2004
Is there any correlation between the confidence level and the voter participation rate? Explain.

Source: U.S. Bureau of the Census, *Statistical Abstract of the United States, 2004–2005* and *Current Population Survey* (November 2004).

How fully do Americans take advantage of the right to vote? In 2004, 58 percent of eligible U.S. voters exercised their right (see Figure 13.2). Just under 29 percent of eligible voters voted for George W. Bush, a proportion comparable to the 27 percent who elected President Reagan in 1980. In fact, the United States has one of the the lowest voter turnout rates in the industrialized world (IDEA, 2005).

The American public's interest in voting is very low, partly because of a relatively low level of confidence in political leaders. Another reason for lower voter turnout is that political parties are no longer as instrumental in getting voters to the polls as they once were. In general, minorities and the lower and working classes tend to vote in smaller proportions than whites and the middle and upper classes. Members of minorities, people with little education, and people with smaller incomes are less likely to vote in both congressional and presidential elections.

Two Models of Political Power

In a democratic society, two major models of political power are evident—*pluralism* and *elitism*. According to **pluralism**, political decisions are the result of bargaining and compromise among special interest groups. No one group holds the majority of power. Rather, power is widely distributed throughout a society or community. In contrast, according to **elitism**, a community or society is controlled from the top by a few individuals or organizations. Power is concentrated in the hands of an elite group whose members have common interests and backgrounds. The masses are very weak politically.

Functionalists think that pluralism based on the existence of diverse *interest groups* best describes the distribution of power in America. While recognizing competition among interest groups, functionalists contend that it is based on an underlying consensus regarding the goals of the entire society. Elitism is based on the conflict perspective. This theory of power distribution assumes that the elites are constantly working to maintain their

- **pluralism**
  system in which political decisions are made as a result of bargaining and compromise among special interest groups

- **elitism**
  system in which a community or society is controlled from the top by a few individuals or organizations

Snapshot of America

Voter Turnout

It is commonly said that the voter holds the power in American politics. What often goes unsaid is that to exercise this power, the voter must actually vote. This map shows the voter turnout, as a percentage of the eligible voting population, in each state for the 2004 presidential election.

2004 Presidential Election

- 70% or more
- 65–69%
- 60–64%
- 55–59%
- 50–54%
- 49% or less

Interpreting the Map

1. Do you see any patterns in the voting rates? Describe them.
2. Identify some reasons for the distribution of rates.
3. What should be done to increase voter turnout rates?

Source: U.S. Bureau of the Census, Current Population Survey, November 2004.

hold on society's major institutions. In so doing, elites force others to help them reach their own goals. These two models are illustrated in Figure 13.3.

Functionalist Perspective: Pluralism

According to pluralists, major political decisions in the United States are not made by an elite few. As an example, they point to the beneficiaries of the 2001 tax-cut bill. Tax breaks came not only to the wealthy, such as Microsoft's Bill Gates, but also to groups with more modest resources, such as churches and mental health care facilities.

Figure 13.3	Characteristics of Two Models of Political Power

This table illustrates the way the functionalist and conflict perspectives view political power. Several key features of the political system are compared. Which theory do you think best describes power in the U.S.? Explain.

Characteristics	Functionalist Perspective (Pluralist Model)	Conflict Perspective (Power Elite Model)
Who exercises power?	Bargaining and compromising interest groups	National political, economic, and military leaders
What is the source of power?	Resources of interest groups	Leadership positions in major institutions
Where is power located?	Spread widely among interest groups	Concentrated in hands of elites
How much influence do nonelites have?	Nonelites have considerable influence on public policy	Nonelites have very little influence on public policy
What is the basis for public policy decisions?	Goals and values are shared by the general public	Preferences of the elites

An **interest group** is a group organized to influence political decision making. Group members share one or more goals. The goals may be specific to the group's own members—as in the case of the National Rifle Association—or may involve a larger segment of society—as in the case of ecology-oriented groups such as the Sierra Club. Figure 13.4 on page 438 lists several current interest groups, sizes, and issues.

Pluralists contend that decisions are made as a result of competition among special interest groups, each of which has its own stake in the issues. In addition to reaching their own ends, interest groups try to protect themselves from opposing interest groups. Responsibility falls to government leaders to balance the public welfare with the desires of various special interests.

Interest groups are not new to American politics. In the nineteenth century they were active in extending women's rights and promoting the abolition of slavery. The twentieth century saw such active interest groups as the Woman's Christian Temperance Union and early labor unions. The 1960s, with controversies surrounding civil rights, the Vietnam War, the environment, the women's movement, and corporate power, strengthened many interest groups and led to the creation of a number of new ones (Clemens, 1997).

● **interest group**
a group organized to influence political decision making

Types of Interest Groups

Organization	Membership	Objectives
ECONOMIC GROUPS		
Business		
U.S. Chamber of Commerce	3,000,000 businesses	Lobby for businesses
National Association of Home Builders	220,000 members	Represent the housing and building industry
Agricultural		
National Farmers Union	Nearly 250,000 farm and ranch families	Represent family farms and ranches
American Farm Bureau Federation	Over 5 million members	Lobby for agribusiness and farm owners
Professional		
American Medical Association (AMA)	Over 750,000 members	Represent physicians and improve the medical system
American Bar Association (ABA)	Over 400,000 members	Improve the legal system
Labor		
AFL–CIO	Over 64 affiliated unions (Over 13 million members)	Protect members from unfair labor practices
United Mine Workers	130,000 members	Represent mine workers and others
NON-ECONOMIC GROUPS		
Public Interest		
League of Women Voters (LWV)	About 1,000 local leagues; 130,000 members and supporters	Promote voter registration and election reform
Common Cause	Nearly 300,000 members	Advocate political reform
Public Citizen	100,000 members	Focus on consumer issues
Single-Issue		
Sierra Club	Over 750,000 members	Protect the natural environment
National Audubon Society	550,000 members	Conserve and restore natural ecosystems
Greenpeace USA	250,000 members	Expose global environmental issues
Ideological		
Americans for Democratic Action (ADA)	65,000 members	Support liberal social, economic, and foreign policies
Christian Coalition	Over 2,000,000 members	Promote Christian values
National Organization for Women (NOW)	Over 500,000 members	Eliminate discrimination and protect the rights of women

Figure 13.4 Types of Interest Groups
The United States government is influenced by a wide variety of interest groups. This figure provides some examples of the most important types. Do you believe that the influence of all these interest groups promotes or hinders democracy? Explain your answers, using conflict theory or functionalism.

New interest groups are born all the time. The environmental lobby is a good example. There were relatively few environmental interest groups before the passage of major environmental legislation (such as the Clean Water Act) in the 1960s. The success of this legislation spawned additional groups, now numbering three times the original total. This added clout produced additional environmental legislation—for example, the 1990 Clean Air Act Amendments—that subsequently led to the creation of other interest groups (Bardes, Schmidt, and Shelley, 2005).

Conflict Perspective: The Power Elite

Sociologist C. Wright Mills was a leading proponent of the elitist perspective. In the 1950s, he claimed that the United States no longer had separate economic, political, and military leaders. Rather, the key people in each area overlapped to form a unified group that he labeled the **power elite.**

According to Mills, members of the power elite share common interests and similar social and economic backgrounds. Elites are educated in select boarding schools, military academies, and Ivy League schools; belong to the Episcopalian and Presbyterian churches; and come from upper-class families. Members of the power elite have known each other for a long time, have mutual acquaintances of long standing, share many values and attitudes, and intermarry. All this makes it easier for them to coordinate their actions to obtain what they want.

● **power elite**
a unified group of military, corporate, and government leaders

Section 2 Assessment

1. What are the major agents of political socialization?

2. How do elitists differ from pluralists in explaining the relationship between racial membership and political power in the U.S.?

3. According to C. Wright Mills, which of the following is not part of the power elite?
   a. military organizations
   b. educational leaders
   c. large corporations
   d. executive branch of the government

Critical Thinking

4. Analyzing Information On page 435, the author writes: "Members of minorities, people with little education, and people with smaller incomes are less likely to vote in both congressional and presidential elections." Do you think that pluralists or elitists are more likely to use advertising to change the political attitudes of individuals in these social categories? Explain.

5. **Drawing Conclusions**
   Is America a pluralist society, or is it controlled by a power elite? Support your conclusion with information from this text and other classes.

3

Economic Systems

Key Terms

- capitalism *(p. 440)*
- monopolies *(p. 440)*
- oligopolies *(p. 440)*
- socialism *(p. 442)*

Section Preview

Capitalist economies are based on private property and the pursuit of profit, and government, in theory, plays a minor role in regulating industry. In socialist economies, the means of production are owned collectively, and government has an active role in planning and controlling the economy.

Capitalism

Economic systems, as suggested earlier, involve the production and distribution of goods and services. **Capitalism** is an economic system founded on two basic premises: the sanctity of private property and the right of individuals to profit from their labors.

Capitalists believe that individuals, not government, deserve to own and to control land, factories, raw materials, and the tools of production. They argue that private ownership benefits society. Capitalists also believe in unrestricted competition with minimum government interference.

How is capitalism thought to benefit society? According to Adam Smith, an eighteenth-century Scottish social philosopher and founder of economics, a combination of the private ownership of property and the pursuit of profit brings advantages to society. Because of competition, Smith stated, individual capitalists will always be motivated to provide the goods and services desired by the public at prices the public is willing and able to pay. Capitalists who produce inferior goods or who charge too much will soon be out of business because the public will turn to their competitors. The public, Smith reasoned, will benefit through economic competition. Not only will the public receive high-quality goods and services at reasonable prices, but also capitalists will always be searching for new products and new technologies to reduce their costs. As a result, capitalist societies will use resources efficiently.

Actually, no pure capitalist economy exists in the world. In practice, there are important deviations from Smith's ideal model. One of these deviations involves the tendency to form *monopolies* and *oligopolies*.

What are monopolies and oligopolies? When capitalist organizations experience success, they tend to grow until they become giants within their particular industries. In this way, capitalism fosters the rise of **monopolies,** companies that control a particular market, and **oligopolies,** combinations of companies working together to control a market. New organizations find it difficult to enter these markets, where they have little hope of competing on an equal basis. Thus, competition is stifled.

Among other problems, the creation of monopolies and oligopolies permits price fixing. Consumers must choose between buying at the "going price" set by the sellers or not buying at all.

A recent example of alleged monopolistic practices in the U.S. economy involves the Microsoft Corporation. Microsoft manufactures, among other

- **capitalism**
  an economic system based on private ownership of property and the pursuit of profit

- **monopolies**
  companies that have control over the production or distribution of a product or service

- **oligopolies**
  combinations of companies that control the production or distribution of a product or service

products, the Windows operating system—by far the most popular operating system for personal computers. Computer manufacturers typically include Windows on the machines they sell. In the 1990s, Microsoft began to insist that manufacturers include its Internet browser, Explorer, on their computers as well. The manufacturers were also instructed not to install another browser in addition to Explorer. If they refused, Microsoft would withhold their license to sell Windows on the machines. Because Microsoft had so much power over computer manufacturers, other makers of Internet browsers, such as Netscape, were essentially excluded from the market (Chandbasekaran, 1999). Eventually, the federal government took Microsoft to court, where it was ruled that Microsoft did indeed engage in monopolistic practices. By 2005, Microsoft had settled its federal case and paid out billions of dollars in antitrust, state, and consumer claims.

The Role of Government in Capitalism

Adam Smith is often misinterpreted as saying that government should have a strictly hands-off approach where the economy is concerned. While Smith strongly opposed overregulation by government, he reserved a place for some regulation. Because one of the legitimate roles of government is to protect its citizens from injustice, Smith knew that the state might have to "step in" to prevent abuses by businesses. In fact, the U.S. government has always been involved in the workings of the economy.

How does the government contribute to the U.S. economy? The Constitution expressly provided a role for the national government in the promotion of a sound economy. Government functions

The enormous success of Bill Gates and Microsoft led to a federal investigation of the software giant's business practices.

The Federal Aviation Administration (FAA) conducts jetliner crash tests as part of the federal government's authority over private business. In what way might cultural values promote such government involvement?

Figure 13.5

Figure 13.5 | Examples of Government Economic and Regulatory Assistance

The government is extensively involved in the U.S. economy. What would Adam Smith say about this?

Public utilities are often owned and operated by state or local governments.

The agricultural industry feels the influence of government through price controls and embargoes on exports to other countries.

Antitrust legislation exists to control the growth of corporations.

The federal government is heavily involved in the defense industry.

Business could not survive without publicly financed roadways, airports, and waterways.

Publicly funded public schools, colleges, and universities supply business with a skilled workforce and provide basic research for product development.

The U.S. military protects American international business interests.

Government supports business through tax breaks.

Legislation requires labor and business to obey labor laws.

include the regulation of commerce, development of a strong currency, creation of uniform standards for commerce, and the provision of a stable system of credit. In 1789, Congress supported our shipping industry through a tariff on goods imported by foreign ships. Since this initial move into the economy, the federal government has continued to help business, labor, and agriculture. For example, the federal government aids private industry through loan guarantees—as in the 1979 government guarantee (up to $1.2 billion) to bail out the Chrysler Corporation. Also, U.S. labor is supported by the government through regulations on such matters as minimum wages, maximum working hours, health and safety conditions, and unemployment support. Then there are the small farmers and agribusinesses that receive financial assistance amounting to billions of dollars each year (Patterson, 2004). See Figure 13.5 for additional examples of government economic and regulatory assistance.

Socialism

● **socialism**
an economic system founded on the belief that the means of production should be controlled by the people as a whole

Socialism is an economic system founded on the belief that the means of production should be controlled by the people as a whole. The state, as the people's representative, should own and control property. Under a socialist system, government directs and controls the economy. The state is expected to ensure all members of society a share in the monetary benefits.

How is socialism thought to benefit society? Socialist theory points to important benefits for workers. Workers under capitalism receive wages below the value their labor produces and have little control over their work. In theory, workers under socialism should profit because both the state and the workplace exist for their benefit. As a result, workers should be able to exert significant control over both their work organizations and the policy directions of the society as a whole.

Does socialism work this perfectly? Cases of pure socialism are as rare as cases of pure capitalism. Strict socialist systems have not been successful in eliminating income inequalities nor have they been able to develop overall economic plans that guarantee sustained economic growth. In the socialistic economy of the former Soviet Union, for example, some agricultural and professional work was performed privately by individuals who worked for a profit. Significant portions of housing were privately owned as well. Managers received salaries that were considerably higher than those received by workers, and managers were eligible for bonuses such as automobiles and housing. Private enterprise existed in Poland under Russian communist rule. Service businesses, such as restaurants and hotels, had a significant degree of private ownership. Hotels, in fact, were typically built and managed by multinational chains. Because Poles could travel abroad, they formed business relationships, learned about capitalist methods, imported goods to fill demand, and brought back hard currency. They then used the hard currency earned abroad to create private businesses (Schnitzer, 2000).

Sweden has a socialist government. What types of market relationships would you expect to find there?

Mixed Economic Systems

Most nations fall between the extremes of capitalism and socialism and include elements of both economic systems. Countries in Western Europe, for example, have developed capitalist economic systems in which both public and private ownership play important roles. In these nations, highly strategic industries (banks, transportation, communications, and some others) are owned and operated by the state. Other industries are privately owned but are more closely regulated than in the United States (Harris, 1997; Ollman, 1998).

As this Shanghai KFC restaurant reflects, elements of capitalism are being introduced into China.

As the former Soviet Union lost control over its republics and Eastern Europe, many of these formerly socialist countries began to move toward capitalism. Czechoslovakia, in several ways, has shifted from public to private ownership of businesses. Private property nationalized after the Russians took over in 1948 has been returned to the original owners or their heirs. These assets moved from the public to the private sector are valued at about $5 billion. Many small shops and businesses have been sold in public auctions. In 1992, Czechoslovakia sold over 1,000 of its bigger state enterprises to its citizens. During 1992–93 as it broke into the Czech Republic and Slovakia, 25 percent of the nations' assets were privatized. In Hungary, state-owned enterprises have been allowed to become privately owned companies. Over one million Hungarians have been given the right to buy land, businesses, buildings, or other property taken over by the Russians in 1949. Nearly all of the state-owned small businesses are now in the hands of private owners. Agricultural cooperatives have also been privatized (Schnitzer, 2000).

In 1993, Cuba's communist party allowed some degree of capitalism by permitting plumbers, carpenters, and other tradespeople to work for profit. China has been successfully incorporating free market reforms into its economy since the late 1970s (Muldavin, 1999; Hart-Landsberg and Burkett, 2005).

Section 3 Assessment

1. Government policies are usually based on cultural values. Can you identify important differences in the cultural values underlying governmental policies that promote either capitalism or socialism?

2. How successful has socialism been as an economic system? Defend your answer.

3. What is meant by a mixed economic system?

Critical Thinking

4. **Making Comparisons** Briefly compare and contrast the advantages of capitalism and socialism.

Cybernews and Democracy

Reporting the news has been part of the United States since its founding. Indeed, freedom of the press is one of the basic guarantees of the Bill of Rights. During the twentieth century, television displaced newspapers as the primary source of news for most Americans. Now, the Internet is promising to make much greater changes in the way news is gathered and delivered.

Central to the changes is the fact that today anyone with access to the Internet is free to "report" the news. Internet journalist Matt Drudge says that now, "any citizen can be a reporter" (Trigaboff, 1998:55). Drudge portrays the Internet as a democratizing institution eliminating differences between reporters and readers.

Many traditional print journalists, however, worry about the negative effects of instant reporting via the Internet. Sources for stories often go unchecked as some citizen journalists, as they are called, sacrifice accuracy for speed. Reporters on the Internet generally do not have editors reviewing their stories, in-house attorneys worrying about lawsuits, or publishers making judgment calls about the appropriateness of news stories. Joseph C. Goulden, former director of media analysis for Accuracy in Media, a non-profit, grassroots citizens watchdog of the news media, describes the reporting style on the Internet as "Ready, fire, aim" (Rust and Danitz, 1998:23).

In the United States, one of the justifications for the freedom of the press is its role in delivering accurate information to voters. If Internet reporting represents a trend toward greater inaccuracy, this traditional contribution of a free press to American democracy could be weakened. What if voters grew to distrust even more the information they received and thus became increasingly cynical about the political process?

The importance of this question is underscored by the fact that the popularity of citizen journalism is growing. One factor encouraging the rapid increase in new citizen journalism sites is the expected growth of online advertising, currently around 20 to 30 percent a year (Gossett, 2005).

To stay competitive with citizen journalism sites, and to reap the benefits of online advertising dollars, most print news media now operate their own online news sites. Some even invite contributions from citizen journalists. At this time no one can be sure what the future holds for journalism. One thing, though, is certain: citizen journalism will have a significant impact on the way news is reported.

Matt Drudge became the symbol of Internet news reporting in the late 1990s. Is Internet journalism good or bad for democracy?

Analyzing the Trends

There is no question that the Internet will affect how democracy is practiced in the U.S. Discuss some ways in which the federal government currently uses the Internet to affect group behavior.

4

The Modern Corporation

Key Terms

- corporation *(p. 446)*
- interlocking direc- torates *(p. 447)*
- conglomerates *(p. 447)*
- multinationals *(p. 447)*

● corporation
an organization owned by shareholders, who have limited liability and limited control

Section Preview

Corporations, especially those with multinational connections, have grown very powerful. Corporate managers affect domestic political decision making and influence the political and economic institutions of countries around the world.

The Nature of Corporations

Sociologists study corporations because of their great importance in modern economic systems. U.S. corporations, for example, not only dominate the American economic system but also influence the economies of nations around the world. Corporations represent massive concentrations of wealth. And because of their economic muscle, corporations such as Microsoft, Verizon, and General Electric command the attention of government decision makers. As a result, government policies regarding such matters as consumer safety, tax laws, and relationships with other nations usually reflect corporate influence.

What are corporations, anyway? A **corporation** is an organization owned by shareholders. These shareholders have limited liability and limited control. Limited liability means they cannot be held financially responsible for actions of the corporation. For example, shareholders are not expected to pay debts the corporation owes. At the same time, they do not have a direct voice in the day-to-day operations of the firm. Shareholders are formally entitled to vote regularly for members of the board of directors. But in practice candidates are routinely approved as recommended by the existing board. The real control of a corporation rests with the board of directors and management.

Corporate Influence

Top corporate officials have tremendous influence on government decisions. This is true for several reasons. Because of their personal wealth and organizational connections, corporate officials are able to reward or punish elected government officials through investment decisions. For example, suppose a town depends on a single large corporation for jobs and other economic advantages. Corporate officials are deciding whether to increase their operation in this town or move some of the facilities to another town, which would endanger local jobs. Town officials are likely to do what they can to make corporate officials happy so that new investment will be made locally.

This agricultural worker is paid by a large corporation rather than a small business/farmer. Which employer would be more secure?

In what other ways do corporations wield power? Such political clout by large corporations is multiplied through **interlocking directorates.** A directorate is another name for the board of directors. Directorates interlock when the heads of corporations sit on one another's boards. Although by law competing corporations may not have interlocking directorates, such directorates are legal for noncompeting corporations. For example, various members of the General Motors board of directors also sit on the boards of many other corporations, including Sony, Sara Lee, and Marriott International. It is not difficult to imagine the political power created by a web of interlocks among already powerful corporations.

The political power of corporations is also enhanced through **conglomerates**—networks of unrelated businesses operating under a single corporate umbrella. RJR Nabisco, Inc., for example, holds companies in such different areas as tobacco, pet foods, candy, cigarettes, food products, bubble gum, research, and technology. A listing of the company's North American subsidiaries covers nearly an entire page in *Who Owns Whom* (2004).

- **interlocking directorates**
  directorates that result when heads of corporations sit on one another's boards

- **conglomerates**
  networks of unrelated businesses operating under one corporate umbrella

Multinational Corporations

The political influence of corporations is not confined to their countries of origin. The world is increasingly being influenced by **multinationals**—firms based in highly industrialized societies with operating facilities throughout the world. Improvements in communication and transportation technology have allowed these companies to exert wide control over their global operations.

- **multinationals**
  firms based in highly industrialized societies with operating facilities throughout the world

How powerful are multinational corporations? Suppose we combined all the political and economic units in the world and then chose the hundred largest units. Of these hundred units, fifty-one would be multinational corporations rather than countries. Several corporations based in the United States—ExxonMobil, IBM, General Motors, Ford Motor Company, AT&T, Wal-Mart Stores, and General Electric—have sales volumes exceeding the annual economic output of some industrialized nations. Figure 13.6 compares some multinational corporations with selected nations.

What are the effects of multinational corporations? Defenders of multinationals argue that the corporations provide developing countries with technology, capital, foreign markets, and products that would otherwise be unavailable to them. Critics claim that multinationals actually harm the economies of the foreign nations in which they locate by exploiting natural resources, disrupting local economies, introducing inappropriate technologies and products, and increasing the amount of income inequality. Multinationals, these critics note, rely on inexpensive labor or abundant raw materials in developing nations while returning their profits to

Wal-Mart Stores, Inc. $258.7 Billion	vs.	Bangladesh $258.8 Billion
Home Depot $64.8 Billion	vs.	Syria $58.0 Billion
IBM International Business Machines Corp. $89.1 Billion	vs.	New Zealand $85.3 Billion
Exxon Mobil $213.2 Billion	vs.	Greece $212.2 Billion
Bank of America $48.1 Billion	vs.	Ethiopia $48.5 Billion
General Electric Company $134.2 Billion	vs.	Israel $120.6 Billion

Figure 13.6 Total Revenue of Multinational Corporations versus National Gross Domestic Products
This table compares the revenue of selected multinational corporations to the gross domestic product (value of all goods produced and consumed domestically) of some countries in 2003. Were you surprised by any of the information?

Source: *The World Almanac and Book of Facts, 2005.*

Sociology Today

Employee Rights

The Supreme Court of the United States has historically granted employers a great deal of power over their employees. In 1878, a New York company posted a list of rules that told employees, among other things, "On the Sabbath, everyone is expected to be in the Lord's House" and "All employees are expected to be in bed by 10:00 P.M." At the turn of the nineteenth century, Henry Ford's automobile workers were carefully watched by management for signs of bad character. Many Ford Motor Company employees lost their jobs for smoking, drinking, or criticizing the firm.

Even today, some employee rights are curtailed at work. The Constitution, for example, protects free speech for all citizens. Employees, however, can be prevented from printing and distributing a critical newsletter to customers of their companies. Of recent concern is the right of employers to track workers' movements on the Internet and to read personal e-mails.

Today, a growing employee rights movement is pushing for greater political and legal protection on the job. Here is a partial list of the rights that many workers feel should be theirs today.

- the right to a job
- the right to protection from arbitrary or sudden termination
- the right to privacy of possessions and person in the workplace, including freedom from arbitrary searches, use of polygraphs, surreptitious surveillance, and intrusive psychological or medical testing
- the right to a clean, healthy, and safe environment on the job, including freedom from undue stress, sexual harassment, cigarette smoke, and exposure to toxic substances
- the right to be informed of records and information kept and to have access to personnel files
- the right to freedom of action, association, and lifestyle when off duty
- the right to freedom of conscience and to inform government or media about illegal or socially harmful corporate actions
- the right to due process for grievances against the employer

Many of these rights already exist; others need to be discussed with employers. There is one thing most employees and employers agree on, however. If employees take a balanced approach to pursuing their rights on the job, both individuals and organizations will benefit.

Doing Sociology

1. Some observers believe that violations of employee rights contradict the rational-legal basis of organizational authority. Do you agree?
2. Discuss the above list of rights with some adult workers. Ask them if they know whether or not these rights exist in their workplaces. Are there any rights not on the list that they believe should be added?

Some multinational corporations are so successful that their products are widely (and illegally) copied around the world. Here, a faked Nike athletic shoe is readied for sale in Shangai, China.

corporate headquarters and shareholders in rich nations. Multinationals' domination of their industries has made it difficult for the economically developing nations to establish new companies that can compete with the multinationals. As a result, multinationals may slow rather than promote economic development in these nations.

Section 4 Assessment

1. Discuss limited liability and limited control in relation to the modern corporation.

2. Describe the influence of the corporation in the world today. Identify some of the benefits and negative consequences for society.

Critical Thinking

3. **Drawing Conclusions** Would you rather work for a large, multinational corporation or for yourself as an independent businessperson? Explain your choice.

Work in the Modern Economy

Key Terms

- primary sector *(p. 450)*
- secondary sector *(p. 450)*
- tertiary sector *(p. 450)*
- occupations *(p. 454)*
- core tier *(p. 454)*
- peripheral tier *(p. 454)*
- downsizing *(p. 455)*
- contingent employment *(p. 455)*

- **primary sector**
  that part of the economy producing goods from the natural environment

- **secondary sector**
  that part of the economy engaged in manufacturing goods

- **tertiary sector**
  that part of the economy providing services

Section Preview

Workers today face a changing job structure. More corporations are downsizing and replacing full-time employees with consultants or temporary workers. Evidence indicates that this trend is having some negative consequences.

The Changing Nature of Work

To understand work in modern society you need to be familiar with the three basic economic sectors. They are the *primary, secondary,* and *tertiary* sectors.

How do the economic sectors differ? The **primary sector** of an economy depends on the natural environment to produce economic goods. The types of jobs in this sector vary widely—farmer, miner, fisherman, timber worker, rancher. In the **secondary sector,** manufactured products are made from raw materials. Occupations in this sector include factory workers of all types, from those who produce computers to those who turn out baseball cards. Those in the secondary sector are popularly known as blue-collar workers. Employees in the **tertiary sector** provide services. If today you went to school, filled your car with gas, stopped by the bank, and visited your doctor, you spent most of your time and someone's money in the tertiary (service) sector. Other service industries include insurance, real estate, retail sales, and entertainment. More and more people in these industries are white-collar workers.

To which sector of the economy does this California logger belong?

Occupational category	Percent of total	Percent male	Percent female
Management, professional, and related occupations	34.9	49.7	50.3
Service occupations	16.3	43.2	56.8
Sales and office occupations	25.4	36.1	63.9
Natural resources, construction, and maintenance occupations	10.5	95.6	4.4
Production, transportation, and material moving occupations	12.9	77.0	23.0

Figure 13.7 Distribution of Workers by Occupational Category
This table shows the percentage of American workers who are employed in each occupational category. It also shows how each occupational category is broken down by gender.

Source: U.S. Department of Labor, Bureau of Labor Statistics, 2004.

Blue-collar workers, such as the longshore workers pictured here, may be an endangered species.

How have the three sectors changed historically?

Obviously, the primary sector dominated the preindustrial economy. At that stage of economic development, physical goods were made by hand. This balance began to change with the mechanization of farming in the agricultural economy. Mechanical inventions (cotton gin, plow, tractor), along with the application of new scientific methods (seed production, fertilization, and crop rotation), drastically increased production. During the 1800s, the average farmer could feed five workers or so. Today, the figure is 130. At the same time production increased, labor demands decreased. Primary sector workers have declined from almost 40 percent of the labor pool in 1900 to about 2 percent today.

With other technological advancements in industry (power looms, motors of all types, electrical power) came the shift of agricultural workers from farms to factories, ushering in the secondary sector. By 1990, the percentage of the U.S. labor force engaged in blue-collar jobs reached almost 40 percent.

Just as in agriculture, technological developments permitted greater production with fewer workers. Since World War II, the fastest-growing occupations in the secondary sector have been white-collar—managers, professionals, sales workers, clerical workers. In 1956, white-collar workers for the first time accounted for a larger proportion of the U.S. labor force than blue-collar workers.

Technological progress did not end with the secondary sector. As relative growth in the proportion of workers in goods-producing jobs was decreasing, the demand for labor in the tertiary sector was increasing. Fueled by computer technology, the United States economy moved from a manufacturing base to a knowledge, or information, base. The current demand is for people who can manage information and deliver services. As shown in Figure 13.7, nearly 77 percent of Americans now work in management, professional, service, sales, and office occupations. The ever-increasing number of women employed outside the home also has influenced the American workplace.

Case Study: The End of the Line

Because she grew up near Chrysler's auto plant in Kenosha, Wisconsin, researcher Kathryn Marie Dudley had a special interest in studying the cultural fallout from the plant's closing in 1988. Dudley's research is a case study of a large plant in a one-industry community experiencing relocations, downsizings, and job eliminations. She offers Kenosha as a typical example of the effect of changing work patterns on midsize towns. As indicated in the excerpt below, the plant changes over the past few decades are seen as part of the shift from an industrial to a postindustrial society:

> What was once a fundamental segment of the American economic structure—heavy industry and durable goods manufacturing—has now become a marginal part of the national portfolio. As this sector of the economy gives way to the new "knowledge industries," workers in this sector are being superseded as well. In America's new image of itself as a postindustrial society, individuals still employed in basic manufacturing industries look like global benchwarmers in the competitive markets of the modern world (Dudley, 1994:161).

When the auto plant was finally shut down, Dudley did in-depth follow-up interviews with autoworkers and with a wide variety of professionals in the Kenosha area. Interview questions were open-ended to give informants freedom to roam where their thoughts and feelings took them. Dudley's only restriction was that the interviews be geared to the cultural meaning of what was happening to the community because of its declining employment base.

For Dudley, the demolition of the auto plant was a metaphor for the dismantling of the way of life created since the early 1950s among U.S. blue-collar workers in core manufacturing industries. These increasingly displaced blue-collar workers, contends Dudley, find themselves caught between two interpretations of success in America. On the one hand, middle-class professionals justify their place in society by reference to their educational credentials and "thinking" jobs. Blue-collar workers, on the other hand, legitimize their place in society on the basis of the high market value society has traditionally placed on their hard labor. One ex-auto worker, whom Dudley calls Al Tirpak, captured the idea beautifully:

> We're worth fifteen dollars an hour because we're producing a product that can be sold on the market that'll produce that fifteen dollars an hour. . . . I don't know if you want to [base a person's value] strictly on education. You can send someone to school for twelve years and they can still be doing something that's socially undesirable and not very worthwhile for society. I don't know if they should get paid just because they had an education. In my mind, yuppie means young

The shift from an industrial to a postindustrial economy will necessarily result in plant shutdowns and layoffs.

unproductive parasite. *We're gonna have an awful lot of yuppies here in Kenosha that say they are doing something worthwhile when, really, they aren't (Dudley, 1994:169).*

Due to the massive loss of high-paying factory jobs, Dudley contends that the blue-collar vision of success is coming to "the end of the line." These workers have lost their cultural niche to a postindustrial world where work is based on education and the application of knowledge.

Dudley documents the blue-collar workers' view of this new reality. From her extensive interviews, she constructs a portrait of their struggle to preserve their cultural traditions in a world in which the type of employment on which these traditions were built is decreasing. The penalty for not creating new cultural supports for a sense of social worth, Dudley concludes, will be life in a state of confusion with a sense of failure.

Working with the Research

1. What is the focus of Dudley's research?

2. What does Dudley's conclusion mean for blue-collar workers in terms of their way of life?

3. Do you think Dudley's research methods are strong enough to support her conclusion?

4. Do you believe that Dudley can be objective in this study of her hometown? Explain your answer.

Occupational Structure

Occupations are categories of jobs that involve similar activities at different work locations. For example, teacher, dental assistant, film producer, and electrician are all occupations because each position requires similar training and involves some standard operations. The United States Department of Labor has identified over 820 occupations with hundreds more specialties within the broader occupation categories.

What is the shape of the U.S. occupational structure? A two-tier occupational structure has developed in the U.S. One tier—the **core tier** —includes jobs with large firms holding dominant positions within their industries. Computer technology, pharmaceutical, and aerospace firms are prime examples. About 35 percent of U.S. workers are in the core. The other level— the **peripheral tier**—is composed of jobs in smaller firms that either are competing for business left over from core firms or are engaged in less profitable industries such as agriculture, textiles, and small-scale retail trade. Most U.S. workers—around 65 percent—are employed in the peripheral tier.

What is the nature of core and peripheral jobs? Historically, jobs in the core paid more, offered better benefits, and provided longer-term employment. This is not surprising since the firms involved are large and highly profitable. Peripheral jobs are characterized by low pay, little or no benefits, and short-term employment. These features follow from the weaker competitive position and the smaller size of the employing firms.

How are the core and peripheral tiers changing? The industries that have supplied most of the core jobs in the U.S. have been scaling back during the last 20 years, laying off experienced workers and not hiring new ones. As early as 1983, for example, a steel mill in Hibbing, Minnesota, that once employed 4,400 people had a payroll of only 650 ("Left Out," 1983). Since 1983, the Weirton Steele Company continued to cut its production capacity by another 30 percent and has laid off more than half of its workforce (Riederer, 1999). In fact, more than 3.2 million jobs in the United States have been eliminated just since 2000 (Birnbaum, 2003). According to one survey, between 2000 and 2003, nearly one out of five workers reported being laid off from a full-time or part-time job (Dixon and Van Horn, 2003). Approximately three-fourths of the jobs lost during this time period were in manufacturing.

The good economic news, fueled by microchip technology, is that the U.S. economy continues its healthy growth and unemployment remains low. The bad economic news is that the new jobs are not as good as the manufacturing jobs they are replacing (Schmitt, 2005). The newer industries provide few jobs suited to the skills and backgrounds of laid-off manufacturing workers. Moreover, most jobs in high-tech industries pay minimal wages and offer few chances for promotion. Responsible positions with high pay are held by a very small proportion of high-tech employees.

To what tier of America's occupational structure do these California aircraft workers belong?

● **occupations**
    categories of jobs that involve similar activities at different work locations

● **core tier**
    an occupational structure composed of large firms dominating their industries

● **peripheral tier**
    an occupational structure composed of smaller, less profitable firms

Thus, reemployment of laid-off workers is a significant problem, particularly for workers laid off from manufacturing jobs. According to the Center for Economic and Policy Research, approximately 33 percent of the manufacturing workers who lost their jobs between 2001 and 2003 still had not returned to work by the start of 2004. Moreover, nearly three-fourths of the workers who had found jobs by 2004 took pay cuts (Schmitt, 2004).

What difference does this make to U.S. workers? As has probably already crossed your mind, this trend makes a huge difference. The U.S. economy has been losing higher-paying jobs and gaining lower-paying jobs. This helps explain why, since the 1970s, the majority of workers have been losing economic ground. While thirty years ago one American worker alone could support a family, the dual-employed married couple has become the norm today.

This process, known as *downwaging*, is expected to continue in the twenty-first century. Of the top ten job categories projected to grow between 2002 and 2012, five pay below the poverty level for a family of four. Only two of the top ten shrinking job categories fall below the poverty threshold (U.S. Bureau of the Census, 2005). Many sociologists believe that the job loss and downwaging trends threaten the American dream (Newman, 1993; Barlett and Steel, 1996; Dixon and Van Horn, 2003).

Downsizing and Contingent Employment

Clearly, the occupational structure in the United States has changed dramatically over the last few decades. *Downsizing* and *contingent employment*, two strategies used by top management, reduce employment in core industries. A discussion of these related practices will help explain why the U.S. occupational structure is changing.

Downsizing is the process by which companies reduce the size of their full-time workforces. **Contingent employment** involves hiring people on a part-time or short-term basis. Although corporate downsizing had been going on since the late 1970s, it accelerated during the 1980s and 1990s. Since 1985, an estimated four million people have lost their jobs to downsizing alone. This trend is expected to continue (Sloan, 1996; Belton, 1999).

Why are downsizing and contingent employment taking place on such a large scale? Part of the motivation for downsizing is based on top management's belief that their companies employ a surplus of people and that, thanks to computers and other labor-saving technology, work can be done by fewer employees without reductions in efficiency and effectiveness. Top management also points to lower profits caused by increasing foreign competition. And it is true that about 20 percent of all U.S. workers are directly exposed to foreign competition (McNamee and Muller, 1998). Companies have responded to increased foreign competition by moving operations overseas and by replacing full-time employees with part-time workers hired to do a limited amount of work for a specified time period.

● **downsizing**
the process by which companies reduce their workforces

● **contingent employment**
the hiring of part-time, short-term workers

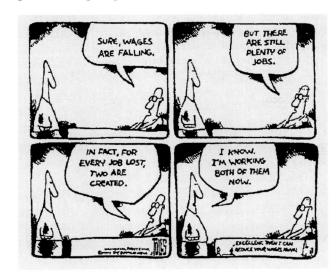

Corporate downsizing is associated with lower pay.

Figure 13.8 Evidence of Declining Trust In Management
According to this graph, employee trust in management is relatively low. Are any of these factors affecting trust more important to you than others?

Source: *The 2003 Towers Perrin Talent Report* (Boston, MA), 2003.w

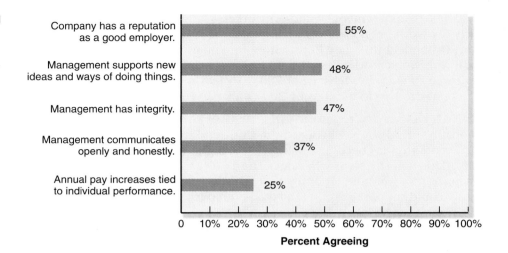

	Percent Agreeing
Company has a reputation as a good employer.	55%
Management supports new ideas and ways of doing things.	48%
Management has integrity.	47%
Management communicates openly and honestly.	37%
Annual pay increases tied to individual performance.	25%

Percent Agreeing

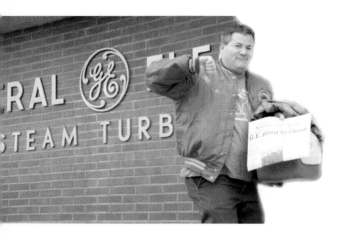

This unhappy worker has been caught in a corporate downsizing. What negative effects is this experience likely to have on him?

Contingent employment is a cost-cutting device. Unlike full-time employees, contingent workers receive lower pay and are not entitled to expensive benefits such as vacation time, health insurance, and retirement benefits.

Does downsizing and contingent employment have a downside? According to Robert Reich, former secretary of the U.S. Department of Labor, downsizing and contingent employment will create greater polarization between those who control capital and those who do not. Some critics believe the "disposable" workforce is the most important trend in business today. They contend that it is fundamentally changing the relationship between Americans and their employers.

A survey of more than 35,000 employees across the United States confirms that employees' attitudes toward their employers are not entirely favorable. Although employees express high job satisfaction, their trust in management appears to be eroding. Workers seem to be losing some faith in management's commitment to them. (See Figure 13.8.) Trust and loyalty are difficult to maintain when employees do not believe company policies treat them fairly. As time passes, additional research will help to focus attention on the full effects of corporate downsizing and contingent employment.

Section 5 Assessment

1. Why have white-collar jobs increased faster than jobs in other sectors of the workforce since the 1930s?

2. What are some immediate benefits of downsizing? Some long-term drawbacks?

Critical Thinking

3. **Drawing Conclusions** Would you like to spend your work life as a contingent employee? Why or why not?

Summary

Section 1: Power and Authority

Main Idea: Political systems can be based on charismatic, traditional, or rational-legal authority. Democratic, totalitarian, and authoritarian are types of political systems.

Section 2: Political Power in American Society

Main Idea: The two major models of political power are elitism and pluralism. The conflict and functionalist theorists have different views of who exercises political power in the United States.

Section 3: Economic Systems

Main Idea: Capitalist and socialist economies differ in terms of the degree of private ownership and in the extent of the government's role in the economy.

Section 4: The Modern Corporation

Main Idea: Corporations, especially those with multinational connections, have grown very powerful, influencing domestic political decisions and the political and economic institutions of countries around the world.

Section 5: Work in the Modern Economy

Main Idea: Workers today face a changing economy, with companies relying more heavily on temporary workers and on foreign labor.

Sociology Online

Self-Check Quiz
Visit the *Sociology and You* Web site at glencoe.com and click on Chapter 13—Self-Check Quizzes to prepare for the chapter test.

Reviewing Vocabulary

Complete each sentence using each term once.

a. charismatic authority
b. monopoly
c. downsizing
d. traditional authority
e. power elite
f. pluralism
g. elitism
h. primary sector
i. interest group
j. corporation
k. rational-legal authority
l. power

1. The ability to control the behavior of others is called _____.

2. _____ is the authority that arises from the personality of an individual.

3. The form of authority in which the power of government officials is based on their offices is called _____ .

4. _____ is the form of authority in which the legitimacy of a leader is rooted in custom.

5. A group organized to influence political decision making is called _____ .

6. _____ is a system in which a community or society is controlled from the top by a few individuals or organizations.

7. The process in which political decisions are made as a result of competition and compromise among special interest groups is called

   _____ .

8. A coalition of top military, corporate, and government leaders is called the _____ .

9. _____ is an organization owned by shareholders who have limited liability and limited control.

10. The reduction of a corporation's workforce is called _____ .

11. A company that has control over the production or distribution of a product or service is called a _____ .

Reviewing the Facts

12. How did Max Weber define power?

13. What is elitism? Give an example.

14. What is socialism? Give an example.

15. The economic system of most nations most closely follows which system?

16. What is downsizing? In general, what can be said about the relationship between the disadvantages of downsizing and the advantages of downsizing?

Thinking Critically

17. Making Inferences

Charismatic leaders such as Adolf Hitler and Branch Davidian cult leader David Koresh show us that the ability to exert control over people has little to do with issues of right and wrong. Why do people embrace men like Hitler or Koresh? What kind of training or education is essential in a democracy to counter the effects of dangerous yet charismatic leaders?

18. Drawing Conclusions

The topic of enforced population control (see Another Place, page 432) is an intriguing one for many Americans. Only ten percent of American families in 2000 had more than two children. Does government ever have a right to legislate how many children couples are allowed to have? Should Americans be encouraged to have only two children for social reasons? Under what circumstances, if any, would government have a legitimate say in the size of families?

19. Analyzing Information

According to conflict theorists, the power elite control many aspects of politics and society at large. A recent book examined the diversity of the power elite—how many women and minorities are in its membership. Discuss the extent to which you think women and minorities are represented in the power elite.

Copyright 2005 J.D. Crowe/Cagle Cartoons

20. Analyzing Visuals

The cartoon above was first published in December 2005. Many cartoons are like this one, that is, they use one dramatic image and have no caption. What effect does this have on the viewer and how well do you think this works? Can you think of a way to alter the cartoon's subject or message by simply changing the label on the hand?

21. Evaluating Information

Many individuals in the history of the United States have been able to influence the political process because of their personal wealth. Examples include Andrew Carnegie, John D. Rockefeller, and—more recently—Microsoft founder Bill Gates. Capitalism encourages the accumulation of wealth. Do you think the government should put limits on how much wealth any one individual or organization can control? Why or why not?

Sociology Projects

22. Political Influence

As an extension of question #21, instead of putting limits on how much wealth any one individual or organization could accumulate, consider the options that the government might use to limit the political influence of the wealthy. Write a brief essay listing and describing those options.

23. Employee Rights

Review the list of employee rights in the Sociology Today feature on page 448. If you have a job, try to find out which of these rights your current employer recognizes. You might ask your manager if your company has a brochure that lists employee rights. If you don't have a job, discuss this activity with a friend who is working.

24. Qualitative Analysis

Study the bar graph below, which reports the percentage of population employed for selected countries. For your project, draw up a list of hypotheses that could explain the differences you see, including the types of sources you might consult to carry out the research project.

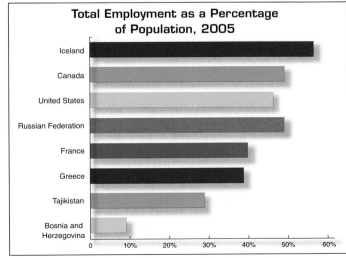

Total Employment as a Percentage of Population, 2005

Source: *United Nations, The Statistical Yearbook of the Economic Commission for Europe 2003*

25. Political Beliefs

On a sheet of paper, write down your own political party affiliation and your parents' political party affiliations. Next, write down your views on some key issues that you feel strongly about, such as immigration or minority rights. Write down your parents' views on these topics. Do you and your parents share the same political beliefs? You might also want to try comparing your views with a friend's. Are your views and your friend's views similar? If so, do you think that this might explain why you are friends? Do you think that people tend to associate more with those who share similar political beliefs?

Technology Activity

26. One of the topics of debate about corporations in America is whether they have any responsibilities beyond making a profit for their shareholders. Some people say that corporations have a "social responsibility" to make their communities better places. Two companies that act on their social responsibilities are Ben & Jerry's and The Body Shop. Go to their web sites at www.benjerry.com/ and www.thebodyshop.ca/.

a. Find their mission statements and read them. What do these companies believe about social responsibility?

b. What specific actions do they take to make their communities better places?

No Shame in My Game
by Katherine S. Newman

Katherine Newman has created a rich portrait of minimum-wage workers employed in four fast-food restaurants in central Harlem. These are the "working poor"—they hold jobs and pay taxes, but they do not earn enough money to buy the basic necessities of life. In the passage below, Newman argues that the working poor share the same basic values as the rest of American society. The shame referred to in the reading lies in society's view that employment in fast-food jobs is somehow degrading.

Swallowing ridicule would be a hardship for almost anyone in this culture, but it is particularly hard on minority youth in the inner city. They have already logged four or five years' worth of interracial and cross-class friction by the time they get behind a [Burger Barn] cash register. More likely than not, they have also learned from peers that self-respecting people don't allow themselves to be "dissed" without striking back. Yet this is precisely what they must do if they are going to survive in the workplace.

This is one of the main reasons why these [fast-food] jobs carry such a powerful stigma in American popular culture: they fly in the face of a national attraction to autonomy, independence, and the individual's "right" to respond in kind when dignity is threatened. In ghetto communities, this stigma is even more powerful because—ironically—it is in these **enclaves** that this mainstream value of independence is most vigorously elaborated and **embellished.** Film characters, rap stars, and local idols base their claim to notoriety on standing above the crowd, going their own way, being free of the ties that bind ordinary mortals. There are white parallels, to be sure, but this is a powerful **genre of icons** in the black community, not because it is a disconnected subculture but because it is an intensified version of a perfectly recognizable American middle-class and working-class fixation.

It is therefore noteworthy that thousands upon thousands of minority teens, young adults, and even middle-aged adults line up for jobs that will subject them, at least potentially, to a kind of character assassination. They do so not because they start the job-seeking process with a different set of values, one that can withstand society's contempt for fast-food workers. They take these jobs because in so many inner-city communities, there is nothing better in the offing. In general, they have already tried to get better jobs and have failed, landing at the door of Burger Barn as a last resort. . . .

The stigma also stems from the low social status of the people who hold these jobs: minorities, teenagers, immigrants who often speak halting English, those with little education, and (increasingly in affluent communities afflicted with labor shortages) the elderly. To the extent that the prestige of a job refracts the social characteristic of its average **incumbents,** fast-food jobs are hobbled by the perception that people with better

- **enclave**
  a territory or cultural unit within a foreign territory

- **embellish**
  to add to; to make more attractive

- **genre of icons**
  category or type of symbols

- **incumbent**
  occupant, job holder

choices would never purposely opt for a "McJob." . . . There is no quicker way to indicate that a person is barely deserving of notice than to point out he or she holds a "chump change" job at Kentucky Fried Chicken or Burger King. . . .

Ghetto youth are particularly sensitive to the status degradation entailed in stigmatized employment. As Elijah Anderson . . . and others have pointed out, a high premium is placed on independence, autonomy, and respect among minority youth in inner-city communities—particularly by young men. No small amount of mayhem is committed every year in the name of injured pride. Hence jobs that routinely demand **displays of deference** force those who hold them to violate "macho" behavior codes that are central to the definition of teen culture. There are, therefore, considerable social risks involved in seeking a fast-food job in the first place, one that the employees and job-seekers are keenly aware of from the very beginning of their search for employment.

It is hard to know the extent to which this stigma discourages young people in places like central Harlem from knocking on the door of a fast-food restaurant. It is clear that the other choices aren't much better and that necessity drives thousands, if not millions, of teens and older job-seekers to ignore the stigma or learn to live with it. But no one enters the central Harlem job market without having to face this **gauntlet.**

Source: Excerpted from Katherine S. Newman, *No Shame in My Game*, New York: Alfred A. Knopf, 1999, pp. 93, 95.

● **display of deference**
acting in a humble or compliant way

● **gauntlet**
ordeal or challenge

Read and React

1. Who are the "working poor"? Give some examples of the types of jobs the working poor would hold.

2. According to Newman, the working poor share the same values as the rest of American society. Discuss the evidence she gives for this. Is she convincing?

3. Why did Newman select *No Shame in My Game* for her book title?

4. Do you think a stigma is attached to being a fast-food worker? Explain.

5. What do you think Newman means by "status degradation" in the context of her research?

Religion

Sections

Learning Objectives

After reading this chapter, you will be able to

- explain the sociological meaning of religion.

- describe the different views of religion as seen by the major theoretical perspectives.

- distinguish the basic types of religious organization.

- discuss the meaning and nature of religiosity.

- define secularization and describe its relationship to religiosity in the United States.

- discuss religious fundamentalism in the United States from the sociological perspective.

Applying Sociology

More than thirty years after the Beatles' last recording session, the group's tapes and CDs are still selling by the millions. But there was a moment when American radio stations banned their music and many teenagers stomped on their records.

The angry reaction was the result of a comment by John Lennon in a 1966 interview: "Christianity will go," Lennon said. "It will vanish and shrink... We're more popular than Jesus now, I don't know which will go first—rock'n'roll or Christianity."

When the interview was published in the United States, there was an uproar that caught some by surprise. If the entire interview had been printed, the response might have been less extreme, but Lennon was forced to apologize. It seemed that many young Americans took their religion very seriously.

The evidence suggests that, unlike people living in many industrialized nations, Americans are fairly religious. This chapter looks at religion as an institution, as well as at the ways that people express their religious beliefs.

Sociology Online

Chapter Overview
Visit the Sociology and You Web site at glencoe.com and click on **Chapter 14— Chapter Overviews** to preview chapter information.

1

Religion and Sociology

Key Terms

- religion *(p. 464)*
- sacred *(p. 464)*
- profane *(p. 464)*

- **religion**
  a unified system of beliefs and practices concerned with sacred things

- **sacred**
  holy; set apart and given a special meaning that goes beyond, or transcends, immediate existence

- **profane**
  nonsacred

Section Preview

Religion is concerned with sacred things. Durkheim concluded that every religion separates the sacred from the profane. Sociologists studying religion face some unique problems. They do not judge the validity of various religions but rather look at those aspects of religion that can be measured and observed in society.

The Sociological Meaning of Religion

A **religion** is a unified system of beliefs and practices concerned with sacred things. This definition comes from Emile Durkheim, whose work was based on studies of the Australian aborigines in the late nineteenth century. According to Durkheim, every society distinguishes between the **sacred** —things and ideas that are set apart and given a special meaning that goes beyond, or transcends, immediate existence—and the **profane**, or nonsacred aspects of life. Profane in this context does not mean unholy. It simply means commonplace and not involving the supernatural. Another word for profane is *secular*.

Sacred things take on a public character that makes them appear important in themselves; profane things do not. The particular things considered sacred vary from culture to culture. For example, Bolivian tin miners attach sacred meaning to figures of the devil and of bulls. Because Americans do not share these religious beliefs, these cultural items are part of their nonsacred, or profane, world. Moreover, some nonreligious aspects of culture can assume a sacred character. Here, two sociologists illustrate the difference between the sacred and the profane:

When Babe Ruth was a living idol to baseball fans, the bat he used to slug his home runs was definitely a profane object. It was Ruth's personal instrument and had little social value in itself. Today, however, one of Ruth's bats is enshrined in the Baseball Hall of Fame. It is no longer used by anyone. It stands, rather, as an object which in itself

Buddhas, like this one in a Korean temple, are sacred objects in the Far East and Southeast Asia, and wherever Buddhists live. What makes an object sacred?

represents the values, sentiments, power, and beliefs of all members of the baseball community. What was formerly a profane object is now in the process of gaining some of the qualities of a sacred object (Cuzzort and King, 1976:27).

Babe Ruth's bat illustrates two particulars about the sociological study of religion. First, a profane object can become sacred, and vice versa. Second, sociologists can deal with religion without becoming involved in theological issues. By focusing on the cultural and social aspects of religion, sociologists avoid questions about the ultimate validity of any particular religion. This point is so important that it needs more explanation.

Is this Ford Mustang convertible a sacred or secular object? Why?

The Sociological Study of Religion

The sociological study of religion involves looking at a set of meanings attached to a world beyond human observation. Because this nonphysical world cannot be directly observed, this task is particularly difficult. Sociologists have to ask themselves hard questions: How can we find evidence for something that can't be seen? How can we remain objective about such a value-laden subject, especially when we have our own beliefs? Is science really the proper tool to evaluate religion?

Obviously, sociologists cannot study the unobservable. Consequently, they approach religion as a human creation and focus on social aspects of religion that can be measured and observed. Sociologists, then, are not in the business of determining which religions people ought to follow. Sociologists keep their own faith personal while investigating the *social* dimensions of religion. Like people in any other occupation, sociologists themselves follow a variety of religions.

Sociologists study the social aspects of religion. One such aspect is the charitable work done by members of different religious organizations.

Section 1 Assessment

1. How does the sociological definition of religion differ from how you previously thought of religion?

2. How do sociologists manage to study religion if they can't see the spiritual world?

Critical Thinking

3. **Evaluating Information** Do you think religion can be studied scientifically? Using the material just presented, make an argument for or against this practice.

Religion at War

As part of studying the effects of religion on society, sociologists note that throughout history, religion has both promoted social stability and led to social conflict. In this excerpt from the article Religion at War, *the conflict aspect is highlighted.*

In virtually every one of the world's 480 major wars since 1700, each side has imagined itself to be exclusively on the side of God, Gött, Allah, Dieu or other names for the deity.

Religion is often so closely linked with ethnic or national identity as to be seen as inseparable from them. Thus a struggle for expressions of ethnic or national identity is experienced as a religious war.

This is so of the current unrest in the Punjab, created by Sikh demands for a separate Sikh state.

Religion evokes powerful emotions and commitments. It is capable of producing believers whose faith moves them to acts of great self-sacrifice and charity. At the same time it can produce believers who feel that their faith calls them to struggle violently in what they believe to be a just cause. One example is the Hindi/Muslim tension in India focused on Ayodhya. Here, a mosque built in the 15th century was destroyed in 1992 by militant Hindus because it is believed to have been built over the birthplace of the Hindu god Rama. While the majority of Hindis and Muslims have lived together peacefully for generations, extremists on both sides are capable of arousing violence through use of powerful religious symbols.

In many faiths, the issue of whether warfare is permissible has given rise to various theories of the just war. Such theories seek to define whether believers can ever engage in the use of violence. The usual conclusion is that violence—including warfare—is only acceptable in pursuit of a greater good. The problem, however, is who defines the greater good?

Source: Joanne O'Brien and Martin Palmer, *The State of Religion Atlas.* New York: Simon & Schuster, 1993, p. 117. Reprinted by permission.

Thinking It Over

Does functionalism or conflict theory best explain the link between strong religious conviction and war? Why?

Activists of a Hindu religious sect demand the right to build a temple on the site of a demolished mosque. Why are wars and conflicts often rooted in religious beliefs and values?

Theoretical Perspectives

Section Preview

Religion has several functions. It legitimates the structure of society, promotes social unity, and provides a sense of meaning and belonging. Marx argued that religion is used to justify and maintain the group in power. Weber believed that religion could promote social change. He connected the Protestant ethic and the rise of capitalism.

Key Terms

- legitimate *(p. 468)*
- spirit of capitalism *(p. 472)*
- Protestant ethic *(p. 472)*

Functionalism and Religion

Religion exists in some form in virtually all societies. (See Figure 14.1 on page 468 and World View on page 469 for a global distribution of major religions.) The earliest evidence of religion and religious customs and taboos has been traced as far back as 50,000 B.C. Humans had by then already begun to bury their dead, a practice based on the belief in existence after death. Evidence of religious practices appears in many ancient cultures. In Rome, there were specific gods for objects and events—a god of trees, a god of money, a goddess of fever. While the early Hebrews believed that pigs were unclean animals whose pollution would spread to all who touched or tasted them, the tribes of New Guinea considered pigs holy creatures worthy of ancestral sacrifice (Harris, 1989).

Emile Durkheim, the first sociologist to examine religion scientifically, wondered why it is that all societies have some form of religion. In one of his books, *The Elementary Forms of Religious Life* (1915), Durkheim offered an

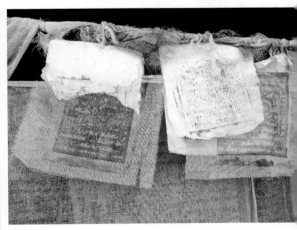

We know that religion is an important part of almost all societies because of the religious artifacts that have been left behind.

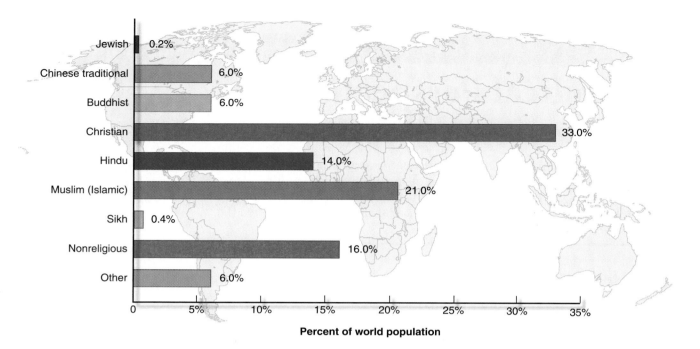

Percent of world population

explanation rooted in the function religion performs for society. The essential function of religion, he believed, was to provide through sacred symbols a mirror for members of society to see themselves. Through religious rituals, people worship their societies and thereby remind themselves of their shared past and future existence.

Following Durkheim's lead, sociologists have identified the following social functions of religion.

● *Religion gives formal approval to existing social arrangements.* Religious doctrine and scripture **legitimate** the status quo. Religion, then, justifies or gives authority to social norms and customs. A society's religion explains why the society is—and should be—the way it is. It tells us why some people have power and others do not, why some are rich and others poor, why some are common and others elite. Many social customs and rituals are based on religion. According to Durkheim, legitimation is the central function of religion.

● *Religion encourages a sense of unity.* Religion, according to Durkheim, is the glue that holds society together. Without religion, society would be chaotic. As Cuzzort and King have stated (1976), Durkheim "provided the greatest justification for religious doctrine ever formulated by a social scientist when he claimed that all societies must have religious commitments. Without religious dedication there is no social order."

In some cases, though, religion causes societies to fragment, even to the point of civil war. Religion divides Catholics and Protestants in Northern Ireland. Thus, while it is accurate to say that religion is usually a source of social unity, it can also divide a society. (See Another Place, page 466.)

● *Religion provides a sense of understanding.* Religion not only explains the nature of social life and encourages social unity, it also provides individuals meaning beyond day-to-day life. People mark important events in life—birth, sexual maturity, marriage, death—with religious ceremonies and explain such events in religious terms. Religion gives believers a sense

World View

Religions of the World

This map displays the worldwide distribution of all religions. Emile Durkheim showed that suicide rates vary according to group characteristics. One of these characteristics is religious background. For example, Durkheim showed that the suicide rate is lower among Catholics than among Protestants.

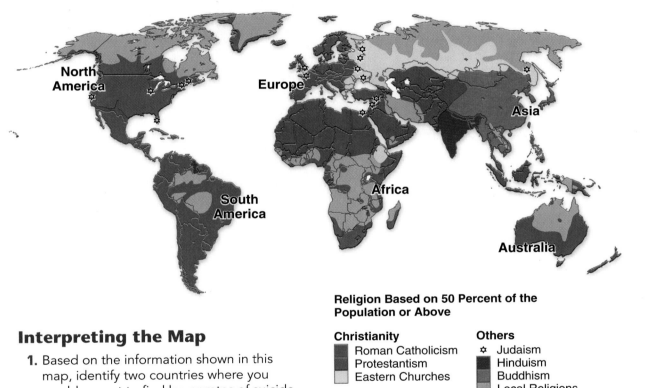

Interpreting the Map

1. Based on the information shown in this map, identify two countries where you would expect to find lower rates of suicide than in England.

2. What information on the map did you use in your analysis?

Religion Based on 50 Percent of the Population or Above

Christianity
- Roman Catholicism
- Protestantism
- Eastern Churches

Islam
- Sunnite
- Shiite

Others
- ✿ Judaism
- Hinduism
- Buddhism
- Local Religions

of their place in the cosmos and gives eternal significance to a short and uncertain earthly existence.

- *Religion promotes a sense of belonging.* Religious organizations provide opportunities for people to share important ideas, ways of life, and ethnic or racial backgrounds. Religion supplies a kind of group identity. People

Religion	Origination	Key Figure	Beliefs	Main Geographic Areas	Number of Followers
Hinduism	Before 2000 B.C.	Unknown	Of many gods, Brahma is the creator of the universe. Life is determined by the law of karma (the spiritual force generated by one's own actions, which determines one's next reincarnation).	India	837,262,000
Judaism	Before 1200 B.C.	Abraham	The one true God has established a covenant with the people of Israel, who are called to lives of justice, mercy, and obedience to God.	Israel, Eastern Europe, USA	14,551,000
Buddhism	About 500 B.C.	Siddhartha Gautama	The existence of God is not assumed. Through adherence to the Eightfold Path (correct thought and behavior), one can escape from desire and suffering and achieve nirvana (a state of bliss reached through extreme denial of the self).	Far East, Southeast Asia	372,974,000
Confucianism	About 500 B.C.	Confucius	The Analects (sayings of Confucius) stress moral conduct and virtuous human relationships.	China	6,425,000
Christianity	About A.D. 1	Jesus Christ	Jesus is the Son of the one true God. Through God's grace and profession of faith, people have eternal life with God.	Europe, North America, South America	2,069,883,000
Islam	About A.D. 600	Muhammad	Muhammad received the Koran (holy scriptures) from the one true God. Believers go to an eternal Garden of Eden.	Africa, Middle East, Southeast Asia	1,254,222,000

Figure 14.2
Major World Religions
This figure summarizes characteristics and beliefs of the major world religions being widely practiced today.

Source: *World Almanac and Book of Facts, 2005.*

usually join religious organizations freely and feel a degree of influence within these organizations. For many people in modern society, membership in a religious organization provides a sense of community. This feeling of belonging helps to counteract depersonalization, powerlessness, and rootlessness.

Conflict Theory and Religion

Conflict theory focuses on how religion works to either inhibit or encourage social change. Two early and important sociologists who looked at religion from these perspectives are Karl Marx and Max Weber.

What did Marx say about religion?
Marx believed that once people have created a unified system of sacred beliefs and practices, they act as if it were something beyond their control. They become "alienated" from the religious system they have set up. People have the power to change (or, better yet, in Marx's mind, to abandon) the religion they have created. They don't do so, however, because they see it as a binding force to which they must conform. Religion, Marx wrote, is used by the ruling class to justify its economic, political, and social advantages over the oppressed. Those in power justify poverty, degradation, and misery as God's will. To eliminate inequalities and injustices is to tamper with God's plan. Religion, then, gives people a sense that all is the way it should be.

Gender Inequality in Religion

Women have been fighting for equal rights in all aspects of society—religion as well as government and business. In some religions women have equal status within their orders. Other religions see feminism as a "Western" issue and irrelevant to their faiths. This map shows how major denominations in each country view the status of women.

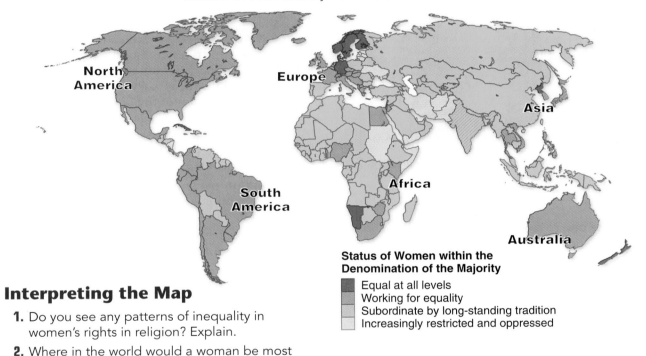

Status of Women within the Denomination of the Majority

- Equal at all levels
- Working for equality
- Subordinate by long-standing tradition
- Increasingly restricted and oppressed

Interpreting the Map

1. Do you see any patterns of inequality in women's rights in religion? Explain.

2. Where in the world would a woman be most likely to head an entire religious organization? Support your answer. Do some research to see if this has occurred. If it has not, explain why.

3. How does the United States compare with the Scandinavian countries in terms of gender equality? Why do you think this difference exists?

4. How would you explain the mixed status of women in India?

Adapted from *The State of Religion Atlas*, New York: Simon & Schuster, 1993.

How did Weber link Protestantism and capitalism? Whereas Marx believed that religion works against social change, Max Weber suggested that religion sometimes encourages social change. He pointed to the relationship between Protestantism and the rise of capitalism. Weber wondered why capitalism emerged in northwestern Europe and America and not in other parts of the world. A possible answer lay in what he termed the *spirit*

The theology of sixteenth-century theologian John Calvin formed the basis for the Protestant ethic.

- **spirit of capitalism**
  the obligation to reinvest money in business rather than to spend it

- **Protestant ethic**
  a set of values, norms, beliefs, and attitudes stressing hard work, thrift, and self-discipline

of capitalism and the *Protestant ethic*. With capitalism, work became a moral obligation rather than a mere necessity. If businesses were to grow, money (capital) had to be put back into the business rather than spent. Investment for the future was more important than immediate consumption. All of this Weber called the **spirit of capitalism.**

Most major religions did not define hard work as an obligation or demand the reinvestment of capital for further profits (rather than for immediate enjoyment). But some Protestant sects did. Here, then, was a religion with a cluster of values, norms, beliefs, and attitudes that favored the emergence of modern capitalism. Weber referred to this cluster of values, norms, beliefs, and attitudes that stressed the virtue of hard work, thrift, and self-discipline as the **Protestant ethic.**

What is the nature of the Protestant ethic?
The Protestant ethic is often associated with John Calvin (1509–1564), an early Protestant theologian. Calvin's followers were known as Calvinists. Calvinist beliefs illustrate several features of the Protestant ethic.

- According to Calvin, God identifies his chosen by rewarding them in this world. Therefore, the more successful people were in this life, the more sure they were of being a member of God's select few.

- Consumption beyond necessity was considered sinful; those who engaged in self-pleasure were agents of the devil.

- Calvinists believed there was an underlying purpose of life: glorification of God on earth through one's occupational calling. Because everyone's material rewards were actually God's, and the purpose of life was to glorify God, profits should be multiplied (through reinvestment) rather than used in the pursuit of personal pleasures.

Symbolic Interactionism and Religion

Sociologist Peter Berger (1990) captured the relationship between religion and symbolic interactionism in his book, *The Sacred Canopy*. In this book, Berger explored the idea that humans create from their religious traditions a canopy, or cover, of symbolic meanings, to "lay" over the secular world. These otherworldly symbolic meanings are used to guide everyday social interaction. Religious beliefs, rituals, and ideas tell people the difference between the sacred and the profane and provide stability and security in a changing and uncertain existence.

Symbolic interactionism, for example, helps us understand the expression "there are no atheists in foxholes." Insecurity and uncertainty, of course, are at a peak in the life-and-death situation of war, and the desire to regain security and certainty is a natural human response. Religious meanings, especially those related to an afterlife, can offer some relief. Japanese kamikaze pilots in World War II and Middle Eastern terrorists infuse their

Figure 14.3 Religion

This table shows that in examining religion the three major perspectives focus on different aspects. Discuss the conclusion of any one of the theories in light of your experience with the institution of religion.

Theoretical Perspective	Focus	Conclusions
Functionalist	Look at contributions of religion to society.	Religion legitimates social arrangements. It promotes social unity. It provides a sense of understanding. It encourages a sense of belonging.
Conflict Theory	Elites use religion to manipulate the masses.	Religion is used by the most powerful to justify their economic, political, and social advantages.
Symbolic Interactionism	People create symbolic meanings from their religious beliefs, rituals, and ideas.	People use their socially created symbolic meanings to guide everyday social interactions.

sometimes suicidal behavior with ultimate meaning by focusing on their reward beyond life. Less dramatically, people enduring troubled marriages can be strengthened by their commitment to uphold their holy vows of matrimony spoken in a place of worship.

Each of the three major theoretical perspectives aids in the sociological study of religion. Figure 14.3 shows the unique light each perspective sheds.

Section 2 Assessment

1. How did Karl Marx view religion?

2. What was Weber's contribution to the sociological study of religion?

3. What did Berger mean by the phrase "the sacred canopy"?

Critical Thinking

4. **Analyzing Information** Does the Protestant ethic still exist in America today? Use Weber's analysis to justify your position.

Is Cloning Humans Ethical?

Aldous Huxley's 1932 novel *Brave New World* describes a society in which babies are created scientifically. Another novel—*The Boys from Brazil*, written by Ira Levin and published in 1976—features a story about German Nazis cloning Adolf Hitler. Both of these books play on our fears about the effects and ethics of human cloning (a nonsexual creation of a genetically identical copy). In February 1997, the potential for cloning technology went from fiction to fact with the birth of a cloned sheep named Dolly. This birth and the subsequent cloning of mice, sheep, and pigs have made the ethical considerations of human cloning much more pertinent today than just a few years ago.

Dr. Brigitte Boisselier, head of a biotechnology company called Clonaid, claims that this company is responsible for the births of at least 14 human clones. Scientists question this claim, however, most particularly because Boisselier is a member of a fringe religious sect that believes humans are descended from clones created 25,000 years ago by space aliens. In addition, two other scientists—a fertility clinic operator in Lexington, Kentucky, and an Italian gynecologist—are offering cloning services to help infertile and gay couples have children. The success that these scientists claim also has not been independently verified.

Although 60 percent of Americans support therapeutic cloning—creating human embryos to harvest their stem cells for medical research—only 9 percent find the reproductive cloning of humans morally acceptable (Gallup, 2005). In 2005, the United Nations gave up on an attempt to create a worldwide ban on human cloning (Biever, 2005). Many member nations were unwilling to ban therapeutic cloning, which supporters believe may help millions of people worldwide suffering from diseases such as diabetes and Parkinson's disease. Other supporters believe that since advances in technology will make human cloning a reality, such cloning should be legalized and regulated to ensure that it is carried out in a safe, scientific manner.

Opponents of human cloning are skeptical that such cloning can be conducted safely and believe that it jeopardizes the health of potential child clones. They point to the fact that experiments in animal cloning have produced few live births, and that many of the animal clones that are born die shortly thereafter from genetic abnormalities. Many traditional religious groups also have expressed serious concerns about cloning. These opponents believe that if humans are cloned, people will be placing themselves in a position only God has occupied.

Human cloning is the latest in a long line of medical technologies that affect the length and quality of life. The ethical considerations of such a procedure, however, will be debated for years to come.

Analyzing the Trends

What role, if any, should religion play in the debate over human cloning? Include some information from this chapter to support your answer.

Religious Organization and Religiosity

Section Preview

The major forms of religious organization are churches, denominations, sects, and cults. Religiosity—the ways people express their religious interests and convictions—can be analyzed in terms of five dimensions: belief, ritual, intellect, experience, and consequences.

Key Terms

- church (p. 475)
- denomination (p. 475)
- sect (p. 478)
- cult (p. 478)
- religiosity (p. 479)

Religious Organization

In Western societies, most people practice religion through some organizational structure. For this reason, the nature of religious organization is an important component of the sociological study of religion. Early scholars identified four basic types of religious organization: *church, denomination, sect*, and *cult*.

How do sociologists distinguish among the basic types of religious organization? To sociologists, a **church** is a life-encompassing religious organization to which all members of a society belong. This type of religious organization exists when religion and the state are closely intertwined. In Elizabethan England, for example, Archbishop Richard Hooker of the Church of England wrote that "there is not any man of the Church of England but the same man is also a member of the commonwealth; nor any man a member of the commonwealth which is not also of the Church of England." As you can see, the sociological definition of *church* is different from the one commonly used in American society. When Americans talk about "churches," they are actually referring to denominations.

A **denomination** is one of several religious organizations that most members of a society accept as legitimate. Because denominations are not tied to the state, membership in them is voluntary, and competition among them

church
a life-encompassing religious organization to which all members of a society belong

denomination
one of several religious organizations that most members of a society accept as legitimate

The Amish are a religious sect. How does a sect differ from a church, denomination, or cult?

Sociology Today

Understanding the Danger of Cults

In late November 1978, news began to arrive in the United States that a semireligious, socialistic colony in Guyana, South America, headed by the Reverend Jim Jones—founder of the California-based People's Temple—had been the scene of a shocking suicide-murder rite in which some nine hundred people died from cyanide poisoning. Many Americans wondered how people could have become involved in something like that.

Some dismissed the participants as ignorant or mentally unbalanced. But as more news came out, it became known that many of the members were fairly well-educated young people and that Jones was trusted and respected by some members of the California political establishment. We also learned that such events, although rare, have occurred before.

Why are people willing to join extremist religious groups? Sociology can help us understand the motivations.

- *Most converts to extremist religious groups seek friendship, companionship, acceptance, warmth, and recognition.* These groups can provide a supportive community that helps overcome past loneliness and isolation. They can provide emotional ties that converts have not found at home, school, church, or work. Many groups even adopt kinship terms to give recruits new identities to separate them from their former lives.

- *Most extremist religious groups emphasize immediate experience and emotional gratification.* Converts "feel" religion rather than merely think about it. Whether by meditation, speaking in tongues, or singing hymns, followers have frequent and intense emotional experiences they have not found elsewhere.

- *Extremist religious groups emphasize security through strict authority.* Under a firm authority structure and a clear, simple set of beliefs and rules, converts have something in which they can believe. Converts think they can exchange uncertainty, doubt, and confusion for trust and assurance through absolute obedience.

The Reverend Jim Jones was the leader of a religious colony in Guyana, South America, where some nine hundred people were involved in a suicide-murder rite.

Friends and family mourn the loss of loved ones who died in Jim Jones's People's Temple mass suicide.

• *Extremist religious groups claim to offer authenticity and naturalness in an "artificial" world.* By emphasizing such things as natural foods, communal living apart from civilization, and a uniform dress code, these groups attempt to show they are not part of the flawed outside world.

Religious movements may not actually be able to meet their followers' needs any better than the outside world. Many of these religious groups lead to disillusionment, frustration, and bitterness when members realize that they cannot completely escape the outside world, which is full of uncertainty, confusion, fuzzy choices, and shades of gray. Moreover, many of these religious groups have joined the consumer society they profess to deplore, attractively packaging and selling themselves to the public. Not only may the new religious groups not solve the problems people in modern society must face, many are as inauthentic as they accuse society of being.

Some key questions exist to evaluate the authenticity of any religious group's claims. For purposes of self-protection, these questions should be answered carefully before committing to an extremist religious group.

• Does it require that you cut yourself off from family and friends?

• Does it consider drugs to be a major vehicle for true religious experiences?

• Is corporal punishment or intensive, hours-long psychological conditioning a part of its program?

• Does it claim to have special knowledge that can be revealed only to insiders?

If the answer to any *one* of these questions is yes, you stand a chance of getting "hooked." If the answers to *several* of these questions are positive, the chances of getting hooked increase dramatically.

Doing Sociology

1. Do you agree or disagree with the reasons given for why people join extremist religious groups? Discuss each reason and explain why you agree or disagree.

2. Can you think of other reasons why people may be attracted to such groups? Show that any reason you identify does not fit into one of the four reasons stated.

3. If you had a friend considering membership in an extremist religious group, how would you use the information in this Sociology Today to discourage him or her?

sect
a religious organization that arises out of a desire to reform an existing religious organization

cult
a religious organization whose characteristics are not drawn from existing religious traditions within a society

Student Web Activity
Visit the *Sociology and You* Web site at glencoe.com and click on **Chapter 14—Student Web Activities** for an activity on religious organizations.

for members is socially acceptable. Being one religious organization among many, a denomination generally accepts the values and norms of the secular society and the state, although it may at times oppose them. As mentioned, most American "churches"—Methodist, Episcopalian, Presbyterian, Baptist, Roman Catholic, and Reform Jew, for example—are actually denominations.

A **sect** is a religious organization formed when members of an existing religious organization break away in an attempt to reform the "parent" group. Generally, sect members believe that some valuable beliefs or traditions have been lost by the parent organization, and they form their own group to save these features. Thus, they see themselves not as establishing a new religious faith but as redeeming an existing one. The withdrawal of a sect from the parent group is usually psychological, but some sects go farther and form communal groups apart from the larger society. The Separatists, or Pilgrims, who landed at Plymouth in 1620, wished to reform the Church of England from which they had separated. Another example is the Amish, a sect formed in 1693 when a Swiss bishop named Jacob Amman broke from the Mennonite church in Europe (Kraybill and Olshan, 1994). Less extreme sects in the United States today include the Seventh-Day Adventists, the Quakers, and the Assemblies of God.

Unlike a sect, a **cult** is a religious organization whose characteristics are not drawn from existing religious traditions within a society. Whether imported from outside the society or created within the society, cults bring something new to the larger religious environment. We often think of cults as engaging in extreme behavior. The world has been shocked twice in recent years. In 1997, reports came of the ritualistic suicides of thirty-nine members of the Heaven's Gate cult in California (Thomas, 1997). Dwarfing this incident was the mass killing of approximately 1,000 members of the Ugandan cult called the

In 1997, thirty-nine members of the Heaven's Gate cult in California committed ritualistic suicide. Most cults are not this dangerous, however.

Calvin and Hobbes are engaged in a conversation about religiosity. Their beliefs are clashing.

Movement for the Restoration of the Ten Commandments of God in March 2000. Cults do not usually appear in such an extreme and bizarre form, however. More conventional examples of cults are the Unification Church, the Divine Light Mission, and the Church of Scientology (Clark, 1993).

Religiosity

Sociologists Charles Glock and Rodney Stark are two sociologists who have studied religion and society. Their work has focused on **religiosity**— the types of religious attitudes and behavior people display in their everyday lives.

religiosity
ways in which people express their religious interests and convictions

How do people display religiosity? Glock and Stark identify five dimensions of religiosity: belief, ritual, an intellectual dimension, experience, and consequences (Glock, 1965; Stark, 1968).

- *Belief* refers to what a person considers to be true. People may, for example, believe that Jesus is the son of God or that there is no God but Allah.

- A *ritual* is a religious practice that the members of a religion are expected to perform. A ritual may be private, such as personal prayer, or public, such as attending mass.

- The *intellectual dimension* of religiosity may involve knowledge of holy or sacred scripture or an interest in such religious aspects of human existence as evil, suffering, and death. Religious persons are expected to be knowledgeable about their faith.

- *Experience* encompasses certain feelings attached to religious expression. This dimension is the hardest to measure. For example, a religious believer may feel "close" to the deity when praying.

The display of religious affiliation varies widely. Golfer Tiger Woods wears a Buddha image, and a Jewish boy reads from the Torah at his Bar Mitzvah.

Snapshot of America

Public Charities

No matter their religion, Americans tend to believe it is important to help people less fortunate than themselves. In 2004 alone, individuals and businesses in the United States contributed nearly $1.4 trillion to more than 820,000 public charities. This map shows the number of public charities based in each state.

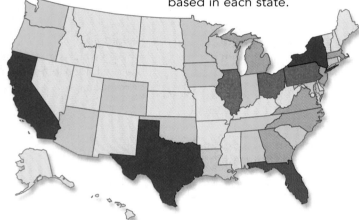

Number of Public Charities

- 50,000 or more
- 40,000–49,999
- 30,000–39,999
- 20,000–29,999
- 10,000–19,999
- 1,000–9,999

Interpreting the Map

1. Which states have the most public charities? Why do you think these states have the most charities?

2. About how many public charities are based in your state? In neighboring states?

Source: National Center for Charitable Statistics, 2004.

- *Consequences* are the decisions and commitments people make as a result of religious beliefs, rituals, knowledge, or experiences. Consequences may be social, such as opposing or supporting capital punishment, or personal, as when practicing sexual abstinence before marriage or telling the truth regardless of the cost.

Section 3 Assessment

1. In your own words, describe the difference between a cult and a sect.

2. Give one example of each of the five dimensions of religiosity, using examples not given in the text.

Critical Thinking

3. **Summarizing Information** Of the dimensions of religiosity discussed in the text, which do you think is most important to denominations today? Give reasons for your answer.

Religion in the United States

Section Preview

Through the process of secularization, the sacred and the profane tend to become intermixed. There has been a revival of religious fundamentalism in the United States. Religious faiths can be analyzed by major social characteristics such as class and political tendencies.

Key Terms

- **secularization** (p. 482)
- **fundamentalism** (p. 485)

The Development of Religion in America

The search for religious freedom was only one of many reasons Puritan colonists came to America—but it was an important one. From the outset, the Puritans viewed themselves as a religious example for the world to follow and admire. Sociologist Robert Bellah has described the American religious connection this way:

> *In the beginning, and to some extent ever since, Americans have interpreted their history as having religious meaning. They saw themselves as being a "people" in the classical and biblical sense of the word. They hoped they were a people of God (Bellah et al. 1992:2).*

The U.S. guarantees religious freedom. Pictured clockwise from the bottom left are a Hindu priest in Ohio, an Islamic prayer group in Maine, a Baptist congregation in Alabama, and a Jewish Chanukah celebration in Maryland.

The framers of the U.S. Constitution seldom raised arguments against religious faith. They were, however, sharply critical of any entanglement between religion and the state. Indeed, the ideas of separation of church and state and freedom of religious expression are cornerstones of American life. Despite this tradition, people in the United States have experienced incidents of religious persecution, including some directed at immigrant groups.

Religion has always been of great importance in American life; but historically, it has played a more active part in some periods than in others. There have been several "Awakenings" in U.S. history when religious principles have guided the development of culture and society. The 1830s, for example, saw new life come to many religious reform movements, including those against slavery and drinking alcohol. Later, the Protestant-led temperance movement resulted in the outlawing of alcohol for a short period during the 1920s.

Secularization in the United States

● **secularization**
process through which the sacred loses influence over society

Countering the growth of religion in U.S. history is **secularization.** Through this process, the sacred loses influence over society, or aspects of the sacred enter into the secular (profane) world of everyday life. For example, formal education originally was a function of religion. Most early teachers and professors were clerics and church members. Over time in the United States, this function was taken over by the state, although many church-sponsored schools still exist.

Is secularization destroying religion in the United States?

Evidence is mixed concerning the relative importance of religion in the United States today. On the one hand, some findings indicate a decline in the importance of religion. The percentage of Americans claiming that religion is very important in their lives fell from 75 percent in 1952 to 57 percent in 2005. (See Figure 14.4.) Scores on the Princeton Religion Index, made up of eight leading indicators, have also declined since the 1940s. In 1957, 14 percent of the public indicated that they believed religion was losing influence on American life. In 2005, 46 percent of the public saw a loss of influence (Gallup, 2005).

On the other hand, some recent research has found Americans today to still be highly committed to religion. Whether measured by the number of churches per capita, the proportion of regular church-goers, or financial support of the churches, sociologist Theodore Caplow observed a trend toward greater involvement in religious affairs (Caplow, 1998).

Figure 14.4 Percentage of Americans Saying Religion Is Very Important in Their Lives: 1952–2005
This figure tracks changes in the percentage of Americans who say that religion is very important in their lives. Why do you think the percentage was so high in the early 1950s? What prediction do you make for the next ten years?

Source: The Gallup Organization, Gallup polls on religion.

Figure 14.5 — Global Comparisons in Religiosity

This table compares the level of religiosity among selected industrialized countries.
Which finding do you think is the most important? Which finding is the most surprising to you? Explain in both cases.

Consider Selves Religious Persons		Attend Church at Least Weekly		Average Ratings of Importance of God*	
Italy	83%	Ireland	82%	United States	8.2
United States	81	United States	43	Ireland	8.0
Ireland	64	Spain	41	Northern Ireland	7.5
Spain	63	Italy	36	Italy	6.9
Great Britain	58	West Germany	21	Spain	6.4
West Germany	58	Czechoslovakia	17	Finland	6.2
Hungary	56	Ethnic Lithuanians	15	Belgium	5.9
France	51	Non-ethnic Lithuanians	12	Great Britain	5.7
Non-ethnic Lithuanians	50	Great Britain	14	West Germany	5.7
Czechoslovaks	49	Hungary	13	Norway	5.4
Scandinavia	46	France	12	Netherlands	5.3
Ethnic Lithuanians	45	Scandinavia	5	Hungary	4.8
				France	4.7
				Denmark	4.4

Source: *Religion in America*, (Princeton, NJ: Princeton Religion Research Center).   *"10" is of highest importance.

In fact, as suggested in the Applying Sociology feature opening this chapter, America still appears to be a religious nation when compared with other industrialized countries (see Figure 14.5). Only 9 percent of the American population is without a religious preference. About 76 percent identify themselves as Protestants, Catholics, or Jews. There are now over three hundred recognized denominations and sects and thousands of independent congregations in the United States (Linder, 2002). About seven in ten Americans belong to a church, a synagogue, or mosque, and over half of these claim to be active in their congregations. Four Americans in ten claim they have attended a church or synagogue in a typical week. (In England, for example, the average weekly church attendance is 14 percent.) Furthermore, although the proportion of Americans belonging to a church, synagogue, or mosque has declined slightly from a high of 76 percent in 1947 to 66 percent in 2005, church attendance has changed very little over the years. Since 1939, weekly church or synagogue attendance in the United States has remained relatively stable—from 41 percent to 44 percent in 2005.

Americans also tend to support traditional religious beliefs. Ninety-four percent of the American population believe in God or a universal spirit, 65 per-

Survey Research: The Electronic Church

Old-time religious evangelists traveled from community to community and preached to the faithful in tents, open fields, or rented meeting halls. Modern-day communications technology has changed all that. To a great extent, radio, television, and the Internet are replacing the traditional meeting places.

Although the "electronic church" (church attendance through telecommunications) has attracted considerable attention, disagreement exists as to the actual size of its audience and the extent of its impact. Many television evangelists claim to have very large audiences, but most rating services estimate the total religious television audience to be of a rather modest size, approximately ten to thirteen million viewers.

William Stacey and Anson Shupe (1982) have advanced sociological understanding of the electronic church by examining the characteristics of its viewers. They surveyed residents of the Dallas–Fort Worth metropolitan area. This area is often referred to as the "buckle" of the southern Bible Belt.

Stacey and Shupe found regular viewers to have relatively low incomes and less than a high school education. Viewers also tended to be female, to be over thirty-five years of age, and to have large families. Blue-collar workers were more likely than white-collar workers to watch, but retired persons and homemakers were more likely to be viewers than people with jobs.

People who attended church regularly tended to watch, an important finding because it contradicted the claim that the electronic church was depriving local churches of members. Fundamentalists were more likely than reformed or moderate believers to tune in. The electronic church preaches to the converted who are already predisposed, or self-selected, to seek out its messages.

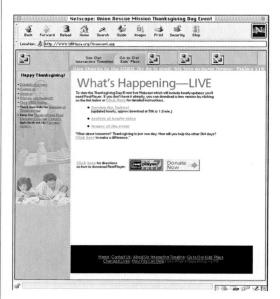

Along with the more "traditional" forms of radio and television, the Internet also offers remote religious services.

Working with the Research

1. According to Stacey and Shupe's research, what demographic groups are most likely to watch religious programming?

2. Would you predict that the electronic church will have greater social impact in the future? Why or why not?

cent believe in life after death, 81 percent believe in heaven, and 70 percent believe in hell. Seventy-eight percent believe in the existence of angels (Gallup, 2004).

Religious Preferences

What are the religious preferences in the U.S.?
Although there are over three hundred denominations and sects in the United States, Americans in the early 2000s were largely Protestant (50 percent) and belonged to a few major denominations—Baptist (16 percent), Methodist (8 percent), Lutheran (5 percent),

Religious Organizations in the U.S.	Number of Members
Roman Catholic Church	66,407,105
Southern Baptist Convention	16,247,736
United Methodist Church	8,251,042
Jewish	6,150,000
Lutheran Church in America	5,038,006
Muslim	4,600,000
Buddist	2,900,000
Episcopal Church	2,333,628
Churches of Christ	1,500,000
Hindu	1,130,000
Jehovah's Witnesses	1,022,397
Seveth-Day Adventist	918,882
Christian Church (Disciples of Christ)	786,334
Church of the Nazarene	643,649
Salvation Army	454,982
Wisconsin Evangelical Lutheran Synod	403.345
Reformed Church in America	281,475

Presbyterian (3 percent), and Episcopalian (2 percent). Sixteen percent prefer various other Protestant denominations. Catholics constitute a relatively large proportion of the American population (24 percent) and Jews a relatively small proportion (2 percent). As noted earlier, only 9 percent of Americans have no religious preference (Gallup, 2004). Figure 14.6 lists many of the religious organizations in the United States with memberships above 300,000.

Figure 14.6 Membership in Selected Religious Organizations in the United States
On the basis of these data, how would you describe the religious composition of the U.S.?

Source: *World Almanac and Book of Facts, 2005.*

Fundamentalism in America

Any careful observer of religion in the United States over the past twenty-five years or so will note the rise of religious *fundamentalism* in the country, especially among Protestant denominations. **Fundamentalism** is based on the desire to resist secularization and to adhere closely to traditional religious beliefs, rituals, and doctrines. It is, of course, inaccurate to limit fundamentalism to Protestants alone. Fundamentalism is found in all religions, including the Roman Catholic, Jewish, and Muslim faiths. This discussion, however, will focus on Protestant fundamentalism.

It is not surprising that most fundamentalists are politically conservative, given that the roots of contemporary religious fundamentalism are in the latter part of the nineteenth century. Two issues disturbed the early fundamentalists. First, fundamentalists were concerned about the spread of secularism. Science was challenging the Bible as a source of truth; Marxism was portraying religion as an opiate for the masses; Darwinism was challenging the biblical interpretation of creation; and religion in general was losing its traditionally strong influence on all social institutions. Second, fundamentalists rejected the movement away from emphasis on the traditional message of Christianity toward an emphasis on social service (Johnstone, 2003).

Since the late 1960s, many of the largest American Protestant denominations—Methodists, Lutherans, Presbyterians, Episcopalians—have either been declining in membership or fighting to hold their own. In contrast, contemporary fundamentalist denominations have been growing. Fundamentalists

● **fundamentalism**
the resistance of secularization and the rigid adherence to traditional religious beliefs, rituals, and doctrines

Figure 14.7
American Church Membership Trends: 1990–1999
Do you believe that this pattern has continued in the twenty-first century? Explain your conclusion using text materials.

Source: *Yearbook of American and Canadian Churches, 1999.*

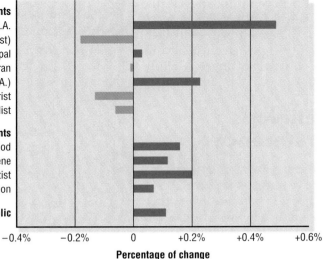

Mainline Protestants		
National Baptist Convention, U.S.A.		
Christian Church (Disciples of Christ)		
Episcopal		
Evangelical Lutheran		
Presbyterian (U.S.A.)		
United Church of Christ		
United Methodist		
Conservative Protestants		
Assembly of God		
Church of the Nazarene		
Seventh-Day Adventist		
Southern Baptist Convention		
Roman Catholic		

−0.4%　−0.2%　0　+0.2%　+0.4%　+0.6%
Percentage of change

This charismatic minister in Atlanta is engaged in faith healing.

exist in all Protestant organizations, but they are predominantly found in such religious bodies as the Mormons, the Assemblies of God, the Seventh-Day Adventists, the Baptists, and the Jehovah's Witnesses. (See Figure 14.7.)

What is the nature of fundamentalism today? The theological agenda of today's fundamentalists is very close to that of their forebears in the nineteenth century.

Fundamentalists believe in the literal truth of the Scriptures, or in taking the Bible at "face value." Protestant fundamentalism involves being "born again" through acceptance of Jesus Christ as the Son of God who was sent to redeem mankind through his sacrifice. Fundamentalist doctrine includes belief in the responsibility of all believers to give witness for God, the presence of Satan as an active force for evil, and the destruction of the world prior to the Messiah's return to establish His kingdom on earth.

Are all fundamentalists alike? Religious organizations that share in much of the fundamentalist theology have some unique beliefs and practices of their own. An example is neo-Pentacostalism—or the *charismatic movement,* as it is sometimes called—which has occurred for the most part within traditional religious organizations, particularly the Roman Catholic and Episcopal churches. Those involved in this movement often speak of receiving "the baptism of the Holy Spirit." But central to most neo-Pentecostal groups is the experience of "speaking in tongues," which believers claim is a direct gift of the Holy Spirit (Cox, 1992, 1996; Hunt, Hamilton, and Walter, 1998).

Why is fundamentalism so strong today? Several reasons for the growth of fundamentalism have been proposed.

- Many Americans feel their world is out of control. The social order of the 1950s was shattered by a string of traumatic events beginning with the civil rights movement and progressing through campus violence, political assassinations, the Vietnam War, and Watergate. Increases in substance abuse, illegitimate births, divorce, and crime are taken as signs of moral decline. Fundamental religion, with its absolute answers and promise of eternal life, provides a strong anchor in a confusing, bewildering world.

- Fundamentalist churches, by emphasizing warmth, love, and caring, provide solace to people who are witnessing and experiencing the weakening of family and community ties. Mainline churches tend to be more formal and impersonal.

- Fundamentalist churches offer what they consider a more purely sacred environment, in contrast to mainline denominations that fundamentalists see as accommodating to secular society.

- The electronic church, in its role as part of the mass media, has been an important contributing factor in the growth of religious fundamentalism. (See Focus on Research on page 484.)

Religion, Class, and Politics

Religious affiliation is related to social class. There are marked differences, for example, in social class (as measured by education and income) among the more traditional religions in the United States. Generally speaking, Presbyterians, Episcopalians, and Jews are at the top of the stratification structure. Below them are Lutherans, Catholics, and Methodists, followed by Baptists. Because these are average figures, there are many individual exceptions to these rankings.

Differences in religiosity exist between the upper and lower classes as well. Religion is important at both ends of the stratification structure, but the upper and lower classes express their beliefs in different ways. The upper classes display their religiosity through church membership, church attendance, and observance of ritual, whereas people in the lower classes more often pray privately and have emotional religious experiences.

Political affiliation, too, is related to religion. Followers of the Jewish faith are particularly aligned with the Democratic Party, followed in strength of support by Catholics and Protestants. This is predictable, because Protestants generally are more politically conservative than Catholics or Jews, and the Democratic Party is generally not associated with political conservatism in the United States today. Of the major Protestant denominations, the greatest support for the Republican Party is found among Episcopalians and Presbyterians. This is hardly surprising, because the upper classes are more likely to be identified with the Republican Party.

There are some contradictions in this general pattern. Despite their affiliation with the more conservative Republican Party, Episcopalians and Presbyterians are less conservative than Baptists, who are the strongest supporters of the Democratic Party of all Protestant denominations, especially in the South.

Religion, Science, and Society

Both science and religion examine humanity's relationship to the world, but they examine it in very different ways. Religion involves matters beyond human observation, while science is all about observation. These fields of study are not mutually exclusive. Many scientists are religious individuals, while many professional clergy appreciate and support the intellectual achievements of the field of science.

Sometimes, however, these two institutions can appear to be in conflict. Depending on the values and norms of the culture, society may favor religious or scientific explanations. In the United States, following the principle

Religion and science sometimes come into heated conflict. One famous case was the 1925 "Monkey Trial" of John Thomas Scopes in Tennessee.

of separation of state and church, it has been common to keep religion apart from government-sponsored institutions. Scientific explanations for natural phenomena, when commonly accepted, have been taught in the schools, leaving religious groups free to teach other interpretations within their organizations.

Strict fundamentalists do not believe that scientific theories such as the theory of evolution and the Big Bang theory of creation should be presented in public schools as facts, while Bible-based explanations such as creationism and intelligent design are not even discussed. In 1999, fundamentalists convinced the Kansas Board of Education to remove any questions about evolution from the state high school exit examination. Until the decision was repealed in 2001, Kansas teachers were not required to teach the theory of evolution. In 2005, the U.S. Supreme Court agreed to hear a case brought against the Dover County, Pennsylvania, School board, which required high school biology teachers to read students a statement questioning Darwin's theory of evolution before discussing it.

Today, many people are questioning whether "pure science" can remain independent of cultural or social norms, as some scientists believe. Scientific discoveries and processes, such as cloning and gene therapy, are moving into ever more ethically debatable areas. The result appears obvious: the interface between science and religion is sure to increase. Society, in particular government, will need to learn how to deal constructively with apparent contradictions in these two areas.

Section 4 Assessment

1. What is secularization and why is it an important process to explore?

2. Describe the relationship between religion and political allegiance in the U.S.

Critical Thinking

3. **Analyzing Information** Analyze how progress in scientific research will affect religious beliefs and practices over the next twenty-five years.

Summary

Section 1: Religion and Sociology

Main Idea: Religion is concerned with sacred things. Sociologists studying religion do not judge the religions but rather look at the societal aspects of religion.

Section 2: Theoretical Perspectives

Main Idea: Religion has several functions. It legitimates the structure of society, promotes social unity, and provides a sense of meaning and belonging.

Section 3: Religious Organization and Religiosity

Main Idea: The major forms of religious organization are churches, denominations, sects, and cults. Religiosity—the ways people express their religious interests and convictions—can be analyzed in terms of five dimensions: belief, ritual, intellect, experience, and consequences.

Section 4: Religion in the United States

Main Idea: Religious faiths can be analyzed by major social charactersitcis, such as social class and political ideology

Self-Check Quiz
Visit the *Sociology and You* Web site at glencoe.com and click on **Chapter 14—Self-Check Quizzes** to prepare for the chapter test.

Reviewing Vocabulary

Complete each sentence using each term once.

a. religion
b. sacred
c. profane
d. legitimate
e. spirit of capitalism
f. Protestant ethic
g. church
h. denomination
i. sect
j. cult
k. religiosity
l. secularization
m. fundamentalism

1. _____ is the word used to describe things and ideas that are set apart and given a special meaning.
2. A religious movement based on the desire to adhere closely to traditional beliefs, rituals, and doctrines is called _____ .
3. The _____ are the nonsacred aspects of life.
4. _____ is the name given to a cluster of values, norms, beliefs, and attitudes that favored the growth of capitalism.
5. _____ means to justify or give official approval to.
6. A religious organization arising out of a desire to reform another religious organization is called _____ .
7. _____ is the obligation to reinvest money rather than spend it.
8. _____ is the name given to a life-encompassing religious organization to which all members of a society belong.
9. A unified system of beliefs and practices concerned with sacred things is called _____ .
10. The ways in which people express their religious interests and convictions is called _____ .
11. A _____ is a religious organization whose characteristics are not drawn from existing religious tradition within a society.

Reviewing the Facts

12. Religious faiths can be analyzed by two major social characteristics. What are those characteristics?

13. Based on Figure 14.4 on page 482, has the percentage of Americans who claim that religion is very important in their lives decreased over time, increased over time, or showed no significant change?

14. How does the upper social class define its religiosity? Use the diagram below to record your answer.

Religiosity as Defined by the Upper Class

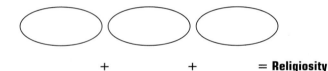

+   +   = **Religiosity**

15. In 1978, the Reverend Jim Jones led hundreds of people who belonged to his group in a mass suicide-murder. What term is used to describe Jones's religious organization?

Thinking Critically

16. Making Inferences

The crucifix is a widely known symbol even to non-Christians. How do the various meanings attached to this symbol relate to an understanding of Durkheim's concept of the sacred and profane? Could the crucifix easily represent other things if it was not for its relationship to Christ? Explain your answer.

17. Drawing Conclusions

Current research says that religion often reflects conventional (traditional) norms. Accordingly, religious clergy tend to address their messages to the more traditional segments of society. Sermons, for example, are aimed at the typical married family arrangement (mother, father, two children). What effect, if any, do you think this could have on general attendance?

David Sipress/Cartoonbank.com

18. Analyzing Visuals

In this chapter, you read about many of the functions religions and religious feeling fulfill in society. How would you describe the function filled by religion depicted in the cartoon above? Do you think the cartoon aims to elevate or bring down the idea of prayer?

19. Analyzing Information

Do you think that economic decisions are influenced by religiously based motivations? Elaborate.

20. Applying Concepts

Many people appear to be less interested in religion during their teenage years. This might be seen in falling church attendance for this age group. Using your sociological imagination, suggest some reasons for this apparent lack of interest. Consider developmental (age) and social factors. Depending on your answers, what suggestions might you make to religious organizations looking for ideas on how to keep teenagers involved and active?

Sociology Projects

21. Survey Research

People have different attitudes toward different religions as demonstrated by the table below. Design a survey that would allow you to conduct an informal study of student attitudes toward religion. Remember that your questions should be directed at social practices and not at the specific beliefs. Be careful to ask questions that respect religious belief. Compare your answers with those in the table below. In class, discuss the results of the survey and whether you found distinctive attitudes toward religions among teens compared to adults.

General Opinions Toward Religious Groups		
	Favorable	Unfavorable
Methodists	90%	10%
Presbyterians	88	12
Jes	88	12
Lutherans	85	15
Episcopalians	85	15
Catholics	85	15
Evangelical Christians	76	24
Muslim Americas	65	35
American Buddhists	60	40
Atheists	34	66

Source: *Pew Research Center, 2001*

22. Researching Religions

Choose a religion, denomination, sect, or cult to research. You can learn about the group by talking with some of its members. You can also find excellent material in libraries and on the Internet. In your research, focus on the following aspects of the group: its origin; fundamental beliefs, important rituals or ceremonies; internal social changes that occurred over time; and membership demographics (social class, ethnicity, and so forth). Based on your research, prepare a report with visual aids that can be given orally.

23. Charitable Organizations

Contact a religious organization in your neighborhood, and arrange to take part in some community service activity in which this organization is involved. Pay close attention to the various ways in which these groups conduct charitable work. Report to the class on the effectiveness of your service—both for the recipient and for yourself. Then consider how your community would be affected if the group stopped providing this service. Would some political or non-governmental organization continue it?

24. Defining and Analyzing Religion

This exercise will help you understand the difficulty social scientists have when it comes to defining and analyzing religion. Take out a piece of paper and answer the following questions:

a. How do you define religion?

b. What does it mean to you?

c. Do you believe in the supernatural?

d. If you do believe in the supernatural, how do you imagine it to be?

After everyone in class has completed these questions, turn to your neighbor and compare your answers with his or her answers. Note the similarities and differences. Share your answers with as many of your classmates as possible.

Technology Activity

25. Using your school or local library and the Internet, research information on the clergy during the middle ages. Based on your research and the material you read in this chapter, how would you classify their religious organization? Some of the characteristics of the clergy might be regarded as a cult. Explain why the clergy in the middle ages were not a cult. Using proper grammar, sentence structure, spelling, and punctuation, write a paragraph defending your conclusion.

Enrichment Reading

India's Sacred Cow
by Marvin Harris

People often take their own religion for granted, overlooking its connections with the rest of society. We are better able to see the link between religious beliefs and culture when we examine an unfamiliar setting. Marvin Harris's analysis of the place of the cow in Hinduism provides such a backdrop.

News photographs that came out of India during the famine of the late 1960s showed starving people stretching out bony hands to beg for food while sacred cattle strolled behind undisturbed. The Hindu, it seems, would rather starve to death than eat his cow or even deprive it of food. The cattle appear to browse unhindered through urban markets eating an orange here, a mango there, competing with people for meager supplies of food.

By Western standards, spiritual values seem more important to Indians than life itself. Specialists in food habits . . . consider Hinduism an irrational **ideology** that compels people to overlook abundant, nutritious foods for scarcer, less healthful foods.

Cow worship . . . carries over into politics. In 1966 a crowd of 120,000 people, led by holy men, demonstrated in front of the Indian House of Parliament in support of the All-Party Cow Protection Campaign Committee. In Nepal, the only **contemporary** Hindu kingdom, cow slaughter is severely punished. As one story goes, the car driven by an official of a United States agency struck and killed a cow. In order to avoid the international incident that would have occurred when the official was arrested for murder, the Nepalese magistrate concluded that the cow had committed suicide. . . .

The easy explanation for India's devotion to the cow, the one most Westerners and Indians would offer, is that cow worship is an integral part of Hinduism. Religion is somehow good for the soul, even it if sometimes fails the body. Religion orders the cosmos and explains our place in the universe. Religious beliefs, many would claim, have existed for thousands of years and have a life of their own. They are not understandable in scientific terms.

But all this ignores history. There is more to be said for cow worship than is immediately apparent. The earliest Vedas, the Hindu sacred texts from the second millennium B.C., do not prohibit the slaughter of cattle. Instead, they ordain it as part of sacrificial rites. The early Hindus did not avoid the flesh of cows and bulls; they ate it at ceremonial feasts presided over by Brahman priests. Cow worship is a relatively recent development in India; it evolved as the Hindu religion developed and changed.

This evolution is recorded in royal **edicts** and religious texts written during the last 3,000 years of Indian history. The Vedas from the first millennium b.c. contain contradictory passages, some referring to ritual

- **ideology**
  a systematic body of thought about human culture or society

- **contemporary**
  modern, current

- **edict**
  official proclamation or law

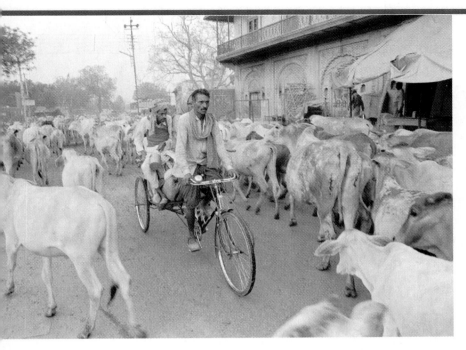

Anthropologist Marvin Harris contends that science and culture can explain the reason cows are sacred to Hindus. How does he attempt to support his claim?

- **exhorted**
  strongly urged

- **venerate**
  worship or revere

- **ascertain**
  determine

- **politically expedient**
  based on practical or advantageous reasons

slaughter and others to a strict taboo on beef consumption. . . . [M]any of the sacred-cow passages were incorporated into the texts by priests of a later period.

By 200 A.D. the status of Indian cattle had undergone a spiritual transformation. The Brahman priesthood **exhorted** the population to **venerate** the cow and forbade them to abuse it or to feed on it. Religious feasts involving the ritual slaughter and consumption of livestock were eliminated and meat eating was restricted to the nobility.

By 1000 A.D., all Hindus were forbidden to eat beef. Ahimsa, the Hindu belief in the unity of all life, was the spiritual justification for this restriction. But it is difficult to **ascertain** exactly when this change occurred. An important event that helped to shape the modern complex was the Islamic invasion, which took place in the eighth century A.D. Hindus may have found it **politically expedient** to set themselves off from the invaders, who were beefeaters, by emphasizing the need to prevent the slaughter of their sacred animals. Thereafter, the cow taboo assumed its modern form and began to function much as it does today.

Source: Excerpted from James M. Henslin, *Down to Earth Sociology: Introductory Readings,* 10th ed., The Free Press, 1999.

Read and React

1. Summarize your understanding (prior to reading this article) of the Hindu religious belief about cows. Has your opinion changed after reading it? Why or why not?

2. How do non-Hindu people's reactions to the sacred cow relate to ethnocentrism and cultural relativism? Explain in each case, drawing on material in the reading.

Chapter

15 Sport

Sections

1. **The Nature of Sport**
2. **Theoretical Perspectives and Sport**
3. **Social Issues in Sport**

Learning Objectives

After reading this chapter, you will be able to

- justify sport as an American institution.
- compare and contrast sport in America from a functionalist, conflict, and symbolic interactionist perspective.
- understand the relationship between American sport and social mobility.
- cite evidence of sexism and racism in American sport.

Applying Sociology

All of a sudden I find I'm stronger than anyone else in the place—all the girls and practically all of the guys . . . . The boys respected me right away, and that's important. They all act like they're so tough, then you go in and lift more than they can. They can't ignore that there's a girl over in the corner doing more than them . . . .

As this quote from a young power lifter shows, participating in a sport can positively affect a girl's self-image. Achieving this benefit was one of the motivations behind passage of Title IX of the 1972 Educational Amendment Act. The law made gender discrimination illegal in any educational institution that received federal funds. Since 1972, more and more girls and young women have participated in athletic programs. Critics argue that male athletic programs have suffered as a result, but others say females can gain opportunities without adversely affecting those of males (Hannon, 2003).

Some sociologists refer to social institutions such as sport and the entertainment industry as *secondary institutions.* This chapter looks at how sport affects American society.

Chapter Overview
Visit the *Sociology and You* Web site at glencoe.com and click on **Chapter 15— Chapter Overviews** to preview chapter information.

The Nature of Sport

Key Terms

- sport *(p. 496)*
- sport subculture *(p. 500)*

- **sport**
  a set of competitive activities in which winners and losers are determined by physical performance within a set of established rules

Section Preview

As a social institution, sport fulfills some important societal needs. One of these is helping individuals identify with other members of society. Sport subcultures have developed around both team and individual sports. For this reason, sport is a reflection of society.

A Definition of Sport

For most people, sport consists of certain leisure activities, exercise, and spectator events. It is actually more complex than that. Sociologists define **sport** as a set of competitive activities in which winners and losers are determined by physical performance within a set of established rules. While sport is an important aspect of recreation, many forms of recreation do not involve sport. Sport sociologist Jay J. Coakley (2004) sees a spontaneous race between two skiers as more of a contest than a sport. Although a contest between skiers involves physical activity and competition, it does not involve definite rules or standardized conditions.

Sport as a Social Institution

Institutions fulfill certain basic needs and reflect the most important aspects of a society. The five most commonly recognized social institutions have been examined in preceding chapters: family, education, government, economic systems, and religion. Although these social institutions take different forms in different societies, they appear in every society because they fulfill needs common to all societies.

What is the difference between a sport and a game?

Sport teaches basic values and aids in socialization.

Because societies have additional needs, there are additional social institutions. Sport is one of these. Sport teaches some of the basic values of society. It also promotes attachment to society. For example, a society requires that its members identify with it. Members must feel that belonging to the society is an important part of who they are. Sport aids in this identification of self with society.

Chariot racing in ancient Rome is a clear illustration of this social identification. Athletes would risk their lives in this dangerous sport in part to reflect their self-identification as Romans.

> *The individual, even when free, did not belong to himself; he was strictly subordinated to the city. His life, his death, were only episodes in the history of the group. To confront death was not an act of exceptional heroism; it was the normal way of proving oneself a Roman (Auguet, 1972:198).*

Sport, Culture, and Society

Sport plays a central role in American society in part because it reflects the culture's emphasis on achievement.

> *People who visit the United States from other countries are often amazed at the extent to which competition [in sport] is used to distribute rewards and evaluate the work of human beings (Coakley, 2004:82).*

As women's place in American society changes, their place in sport also changes. Women's soccer and basketball teams in particular have received a great deal of attention in recent years.

The prevailing American view of sport is the one reportedly expressed by the late Vince Lombardi, coach of the Green Bay Packers of the National Football League during the 1960s: "Winning is not everything. It is the only thing." For the most part, sport continues to be dominated by achievement-oriented values.

Sport reflects society, so it is not surprising that males dominate the sports world just as they do many other aspects of American society. Females are second to men overall in power, income, and job opportunities in sports just as they are in business, education, medicine, and law (Eitzen, 2003).

Some progress toward equality is being made, however, especially on the college level. The women's basketball teams at both the University of Tennessee and the University of Connecticut have at different times held the best single season record in men's or women's basketball history. Women are making inroads in professional golf and tennis, and the women's professional basketball league (WNBA) has many fans. Women's place in athletics was given a healthy boost in 1999 when Mia Hamm and her teammates won soccer's World Cup. Equality of opportunity for women in sports, though, remains a distant goal.

Racing in Rome

The chariot races of the Roman Empire, made famous in America by the movie Ben Hur, *involved considerable skill and courage. Charioteers delivered the violence required to please the crowd.*

At the end of a race, the charioteers drove abreast, wheel against wheel, for the whole length of the track, whipping their horses madly to gain the half-length which might assure their victory. At this point skill turned into pure violence; each charioteer was no longer content merely to hamper his adversary but took the risk of overturning him by driving his chariot against him in order to break its axle, or of destroying him by whipping his horses into the rear of his chariot. To ward off his maneuver the charioteer so threatened no longer leaned forward but literally "hung on the necks of his horses." He had no need to turn round to see what was happening. He could already feel the breath of his pursuers and the rhythmic shock of their hooves shaking the back of his chariot. A few seconds later, if he had not succeeded in gaining a little ground, there would no longer be either rival, chariot or team, but only an amorphous mass littering the middle of the track.

It was the most spectacular and most popular of all the events of the circus; so much that charioteers did their utmost to involve their rivals in this maneuver in front of the imperial box. For a Roman it summed up all the poetry of the circus; with a sharp, dry crack the fragile box carrying a man was reduced to powder at full speed; the overheated axle collapsed and splinters flew in all directions; the horses crashed into the sand head over heels in a clutter of straps or, seized with panic, broke away from the harness which held them. Before the final catastrophe, the charioteer had to draw the dagger at his waist and cut the reins which, wound about him, bound him to his team; if he succeeded in doing this he had a chance of emerging from the wreck merely bruised, his body full of splinters.

But sometimes he was pitched out head first by the violence of the impact. Then he had no time for this simple act and, if the horses did not fall, was dragged across the circus. As he wore nothing but a tunic held by a set of straps across the chest, his only protection was a leather helmet, insufficient to save his life in such circumstances. But the aggressor did not always emerge unscathed; at the moment of impact his horses reared up and came down again with their forefeet between the spokes of the wheel of the damaged chariot which was turning in the air; they crashed down, their bones broken, whinnying with pain, and the charioteer, halted in full career, ran the same risks as his rival.

Source: Roland Auguet, *Cruelty and Civilization: The Roman Games* (London: George Allen and Unwin Ltd., 1972), pp. 131–132. Reprinted by permission.

Thinking It Over

Some athletes today engage in "extreme sports" such as sky surfing, street luge, and snowboarding. The criteria for an extreme sport is that it is nonmotorized; has a sanctioning body; is deemed as extreme or unusual; and requires learned skills, conditioning, and practice. Do you think chariot racing of ancient Rome is similar to the extreme sports of today? Why or why not?

Sport Subcultures

sport subculture
a group with distinct roles, values, norms, and beliefs that is organized around a sport activity

The relationship between sport, society, and culture can also be seen in *sport subcultures*. A **sport subculture** is a group within the larger context of sport that has some of its own distinct roles, values, and norms. These subcultures are organized around a sport activity and beliefs vary widely. Sociologist Michael Smith (1979) wanted to know if violence among hockey players is due to involvement in a "subculture of violence." In this kind of subculture, violence is the expected response to a perceived challenge or insult—a jostle, a glance, or an offensive remark. Following this norm is essential in acquiring and maintaining honor, especially when challenges are associated with masculinity.

Smith found that hockey players favor violence more than nonplayers. Because of the expectations of coaches and teammates, many hockey players act violently during games. In fact, players criticize teammates who aren't violent. As one National Hockey League player put it:

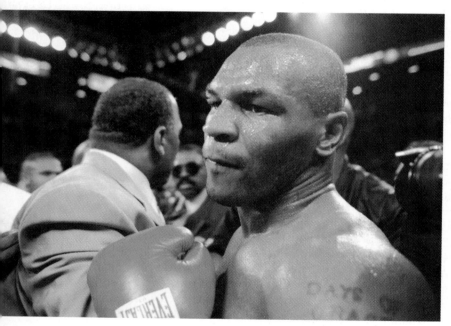

Even though boxing is the essence of a violent sport, former heavyweight champion Mike Tyson broke the rules when he bit opponent Evander Holyfield on the ear. After the incident, boxing officials fined Tyson $3 million and revoked his license.

I don't think that there's anything wrong with guys getting excited in a game and squaring off and throwing a few punches. That's just part of the game. It always has been. And you know if you tried to eliminate it, you wouldn't have hockey any more. You look at hockey from the time it was begun, guys gets excited and just fight, and it's always been like that (Eitzen, 1996:165).

Kent Pearson (1981) researched subcultures involving water-related sports in Australia and New Zealand. He found major cultural differences between surfboard riders and surf lifesavers. Surfboard riders avoid formal organizations, work with loose and flexible definitions of the territory in which their sport will occur, place a heavy emphasis on physical prowess and individualism, and generally oppose the larger society. In contrast, surf lifesaving clubs are highly organized entities that stage competitions involving swimming, boating, and lifesaving. The territory for such competitions is precisely defined, and formal rules are employed.

Even in nonteam sports, subcultures emerge. Thoroughbred jockeys have developed a subculture with a strong emphasis on displaying dignity, poise, and integrity. The ideal within the subculture of jockeys is a fiery animal with a cool rider.

The cool jockey can wait patiently with a horse in a pocket and get through on the inside, risking the possibility that there will be no opening. Coolness is waiting far back in the pack, risking the possibility that his horse will not "get up" in time. Coolness is sparing the whip on a front-running horse when another animal has pressed into the lead, risking the possibility that once his horse is passed he will not get started again. All these activities are taken by observers as instances of a jockey's character. In short, moral character is coolness in risky situations (Scott, 1981:146–147).

What values are at the center of the unique jockey subculture?

Jockeys take such chances partly because their subculture requires it. Jockeys who fail to display gallantry, integrity, and coolness—qualities expected of them by horse owners, trainers, and other jockeys—do not receive their choice of horses and therefore win few races. Failing to take risks leads to lost opportunities.

Section 1 Assessment

1. Do you agree that in order for an activity to be a sport, it should include a defined set of rules? Why or why not?

2. Which of the following is not an example of sport?
   a. a baseball game between two major league teams
   b. a baseball game between two minor league teams
   c. a spontaneous race between two cyclists
   d. a swim meet involving amateur athletes

Critical Thinking

3. **Analyzing Information** Think about sports in your school. How is the cultural value of achievement reflected in the behavior of athletes, peers, teachers, and parents? Give some specific examples.

TECH TRENDS

Mass Media and Sports

Sport fulfills two functions. It teaches some of the basic values of society, and it promotes attachment to society. During televised sports events, the National Collegiate Athletic Association (NCAA) and the National Football League (NFL) regularly show student athletes and professional sports stars working with children and disadvantaged persons, behavior reflecting both of these functions.

How do we square this positive picture of sport with the "dark" side of sport that is continuously fed the public by the mass media? Much of the media coverage of modern sports now focuses on the bad, tough-guy image of athletes, coaches, and owners. Not only is "winning the only thing," as Vince Lombardi, legendary coach of the Green Bay Packers, said. Now, the winners are expected to have an attitude.

Dennis Rodman, a former forward in the National Basketball Association (NBA), gained fame from media attention of his cross-dressing and physical assaults. Former heavyweight boxing champion Mike Tyson achieved negative recognition when he bit off a chunk of an opponent's ear and for a number of other physical attacks.

It is hard to believe that these are the "respectable" sports! The newer events covered by the mass media—such as Roller Derby and Wrestle Mania—are going much further. Look at the names of events that World Wrestling Entertainment (WWE), formerly known as the World Wrestling Federation (WWF), has recently sponsored: "Road Rage Tour" and "Smack-Down." Its biggest television draws include individuals with stage names such as "Boogeyman," "Road Warrior Animal," and "The Undertaker." Women have also achieved star status in wrestling. Former wrestler Chyna was known as "the ninth wonder of the world," and Jacquelyn, two-time women's champion, draws many fans.

So, does mass-media sports coverage reflect basic social values and promote societal identification? Where is the coverage of teamwork, sportsmanship, and character development? Do we simply celebrate with the media the message of unrivaled competition and winning at any cost? At times, it appears the latter is the case, especially when everyday behavior seems to mirror the negative presentation of sport.

Some critics fear that the mass media and entertainment promoters are ruining the integrity of sport in America.

Analyzing the Trends

1. Based on how they are presented in the media, would you analyze sports in America from the functionalist or the conflict theory perspective? What perspective do you believe is reflected in the media presentation of sports?

2. "Fake" wrestling grew in popularity after it began being marketed as sports entertainment. In what ways is the role WWE wrestling plays in society similar to and different from the Roman chariot races?

Theoretical Perspectives and Sport

Section Preview

Functionalists see sport positively, as a means for socializing young people, promoting social integration, providing a release for tensions, and developing sound character. Conflict theorists believe that organized sports can be harmful to character development. Symbolic interactionists focus on the self-concepts and relationships developed through sport activities.

Culture and Sport

S port is a major social activity through which culture is created and reinforced. As noted earlier, sociologists recognize this important aspect of sport.

> *American sport embodies American values—striving for excellence, winning, individual and team competition, and materialism. Parents want their children to participate in sport because participation teaches them the basic values of American society and builds character (Eitzen, 1999:3).*

Although sociologists agree that sport mirrors society, and that the relationship is complex, they disagree over the social implications of sport. Sport sociologist Stanley Eitzen has written a book on the paradoxes, or contradictions, of sport in America. (See Figure 15.1 on page 504.) Functionalists, who tend to concentrate on the benefits of sport, are represented in Eitzen's book. So are conflict theorists, who see a social downside to sport. Symbolic interactionists focus on personal meanings derived from sport.

"WE'RE IN BIG TROUBLE.. THEY PLAY LIKE GIRLS!"

Sport has long been an important basis for stratification in high schools.

Figure 15.1 | Sport Paradoxes

Stanley Eitzen, a highly respected sport sociologist, argues that sport is inherently contradictory. Here are a few of the paradoxes Eitzen identifies. Do you agree with Eitzen that these paradoxes exist?

Social Integration
- Sport can unite different social classes and racial/ethnic groups
  but
- sport can heighten barriers that separate groups.

Fair Play
- Sport promotes fair play by teaching the importance of following the rules
  but
- sport's emphasis on winning tempts people to cheat.

Physical Fitness
- Sport promotes muscle strength, weight control, endurance, and coordination
  but
- sport can lead to the use of steroids and other drugs, excessive weight loss or gain, and injuries.

Academics
- Sport contributes to higher education through scholarships and fund raising
  but
- sport takes money away from academics and emphasizes athletic performance over learning and graduation.

Social Mobility
- Sport allows athletes who might otherwise not attend college to obtain an education
  but
- only a few can achieve the promise of fame and wealth in the professional ranks.

Source: D. Stanley Eitzen, *Fair and Foul* (Lanham, MD: Rowman & Littlefield Publishers, Inc. 2003), pp. 4–7.

Functionalism

How do functionalists view the role of sport in society?
Functionalists think sport is important primarily because it helps society work more smoothly. It does this by performing the following functions (Eitzen and Sage, 2002).

- *Sport teaches basic beliefs, norms, and values.* Sport readies us for adult roles. Games, for instance, prepare participating athletes for work in organizations. Young people who are exposed to competitive sport become more achievement motivated than those who are not. And the earlier the exposure occurs, the higher the orientation towards achievement. This is important because achievement-motivation is essential to productivity in the modern economy.

- *Sport promotes a sense of social identification.* A team binds people to their community and nation. Clevelanders are united in their love of the Browns, Indians, and Cavaliers. During recent baseball seasons, Americans seemed to divide into Red Sox and Yankee fans. The Atlanta Braves have become "America's team." Higher social integration results.

Cleveland Browns fans identified so strongly with their city's football team that the city brought suit to keep the team name and colors from leaving town.

- *Sport offers a safe release of aggressive feelings generated by the frustrations, anxieties, and strains of modern life.* It is socially acceptable to yell and scream for an athletic team. Similar behavior directed at a teacher, principal, parent, or employer can have negative consequences.

- *Sport encourages the development of character.* Coaches, school officials, and parents often draw a parallel between sport and "life." "When the going gets tough, the tough get going" is a sentiment expressed in most locker rooms. The hard work, discipline, and self-sacrifice demanded by team sports become part of an athlete's value system.

What are the social dysfunctions of sport? Functionalists have identified some drawbacks to sport. Because sport reflects society, it draws on achievement-oriented values that can be intensified to an extreme degree (Kohn, 1992). When achievement and winning come to be seen as the primary goals of sport, any method of winning—including violence and cheating—may be encouraged.

We need not look far to see examples of violence in sport. Coaches and fans expect athletes to place their physical well-being on the line. Players in many sports are expected to resort to violence. In high school football, aggressive behavior is defended as preparation for "real-life" competition. Pressures are intensified at the professional level, where many sports have developed the informal role of *enforcer*—a team member whose major responsibility is to intimidate, provoke, and even injure opponents (Coakley, 2004). Boston Bruins hockey player Marty McSorley used his hockey stick to deliver a vicious blindside slash to the head of opposing player Donald Brashear in February of 2000. The attack was the culmination of a game marked by injuries and was the result of the long-standing rivalry between two "top enforcers."

Olympic Success

Sport also plays an important role in today's global society. For some time, the winning of Olympic medals has been a source of regional and global prestige. This map shows the number of medals earned by each country in the 2004 Summer Olympic Games.

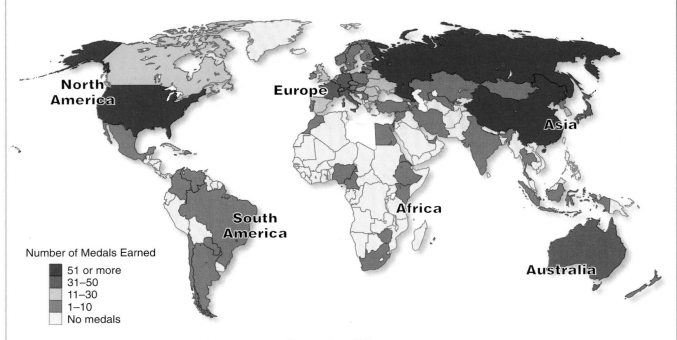

Number of Medals Earned

- 51 or more
- 31–50
- 11–30
- 1–10
- No medals

Source: *The World Almanac and Book of Facts, 2005.*

Interpreting the Map

1. Why do you think there is such wide variation in the number of Olympic medals earned?

2. Do the Olympics illustrate a connection between sport and politics? Explain.

Cheating may not be as easy as violent behavior to identify, but is often present, nonetheless. Cheating was no doubt involved when American Olympic skater Nancy Kerrigan was struck on the right leg with a metal rod by an assailant later linked to her competitor, Tonya Harding. In 2000, the Atlanta Braves were penalized for signing a player before his sixteenth birthday. The use of steroids by professional athletes in any sport is cheating. Cheating can even extend beyond players, as when a Utah state committee used illegal inducements to attract the 2002 Winter Olympics.

Conflict Theory

Some sociologists have raised disturbing questions about the effects of sport on society. These questions are best understood through the conflict perspective. Conflict theorists are interested in who has the power and how elites use power to satisfy their own interests. To conflict theorists, sport is a social institution in which the most powerful oppress, manipulate, coerce, and exploit others. Conflict theorists highlight the ways in which sport mirrors the unequal distribution of power and money in society. They also emphasize the role of sport in maintaining inequality (Cozzillio, 2005).

While functionalists see sport as contributing to the unification of society, conflict theorists do not. While people from all major segments of a community or society may join in cheering for the same team, their union is only temporary.

> *When the game is over, the enthusiasm dies, the solidarity runs short, and disharmony in other relations reasserts itself. Much as one hour a week cannot answer to the religious impulse, one game a week cannot answer to the solidarity needs of a racist, sexist, or elitist society (Young, 1986).*

Basic social class divisions, in other words, will continue to exist and to affect social relationships in a community even if the local team has just won the World Series or the Super Bowl.

The contribution sport makes in forming good character is also questioned by conflict theorists. Among college athletes, studies have shown that the degree of sportsmanship apparently declines as athletes become more involved in the sports system. As sociologist Stanley Eitzen (2004) notes, nonscholarship athletes display greater sportsmanship than those with athletic scholarships, and those who have not earned letters exhibit more sportsmanship than letter winners.

Conflict theorists can point to any number of past and present scandals in both the college and professional ranks. Americans are constantly reading in the sports section of the daily newspaper about athletes, from high school to the professional level, who are taking drugs, cheating in school, or accepting illegitimate cash "gifts." One university after another is being investigated and penalized by the National Collegiate Athletic Association. Coaches as well as players are involved in misconduct.

> *Athletes may use performance-enhancing drugs such as steroids and amphetamines to achieve a "competitive edge." . . . Big-time college coaches in their zeal to win have been found guilty of exploiting athletes, falsifying transcripts, providing illegal payments, hiring surrogate test takers, paying athletes for nonexistent summer jobs, and illegally using government Pell grants and work study monies for athletes. So much, I would argue, for the myth that "sport builds character" (Eitzen, 1996:189).*

In some cultures, sport is so important lives may depend on it. In 1994, Colombian soccer player Andres Escobar was gunned down, apparently for scoring against his own team in the World Cup soccer match against the United States. (Colombia lost, 2–1.)

Symbolic Interactionism

Symbolic interactionism also contributes to our understanding of sport as a social institution. This theoretical perspective concentrates on personal meanings, social relationships, and self-identity processes. Symbolic interactionists are concerned with the symbols of sports. The meanings and interpretations of these symbols are important because they affect the self-concepts, as well as the relationships, of those involved.

The social context of Little League baseball illustrates this perspective. For three years, Gary Alan Fine (1987) studied American adolescent suburban males who played Little League baseball. He discovered and documented a variety of ways in which the boys assigned meanings to their team activities. In addition, he described how these meanings and interpretations influenced the boys' social interactions and affected their self-definitions.

What were these meanings? Much of the activity of coaches and parents centered on teaching the rules of the game and teaching values, such as team play, hard work, fair play, competition, and winning. But these ten- to twelve-year-old boys formed their own interpretations of these messages. The boys misinterpreted the adult values of hard work, competition, and so forth as the "masculine" values of dominance, "toughness," and risky behavior.

How were social interaction and self-concepts affected?
In the first place, the boys' behavior convinced coaches and parents that the youngsters understood and accepted their values. For example, the aggressive behavior that the boys considered as evidence of their masculinity was seen by the coaches and parents as evidence of "hustle," dedication to competition, and the desire to win. The boys were praised for this behavior, which encouraged them to continue it. "Weaker" peers, younger children, and girls in general frequently experienced the disdain of these Little Leaguers. This disrespect often led to a loss of self-esteem for children who suffered the brunt of the Little Leaguers' scorn.

What are some limitations of each perspective? The functionalist perspective makes important points regarding the positive and negative role of sport in society. Its critics, however, contend that many sports have become so closely tied to elite interests that they contribute more to private profit than to the general well-being of society. To investigate this point, the conflict perspective concentrates on some major concerns of sport, such as racism and sexism (discussed in the next section). On the other hand, conflict theorists tend to overlook the positive contributions of sport to society. They are accused of placing too much emphasis on the extent to which sport is manipulated and controlled by the elite. Their critics also claim that

This young boy might be misinterpreting what his coach is trying to teach him about sportsmanship.

Figure 15.2   Social Effects of Sport

This table illustrates how each theoretical perspective might study an issue involving sport. For each assumption, provide a specific example from your own experience or from a team you follow.

Theoretical Perspective	Concept	Assumption	
Functionalism	Social integration	Athletic teams promote togetherness and belonging in a community.	
Conflict Theory	Social conflict	Deep social conflict exists within a community and persists despite widespread attachment to athletic teams.	
Symbolic Interactionism	Social concept	Participation in a team sport may promote or harm self-esteem depending upon factors such as emphasis on winning and fair play.	

conflict theorists underestimate the character-building benefit of team sports. Symbolic interactionism contributes greatly to understanding the socialization process in sport. But, because it concentrates on social interaction, it fails to include the broader social and cultural context. For example, symbolic interactionism does not address the functions of sport in society or explore sport within the context of power and social inequality.

Section 2 Assessment

1. What is the relationship between sport and achievement-oriented values?

2. Name three roles that sport plays in society, according to functionalists.

3. Summarize in one sentence the overall attitude of the conflict perspective toward sport.

Critical Thinking

4. **Finding the Main Idea** Has your self-concept been affected by sports? Explain the effects from the symbolic interactionist viewpoint.

Focus on Research

Case Study: Tough Guys, Wimps, and Weenies

Remember Donna Eder's study of middle-school stratification? (See pages 66–67.) She also researched the nature of middle-school sports. Using the framework of symbolic interactionism, Eder assumes that the social world of teenagers is constructed through interaction with others. Thus, everyday exchanges—insults, greetings, gossip—give teenagers a sense of their social world.

Middle-school coaches accented the value of toughness. In the world of athletics, having a "mean" attitude is masculine, and being nice is effeminate. Wrestlers, for example, were told to make opponents "suffer." Football coaches did not tolerate fighting off the field, but as a means to handle conflict among athletes, these same coaches encouraged physical force on the field.

> I said that I had heard that Coach Paulson wasn't pleased with the way the team played. Walter and Carl both agreed. Walter [the team manager] said that the team didn't hit like they should have and that made the coach mad. Carl said, "Yeah, but I really socked that guy. Man, I threw him down on the concrete. Did you hear Coach James yelling, "Way to go, Orville"? (Eder, 1995:62)

Evidence of weakness was greeted by derogatory names like "wuss," "wimp," and "girl." Ritual insults promoted stereotypically masculine behavior, particularly among higher-status boys. Stories of physical force in sports were repeated with pride. Even soccer players bragged about kicking opponents in the shins or throwing a ball into an opponent's face.

The most forcefully combative boys were the most respected. Although the coaches tried to curb physical violence outside of games and matches, many players considered fighting an appropriate way to handle all peer conflicts.

> [The] importance of being tough extended to behavior off the playing field as well as on it. Boys were continually challenged to develop more aspects of toughness, including the ability to deny pain and suppress feelings as well as respond combatively to verbal and physical attacks. Boys who rejected these messages were sometimes subject to ridicule by girls as well as boys, showing the difficulty boys faced when trying to escape the pressures of being masculine within this school setting (Eder, 1995:72).

SIDELINES

"When are you gonna learn when it's necessary to use unnecessary roughness?"

Future sociologists may study the effect that team sports plays on women's aggression.

Insult exchanges could be won by getting another boy to become angry. By losing his cool, the other boy lost his image of toughness. Some boys would insult another boy just to look good to others. An example is provided by one of the researcher's notes on Hank, the highest-status boy in the seventh grade, who had a reputation for verbal assault.

Hank does seem to enjoy conflict or competition on a one-on-one basis. A couple of times today he left the table just to go down and abuse some kid at the end of the table, calling him a pud, a squirt, or a wimp. Then he would come back and tell the group how the guy had done nothing when he had said this. Hank would get a big smile on his face and was really pleased (Eder, 1995:73–74).

Insults and counter-insults delivered several messages. First, boys learned not to care about the feelings of others. Second, insulting, or even humiliating, their peers was a socially approved means of achieving or displaying higher status. Third, boys who humiliated low-status peers were rewarded with social recognition. This was true even if the target of ridicule had a disability or was overweight.

Working with the Research

1. Do you think this study describes sports at your school? Explain.
2. Do female athletes treat each other differently from the way boys treat each other? Explain.

3

Social Issues in Sport

Key Term

- stacking *(p. 514)*

Section Preview

Sport contributes to upward mobility among collegiate athletes, but the opportunities are too few. Minorities still face discrimination in sport. Women in sport suffer from gender-based stereotypes. Intercollegiate female athletes do not receive treatment equal to the treatment received by males, although this situation is slowly improving.

Sport and Social Mobility

The autobiographies of star athletes often point to sport as their way out of poverty. One educator once predicted that "football would enable a whole generation of young men in the coal fields of Pennsylvania to turn their backs on the mines that employed their fathers" (Rudolph, 1962:378). Many athletes do use sport as a means out of their equivalent "coal fields," and many minority members work their way out of poverty through sport. It is also true that the average salaries of professional athletes are very high (Leonard, 1998). Even so, let's examine this alleged relationship between sport and social mobility.

Does sport really promote social mobility? Participating in sport increases the likelihood of improving a person's place in the stratification structure. Whatever sport they play, college athletes tend to be better educated, earn more money, and have higher occupational prestige than their fathers. This is the very definition of upward social mobility. And in these terms, college athletes as a whole are more successful than college students who do not participate in sports (Leonard, 1998). Although this finding is meaningful, it has not settled the debate regarding how much sport promotes upward mobility for minorities.

Sports have long been an important basis for stratification in high schools.

Does sport promote upward mobility for minorities?

Some people argue that sport is a social class escalator for minorities. They point to Tiger Woods, Michael Vick, and Venus and Serena Williams, among others. A different viewpoint argues that the emphasis on sport is harmful because it diverts attention away from learning the academic and business-related skills necessary for success in main-stream American society. Because of the lure of high salaries and prestige, many aspiring minority athletes fail to develop alternative career plans. Minority members who spend their youth sharpening their athletic skills at the expense of their general education will very likely be casualties of an unrealizable dream of wealth and glory (Lapchick and Matthews, 1999; Lapchick, 2004).

Some convincing evidence supports those who see sport as a barrier to upward mobility for minorities. Figure 15.3 shows that there are over one million high school football players. Just under 60,000 of these players become college football players. And 1,600 of these college players become professional players. Thus, the probability that a high school football player will make it to the pros is less than two-tenths of one percent. Similarly, a high school baseball player has a 0.2 percent chance of becoming a major leaguer. The odds are even worse for a high school basketball player, who has a 0.1 percent probability of making it to the National Basketball Association. Moreover, those who become professional athletes have short careers on the average: one to seven years for baseball players, four to six years for basketball players, and four and one-half years for football players.

Of course, this does not mean minority athletes should not enjoy the benefits of a collegiate sport. To be sure, some athletes have received good college educations who may otherwise not have had the chance. It does argue, however, that no high school athlete—minority or white, for that matter—should rely solely on sport as a ticket up the stratification structure.

The phenomenal success of basketball star Michael Jordon is frequently used to prove that sport is a path of upward mobility for minorities. Is Jordon a typical example?

Figure 15.3
High School Athletes' Chances of Advancing to the Pros
This table shows the slim chance that high school athletes have to play a professional sport. Does this surprise you?

Sources: National Federation of State High School Associations, 1999–2000.

	Number of Players in High School	Percentage Advancing from High School to College	Number of Players in College	Percentage Advancing from College to Professional Level	Number of Players at Professional Level	Percentage Advancing from High School to Professional Level
MALES						
Football	1,002,734	6%	57,593	3%	1,643	0.16%
Basketball	541,130	3%	15,874	2%	348	0.06%
Baseball	451,701	6%	25,938	3%	750	0.17%
Ice hockey	27,245	13%	3,647	18%	648	2.38%
Total	2,022,811	5%	103,052	3%	3,389	0.17%
FEMALES						
Basketball	451,600	3%	14,445	1%	132	0.03%
Golf	49,690	6%	3,108	2%	52	0.10%
Tennis	159,740	5%	8,314	2%	150	0.09%
Total	661,030	4%	25,867	1%	334	0.05%
Grand Total	2,683,841	5%	128,919	3%	3,723	0.14%

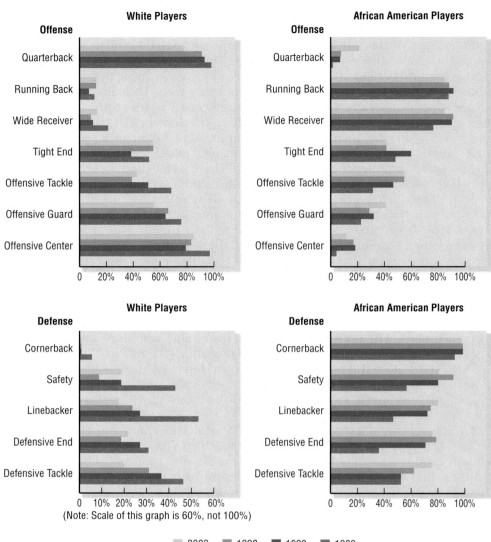

Figure 15.4 National Football League Positions, by Race
Do you think that these data support the presence of stacking in the NFL?

Source: The Institute for Diversity and Ethics in Sport, 2004.

Sport and Racism

One sign of systematic discrimination shows up in what is called stacking. In **stacking,** players are assigned to less central positions on the basis of race or ethnicity. "Central" positions are those that involve leadership and decision-making responsibilities and thus offer a greater likelihood of influencing the outcome of the game. Historically, minorities have more often been assigned to positions requiring relatively little interaction and coordination with other players. In football, for example, African American quarterbacks traditionally have been rare, while the proportions of African Americans in many defensive and other less central positions have been high. (See Figure 15.4.)

Such discrimination has important economic consequences, because the positions occupied by most African Americans have high injury rates that cut careers short. Both salaries and pension benefits are reduced as a result.

Is there salary fairness in professional sports? Discrimination in salary at the professional level exists. African Americans in the major professional sports are, on the average, paid as much as or more than their white counterparts. It is only when level of performance is controlled that discrimination appears—African Americans have lower average salaries than whites for the same level of performance. In other words, African Americans must perform better than whites to avoid pay discrimination (Eitzen and Sage, 2002).

What other areas of discrimination have been found? Minority former athletes profit much less than their white colleagues from personal appearances and commercial endorsements. They also lose out in sports-related careers when their playing days are over. While approximately 76 percent of players in the National Basketball Association (NBA) are black, only about 17 percent of radio and television NBA sports announcers are African American, and only about 8 percent of the announcers are Latino.

At the professional level, there are few minorities represented in the power structure—head coaches, general managers, owners, executives, commissioners. In 1989, Bill White became the first African American to head a major professional sports league. As of 2004, only two major sport franchises in the U.S. were owned by minorities. And only four minorities in the NFL and Major League Baseball were general managers, presidents, or CEOs. In 2000, Michael Jordan became president of basketball operations for the NBA's Washington Wizards. In the following year, despite the fact that the deal would give him partial ownership of the team, Jordan resigned and signed a player's contract. There were only three African American head coaches in professional football in 2003, and only three African American baseball managers and four Latino baseball managers in 2004. However, 37 percent of NBA head coaches were members of minority groups in 2004.

Student Web Activity
Visit the *Sociology and You* Web site at glencoe.com and click on **Chapter 15—Student Web Activities** for an activity on sport and sexism.

Minorities are well represented as players in major U.S. sports. However, after their playing days are over, minorities are underrepresented in positions of power within their sport.

Snapshot of America

Who Are the Biggest Baseball Fans?

Baseball fans used to be young working-class white males. Today's fans are older and more affluent but still predominantly white and male. The relative lack of African American fans might be traced to baseball's traditional racist policies on the field and in the front office.

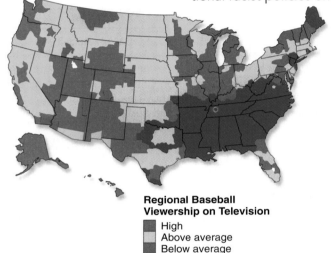

**Regional Baseball
Viewership on Television**

- High
- Above average
- Below average
- Low

Interpreting the Map

1. Do you see any regional patterns in the rates of baseball viewership? Describe.
2. How do you explain these patterns?
3. As a baseball fan, are you similar to or different from the general pattern in your state? Why?

Adapted from *Latitudes and Attitudes: An Atlas of American Tastes, Trends, Politics, and Passions.* Boston: Little, Brown.

Sexism in Sport

Racial and ethnic minorities have not been the only victims of prejudice and discrimination in sport. Women have experienced sexism in athletics. The cultural roots of sexism date back at least as far as the ancient Greeks. Greek gods were depicted as athletic, strong, powerful, competitive, rational, physical, and intellectual. Many Greek goddesses were passive, beautiful, physically weak, supportive, unathletic, and sexually attractive. (The few active, strong goddesses were usually not attractive to nor attracted by men. To Greek males, women who were physically or intellectually superior to them were unfeminine.) These gender definitions have survived in large part for the past 2,500 years. Their influence is felt in sport just as it is in other aspects of social life.

What are some of the consequences of sexism? Stereotypes have traditionally discouraged females from playing sports. For centuries, the idea that playing sports makes females more masculine has been widespread. To be an athlete, females were told, is to be unfeminine. This stigma discouraged many females from participating in athletics and tyrannized many of those who did. Another barrier was the old, discredited argument that sports harm a woman's health, particularly her ability to have children.

Sexism has denied females equal access to organized sports. At the local level, resistance to female participation in sports continues to exist. It was not until the mid-1970s that, under legal threat, the national Little League organization ended its males-only policy. Only when the 1972 Educational Amendment Act (Title IX) was passed were public high schools and colleges required to offer females equal access to sports. Originally, Title IX was interpreted as providing equal opportunity in "all" sport programs of institutions receiving federal funds. Ambiguities in Title IX have led to many legal suits. Important issues remain unresolved. Currently, the courts favor matching the ratio of males and females in a school's athletic programs to their proportionate numbers in the student body of that school (Hannon, 2003).

Why has the percentage of women coaching women's programs declined?
Women are still denied equal access to the power structure of sport (Lapchick and Matthews, 2001). What's more, although Title IX increased equality for female athletes, it led to a decrease in the number of coaching and administrative positions held by women. In the early 1970s, women's intercollegiate teams were headed almost entirely by women. As of 2004, more than half of the NCAA women's teams were coached by men. (See Figure 15.5 on page 518.) Less than 19 percent of all women's programs were headed by a female administrator, and females held only 41 percent of all administrative jobs in women's programs (Acosta and Carpenter, 2004).

Ironically, Title IX may be one reason for this decline. As the money and prestige associated with women's programs have increased, men have found these coaching jobs much more attractive. And conflict theorists believe that men, who are overwhelmingly in charge of athletic programs and who have the power to make hiring decisions, are more likely to choose men as coaches (Nixon and Frey, 1996; Fazioli, 2004).

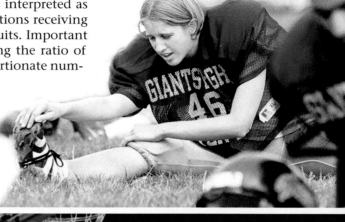

Although sexism in sports has been decreasing, women athletes continue to suffer from inequalities.

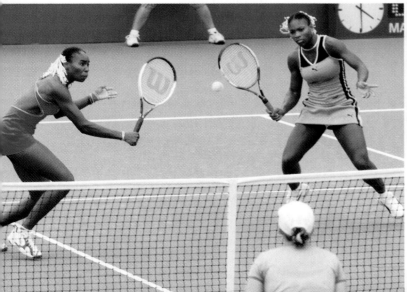

Figure 15.5 Percentage of College Women's Athletic Teams Coached by Women
What is most interesting to you about these data?

Source: R. Vivian Acosta and Linda Jean Carpenter, "Women in Intercollegiate Sport." Brooklyn College, 2004.

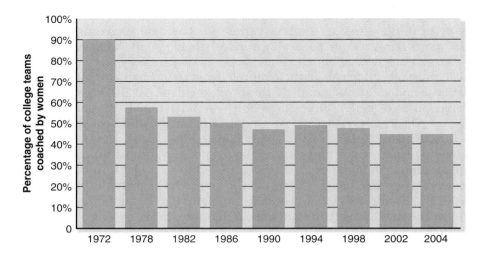

Are women represented at the national level? Currently, professional sports for women include a Women's National Basketball Association (WNBA), a volleyball league, a golf tour, and a tennis circuit. As we have already seen, few women athletes make it to the professional ranks. Even those women who become professionals earn significantly less than their male counterparts (Levin, 1996; Fazioli, 2004). Golf, for example, is one of the few professional sports offering significant opportunities for women. Still, the leading money winner on the men's tour earns far more than twice as much as the leading money winner on the women's tour. This disparity is reflected in the total prize money for the Professional Golfers' Association (PGA) and the Ladies Professional Golf Association (LPGA) tours—$250 million for men in 2005; $45 million for women.

There are some positive, if small, signs of change. In addition to her Nike endorsement, U.S. soccer star Mia Hamm has a lucrative deal with Gatorade. Tennis sensation Venus Williams has product endorsement contracts with American Express, McDonald's, and Wilson Racquet Sports. In 2003, Serena Williams signed a five-year contract with Nike worth close to $40 million. And shortly after 16-year-old golfer Michelle Wie turned professional in 2005, she signed endorsement deals worth $10 million a year.

Section 3 Assessment

1. What advice would you give to a young man or woman planning to become a professional athlete? Use the information in this chapter in your response.

2. How did the Educational Amendment Act of 1972 (Title IX) affect women's sport programs?

Critical Thinking

3. **Analyzing Information** "American females experience more prejudice and discrimination in sport than males." Explain why you agree or disagree with this statement.

How to Avoid Bigotry in Sport

Sports sociologist J. Coakley supports the concerns of many Native Americans on the issue of team names. He wrote the following article about this issue.

Most of us are not very concerned about the use of Native American names by many athletic teams. But to Native Americans, war whoops and tomahawk chopping portray negative stereotypes.

Using stereotypes to characterize Native Americans in the U.S. is so common that most people don't even realize they are doing it. . . . When these stereotypes are used as a basis for team names, mascots, and logos, sports become a way of perpetuating an ideology that exploits, trivializes, and demeans the history and cultural heritage of Native Americans.

If teachers, administrators, and students in U.S. schools had a deep knowledge of the rich and diverse cultures of Native Americans and realized the discrimination native peoples currently face, they would not use names such as Indians, Redskins, Chiefs, Braves, Savages, Tribe, and Redmen for their teams; they would not allow Anglo students to entertain fans by dressing up as caricatures of Native Americans; and they would not allow fans to mimic Native American chants or act out demeaning stereotypes of war-whooping, tomahawk-chopping Native Americans.

Schools should not use any Native American name or symbol in connection with sport teams unless they do the following:

1. Sponsor a special curriculum to inform students of the history, cultural heritage, and current living conditions of the native group after which their sport teams are named. Unless 70 percent of the students can pass annual tests on this information, schools should drop the names they say are used to "honor" native people.

2. Publish two press releases per year in which information about the heritage and current circumstances of the native peoples honored by their team names is described and analyzed; publish similar materials annually in school newspapers and yearbooks.

3. Once per year, during homecoming or a major sport event, sponsor a special ceremony designed by and for native peoples in the local area, with the purpose of informing students and parents about the people they say they honor with their team names.

Source: Jay J. Coakley, *Sport in Society.* 6th ed. Boston: Irwin McGraw-Hill, 1998, pp. 272–273.

Doing Sociology

Is there a sport symbol in your community or state that might be offensive to Native Americans? Has the existence of this offensive symbol hurt your community or state economically? Explain.

Summary

Section 1: The Nature of Sport

Main Idea: As a social institution, sport fulfills some important societal needs. One of these is helping individuals identify with others members of society. Sport subcultures have developed around both team and individual sports. For this reason, sport is a reflection of society.

Section 2: Theoretical Perspectives and Sport

Main Idea: Functionalists see sport positively, as a means for socializing young people, promoting social integration, providing a release for tensions, and developing sound character. Conflict theorists believe that organized sports can be harmful to character development. Symbolic interactionists focus on the self-concepts and relationships developed through sport activities.

Section 3: Social Issues in Sport

Main Idea: Sport contributes to upward mobility among collegiate athletes, but the opportunities are too few. Minorities still face discrimination in sport. Women in sport suffer from gender-based stereotypes. Intercollegiate female athletes do not receive treatment equal to the treatment received by males, although this situation is slowly improving.

Sociology Online

Self-Check Quiz
Visit the *Sociology and You* Web site at glencoe.com and click on **Chapter 15—Self-Check Quizzes** to prepare for the chapter test.

Reviewing Vocabulary

Complete each sentence using each term once.

a. sport
b. Title IX
c. sports subculture
d. functionalist perspective on sport
e. conflict perspective on sport
f. symbolic interactionist perspective on sport
g. social mobility in sport
h. stacking
i. salary equity
j. sexism in sport

1. The assumption that all athletes are paid based on level of performance is known as _____ .
2. The perspective that is most concerned with the relationships of those involved is called _____ .
3. Using sport to improve a position in the stratification structure is known as _____ .
4. is the assigning of less central positions to minorities.
5. _____ is the perspective that emphasizes the positive contributions of sport to society.
6. A set of norms that surround a particular sport is called _____ .
7. _____ is the perspective that sees sport as an institution in which the most powerful oppress, manipulate, coerce, and exploit others.
8. _____ is a set of competitive activities in which winners and losers are determined by physical performance within a set of established rules.
9. _____ was established with the intent of increasing opportunity for female athletes in school settings.
10. The defining of sport as a masculine activity is known as _____ .

Reviewing the Facts

11. Why does sport play an important role in American society?
12. According to the functionalists, what is one purpose of sport?
13. What is the conflict theorists' view of sport as an institution?

14. Outline and summarize sport from the three sociological perspectives. Create a diagram similar to the one below to record your answer.

Perspective	Summary
Functionalist	
Conflict Theorist	
Symbolic Interactionist	

15. Identify the relationship between sport and social mobility.

Thinking Critically

16. Drawing Conclusions

High school athletes with superior skills are often given extraordinary help in meeting college entrance requirements. Many students feel this is unfair to those who have higher grades but aren't accepted. Others point out that athletics bring in lots of money for colleges. They also say that athletes have skills as rare as high intelligence and so deserve their sports scholarships. What do you think?

17. Analyzing Information

Some schools have made efforts to change their school nicknames and mascots so as not to offend various groups that might have been negatively portrayed by these mascots and nicknames. Do you think that schools and teams have an obligation to take such actions? Or should teams be allowed to retain their traditional nicknames and mascots?

18. Evaluating Information

In the National Basketball Association draft, the best players go to the teams that completed the previous season with the worst records. Why do you think the NBA uses this approach instead of allowing the best players to go to the teams with the most prestige, status, and monetary resources?

Copyright 2006 Mike Lester/Cagle Cartoons

19. Analyzing Visuals

In this chapter, you read about how two different sociological perspectives—the functionalists and the conflict theorists—see sports in American culture. Patrick Chappatte's cartoon could be said to represent both of these perspectives. How might a functionalist "read" the cartoon? And how might a conflict theorist see it?

20. Applying Concepts

Here's a thought experiment to try. Using your answer to number 18 above, see if you can apply your reasoning to the institution of the family. Imagine that NBA teams are like families in various social classes and that each generation is like a season of professional basketball. Wouldn't it be fair to ask the winning families (those at the top of the social class ladder) not to pass on their advantages to their offspring? In other words, for the competition to be fair, wealthier families should not be allowed to go to the best schools but instead should be sent to the schools with the fewest resources. The logic used here is that the best and most talented succeed anywhere. What is the fallacy in this argument?

21. Drawing Conclusions

In referring to the way a crowd of people can motivate a team of players, Emile Durkheim once said, "There are occasions when this strengthening and vivifying action of society is especially apparent. In the midst of an assembly animated by a common passion, we become susceptible of acts and sentiments of which we are incapable when reduced to our own forces." Do you believe that a home court or home field advantage really exists? Do players rise to the occasion when cheered on by the home crowd? Are there ever times when athletes might play better when not at home?

22. Evaluating Information

Pretend that you are attending a professional tennis match with an economist, a political scientist, a psychologist, and a sociologist. Link each of the questions below to the discipline most likely to give a complete answer.

a. How did the hot dogs get to be five dollars?

b. Why do some athletes fall apart after a bad call?

c. What is the socioeconomic status of the players?

d. Does tennis reflect mainstream values?

e. How did Americans lose their dominance in this sport?

f. Why does it seem that all tennis courts are located in wealthy neighborhoods?

Sociology Projects

23. Sports and Statistics

The sports section is a great place to examine how statistics are used. For one week follow a team in any sport that is currently in season. Track several team and individual statistics. Do dramatic changes occur in the statistics, or are the changes insignificant? Can you offer any reason for the change or lack of change? Compare your team's statistics with those of a classmate's team. Analyze the validity of the statistics. Do they accurately tell the story, or can statistics deceive us?

24. Analyzing the Effects of Sport Attendance

The table below provides information on attendance for some of the most popular sports in the United States. Work with another student to develop a list of the positive and negative effects of people's attending high school sporting events. Next develop a list of possible effects for other sports in the table. To stimulate your thinking, look at community and national media sources. (Your list might include community spirit, violence, television time, and advertising dollars.) As a class, discuss your lists. Try to see if there are any major differences for effects among different sports.

Adult Attendance at Sports Events, 2004 (in thousands)		
Sports Event	Attend once or more often a month	Attend once a month or less
NASCAR	2,251	6,653
Baseball	8,524	16,217
Professional Basketball	2,853	7,397
Professional Football	5,730	11,330
High School Sports	11,578	6,658
Ice Hockey	2,576	5,731
Soccer	2,848	2,929
Tennis	841	2,291
Golf	1,737	3,629
Professional Wrestling	1,158	2,387

Source: *Statistical Abstract of the United States*, 2006

25. Minorities in Coaching and Management

The text discusses underrepresentation of minorities in coaching and management positions. To find out whether this pattern still holds, conduct a quick survey of your own. Concentrating on professional sports, what are the names of coaches and managers from all the teams in a national league? Use the Internet to find answers to these questions. Identify as many of the coaches and managers as possible by race and ethnicity. What is the proportion of minority coaches and managers in your sample?

26. The Home Court Advantage

Interview athletes who participate in several of your school's sports. Ask the following questions.

a. What are the advantages of playing at home?

b. What are the disadvantages of playing on the road?

c. What factors contribute to home court advantage?

d. What factors hinder better performances on the road?

e. Do you ever prefer to play at home?

f. Compare your notes with those of your classmates to see if there is consensus.

27. The Cost of Sports

Research suggests that participation in sports reflects geographic location and economic conditions. For instance, basketball is an urban game that does not require a lot of money to play. All one needs is a ball and a place to shoot. Conduct research on other major sports—football, baseball, hockey, skiing, tennis, and golf. Try to determine where and by whom these sports tend to be played. How much does it cost an individual who is not professional to play these sports? Share your results with the class.

28. Sports in Film

Numerous movie videos deal with sports themes. Select a video, and write a report on it using concepts discussed in the chapter. For example, the film *Jerry McGuire* touches on player salaries and issues of race, among other themes. Present your report to the class.

Technology Activity

29. Using your favorite search engine, do a search for "sociology of sport."

a. How many web page matches did your search find? What does that indicate to you about the importance of this subject?

b. Go to the Web site for the North American Society for the Sociology of Sport at www.nass.org. Find the link to NASSS newsletters and reveiew a recent issue. From what you can see there, what types of topics interest sports sociologists?

c. Click on Overview. Where is this journal published? Why was it started?

We Don't Like Football, Do We?

by D. Stanley Eitzen

● **relishing**
being pleased with or gratified by

● **prerequisite**
required as a prior condition to something

● **insidiously**
developing in a stealthy and harmful manner so gradually as to become established before being apparent

If you grew up female in America, you heard this: Sports are unfeminine. And this: Girls who play sports are tomboys. You got this message: Real women don't spend their free time sliding feet-first into home plate or smacking their fists into soft leather gloves.

So you didn't play or you did play and either way you didn't quite fit. You didn't fit in your body—didn't learn to live there, breathe there, feel dynamic and capable. Or maybe you fell madly, passionately in love with sports but didn't quite fit in society, never saw yourself—basketball player, cyclist, golfer—reflected in movies, billboards, magazines.

Or you took a middle ground, shying away at first but then later sprinting toward aerobics and weight lifting and in-line skating, relishing your increasing endurance and grace and strength. Even then, though, you sensed that something was wrong: all the ads and articles seemed to focus on weight loss and beauty. While those may have inspired you to get fit in the first place, there are more important things, you now know, than how you looked. No one seemed to be talking about pride, pleasure, power, possibility.

If you grew up male in America, you heard this: Boys who don't play sports are sissies or . . . [homosexuals]. And this: Don't throw like a girl. You got this message: Sports are a male initiation rite, as fundamental and natural as shaving and deep voices—a prerequisite, somehow, to becoming an American man. So you played football or soccer or baseball and felt competent, strong, and bonded with your male buddies. Or you didn't play and risked ridicule.

Whether we were inspired by Babe Ruth or Babe Didrikson or neither, and whether we played kickball with our brothers or sisters or both, all of us, female and male, learned to associate sports prowess and sports privilege with masculinity. Even if the best athlete in the neighborhood was a girl, we learned from newspapers, television, and from our own parents' prejudices that batting, catching, throwing, and jumping are not neutral, human activities, but somehow more naturally a male domain. Insidiously our culture's reverence for men's professional sports and its silence about women's athletic accomplishments shaped, defined, and limited how we felt about ourselves as women and men.

. . . You may have noticed that boys are no longer the only ones shooting baskets in public parks. One girl often joins the boys now, her hair dark with sweat, her body alert as a squirrel's. Maybe they don't pass her the ball. Maybe she grabs it anyway, squeezes mightily through the barricade of bodies, leaps skyward, feet flying.

Or she teams with other girls. Gyms fill these days with the rowdy sounds of women hard at play: basketballs seized by calloused hands, sneakers squealing like shocked mice. The players' high, urgent voices

This West Virginia high school student is a starter on her school's only varsity basketball team.

resonate, too—"Here!" "Go!"—and right then nothing exists for them except the ball, the shifting constellation of women, the chance to be fluid, smooth, alive.

What does this mean? What does it mean that everywhere, women are running, shooting baskets, getting sweaty and exhausted and euphoric? What changes when a woman becomes an athlete?

Everything.

On playing fields and in gyms across America, women are engaged in a contest with higher stakes than trophies or ribbons or even prize money. Through women's play, and through their huddles behind the scenes, they are deciding who American women will be. Not just what games they will play, but what role they will play in this still-young nation. Not only what their bodies will look like, but what their bodies can do.

Adapted from Mariah Burton Nelson. "We Don't Like Football, Do We?" in D. Stanley Eitzen, *Sport in Contemporary Society: An Anthology,* 5th ed., St. Martin's Press, Inc., 1996, pp. 25–26.

Read and React

1. State briefly the main point of this article.
2. What do you think is the author's viewpoint on the relationship between gender and sport? Do you agree with him?
3. Do you believe that attitudes in the United States regarding female participation in sport are changing? Explain.
4. From which theoretical perspective is the author writing? Use examples to illustrate that perspective.

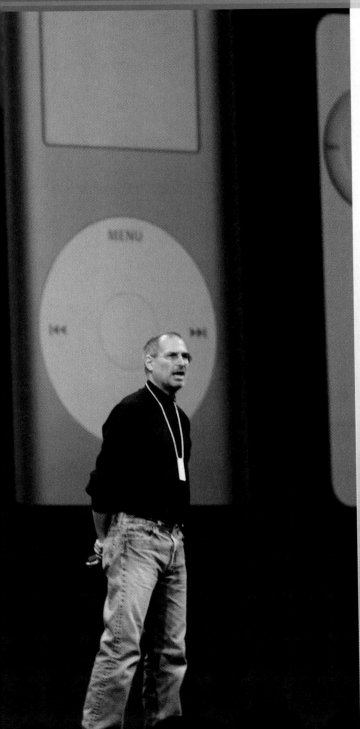

Chapter 16
Population and Urbanization

Chapter 17
Social Change and Collective Behavior

527

Sections

1. **The Dynamics of Demography**
2. **World Population**
3. **The Urban Transition**
4. **Urban Ecology**

Learning Objectives

After reading this chapter, you will be able to

- identify the three population processes.
- relate the ideas of Thomas Malthus to population changes.
- predict world population trends.
- trace the development of pre-industrial and modern cities.
- compare and contrast four theories of city growth.

Applying Sociology

Suppose you read the following paragraph in your history textbook.

On October 12, 1999, the United Nations officially declared that the world's population had reached six billion. United Nations Secretary-General Kofi Annan was visiting Sarajevo, Bosnia, when the historic milestone was reached. To symbolize the event, he chose a baby boy born in a local clinic at two minutes after midnight to be named "Baby Six Billion."

Overall, the world population doubled in the 40 years from 1959 to 1999. World population growth is expected to continue, though at a slightly slower rate. If someone were to ask you about this growth, you would probably refer to the high birthrate in developing countries. You could point out that every year, 137 million infants are born—equal to the population of Nigeria.

This explanation is only half of the story. It leaves out the other side of the equation—the death rate. The population in these countries is growing rapidly because their birthrates remain high while their death rates have dropped sharply, thanks to modern medicine, improved sanitation, and better hygiene. In this chapter, we look at demography and discuss why this issue is important to sociologists.

Sociology Online

Chapter Overview
Visit the *Sociology and You* Web site at <u>glencoe.com</u> and click on **Chapter 16— Chapter Overviews** to preview chapter information.

The Dynamics of Demography

Key Terms

- population *(p. 530)*
- demography *(p. 530)*
- fertility *(p. 531)*
- fecundity *(p. 531)*
- crude birthrate *(p. 531)*
- fertility rate *(p. 531)*
- total fertility rate *(p. 532)*
- mortality *(p. 533)*
- life span *(p. 533)*
- life expectancy *(p. 533)*
- crude death rate *(p. 533)*
- infant mortality rate *(p. 533)*
- migration *(p. 534)*
- gross migration rate *(p. 534)*
- net migration rate *(p. 534)*

- **population**
  a group of people living in a particular place at a specified time

- **demography**
  the scientific study of population

Section Preview

Demography is the scientific study of population. The collection of population data is very important today, in part because of its use by government and industry. Demographers consider three population processes when looking at population change: fertility, mortality, and migration.

The Changing Population

Sociologists study population because it affects social structure, especially in crowded areas. They look for patterns that will help them understand and predict how groups of people will behave. For example, they might examine the relationship between population growth and politics. We know that historically the growth of minorities in the United States has benefited Democrats more than Republicans (Tilove, 1999). But the situation today is different with respect to Latinos. Now the largest minority in the United States, Latinos are not firmly aligned with either political party. Regardless of political affiliation, the growth of minority populations affects how congressional districts are drawn and is one reason why census taking can be a controversial topic. Or sociologists might study trends in population shifts, such as the aging baby boomers, to help plan for hospitals and long-term nursing facilities.

How do sociologists define population? A **population** is a group of people living in a particular place at a specified time. The scientific study of population is called **demography** (*demos* is a Greek word that means "people"). To study population, demographers look at many factors, including the number of people (size); how and where they are located (distribution); what groups make up the population (composition); and the ages represented in the population (age structure). Demographers also analyze three processes: birth (*fertility*), death (*mortality*), and movement from one place to another (*migration*). Major changes in populations come from one or all of these three processes. In the following sections, we look at the factors and processes that affect populations.

Social structures reflect the ability of the land to support people.

How might fertility drugs affect the crude birthrate?

Fertility

Fertility measures the actual number of children born to a woman or to a population of women. **Fecundity** is the potential number of children that could be born if every woman reproduced as often as biology allowed. Obviously, fertility rates are much lower than fecundity rates. The highest realistic fecundity rate you could expect from a society would be about fifteen births per woman. The record fertility rate for a group probably is held by the Hutterites, who migrated a century ago from Switzerland to North and South Dakota and Canada. Hutterite women in the 1930s were giving birth to an average of more than twelve children each (Westoff and Westoff, 1971). The Hutterites give us a good estimate of fecundity, because they are the best example of *natural fertility*—the number of children born to women in the absence of conscious birth control (Weeks, 2004).

How is fertility measured?
The **crude birthrate** is the annual number of live births per one thousand members of a population. The crude birthrate varies considerably from one country to another. The crude birthrate for the United States is fourteen per one thousand. Niger, in West Africa, experiences a very high crude birthrate of fifty-six per one thousand; and Germany, a very low rate of nine per one thousand.

To calculate the crude birthrate, divide the annual number of live births by the total population and multiply that number by 1,000.

$$\text{Crude Birthrate} = \frac{\text{Number of Live Births}}{\text{Total Population}} \times 1{,}000$$

The term *crude* in this case means rough, or approximate. The crude birthrate is approximate because it is based on the entire population rather than just women of childbearing age. It also ignores the age structure of the population. Both sex and age affect the number of live births in any given year. Consequently, in addition to crude birthrate, demographers use the **fertility rate**— the annual number of live births per one thousand women aged fifteen to

- **fertility**
  a measure of the number of children born to a woman or a population of women

- **fecundity**
  the maximum rate at which women can physically produce children

- **crude birthrate**
  the annual number of live births per one thousand members of a population

- **fertility rate**
  the annual number of live births per one thousand women aged fifteen to forty-four

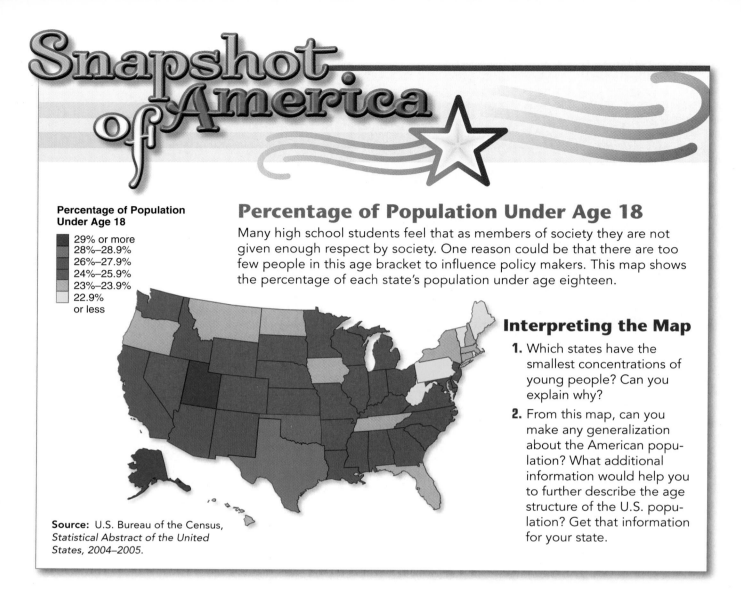

Snapshot of America

Percentage of Population Under Age 18

■	29% or more
■	28%–28.9%
■	26%–27.9%
■	24%–25.9%
■	23%–23.9%
□	22.9% or less

Percentage of Population Under Age 18

Many high school students feel that as members of society they are not given enough respect by society. One reason could be that there are too few people in this age bracket to influence policy makers. This map shows the percentage of each state's population under age eighteen.

Source: U.S. Bureau of the Census, *Statistical Abstract of the United States, 2004–2005.*

Interpreting the Map

1. Which states have the smallest concentrations of young people? Can you explain why?

2. From this map, can you make any generalization about the American population? What additional information would help you to further describe the age structure of the U.S. population? Get that information for your state.

● **total fertility rate**
average number of children born to a woman during her lifetime

forty-four. The rate that is easiest to use is the **total fertility rate,** or the average number of children born to a woman during her lifetime. Currently, total fertility rates in the world range from 8.0 in Niger to 1.2 in Ukraine.

What other factors influence birthrate? The birthrate of a population is influenced by both health and social factors. For example, widespread disease (especially rubella, or German measles) causes the birthrate to decline because many pregnancies end in miscarriages. Social factors affecting the birthrate include the average age at marriage, the level of economic development, the availability and use of contraceptives and abortion, the number of women in the labor force, the educational status of women, and social attitudes toward reproduction.

The U.S. birthrate in recent years has shown a steady decline. More couples today consider two children—or even one child—a desirable number. Work patterns have affected the birthrate as well. More American women today are postponing having children until their late twenties and early thirties. As a result, women are having fewer children.

Mortality

Mortality refers to death. To analyze patterns of mortality within a population, sociologists look at *life span* and *life expectancy*. **Life span** is the most advanced age to which humans can survive. We know for sure of a Japanese man who lived nearly 121 years, but few people even approach this age. **Life expectancy** is the average number of years that persons in a given population born at a particular time can expect to live. World life expectancy ranges from 82 years in Japan to 42 years in Afghanistan (*World Population Data Sheet*, 2005).

How is mortality measured? The **crude death rate** is figured by dividing the annual number of deaths by the total population and multiplying by 1,000. Like the crude birthrate, the crude death rate varies widely throughout the world. The worldwide average crude death rate is nine per one thousand persons. Looking at specific regions of the world, the death rate varies from a low of six per thousand in Latin America and the Caribbean to a high of fifteen per thousand in Africa. The death rate in the United States is about eight per thousand (*World Population Data Sheet*, 2005).

Demographers are also interested in the variations in death rates for specific groups. They have devised *age-specific death rates* to measure the number of deaths per thousand persons in a specific age group, such as fifteen- to nineteen-year-olds or sixty- to sixty-four-year-olds. This allows them to compare the risk of death to members of different groups. Although death eventually comes to everyone, the rate at which it occurs depends on many factors, including age, sex, race, occupation, social class, standard of living, and health care.

The **infant mortality rate**—the number of deaths among infants under one year of age per one thousand live births—is considered a good indicator of the health status of any group. This is because infants are the first to suffer

- **mortality**
  deaths within a population

- **life span**
  the most advanced age to which humans can survive

- **life expectancy**
  the average number of years that persons in a given population born at a particular time can expect to live

- **crude death rate**
  the annual number of deaths per thousand members of a population

- **infant mortality rate**
  the annual number of deaths among infants under one year of age per one thousand live births

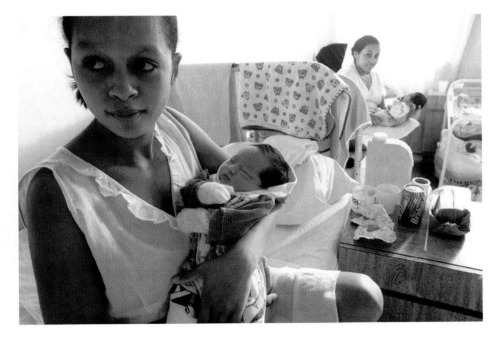

This Brazilian mother attends a local clinic to get health care for her infant.

Figure 16.1 World Population Growth

This figure shows estimated world population growth to 2150. What factors do you think led to the sharp rise in population around 1850?

Source: Washington, DC: Population Reference Bureau.

from a lack of good medical care and sanitation. Infants in less developed countries are almost ten times more likely to die before their first birthday than infants in more developed nations. Working together, birthrates, fertility rates, and mortality rates determine world population growth. (See Figure 16.1.)

Migration

● **migration**
the movement of people from one geographic area to another

Migration refers to the movement of people from one geographic area to another. Migration can occur within a country or between countries. An example of migration from country to country is the resettlement of Asian refugees from Vietnam and Cambodia in countries around the world. Many of the refugees who settle in the United States in one particular city or region later move to another region, thus becoming internal migrants. Anyone who moves from one part of the country to another—say, from New York to Arizona—is engaging in internal migration.

● **gross migration rate**
the number of persons per year per one thousand members of a population who enter or leave a geographic area

● **net migration rate**
the annual increase or decrease per one thousand members of a population resulting from migration into and out of the population

How is migration measured? The **gross migration rate** into or out of an area is the number of persons per one thousand members of a population who enter or leave a geographic area in a given year. *Net migration* is the difference between the number of people entering and leaving an area. Thus, the **net migration rate** is the annual increase or decrease per one thousand members of a population resulting from movement into and out of the population. In 2003, for example, the United States had a net migration rate of about 4.4 per one thousand population. That is, 4.4 more persons per one thousand population entered the country than left the country. It is also possible of course, to have a negative net migration rate showing more people overall left an area than entered it.

When the U.S. Census Bureau reports migration rates, it refers only to the number of legal immigrants. Many people violate immigration laws to enter the United States. In the 1970s, the issue of illegal immigration—primarily from Latin American and Caribbean countries—became a major concern and continues to be controversial today. There are no precise statistics on either the illegal immigration rate or the total number of illegal aliens living in the United States. Currently, the U.S. Census Bureau estimates that there are about seven million unauthorized immigrants living in the United States.

Another Place

The Graying of Japan

Birthrates and death rates have important social and cultural consequences. In Japan, elders have traditionally been held in high esteem. This tradition is threatened by a combination of two factors: People are generally living longer, and there are fewer young people to support the elders' existence. As they lose respect, many older Japanese now pray in their temples for a quick death.

The population of Japan is aging faster than any on earth, a result of declining birth and death rates. The situation of the elderly of Japan is like the proverbial glass of water that is either half full or half empty, depending on whether the positive or negative aspects of their lives are emphasized. In some ways, elderly Japanese are better off than the elderly of the other developed countries. They hold the position of "honorable elders," a reflection of the Confucian precept of duty owed to parents. Japan even has a national holiday, "Respect for the Aged Day," September 15th, when most offices and factories are closed. Furthermore, a relatively high proportion of elderly Japanese live with their adult children, which is often cited as evidence of the reverence this country pays to the aged.

However, it can also be argued that elderly Japanese are not really so well off and that the "ecstasy years" of old age are losing their rosy glow—if they truly ever had one. Among the more sensational evidence cited are the supposedly high rate of suicide among elderly Japanese and the existence of temples where the elderly go to pray for a quick death. Also, in recent years, the number of activities for or honoring the elderly on their special day have been few and far between. For most Japanese, September 15th is just another holiday.

The particularly rapid pace of aging in Japan and the potential consequences have captured the attention of policymakers and officials. [A major government report] listed population aging along with internationalization and maturation of the economy as the three major challenges for twenty-first-century Japan. Japanese prime ministers have regularly referred to aging as they have set the policy agenda, recognizing that population aging affects many aspects of the society and the economy.

Source: Linda G. Martin, "The Graying of Japan," *Population Bulletin* (Washington, DC).

Thinking It Over

What theoretical perspective best explains the effect of the graying of Japan?

Section 1 Assessment

1. What three major processes affect the way populations change?

2. How might data about age-specific death rates or population shifts be of use?

3. Why is the infant mortality rate a key statistic for health workers?

Critical Thinking

4. **Drawing Conclusions** Why is demography increasingly important? Think of a way in which the federal government could use some specific piece of demographic data. State how this information would help the government make a policy decision.

2

World Population

Key Terms

- census *(p. 536)*
- doubling time *(p. 537)*
- exponential growth *(p. 538)*
- demographic transition theory *(p. 540)*
- zero population growth *(p. 541)*
- population momentum *(p. 541)*
- replacement level *(p. 541)*
- population control *(p. 541)*
- family planning *(p. 542)*
- population pyramid *(p. 545)*
- dependency ratio *(p. 545)*

- **census**
  regularly occurring count of a particular population

Section Preview

Thomas Malthus (1798) predicted that population size would ultimately outstrip the food supply, resulting in mass starvation and death. The demographic transition theory looks at economic development to predict population patterns. While the rate of world population growth is slowing, the world's population will continue to increase for many years. Population control has become a concern of many governments worried about providing for their future citizens.

The Problem of Population Growth

No organization has actually ever counted all the people in the world. World population figures are a composite of best estimates and national **census** figures where available. While many countries count and categorize people living in those countries, the quality of census data varies a great deal and can be very unreliable. Nevertheless, world population growth patterns can be identified.

Rapid world population growth is a relatively recent phenomenon. In fact, your grandparents have seen more population growth during their lifetimes

HOW MANY STARS ARE IN THE SKY?

HOW MANY GRAINS OF SAND LIE ON THE BEACH?

HOW MANY FISH SWIM IN THE SEA?

HOW MANY PEOPLE LIVE IN THE CITIES?

SIGH

U.S. CENSUS BUREAU

THAT'S ENOUGH WORK FOR ONE DAY

If the counting of the population is a problem in more developed societies, imagine the difficulty with obtaining accurate counts in less developed societies.

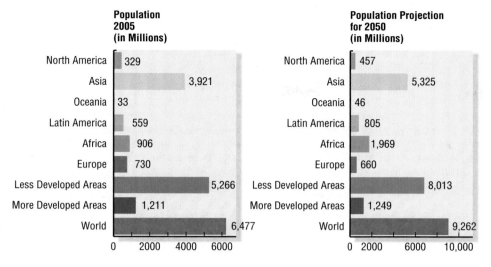

Population 2005 (in Millions)

Region	Population
North America	329
Asia	3,921
Oceania	33
Latin America	559
Africa	906
Europe	730
Less Developed Areas	5,266
More Developed Areas	1,211
World	6,477

Population Projection for 2050 (in Millions)

Region	Population
North America	457
Asia	5,325
Oceania	46
Latin America	805
Africa	1,969
Europe	660
Less Developed Areas	8,013
More Developed Areas	1,249
World	9,262

Figure 16.2 **Population Projections by Regions of the World** This graph displays population projections, by regions of the world, from 2005 to 2050. Note the dramatic difference in population doubling time between less developed areas and more developed areas.

Source: Adapted from *World Population Data Sheet*, 2005.

Projected Population Change Between 2005 and 2050

Region	Change
North America	39%
Asia	36%
Oceania	39%
Latin America	44%
Africa	117%
Europe	−10%
Less Developed Areas	52%
More Developed Areas	3%
World	43%

Doubling Time (in Years)

Region	Years
North America	125
Asia	55
Oceania	70
Latin America	44
Africa	30
Europe	*
Less Developed Areas	46
More Developed Areas	680
World	56

*Doubling not projected to occur.

than occurred during the preceding four million years. An estimated 250 million people were on the earth in A.D. 1. (Refer back to Figure 16.1 on page 534.) It was not until 1650 that the world's population doubled, to half a billion. The second doubling occurred in 1800, bringing the world population to one billion. By 1930, another doubling had taken place. Less than fifty years after that, in 1976, a fourth doubling raised the world's population to four billion. At the current growth rate, the world's population is expected to double again in about fifty-six years and will approach eight billion persons by the year 2025. As you can see, the number of years between each doubling of the population—called, for obvious reasons, the **doubling time**—is getting shorter and shorter (*World Population Data Sheet*, 2005). Figure 16.2 breaks down world population projections by region. Figure 16.3 on the next page looks at key demographic statistics by world regions.

● **doubling time**
number of years needed to double the base population size

Figure 16.3 World Birthrates, Death Rates, and Infant Mortality Rates

Would you always expect to see a correlation between crude birthrates and total fertility rates for a country? Between crude death rates and infant morality rates?

Source: Washington, DC: Population Reference Bureau, 2005.

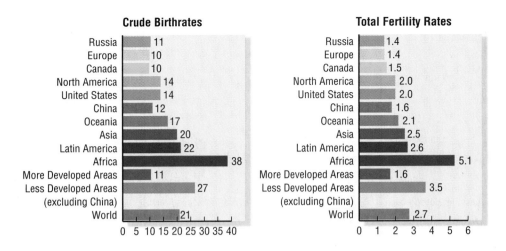

Crude Birthrates

Russia	11
Europe	10
Canada	10
North America	14
United States	14
China	12
Oceania	17
Asia	20
Latin America	22
Africa	38
More Developed Areas	11
Less Developed Areas (excluding China)	27
World	21

0 5 10 15 20 25 30 35 40

Total Fertility Rates

Russia	1.4
Europe	1.4
Canada	1.5
North America	2.0
United States	2.0
China	1.6
Oceania	2.1
Asia	2.5
Latin America	2.6
Africa	5.1
More Developed Areas	1.6
Less Developed Areas (excluding China)	3.5
World	2.7

0 1 2 3 4 5 6

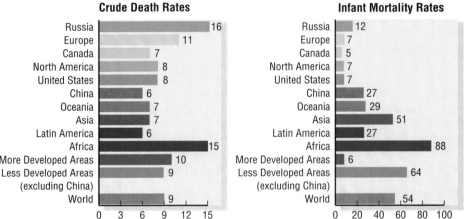

Crude Death Rates

Russia	16
Europe	11
Canada	7
North America	8
United States	8
China	6
Oceania	7
Asia	7
Latin America	6
Africa	15
More Developed Areas	10
Less Developed Areas (excluding China)	9
World	9

0 3 6 9 12 15

Infant Mortality Rates

Russia	12
Europe	7
Canada	5
North America	7
United States	7
China	27
Oceania	29
Asia	51
Latin America	27
Africa	88
More Developed Areas	6
Less Developed Areas (excluding China)	64
World	54

0 20 40 60 80 100

● **exponential growth**
growth in which the amount of increase is added to the base figure each time period

Why is the world's population growing so fast? The population has increased so dramatically in part because of the way population increases. We are accustomed to thinking in terms of *linear growth,* whereby amounts increase arithmetically (as in the progression 1, 2, 3, 4, 5 . . .). Population, however, does not grow linearly. It follows the principle of **exponential growth,** and increases geometrically (as in the progression 2, 4, 8, 16, 32). With exponential growth, the *amount* of increase is greater each time period even though the *rate* of increase remains the same. This is because each increase is added to the base amount and becomes part of the calculation for the next rise.

A classic example of exponential growth follows: The story tells of a clever minister who presented a beautiful chess set to his king. In return, he asked only that the king give one grain of rice for the first square on the chessboard; two grains, or double the amount, for the second square; four (doubling again) for the third; and so forth. The king, not being mathematically minded, agreed and ordered the rice brought forth. The eighth square required 128 grains, and the twelfth took more than a pound of rice. Long before reaching the sixty-fourth square, the king's coffers were depleted. Even today, the world's richest king could not produce enough rice to fill the final square. It would require more than 200 billion tons, or the equivalent of the world's current total production of rice for the next 653 years.

If a population is growing at 1 percent per year, it takes seventy years to double. For example, suppose the population of a city was 50,000 in 1800. At a growth rate of 1 percent, that population would grow to 100,000 in 1870. By 1940 it would reach 200,000; by 2010, 400,000. Recalling the chessboard example, you can see that even a 1 percent growth rate can have serious consequences. The number of people added each year becomes part of the total population, which then increases by another 1 percent in the following year.

Malthus and Population Growth

Concern about population is not new. In 1798, Thomas Robert Malthus, an English minister and economist, published *An Essay on the Principle of Population.* In his essay, Malthus described relationships between population growth and economic development. Here are the key concepts in his theory.

English minister and economist Thomas Malthus wrote about the ability of the food supply to keep up with population growth.

- Population, if left unchecked, will exceed the food supply. This is because population increases exponentially, while the food supply does not.

- Checks on population can be *positive* or *preventive*. Positive factors are events or conditions that increase mortality. They include famine, disease, and war. Preventive factors decrease fertility and include sexual abstinence and marrying at a later age. (Remember that at the time Malthus wrote there was no reliable birth control. For this conservative minister, sexual abstinence was the only acceptable way to reduce the number of births.)

- For the poor, any improvement in income is eaten up in additional births. This leads to lower per-person food consumption, lower standards of living, and eventually death.

- The wealthy and well educated already exercise preventive checks.

How did Malthus apply his theory to population control?

Malthus believed that positive checks on population growth could be avoided through education of the poor. With education, he wrote, the poor would raise their standard of living and choose to have smaller families. That part of Malthus's theory is not generally known, however, because he is most remembered for his dire predictions that overpopulation would result in famine and poverty.

The Demographic Transition

Although wrong in some of his key assumptions, Malthus had a lasting impact on population study. His is not the only theory, however. Developed nations have followed a pattern of population growth different from that

Figure 16.4 Stages of the Demographic Transition
This figure illustrates the demographic transition. Stage 1 begins with small population growth due to a balance between birthrates and death rates (both at high levels). In Stage 2, population grows dramatically because the death rate decreases so much faster than the birthrate. Population growth begins to slow in Stage 3, when the birthrate belatedly drops sharply. Stage 4 is again a condition of smaller population growth because birthrates and death rates come into balance (both at low levels).

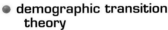

demographic transition theory
theory that population growth is a function of the level of economic development in a country

predicted by Malthus's theory. The **demographic transition theory** looks at the stages of economic development in a country to make predictions about population growth. This theory takes into consideration two things Malthus did not predict—agricultural productivity and reliable methods of birth control. Demographic transition theory describes four stages of population growth. (See Figure 16.4 shown above.)

- Stage 1. Both the birthrate and the death rate are high. Population growth is slow. No countries are at this stage today.

- Stage 2. The birthrate remains high, but the death rate drops sharply because of modernizing factors such as sanitation, increased food production, and medical advances. The rate of population growth is very high. Most sub-Saharan African countries are presently at this stage.

- Stage 3. The birthrate declines sharply, but because the death rate continues to go down, population growth is still rapid. Many Latin American countries are currently at this stage.

- Stage 4. Both the birthrate and the death rate are low, and the population grows slowly if at all. Anglo America, Europe, and Japan are at this stage today.

Future World Population Growth

World population growth has reached a turning point. After more than two hundred years of increase, the annual population growth rate is declining. The current growth rate is 1.2 percent, compared with the peak of 2.04 percent in the late 1960s. Moreover, the rate is projected to drop to zero by the year 2100.

But as we have seen, despite the reduction in the annual growth rate and birthrate, the world's population will continue to increase. Nearly eight billion people are expected to inhabit the globe by 2025. Throughout the first half of the twenty-first century, the annual growth rate is expected to decline until world population stabilizes at about eleven billion people. (See Figure 16.5.)

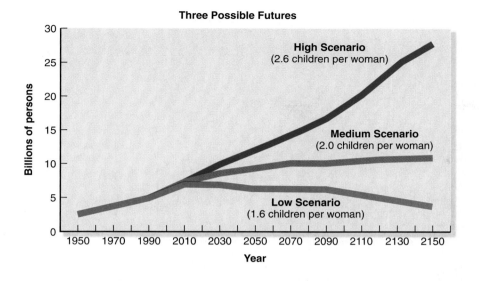

Three Possible Futures

High Scenario
(2.6 children per woman)

Medium Scenario
(2.0 children per woman)

Low Scenario
(1.6 children per woman)

Billions of persons

1950 1970 1990 2010 2030 2050 2070 2090 2110 2130 2150

Year

Figure 16.5 Long-Range Projections of World Population: 2000–2150
The United Nations' estimate of future growth is based on three different assumptions. The high scenario would push world population growth to over 27 billion. The medium scenario would result in a world population of about 11 billion. The low scenario would leave the world population at about 4 billion.

Source: United Nations, *Long-Range World Population Projections*, 1999.

At this point, the world will have reached **zero population growth**—when deaths are balanced by births so that the population does not increase (*World Population Data Sheet*, 2005).

Contrary to popular belief, limiting the average family size to two children does not immediately produce zero population growth. There is a time lag of sixty to seventy years because of the high proportion of young women of childbearing age in the world's population. Even if each of these women had only two children, the world population would grow.

The time lag is what demographers call **population momentum.** The growth of the world's population, like a huge boulder rolling down a mountain, cannot be stopped immediately. But the sooner the momentum of current population growth is halted, the better. The sooner the world fertility rate reaches the **replacement level** (the rate at which people replace themselves without adding to the population) the sooner zero population growth will be reached. The ultimate size of the world's population, when it does stop growing, depends greatly on the timing of reaching replacement level. To state it another way, for each decade it takes to reach replacement level, the world's population will increase by 15 percent.

- **zero population growth**
  situation in which deaths are balanced by births so that the population does not increase

- **population momentum**
  inability to stop population growth immediately because of previous high rate of growth

- **replacement level**
  birthrate at which a couple replaces itself without adding to the population

Population Control

As discussed earlier, death rates in both less developed and more developed nations have already dropped dramatically. Any significant progress in curbing world population growth must concentrate on lowering birthrates. **Population control** refers to the conscious attempt to regulate population size through national birth control programs.

Is government-sponsored population control new? Historically, most societies were more concerned with increasing the population than with overpopulation. Many births were needed to offset the high death rates from disease and poor hygiene. With surplus populations, aggressive nations were able to maintain larger armies. Agricultural societies needed large numbers of people to work the land. Aging parents wanted to be more secure in old age. High birthrates were also encouraged in countries with religious laws against birth control.

- **population control**
  attempts by government to control birthrates

European countries, such as Germany, have been very successful in controlling population growth through family planning.

● **family planning**
the voluntary use of population control methods

Since the middle of the twentieth century, however, more (but certainly not all) governments have come to view high birthrates as a threat to their national well-being. By 1990, most countries had in place formal programs to reduce birthrates. Government policies for population control range from voluntary to compulsory.

What is voluntary population control? The voluntary use of population control methods is generally known as **family planning.** Governments that support family planning provide information and services that help couples have only the number of children they want. Voluntary government policies range from indirect means such as family planning education to direct means such as distributing birth control materials at health clinics.

Even when effective, however, family planning programs merely enable families to achieve their *desired* family size. Unfortunately for effective population control, the desired family size in many nations is quite high. The average preferred family size (number of children) in African nations is 7.1; in Middle-Eastern nations, 5.1; in Latin American nations, 4.3; and in Asian Pacific nations, 4.0. In European countries, the average preferred family size ranges from 2.1 to 2.8.

How successful is voluntary population control? Family planning has succeeded in Taiwan, where the birthrate had fallen below replacement level by 2000. Taiwan's family planning efforts were launched under very favorable conditions. When the Japanese withdrew from Taiwan after World War II, they left behind a labor force trained for industrial work. Consequently, the Taiwanese were able to use this advantage to build an expanding economy. With economic development came a decline in both birth and death rates. In short, the Taiwanese went through the demographic transition fairly rapidly.

India was a different story. Family planning there got off to a very slow start, and the country has been unable to reduce the rate of population growth through voluntary means. Family planning efforts failed because government officials and family planners did not take the broader social context into account. For one thing, India did not have Taiwan's advantage of relatively rapid economic development. In addition, the Indian officials and planners did not make enough efforts to overcome cultural and religious opposition to birth control. Nor did they find enough ways to effectively communicate birth control information and technology. Finally, the national birth control program was left in the hands of individual state governments to implement.

Efforts to control population began to succeed in India only after the government turned to a sterilization program in 1976. Although the government did not use the force of law, a system of *disincentives* had the effect of compulsion. Those who could not produce official proof of a sterilization were denied such things as business permits, gun licenses, and ration cards for the purchase of basic goods (Weeks, 2004).

Have compulsory population control methods ever been used successfully?

Both China and Singapore have forced population control policies that seem to achieve their goals. China has been successful in reducing its total fertility rate from 7.5 in 1963 to 1.6 in 2005 through a system of rewards and punishments that includes a "one-child" policy. One-child families receive a larger retirement pension and enjoy preference in housing, school admission for their children, and employment. Families with more than one child are subject to an escalating tax on each child, and they get no financial aid from the government for the medical and educational costs of their extra children.

The island city-state of Singapore began formally discouraging large families in 1969. The government passed laws that penalized parents with large families (Weeks, 2004). These measures included

- denial of a paid eight-week maternity leave;
- loss of an income tax allowance;
- diminished access to public housing;
- increased maternity costs for each additional child;
- a lower likelihood of children's entering good schools.

India's population control programs have been only moderately successful at best. Consequently, India's population size is expected to exceed that of China within the next several decades.

China's population control efforts have been very effective. This poster of a mother and baby was designed to promote small families.

These policies worked so well that the total fertility rate in Singapore dropped from 4.5 children per woman to 1.4 between 1966 and 1987. In fact, the government became worried about the reduction in population size and, in 1986, reversed some of its earlier policies. The government of Singapore now supports three or more children for people able to afford them (Yap, 1995). Despite this effort, Singapore's current total fertility rate of 1.3 is far below replacement level.

Does one child make a difference? The importance of limiting family size, even by one child, can be illustrated by population projections for the United States. Even though the United States is unlikely to increase to a three-child average in the future, the hypothetical American case can help us understand the importance of population control. Figure 16.6 contrasts the projected population of the United States in the year 2070 for an average family size of two children and an average family size of three children. When small decreases in the death rate and net migration at the present level are assumed, an average two-child family size would result in a population of 300 million in 2015. Taking the hypothetical average family size of three children, the U.S. population would grow to 400 million by 2015. As time passed, the difference of only one extra child per family would assume added significance. By 2070, the two-child family would produce a population of 350 million, but the three-child family would push the population close to one billion! To say it another way, with an average family of two children, the U.S. population would not quite double itself between 1970 and 2070. But should the three-child family have been the average, the population would have doubled itself twice during this same period.

The consequences of limiting population in less developed regions becomes clearer when the effect of even one child added to the average number of children in a family is recognized. Moreover, the addition of one child per family has a greater effect as the population base gets larger; not only is one extra person added, but theoretically that one person will be involved with the reproduction of yet another three, and on it goes. The largest populations are found in less developed countries, which also have the largest average number of children per family.

Figure 16.6 Projected Populations of the United States
This graph illustrates the importance of reaching the population replacement level (two children per family). Are you surprised at the difference in U.S. population growth caused by an average of three children per family versus two children?

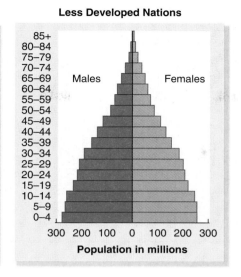

More Developed Nations

Age in years

Males   Females

85+
80–84
75–79
70–74
65–69
60–64
55–59
50–54
45–49
40–44
35–39
30–34
25–29
20–24
15–19
10–14
5–9
0–4

300 200 100 0 100 200 300
Population in millions

Less Developed Nations

Males   Females

85+
80–84
75–79
70–74
65–69
60–64
55–59
50–54
45–49
40–44
35–39
30–34
25–29
20–24
15–19
10–14
5–9
0–4

300 200 100 0 100 200 300
Population in millions

Figure 16.7
Age-Sex Pyramids in More Developed and Less Developed Countries
This figure shows general population patterns by age and sex in more developed and less developed countries. Using the dependency ratio, explain why children in more developed countries are economically better off than those in less developed nations.

Source: United Nations Population Division.

Population Pyramids

Population pyramids allow you to see at a glance the age and sex composition of a population. Age and sex are key indexes to fertility and mortality rates, which in turn are used to project school and housing needs, health resources, and other key social services. Population pyramids illustrate the *dependency ratio* that results from different rates of population growth. The **dependency ratio** is the ratio of persons in the dependent ages (under fifteen and over sixty-four) to those in the "economically active" ages (fifteen to sixty-four). The two aspects of the dependency ratio are *youth dependency* and *old-age dependency.* Less developed nations have much higher youth dependency than more developed nations. More developed nations have significantly higher old-age dependency. Figure 16.7 displays typical age-sex pyramids for more developed and less developed nations.

Why is the dependency ratio important? For less developed countries such as Mexico, a high youth dependency means that national income must be diverted from economic development to provide food, housing, and education for its large young population. In more developed countries such as the United States, rising old-age dependency creates a different set of problems. With a larger older population, there are fewer young people in the labor force to support the growing number of older people.

- **population pyramid**
  a graphic representative of the age and sex composition of a population

- **dependency ratio**
  the ratio of dependent persons to economically active

America's aging population is raising the dependency ratio. Why should that concern you?

This graph illustrates the rising old-age dependency occurring in the United States.

Source: U.S. Bureau of the Census, *Statistical Abstract of the United States, 2004–2005.*

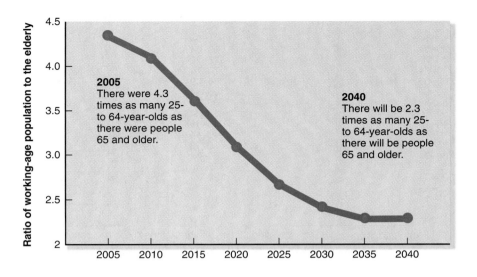

2005
There were 4.3 times as many 25- to 64-year-olds as there were people 65 and older.

2040
There will be 2.3 times as many 25- to 64-year-olds as there will be people 65 and older.

For example, in the United States in 2005 there were just over four times as many people age 25 to 64 as people 65 and over. By 2040, there will be only 2.3 times as many. (See Figure 16.8.) This shift will increase the burden on the young to pay for Social Security and Medicare. Other problems will include the need for increasing health care services and institutional arrangements for the long-term care of elderly people.

Section 2 Assessment

1. Briefly explain the difference between exponential and linear growth.
2. What are positive checks?
3. How does the demographic transition theory reflect the development of Western nations?

4. Which of the following figures is the world's population most likely to reach before it stops growing?
   a. four billion
   b. eight billion
   c. eleven billion
   d. twenty-five billion

Critical Thinking

5. **Evaluating Information** Given the exponential rate at which population grows, discuss the effect of zero population growth on the size of the world's population in 2020.

Sociology Today

Demography for Businesses

Businesses have discovered that they can grow bigger by targeting smaller groups of consumers. These groups, called generations, or cohorts, are defined by important life experiences. Events occurring when people first become economic adults (usually between ages 17 and 21) affect their lifelong attitudes and values. These attitudes and values are unlikely to change as a person ages. So the kind of music that is popular during these formative years often remains the preferred type of music for life. Similarly, early lifetime experiences influence preferences in many other product and service categories.

Studies of the U.S. population have identified seven distinct groups described in the table below. Which cohort are you? Your parents?

Cohort	Description	Born	Popular Music Styles
The Depression cohort	The G.I. generation	1912–1921	Big band
The World War II cohort	The Depression generation	1922–1927	Swing
The Postwar cohort	The silent generation	1928–1945	Frank Sinatra/Rat Pack
The Boomers I cohort	The Woodstock generation	1946–1954	Rock and roll
The Boomers II cohort	The zoomer generation	1955–1965	Rock and roll, disco
The Generation X cohort	The baby-buster generation	1966–1976	Grunge, rap, country western
The Boomlet cohort	The echo-boom generation	1977–	Retro-swing, Latin

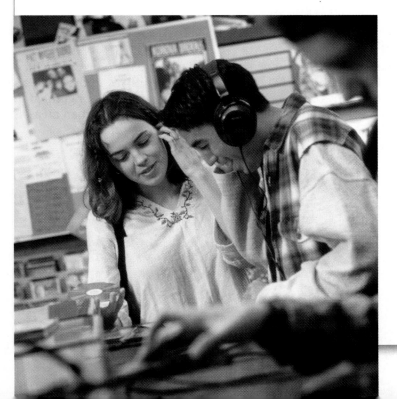

Doing Sociology

Have short interviews with members of at least two of the demographic business cohorts profiled above. Identify a number of differences in preferences for products between the members of different cohorts.

Source: Berkowitz, Kerin, Hartley, and Rudelius, *Marketing*, 5th ed. Chicago: Irwin, 1997.

The products in this mall store have been selected by taking into account the buying preferences of teenagers.

3

The Urban Transition

Key Terms

- city *(p. 548)*
- urbanization *(p. 548)*
- overurbanization *(p. 552)*
- suburbanization *(p. 552)*
- central-city dilemma *(p. 554)*
- gentrification *(p. 554)*
- edge city *(p. 554)*

- **city**
  dense and permanent concentration of people living in a specific area and working primarily in nonagricultural jobs

- **urbanization**
  process by which an increasingly larger portion of the world's population lives in cities

Crowded inner cities and sprawling suburbs appear in all American cities.

Section Preview

The first preindustrial cities developed in fertile areas where surplus food could be grown. With the Industrial Revolution came a major increase in the rate of urbanization. The development of factories was an especially important influence on the location of cities. Urbanization in more developed and less developed nations has occurred at different speeds. The United States is now primarily a suburban nation.

Defining a City

When does a village become a city? In Denmark and Sweden, an area with 200 inhabitants officially qualifies as a city. Populous Japan uses a much higher number—30,000. The cutoff point used by the U.S. Census Bureau to define a city is a population of 2,500. This number was set at a time when urbanization had just begun and population concentrations were small. It is obviously low for modern times.

A city is more than just a reasonably large number of people, however. Cities are also long-lasting. The periodic Woodstock rock festivals gather a large number of people in one place, but only for short periods of time. Clearly, large gatherings alone do not make a city. Cities also have a centralized economic focus. That is, they provide people with a chance to work in commerce, industry, or service. In summary, a **city** is a dense and permanent concentration of people living in a limited geographic area who earn their living primarily through nonagricultural activities.

Urbanization

The world has been greatly changed by **urbanization**—the process by which an increasingly larger portion of the world's population lives in or very near to cities. Urbanization has been so common that it is now taken for granted in many parts of the world. Today, almost as many people live in urban areas as in rural areas. This is a fairly recent development in human history.

What were early cities like? The first cities appeared about five or six thousand years ago and were quite small by modern standards. One of the world's first major cities was Ur, located at the point where the Tigris and Euphrates Rivers meet (in modern-day Iraq). At its peak, Ur held only about 24,000 people. Later, during the time of the Roman Empire, only a few cities had populations over 100,000. The population of Rome itself was probably between 500,000 and 1 million.

In addition to their small size, the cities of ancient and medieval periods contained only a small portion of the world's population. As recently as 1800, less than 3 percent of the world's population lived in cities of 20,000 or more. By contrast, today, 47 percent of the world's population live in urban areas. In North America, 79 percent of the population live in cities (*World Population Data Sheet*, 2005). How did cities develop so quickly and why have cities replaced rural living for most people?

Preindustrial Cities

Many of the first urban settlements were located in Mesopotamia and were established around 3500 B.C. This was after people learned how to cultivate plants and domesticate animals, a period known as the *agricultural revolution*. The Mesopotamian region is among the world's most fertile areas and the farmers in the area were able to provide enough extra, or surplus, food to feed people in the cities. A surplus food supply is necessary for urbanization to occur.

Who lived in preindustrial cities? Besides available food, people needed other reasons to gather in cities. Cities tended to attract four basic types of people: elites, functionaries, craftspeople, and the poor and destitute. For elites, the city provided a setting for consolidating political, military, or religious power. The functionaries were the political or religious officials who carried out the plans of the elites. Their lives were undoubtedly easier than those of the peasant-farmers in the countryside. Craftspeople, still lower in the stratification structure, came to the city to work and sell their products to the elites and functionaries. The poor came hoping to find work but were seldom able to improve their condition.

Calcutta, India, remains essentially a preindustrial city.

Do preindustrial cities still exist today? Africa, Asia, and Latin America are only partly industrialized. For this reason, many of their cities still have some preindustrial characteristics. This is particularly true in capital cities because they are a magnet to the rural poor seeking a better life. Rural migrants are attracted to these cities because there are limited opportunities for making a living in the rural areas and the city promises a better life. Unfortunately, most of those who migrate to the cities are disappointed, because the expected employment opportunities do not exist. The migrants end up living in terrible slums.

In Calcutta, India, for example, over 13 million people are crowded into a city whose last major sewer line was built in 1896. Epidemics are frequent, and disease is commonplace. Calcutta's housing supply, waterworks, electrical system, and other facilities are not sufficient to cope with the city's rapid growth.

Urban Population as a Proportion of Total Population

As discussed in the text, the Industrial Revolution encouraged the rapid growth of cities. The map below shows that many countries now have urban populations that comprise 60 percent or more of their total populations.

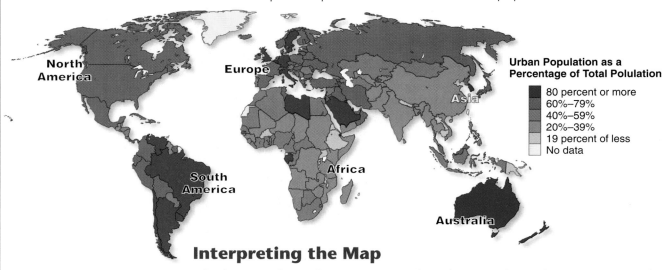

Urban Population as a Percentage of Total Polulation

- 80 percent or more
- 60%–79%
- 40%–59%
- 20%–39%
- 19 percent of less
- No data

Source: Population Reference Bureau, *2005 World Population Data Sheet*

Interpreting the Map

1. The map shows that countries such as the United Kingdon, Germany, and Sweden have urban populations that make up over 80 percent of their total populations. This can be explained by the effects of the Industrial Revolution, since these countries' economies are highly developed. However, other countries, such as Venezuela, Argentina, and Libya, which are not highly developed, also have urban populations that comprise over 80 percent of their totals. Can you think of reasons why this is so? Explain.

2. What effects will increased urbanization have on countries and the world?

The Rise of the Modern City

Beginning in the 1700s, the Industrial Revolution created major changes in transportation, agriculture, commerce, and industry. Technological developments led to better agricultural productivity and more efficient transportation systems. Farmworkers were free to leave rural areas and move into cities. More important, however, was the spread of factories.

Factories were not established to encourage the growth of cities, but they had that effect. Factory owners tended to build in the same area to share raw materials and to take advantage of natural features such as water power and river transport. Machinery and equipment makers located their plants

Figure 16.9	Urban Society

This table illustrates how functionalism and conflict theory might approach the study of urban society. Symbolic interactionism was not included. Why do you think it was excluded? Can you suggest a research topic in either population or urbanization for which symbolic interactionism would be appropriate?

Theoretical Perspectives	Concepts	Sample Research Topic
Functionalism	Urbanization	Study of the relationship between population density and the suicide rate
Conflict Theory	Overurbanization	Investigation of the relationship between the distribution of scarce resources and social class

next to the factories they would be supplying. All these businesses in turn attracted retailers, innkeepers, entertainers, and a wide range of people offering services to city dwellers. The more services offered, the more people were attracted, maintaining the cycle of urban growth. The industrial world was becoming an urbanized world.

World Urbanization

Urbanization is a worldwide movement. From 1800 to the mid-1980s, the number of urban dwellers increased one hundred times, while the population increased only about fivefold. Over 3 billion people—47 percent of the world's population—now live in urban areas. In more developed countries, 76 percent of the population lives in urban areas compared to 41 percent in less developed countries. (See Figure 16.10 on page 553.)

What are the patterns for urbanization? More developed and less developed countries have distinct patterns of urbanization. Most of the urban growth in less developed countries before the turn of the century occurred through colonial expansion. Western countries, which had been involved in colonial expansion since the late fifteenth century, held half the world under colonial rule by the latter part of the nineteenth century. It has been only since World War II that many of these colonial countries have become independent nations (Bardo and Hartman, 1982).

Since gaining independence, these former colonies have been experiencing rapid urbanization and industrialization. In fact, urbanization in these areas is now proceeding nine times faster than it did in the West during its urban expansion period. The rate of urbanization for major industrial nations in the West was 15 percent each decade throughout the nineteenth century. In the 1960s, the rate of urbanization in major less developed countries was 20 percent per decade (Light, 1983).

What are some other differences in the pattern of world urbanization? In the first place, industrialization in less developed countries, unlike the Western experience, has not kept pace with urbanization. Cities of North America and Europe had jobs for all migrants from rural areas. In the cities of less developed nations, the supply of labor from the countryside is greater than the demand for labor in the cities. A high rate of urban unemployment is the obvious result. The term **overurbanization** has been created to describe a situation in which a city is unable to supply adequate jobs and housing for its inhabitants.

Another difference between urbanization in more developed and less developed countries is the number and size of cities. When grouped by size, cities in more developed countries form a pyramid: a few large cities at the top, many medium-sized cities in the middle, and a large base of small cities. In the less developed world, in contrast, many countries have one tremendously big city that dwarfs a large number of villages. Calcutta, India, and Mexico City are examples. Of the world's ten largest cities, only three—Shanghai, Buenos Aires, and Calcutta—were in less developed countries in 1950. By 2003, as you can see in Figure 16.10 on the opposite page, seven of the top ten largest urban areas were in less developed countries. By the year 2015, it is predicted that there will be twenty-one "megacities" with populations of ten million or more. Seventeen of these will be in less developed countries, including the most impoverished societies in the world.

What are "push" and "pull" factors? In explaining why people in less developed countries move to large cities with inadequate jobs and housing, urban sociologists point to the operation of "push" and "pull" factors. People are pushed out of their villages because expanding rural populations cannot be supported by the existing agricultural economy. They are forced to migrate elsewhere, and cities are at least an alternative. Poor people are also attracted to cities in the belief there are opportunities for better education, employment, social welfare support, and good medical care. Unfortunately, they are likely to be disappointed.

Suburbanization in the United States

Unlike cities in the less developed world, cities in the United States have recently been losing population, not gaining. Since 1950, the proportion of the population living in suburbs has more than doubled. **Suburbanization** occurs when central cities lose population to the surrounding areas. The United States is now predominantly suburban.

What makes suburbanization possible? Suburbanization has become an important trend partly because of technological developments. Improvements in communication (such as telephones, radios, and television and later computers, fax machines, and the Internet) have allowed people to live away from the central city without losing touch with what is going on there.

● **overurbanization**
situation in which a city cannot supply adequate jobs and housing for its inhabitants

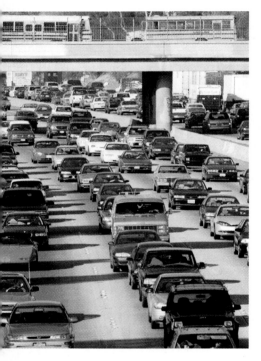

Los Angeles drivers spend about 82 hours a year, two full weeks of work, waiting in traffic. Does this mean that Los Angeles is overurbanized?

● **suburbanization**
loss of population of a city to surrounding areas

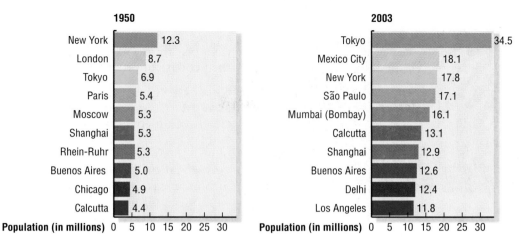

1950	
New York	12.3
London	8.7
Tokyo	6.9
Paris	5.4
Moscow	5.3
Shanghai	5.3
Rhein-Ruhr	5.3
Buenos Aires	5.0
Chicago	4.9
Calcutta	4.4

Population (in millions) 0 5 10 15 20 25 30

2003	
Tokyo	34.5
Mexico City	18.1
New York	17.8
São Paulo	17.1
Mumbai (Bombay)	16.1
Calcutta	13.1
Shanghai	12.9
Buenos Aires	12.6
Delhi	12.4
Los Angeles	11.8

Population (in millions) 0 5 10 15 20 25 30

Developments in transportation (especially trains, highways, automobiles, and trucks) have made it possible both for people to commute to work and for many businesses to leave the central city for suburban locations.

Technology is not the only cause of suburbanization. Both cultural and economic pressures have encouraged the development of suburbs. Partly because of America's frontier heritage, American culture has always had a bias against urban living. Some Americans prefer urban life, but most report that they would rather live in a rural setting. Even those who choose to live in the city believe they are giving up some advantages. Suburbs, with their low-density housing, have allowed many people to escape the problems of urban living without leaving the urban areas completely. Suburbs are attractive because of decreased crowding and traffic congestion, lower taxes, better schools, less crime, and reduced pollution.

The scarcity and high cost of land in the central city also encourages suburbanization. Developers of new housing, retail, and industrial projects often find suburban locations far less expensive than those near the central city. Finally, government policy has often increased the impact of economic forces. Federal Housing Administration regulations, for example, have favored the financing of new houses (which can be built most cheaply in suburban locations) rather than the refurbishing of older houses in central cities. Among other things, this has led to the *central-city dilemma*.

What is the central-city dilemma?

When suburbanization first became noticeable in the 1930s, only the upper and middle classes could afford to leave the central city. Not until the 1950s did the white working class follow them. Despite federal legislation prohibiting housing discrimination, the suburbs remained largely white until the 1970s. Since then, central-city minorities have moved to the suburbs in greater numbers. Still, the percentage of African Americans living in central cities has declined only slightly since 1970 (Farley, 1998; Palen, 2004).

The problem is not merely that minorities remain trapped in inner cities. Businesses have followed the more affluent people to the suburbs where they can find lower tax rates, less expensive land, less congestion, and their customers who have already left the city. Accompanying the exodus of the middle class, manufacturers, and retailers is the shrinking of the central-city tax base. As a result, the central city has become increasingly populated by the poor, the unskilled, and the uneducated. This has created the

Figure 16.10 World's Largest Urban Areas: 1950, 2003
This figure compares the world's largest urban areas in 1950 and 2003. What is the most surprising aspect of these data to you?

Source: *The World Almanac and Book of Facts, 2005.*

Sociology Online

Student Web Activity
Visit the *Sociology and You* Web site at glencoe.com and click on **Chapter 16—Student Web Activities** for an activity on suburbanization.

This view of Dallas was taken from the rooftop pool area of an old garment factory converted into luxury apartments.

● **central-city dilemma**
concentration of people in need of public services without tax base–generated money to provide for them

● **gentrification**
the development of low-income areas by middle-class homebuyers, landlords, and professional developers

● **edge city**
a suburban unit specializing in a particular economic activity

central-city dilemma—the concentration of a large population in need of public services (schools, transportation, health care) without the tax base to provide them.

Can the central-city dilemma be solved? Some countertrends exist. There are city governments now requiring certain public employees to live in the city. Some parts of inner cities are being restored through **gentrification**—the development of low-income areas by middle-class home buyers, landlords, and professional developers. Finally, there is a fairly significant movement of whites back to the central city. This movement is particularly evident among baby boomers who are remaining single or establishing childless or two-income families. Because these people are not as heavily involved in child rearing, they prefer central-city living more than the previous generation did (Palen, 2004). The importance of these countertrends for easing the central-city dilemma remains to be seen. They certainly have not been sufficiently important to stop the emergence of *edge cities*.

What are edge cities? As stated, increasing numbers of businesses and jobs have followed people to the suburbs. In fact, "suburban downtowns" are changing the face of urban America. An **edge city** is a smaller, more focused, version of an urban downtown. It is a suburban unit that specializes in a particular economic activity (Garreau, 1991). Employment in one edge city may focus on computer technology; employment in another, on financial services or health care. A specialized edge city, of course, will have many other types of economic activities as well, such as industrial tracts, office parks, distribution and warehousing clusters, and home offices of national corporations. Edge cities are actually little cities in themselves with a full range of services, including schools, retail sales, restaurants, malls, recreational complexes, medical facilities, and hotels and motels.

Edge cities do not have legal and physical boundaries separating them from the larger urban area in which they are located. This has not prevented names from being attached to several of them. Tyson's Corner is located in northern Virginia near Washington, D.C., Los Colinas is close to the Dallas-Fort Worth airport, and King of Prussia is northwest of Philadelphia. Another recent trend is *new urbanism*. This trend involves new housing and shopping areas built to mimic old-style neighborhoods. New older-style houses are built close together in walkable neighborhoods, with front porches that encourage interaction.

Section 3 Assessment

1. Give a brief definition of *urbanization*.

2. What are two conditions necessary for the development of modern cities?

3. Where are preindustrial cities located today?

4. What term describes mass migration to the suburbs?

Critical Thinking

5. **Analyzing Information** Do you think preindustrial cities can continue to exist? Why or why not?

TECH TRENDS

Virtual Communities

Some people find life in the big city so impersonal that they feel no sense of belonging to a community. In recent years, organizers throughout the country have used the Internet to rebuild community relationships through electronic networks. These *dedicated*—specialized—virtual communities use communications technology to link people who live in the same area, city, or neighborhood.

Organizers of community networks share the goals of local participation, community building, and democracy. As with the New England colonies' town meetings, the ideal of the new community networks is to include everyone. Supporters of the new technology claim that electronic communications will allow people to reestablish more personal relationships.

As with all projects involving technology, though, the problem of "electronic stratification" arises. Because of the costs involved, access to technological advances is not equally distributed throughout the community. Low-income individuals and families cannot afford computers or Internet access, and public agencies are not ready to supply sufficient funding. Furthermore, as computers become more sophisticated, people who are not already computer literate (especially lower-income people) will have an increasingly difficult time catching up. The technologically poor will become technologically poorer.

myspace.com is a Web site offering a virtual community for friends to stay in touch.

The Boulder (Colorado) Community Network (BCN), established in the mid-1990s, experienced many of these problems. The founders of BCN trained many different Boulder groups to use community networks. They found that acceptance varied widely among the groups. For example, residents at a local senior citizens' home became avid users of the community computers placed in their facility. In contrast, a group of low-income single parents virtually ignored the existence of the computers and the Internet, even after extensive training (Virnoche, 1998).

One national survey of Internet users found that virtual communities help individuals feel a closer connection to their local communities (Horrigan, 2001). Hence, ensuring that all segments of society have access to technological advancements may one day make the impersonal nature of big-city life a thing of the past.

Analyzing the Trends

What do you think will be the most significant effects of virtual communities on social roles?

4

Urban Ecology

● **urban ecology**
the study of the relationships between humans and city environments

● **concentric zone theory**
theory that describes urban growth in terms of circular areas that grow from the central city outward

Section Preview

Urban ecologists have developed four major theories of city growth: concentric zone theory, sector theory, multiple nuclei theory, and peripheral theory. Combining insights from all four theories is useful to our understanding of how humans relate to city environments.

The Nature of Urban Ecology

Although every city is unique, patterns have been found in the way humans interact with the cities they inhabit. **Urban ecology** is the study of the relationships between humans and their city environments.

In the 1920s and 1930s, sociologists at the University of Chicago studied the effects of the city environment on city residents. They asked such questions as why there are differences between areas of a city, how do different areas affect one another, and what processes change an area. To answer these and other questions, the University of Chicago sociologists developed theories of urban ecology, including theories of city growth (Flanagan, 1993; Micklin and Poston, 1998; Kleniewski, 2005).

Theories of City Growth

Sociologists focus on four major theories of city growth. *Concentric zone theory* describes urban growth in terms of circular areas that grow from the central city outward. *Sector theory* emphasizes the importance of transportation routes in the process of urban growth. *Multiple nuclei theory* focuses on specific geographic or historical influences. *Peripheral theory* emphasizes the growth of suburbs around the central city. The four approaches lead to quite different images of urban space. (See Figure 16.11 on the facing page.) No city exactly fits any of these images, however. Indeed, the theories tell us more when considered together than they tell us separately. To understand why this is so, we must first examine each theory.

What is concentric zone theory? Ernest Burgess (1925), like other early sociologists at the University of Chicago, was interested in the causes and consequences of Chicago's growth. His work led to the **concentric zone theory**, which describes city growth in terms of distinctive zones—zones that develop from the central city outward in a circular pattern. Many northern cities that experienced a great deal of immigration and rapid growth developed this way.

As illustrated in Figure 16.11, the innermost circle is the *central business district,* the heart of the city. This district contains major government and private office buildings, banks, retail and wholesale stores, and entertainment and cultural facilities. Because land values in the central city are high, space is at a premium. The central business district contains a large proportion of a city's important businesses partly because the less important ones are unable to compete for the expensive space in the central business district.

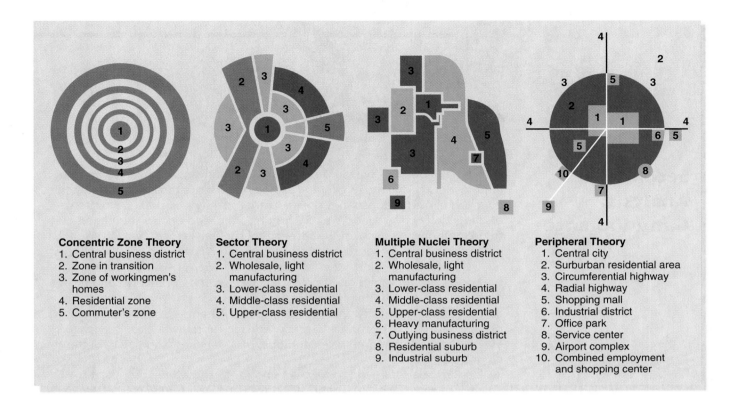

Concentric Zone Theory
1. Central business district
2. Zone in transition
3. Zone of workingmen's homes
4. Residential zone
5. Commuter's zone

Sector Theory
1. Central business district
2. Wholesale, light manufacturing
3. Lower-class residential
4. Middle-class residential
5. Upper-class residential

Multiple Nuclei Theory
1. Central business district
2. Wholesale, light manufacturing
3. Lower-class residential
4. Middle-class residential
5. Upper-class residential
6. Heavy manufacturing
7. Outlying business district
8. Residential suburb
9. Industrial suburb

Peripheral Theory
1. Central city
2. Surburban residential area
3. Circumferential highway
4. Radial highway
5. Shopping mall
6. Industrial district
7. Office park
8. Service center
9. Airport complex
10. Combined employment and shopping center

The central business district strongly influences other parts of a city. Its influence is especially clear in the zone immediately surrounding it. Burgess called this the *zone in transition* because it is in the process of change. As new businesses and activities enter the central business district, the district expands by invading the next zone. This area may have been a residential area inhabited by middle- or upper-class families, who left because of the invasion of business activities. Most of the property in this zone is bought by those with little interest in the area. Rather than investing money in building maintenance, landowners simply extract rent from the property or sell it at a profit after the area has become more commercialized. Until the zone in transition is completely absorbed into the central business district (which may never occur), it is used for slum housing, warehouses, and marginal businesses that are unable to compete economically for space in the central business district itself. In short, the invasion of business activities creates deterioration for the zone in transition.

Surrounding the zone in transition are three zones devoted primarily to housing. The *zone of workingmen's homes* contains modest but stable neighborhoods populated largely by blue-collar workers. In the northern United States, the zone of workingmen's homes is often inhabited by second-generation immigrants who have had enough financial success to leave the deteriorating zone in transition. Next comes a *residential zone* containing mostly middle-class and upper-middle-class neighborhoods. Single-family dwellings dominate this zone, which is inhabited by managers, professionals, white-collar workers, and some well-paid factory workers. On the outskirts of the city, often outside the official city limits, is the *commuter's zone,* which contains upper-class and upper-middle-class suburbs.

Figure 16.11
Theories of City Growth
This figure diagrams the four major theories of city growth. Discuss one important contribution each theory makes to our understanding of urban growth.

Source: Adapted from Chauncy D. Harris, *Urban Geography*, 1997.

Secondary Analysis: Gang Violence

Gangs have been a constant feature of the American urban landscape during most of the twentieth century. James Hagedorn's research (1998), however, led him to propose that postindustrial society has changed patterns of gang violence. Hagedorn's conclusions are based on a combination of three methods: a review of the research of others, secondary analysis of data collected by other researchers, and original data gathered himself.

Gangs (mostly male) in the industrial period were tied to specific neighborhoods and new immigrant groups. Gang violence primarily centered on "turf" battles among neighborhood peer groups. Pride in violence came from defending territory. Violence provided excitement and a sense of place in a group. Nevertheless, these working- and lower-class boys would eventually move on to hold decent jobs, have families, and live in better neighborhoods.

Gangs today still tend to form around racial and ethnic groups and neighborhoods. Currently, gangs tend to be African American, Latino, or Asian, just as earlier gangs were formed mostly by European immigrants, such as those from Ireland, Italy, or Eastern Europe. According to Hagedorn, however, postindustrial gangs are different in important ways. First, gang violence has significantly increased. Second, gang-related homicides have risen dramatically. Gang violence, he notes, skyrocketed at the same time American corporations were moving well-paying jobs away from the central city. As legitimate work disappeared in inner cities, gangs turned from their earlier territorial emphasis to participation in the illegitimate drug market. The common outlook of gang members today is expressed by this gang member:

> I got out of high school and I didn't have a diploma, wasn't no jobs, wasn't no source of income, no nothing. That's basically the easy way for a . . . young man to be—selling some dope—you can get yourself some money real quick, you really don't have nothing to worry about, nothing but the feds. You know everybody in your neighborhood. Yeah, that's pretty safe just as long as you don't start smoking it yourself (Hagedorn, 1998:390).

Significantly, this gang member was not a teenager. While a minority of gang members remain committed to the drug economy, most seek "legit" jobs as they approach their thirties.

Working with the Research

1. Explain why urban gangs tend to form around minority groups.
2. Relate Hagedorn's findings on urban gang violence to Merton's strain theory, discussed in Chapter 7.

What is sector theory? Not everyone agreed with Burgess's theory of how cities grow. The sociologist Homer Hoyt (1939) offered another model—**sector theory.** Hoyt's work indicated that growth patterns do not necessarily spread out in rings from the central business district. Instead, growth is more strongly affected by major transportation routes.

As Figure 16.11 shows, sectors tend to be pie-shaped, with wedges radiating from the central business district to the city's outskirts. Each sector is organized around a major transportation route. Once a given type of activity is organized around a transportation route, its nature tends to be set. Thus, some sectors will be predominantly industrial, others will contain stores and professional offices, others will be "neon strips" with motels and fast-food restaurants, and still others will be residential sectors, each with its own social class and ethnic composition.

As in concentric zone theory, cities are generally circular in shape. But because of the importance of transportation routes extending from the central business district, the boundaries of many cities form a starlike pattern, rather than a uniformly circular shape. The exact shape of a city, however, is not a major issue in sector theory. Emphasis here is on how patterns of growth are organized around transportation routes. Cities that follow this pattern include Seattle, Richmond, and San Francisco.

What is multiple nuclei theory? Many cities have areas that cannot be explained by either concentric zone or sector theory. Chauncy Harris and Edward Ullman (1945) suggested that cities do not always follow a pattern dependent on a central district. The **multiple nuclei theory** states that a city may have several separate centers, some devoted to manufacturing, some to retail trade, some to residential use, and so on. These specialized centers can develop because of the availability of automobiles and highways. They reflect such factors as geography, history, and tradition. The city of Boston fits this model.

What is peripheral theory? The three theories of urban growth just discussed were originally developed more than sixty years ago. Despite their age, the insights of each theory still help us to understand how cities have expanded from the center outward. This is especially the case for older cities such as Chicago and San Francisco. Many cities today, however, no longer have a central city core to which other parts of the metropolitan area are oriented all of the time.

Dependence on shipping, railroads, and heavy manufacturing has been replaced by more flexible means of transportation, such as cars and trucks. And large urban areas are now encircled by highways. New technologies (fax machines, cell phones, computers, the Internet) are also loosening the ties of most parts of the city to the central city core. As a result, many cities are now oriented *away* from the older urban core.

As noted earlier, many Americans have moved from the city to the suburbs. They have done so in part because many businesses— offices, factories, schools, retail stores, restaurants, health centers—are also in the suburbs. To describe changes in urban areas today, urban geographer Chauncy Harris (1997) has formulated the **peripheral theory.** The dominant feature of this model is the growth of suburbs (and edge

---

● **sector theory**
theory that emphasizes the importance of transportation routes in the process of urban growth

● **multiple nuclei theory**
theory that focuses on specific geographic or historical influences on urban growth

● **peripheral theory**
theory that emphasizes the growth of suburbs around the central city

Explain which theory of urban growth best accounts for this suburban office building.

cities) around and away from the central cities. (See Figure 16.11.) Peripheral theory brings urban growth research up to date.

Which of these theories of city growth is correct? As suggested earlier, no single theory covers the dynamics of city growth for all cities. But each theory emphasizes the importance of certain factors that cannot be overlooked by anyone interested in city growth.

- Concentric zone theory emphasizes the fact that growth in any one area of a city is largely influenced by politics and economics. According to this theory, the distribution of space is heavily influenced by those with the money to buy the land they want for the purposes they have in mind.

- Sector theorists have also contributed to an understanding of urban growth. As they have noted, transportation routes have a strong influence on cities. Decisions about the placement of railroad lines had important effects on the growth of cities in the nineteenth and early twentieth centuries. Highways and major streets have an even larger impact now.

- Although multiple nuclei theory is vague in its predictions, the types of geographic and historical factors it emphasizes are also important for understanding any specific city.

- Peripheral theory has brought urban growth research up to date by emphasizing the development of suburbs around the central city.

Section 4 Assessment

1. Provide a brief description of each of the following zones.
   a. central business district
   b. commuter's zone
   c. residential zone
   d. zone in transition
   e. zone of workingmen's homes

2. What is the driving force behind the sector theory?

3. Why is the multiple nuclei theory considered more flexible than the concentric zone theory or the sector theory?

Critical Thinking

4. **Summarizing Information** Summarize the evolution of cities, focusing on the differences between life in preindustrial cities and life in industrial and suburban cities.

5. **Applying Concepts** Discuss the major contributions the four theories of city growth have made to our understanding of city growth.

Summary

Section 1: The Dynamics of Demography

Main Idea: Demography is the scientific study of population. Demographers consider three population processes when looking at population change: fertility, mortality, and migration.

Section 2: World Population

Main Idea: Thomas Malthus (1798) predicted that population size would ultimately outstrip the food supply, resulting in mass starvation and death. The demographic transition theory looks at economic development to predict population patterns. While the rate of world population growth is slowing, the world's population will continue to increase for many years.

Section 3: The Urban Transition

Main Idea: The first preindustrial cities developed in fertile areas where surplus food could be grown. With the Industrial Revolution urbanization increased dramatically. Urbanization in developed and developing nations has occurred at different speeds.

Section 4: Urban Ecology

Main Idea: Urban ecologists have developed four major theories of city growth: concentric zone theory, sector theory, multiple nuclei theory, and peripheral theory.

Sociology Online

Self-Check Quiz
Visit the *Sociology and You* Web site at glencoe.com and click on **Chapter 16—Self-Check Quizzes** to prepare for the chapter test.

Reviewing Vocabulary

Complete each sentence using each term once.

a. demography
b. fertility
c. fecundity
d. crude birthrate
e. fertility rate
f. mortality
g. crude death rate
h. infant mortality rate
i. migration
j. doubling time
k. replacement level
l. urban ecology

1. _____ is the number of children born to a woman or a population of women.
2. The annual number of live births per one thousand women aged fifteen to forty-four is called _____ .
3. _____ refers to the deaths within a population.
4. The annual number of deaths per one thousand members of a population is called _____ .
5. _____ is the annual number of deaths among infants under the age of one per one thousand live births.
6. The number of years needed to double the base population is known as the _____ .
7. _____ is the birthrate at which a couple replaces itself without adding to the population.
8. The scientific study of population is called _____ .
9. The study of relationships between humans and their city environments is called _____ .
10. _____ is the movement of people from one geographic area to another.
11. The annual number of live births per one thousand members of a population is called _____ .
12. _____ is the maximum rate at which women can physically produce children.

Reviewing the Facts

13. Identify and describe the three population processes. Use a diagram similar to the one below to record your answers.

Process	Description
1.	
2.	
3.	

14. What is suburbanization?

15. What was Thomas Malthus' solution for overpopulation?

16. In your own words, explain population momentum.

17. What is the difference between replacement level and zero population growth?

18. List and explain the four major theories of city growth.

Thinking Critically

19. Making Generalizations

The United States is actually nearing zero population growth—except for the influx of immigrants. Recall from your history or government classes as many of the benefits and disadvantages of open immigration as you can and discuss them in class. Do you think immigration should be a factor in considering methods of controlling population? Why or why not?

20. Drawing Conclusions

Sometime in October 1999, the world population reached six billion. As you read in the chapter, the population is expected to reach seven billion by 2010. How are technological improvements contributing to this rapid growth?

21. Analyzing Information

Technology has been credited with increasing population growth. In what ways might it be employed to slow down the rate of population growth?

Best of Latin America/Cagle Cartoons

22. Analyzing Cartoons

This cartoon was published in Brazil. As your chapter notes, in developing nations, it is often the case that there is on gargantuan city (upwards of 10 million population), and many smaller towns and villages in the rest of the country. How does the cartoonist's art help convey his message about the effects? What nationality do you suppose the person is in the center?

23. Making Inferences

Emile Durkheim was concerned about the changes brought on by the Industrial Revolution. He studied suicide rates and found them to be higher in urban areas. What factors might contribute to higher suicide rates in urban areas that would not be factors in rural areas? Do you think Durkheim's findings hold today, or is the likelihood of suicide just as great in rural and suburban areas?

Sociology Projects

24. Theories of Urban Growth

Obtain a map of a large city in your area. (If you live in a fairly large city, use a map of it.) By looking at the map, can you determine if patterns of growth in this city proceeded according to one of the theories of urban growth described in the chapter? If so, take a marker and illustrate the patterns on the map. You might also talk with people in the city who have some knowledge of how the city changed over time, such as the local historical society, city clerks, or a local sociologist.

25. Analyzing Trends

In this chapter, you read about migration. Study the table below, which presents immigration statistics for the past 25 years: the first two columns give data for a ten-year increment, while the second two columns give data for three-year and one-year increments respectively. Based on the information, is the next decade on track to sustain immigration growth at the same rate for each world region? Conduct further research by finding a recent newsmagazine article on immigration. Then summarize this information and determine whether it reflects the data in this table. In class, share your article and conclusions with others.

Immigrants to the U.S., 1981–2004 (in thousands)				
Place of Birth	1981–1990	1991–2000	2001–2003	2004
Europe	705.6	1,311.4	450.3	127.7
Asia	2,817.4	2,892.2	936.6	330.0
Arica	192.3	383.0	163.0	66.3
Oceania	NA	48.0	16.0	6.0
North America	3,125.0	3,917.4	1,063.1	341.2
South America	455.9	539.9	198.6	71.8
All Other	7,338.1	9,095.4	2,833.9	946.1

Source: *Statistical Abstract of the United States, 2006*

26. Demographic Transition

Pick another country. Of the four stages of demographic transition described on pages 539–540, which one best reflects the country you chose? What are the factors that caused you to place the country at this stage?

27. Urban Planning

Choose three classmates to join you as members of the Urban Planning Board of Betterville, USA. As members of the Urban Planning Board, it is your task to jointly design the city for redevelopment. Examine the four major theories of city growth. Determine which theory or combination of theories you would use to design Betterville. Create a visual representation of your city design (e.g., blueprint, chart, artist rendering, etc.). Write a one-page essay explaining the theory or combination of theories that you chose and the rationale for your choice.

Technology Activity

28.

William Julius Wilson, a sociologist at Harvard University, has done extensive research on what the text calls the central-city dilemma. The Public Broadcasting System (PBS) sponsored an on-line forum with Dr. Wilson, called "A Look at the Truly Disadvantaged." Go to this web site at http://www.pbs.org/newshour/forum/november96/wilson10.html and select "Why is inner city education so poor?"

a. What is to blame for the poor results often obtained in inner city schools, according to Dr. Wilson?

b. Now select "How can inner cities be reconnected to the rest of American society?" What are Dr. Wilson's recommendations for solving the central-city dilemma?

Enrichment Reading

HIV/AIDS and the Global Population

from the Population Reference Bureau

- **epidemic**
  widespread outbreak of disease

- **prematurely**
  before the usual time

- **ravages**
  affects destructively

Now in its third decade, HIV/AIDS may become one of the deadliest **epidemics** in human history. Experts estimate that at least 20 million people have already died of AIDS, and that most of the 40 million people now living with HIV are likely to die a decade or more **prematurely.** In 2003, an estimated 5 million people were newly infected with HIV, about 95 percent of whom live in developing countries. The UN projects 45 million new HIV infections by 2010 unless the international community launches massive, coordinated measures to combat the epidemic.

In developing countries, AIDS is reversing hard-earned improvements in health over the last 50 years as the disease claims the lives of millions of young adults in their most productive years. Indicators of human development, such as child mortality, literacy, and food production, are slipping. The disease **ravages** families, communities, and health systems, and in severely affected countries, the economy and political stability are also threatened.

Areas Most Affected

Sub-Saharan Africa is the hardest hit region in the world, accounting for almost two-thirds of all people infected with HIV. In this region, where the disease is mainly transmitted heterosexually, more people die of AIDS-related illnesses than of any other cause. South Africa has the highest absolute number of infections of any country in the world: 5 million. Botswana has the highest adult HIV prevalence rate: An estimated 39 percent of the country's adults are infected with HIV.

Other regions face serious HIV/AIDS epidemics as well, though the main mode of transmission varies from one region to another.... HIV prevalence is already high in the Caribbean and is rising rapidly in Eastern Europe, the former Soviet republics, and many parts of eastern and southern Asia. Demographic billionaires China and India have relatively low prevalence rates, but the numbers of infected people are staggering: An estimated 1 million in China and 4.5 million in India are living with the disease. These two countries will see millions of additional infections unless they launch large-scale, effective prevention programs.

Health and Life Expectancy

In sub-Saharan Africa and elsewhere, HIV infection has triggered an upsurge in several other infectious diseases and is contributing to an explosive tuberculosis epidemic. In heavily affected countries, HIV has overwhelmed public health systems, stretching health care providers, infrastructure, and budgets beyond capacity.

HIV/AIDS is now the fourth leading cause of death worldwide. In 2003, an estimated 3 million adults and children died of AIDS, of whom 2.3 million were in sub-Saharan Africa. In a few countries, such as Brazil, where drugs are available to treat HIV/AIDS, AIDS deaths have fallen, but in most countries the drugs are not widely available or affordable. . . . .

The excess deaths are contributing to a rapid drop in life expectancy: In the 38 most-affected African countries, nearly 10 years of life expectancy will have been lost by 2020–2025. Average life expectancy has dropped to age 40 or less in Botswana, Mozambique, and six other countries.

Population Growth and Structure

Despite large numbers of AIDS deaths, populations continue to grow in many heavily affected countries, although the growth is less than it would be in the absence of AIDS. Africa's population will grow to 1 billion by 2050 because of continued high fertility in the region, but this is about 350,000 less than projected without AIDS. In South Africa, one of the hardest-hit countries, the current population of 44 million is projected to be 33 million in 2050, almost one-half what it would have been without AIDS. AIDS will trigger population decline in a few African countries in addition to South Africa—Botswana, Lesotho, Mozambique, and Swaziland. Population growth is expected to halt in Malawi, Namibia, and Zimbabwe.

Because HIV/AIDS tends to strike the young and sexually active, AIDS deaths have **distorted** the age and sex profiles of the populations in heavily affected communities and countries. Individuals are often infected as young adults and can survive an average of about 10 years after infection; thus, AIDS deaths tend to be high among women in their 30s and among men in their 40s and 50s. The unbalanced ratios affect population growth as well as the social and economic well-being of the heavily infected areas.

Toll on Societies

Households bear most of the burden of the disease, as families must care for the ill or for orphans whose parents **succumbed** to AIDS, and cope with a loss of income when breadwinners die. In addition, HIV/AIDS exacts a particular toll on a country's health sector, educational system and other public services, and industry and agriculture.

The global HIV/AIDS **pandemic** shows little sign of slowing despite stepped-up efforts to control it. The future course of the epidemic is difficult to predict and will depend on several factors: the effectiveness of prevention programs in educating people about HIV/AIDS and persuading them to change their behavior; the availability of treatments for those who have the disease; the future availability of an effective vaccine (now still distant); and the financial and human resources devoted to these efforts worldwide.

Read and React

1. What area of the world accounts for the majority of HIV infections?
2. How many people in China and India have HIV?
3. How has average life expectancy been affected in Botswana and Mozambique?
4. How is AIDS affecting population projections for South Africa?

- **distorted**
  twisted out of a natural, normal, or original shape or condition

- **succumbed**
  died by the effect of destructive forces

- **pandemic**
  worldwide spread of disease

Source: Population Reference Bureau staff, "Transitions in World Population," Population Bulletin 59, no. 1 Washington, DC: Population Reference Bureau, 2004.

Social Change and Collective Behavior

Learning Objectives

After reading this chapter, you will be able to

- illustrate the three social processes that contribute to social change.

- discuss how technology, population, natural environment, revolution, and war cause cultures to change.

- describe social change as viewed by the functionalist and conflict perspectives.

- discuss rumors, fads, and fashions.

- compare and contrast theories of crowd behavior.

- compare and contrast theories of social movements.

Applying Sociology

Social change occurs in all societies and in many ways. Today, many Americans may be especially aware of the changes technology brings. News stories tell of workers losing their jobs in the steel industry or of others who must learn computer skills to survive.

The photo at left shows a dramatic example of social change in action: the March on Washington of August 28, 1963. That day, more than 250,000 people gathered to demand that the government pass a major civil rights bill and take other actions to end racial discrimination. Since that day, Americans have seen other groups organize to bring about social change—women, Latinos, gay men and women, and other groups, as well.

We often assume that the societies of the past stood still. Sociology teaches us, however, that change comes to all societies. Whether by borrowing from other cultures or discovering new ways of doing things, societies change—though industrialized societies tend to change at a faster pace. In this chapter you will read about the many ways change is introduced in a culture and how its effects ripple through a society.

Sociology Online

Chapter Overview
Visit the *Sociology and You* Web site at glencoe.com and click on **Chapter 17— Chapter Overviews** to preview chapter information.

Social Change

● **social change**
  new societal behaviors with important long-term consequences

Section Preview

Social change refers to new behaviors that have long-term and relatively important consequences. Discovery, invention, and diffusion are the major social processes through which social change occurs. Important agents of social change are technology, population, the natural environment, revolution, and war.

Defining Social Change

Change is one of the most constant features of American society. This is so true that it is almost a cliché. In fact, all societies change—some rapidly, others more slowly. For sociologists, **social change** occurs when many members of the society adopt new behaviors. The behaviors must have long-term and important consequences.

How fast has social change occurred?
Scientists use an analogy to help people understand the pace of social change. Imagine for a moment the entire history of Earth as a 365-day period. Midnight of January 1 is the starting point. Today's date is December 31. Each Earth "day" represents about twelve million years. The first form of life, a simple bacterium, appeared in February. More complex life, such as fish, appeared about November 20. On December 10, the dinosaurs appeared; by Christmas they were extinct. The first recognizable human beings did not appear until the afternoon of December 31. Modern humans (*homo sapiens*) emerged shortly before midnight that day. All of recorded history occurred in the last sixty seconds of the year (Ornstein and Ehrlich, 2000). In the scheme of history, then, human social changes occur in the "blink of an eye." Only when we look at social change from the perspective of the human life span does it sometimes seem to be a slow process.

Can social change be predicted?
It is difficult to predict how a society will change. This is partly because the course of change in a society depends on the nature of the existing culture. For example, two societies that adopt a democratic form of government may develop in very different ways. Both Britain and the United States are democracies. But their histories prior to becoming democracies were different, since Britain had a royal tradition. As a result, democratic government took different forms in these two nations.

Figure 17.1 Key Assumptions in Predicting Social Change in America

The most accurate predictor of trends in American society has been the Frenchman Alexis de Tocqueville. Tocqueville's *Democracy in America*, which was published in the 1830s, displayed an amazing grasp of American society. Tocqueville's success has been attributed to several key assumptions he made. Do you think that any of these assumptions are less important today in predicting social change than the others?

1. **Major social institutions would continue to exist.**
   Unlike many of his contemporaries—and many of ours—Tocqueville did not expect the family, religion, or the state to disappear or to be greatly changed.

2. **Human nature would remain the same.** Tocqueville did not expect men and women to become much better or worse or different from what history had shown them to be.

3. **Equality and the trend toward centralized government would continue.**

4. **The availability of material resources (such as land, minerals, and rich soils) limits and directs social change.**

5. **Change is affected by the past, but history does not strictly dictate the future.**

6. **There are no social forces aside from human actions.**
   Historical events are not foreordained by factors beyond human control.

Adapted from Theodore Caplow, *American Social Trends* (New York: Harcourt Brace Jovanovich, 1991), p. 216.

In addition, change does not merely "happen" to people. People in a society can consciously decide for themselves how change will occur. They can, for example, deliberately avoid a predicted state of affairs (Caplow, 1991).

These facts should not discourage people from attempting to understand changes in society. Alexis de Tocqueville was a Frenchman who published a remarkably penetrating study of American society after a tour in the early 1830s. The accuracy of his predictions was based upon sound assumptions he made about American society. Figure 17.1 discusses these basic premises.

Why do some societies change faster than others? Understanding why some societies change faster than others is another difficult task. Sociologists have identified several important social processes that influence the pace of social change. In addition, several specific factors play important roles. We turn first to the social processes and then to the specific agents, or factors, that affect rates of change.

Social Processes

A process is a series of steps that lead gradually to a result. As you get closer to graduation from high school, you may decide to continue your formal education. You will then begin a process of applying for acceptance to various colleges. If you follow all the steps in the necessary order and meet the colleges' criteria for entrance, the end result of your application process will be an acceptance letter.

Cultures and societies experience **social processes** that result in significant changes. Three important social processes are *discovery*, *invention*, and *diffusion*.

● **social processes**
series of steps leading to change on a societal level

Rapid social change means that generations do not share certain knowledge. Besides "snail-mail," what are some other products or technologies that might become obsolete?

discovery
process by which something is learned or reinterpreted

How does discovery promote social change? In the **discovery** process, something is either learned or reinterpreted. When early ocean explorers did not fall off the end of the world, they changed what all but a few people believed about the shape of the earth. With this geographical knowledge came new patterns of migration, commerce, and colonization. Salt, another early discovery, was first used to flavor food. Because it was so highly valued, it also came to be used as money in Africa and as a religious offering among early Greeks and Romans. Fire was used at first by prehistoric peoples for warmth and cooking. Later, people discovered that fire could be used to clear fields, to create ash for fertilizer, and to melt ores to combine into new metals.

invention
the creation of something new from previously existing items or processes

What is the role of invention in social change? **Invention** is the creation of something new from items or processes that already exist. Examples of physical inventions come easily to mind. Consider the airplane. It was not so much the materials Orville and Wilbur Wright used—most of the parts were available—but the way the brothers combined these materials that enabled them to make their successful flight at Kitty Hawk.

The pace of social change through invention is closely tied to how complex the society or culture already is. The greater the number of existing items, or elements, the more ways they can be combined into inventions. Thus, the more complex and varied a society, the more rapidly it will change. This helps to explain why people reached the moon less than seventy years after the Wright brothers' first flight, even though scientists believe that several million years had passed between the appearance of the human species and the invention of the airplane. NASA was able to reach the moon relatively quickly because the United States had become advanced in such areas as physics, aerodynamics, and the manufacturing of specialized materials.

diffusion
process by which one culture or society borrows from another culture or society

How important is diffusion in social change? When one group borrows something from another group—norms, values, foods, styles of architecture—change occurs through the process of **diffusion.** The extent and rate of diffusion depend on the degree of social contact. The more contact a group has with another group, the more likely it is that objects or ideas will be exchanged. In other words, social contact has the same effect on diffusion that complexity has on invention.

By which social process did this image of Elvis reach Jerusalem, Israel?

Borrowing may involve entire societies. The American colonists learned methods of growing cotton that were first developed in India. Potatoes from South America were transplanted across the Atlantic to become Ireland's most important food crop. Diffusion may also take place between groups within the same society. African American musicians were the creators of a jazz subculture that spread throughout white America (and into other countries as well).

Before it is widely accepted, a borrowed element must harmonize with the group culture. In spite of the fact that unisex fashion is popular in America today, wearing a Scottish kilt on the job could get a construction worker laughed off the top of a skyscraper. Wearing kilts still clashes with the American definition of manhood. If skirts are ever to become as acceptable for American men as pants are for women, either their form will have to be modified or the cultural concept of masculinity will have to change.

Diffusion may involve using only part of a borrowed characteristic or trait. The Japanese, for example, accept capitalism but resist the American form of democratic government, style of conducting business, and family structure. Diffusion almost always involves picking and choosing.

In modern society, most aspects of culture are borrowed rather than created. The processes of discovery and invention are important, but usually far more elements enter a society through cultural diffusion.

Technology

Besides the three processes for social change, sociologists have identified some major forces that lead to change. **Technology** includes knowledge and hardware (tools) that are used to achieve practical goals. The appearance of new technology is generally a sign that social change will soon follow (MacKenzie and Wajcman, 1998).

How important is technology to social change? Technology is a prime promoter of social change. *Time* magazine's selection of Albert Einstein as the person of the century reflected the magazine's conclusion that the twentieth century will be remembered most for its advances in science and technology (Golden, 1999).

● **technology**
knowledge and tools used to achieve practical goals

These students seem very comfortable with the fast pace of technological change in American society.

The creation of the silicon chip, which led to the computer revolution, has brought about technological change at an astounding rate. It took more than a century for telephones to spread to 94 percent of the homes in the United States. In contrast, in less than five years the Internet had reached over 25 percent of Americans. (See page 29 for a comparison of the number of years it took for various technologies to be adopted in U.S. households.)

The changes that resulted from the use of computers are almost impossible to list. In 1999, social historian Francis Fukuyama described a workplace undergoing a transformation. The effects of these changes, he claims, will be as great as those of the Industrial Revolution. Telecommunications technology, for example, will allow many to work from their homes, but it will result in far less human interaction (McGinn and Raymond, 1997–98). In the field of medicine, computer technology has radically changed many surgical techniques. Microsurgeries and radio wave therapy are examples (Cowley and Underwood, 1997–98). Drivers in Germany can get real-time computer-generated information on traffic problems on the autobahn by using cell phones or electronic consoles in their cars.

Population

Changing demographics are another important factor for creating social change. A classic example is the huge increase in the birth of babies following the return of American soldiers at the end of World War II (the so-called baby boom). Americans born between 1946 and 1964 caused the expansion of child healthcare facilities and created the need for more teachers and schools in the 1950s and 1960s. On the other hand, the generation following baby boomers now in their thirties and forties and in the labor market are experiencing increased competition for jobs and fewer opportunities to move up the career ladder. As the baby boomers retire, problems of health care and Social Security loom large. Longer working hours, retraining programs, and reeducation for older people will probably become political issues for future elections. As America's population continues to age, more attention is being paid to our senior citizens. Already, there are more extended-care homes, an increase in geriatric emphasis in medicine, and more television advertising and programming targeting the aging elderly population.

The Natural Environment

Interaction with the natural environment has, from the earliest times, also transformed American life. The vast territory west of the thirteen colonies permitted the nation to expand, ultimately to the Pacific Ocean. This western movement helped shape our cultural identity and values. It also caused untold changes, most tragically the destruction of many Native American cultures.

The environment continued to shape historical events, especially when natural disasters occurred. The Great Depression of the 1930s was due in part to a long drought that hit the Midwestern plains states. Overplanting and plowing had upset the fragile ecosystem and turned the prairies into a giant "dust bowl."

In 1986, the Chernobyl nuclear plant in Ukraine had a meltdown. This event added to opposition in the U.S. to using nuclear power as an energy source.

Another Time

The Horse Among the Plains Indians

Diffusion is one of the social processes that creates social change. The society of the Plains Indians in the west central United States was altered drastically by the European introduction of the horse—an example of diffusion.

In the nineteenth century, horses were the primary means of transportation and as such were an integral part of Plains Indian culture. The modern horse, however, was not native to the Americas, but was first brought by the Spanish. It was not until the late 1600s and early 1700s that horses in any numbers became available to the tribes of the Great Plains. . . .

The horse truly revolutionized life among the Plains tribes. The horse drastically altered the economic base and changed the lifestyle of these peoples. On horseback a hunter armed with bow and arrow could find and kill enough bison within a few months to feed his family for the year. Not only could he kill larger numbers of game animals, but he could pack the meat onto horses and readily transport it vast distances. Horses also allowed for the transporting of increased quantities of material goods. Teepees increased in size, and clothing and other material items became increasingly abundant and elaborate in decoration. For the first time these widely scattered groups could gather together in large camps, sometimes numbering in the thousands, for at least a portion of the year. In short, the horse quickly elevated the Plains tribes to relative prosperity.

The horse also sharply altered the relationship between these peoples and the neighboring farming tribes. The once relatively inoffensive nomads were now transformed into aggressive, predatory raiders. The Plains tribes were now capable of quickly assembling large parties of horse-mounted warriors who could raid the sedentary farming villages with impunity. The military balance of power had shifted.

In the decades immediately after the acquisition of the horse, the original Plains tribes flourished. Attacks on the neighboring farming peoples had a devastating effect, and many villages were abandoned. It was not long, however, before many cultivators saw both the economic and the military advantages derived from being horse-mounted nomadic bison hunters. The Cheyenne and some of the Dakota abandoned the life of settled farmers and moved westward to the plains to become nomadic, teepee-dwelling, bison hunters themselves. As they moved onto the plains, they came to challenge directly the original Plains tribes for dominance over critical hunting resources, which intensified warfare. As a result, warfare and the warrior tradition became an integral part of Plains Indian values, social organization, and behavior.

Source: Adapted from James Peoples and Garrick Bailey, *Humanity,* 5th ed. Belmont, CA: Wadsworth, 2000, p. 284.

Thinking It Over

1. List at least five major changes that resulted from the introduction of the horse to the culture of the Plains Indians.

2. Identify an item that has been introduced to your culture from another place. (This item could be food, clothing, an invention, or even an idea.) What effect has it had on your life?

World View

Internet Connections

As this map shows, the number of people connected to the Internet varies widely from country to country. As of 2004, over 74 percent of Internet connections were on the North American continent. This map shows the number of computers connected to the Internet per 10,000 people.

Computers Connected to the Internet per 10,000 People

- 5,000 or more
- 3,000–4,999
- 1,000–2,999
- 500–999
- 250–499
- 50–249
- 49 or less
- No Data

Source: International Telecommunication Union, 2004.

Interpreting the Map

1. Do you see a pattern in the number of connections to the Internet? Explain.
2. What implications might this distribution have for future social change?

In the early 1970s, OPEC (an organization of oil-producing nations) launched an embargo, refusing to sell its oil to other countries. Because of the natural short supply of oil without the contribution of the oil-rich Mideastern countries, oil products became scarce and expensive, contributing to economic inflation in the United States in the 1970s and early 1980s. As a result, Americans began driving smaller, more fuel-efficient automobiles.

Revolution and War

Revolution and war are related factors that lead to social change. A **revolution** involves the sudden and complete overthrow of an existing social or political order. A revolution is often, but not always, accompanied by violence. Most revolutionaries expect that the revolution will bring about fundamental changes. Karl Marx, for example, expected workers' revolutions

● **revolution**
sudden and complete overthrow of a social or political order

to eliminate class-based inequality and therefore to have a profound effect on the social and economic structures of the societies in which they occurred.

Are revolutions normally followed by radical changes? According to Charles Tilly, a revolution results in the replacement of one set of power holders by another (Tilly, 1978, 1997). In the view of another respected sociologist, a post-revolutionary society is eventually replaced by a society that looks much like the original one (Brinton, 1990). Radical changes are rarely permanent because people tend to revert to more familiar customs and behaviors. They do so in part because continuity with the past provides security and a blueprint for behavior.

What sorts of changes do follow revolutions? In most cases, the new social order created by a successful revolution is likely to be a compromise between the new and the old. Consider the example of China, the site of a communist revolution in 1949. The revolution did not result in the wholesale changes promised by its leaders. One of the revolutionary reforms, for example, promised liberation from sexism. The situation for Chinese women has improved, but sexual equality is a far-distant dream in that country ("Closing the Gap," 1995; Yuan, 2005).

How does war promote social change? **War** is organized, armed conflict that occurs within a society or between nations. Sociologist Robert Nisbet (2003) described how war brings about social change through diffusion, discovery, and invention. Social change is created through diffusion because wars break down barriers between societies, bringing people from different societies together. This association leads to the adoption of new ways of thinking, feeling, and behaving.

Wars also promote invention and discovery. For example, during World War II (1939–1945), the pressure of war enabled the U.S. government to promote and finance the development of such technologies as the atomic bomb, synthetic rubber, and antibiotics. Each contributed to a cultural revolution after the war. And America's culture, both during and after World War I, was imported by societies all over the world.

Wars often bring about social change because culturally dissimilar societies, such as the U.S. and Iraq, come into increased contact.

● **war**
organized, armed conflict that occurs within a society or between nations

Section 1 Assessment

1. Briefly describe three important processes for social change.

2. Provide one example each (not given in the text) of how population and interaction with the natural environment have caused social change.

3. Explain how war can be both a positive and a negative force for social change.

Critical Thinking

4. **Drawing Conclusions** Identify a major social change that has occurred in your lifetime. What do you think are the major sources of this change—discovery, diffusion, or invention? Be careful to relate the manner of change to the nature of the change itself.

Focus on Research

Case Study: Is the American Dream Dying?

Americans have long expected to achieve a higher standard of living than their parents. Instead, according to Katherine Newman (1994), social and economic change are placing the American Dream in jeopardy. The downscaling of jobs and pay that occurred during the 1980s and 1990s has replaced earlier optimism with anger, doubt, and fear.

Newman spent two years conducting personal interviews with 150 Americans living in "Pleasanton," a suburban community representative of much of America. Pleasanton is a mix of skilled blue-collar workers and white-collar professionals from a variety of ethnic and religious origins. Her respondents were schoolteachers, guidance counselors, and sixty families whose children were then grown.

The residents of Pleasanton believed that the promise of America had taken an unexpected wrong turn, and they were trying to make sense of it. Newman attempted to understand the residents' view of this downward mobility. The stresses associated with changing economic conditions, she believed, would bring cultural expectations, disappointments, and conflicts close enough to the surface for a trained social scientist to see. As the study progressed, she did, in fact, see conflict between parents and grown children, disagreements along lines of race and ethnicity, and unhappy marriages. The following statement reveals a baby boomer's shattered confidence in the American Dream.

> I'll never have what my parents had. I can't even dream of that. I'm living a lifestyle that's way lower than it was when I was growing up and it's depressing. You know it's a rude awakening when you're out in the world on your own. . . . I took what was given to me and tried to use it the best way I could. Even if you are a hard worker and you never skipped a beat, you followed all the rules, did everything they told you you were supposed to do, it's still horrendous. They lied to me. You don't get where you were supposed to wind up. At the end of the road it isn't there. I worked all those years and then I didn't get to candy land. The prize wasn't there . . . (Newman, 1994:3).

After a detailed and often personal exploration of what Newman calls the "withering American Dream," she turns to the larger social and political implications for society. She explores the transition from a society of upward mobility based on effort and merit to a society in which social classes of birth increasingly dictate future social and economic positions.

According to Newman, the soul of America is at stake. She raises these questions: Will Americans turn to exclusive self-interest, or will they care for others as well as themselves? Will suburbanites turn a blind eye to the rapidly deteriorating inner cities? Will the generational, racial, and ethnic groups turn inward, or will they attempt to bridge the divides that threaten to separate them further?

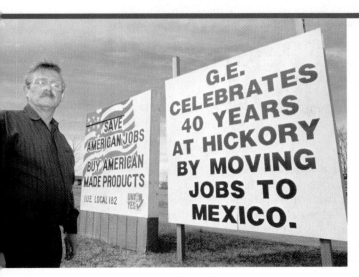

G.E. CELEBRATES 40 YEARS AT HICKORY BY MOVING JOBS TO MEXICO.

SAVE AMERICAN JOBS BUY AMERICAN MADE PRODUCTS
I.U.E. LOCAL 182 UNION YES

A former G.E. worker stands in front of signs lamenting the move of a plant from North Carolina to Mexico. This thirty-year veteran of the closing plant would agree that the American dream is dying.

A partial answer to these questions is reflected in public opinion about federal, state, and local tax revenues. If the residents of Pleasanton are any guide, Americans do not wish to invest in the common good. Public schools, colleges, universities, and inner cities, for example, are receiving a rapidly declining share of public economic support. In conclusion, Newman states:

This does not augur well for the soul of the country in the twenty-first century. Every great nation draws its strength from a social contract, an unspoken agreement to provide for one another, to reach across the narrow self-interests of generations, ethnic groups, races, classes, and genders toward some vision of the common good. Taxes and budgets—the mundane preoccupations of city hall—express this commitment, or lack of it, in the bluntest fashion. Through these mechanistic devices, we are forced to confront some of the most searching philosophical questions that face any country: What do we owe one another as members of a society? Can we sustain a collective sense of purpose in the face of the declining fortunes that are tearing us apart, leaving those who are able to scramble for advantage and those who are not to suffer out of sight? (Newman, 1994:221)

Working with the Research

1. Think about your past experiences at home and in other social institutions (such as schools and churches). What is your conception of the American dream, based on these experiences? Critically analyze the ways in which society shaped your conception.

2. Newman's research was done in the early 1990s. Do you believe that she is right about the fate of the American dream? Explain.

3. If the American dream is withering, many social changes are in store. Describe the major changes you foresee.

4. Suppose Katherine Newman had decided to place her study in the context of sociological theory. Write a conclusion to her book from the theoretical perspective—functionalist or conflict theorist—that you think is most appropriate.

2

Theoretical Perspectives on Social Change

Key Terms

- equilibrium *(p. 578)*
- urbanism *(p. 580)*

Section Preview

The functionalist and conflict perspectives view social change in very different ways. The functionalist perspective depicts societies as relatively stable. Following a major change, these integrated systems seek a new equilibrium. According to the conflict perspective, societies are unstable systems that are constantly undergoing change. Symbolic interactionism identifies decreasing shared values as a source of social instability.

The Functionalist Perspective

Because functionalism emphasizes social stability and continuity, it may seem contradictory to refer to a functionalist theory of social change. There are, however, two functionalist theories of social change—proposed by William Ogburn and Talcott Parsons—that are especially interesting. Both of these theories are based on the concept of *equilibrium*.

Close your eyes and imagine a tightrope walker inching his way across a deep chasm on a narrow rope. If you have an active imagination, you will picture him continually shifting his body and using a pole to counterbalance the effects of the wind as well as the effects of his own motions. The tightrope walker is concerned with maintaining equilibrium. When used by sociologists, **equilibrium** describes a society's tendency to react to changes by making small adjustments to keep itself in a state of functioning and balance.

A society in change, then, moves from stability to temporary instability and back to stability. Sociologists refer to this as a dynamic, or moving, equilibrium. For example, in 1972, a broken dam led to the destruction of the community of Buffalo Creek, West Virginia. The physical destruction of the community was accompanied by death and the loss of the old way of life.

- **equilibrium**
  a state of functioning and balance, maintained by a society's tendency to make small adjustments to change

Social equilibrium was shaken for a while, after an earthquake caused the collapse of this Los Angeles area freeway.

Figure 17.2 Social Change

This table provides one example each of how the functionalist, conflict, and symbolic interactionist perspectives view social change. Describe how a functionalist would look at an interest group and how a conflict theorist would view equilibrium.

Theoretical Perspectives	Concepts	Example
Functionalism	Equililbrium	Continuity in the nature of the presidency despite scandals in the Nixon and Clinton administrations
Conflict Theory	Interest Group	Enactment of civil rights laws in the 1960s as a result of the struggle over racial equality
Symbolic Interactionism	Urbanism	The smaller proportion of social interaction in a large city compared to a small town is based on a decrease in the number of shared meanings

Despite the ensuing chaos, residents slowly pulled their lives together again. Although things were not the same as before, a new equilibrium was built out of the wreckage. In time, we will see how this tendency toward equilibrium unfolds in New Orleans, which was devastated by Hurricane Katrina in 2005.

The 1960s saw the norms of sexual behavior change radically. After skyrocketing, for example, teenage pregnancy is declining. Although Americans do not follow the norms of the 1950s, a retreat from extremes is occurring as new norms of sexual behavior are being established.

The Conflict Perspective

According to the conflict perspective, social change is the result of struggles among groups for scarce resources. Social change is created as these conflicts are resolved. Many of the basic assumptions of the conflict perspective emerge from the writings of Karl Marx about social class conflicts (see page 16). Marx wrote that "without conflict, no progress: this is the law which civilization has followed to the present day."

Sociologists such as Ralf Dahrendorf have adapted many of Marx's ideas. Dahrendorf believes that the resources at stake are more than economic. The quest for power is the source of social change in his view. Whereas Marx saw conflict between two opposing social classes, Dahrendorf sees conflict among groups at all levels of society. Social change thus comes from a multitude of competing interest groups. These groups can be political, economic, religious, racial, ethnic, or gender based. Society changes as power relationships among interest groups change.

History seems to favor Dahrendorf's viewpoint over Marx's. Class conflict has not occurred in any capitalist society; social classes have not been polarized into major warring factions. Rather, capitalist societies are composed of countless competing groups. In America, racial groups struggle over the issue of equal economic opportunity, environmentalists and industrialists argue about environmental protection and economic development, and so on, with many other groups at odds with opposing groups over their own special issues.

Symbolic Interactionism

Human beings, according to symbolic interactionism, interact with others on the basis of commonly shared symbols. The nature and frequency of social interaction are affected by the extent to which people share meanings. As shared interpretations of the world decrease, social ties weaken and social interaction becomes more impersonal.

The relationship between shared meanings and the nature of social interaction can be illustrated within the context of the change from an agricultural economy to an industrial one. Accompanying this shift is the emergence of urbanization and its distinctive way of life. This distinctive way of life is known as **urbanism.**

What is the way of life associated with urbanism?

According to German sociologist Ferdinard Tönnies (1957), social interaction prior to the Industrial Revolution was based on shared tradition. In rural settings, daily life revolved around family, common norms and values, and an interest in the welfare of all community members. Tönnies thought that urbanization creates a very different way of life. In urban society, he wrote, social interaction is impersonal and fragmented because most people with whom one interacts are strangers who share little common tradition.

Sociologists have both agreed and disagreed with Tönnies ever since he introduced this view of urbanism in 1887. According to Tönnies's critics, the way of life in urban society is much more varied than he described it (Gans, 1968). While some urbanites may have hardly any shared meanings on which to base social interaction with others (poor people, elderly people), many others share meanings on which they interact (members of ethnic neighborhoods, members of artistic subcultures).

We need not worry about the outcome of this ongoing debate. It has been the subject of research for sociologists for a long time. What matters here is that this research is guided by ideas of symbolic interactionism.

Student Web Activity
Visit the *Sociology and You* Web site at glencoe.com and click on **Chapter 17—Student Web Activities** for an activity on urbanism.

● **urbanism**
the distinctive way of life shared by the people living in a city

Section 2 Assessment

1. Describe an area of your life that would benefit from having more equilibrium. How might you achieve this?

2. How did Dahrendorf's interpretation differ from Marx's theory of social change?

3. What theory of social change best explains the enactment of civil rights laws in the 1960s?

Critical Thinking

4. **Finding the Main Idea** Are functionalism and conflict theory compatible as explanations for social change? Clearly distinguish the two perspectives in formulating your answer.

Collective Behavior

Section Preview

Collective behavior describes how people behave when they are united by a single short-term goal. Rumors, fads, fashions, mass hysteria, and panics are examples of collective behaviors. Crowds gather and behave in different ways depending on the stimuli and conditions present. Contagion theory and emergent norm theory describe crowd behavior.

Defining Collective Behavior

The term **collective behavior** refers to the spontaneous behavior of people who are responding to similar stimuli. Let's look more closely at some of the terms in this definition. First, what is meant by *collective*? When sociologists use this term, they are referring to a large number of people who do not normally interact and who do not necessarily share clearly defined norms. Sociologists call such a gathering of people a **collectivity**. Stimuli are outside events or persons that cause a response. Putting it all together, collective behavior involves spontaneous social interaction in which loosely connected participants influence one another's behavior.

The study of collective behavior poses a large problem. Sociologists are used to studying structured, not unplanned, behavior. How are researchers going to investigate a social phenomenon that occurs spontaneously? In spite of this difficulty, sociologists have developed fascinating theories of collective

Key Terms

- collective behavior *(p. 581)*
- collectivity *(p. 581)*
- dispersed collectivity *(p. 582)*
- rumor *(p. 582)*
- urban legend *(p. 582)*
- fad *(p. 583)*
- fashion *(p. 583)*
- mass hysteria *(p. 584)*
- panic *(p. 586)*
- crowd *(p. 586)*
- mob *(p. 587)*
- riot *(p. 587)*
- contagion theory *(p. 587)*
- emergent norm theory *(p. 588)*
- convergence theory *(p. 588)*

- **collective behavior**
  the spontaneous behavior of a group of people responding to similar stimuli

- **collectivity**
  collection of people who do not normally interact and who do not share clearly defined norms

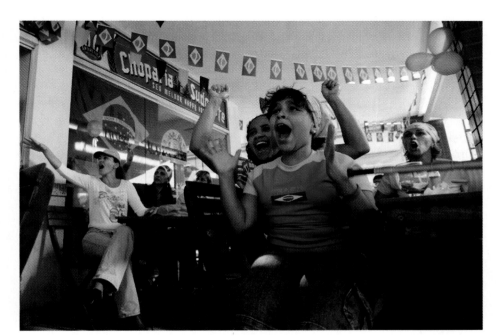

These Brazilian soccer fans may be influencing each other's behavior.

- **dispersed collectivity**
  collectivity made up of people who are not physically connected but who follow common rules or respond to common stimuli

Salsa dancing has become popular again.

- **rumor**
  a widely circulating piece of information that is not verified as being true or false

- **urban legend**
  a moralistic tale that focuses on current concerns and fears of the city or suburb dweller

behavior. It turns out that collective behavior involves more structure and rationality than appear on the surface. Sociologists identify several types of collective behavior. In the more structured forms, such as crowds and social movements, people are in physical contact. We will look at these interactions in the following sections. In a **dispersed collectivity** people are widely scattered. Nevertheless, they are in some way following common rules or responding to common stimuli. Behavior among members of dispersed collectivities is not highly individualized:

> When people are scattered about, they can communicate with one another in small clusters of people; all of the members of a public need not hear or see what every other member is saying or doing. And they can communicate in a variety of ways—by telephone, letter, Fax machine, computer linkup, as well as through second-, or third-, or fourth-hand talk in a gossip or rumor network (Goode, 1992:255).

Rumors, Legends, Fads, and Fashions

People will typically respond to certain information in similar ways, even when physically separated. *Rumors, fads,* and *fashions* are collective behaviors characteristic of dispersed collectivities.

What is a rumor? A **rumor** is a widely circulating story of questionable truth. Rumors are usually spread by people about events or other people that are of great interest to themselves. The mass media exploit the public's fascination with rumors. Entertainment magazines devote themselves exclusively to rock idols and movie stars; tabloid newspapers are loaded with suggestive guesswork, half-truths, and innuendos; even mainstream news publications offer accounts of the rich, famous, and offbeat. As these examples suggest, rumors and gossip are closely related.

You probably heard many rumors about what would happen when the clock struck midnight on the last day of 1999. According to these rumors, power grids would fail, elevators would stop working, and the stock market would crash as the year 2000 began. According to another rumor, a fast-food restaurant chain was increasing the protein content of its hamburgers by adding ground worms. The media told us of murders, rapes, and beatings in the New Orleans Superdome following Hurricane Katrina. There were also rumors of anthrax, monkeypox, and various rashes. None of these rumors proved true; but they were spread and believed, in part, because they touched on people's insecurities and anxieties.

How are urban legends started? Related to rumors are what Jan Harold Brunvand calls *urban legends* (Brunvand, 1989). **Urban legends** are moralistic tales passed along by people who swear the stories happened to someone they know or to an acquaintance of a friend or family member. Instead of fairy tales that take place in the far-distant past, urban legends take place in shopping malls, on city subways, and in schools. The tales often focus on current concerns and fears, such as AIDS and inner-city gangs. A typical story tells about a man who wakes up in a hotel room missing a kidney. Another describes alligators roaming the sewer systems of big cities. As cautionary tales, urban legends warn us against engaging in risky behaviors by pointing out what has supposedly happened to others who did what we might be tempted to try. Like rumors, urban legends permit us to play out some of our hidden fears and guilt feelings by being shocked and horrified at others' misfortune.

Are fads long lasting? A **fad** is an unusual behavior pattern that spreads rapidly, is embraced zealously, and then disappears after a short time. The widespread popularity of a fad rests largely on its novelty. Students in the early 1970s introduced the "streaking" fad—running naked across college grounds or through occupied classrooms. More recent fads include body piercing, tattoos, snowboarding, and oversized plain white T-shirts.

What are fashions? Fads are adopted by a particular group; fashions are much more widespread. A **fashion** is a behavior pattern that is widely approved but is expected to change periodically. In the United States today, the "in" fashions for clothing are introduced seasonally and usually involve changes in such features as skirt length and lapel width. High school students wishing to be fashionable wear the labels of Tommy Hilfiger, FUBU, Abercrombie & Fitch, Gap, and Nike.

Fashion changes show up most often in items that involve personal appearance such as clothing, jewelry, and hairstyles; but automobile design, home decorating, architecture, and politics are also subject to fashion. Slang is a language-based fashion. Slang terms go in and out of favor very quickly (Lofland, 1993). *Cool, the cat's pajamas, groovy, tubular, neat, tough, fine, awesome, rad, bad, phat,* and *sick* are all slang terms of approval that were popular among young people of various decades.

● **fad**
an unusual behavior pattern that spreads rapidly and disappears quickly

● **fashion**
a widely accepted behavior pattern that changes periodically

Fashion in dress is constantly changing. Can you identify each of these styles with a decade between 1960–2000?

Sociology Today

Terrorist Attacks and Disaster Myths

You fail a test, lose a boyfriend, have a minor auto accident, or suffer defeat by an archrival's basketball team. You might well describe each of these occasions as a "disaster." For sociologists, however, the term disaster is limited to events with the following characteristics:

- Extensive damage to property
- Great loss of human life
- Massive disruption to everyday living
- Unpredictability and suddenness of a short-term event

Researchers typically divide disasters into "natural disasters" such as floods, earthquakes, hurricanes and "technological accidents" such as airline crashes, nuclear plant meltdowns, and ship sinkings. But how can we classify the September 11, 2001, attacks on the World Trade Center in New York City and the Pentagon in Washington, D.C.? It was neither natural nor an accident. But, it had all the characteristics of a disaster. In fact, terrorism is introducing a new type of disaster, one that involves technology and is intentionally caused by humans.

The World Trade Center and Pentagon attacks obviously met the criteria of a disaster. Less obviously, they also exposed as false many popular beliefs about human behavior in disasters. Let's consider four such myths within the context of this national tragedy.

- **Victims of disasters panic.** Contrary to this myth, disaster victims do not generally panic. While some individuals in disasters may panic and while mass panics may follow disasters, the prevailing response is one of general composure and problem-solving behavior. Some inside the

Firefighters raising the flag at the World Trade Center rescue site.

● **mass hysteria**
collective anxiety created by the acceptance of one or more false beliefs

Mass Hysteria and Panics

Mass hysteria exists when collective anxiety is created by acceptance of one or more false beliefs. Orson Welles's famous "Men from Mars" radio broadcast in 1938, though based entirely on H. G. Wells's novel *The War of the Worlds,* caused nationwide hysteria. About one million listeners became frightened or disturbed, and thousands of Americans hit the road to avoid the invading Martians. Telephone lines were jammed as people shared rumors, anxieties, fears, and escape plans (Houseman, 1948; Cantril, 1982; Barron, 1988).

A classic example of mass hysteria was the response to imagined witches in seventeenth-century Salem, Massachusetts, chronicled in Arthur Miller's famous play, *The Crucible.* Twenty-two people labeled witches died—twenty by hanging—before the false testimony of several young girls began to be

584 **Unit 5** Social Change

World Trade Center did respond with incapacitating emotion. One secretary in shock, for example, had to be carried out by a fellow worker. Some people jumped from the towers. But the disaster failed to set off a widespread panic. Many who heeded the first building-wide instructions died after calmly remaining in their offices. And many of the survivors remained as interested observers, forcing police to broadcast an urgent plea for them to hurry away for their own safety.

- **Disaster victims respond as isolated individuals.** Typically, we picture disaster victims as individuals trying to save only themselves. Actually, according to research, people immediately engage in group efforts to help others. People in the World Trade Center with cell phones offered them to other victims desperate to call family or friends. Scores of New York police and over 300 firefighters died while working together to rescue trapped victims.

- **Disaster victims leave the scene as soon as possible.** Contrary to this myth, the majority of victims remain near the disaster site. Rather than fleeing, most victims remained to help others, to witness the fire and rescue efforts, or to think about returning to their offices. Large numbers of volunteers and off-site emergency personnel actually rushed to the scene. Bellevue Hospital at one point had five doctors for each emergency ward patient. Four firefighters who were playing golf on Staten Island saw the first plane hit the north tower. Three of

those four lost their lives in rescue efforts, and they were just a few of the hundreds of firefighters who died after *entering* the disaster site. To help rescuers searching for survivors under the rubble, ironworkers, many of whom had built the World Trade Center, labored together in 12-hour volunteer shifts clearing away twisted steel.

- **Crime is prevalent during disasters.** Rather than increasing, crime actually decreases after a disaster. While some isolated instances of criminal behavior occur, the crime rate in a disaster falls. After the World Trade Center disaster, some looting in surrounding buildings was reported, and a Picasso drawing valued at $320,000 was stolen from a Madison Avenue art gallery. More importantly, the overall crime rate in New York City declined 34 percent in the week following the disaster. According to the NYPD, arrests were down 64 percent compared to the same seven days the previous years.

Doing Sociology

1. Think of some event you formerly considered a disaster. Explain why it was not a disaster from a sociological viewpoint.

2. Do you think that the behavior following the terrorist attack on the World Trade Center is best explained by functionalism, conflict theory, or symbolic interactionism? Explain your choice.

questioned. The mass hysteria dissipated only after the false beliefs were discredited. There has been some hysteria in the United States regarding AIDS. A 1987 Gallup poll showed that a substantial proportion of Americans held false beliefs regarding the spread of AIDS—30 percent believed insect bites could spread the disease, 26 percent related the spread to food handling or preparation, 26 percent thought AIDS could be transmitted via drinking glasses, 25 percent saw a risk in being coughed or sneezed upon, and 18 percent believed that AIDS could be contracted from toilet seats (Gallup, 1988). These mistaken ideas persisted on a widespread basis despite the medical community's conclusion that AIDS is spread through sexual contact, by sharing hypodermic needles, and by transfusion of infected blood. By the late 1990s, knowledge, tolerance, compassion, and understanding of AIDS had increased enough that the frequency of these rumors dropped off.

- **panic**
  reaction to a real threat in fearful, anxious, and often self-damaging ways

- **crowd**
  a temporary collection of people who share an immediate common interest

Each of these photos can be associated with a type of crowd. Which photo shows an *acting crowd*?

What is the difference between mass hysteria and a panic?

A **panic** occurs when people react to a real threat in fearful, anxious, and often self-damaging ways. Panics usually occur in response to such unexpected events as fires, invasions, and ship sinkings. Over 160 people, for example, died in the Kentucky Beverly Hills Supper Club in 1977 when a panic reaction to a fire caused a jamming of the escape routes. Interestingly enough, people often do not panic after natural disasters such as earthquakes and floods. Although panics may occur at the outset, major natural catastrophes usually lead to highly structured behavior (Erikson, 1976; Dynes and Tierney, 1994).

Crowds

A **crowd** is a temporary collection of people who share an immediate common interest. The temporary residents of a large campground, each occupied with his or her own activities, would not be considered a crowd. Sociologists would call this kind of gathering an *aggregate*. But if some stimulus, such as the landing of a hot-air balloon or the sudden appearance of a bear, drew the campers together, the aggregate would become a crowd.

People in a crowd often have no predefined ideas about the way they should behave. They do, however, share the urgent feeling that something either is about to happen or should be made to happen.

Are there different types of crowds? Sociologist Herbert Blumer (1969a) has distinguished four basic types of crowds.

1. A *casual crowd* is the least organized, least emotional, and most temporary type of crowd. Although the people in a casual crowd share some point of interest, it is minor and fades quickly. Members of a casual crowd may gather with others to observe the aftermath of an accident, to watch someone threatening to jump from a building, or to listen to a street rap group.

2. A *conventional crowd* has a specific purpose and follows accepted norms for appropriate behavior. People watching a film, taking a chartered flight to a university ball game, or observing a tennis match are in conventional crowds. As in casual crowds, there is little interaction among members of conventional crowds.

3. *Expressive crowds* have no significant or long-term purpose beyond unleashing emotion. Their members are collectively caught up in a dominating, all-encompassing mood of the moment. Free expression of emotion—yelling, crying, laughing, jumping—is the main characteristic of this type of crowd. Hysterical fans at a rock concert, the multitude gathered at Times Square on New Year's Eve, and the some 250,000 Americans at the Woodstock music festival in 1999 are all examples of expressive crowds.

4. Finally, a crowd that takes some action toward a target is an *acting crowd*. This type of crowd concentrates intensely on some objective and engages in aggressive behavior to achieve it. Protestors at the 2005 Group of Eight economic summit in Edinburgh, Scotland, were an acting crowd. Although the protests involved many groups with various objectives, they all shared the goal of putting an end to poverty (Gardiner, 2005). A conventional crowd may become an acting crowd, as when European soccer fans abandon the guidelines for spectators in order to attack the officials. Similarly, an expressive crowd may become an acting one, as in the case of celebrating Super Bowl fans who wind up overturning cars and destroying property. Mobs are acting crowds, as are crowds engaging in riots.

What are mobs and riots? A **mob** is an emotionally stimulated, disorderly crowd that is ready to use destructiveness and violence to achieve a purpose. A mob knows what it wants to do and considers all other things distractions. In fact, individuals who are tempted to deviate from the mob's purpose are pressured to conform. Concentration on the main event is maintained by strong leadership.

Mobs have a long and violent history. Many students are familiar with the scenes of mob actions described by Charles Dickens in the classic story *A Tale of Two Cities*. The formation of mobs is not limited to revolutions, however. During the mid-1700s, American colonists mobbed tax collectors as well as other political officials appointed by the British. During the Civil War, hundreds of people were killed or injured as armed mobs protested against the Union Army's draft. Mobs in the United States have acted as judges, juries, and executioners in the lynching of African Americans (as well as some whites) since the end of the nineteenth century.

Some acting crowds, although engaged in deliberate destructiveness and violence, do not have the mob's sense of common purpose. These episodes of crowd destructiveness and violence are called **riots.** Riots involve a much wider range of activities than mob action. Whereas a mob surges to burn a particular building, to lynch an individual, or to throw bombs at a government official's car, rioters often direct their violence and destructiveness at targets simply because they are convenient. People who participate in riots typically lack power and engage in destructive behavior as a way to express their frustrations. A riot, usually triggered by a single event, is best understood within the context of long-standing tensions.

Ghetto riots tore through many large American cities during the summer of 1967. The riots occurred against a background of massive unemployment, uncaring slum landlords, poverty, discrimination, and charges of police brutality. In 1989, thousands of angry citizens stormed the secret police headquarters in East Berlin. Although no one was killed or injured, the protest aroused widespread fear that the country was about to drop into anarchy (Bierman, 1990). In 1992, police officers charged in the beating of Rodney King in Los Angeles were acquitted by a jury. In the aftermath of the acquittals, Los Angeles experienced America's deadliest riots in twenty-five years. Two days of rioting left the City of Angels with at least 53 dead, over 2,000 injured, over 16,000 arrested, and an estimated $800 million in damage from looting and burning (Duke and Escobar, 1992; Mathews, 1992).

Theories of Crowd Behavior

Theories have been developed to explain crowd behavior. The three most important are *contagion theory, emergent norm theory* and *convergence theory*.

What is contagion theory? *Contagion* often refers to the spread of disease from person to person. Accordingly, **contagion theory** focuses on the spread of emotion in a crowd. As emotional intensity in the crowd increases, people temporarily lose their individuality to the "will" of the crowd. This makes it possible for a charismatic or manipulative leader to direct crowd behavior, at least initially.

Contagion theory has its roots in the classic 1895 work of Gustave Le Bon (originally published in 1895). Le Bon was a French aristocrat who disdained crowds made up of the masses. People in crowds, Le Bon thought, were reduced to a nearly subhuman level.

- **mob**
  emotional crowd ready to use violence for a specific purpose

- **riot**
  episode of largely random destruction and violence carried out by a crowd

Riots occurred in 1992 in Los Angeles after the acquittals of four white officers accused of the beating of African American motorist Rodney King. This looter took advantage of the riot to add to her wardrobe.

- **contagion theory**
  theory stating that members of crowds stimulate each other to higher and higher levels of emotion and irrational behavior

Riot police officers look at a fire set by fans during a 1996 soccer game in Athens. How does contagion theory describe the behavior that led to the fire?

● **emergent norm theory**
theory stating that norms develop to guide crowd behavior

● **convergence theory**
theory that states that crowds are formed by people who deliberately congregate with like-minded others

By the mere fact that he forms part of an organized crowd, a man descends several rungs in the ladder of civilization. Isolated, he may be a cultivated individual; in a crowd, he is a barbarian—that is, a creature acting by instinct. He possesses the spontaneity, the violence, the ferocity, and also the enthusiasm and heroism of primitive beings (Le Bon, 1960:32).

Herbert Blumer (1969a) has offered another version of contagion theory. Blumer avoids Le Bon's elitist bias but still implies that crowds are irrational and out of control. For Blumer, the basic process in crowds is a "circular reaction"—people mutually stimulating one another. This process includes three stages. In *milling,* the first stage, people move around in an aimless and random fashion, much like excited herds of cattle or sheep. Through milling, people become increasingly aware of and sensitive to one another; they enter something akin to a hypnotic trance. All of this prepares the crowd to act in a concerted and spontaneous way.

The second stage, *collective excitement,* is a more intense form of milling. At this stage, crowd members become impulsive, unstable, and highly responsive to the actions and suggestions of others. Individuals begin to lose their personal identities and take on the identity of the crowd.

The last stage, *social contagion,* is an extension of the other stages. Behavior in this stage involves rigid, unthinking, and nonrational transmission of mood, impulse, or behavior. We see such behavior, for example, when fans at soccer games in Europe launch attacks on referees that disrupt games and leave people injured or even killed. Taking a less extreme case, people at auctions can find themselves buying objects of little or no value to them because they have become caught up in the excitement of bidding.

What is emergent norm theory? Sociologists today realize that much crowd behavior, even in mobs, is actually very rational (McPhail, 1991). **Emergent norm theory** stresses the similarity between daily social behavior and crowd behavior. In both situations, norms guide behavior (Turner, 1964; Turner and Killian, 1987). So even within crowds, rules develop. These rules are *emergent* norms because the crowd participants are not aware of the rules until they find themselves in a particular situation. The norms develop on the spot as crowd participants pick up cues for expected behavior.

Contagion theory proposes a collective mind that motivates members of the crowd to act. According to emergent norm theory, people in a crowd are present for a variety of reasons. Hence, they do not all behave in the same way. Conformity may be active (some people in a riot may take home as many watches and rings as they can carry) or passive (others may simply not interfere with the looters, although they take nothing for themselves). In Nazi Germany, for instance, some people destroyed the stores of Jewish merchants, while others watched silently.

What is convergence theory? Both the contagion and emergent norm theories of crowd behavior assume that individuals are merely responding to those around them. It may be a more emotional response (as in contagion theory) or a more rational response (as in emergent norm theory). In other words, the independent variable in crowd behavior is the crowd itself. In contrast, in **convergence theory,** crowds are formed by people who deliberately congregate with others who they know to be like-minded. According to convergence theory the independent variable in crowd behavior is the desire of people with a common interest to come together.

Many Americans have visited the memorial site in Oklahoma City. It commemorates the 1995 terrorist bombing that destroyed a U.S. government complex, killing 168 people. How does this behavior relate to convergence theory for crowd behavior?

There have been many instances of crowds gathering in front of clinics to discourage abortions. This behavior, say convergence theorists, does not simply occur because people happened to be at the same place and are influenced by others. Such a crowd is motivated to form because of shared values, beliefs, and attitudes (Berk, 1974).

Section 3 Assessment

1. How is a dispersed collectivity different from other types of collectivities?

2. Some observers at a lynching do not participate but do not attempt to stop the lynching. Which of the following theories of crowd behavior best explains this?
   a. contagion theory
   b. crowd decision theory
   c. emergent norm theory
   d. convergence theory

Critical Thinking

3. **Making Generalizations** Rumors may or may not be true. Do you think most rumors turn out to be false? Why or why not?

4. **Applying Concepts** Identify a current rumor, fad, or fashion. Explain why it is part of a dispersed collectivity.

5. **Applying Concepts** Think of a crowd you have been part of, and identify it as one of the four types of crowds described in the text. Provide examples of behavior within the crowd (yours or someone else's) that illustrate why it was that particular type.

TECH TRENDS

Rumors at Warp Speed

Even before e-mail and the Internet, rumors spread like wildfire. Now, with instantaneous and multiple communications, there is virtually no limit to how fast a rumor can travel. A recent example demonstrates how quickly rumors can spread through the Internet.

The "gangsta" rapper Tupac Shakur was shot four times while riding in a car on the Las Vegas strip. A week after his death, a rumor surfaced that he was still alive. This rumor became so widespread on the Internet that the television show *Nightline* reported it. *Nightline* gave no credence to the story, but it found the rumor itself worth reporting. The rumor is still believed by many of Shakur's fans.

The Internet has rumors, gossip, and conspiracy theories to satisfy almost any taste. *Conspiracy Nation*, a magazine devoted to conspiracy theories, has a Web site that describes dozens of rumors about plots. A recent offering, for example, asserts that the newly designed $20 bill contains a tiny "chip" that will allow the "surveillance society" to track Americans' activities. Other articles have examined a variety of theories on political assassinations and suicides. E-mail chain letters spread rumors ranging from impending doom caused by various computer viruses to tales of free vacations and cash prizes (Long, 2005). Clearly the Internet can accelerate and magnify the effects of such rumors.

And the effects of rumors can be serious. One recent Internet rumor charged that a floor-cleaning product sold by one of the nation's largest and most well-known consumer product manufacturers was responsible for the deaths of some household pets. Even though poison experts at the American Society for the Prevention of Cruelty to Animals later proved this charge false, it has not

The rapper Tupac Shakur was widely rumored to still be alive a week after he was shot to death on the Las Vegas strip. This rumor was spread on the Internet.

been easy for the company to put the rumor to rest (O'Donnell, 2005).

Such damage can now occur overnight, be long lasting, and even become irreversible. Some companies fear that trying to disprove rumors can actually make matters worse. And rumors have become so rampant on the Internet that there now exist a number of sites whose sole purpose is to debunk them, including Snopes.com and Hoaxbusters.org. Still, perhaps the best advice to follow when there is no clear line between fact and fiction on the Internet is, "Let the reader beware!"

Analyzing the Trends

How credible are Internet sources? What criteria can you use to evaluate them?

Social Movements

Section Preview

Social movements are more permanent and more organized than other types of collectivities. Theories to explain how social movements develop include value-added theory and resource mobilization theory.

The Nature of Social Movements

The **social movement** is the most highly structured, rational, and enduring form of collective behavior. Several defining elements characterize social movements.

- a large number of people
- a common goal to promote or prevent social change
- structured organization with commonly recognized leaders
- activity sustained over a relatively long time period

Examples of past and present social movements include the American Revolution, abolitionism, the suffragist movement, the pro-life and pro-choice movements, and the environmental movement.

Most social movements are started to stimulate change. As the definition indicates, however, a social movement may instead oppose change. Conservative political and fundamentalist religious organizations, for example, are engaged in a concerted effort to oppose abortion (Hull et al., 2004). The National Rifle Association has focused its resources and membership on blocking certain gun control legislation (Walsh and Suro, 1999; Patrick, 2003).

A very human need to belong is a prime motivator for joining social movements. What other motivations might be responsible for causing a person to join a social movement?

Key Terms

- **social movement** (p. 591)
- **revolutionary movement** (p. 592)
- **reformative movement** (p. 592)
- **redemptive movement** (p. 592)
- **alternative movement** (p. 593)
- **value-added theory** (p. 593)
- **resource mobilization theory** (p. 596)

- **social movement** movement whose goal is to promote or prevent social change; the most structured and rational form of collective behavior

Listen—just take one of our brochures and see what we're all about . . . In the meantime, you may wish to ask yourself, "Am I a happy cow?"

Figure 17.3	Major Forms of Collective Behavior	
Behavior	**Definition**	**Example**
Rumor	A widely circulating piece of information that is not verified as being true or false	Continuously repeated prediction that airplanes would crash on a massive scale on January 1, 2000
Urban legend	A moralistic tale that focuses on current concerns and fears of the city or suburban dweller	Fierce alligators in New York City's sewer system
Fad	An unusual behavior pattern that spreads rapidly and disappears quickly (although it may reappear)	Body piercing
Fashion	A widely accepted behavior pattern that changes periodically	Nike shoes
Crowd	A temporary collection of people who share an immediate interest	New Year's celebrants at Times Square in New York City
Mob	An emotional crowd ready to use violence for a specific purpose	Lynch mob
Riot	An episode of largely random destruction and violence carried out by a crowd	Destructive behavior following the acquittal of police officers who were filmed using extreme force against Rodney King
Social movement	Movement whose goal is to promote or prevent social change	Civil Rights movement

Primary Types of Social Movements

Despite commonalities, various social movements have unique characteristics. It is difficult to compare the civil rights movement with the environmental movement. This has led sociologists to study differences between social movements. David Aberle (1991) has identified four basic types of social movements.

- A **revolutionary movement** attempts to change a society totally. The American Revolution was one of the most successful revolutionary movements in history. Another example is the revolutionary movement led by Mao Zedong in China. As a result of Mao's revolutionary movement, a communist government was instituted.

- A **reformative movement** aims to effect more limited changes in a society. The Woman's Christian Temperance Union (an anti-alcohol organization founded in 1874) and the antiwar movement of the 1960s illustrate this type of social movement.

- A **redemptive movement** focuses on changing people completely. The religious cult of David Koresh (the Branch Davidians) was a redemptive movement.

● **revolutionary movement**
a social movement that attempts to change the total structure of society

● **reformative movement**
a social movement that attempts to make limited changes in society

● **redemptive movement**
a social movement that seeks to change people completely

Demonstrators, with banners in hand, ride a truck en route to Tiananmen Square to protest for democracy and human rights in Beijing, China, in 1989. Explain the type of social movement this demonstration best illustrates.

- An **alternative movement** seeks only limited changes in people. Zero Population Growth (renamed Population Connection), an organization that first began in the late 1960s, illlustrates such a movement. It attempts to persuade people to limit the size of their families. It does not advocate sweeping lifestyle changes, however; nor does it advocate legal penalties for large families.

● **alternative movement**
a social movement that focuses on bringing about limited changes in people

Theories of Social Movements

Because of the highly structured nature of social movements, sociologists have been able to analyze this form of collective behavior. Two major theories of social movements have evolved. One is *value-added theory,* and the other is *resource mobilization theory.*

What is value-added theory?
Before discussing value-added theory, we need to understand the concept of adding value. In the value-added process, each step in the creation of a product contributes, or adds value, to the final entity. Neil Smelser, the sociologist who originated the value-added theory of social movements, gives an example involving automobile production.

> An example of [the value-added process] is the conversion of iron ore into finished automobiles by a number of stages of processing. Relevant stages would be mining, smelting, tempering, shaping, and combining the steel with other parts, painting, delivering to retailer, and selling. Each stage "adds its value" to the final cost of the finished product. The key element in this example is that the earlier stages must combine according to a certain pattern before the next stage can contribute its particular value to the finished product, an automobile. Painting, in order to be effective as a "determinant" in shaping the product, has to "wait" for the completion of the earlier processes. Every stage in the value-added process, therefore, is a necessary condition for the appropriate and effective condition of value in the next stage (Smelser, 1971:13–14).

Smelser used this process as a model to understand social movements. The **value-added theory** identifies six conditions that must exist in order for social movements to occur.

● **value-added theory**
theory holding that certain conditions must exist for social movements to occur

1960s	1970s	1980s	1990s	2000s
Hot Topics	**Hot Topics**	**Hot Topics**	**Hot Topics**	**Hot Topics**
Vietnam War	Clean Air and	International	Gay Rights	Globalization
Civil Rights	Water	Human Rights	Sweatshop Labor	Corporate
	Female	Endangered	Medical Use of	Dominance
	Empowerment	Species	Marijuana	Immigration
		Sexual		
		Harassment		

Figure 17.4 Hot Buttons for College Activists
According to Robert Merton, protest movements are reactions on structural strains of burning importance. College activists have been moved to action by different structural strains since the 1960s.

Source: U. *The National College Magazine* (February, 2000).

This famous photograph of the tragic antiwar demonstrations at Kent State University in 1970 captured the attention of the nation.

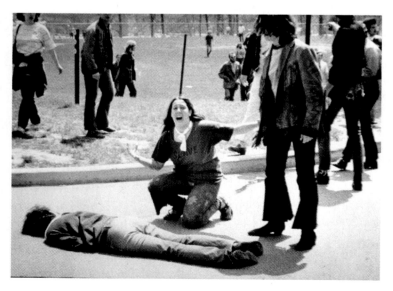

1. *Structural conduciveness.* The environment must be social-movement friendly. The college student demonstrations in the 1960s and 1970s occurred because of the war in Vietnam, yes, but also because most college campuses had convenient sites for rallies and protest meetings.

2. *Structural strains.* A second condition promoting the emergence of a social movement is the presence of conflicts, ambiguities, and discrepancies within a society. Without some form of strain, there is no stimulus for change. A key discrepancy in the antiwar movement case was the government's continued stance that there was no war (no legal war had been declared), despite the vast resources being devoted to battle and the obvious combat casualties. (Figure 17.4 identifies major structural strains that have mobilized college students since the 1960s.)

3. *Generalized beliefs.* Generalized beliefs include a general recognition that there is a problem and agreement that something should be done to fix it. Two shared beliefs were crucial to the antiwar movement. One was the belief that the Johnson and Nixon administrations were not telling the truth about the war. Another was that the Vietnam War was so morally wrong that it had to be stopped.

4. *Precipitating factors.* One or more significant events must occur to galvanize people into action. On April 30, 1970, President Nixon ordered the invasion of the neutral country of Cambodia. This event was a show of force to the North Vietnamese government with which the United States government was negotiating to end the war.

5. *Mobilization of participants for action.* Once the first four conditions exist, the only remaining step is to get the people moving. Massive demonstrations were part of the political furor the Cambodian invasion provoked. More than 100,000 opponents of the Vietnam War marched on Washington, D.C. Hundreds of colleges were forced to close as a result of strikes by 1.5 million students.

Women in the Workplace

The number of women in the U.S. workplace is related to social change and social movements. The U.S. female workforce shot up during World War II. Once the soldiers returned home, however, a large percentage of those working women quit work to raise families. Owing in part to the women's rights movement, the U.S. has seen a resurgence of women entering the workforce. This map shows the percentage of women in each state who are active in the labor force.

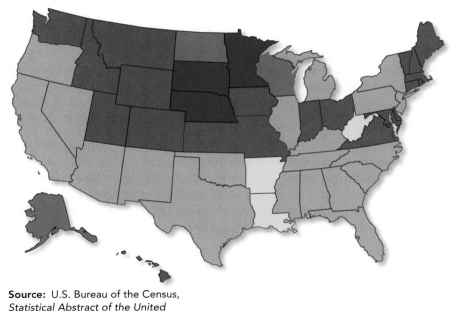

Source: U.S. Bureau of the Census, *Statistical Abstract of the United States, 2006*

Interpreting the Map

1. Relate strain theory, the women's movement, and increased female labor force participation.

2. How does your state compare with other states in terms of female employment? Describe.

Percentage of Women in the Workforce, 2004

- 68% or more
- 66%–67.9%
- 62%–65.9%
- 60%–61.9%
- 55%–59.9%
- 54.9% or less

6. *Social control.* The sixth determinant of a social movement is ineffective social control. Actions of the media, police, courts, community leaders, and political officials can lead to the success or failure of a social movement. If the right kind of force is applied, a potential social movement may be prevented, even though the first five determinants are present. Efforts to control the situation may block the social movement, minimize its effects, or make matters worse. Efforts to control the antiwar movement, for example, were actually counterproductive. During the student antiwar protests following the Cambodian invasion, the Ohio National Guard, mobilized by the governor of Ohio, killed four students

People throughout the United States donated money to help the victims of Hurricane Katrina in 2005. Relate this behavior to resource mobililzation theory.

and wounded at least nine others on the Kent State University campus. Two African American students were killed during an antiwar protest at Jackson State University in Mississippi. Such heavy-handedness on the part of politicians and law enforcement officials only stimulated further protest that hastened the ending of the war.

- **resource mobilization theory**
  theory of social movements that focuses on the use of resources to achieve goals

What is resource mobilization theory? Resource mobilization theory focuses on the process through which members of a social movement secure and use the resources needed to advance their cause. Resources include human skills such as leadership, organizational ability, and labor power, as well as material goods such as money, property, and equipment (Cress and Snow, 1996; McCarthy and Wolfson, 1996).

The civil rights movement of the 1960s succeeded primarily because of the leadership and commitment of African Americans, but white Americans also contributed time, money, and energy to the cause. In recent years, gays, too, have achieved greater equality. This achievement can be traced to active support from a broad segment of American society. Today, many more Americans support equal rights for gays than did so in the 1950s.

Section 4 Assessment

1. How would a sociologist define the term *social movement?*

2. Which of the following is an example of a reformative social movement?
   a. the French Revolution
   b. Zero Population Growth (Population Connection)
   c. the Branch Davidians
   d. Woman's Christian Temperance Union

3. How is Smelser's theory of social movements an example of the value-added process?

4. Briefly explain the resource mobilization theory of social movements.

Critical Thinking

5. **Synthesizing Information** If you wished to mount a social movement to change some U.S. policy (i.e., air pollution limits), which theory of social change would most likely guide your strategy? Explain why you would select a particular theory and how it would guide your approach.

17

Assessment

Summary

Section 1: Social Change

Main Idea: Social change refers to new behaviors that have long-term and relatively important consequences. Discovery, invention, and diffusion are the major social processes through which social change occurs. Important agents of social change are technology, population, the natural environment, revolution, and war.

Section 2: Theoretical Perspectives on Social Change

Main Idea: The functionalist perspective depicts societies as relatively stable. According to the conflict perspective, societies are unstable systems that are constantly undergoing change. Symbolic interactionism identifies decreasing shared values as a source of social instability.

Section 3: Collective Behavior

Main Idea: Collective behavior describes how people behave when they are united by a single short-term goal. Rumors, fads, fashions, mass hysteria, and panics are examples of collective behaviors. Contagion theory and emergent norm theory describe crowd behavior.

Section 4: Social Movements

Main Idea: Social movements are more permanent and more organized than other types of collectives. Theories to explain how social movements develop include value-added theory and resource mobilization theory.

Sociology Online

Self-Check Quiz
Visit the *Sociology and You* Web site at glencoe.com and click on **Chapter 17— Self-check Quizzes** to prepare for the chapter test.

Reviewing Vocabulary

Complete each sentence using each term once.

a. social movement
b. contagion theory
c. rumor
d. revolution
e. fashions
f. fads
g. crowd
h. collective behavior
i. emergent norm theory
j. social change
k. technology

1. New societal behaviors with long-term and relatively important consequences are called _____ .

2. _____ is the knowledge and hardware used to achieve practical goals.

3. _____ is a type of social movement that may involve the violent toppling of a political regime.

4. The spontaneous and unstructured social behavior of people who are responding to similar stimuli is known as _____ .

5. _____ is a widely circulating story of questionable truth.

6. The unusual behavior patterns that spread rapidly, are embraced zealously, and then disappear in a short time are called _____ .

7. _____ are behavior patterns that are widely approved but expected to change periodically.

8. A temporary collection of people who share a common interest is known as a _____ .

9. _____ emphasizes the irrationality of crowds, created when members stimulate one another to higher and higher levels of emotional intensity.

10. _____ stresses the similarity between daily social behavior and crowd behavior.

11. The form of collective behavior that has the most structure is called _____ .

Reviewing the Facts

12. Use a diagram similar to the one below to show the cause and effect relationship between the three major social processes and social change.

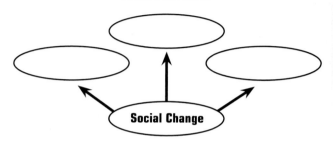

Social Processes

Social Change

13. Identify and describe the three theories of crowd behavior.

14. What are the five important agents of social change?

15. In your own words explain the value-added theory of social movements.

16. List and describe the four primary types of social movements.

17. Explain the resource mobilization theory of social movements.

Thinking Critically

18. Applying Concepts

Once upon a time, a family decided to grow orange trees. After several years of hard work, the first oranges appeared. Every year after that, when the oranges appeared, the father would say, "Everyone is entitled to choose one orange from the crop." The business thrived and expanded. The children were puzzled that even when the orange grove had grown, they were allowed only one orange a year. Finally, when there were grandchildren, one of them said, "Grandpa, every year we produce hundreds of thousands of oranges, and every year you tell us that we can have only one orange. Why is that?" Grandpa replied, "Because that's the way it's always been." How is this story a metaphor for society?

Pat Bagley/Salt Lake Tribune/Cagle Cartoons

19. Analyzing Visuals

Social change follows from many different types of causes—a political policy, a social movement, or new technology. Analyze this cartoon in view of what your chapter has explained about the agents of social change. What feeling about this change does the cartoonist convey by his drawing? Write a short paragraph that explains how the specific change depicted in the cartoon might affect other aspects of American life.

20. Evaluating Information

In this country, it is common to read about rumors, especially in tabloid newspapers and television programs. How justified are newspapers and news reporters in publicizing unverified information? Should viewers be responsible for evaluating the information themselves? Should the news sources be penalized for not investigating or verifying rumors? What are the consequences for society if news sources are not reliable?

21. Analyzing Information

Television shows often mirror social changes. Sometimes, these changes have not yet reached the mainstream culture. What role do you think television has in changing society? Do you think its influence is more positive or negative?

22. Drawing Conclusions

Twenty years ago, body piercing (other than for earrings) was considered deviant behavior. Today, it is fast becoming a social norm. Is body piercing a fad or a fashion? What factors might cause a behavior that is not desirable in one generation become acceptable?

Sociology Projects

23. Fads

Look through old and new magazines for examples of fads that have appeared since you were born. Create a collage illustrating those fads. Are some of them still around? Ask your parents or grandparents what some fads were when they were teenagers. Find pictures and make a poster to explain the fads.

24. Social Movements

In the chapter, you read about the primary types of social movements. The table below reports a 1999 survey of public opinion about seven social changes. On a sheet of paper, identify which type of social movement each one represents and why you think so. Then in small groups develop a list of current social changes. Conduct an informal survey on students' attitudes towards them. Finally, share your findings with the rest of the class.

A Change for the...	Better	Worse	No Difference	Don't Know
Civil rights movement	85%	5%	8%	3%
Women in the workplace	83	10	6	1
Growth of suburbs	52	21	21	6
Rock and roll	45	23	27	5
Legalized abortion	34	42	17	7
More acceptance of divorce	30	53	13	4
Wide use of credit cards	22	68	7	3

25. Technology

Over the next few days, look for new technologies that have initiated social changes within the last five years. For example, podcasting is a fairly new technological invention. Make a list of such items, including things that you have heard are coming but have not yet been released. For each item write down what earlier development made the new item possible. For example, high-definition TV was a result of knowledge gained from aerospace satellite projects. Share your findings with classmates. You will probably be amazed at how extensive your list is. Post it in the classroom, and add to it as you hear about more changes.

26. Rumors and the Media

As an extension to "Thinking Critically," question 20, consider and list the options that a news reporter has when he or she receives unverified stories to report. Suggest possible consequences associated with each option.

Technology Activity

27. Jan Harold Brunvand coined the term *urban legend* to describe a type of rumor that is long lasting and widely believed. This term is commonly used now, and if you search the Internet, you will find many sites devoted to this subject.

   a. Select a few of the web sites (two good ones are at www.urbanlegends.com/ and www. snopes2.com/) and review them. Be prepared to share one or two of them with your class.

   b. What common elements do these urban legends have? Do your observations correspond with those of Urbanlegends.com?

   c. What role do you think the Internet plays in spreading these urban legends?

The Internet and Social Change

Since 2000, the Pew Internet & American Life Project has conducted surveys of Americans concerning their Internet experiences. Here are some of the latest findings.

● **parity**
state of being equivalent

On a typical day at the end of 2004, some 70 million American adults logged onto the internet to use email, get news, access government information, check out health and medical information, participate in auctions, book travel reservations, research their genealogy, gamble, seek out romantic partners and engage in countless other activities. That represents a 37% increase from the 52 million adults who were online on an average day in 2000 when the Pew Internet & American Life Project began its study of online life. . . .

The New Normal

The Web has become the "new normal" in the American way of life; those who don't go online constitute an ever-shrinking minority. And as the online population has grown rapidly, its composition has changed rapidly. At the infant stage, the internet's user population was dominated by young, white men who had high incomes and plenty of education. As it passed into its childhood years in 1999 and 2000, the population went mainstream; women reached **parity** with men online, lots more minority families joined the party, and more people with modest levels of income and education came online.

This transition altered the internet's social environment. These early adopters loved the liberation they got from being online. They liked the fact that they could get news from nontraditional sources. . . . These early adopters wanted to topple all manner of institutions and establish a new order in virtual space. They had a utopian sense of the transformative power of the new technology.

The later adopters are not looking to this technology to overturn the existing order. They like the internet because it can make them more productive and more connected. Theirs is an unsentimental outlook. . . .

Now we are in the midst of yet another important change in the internet—the rapid switchover from dial-up access to high-speed broadband connections. More than half of Americans who go online now have access to always-on connections at home or work, and they are different kinds of users than those with dial-up connections. They spend more time online. They do more online activities, especially those that exploit bigger information "pipelines," such as accessing streaming video. They are much more likely to create content and share it with the rest of the online population. And they report greater levels of satisfaction with the role of the internet in their lives.

Who Goes Online—and Why

No matter how fast an online connection they have, different people still use the internet in different ways. For example, online men are more likely than online women to use the internet to get news, check out sports and execute financial transactions. In contrast, online women are more likely to get health information and religious news and to use email to maintain and deepen personal relationships. African-Americans are among the most likely to get religious and spiritual information, while Latinos are among the most likely to access cultural material, such as information about music. . . .

Social Impact of the Internet

Over the years the Pew Internet & American Life Project has regularly asked people to describe what impact the internet has had on the way they lead their lives. Here is what they have told us:

The internet enhances social interaction. People use email to deepen their connection to the people they like and love and increase the volume of communication they have with them. Email users, especially women, feel they are working on relationships and tending to their social networks as they exchange email.

The internet is more than a bonding agent; it is also a bridging agent for creating and sustaining community. Some 84% of internet users, or close to 100 million people, belong to groups that have an online presence. More than half have joined those groups since getting internet access; those who were group members before getting access say their use of the internet has bound them closer to the group. Members of online groups also say the internet increases the chances that they will interact with people outside their social class, racial group or generational cohort. . . .

The internet changes the way people deal with health issues. E-patients are creating a new health-care environment in which the traditional medical model—ruled by the all-wise doctor who tells patients what is best for them—is being challenged by a new model in which empowered patients can access large amounts of medical information, advice and support online, and act as partners with their doctors in making health-care decisions for themselves and their loved ones.

The internet creates new online town squares and civic storms. The widely varying information sources that are available online, combined with the new opportunities that the internet creates for civic participation, have begun to reshape politics and community life. Nowhere was that more evident than in the rapid rise of blogs during the 2004 campaign. Political bloggers serve up a boiling **caldron** of facts, rumors, commentaries, conspiracy theories, ideological **screeds** and media criticisms. The new-found importance of blogs was also illustrated early in 2005 by their use in linking communities in Southeast Asia with the rest of the world after the devastation caused by the year-end tsunami.

The internet enhances the relationship of citizens to their government. E-government applications are growing in popularity with online Americans. For instance, 38 million have sent email to government officials to try to influence policy decisions and another 29 million have researched or applied for government benefits on government Web sites. Many report that the convenience and usefulness of these sites have improved their perceptions of how government functions.

● **caldron**
cauldron; large kettle

● **screed**
informal piece of writing

Read and React

1. How do men and women tend to differ in their use of the Internet?

2. How has the Internet changed the way people deal with health issues?

3. How has the Internet changed people's perceptions of how government functions?

Source: Lee Rainie and John Horrigan, "A Decade of Adoption: How the Internet Has Woven Itself into American Life." Pew Internet & American Life Project, January 25, 2005, http://207.21.232.103/PPF/r/148/report_display.asp

Sociology Databank

Contents

The Family

For sociologists, a *family* is a group of people related by marriage, blood, or adoption.

Percentage of Children Living with Grandparents as Caregivers

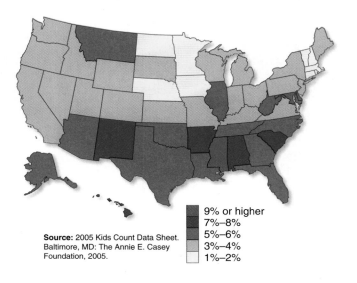

- 9% or higher
- 7%–8%
- 5%–6%
- 3%–4%
- 1%–2%

Source: 2005 Kids Count Data Sheet. Baltimore, MD: The Annie E. Casey Foundation, 2005.

Americans Who Identified With More Than One Race, 2000

- White + Asian 13%
- White + American Indian 16%
- White + Some other race 32%
- White + African American 11%
- African American + Some other 6%
- Asian + Some other 4%
- African American + American Indian 3%
- Other two races 8%
- Three or more races 7%

Total multiracial Americans = 6,826,228

Source: First Glimpses From the 2000 U.S. Census Population Bulletin Vol. 56, No. 2 June 2001.

Child Abuse and Neglect Cases 1990–2003, by Type

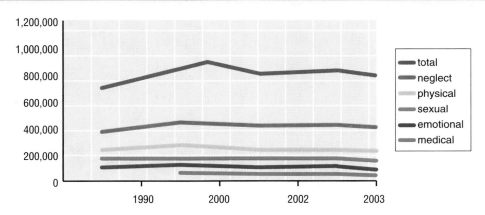

Legend:
- total
- neglect
- physical
- sexual
- emotional
- medical

Source: U.S. Bureau of the Census. Statistical Abstract of the United States 2006. Washington DC: U.S. Government Printing Office.

Education

Education is the social institution responsible for the transmission of knowledge to its members. This includes academic knowledge, vocational skills, and a society's beliefs, norms, and values.

How Educated Are Young Workers?

Percentage of 25 to 29-year-olds with college degrees

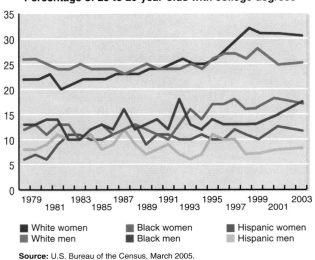

- White women
- White men
- Black women
- Black men
- Hispanic women
- Hispanic men

Source: U.S. Bureau of the Census, March 2005.

Percentage of Postsecondary Graduates by Sex, 1960 to 2003

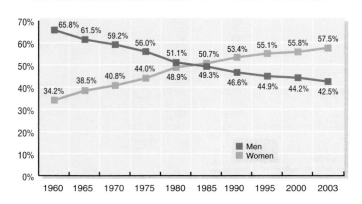

Men: 65.8%, 61.5%, 59.2%, 56.0%, 51.1%, 50.7%, 46.6%, 44.9%, 44.2%, 42.5%

Women: 34.2%, 38.5%, 40.8%, 44.0%, 48.9%, 49.3%, 53.4%, 55.1%, 55.8%, 57.5%

- Men
- Women

Source: Digest of Education Statistics. Washington DC: U.S. National Center for Education Statistics, 2004. www.nces.ed.gov.

Education Spending

Median Household Income by State, 2003

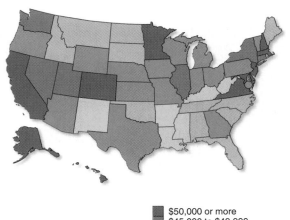

- $50,000 or more
- $45,000 to $49,999
- $40,000 to $44,999
- $35,000 to $39,999
- $30,000 to $34,999

Source: U.S. Bureau of the Census, *Statistical Abstract of the United States, 2006.*

School Expenditures, 2004

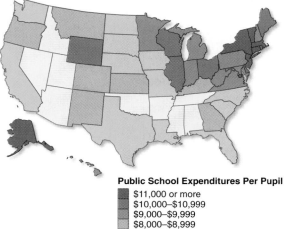

Public School Expenditures Per Pupil

- $11,000 or more
- $10,000–$10,999
- $9,000–$9,999
- $8,000–$8,999
- $7,000–$7,999
- $6,999 or less

Educational Attainment of the Population by Age Group (2003)

At Least Upper Secondary Education

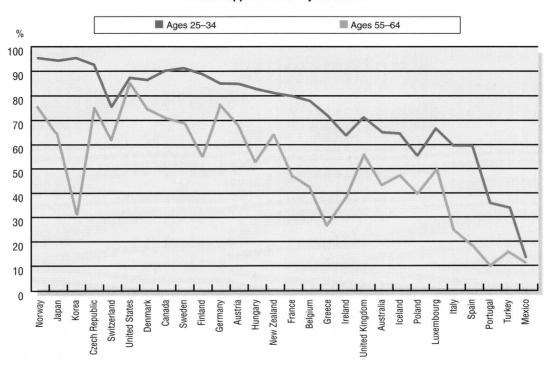

Legend: ■ Ages 25–34   ▨ Ages 55–64

(Countries along x-axis: Norway, Japan, Korea, Czech Republic, Switzerland, United States, Denmark, Canada, Sweden, Finland, Germany, Austria, Hungary, New Zealand, France, Belgium, Greece, Ireland, United Kingdom, Australia, Iceland, Poland, Luxembourg, Italy, Spain, Portugal, Turkey, Mexico)

At Least Tertiary Education

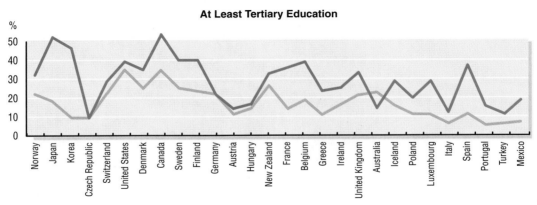

(Countries along x-axis: Norway, Japan, Korea, Czech Republic, Switzerland, United States, Denmark, Canada, Sweden, Finland, Germany, Austria, Hungary, New Zealand, France, Belgium, Greece, Ireland, United Kingdom, Australia, Iceland, Poland, Luxembourg, Italy, Spain, Portugal, Turkey, Mexico)

Source: Education at a Glance 2005. Paris: Organization for Education Cooperation and Development.

The Political Institution

The *political institution* is the body through which power is obtained and exercised to maintain order and handle conflict in the society.

Electoral Votes by State, 2000

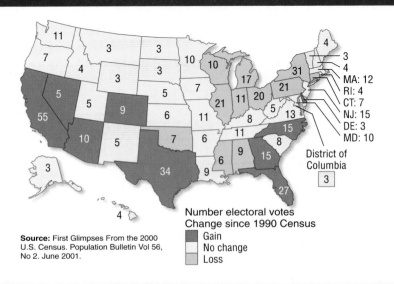

Source: First Glimpses From the 2000 U.S. Census. Population Bulletin Vol 56, No 2. June 2001.

Number electoral votes
Change since 1990 Census
- Gain
- No change
- Loss

U.S. House of Delegations

(As determined by the 2004 elections)

- Other (Independent)
- Majority Republican
- Majority Democratic
- Equal Party Representation

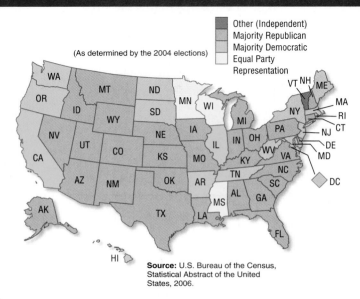

Source: U.S. Bureau of the Census, Statistical Abstract of the United States, 2006.

Political Action Committee (PAC) Count—1980 to Present

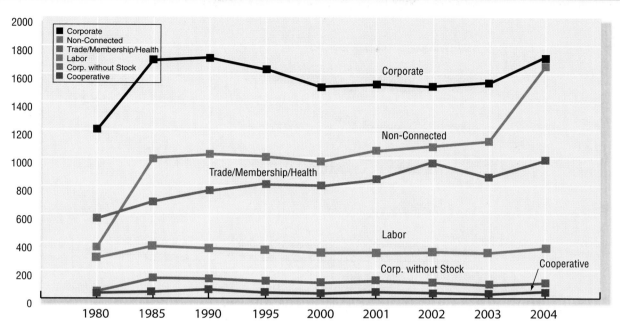

Legend:
- Corporate
- Non-Connected
- Trade/Membership/Health
- Labor
- Corp. without Stock
- Cooperative

Source: U.S.Bureau of the Census, Statistical Abstract of the United States, 2006.

Number of Women Holding State Public Offices, 2004

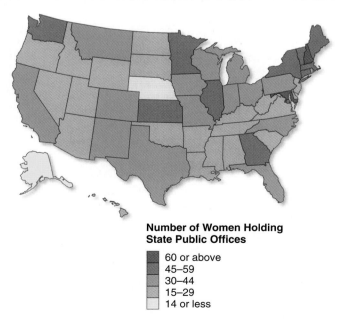

Number of Women Holding State Public Offices
- 60 or above
- 45–59
- 30–44
- 15–29
- 14 or less

Source: U.S. Bureau of the Census,
Statistical Abstract of the United States, 2006.

Reported Voting by Age Group—Presidential Elections, 1984-2004

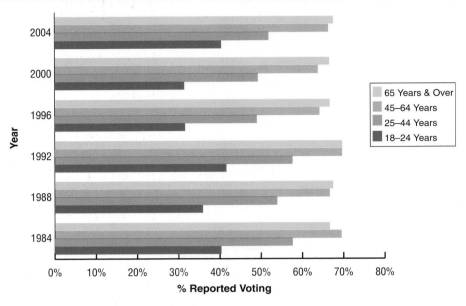

Source: U.S. Bureau of the Census, Current Populationi Surveys.

Average Voter Turnout in All National Elections Since 1945

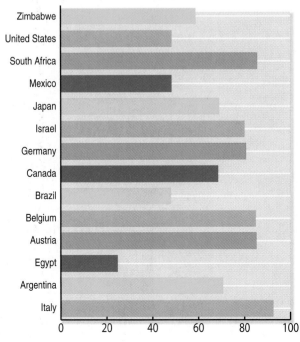

Source: Federal Election Commission

The Economy

The *economy* is the social institution that regulates the production and distribution of goods and services for a society.

What Jobs Do Women Have?

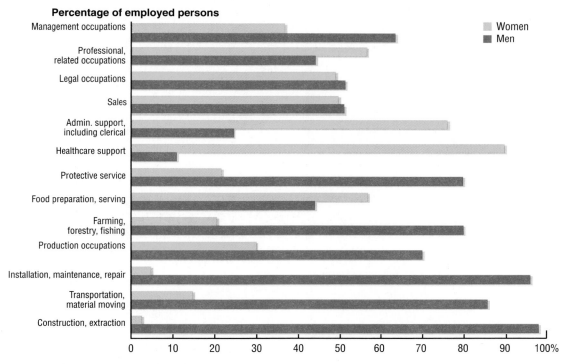

Percentage of employed persons

Legend: Women, Men

- Management occupations
- Professional, related occupations
- Legal occupations
- Sales
- Admin. support, including clerical
- Healthcare support
- Protective service
- Food preparation, serving
- Farming, forestry, fishing
- Production occupations
- Installation, maintenance, repair
- Transportation, material moving
- Construction, extraction

Axis: 0, 10, 20, 30, 40, 50, 60, 70, 80, 90, 100%

Source: U.S. Bureau of Labor Statistics, Women in the Labor Force: A Databook, 2005.

Sociology Databank

The Ten Fastest-Growing Occupations

Occupation	Employment (in thousands)		Growth 2002–2012	
	2002	2012	(1000s)	Percent
Medical assistants	365	579	215	59%
Network systems/data communications analysts	186	292	106	57%
Physician assistants	63	94	31	49%
Social/human service assistants	305	454	149	49%
Home health aides	580	859	279	48%
Medical records/health information technicians	147	216	69	47%
Physician therapist assistants	50	73	22	45%
Fitness trainers/aerobics instructors	183	264	81	44%
Database administrators	110	159	49	44%
Veterinary technologists/technicians	53	76	23	44%

Source: U.S. Bureau of the Census, Statistical Abstract of the United States, 2006.

Average Annual Salary, by State

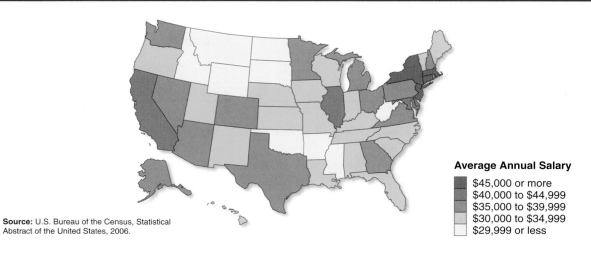

Source: U.S. Bureau of the Census, Statistical Abstract of the United States, 2006.

Average Annual Salary
- $45,000 or more
- $40,000 to $44,999
- $35,000 to $39,999
- $30,000 to $34,999
- $29,999 or less

Gross National Income in Purchasing Power Parity Per Capita for Selected Countries, 2004

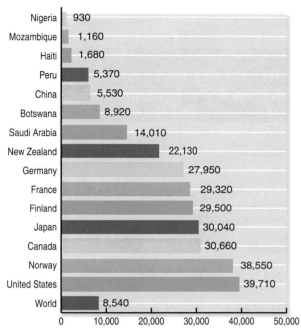

Country	GNI PPP Per Capita
Nigeria	930
Mozambique	1,160
Haiti	1,680
Peru	5,370
China	5,530
Botswana	8,920
Saudi Arabia	14,010
New Zealand	22,130
Germany	27,950
France	29,320
Finland	29,500
Japan	30,040
Canada	30,660
Norway	38,550
United States	39,710
World	8,540

Source: 2005 World Population Data Sheet.
Washington DC: Population Reference Bureau, 2005.
Note: Figures given in U.S. dollars

Percentage of Income Paid in Taxes by Individuals in Selected Countries

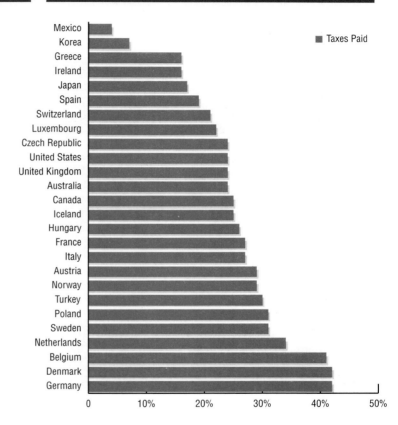

■ Taxes Paid

Mexico, Korea, Greece, Ireland, Japan, Spain, Switzerland, Luxembourg, Czech Republic, United States, United Kingdom, Australia, Canada, Iceland, Hungary, France, Italy, Austria, Norway, Turkey, Poland, Sweden, Netherlands, Belgium, Denmark, Germany

Source: The World Almanac and Book of Facts, 2005.

Religion

Religion is a unified system of beliefs and practices concerned with sacred things.

Percentage of Americans Who Think Religion Is Increasing or Losing Its Influence

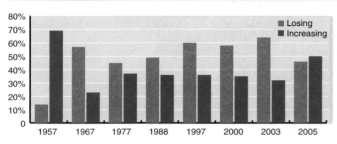

Source: The Gallup Organization.

U.S. Per Capita Income/Per Member Giving as a Percentage of Income

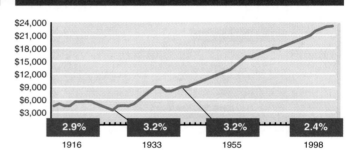

Percentage of Americans Who Believe That Religion Can Answer All of Today's Problems or Is Old-Fashioned

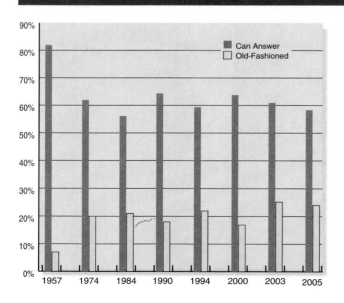

Source: The Gallup Organization.

Christian Church Adherents, by State

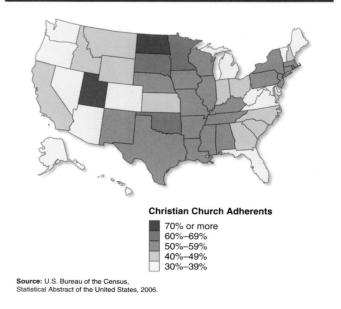

Christian Church Adherents

- 70% or more
- 60%–69%
- 50%–59%
- 40%–49%
- 30%–39%

Source: U.S. Bureau of the Census, Statistical Abstract of the United States, 2006.

Sport

Sport is a set of competitive activities in which winners and losers are determined by physical performance within a set of established rules.

Participation in High School Athletic Programs, 1973–2003

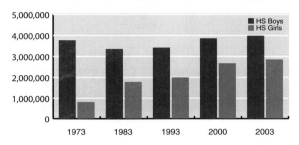

Source: U.S. Bureau of the Census, Statistical Abstract of the United States, 2006.

Interest in Professional Sports Based on Attendance At Professional Sporting Events: United States by Demographics

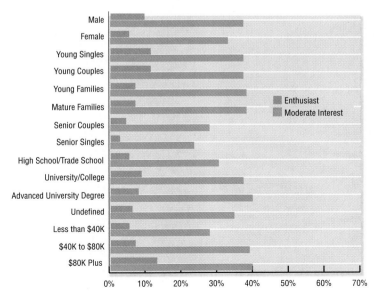

Source: Lang, David. "Interest in Professional Sports (As a Spectator) Profile Report." April 2001.

Sociology Databank

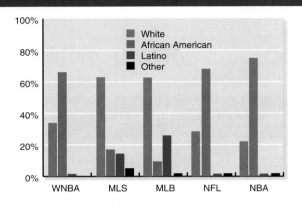

Source: Richard E. Lapchick (2004). "2004 Racial and Gender Report Card." The Institute for Diversity and Ethics in Sport.

Participation in NCAA Sports

NCAA Sport	Male Athletes	Female Athletes	NCAA Sport	Male Athletes	Female Athletes
Baseball	27,262	N/A	Sailing	259	N/A
Basketball	16,028	14,596	Skiing	467	457
Bowling	25	358	Soccer	18,512	20,437
Cross country	11,273	12,678	Softball	N/A	16,079
Equestrian	49	1,120	Squash	325	389
Fencing	610	653	Swimming/ Diving	7,333	10,539
Football	59,980	N/A	Synchronized swimming	N/A	104
Golf	7,738	3,628	Tennis	7,219	8,448
Gymnastics	326	1,380	Track, indoor	18,157	18,065
Ice hockey	3,782	1,600	Track, outdoor	20,869	19,658
Lacrosse	7,103	5,545	Volleyball	1,195	13,310
Rifle	192	205	Water polo	865	1,126
Rowing	1,758	6,805	Wrestling	5,943	N/A

Source: U.S. Bureau of the Census, Statistical Abstract of the United States, 2006.

American Sociological Association's Code of Ethics

The American Sociological Association's (ASA's) Code of Ethics sets forth the principles and ethical standards that underlie sociologists' professional responsibilities and conduct. These principles and standards should be used as guidelines when examining everyday professional activities. They constitute normative statements for sociologists and provide guidance on issues that sociologists may encounter in their professional work.

The Preamble and General Principles of the Code are aspirational goals to guide sociologists toward the highest ideals of sociology. Although the Preamble and General Principles are not enforceable rules, they should be considered by sociologists in arriving at an ethical course of action and may be considered by ethics bodies in interpreting the Ethical Standards.

The Ethical Standards set forth enforceable rules of conduct by sociologists. Most of the Ethical Standards are written broadly in order to apply to sociologists in varied roles, and the application of an Ethical Standard may vary depending on the context. The Ethical Standards are not exhaustive. Any conduct that is not specifically addressed by this Code of Ethics is not necessarily ethical or unethical.

Preamble

This Code of Ethics articulates a common set of values upon which sociologists build their professional and scientific work. The Code is intended to provide both the general principles and the rules to cover professional situations encountered by sociologists. It has as its primary goal the welfare and protection of the individuals and groups with whom sociologists work. It is the individual responsibility of each sociologist to aspire to the highest possible standards of conduct in research, teaching, practice, and service.

The development of a dynamic set of ethical standards for a sociologist's work-related conduct requires a personal commitment to a lifelong effort to act ethically; to encourage ethical behavior by students, supervisors, supervisees, employers, employees, and colleagues; and to consult with others as needed concerning ethical problems. Each sociologist supplements, but does not violate, the values and rules specified in the Code of Ethics based on guidance drawn from personal values, culture, and experience.

General Principles

The following General Principles are aspirational and serve as a guide for sociologists in determining ethical courses of action in various contexts. They exemplify the highest ideals of professional conduct.

Principle A: Professional Competence Sociologists strive to maintain the highest levels of competence in their work; they recognize the limitations of their expertise; and they undertake only those tasks for which they are qualified by education, training, or experience. They recognize the need for ongoing education in order to remain professionally competent; and they utilize the appropriate scientific, professional, technical, and administrative resources needed to ensure competence in their professional activities. They consult with other professionals when necessary for the benefit of their students, research participants, and clients.

Principle B: Integrity Sociologists are honest, fair, and respectful of others in their professional activities—in research, teaching, practice, and service. Sociologists do not knowingly act in ways that jeopardize either their own or others' professional welfare. Sociologists conduct their affairs in ways that inspire trust and confidence; they do not knowingly make statements that are false, misleading, or deceptive.

Principle C: Professional and Scientific Responsibility Sociologists adhere to the highest scientific and professional standards and accept responsibility for their work. Sociologists understand that they form a community and show respect for other sociologists even when they disagree on theoretical, methodological, or personal approaches to professional activities. Sociologists value the public trust in sociology and are concerned about their ethical behavior and that of other sociologists that might compromise that trust. While endeavoring always to be collegial, sociologists must never let the desire to be collegial outweigh their shared responsibility for ethical behavior. When appropriate, they consult with colleagues in order to prevent or avoid unethical conduct.

Principle D: Respect for People's Rights, Dignity, and Diversity Sociologists respect the rights, dignity, and worth of all people. They strive to eliminate bias in their professional activities, and they do not tolerate any forms of discrimination based on age; gender; race; ethnicity; national origin; religion; sexual orientation; disability; health conditions; or marital, domestic, or parental status. They are sensitive to cultural, individual, and role differences in serving, teaching, and studying groups of people with distinctive characteristics. In all of their work-related activities, sociologists acknowledge the rights of others to hold values, attitudes, and opinions that differ from their own.

Principle E: Social Responsibility Sociologists are aware of their professional and scientific responsibility to the communities and societies in which they live and work. They apply and make public their knowledge in order to contribute to the public good. When undertaking research, they strive to advance the science of sociology and to serve the public good.

Ethical Standards

The complete text of the Ethical Standards can be found at the ASA Web site. Excerpts from this code are reproduced here.

1. Professional and Scientific Standards: Sociologists adhere to the highest possible technical standards that are reasonable and responsible in their research, teaching, practice, and service activities.

2. Competence: Sociologists conduct research, teach, practice, and provide service only within the boundaries of their competence, based on their education, training, supervised experience, or appropriate professional experience.

3. Representation and Misuse of Expertise: Because sociologists' scientific and professional judgments and actions may affect the lives of others, they are alert to and guard against personal, financial, social, organizational, or political factors that might lead to misuse of their knowledge, expertise, or influence.

4. Delegation and Supervision: Sociologists provide proper training and supervision to their students, supervisees, or employees and take reasonable steps to see that such persons perform services responsibly, competently, and ethically.

5. Nondiscrimination: Sociologists do not engage in discrimination in their work based on age; gender; race; ethnicity; national origin; religion; sexual orientation; disability; health conditions; marital; domestic, or parental status; or any other applicable basis proscribed by law.

6. Non-exploitation: Whether for personal, economic, or professional advantage, sociologists do not exploit persons over whom they have direct or indirect supervisory, evaluative, or other authority such as students, supervisees, employees, or research participants.

7. Harassment: Sociologists do not engage in harassment of any person, including students, supervisees, employees, or research participants. Harassment consists of a single intense and severe act or of multiple persistent or pervasive acts which are demeaning, abusive, offensive, or create a hostile professional or workplace environment. Sexual harassment may include sexual solicitation, physical advance, or verbal or non-verbal conduct that is sexual in nature. Racial harassment may include unnecessary, exaggerated, or unwarranted attention or attack, whether verbal or non-verbal, because of a person's race or ethnicity.

8. Employment Decisions: Sociologists have an obligation to adhere to the highest ethical standards when participating in employment-related decisions, when seeking employment, or when planning to resign from a position.

9. Conflicts of Interest: Sociologists maintain the highest degree of integrity in their professional work and avoid conflicts of interest and the appearance of conflict. Conflicts of interest arise when sociologists' personal or financial interests prevent them from performing their professional work in an unbiased manner.

10. Public Communication: Sociologists adhere to the highest professional standards in public communications about their professional services, credentials and expertise, work products, or publications, whether these communications are from themselves or from others.

10.02 In working with the press, radio, television, or other communications media or in advertising in the media, sociologists are cognizant of potential conflicts of interest or appearances of such conflicts (e.g., they do not provide compensation to employees of the media), and they adhere to the highest standards of professional honesty (e.g., they acknowledge paid advertising).

11. Confidentiality: Sociologists have an obligation to ensure that confidential information is protected. They do so to ensure the integrity of research and the open communication with research participants and to protect sensitive information obtained in research, teaching, practice, and service. When gathering confidential information, sociologists should take into account the long-term uses of the information, including its potential placement in public archives or the examination of the information by other researchers or practitioners.

11.02 Sociologists may confront unanticipated circumstances where they become aware of information that is clearly health- or life-threatening to research participants, students, employees, clients, or others. In these cases, sociologists balance the importance of guarantees of confidentiality with other principles in this Code of Ethics, standards of conduct, and applicable law.

Confidentiality is not required with respect to observations in public places, activities conducted in public, or other settings where no rules of privacy are provided by law or custom. Similarly, confi-dentiality is not required in the case of information available from public records.

11.06 Sociologists do not disclose in their writings, lectures, or other public media confidential, personally identifiable information concerning their research participants, students, individual or organizational clients, or other recipients of their services which is obtained during the course of their work, unless consent from individuals or their legal representatives has been obtained.

When confidential information is used in scientific and professional presentations, sociologists disguise the identity of research participants, students, individual or organizational clients, or other recipients of their services.

12. Informed Consent: Informed consent is a basic ethical tenet of scientific research on human populations. Sociologists do not involve a human being as a subject in research without the informed consent of the subject or the subject's legally authorized representative, except as otherwise specified in this Code. Sociologists recognize the possibility of undue influence or subtle pressures on subjects that may derive from researchers' expertise or authority, and they take this into account in designing informed consent procedures.

12.04 In undertaking research with children, sociologists obtain the consent of children to participate, to the extent that they are capable of providing such consent, except under circumstances where consent may not be required.

12.05 Sociologists never deceive research participants about significant aspects of the research that would affect their willingness to partici-pate, such as physical risks, discomfort, or unpleasant emotional experiences.

12.06 Sociologists obtain informed consent from research participants, students, employees, clients, or others prior to videotaping, filming, or recording them in any form, unless these activities involve simply naturalistic observations in public places and it is not anticipated that the recording will be used in a manner that could cause personal identification or harm.

13. Research Planning, Implementation, and Dissemination: Sociologists have an obligation to promote the integrity of research and to ensure that they comply with the ethical tenets of science in the planning, implementation, and dissemination of research. They do so in order to advance knowledge, to minimize the possibility that results will be misleading, and to protect the rights of research participants.

13.01 Planning and Implementation: In planning and implementing research, sociologists minimize the possibility that results will be misleading.

　　Sociologists take steps to implement protections for the rights and welfare of research participants and other persons affected by the research.

　　In their research, sociologists do not encourage activities or themselves behave in ways that are health- or life-threatening to research participants or others.

　　In planning and implementing research, sociologists consult those with expertise concerning any special population under investigation or likely to be affected.

13.04 Reporting on Research: Sociologists do not fabricate data or falsify results in their publications or presentations.

In presenting their work, sociologists report their findings fully and do not omit relevant data. They report results whether they support or contradict the expected outcomes.

Sociologists report sources of financial support in their written papers and note any special relations to any sponsor. In special circumstances, sociologists may withhold the names of specific sponsors if they provide an adequate and full description of the nature and interest of the sponsor.

14. Plagiarism: In publications, presentations, teaching, practice, and service, sociologists explicitly identify, credit, and reference the author when they take data or material verbatim from another person's written work, whether it is published, unpublished, or electronically available.

15. Authorship Credit: Sociologists take responsibility and credit, including authorship credit, only for work they have actually performed or to which they have contributed.

Sociologists ensure that principal authorship and other publication credits are based on the relative scientific or professional contributions of the individuals involved, regardless of their status. In claiming or determining the ordering of authorship, sociologists seek to reflect accurately the contributions of main participants in the research and writing process.

A student is usually listed as principal author on any multiple-authored publication that substantially derives from the student's dissertation or thesis.

20. Adherence to the Code of Ethics: Sociologists have an obligation to confront, address, and attempt to resolve ethical issues according to this Code of Ethics.

20.01 Familiarity with the Code of Ethics: Sociologists have an obligation to be familiar with this Code of Ethics, other applicable ethics codes, and their application to sociologists' work. Lack of awareness or misunderstanding of an ethical standard is not, in itself, a defense to a charge of unethical conduct.

20.02 Confronting Ethical Issues: When sociologists are uncertain whether a particular situation or course of action would violate the Code of Ethics, they consult with other sociologists knowledgeable about ethical issues, with ASA's Committee on Professional Ethics, or with other organization entities such as institutional review boards.

When sociologists take actions or are confronted with choices where there is a conflict between ethical standards enunciated in the Code of Ethics and laws or legal requirements, they make known their commitment to the Code and take steps to resolve the conflict in a responsible manner by consulting with colleagues, professional organizations, or the ASA's Committee on Professional Ethics.

20.03 Fair Treatment of Parties in Ethical Disputes: Sociologists do not discriminate against a person on the basis of his or her having made an ethical complaint.

   Sociologists do not discriminate against a person based on his or her having been the subject of an ethical complaint. This does not preclude taking action based upon the outcome of an ethical complaint.

20.04 Reporting Ethical Violations of Others: When sociologists have substantial reason to believe that there may have been an ethical violation by another sociologist, they attempt to resolve the issue by bringing it to the attention of that individual if an informal resolution appears appropriate or possible, or they seek advice about whether or how to proceed based on this belief, assuming that such activity does not violate any confidentiality rights. Such action might include referral to ASA's Committee on Professional Ethics.

20.05 Cooperating with Ethics Committees: Sociologists cooperate in ethics investigations, proceedings, and resulting requirements of the American Sociological Association. In doing so, they make reasonable efforts to resolve any issues of confidentiality. Failure to cooperate may be an ethics violation.

20.06 Improper Complaints: Sociologists do not file or encourage the filing of ethics complaints that are frivolous and are intended to harm the alleged violator rather than to protect the integrity of the discipline and the public.

Glossary–Glosario

A

absolute poverty the absence of enough money to secure life's necessities

achieved status a position that is earned or chosen

actuarial tables statistics of life expectancies; used as basis for life insurance costs

age stratification the unequal distribution of scarce resources based on age

ageism a set of beliefs, attitudes, norms, and values used to justify age-based prejudice and discrimination

agricultural society a society that uses plows and draft animals in growing food

alternative movement a social movement that focuses on bringing about limited changes in people

anomie a social condition in which norms are weak, conflicting, or absent

anticipatory socialization the voluntary process of preparing to accept new norms, values, attitudes, and behaviors

ascribed status a position that is neither earned nor chosen but assigned

assimilation the blending or fusing of minority groups into the dominant society

authoritarianism a political system controlled by nonelected rulers who usually permit some degree of individual freedom

authority the legitimate or socially approved use of power

averting turning aside; prevention

pobreza absoluta falta de dinero suficiente para cubrir las necesidades de la vida

estado logrado posición que se gana o elige

cuadros actuariales estadísticas de expectativas de vida, usadas como bases para los costos de los seguros de vida

estratificación por edad distribución desigual de recursos escasos basada en la edad

discriminación por edad conjunto de creencias, actitudes, normas y valores usados para justificar la discriminación y prejuicios basados en la edad

sociedad agrícola una sociedad que usa el arado y animales de tiro para cultivar los alimentos

movimiento alternativo movimiento social que se enfoca hacia el logro de obtener cambios limitados en las personas

desmandado condición social en la cual las normas son débiles, conflictivas o ausentes

socialización anticipadora el proceso voluntario de prepararse para aceptar nuevas normas, valores, actitudes y comportamientos

estado adscrito posición que no es ganada ni elegida sino asignada

asimilación la mezcla o fusión de grupos minoritarios con la sociedad dominante

autoritarismo sistema político controlado por mandatarios no elegidos quienes generalmente permiten algún grado de libertad individual

autoridad poder aceptado como legítimo o aprobado socialmente por aquellos sometidos a él

evitando dejado a un lado, prevención

B

beliefs ideas about the nature of reality

bilateral family arrangement where descent and inheritance are passed equally through both parents

biological determinism principle that behavioral differences are the result of inherited physical characteristics

creencias ideas sobre la naturaleza de la realidad

arreglos familiares bilaterales cuando la descendencia y la herencia se transmite a través de ambos padres

determinismo biológico principio que sostiene que las diferencias en comportamiento son el resultado de características físicas heredadas

bourgeoisie class owning the means for producing wealth

bullish optimistic; hopeful

bureaucracy a formal organization based on rationality and efficiency

burguesía clase que posee los medios para producir riquezas

alcista optimista, esperanzado

burocracia organización formal basada en la racionalidad y eficiencia

C

canon an accepted principle or rule

capitalist person who owns or controls the means for producing wealth

capitalism an economic system based on private ownership of property and the pursuit of profit

case study intensive study of a single group, incident, or community

caste system a stratification structure that does not allow for social mobility

causation the belief that events occur in predictable ways and that one event leads to another

census regularly occurring count of a particular population

central-city dilemma concentration of people in need of public services without tax base–generated money to provide for them

charismatic authority authority that arises from the personality of an individual

charter schools public schools that are operated like private schools by public school teachers and administrators

church a life-encompassing religious organization to which all members of a society belong

city dense and permanent concentration of people living in a specific area and working primarily in nonagricultural jobs

class conflict the ongoing struggle between the bourgeoisie (owners) and the proletariat (working) classes

class consciousness identification with the goals and interests of a social class

closed-ended questions questions a person must answer by choosing from a limited, predetermined set of responses

coercion interaction in which individuals or groups are forced to behave in a particular way

cognitive ability capacity for thinking abstractly

canon principio o regla aceptado

capitalismo sistema económico basado en la posesión privada de la propiedad y la persecución del lucro

persona capitalista persona que posee o controla los medios para producir riquezas

estudio de caso estudio intensivo sobre un grupo, incidente o comunidad

sistema de castas estratificación de estructura que no permite la movilidad social

causalidad creencia que los sucesos ocurren de manera predecible y que un hecho lleva a otro

censo cuenta periódica de una población en particular

dilema de ciudad principal concentración de personas en necesidad servicios públicos sin contar con los medios producidos por los impuestos para proporcionarlos

autoridad carismática autoridad que emana de la personalidad de un individuo

escuelas diferenciadas escuelas públicas que operan como escuelas privadas pero con profesores y administradores del Estado

iglesia organización religiosa que abarca un sistema de vida a la cual pertenecen todos los miembros de una sociedad

ciudad área específica donde habita una densidad y concentración permanente de personas que mantienen empleos primariamente no agrícolas

conflicto de clases lucha permanente entre la clase burguesa (propietarios) y la proletaria (trabajadores)

conciencia de clase identificación con las metas e intereses de una clase social

preguntas limitadas preguntas que una persona debe contestar eligiendo entre una variedad limitada y predeterminada de respuestas

coerción interacción en la cual individuos o grupos están forzados a actuar de una manera determinada

habilidad cognoscitiva capacidad de pensar en forma abstracta collective behavior the spontaneous behavior of a group of people responding to similar stimuli

collectivity collection of people who do not normally interact and who do not share clearly defined norms

compensatory education specific curricular programs designed to overcome a deficiency

competition system in which rewards are based on relative performance

concentric zone theory theory that describes urban growth in terms of circular areas that grow from the central city outward

conflict interaction aimed at defeating an opponent

conflict perspective approach emphasizing the role of conflict, competition, and constraint within a society

conformity behavior that matches group expectations

conglomerates networks of unrelated businesses operating under one corporate umbrella

contagion theory theory stating that members of a crowd stimulate each other to higher and higher levels of emotion and irrational behavior

contingent employment the hiring of part-time, short-term workers

control theory theory that compliance with social norms requires strong bonds between individuals and society

convergence theory theory that states that crowds are formed by people who deliberately congregate with like-minded others

cooperation interaction in which individuals or groups combine their efforts to reach a goal

cooperative learning instructional method that relies on cooperation among students

core tier an occupational structure composed of large firms dominating their industries

corporation an organization owned by shareholders, who have limited liability and limited control

correlation a measure of the relationship between two variables

conducta colectiva el comportamiento espontáneo de un grupo de personas que responden a estímulos similares

colectividad conjunto de personas que normalmente no interactúan y que no comparten normas claramente definidas

educación compensatoria programas específicos de educación diseñados para superar una deficiencia

competencia sistemas en los cuales las recompensas están basadas en desempeños relativos

teoría de zona concéntrica teoría que describe el crecimiento urbanístico en términos de áreas circulares que crecen desde la ciudad principal a la periferia

conflicto interacción dirigida hacia la derrota de un oponente

perspectiva de conflicto enfoque que enfatiza el papel que juega el conflicto, la competencia y la restricción dentro de una sociedad

conformidad conducta acorde a las expectativas de grupo

conglomerados redes de firmas no relacionadas que operan bajo la protección de una corporación

teoría de contagio teoría que sostiene que los miembros de una multitud se estimulan mutuamente para alcanzar niveles cada vez más altos de emoción y conducta irracional

empleo contingente la contratación de empleados a medio tiempo por períodos cortos

teoría de control teoría que sostiene que la adhesión a las normas sociales requiere de fuertes lazos entre los individuos y la sociedad

teoría de convergencia teoría que sostiene que las multitudes están formadas de personas que deliberadamente se juntan con otras que piensan lo mismo

cooperación interacción mediante la cual individuos o grupos combinan sus esfuerzos para alcanzar un objetivo

aprendizaje cooperativo método de instrucción que se basa en la cooperación entre estudiantes

primera línea estructura ocupacional compuesta de grandes firmas que dominan a sus industrias

corporación organización que es propiedad de los accionistas quienes tienen responsabilidad y control limitado

correlación medida de la relación entre dos variables

counterculture a subculture deliberately and consciously opposed to certain central beliefs or attitudes of the dominant culture

anticultura subcultura que deliberada y conscientemente se opone a ciertas creencias y actitudes esenciales de la cultura dominante

crime acts committed in violation of the law

crímenes actos cometidos en violación de la ley

criminal justice system system comprising institutions and processes responsible for enforcing criminal statutes

sistema de justicia criminal sistema que comprende las instituciones y procesos responsables de hacer cumplir los estatutos criminales

crowd a temporary collection of people who share an immediate common interest

multitud número temporal de personas que comparten un interés común inmediato

crude birthrate the annual number of live births per one thousand members of a population

tasa bruta de nacimientos número anual de nacimientos con vida por cada mil miembros de una población

crude death rate the annual number of deaths per one thousand members of a population

tasa bruta de fallecimientos número anual de defunciones por cada mil miembros de una población

cult a religious organization whose characteristics are not drawn from existing religious traditions within a society

culto organización religiosa cuyas características no se originan de las tradiciones religiosas existentes en una sociedad

cultural bias the unfair measurement of the cognitive abilities of people in some social categories

prejuicio cultural la medición injusta de las habilidades cognoscitivas de las personas pertenecientes a ciertas categorías sociales

cultural particulars the ways in which a culture expresses universal traits

peculiaridades culturales la forma en que una cultura expresa características universales

cultural pluralism desire of a group to maintain some sense of identity separate from the dominant group

pluralismo cultural deseo de un grupo de mantener algún sentido de identidad distinto al del grupo dominante

cultural universals general cultural traits that exist in all cultures

manifestaciones culturales universales características culturales generales que existen en todas las culturas

culture knowledge, values, customs, and physical objects that are shared by members of a society

culture conocimientos, valores, costumbres y objetos físicos que comparten los miembros de una sociedad

D

de facto segregation denial of equal access based on everyday practice

segregación de facto negación a igualdad de acceso basado en la práctica

de jure segregation denial of equal access based on the law

segregación legal negación a igualdad de acceso basado en la ley

demographic transition theory theory that population growth is a function of the level of economic development in a country

teoría de transición demográfica teoría que sostiene que el aumento de la población es una función relacionada al nivel del desarrollo económico de un país

demography the scientific study of population

demografía el estudio científico de la población

denomination one of several religious organizations that most members of a society accept as legitimate

creencia una de varias organizaciones religiosas que la mayoría de los miembros de una sociedad aceptan como legítima

dependency ratio the ratio of dependent persons to economically active persons

porcentaje de dependientes la relación de personas dependientes de alguien con respecto a las económicamente activas dependent variable a characteristic that reflects a change

desocialization the process of giving up old norms, values, attitudes, and behaviors

deterrence discouraging criminal acts by threatening punishment

deviance behavior that departs from societal or group norms

deviant a person who breaks significant societal or group norms

differential association theory theory that individuals learn deviance in proportion to the number of deviant acts to which they are exposed

diffusion process by which one culture or society borrows from another culture or society

discovery process by which something is learned or reinterpreted

discrimination treating people differently based on ethnicity, race, religion, or culture

dispersed collectivity collectivity made up of people who are not physically connected but who follow common rules or respond to common stimuli

doubling time number of years needed to double the base population size

downsizing the process by which companies reduce their workforces

dramaturgy approach that depicts human interaction as theatrical performances

drive impulse to reduce discomfort

dysfunction negative consequence of an aspect of society

variable dependiente característica que refleja un cambio

desocialización el proceso de renunciar a antiguas normas, valores, actitudes y conductas

disuasión disuadir de cometer actos criminales amenazando con el castigo

desviación conducta que se aleja de normas sociales o de grupos sociales

desviado persona que quiebra normas importantes de la sociedad o de grupos sociales

teoría diferencial de asociación teoría que sostiene que la proporción de individuos que se convierten en desviados guarda relación con el número de desviaciones a las que han estado sometidos

difusión proceso por el cual una cultura o sociedad toma prestado de otra cultura o sociedad

descubrimiento proceso mediante el cual algo es aprendido o vuelto a interpretar

discriminación trato diferente a las personas basado en la etnia, raza, religión o cultura

colectividad dispersa colectividad formada por personas que no están conectadas físicamente pero que siguen reglas comunes o responden a estímulos comunes

momento de duplicación número de años necesarios para duplicar el tamaño de la población base

reducirse el proceso mediante el cual las empresas reducen su fuerza laboral

dramaturgia enfoque que describe las interacciones humanas como representaciones teatrales

empuje impulso para reducir el malestar

disfunción consecuencia negativa de un aspecto de la sociedad

E

economic institution institution that determines how goods and services are produced and distributed

edge city a suburban unit specializing in a particular economic activity

educational equality condition in which schooling produces the same results for lower-class and minority children as it does for other children

instituciones de economía instituciones que determinan como se deben producir y distribuir los bienes y servicios

ciudad satélite unidad suburbana que se especializa en una actividad económica determinada

igualdad educacional condición en la cual la enseñanza produce los mismos resultados en los niños de clases sociales más bajas o pertenecientes a las minorías que en el resto de los niños

elitism system in which a community or society is controlled from the top by a few individuals or organizations

emergent norm theory theory stating that norms develop to guide crowd behavior

endogamy marriage within one's own group as required by social norms

equalitarian family structure where authority is evenly shared between the husband and wife

equilibrium a society's tendency to react to changes by making adjustments to keep itself in a state of functioning and balance

ethnic minority group identified by cultural, religious, or national characteristics

ethnocentrism judging others in terms of one's own cultural standards

exogamy the practice of marrying outside one's group

exponential growth growth in which the amount of increase is added to the base figure each time period

extended family two or more adult generations of the same family whose members share economic resources and a common household

extrapolating predicting based on past experiences

elitismo sistema en el cual una comunidad o sociedad está controlada desde arriba por unos pocos individuos u organizaciones

teoría de normas emergentes teoría que sostiene que las normas se desarrollan para guiar la conducta de las multitudes

endogamia matrimonio dentro de su grupo social, como lo exigen las normas sociales

estructura familiar igualitaria es en la que la autoridad está distribuida en forma pareja entre el marido y la esposa

equilibrio la tendencia de una sociedad de reaccionar a los cambios haciendo ajustes para mantenerse en un estado balanceado de funcionamiento

minoría étnica grupo identificado por características culturales, religiosas o nacionales

etnocentrismo juzgar a los demás en términos de sus propios estándares culturales

exogamia práctica de casarse con alguien de fuera de su grupo social

crecimiento exponencial crecimiento en el cual la cantidad de aumento es agregada a la cifra base en cada período de tiempo

prolongación familiar dos o más generaciones adultas de la misma familia cuyos miembros comparten los recursos económicos en una vivienda común

extrapolación predicciones basadas en experiencias pasadas

F

fad an unusual behavior pattern that spreads rapidly and disappears quickly

false consciousness adoption of the ideas of the dominant class by the less powerful class

family a group of people related by marriage, blood, or adoption

family planning the voluntary use of population control methods

fashion a widely accepted behavior pattern that changes periodically

fecundity the maximum rate at which women can physically produce children

feminization of poverty a trend in U.S. society in which women and children make up an increasing proportion of the poor

furor forma de comportamiento inusual que se extiende rápidamente y desaparece rápido

falsa conciencia adopción de ideas de la clase dominante por la clase menos poderosa

familia grupo de personas relacionadas por matrimonio, sangre, o adopción

planificación familiar el uso voluntario de métodos de control de la población

moda patrón de comportamiento generalmente aceptado que cambia periódicamente

fecundidad la tasa máxima en la cual las mujeres pueden físicamente producir niños

feminización de la pobreza tendencia de la sociedad estadounidense en la cual las mujeres y los niños representan una proporción en el aumento de la pobreza

fertility a measure of the number of children born to a woman or a population of women

fertility rate the annual number of live births per one thousand women aged fifteen to forty-four

field research research that takes place in a natural (nonlaboratory) setting

folkways norms that lack moral significance

for-profit schools schools run by private companies on government funds

formal organization a group deliberately created to achieve one or more long-term goals

formal sanctions sanctions imposed by persons given special authority

formal schooling education that is provided and regulated by society

fundamentalism the desire to resist secularization and to adhere closely to traditional religious beliefs, rituals, and doctrines

fertilidad medición de los hijos nacidos a una mujer o a una población de mujeres

asa de fertilidad el número anual de nacimientos vivos por mil mujeres entre las edades de quince a cuarenta y dos

investigación en terreno investigación que tiene lugar en ambientes naturales (no de laboratorio)

costumbres populares normas que no tienen significado moral

organización formal grupo creado específicamente para lograr una o más metas a largo plazo

sanciones formales sanciones impuestas por personas a quienes se les ha dado autoridad especial

educación formal educación proporcionada y regulada por la sociedad

colegios gananciales colegios administrados por compañías privadas con fondos del gobierno

fundamentalismo deseo de resistir a la secularización y adherir estrictamente a creencias religiosas tradicionales, rituales y doctrinas

G

game stage Mead's third stage in the development of role taking; children anticipate the actions of others based on social rules

gemeinschaft "community"; preindustrial society based on tradition, kinship, and close social ties

gender identity a sense of being male or female based on learned cultural values

gender socialization the social process of learning how to act as a boy or girl

generalized other integrated conception of the norms, values, and beliefs of one's community or society

genocide the systematic effort to destroy an entire population

gentrification the development of low-income areas by middle-class homebuyers, landlords, and professional developers

gesellschaft "society"; industrial society characterized by weak family ties, competition, and impersonal social relationships

gross migration rate the number of persons per year per one thousand members of a population who enter or leave a geographic area

etapa de juego la tercera etapa de Mead en el desarrollo de adoptar roles, los niños anticipan las acciones de terceros basados en las leyes sociales

comunidad de "clan" sociedad preindustrial basada en la tradición, parentesco y estrechos vínculos sociales

identidad de género sentido de ser hombre o mujer basado en valores culturales aprendidos

socialización del género el proceso social de aprender la forma de actuar de un niño o niña

generalización otra forma integrada de concepción de las normas, valores y creencias de la propia comunidad o sociedad

genocidio esfuerzo sistemático de destruir una población completa

incorporación de áreas populares el desarrollo de áreas de bajos ingresos por compradores de casas de la clase media, rentistas o corredores profesionales de propiedades

sociedad de firmas sociedad industrial carente de lazos familiares y caracterizada por la competencia y relaciones sociales impersonales

tasa bruta de migración el número de personas por cada mil miembros de una población que entra o sale de un área geográfica group at least two people who have one or more goals in common and share common ways of thinking and behaving

groupthink when thinking in a group is self-deceptive, based on conformity to group beliefs, and created by group pressure to conform

grupo al menos dos personas que tienen uno o más objetivos en común y que comparten formas de pensar o de comportarse

pensamiento de grupo cuando el pensamiento en grupo es engañoso pues está basado en la conformidad a las creencieas del grupo creada bajo la presión ejercida por el mismo grupo para concordar

H

hate crime a criminal act motivated by prejudice

crimen de odio acto criminal provocado por el prejuicio

hidden curriculum the informal and unofficial aspects of culture that children are taught in school, such as conformity or cooperation

curriculum oculto los aspectos culturales informales y extraoficiales que se les enseña a los niños en el colegio tales como la cooperación y conformidad

hidden unemployment unemployment that includes people not counted in the traditional unemployment categories

desempleo oculto desempleo que incluye a personas que no forman parte de las categorías tradicionales de desempleo

horizontal mobility a change in occupation within the same social class

movilidad horizontal cambios en la ocupación dentro de una misma clase social

horticultural society a society that survives primarily through the growing of plants

sociedad hortícola sociedad que sobrevive primariamente a través del cultivo de plantas

hunting and gathering society a society that survives by hunting animals and gathering edible foods

sociedad de caza y recolección sociedad que sobrevive por medio de la caza y recolección de alimentos

hypothesis testable statement of relationships among variables

hipótesis verificable enunciación de las relaciones entre variables

hypothesis of linguistic relativity theory stating that our idea of reality depends largely upon language

hipótesis de relatividad lingüística teoría que sostiene que nuestra idea de la realidad depende en gran medida del lenguaje

I

"I" the part of the self that accounts for unlearned, spontaneous acts

él Yo parte de la personalidad responsable de los actos espontáneos no aprendidos

ideal culture cultural guidelines that group members claim to accept

cultura ideal pautas culturales que los miembros del grupo dicen aceptar

imitation stage Mead's first stage in the development of role taking; children begin to imitate behaviors without understanding why

etapa de imitación la primera etapa de Mead en el desarrollo de toma de roles: los niños empiezan a imitar conductas sin saber por qué

in-group exclusive group demanding intense loyalty

grupo exclusivo grupo exclusivo que exige lealtad incondicional

incarceration a method of protecting society from criminals by keeping them in prisons

incarcelamiento método de protección a la sociedad de los criminales manteniéndolos en prisiones

incest taboo a norm forbidding marriage between certain kinds of relatives

tabú de incesto norma que prohibe el matrimonio entre cierto nivel de parentesco

income amount of money received by an individual or group over a specific time period

ingreso cantidad de dinero recibido por un individuo o grupo en un período específico de tiempo independent variable a characteristic that causes something to occur

industrial society a society that depends on science and technology to produce its basic goods and services

infant mortality rate the annual number of deaths among infants under one year of age per one thousand live births

informal organization groups within a formal organization in which personal relationships are guided by norms, rituals, and sentiments that are not part of the formal organization

informal sanctions rewards or punishments that can be applied by most members of a group

instincts innate (unlearned) patterns of behavior

institutionalized discrimination unfair practices that grow out of common behaviors and attitudes and that are a part of the structure of a society

integrative curriculum an approach to education based on student-teacher collaboration

interest group a group organized to influence political decision making

intergenerational mobility a change in status or class from one generation to the next

interlocking directorates directorates that result when heads of corporations sit on one another's boards

intervening variable a variable that changes the relationship between an independent and a dependent variable

interview a survey method in which a trained researcher asks questions and records the answers

invention the creation of something new from previously existing items or processes

iron law of oligarchy theory that power increasingly becomes concentrated in the hands of a few members of any organization

variable independiente característica que hace que algo ocurra

sociedad industrial sociedad que depende de la ciencia y la tecnología para producir sus bienes y servicios básicos

tasa de mortalidad infantil el número anual de muertes de niños menores de un año por cada mil nacimientos vivos

organizaciones informales grupos dentro de organizaciones formales en los cuales las relaciones personales están guiados por normas, rituales y sentimientos que no forman parte de las organizaciones formales

sanciones informales recompensas o castigos que pueden ser aplicados por la mayoría de los miembros de un grupo

instintos cánones innatos (no aprendidos) de conducta

discriminación institucionalizada prácticas injustas que emanan de conductas y actitudes comunes y que forman parte de la estructura de una sociedad

programa integrante un enfoque educativo basado en la colaboración profesor-alumno

grupo de interés grupo organizado para influir las decisiones políticas

movilidad intergeneracional cambio en el estado o clase de una generación a la otra

directorios entrelazados los directorios que resultan cuando las cabezas de algunas corporaciones forman parte de los directorios de otras

variable interviniente variable que cambia la relación entre una variable independiente y una dependiente

entrevista método de encuesta en el cual un investigador entrenado formula preguntas y registra las respuestas

invención creación de algo nuevo de ítems o procesos que existían previamente

ley del hierro de la oligarquía teoría que sostiene que el poder se concentra cada vez más en las manos de unos pocos miembros de cualquier organización

L

labeling theory theory that society creates deviance by identifying particular members as deviant

latent function an action that produces an unintended and unrecognized result

teoría de etiquetado teoría que sostiene que la sociedad crea la desviación identificando a ciertos miembros como desviados

acción latente que produce un resultado no deseado y no admitido

law a norm that is formally defined and enforced by officials

legitimate justify or give official approval to

life expectancy the average number of years that persons in a given population born at a particular time can expect to live

life span the most advanced age to which humans can survive

looking-glass self an image of yourself based on what you believe others think of you

ley norma formalmente definida e impuesta por funcionarios públicos

legitimar justificar o dar aprobación oficial a algo o alguien

expectativa de vida el número promedio de años de esperanza de vida de personas de una población determinada, nacidas en un tiempo determinado

período de vida la edad más avanzada que pueden alcanzar los seres humanos

espejo de sí mismo imagen que uno tiene de sí mismo basado en lo que cree que los otros piensan de él

M

magnet schools public schools that focus on particular disciplines or areas, such as fine arts or science

manifest function an action that produces an intended and recognized result

marriage a legal union based on mutual rights and obligations

mass media means of communication designed to reach the general population

master status a position that strongly affects most other aspects of a person's life

material culture the concrete, tangible objects of a culture

matriarchy the pattern in which the oldest woman living in the household has authority over all other family members

matrilineal family arrangement where descent and inheritance are passed through the female line

matrilocal the pattern in which married couples live with or near the wives' parents

"me" the part of the self formed through socialization

mechanical solidarity social dependency based on a widespread consensus of values and beliefs, enforced conformity, and dependence on tradition and family

mechanization the process of replacing animal and human power with machine power

meritocracy a society in which social status is based on ability and achievement

escuelas imán escuelas públicas enfocadas hacia disciplinas o áreas específicas, como ser las bellas artes o la ciencia

función declarada acción que produce un efecto deseado y admitido

matrimonio unión legal basada en derechos y obligaciones mutuas

medios de comunicación conjunto de medios de comunicación diseñados para llegar a la población en general

condición dominante estado social que afecta fuertemente la mayoría de los otros aspectos de la vida de una persona

cultura material los objetos concretos y tangibles de una cultura

matriarcado forma de organización en la cual la mujer de más edad que vive en una casa tiene autoridad sobre todos los otros miembros de la familia

por línea materna arreglo familiar según el cual la descendencia y la herencia se transmiten por línea materna

cerca de la madre modelo en el cual las parejas casadas viven cerca o con los padres de la esposa

"Yo" la parte de uno mismo formada a través de la socialización

solidaridad mecánica dependencia social basada en un consenso muy divulgado de valores y creencias, conformidad impuesta y dependencia de la tradición y la familia

mecanización el proceso de reemplazar la potencia humana y animal por potencia mecánica

meritocracia sociedad en la cual el estado social está basado en la habilidad y logros

migration the movement of people from one geographic area to another

minority a group of people with physical or cultural traits different from those of the dominant group in the society

mob emotional crowd ready to use violence for a specific purpose

monogamy a marriage consisting of one man and one woman at a time

monopolies companies that have control over the production or distribution of a product or service

mores norms that have moral dimensions and that should be followed by members of the society

mortality deaths within a population

multicultural education an educational curriculum that emphasizes differences among gender, ethnic, and racial categories

multinationals firms based in highly industrialized societies with operating facilities throughout the world

multiple causation the belief that an event occurs as a result of several factors working in combination

multiple nuclei theory theory that focuses on specific geographic or historical influences on urban growth

migración el movimiento de personas de un área geográfica a otro

minoría grupo de personas con peculiaridades físicas o culturales diferentes de las del grupo dominante de la sociedad

masas multitud emocional lista a ejercer la violencia para un propósito específico

monogamia matrimonio consistente de un solo hombre y mujer por vez

monopolios compañías que tienen el control de la producción o distribución de un producto o servicio

mases normas que tienen dimensiones morales y que los miembros de una sociedad debería cumplir

mortalidad muertes dentro de una población

educación multicultural un programa de estudios que enfatiza las diferencias existentes entre los géneros, las etnias y las categorías raciales

firmas multinacionales basadas en sociedades altamente industrializadas con instalaciones operativas en todo el mundo

causalidad múltiple la creencia que un suceso ocurre como resultado de varios factores operando en combinación

teoría de núcleos múltiples teoría que se enfoca en influencias específicas geográficas o históricas sobre el crecimiento urbano

N

negative deviance involves behavior that underconforms to accepted norms

neolocal the pattern in which newly married couples set up their own households

net migration rate the annual increase or decrease per one thousand members of a population resulting from migration into and out of the population

nonmaterial culture ideas, knowledge, and beliefs that influence people's behavior

norms rules defining appropriate and inappropriate behavior

nuclear family family structure composed of one or both parents and children

nullifying causing to have no value or force; negating

desviación negativa involucra una actitud inconformista hacia las normas aceptadas

nuevos hogares la forma en que los recién casados establecen sus propios hogares

tasa neta de migración el incremento o disminución anual por cada mil integrantes de una población resultante de población migrante que entra o sale

cultura no material ideas, conocimientos y creencias que influencian la conducta de las personas

normas reglas que definen un comportamiento adecuado e inadecuado

núcleo familiar estructura familiar compuesta de uno o los dos padres y sus hijos

anulación causando que no tenga valor ni fuerza: negando

O

obligations behaviors that individuals are expected to perform toward others

occupational sex segregation the concentration of women in lower-status positions

occupations categories of jobs that involve similar activities at different work locations

oligopolies combinations of companies that control the production or distribution of a product or service

open class system a system in which social class is based on merit and individual effort; movement is allowed between classes

open classroom a nonbureaucratic approach to education based on democracy, flexibility, and noncompetitiveness

open-ended questions questions a person is to answer in his or her own words

organic solidarity social interdependency based on a high degree of specialization in roles

out-group group targeted by an in-group for opposition, antagonism, or competition

overurbanization when a city cannot supply adequate jobs and housing for its inhabitants

obligaciones conducta que se espera que tengan los individuos

segregación ocupacional por sexo a concentración de mujeres en posiciones de menor importancia

ocupaciones categorías de trabajos que involucran actividades similares en diferentes ubicaciones de trabajo

oligopolios combinación de compañías que controlan la producción o distribución de un producto o servicios

sistema social abierto sistema en el cual las clases sociales están basadas en el mérito y el esfuerzo individual; el movimiento entre clases sociales está permitido

educación abierta un enfoque no burocrático de la educación basado en la democracia, la flexibilidad y carente de competencia

preguntas libres preguntas que una persona debe responder en sus propias palabras

solidaridad de cuerpo interdependencia social basada en un alto grado de especialización en los diferentes roles

grupo externo grupo dirigido por un grupo exclusivo para fines de oposición, antagonismo o competencia

sobreurbanización cuando una ciudad no es capaz de proporcionar trabajos y habitación adecuados a sus habitantes

P

Pandora's box a source of trouble

participant observation a case study where the researcher becomes a member of the group being studied

pastoral societies societies where food is obtained primarily by raising and taking care of animals

patriarchy the pattern in which the oldest man living in the household has authority over the rest of the family members

patrilineal family arrangement where descent and inheritance are passed through the male line

patrilocal the pattern in which married couples live with or near the husbands' parents

peer group set of individuals of roughly the same age and interests

la caja de Pandora fuente de conflictos

observación del participante en un estudio de caso, cuando el investigador se convierte en miembro del grupo estudiado

sociedades pastorales sociedades en las cuales se obtiene el alimento de la crianza y cuidado de los animales

patriarcado modelo en el cual el hombre de más edad que habite en una casa tiene autoridad sobre el resto de los miembros de la familia

por línea paterna arreglos familiares mediante el cual la descendencia y la herencia se transmiten por la línea paterna

cerca del padre modelo en el cual las parejas casadas viven con o cerca de los padres del esposo

grupo de pares grupo de individuos de aproximadamente la misma edad e intereses

Glossary–Glosario

peripheral theory theory that emphasizes the growth of suburbs around the central city

peripheral tier an occupational structure composed of smaller, less profitable firms

perspective a particular point of view

play stage Mead's second stage in the development of role taking; children act in ways they imagine other people would

pluralism system in which political decisions are made as a result of bargaining and compromise among special interest groups

political institution institution that determines how power is obtained and exercised

political socialization informal and formal processes by which a person develops political opinions

polyandry the marriage of one woman to two or more men at the same time

polygamy the marriage of a male or female to more than one person at a time

polygyny the marriage of one man to two or more women at the same time

population a group of people living in a particular place at a specified time or a group of people with certain specified characteristics

population control attempts by government to control birthrates

population momentum inability to stop population growth immediately because of previous high rate of growth

population pyramid a graphic representative of the age and gender composition of a population

positive deviance involves behavior that overconforms to social expectations

positivism the belief that knowledge should be derived from scientific observation

postindustrial society a society in which the economic emphasis is on providing services and information

power the ability to control the behavior of others

power elite a unified group of military, corporate, and government leaders

prejudice widely held negative attitudes toward a group (minority or majority) and its individual members

teoría periférica teoría que enfatiza el crecimiento de los suburbios alrededor de una ciudad principal

línea periférica estructura ocupacional compuesta por firmas más pequeñas con menores ganancias

perspectiva un punto de vista particular

etapa de juego segunda etapa de Mead en el desarrollo de la toma de roles, los niños actúan de la forma en que se imaginan actuarían otras personas

pluralismo sistema en el cual las decisiones políticas se toman como resultado de negociaciones y compromisos entre grupos de intereses determinados

instituciones políticas instituciones que determinan como se obtiene y se ejerce el poder

socialización política procesos formales e informales mediante los cuales una persona desarrolla sus opiniones políticas

poliándrico el matrimonio de una mujer a uno o dos hombres al mismo tiempo

poligamia el matrimonio de un hombre o mujer a más de una persona al mismo tiempo

poligenia el matrimonio de un hombre a dos o más mujeres al mismo tiempo

población grupo de personas que viven en un lugar específico en un tiempo determinado ó grupo de personas con ciertas características específicas

control de la población intentos del gobierno de controlar la tasa de nacimientos

ímpetu de poblamiento incapacidad de detener de inmediato el crecimiento de la población debido a una previa alta taza de crecimiento

pirámide de la población gráfico representativo de la composición de una población por edad y sexo

desviación positiva involucra un comportamiento que se conforma excesivamente a las expectativas de la sociedad

positivismo creencia que el conocimiento debe derivar de la observación científica

sociedad post-industrial sociedad en la cual el énfasis está puesto en proporcionar servicios e información

poder habilidad para controlar el comportamiento de otros

elite de poder grupo unificado de líderes del gobierno, militares y de la industria

prejuicio actitudes negativas muy difundidas hacia un grupo (mayoritario o minoritario) y sus miembros individuales

prestige recognition, respect, and admiration attached to social positions

primary deviance deviance involving occasional breaking of norms that is not a part of a person's lifestyle or self-concept

primary group people who are emotionally close, know one another well, and seek one another's company

primary relationships interactions that are intimate, personal, caring, and fulfilling

primary sector that part of the economy producing goods from the natural environment

profane nonsacred aspects of life

proletariat class that labors without owning the means of production; those who labor for the bourgeoisie

Protestant ethic a set of values, norms, beliefs, and attitudes stressing hard work, thrift, and self-discipline

prestigio reconocimiento, respeto y admiración ligados a posiciones sociales

desviación primaria desviación que comprende un rompimiento ocasional de las normas y no forma parte del estilo de vida o autoconcepto de la persona

grupo primario grupo de personas unidas por lazos emocionales, con relaciones íntimas, personales, y satisfactorias

relaciones primarias interacciones íntimas, personales, afectuosas y satisfactorias

sector primario la parte de la economía que produce bienes procedentes del medio ambiente natural

profano los aspectos no sagrados de la vida

proletariado clase social que trabaja sin poseer los medios de producción; aquéllos que trabajan para la burguesía

ética protestante conjunto de valores, normas, creencias y actitudes que enfatizan el trabajo duro, la frugalidad y la autodisciplina

Q

qualitative variable a characteristic that is defined by its presence or absence in a category

quantitative variable a characteristic that can be measured numerically

questionnaire a written set of questions to be answered by a research participant

variable cualitativa característica que se define por su presencia o ausencia en una categoría

variable cuantitativa característica que se puede medir numéricamente

cuestionario conjunto de preguntas escritas que deben ser respondidas por un participante de una investigación

R

race people sharing certain inherited physical characteristics that are considered important within a society

racism an extreme form of prejudice that assumes superiority of one group over others

rational-legal authority form of authority in which the power of government officials is based on the offices they hold

rationalization the mind-set emphasizing knowledge, reason, and planning

real culture actual behavior patterns of members of a group

recidivism a repetition of or return to criminal behavior

raza personas que comparten ciertas características físicas heredadas que son consideradas importantes dentro de una sociedad

racismo forma extrema de prejuicio que asume superioridad de un grupo sobre otros

autoridad racional legal forma de autoridad en la cual el poder de los funcionarios de gobierno está basado en el cargo que ocupan

racionalización estado de la mente que enfatiza el conocimiento, la razón y la planificación

cultura real pautas efectivas de comportamiento de los miembros de un grupo

reincidencia repetición o vuelta a una conducta criminal

redemptive movement a social movement that seeks to change people completely

reference group group used for self-evaluation and the formation of attitudes, values, beliefs, and norms

reflex automatic reaction to physical stimulus

reformative movement a social movement that attempts to make limited changes in society

rehabilitation process of changing or reforming a criminal through socialization

relative poverty a measure of poverty based on the economic disparity between those at the bottom of a society and the rest of the society

religion a unified system of beliefs and practices concerned with sacred things

religiosity ways in which people express their religious interests and convictions

replacement level birthrate at which a couple replaces itself without adding to the population

representative democracy a system of government that uses elected officials to fulfill majority wishes

representative sample a sample that accurately reflects the characteristics of the population as a whole

resocialization the process of adopting new norms, values, attitudes, and behaviors

resource mobilization theory theory of social movements that focuses on the use of resources to achieve goals

retribution punishment intended to make criminals pay compensation for their acts

revolution sudden and complete overthrow of a social or political order

revolutionary movement a social movement that attempts to change the total structure of society

rights behaviors that individuals can expect from others

riot episode of largely random destruction and violence carried out by a crowd

role expected behavior associated with a particular status

role conflict condition in which the performance of a role in one status interferes with the performance of a role in another status

movimiento redentor movimiento social que busca el cambio completo de las personas

grupo de referencia grupo utilizado como autoevaluación y desarrollo de actitudes, valores, creencias, y normas

reflejo reacción automática a estímulos físicos

movimiento reformista movimiento social que intenta efectuar cambios limitados en la sociedad

rehabilitación proceso para cambiar o reformar a un criminal por medio de la socialización

pobreza relativa sistema para medir la pobreza basado en la desigualdad económica existente entre aquéllos que se encuentran en el extremo inferior de la escala social y el resto de la sociedad

religión sistema unificado de creencias y prácticas relativas a cosas sagradas

religiosidad formas en que las personas expresan sus intereses y convicciones religiosas

nivel de reemplazo tasa de nacimientos en la cual la pareja se reemplaza a sí misma sin aumentar la población

democracia representativa sistema de gobierno que usa a funcionarios elegidos para satisfacer los deseos de la mayoría

muestra representativa muestra que refleja con exactitud las características de la población tomada en su totalidad

resocialización el proceso de adoptar nuevas normas, valores, actitudes, y conductas

movilización de recursos teoría de movimiento social que se centra en el uso de los recursos para lograr metas

punición castigo que tiene como objetivo que los criminales paguen compensación por sus actos

revolución derrocamiento repentino y total de un orden político o social

movimiento revolucionario movimiento social que intenta cambiar la estructura total de la sociedad

derechos conductas que los individuos pueden esperar de otros

disturbio episodio de violencia y destrucción aleatoria llevada a cabo por una multitud

rol la conducta esperada asociada a un estado social determinado

conflicto de roles condición en la cual la ejecución del rol de un estado social interfiere con la ejecución del rol de otro estado social

role performance the actual behavior of an individual in a role

role strain condition in which the roles of a single status are inconsistent or conflicting

role taking assuming the viewpoint of another person and using that viewpoint to shape the self-concept

rumor a widely circulating piece of information that is not verified as being true or false

desempeño de un rol la conducta real de un individuo en un rol

tensión de rol condición en la cual los roles de un solo estado social son inconsistentes o conflictivos

tomar un rol asumir el punto de vista de otra persona y usar ese punto de vista para moldear el concepto de sí mismo

rumor trozo de información de gran difusión que no ha sido verificada como verdadera o falsa

S

sacred things and ideas that are set apart and given a special meaning that goes beyond, or transcends, immediate existence

sample a group of people that represents a larger population

sanctions rewards and punishments used to encourage people to follow norms

school desegregation the achievement of a racial balance in the classroom

scientific method the recognition and formulation of a problem, the collection of data through observation and experiment, and the formulation and testing of hypotheses

secondary analysis using precollected information for data collection and research purposes

secondary deviance deviance in which an individual's life and identity are organized around breaking society's norms

secondary group people who share only part of their lives while focusing on a goal or task

secondary relationships impersonal interactions involving limited parts of personalities

secondary sector that part of the economy engaged in manufacturing goods

sect a religious organization that arises out of a desire to reform an existing religious organization

sector theory theory that emphasizes the importance of transportation routes in the process of urban growth

secularization process through which the sacred loses influence over society

self-concept an image of yourself as having an identity separate from other people

sagrado objetos e ideas que se ponen aparte y a las cuales se les da un significado especial que va más allá o trasciende la existencia inmediata

muestra grupo de personas que representan una población mayor

sanciones recompensas o castigos usados para estimular a las personas que sigan las normas

integración escolar el logro del equilibrio racial en una sala de clases

método científico el reconocimiento y formulación de un problema, la recolección de datos a través de la información y la experiencia y la formulación y comprobación de hipótesis

análisis secundario la utilización de información prerrecolectada para propósitos de recolección de datos e investigación

desviación secundaria desviación en la cual la vida e identidad de un individuo están organizadas en torno al rompimiento de las normas sociales

grupo secundario personas que comparten sólo parte de sus vidas mientras se centran en una meta o labor

relaciones secundarias interacciones impersonales que involucran porciones limitadas de las personalidades

sectores secundarios aquella parte de la economía que se ocupa de los bienes manufacturados

secta organización religiosa que proviene de un deseo de reformar una organización religiosa ya existente

teoría de sector teoría que enfatiza la importancia de las rutas de transporte en el proceso de crecimiento urbano

secularización el proceso a través del cual lo sagrado pierde influencia sobre la sociedad

autoconcepto imagen de sí mismo como teniendo una identidad separada de la de otras personas self-fulfilling prophecy an expectation that leads to behavior that causes the expectation to become reality

sex classification of people as male or female based on biological characteristics

sexism a set of beliefs, attitudes, norms, and values used to justify sexual inequality

significant others those people whose reactions are most important to your self-concept

social aggregate people temporarily in the same place at the same time

social category a group of people who share a social characteristic

social change new societal behaviors with important long-term consequences

social class segment of society whose members hold similar amounts of resources and share values, norms, and an identifiable lifestyle

social control ways to encourage conformity to society's norms

social dynamics the study of social change

social exchange a voluntary action performed in the expectation of getting a reward in return

social interaction the process of influencing each other as people relate

social mobility the movement of individuals or groups between social classes

social movement movement whose goal is to promote or prevent social change; the most structured and rational form of collective behavior

social network a web of social relationships that joins a person to other people and groups

social processes series of steps leading to change on a societal level

social sanctions rewards or punishments that encourage conformity to social norms

social solidarity the degree to which a society is unified

social statics the study of social stability and order

social stratification ranking of people or groups according to their unequal access to scarce resources

social structure the patterned interaction of people in social relationships

profecía autocumplida predicción que tiene como resultado una conducta que hace que lo esperado se convierta en realidad

sexo clasificación de las personas en masculino o femenino basada en características biológicas

sexismo conjunto de creencias, actitudes, normas y valores usados para justificar la desigualdad de los sexos

personas importantes aquéllas personas cuyas reacciones son las más importantes para su autoconcepto

agregado social agrupaciones de personas al mismo tiempo en el mismo lugar

categorías sociales grupos de personas que comparten una característica social

cambio social nuevas conductas sociales con consecuencias importantes en el largo plazo

clase social segmento de la sociedad cuyos miembros poseen cantidades similares de recursos y comparten valores, normas y un estilo de vida identificable

control social formas para estimular la conformidad a las normas sociales

dinámica social el estudio del cambio social

intercambio social acción voluntaria llevada a cabo con la esperanza de obtener una recompensa a cambio

interacción social el proceso de influenciar a otras personas mientras las personas se relacionan entre sí

movilidad social el movimiento de individuos o personas entre clases sociales

movimiento social movimiento cuyo objetivo es promover o prevenir los cambios sociales; la forma mejor estructurada y racional de conducta colectiva

red social red de relaciones sociales que unen una persona a otras personas y grupos

procesos sociales serie de pasos que llevan a un cambio en el nivel social

sanciones sociales premios o castigos que incentivan la conformidad con las normas sociales

solidaridad social el grado en que una sociedad está unida

estática social el estudio de la estabilidad y orden social

estratificación social la clasificación de personas o grupos de acuerdo a su acceso desigual a los recursos escasos

estructura social las interacciones moldeadas de las personas en las relaciones sociales

socialism an economic system founded on the belief that the means of production should be controlled by the people as a whole

socialization the process of learning to participate in a group

society a specific territory inhabited by people who share a common culture

sociobiology the study of the biological basis of human behavior

sociological imagination the ability to see the link between society and self

sociological perspective a view that looks at the behavior of groups, not individuals

sociology the scientific study of social structure (patterned social behavior)

spirit of capitalism the obligation to reinvest money in business rather than to spend it

sport a set of competitive activities in which winners and losers are determined by physical performance within a set of established rules

sport subculture a group with distinct roles, values, norms, and beliefs that is organized around a sport activity

spurious correlation a relationship between two variables that is actually caused by a third factor

stacking assignment of players to less central positions on the basis of race or ethnicity

status a position a person occupies within a social structure

status set all of the statuses that a person occupies at any particular time

stereotype a distorted, exaggerated, or oversimplified image applied to a category of people

stigma an undesirable trait or label that is used to characterize an individual

strain theory theory that deviance is more likely to occur when a gap exists between cultural goals and the ability to achieve these goals by legitimate means

subculture a group that is part of the dominant culture but that differs from it in some important respects

subjugation process by which a minority group is denied equal access to the benefits of a society

socialismo sistema económico basado en la creencia que los medios de producción deben ser controlados por las personas como un todo

socialización el proceso de aprendizaje a participar en un grupo

sociedad territorio específico habitado por personas que comparten una cultura en común

sociobiología el estudio de la base biológica del comportamiento humano

imaginación sociológica habilidad para ver el vínculo entre la sociedad y uno mismo

perspectiva sociológica punto de vista que mira el comportamiento de grupos, no de individuos

sociología el estudio científico de la estructura social (conducta social humana)

espíritu del capitalismo la obligación de reinvertir el dinero en negocios en vez de gastarlo

deporte conjunto de actividades competitivas en las cuales los ganadores y los perdedores se determinan por el desempeño físico, bajo un conjunto de reglas establecidas

subcultura deportiva grupo que desempeña roles determinados, valores y creencias organizadas alrededor de una actividad deportiva

correlación espuria relación entre dos variables que es realmente ocasionada por un tercer factor

relegación designación de jugadores a posiciones menos importantes sobre una base de raza o etnicidad

estado posición que ocupa una persona dentro de la estructura social

conjunto de estados todas las posiciones que ocupa una persona en un tiempo específico

estereotipo imagen distorsionada, exagerada o demasiado simplificada aplicada a una categoría de personas

estigma rasgo o calificación no deseada que se usa para caracterizar a un individuo

teoría de tensión teoría que sostiene que las desviaciones ocurren cuando existe un espacio entre las metas culturales y la habilidad para lograr esas metas por medios legítimos

subcultura grupo que forma parte de la cultura dominante pero que difiere de ella en algunos aspectos importantes

subyugación proceso por medio del cual se le niega a un grupo minoritario el acceso a los beneficios de una sociedad

Glossary–Glosario

suburbanization loss of population of a city to surrounding areas

survey research method in which people respond to questions

symbol anything that stands for something else and has an agreed-upon meaning attached to it

symbolic interactionism approach that focuses on the interactions among people based on mutually understood symbols

suburbanización pérdida de población de una ciudad a las áreas circundantes

investigación por encuesta método en el cual las personas responden a preguntas

símbolo cualquier cosa que representa otra cosa y que tiene un significado acordado

interacción simbólica enfoque que se centra en las interacciones entre las personas basadas en símbolos que ambas entienden

T

taboo a rule of behavior, the violation of which calls for strong punishment

technology knowledge and tools used to achieve practical goals

tertiary sector that part of the economy providing services

theoretical perspective a set of assumptions accepted as true

total fertility rate average number of children born to a woman during her lifetime

total institutions places in which people are separated from the rest of society and controlled by officials in charge

totalitarianism a political system in which a ruler with absolute power attempts to control all aspects of a society

tracking placement of students in programs according to academic ability levels

traditional authority forms of authority in which the legitimacy of a leader is rooted in custom

tabú regla de conducta cuya violación exige de un castigo severo

tecnología conocimiento y herramientas utilizados par lograr metas prácticas

sector terciario la parte de la economía que proporciona servicios

perspectiva teórica conjunto de suposiciones que se aceptan como verdaderas

tasa de fertilidad total promedio de niños que tiene una mujer durante su vida

instituciones absolutas lugares en que las personas son separadas del resto de la sociedad y controladas por los funcionarios a cargo

totalitarismo sistema político en el cual un gobernante con poderes absolutos trata de controlar todos los aspectos de una sociedad

clasificación colocación de los alumnos en programas acordes a sus niveles de habilidad académica

autoridad tradicional formas de autoridad en las cuales la legitimidad de un líder tiene sus raíces en la costumbre

U

underclass people typically unemployed who came from families that have been poor for generations

urban ecology the study of the relationships between humans and city environments

urban legend a moralistic tale that the teller swears happened to someone he or she knows

urbanism the idea that urbanization involves a distinctive way of life

clase inferior personas típicamente desempleadas que provienen de familias que han sido pobres por generaciones

ecología urbans el estudio de las relaciones entre los seres humanos y el medio ambiente de las ciudades

leyenda urbana una historia moralista que el narrador jura que le pasó a alguien que él o ella conocen

urbanismo la idea que la urbanización involucra un estilo particular de vida urbanization the shifting of population from farms and villages to large cities

urbanización proceso por medio del cual una porción más grande de la población mundial vive en las ciudades

V

value-added theory theory holding that certain conditions must exist for social movements to occur

teoría de valor agregado teoría que sostiene que ciertas condiciones deben estar dadas para que los movimientos sociales ocurran

values broad ideas about what is good or desirable shared by people in a society

valores idea amplia sobre lo que es bueno o deseable compartida por muchos integrantes de una sociedad

variable a characteristic that is subject to change

variable característica sujeta a cambios

verstehen understanding social behavior by putting yourself in the place of others

empatía la comprensión de la conducta humana poniéndose uno mismo en el lugar de otros

vertical mobility a change upward or downward in occupational status or social class

movilidad vertical cambio hacia arriba o hacia abajo del estado ocupacional o clase social

victim discounting process of reducing the seriousness of the crimes that injure people of lower status

clasificación de víctimas procedimiento mediante el cual se reduce la gravedad de los crímenes que dañan a personas de estratos bajos

voucher system system in which public school funds may be used to support public, private, or religious schools

sistema de comprobantes sistema en el cual los fondos de las escuelas fiscales pueden utilizarse para subsidiar a escuelas públicas, privadas, o religiosas

W

war organized, armed conflict that occurs within a society or between nations

guerra conflicto armado organizado que ocurre dentro de una sociedad o entre naciones

wealth total economic resources held by a person or group

riqueza el total de los recursos económicos que posee una persona o grupo

white-collar crime job-related crimes committed by high-status people

crimen de ejecutivos crímenes relacionados al trabajo cometido por personas de condición alta

working poor people employed in low-skill jobs with the lowest pay who do not earn enough to rise out of poverty

trabajadores pobres personas empleadas en trabajos que requieren de un grado elemental de habilidad con los sueldos más bajos y que no ganan lo suficiente para salir de la pobreza

Z

zero population growth situation in which deaths are balanced by births so that the population does not increase

crecimiento cero de la población situación en la cual las muertes están equilibradas con los nacimientos de modo que no crece la población

References

A

Acosta, R. Vivian, and Linda Jean Carpenter (2004). "Women in Intercollegiate Sport: A Longitudinal Study—Twenty Seven Year Update, 1977–2004." Department of Physical Education, Brooklyn College.

Adelmann, P. K., T. C. Antonucci, S. E. Crohan, and L. M. Coleman (1989). "Empty Nest, Cohort, and Employment in the Well-Being of Midlife Women." *Sex Roles,* 173–189.

Adler, Emily Stier, and Roger Clark (1999). *How It's Done: An Invitation to Social Research.* Belmont, CA: Wadsworth Publishing Company.

Adler, Patricia A., and Peter Adler (1998). *Peer Power.* New Brunswick: Rutgers University Press.

Administration for Children and Families, U.S. Department of Health & Human Services (2003). *Child Maltreatment 2003.*

Allport, Gordon (1979). *The Nature of Prejudice.* Garden City, NY: Doubleday.

American Sociological Association (2006). "Careers in Sociology." Washington, DC.

Andersen, Margaret L. (2005). *Thinking About Women.* 7th ed. Boston: Allyn and Bacon.

Asch, Solomon E. (November 1955). "Opinions and Social Pressure." *Scientific American 193,* 31–35.

Atchley, Robert C. (2003). *Social Forces and Aging.* 10th ed. Belmont, CA: Wadsworth.

Auguet, Roland (1972). *Cruelty and Civilization.* London: George Allen and Unwin, Ltd.

____. (1972). *Crueldad y Civilización: Los Juegos Romanos.* Barcelona: Aymá.

B

Baca Zinn, Maxine, and D. Stanley Eitzen (1998). "Economic Restructuring and Systems Inequality." In Margaret L. Andersen and Patricia Hill. (eds.), *Race, Class, and Gender: An Anthology.* 3rd ed. Belmont, CA: Wadsworth Publishing Co., pp. 233–237.

Bai, Matt, and Andrew Murr (January 25, 1999). "Go for the Greed." *Newsweek.*

Bailey, Susan M. (2002). *Gender in Education.* San Francisco, CA: Jossey-Bass.

Ballantine, Jeanne H. (2001). *The Sociology of Education.* 5th ed. Englewood Cliffs, NJ: Prentice Hall.

Bardes, Barbara A., Mack C. Shelley, and Steffen W. Schmidt (2005). *American Government and Politics Today.* 12th ed. Belmont, CA: Wadsworth.

Bardo, John W., and John J. Hartman (1982). *Urban Sociology.* Itasca, IL: Peacock.

Barlett, Donald L., and James B. Steele (1996). *America: Who Stole the Dream?* Kansas City, MO: Andrews McMeel.

Barner, Robert (1996). "The New Millennium Workplace: Seven Changes That Will Challenge Managers—and Workers." *The Futurist 30,* 14–19.

Baron-Cohen, Simon (2003). *The Essential Difference: The Truth about the Male and Female Brain.* New York: Perseus Books.

Barr, C. (1995). "Pushing the Envelope: What Curriculum Integration Can Be." In E. Brazee and J. Capelluti. (eds.), *Dissolving Boundaries: Toward an Integrative Curriculum.* Columbus, OH: National Middle School Association.

Barron, James (September 16, 1988). "Fondly Recalling a Martian Invasion." *New York Times,* B1, B3.

Barry, Norman P. (1999). *Welfare.* 2nd ed. Minneapolis: University of Minnesota Press.

Beaton, Rod (February 25–27, 2000). "Braves Penalized for Illegal Signing." *USA Today* :1A.

Becker, Howard S. (1991). *Outsiders.* New York: Free Press.

Begley, Sharon (November 1, 1993). "Not Just a Pretty Face." *Newsweek,* 63–67.

____. (February 28, 2000). "Getting Inside a Teen Brain." *Newsweek,* 58–59.

Bell, Daniel (1999). *The Coming of Post-Industrial Society.* New York: Basic Books.

Bellah, Robert N., et al. (1992). *The Good Society.* New York: Vintage.

Belton, Beth (March 2, 1999). "Fear Forces Employees to Take Initiative." *USA Today.*

Benokraitis, Nijole V. (1999). *Subtle Sexism.* Thousand Oaks, CA: Sage.

____. (2004). *Marriages and Family.* 5th ed. Englewood Cliffs, NJ: Prentice Hall.

Berger, Peter L. (1990). *The Sacred Canopy: Elements of a Sociological Theory of Religion.* New York: Doubleday & Co.

Berk, Richard A. (1974). *Collective Behavior.* Dubuque, IA: William C. Brown.

Bernt, Phyllis W., Sandra V. Turner, and Joseph P. Bernt (September 2005). "Middle School Students are Co-Researchers of Their Media Environment." *Middle School Journal 37*, 38–44.

Bianchi, Suzanne M. (June 1990). "America's Children: Mixed Prospects." *Population Bulletin 45*, 3–41.

Bierman, John (January 29, 1990). "Frustration and Fury." *Maclean's* 29.

Biever, Celeste (March 9, 2005). "UN Abandons Legal Ban on Human Cloning." *Newscientist.com.*

Birnbaum, Jane (September 2003). "America at Work." AFL-CIO.

Blum, Debra E. (August 11, 1993). "Men Turn to Federal Anti-Bias Laws to Protect Teams from the Chopping Block." *Chronicle of Higher Education*, A33–A34.

Blumer, Herbert (1969). "Collective Behavior." In Alfred M. Lee (ed.), *Principles of Sociology*. 3rd ed. New York: Barnes & Noble, pp. 65–121.

____. (1986). *Symbolic Interactionism*. Berkeley, CA: University of California Press.

Booth, Alan, and Ann C. Crouter. (eds.). (1998). *Men in Families: When Do They Get Involved? What Difference Does It Make?* Mahwah, NJ: Lawrence Erlbaum Associates.

Boushey, Heather, and David Rosnick (September 5, 2003). "Jobs Held by Former Welfare Recipients Hit Hard by Economic Downturn." Center for Economic and Policy Research.

Bowen, William G., and Derek Bok (2000). *The Shape of the River: Long-Term Consequences of Considering Race in College and University Admissions*. Princeton, NJ: Princeton University Press.

Bracey, Gerald W. (2003). *On the Death of Childhood and the Destruction of Public Schools*. Portsmouth, IL: Heinemann.

Brajuha, Mario, and Lyle Hallowell (January 1986). "Legal Intrusion and the Politics of Fieldwork: The Impact of the Brajuha Case." *Urban Life 14*, 454–478.

Brinton, Crane (1990). *The Anatomy of Revolution*. New York: Knopf.

Brodie, Mollyann (1995). *The Four Americas: Government and Social Policy Through the Eyes of America's Multi-Racial and Multi-Ethnic Society*. A report of the Washington Post/Kaiser Family Foundation/Harvard Survey Project. Menlo Park, CA: Kaiser Family Foundation.

Bruner, Jerome (January 1982). "Schooling Children in a Nasty Climate." *Psychology Today*, 57–63.

Brunvand, Jan Harold (1989). *Curses! Broiled Again!* New York: Norton.

Burgess, Ernest W. (1925). "The Growth of the City." In Robert E. Park, Ernest W. Burgess, and Robert D. McKenzie (eds.). *The City*. Chicago: University of Chicago Press, pp. 47–62.

Buss, David M., Neil M. Malamuth, and Barbara A. Winstead (1998). "Sex, Power, Conflict: Evolutionary and Feminist Perspectives." *Contemporary Psychology 43*.

C

Campbell, Frances A., and Craig T. Ramey (1994). "Effects of Early Intervention on Intellectual and Academic Achievement: A Follow-Up Study of Children from Low-Income Families." *Child Development 65*, 684–698.

Cantril, Hadley (1982). *The Invasion from Mars*. Princeton, NJ: Princeton University Press.

Caplow, Theodore (1991). *American Social Trends*. New York: Harcourt Brace Jovanovich.

____. (February 1998). "The Case of the Phantom Episcopalians." *American Sociological Review 63*, 137–145.

Casbergue, Renee M., and Judith Kieff (Spring 1998). "Marbles Anyone? Traditional Games in the Classroom." *Childhood Education*, 143–147.

Casler, Lawrence (1965). "The Effects of Extra Tactile Stimulation on a Group of Institutionalized Infants." *Genetic Psychology Monographs 71*, 137–175.

Casper, Lynne M., and Kristin E. Smith (May 31, 2004). "Self Care: Why Do Parents Leave Their Children Unsupervised?" *Demography 41*, 285–301.

Center for American Women and Politics. "Fact Sheet." November 2005.

Chagnon, Napoleon A. (1997). *Yanomamö*. 5th ed. Fort Worth: Harcourt Brace College Publishers.

Chamberlain, Gary (October 4, 1999). "Metal Wars." *Design News 115*.

Chambliss, William J. (November/December 1973). "The Saints and the Roughnecks." *Society 11*, 24–31.

Chandbasekaran, Rajiv (June 25, 1999). "Microsoft Trial Ends After 8 Months," *The Washington Post*, A1, A20.

Chang, Iris (1998). *The Rape of Nanking: The Forgotten Holocaust of World War II*. New York: Viking Penguin.

Children's Defense Fund (1991). *The State of America's Children—1991*. Washington, DC: Children's Defense Fund.

Clark, Charles S. (May 7, 1993). "Cults in America." *CQ Researcher 3*, 385–408.

"Closing the Gap." (September 2, 1995) *The Economist 74*.

Coakley, Jay J. (ed.). (1998). *Sport in Society*. 6th ed. Boston: Irwin/McGraw-Hill.

____. (2004). *Sports in Society*. 8th ed. New York: McGraw-Hill.

Cohen, David, and Marvin Lazerson (March/April 1972). "Education and the Corporate Order." *Socialist Revolution 2*, 47–72.

Coleman, James S., et al. (1966). *Equality of Educational Opportunity*. Washington, DC: U.S. Government Printing Office.

Coleman, James W. (September 1987). "Toward an Integrated Theory of White-Collar Crime." *American Journal of Sociology 93*, 406–439.

Cooley, Charles Horton (1902). *Human Nature and the Social Order*. New York: Scribner's.

Cowgill, Donald O., and Lowell D. Holmes (eds.). (1972). *Aging and Modernization*. New York: Appleton-Century-Crofts.

Cowley, Geoffrey, and Anne Underwood (Winter, 1997–98). "Surgeon, Drop that Scalpel." *Newsweek* 77–78.

Cox, Frank D. (2005). *Human Intimacy: Marriage, the Family, and Its Meaning*. 10th ed. Belmont, CA: Wadsworth Publishing Company.

Cox, Harvey (1977). *Turning East: The Promise and Peril of the New Orientalism*. New York: Simon and Schuster.

____. (1992). *Religion in the Secular City*. New York: Simon & Schuster.

____. (1996). *Fire from Heaven*. London: Cassell.

____. (1996). *Fire from Heaven: The Rise of Pentecostal Spirituality and the Reshaping of Religion in the Twenty-First Century*. Reading, MA: Addison Wesley Longman, Inc.

Cozzillio, Michael J. (2005). *Sports and Inequality*. Durham, NC: Carolina Academic Press.

Crain, Robert L. (January 1970). "School Integration and Occupational Achievement of Negroes." *American Journal of Sociology 75*, 593–606.

Crain, Robert L., and Carol S. Weisman (1972). *Discrimination, Personality and Achievements*. New York: Seminar Press.

Cress, Daniel M., and David A. Snow (December 1996). "Mobilization at the Margins: Resources, Benefactors, and the Viability of Homeless Social Movement Organizations." *American Sociological Review 61*, 1089–1109.

Crewdson, John (March 13, 1994). "Fraud in Breast Cancer Study." *Chicago Tribune 1*.

Crosby, F. E. (1993). *Juggling*. New York: Free Press.

Crosby, John F. (1985). *Reply to Myth: Perspectives on Intimacy*. New York: Wiley.

CRS Report for Congress (November 7, 2005). "Topics in Aging: Income and Poverty Among Older Americans in 2004." Washington, DC: Congressional Research Service.

Cuzzort, R. P., and E. W. King (1976). *Humanity and Modern Social Thought*. 2nd ed. Hinsdale, IL: Dryden Press.

D

Daniels, Cynthia R. (2000). *Lost Fathers*. New York: Palgrave Macmillan.

Darder, Antonia, and Rodolfo D. Torres (1997). *The Latino Reader*. Malden, MA: Blackwell.

Davies, Bronwyn (2003). *Frogs and Snails and Feminist Tales*. New York: Hampton Press.

Deak, JoAnn (1998). *How Girls Thrive*. Washington, DC: National Association of Independent Schools.

DeBare, Ilana (2004). *Where Girls Come First*. New York: Tarcher.

Degler, Carl N. (1991). *In Search of Human Nature*. New York: Oxford University Press.

DeYoung, Alan J. (1989). *Economics and American Education*. White Plains, NY: Longman.

DiIulio, John J., Jr., and Anne Morrison Piehl (Fall 1991). "Does Prison Pay?: The Stormy National Debate Over the Cost-Effectiveness of Imprisonment." *The Brookings Review* 28–35.

Dixon, K.A., and Carl E. Van Horn (July 2003). "The Disposable Worker." John J. Heldrich Center for Workforce Development, Rutgers University.

Donnerstein, Ed (2004). "Violence in the Media." *University of Arizona Alumnus Magazine*.

Doreian, Patrick, and Frans N. Stokman (1997). *Evolution of Social Networks*. Amsterdam: Gordon & Breach Publishers.

Dornbush, Sanford M., et al. (1985). "Single Parents, Extended Households, and the Control of Adolescents." *Child Development 56*, 326–341.

Dudley, Kathryn Marie (1997). *The End of the Line: Lost Jobs, New Lives in Postindustrial America*. Chicago: The University of Chicago Press.

Dudley, William (ed.) (1999). *Media Violence*. San Diego, CA: Greenhaven Press.

Duke, Lynne, and Gabriel Escobar (May 10, 1992). "A Looting Binge Born of Necessity, Opportunity." *Washington Post* Al, A23.

Durkheim, Emile (1964a). *The Division of Labor in Society*. New York: Free Press.

____. *Suicide*. Translated by John A. Spaulding and George Simpson (1964b). Edited by George Simpson. New York: Free Press.

____. *The Elementary Forms of the Religious Life* (1995). New York: Free Press.

Dynes, Russell R., and Kathleen J. Tierney (eds.) (1994). *Disasters, Collective Behavior, and Social Organization.* Newark: University of Delaware Press.

E

Eccles, Jacquelynne, et al. (February, 1993). "Development During Adolescence: The Impact of Stage-Environment Fit on Young Adolescents' Experiences in Schools and in Families." *American Psychologist 48,* 90–101.

Eder, Donna (1995). *School Talk.* New Brunswick, NJ: Rutgers University Press.

Eitzen, D. Stanley (2004). *Sport in Contemporary Society: An Anthology.* 7th ed. New York: St. Martin's Press.

____. "The Dark Side of Competition." In D. Stanley Eitzen (ed.) (1996), *Sport in Contemporary Society.* 5th ed. New York: St. Martin's Press, pp. 185–192.

____. *Fair and Foul: Beyond the Myths and Paradoxes of Sport.* 2nd ed. Lanham, MA: Rowman & Littlefield Publishers, 2003.

Eitzen, D. Stanley, and George H. Sage (2002). *Sociology of North American Sport.* 7th ed. Boston: WCB McGraw-Hill.

El Nasser, Haya (June 25, 1996). "Judges Say 'Scarlet Letter' Angle Works." *USA Today* 1A–2A.

Elikann, Peter T. (1996). *The Tough-On-Crime Myth: Real Solutions to Cut Crime.* New York: Plenum.

Elkin, Frederick, and Gerald Handel (1991). *The Child and Society.* 5th ed. New York: McGraw-Hill.

Ember, Carol R., and Melvin Ember (1999). *Anthropology.* 9th ed. Upper Saddle River, NJ: Prentice Hall.

Erikson, Erik H. (1964). *Childhood and Society.* 2nd ed. New York: Norton.

____. (1982). *The Life Cycle Completed.* New York: Norton.

Erikson, Kai. *Sociological Visions.* Blue Ridge Summit, PA: Rowman & Littlefield Publishers, 1997.

Erikson, Kai T. (1976). *Everything in Its Path.* New York: Simon & Schuster.

Espiritu, Yen Le (1996). *Asian American Men and Women.* Thousand Oaks, CA: Sage.

Etzioni, Amitai (October 1982). "Education for Mutuality and Civility." *Futurist 16,* 4–7.

Evans, Jean. *Three Men.* New York: Knopf, 1954.

F

Farley, Reynolds (1998). *The New American Reality: Who We Are, How We Got There, Where We Are Going.* New York: Russell Sage Foundation.

Fausto-Sterling, Anne (1987). *Myths of Gender.* New York: Basic Books.

Fazioloi, Jennifer K. (2004). "The Advancement of Female Coaches in Intercollegiate Athletics." Department of Labor Studies and Industrial Relations, Pennsylvania State University.

Feagin, Joe R. (February 1991). "The Continuing Significance of Race: Antiblack Discrimination in Public Places." *American Sociological Review 56,* 101–115.

Fedarko, Kevin (December 6, 1993). "Bodies of Evidence." *Time 70.*

Federal Bureau of Investigation (2004). *Uniform Crime Reports, 2003.* Washington, DC.

____. (November 2004). *Hate Crime Statistics, 2003.* Washington, DC.

Federal Election Commission. (2001) "International Voter Turnout." www.fec.gov/.

Fine, Gary Alan (1987). *With the Boys: Little League Baseball and Preadolescent Culture.* Chicago: University of Chicago Press.

____. (1996). *The Culture of Restaurant Work.* Berkeley and Los Angeles: University of California Press.

Fischer, David Hackett (1977). *Growing Old in America.* New York: Oxford University Press.

Fishman, Mark, and Gray Cavender. (eds.) (1998). *Entertaining Crime.* Hawthorne, NY: Aldine de Gruyter.

Flanagan, William G. (1993). *Contemporary Urban Sociology.* New York: Cambridge University Press.

Freedom House (2005). *Freedom in the World, 2005.* Washington, DC.

Fukuyama, Francis (May 1999). "The Great Disruption: Human Nature and the Reconstitution of Social Order." *Atlantic Monthly 283,* 55–80.

G

Galloway, Joseph L. (March 3, 1999). "In the Heart of Darkness." *U.S. News & World Report.*

Gallup, George H., Jr. (2005). *The Gallup Poll.* www.gallup.com/poll/.

Gallup, George H., Jr. (1988). *The Gallup Poll.* Wilmington, DE: Scholarly Resources.

____. (1994). *The Gallup Poll, Public Opinion 1993.* Wilmington, DE: Scholarly Resources.

____. (1996). *Religion in America 1996.* Princeton, NJ: The Princeton Religion Research Center.

Game, Ann, and Andrew W. Metcalfe (1996). *Passionate Sociology.* Thousand Oaks, CA: Sage.

Gamst, Glenn, and Charles M. Otten (Summer 1992). "Job Satisfaction in High Technology and Traditional

Industry: Is There a Difference?" *The Psychological Record*, 413–425.

Gans, Herbert J. (1968). *People and Plans*. New York: Basic Books.

____. (July/August 1971). "The Uses of Poverty: The Poor Pay All." *Social Policy 2*, 20–24.

Gardiner, Beth (July 5, 2005). "Activists Keep Up Pressure on G-8 Leaders." Associated Press.

Gardner, David Pierpont (1983). *A Nation at Risk: The Imperative for Educational Reform*. Report of the National Commission on Excellence in Education. Washington, DC: U.S. Government Printing Office.

Garreau, J. (1991). *Edge City: Life on the New Frontier*. New York: Doubleday.

Gegax, T. Trent, and Matt Bai (May 10, 1999). "Searching for Answers." *Newsweek*, 30–34.

Gelles, Richard J. (1997). *Intimate Violence in Families*. 3rd ed. Thousand Oaks, CA: Sage.

Gerstel, Naomi, and Harriet Engel Gross (1995). "Gender and Families in the United States: The Reality of Economic Dependence." In Jo Freeman (ed.), *Women: A Feminist Perspective*. 5th ed. Mountain View, CA: Mayfield, pp. 92–127.

Gerth, H. H., and C. Wright Mills (eds.) (1958). *From Max Weber*. New York: Oxford University Press.

Gertzen, Jason (May 17, 2003). "Company Spy: More Firms Monitoring Employees' Surfing." *Milwaukee Journal Sentinel*.

Gibbons, Tom (February 24, 1985). "Justice Not Equal for Poor Here." *Chicago Sun-Times* 1, 18.

Gibson, Margaret A., and John V. Ogbu (1991). *Minority Status and Schooling*. New York: Garland Publishing.

Giddens, Anthony (1987). *Social Theory and Modern Sociology*. Stanford, CA: Stanford University Press.

____. (2005). *Essentials of Sociology*. New York: Norton.

Gilbert, Dennis (2003). *The American Class Structure*. 6th ed. Belmont, CA: Wadsworth Publishing Company.

Glazer, Nathan (1999). "The End of Meritocracy." *The New Republic*.

Glick, P., and S. L. Lin (February 1986). "More Young Adults Are Living with Their Parents: Who Are They?" *Journal of Marriage and the Family*, 107–112.

Goffman, Erving (1961). *Encounters*. Indianapolis: Bobbs-Merrill.

____. (1963). *Stigma*. Englewood Cliffs, NJ: Prentice Hall.

____. (1974). *The Presentation of Self in Everyday Life*. New York: Overlook Press.

____. (1979). *Gender Advertisements*. New York: Harper & Row.

____. (February 1983). "The Interaction Order." *American Sociological Review 48*, 1–17.

Golden, Frederic (December 31, 1999). "Albert Einstein: Person of the Century." *Time*, 62–65.

Goode, Erich (1992). *Collective Behavior*. Fort Worth, TX: Sanders College Publishing.

Goode, William J. (1970). *World Revolution and Family Patterns*. New York: Free Press.

Gossett, Sherrie (June 28, 2005). "Citizen Journalism Growing." Accuracy in Media. www.aim.org.

Gould, Stephen Jay (1996). *The Mismeasure of Man*. rev. ed. New York: Norton.

Graham, Patricia Albjerg (2005). *Schooling America*. New York: Oxford University Press.

Greenwald, Elissa A., Hilary R. Persky, Jay R. Campbell, and John Mazzeo (1999). *NAEP 1998 Writing: Report Card for the Nation and the States*. Washington, DC: National Center for Education Statistics.

Greenya, John (February 4, 2005). "Bullying." *CQ Researcher Online*, 101–124.

Griffin, John Howard (2003). *Black Like Me*. Boston: Houghton Mifflin.

H

Hagan, Frank E. (1994a). *Introduction to Criminology*. 3rd ed. Chicago: Nelson-Hall Publishers.

Hagan, John (1994b). *Crime and Disrepute*. Thousand Oaks, CA: Pine Forge Press.

Hagedorn, John M. (1998). "Gang Violence in the Postindustrial Era." In Michael Tonry and Mark H. Moore (eds.), *Youth Violence*. Chicago: The University of Chicago Press, pp. 365–419.

Hammel, Sara, and Anna Mulrine (July 12, 1999). "They Get More than Just Game." *U.S. News and World Report*.

Handel, Gerald (ed.). (June 1990). "Revising Socialization Theory." *American Sociological Review 55*, 463–466.

Hannon, Kelly (August 8, 2003). "Title IX: History of the Civil Rights Legislation." *Lynchburg News & Advance*.

Harlow, Harry F. (1967). "The Young Monkeys." *Psychology Today 5*, 40–47.

Harlow, Harry F., and Margaret Harlow (November 1962). "Social Deprivation in Monkeys." *Scientific American 207*, 137–146.

Harlow, Harry F., and Robert R. Zimmerman (August 1959). "Affectional Responses in the Infant Monkey." *Science 21*, 421–432.

Harris, Chauncy D. (1997). "'The Nature of Cities' and Urban Geography in the Last Half Century." *Urban Geography*, 15–35.

Harris, Judith Rich (1998). *The Nurture Assumption: Why Children Turn Out the Way They Do*. New York: Free Press.

Harris, Marvin (1989). *Cows, Pigs, Wars, and Witches*. New York: Random House.

Hart-Landsberg, Martin, and Paul Burkett (2005). *China and Socialism: Market Reforms and Class Struggle*. New York: Monthly Review Press.

Hawking, Stephen W. (2005). *A Briefer History of Time*. New York: Bantam Books.

Hawley, W. D. (1985). "Achieving Quality Integrated Education—With or Without Federal Help." In F. Schultz (ed.). *Annual Editions: Education 85/86*. Guilford, CT: Dushkin Publishing, pp. 142–145.

Hawley, W. D., and M. A. Smylie (1988). "The Contribution of School Desegregation to Academic Achievement and Racial Integration." In P. A. Katz and D. A. Taylor (eds.), *Eliminating Racism*. New York: Plenum Press, pp. 281–297.

Heller, Mary Edna, Ruth S. Kempe, and Richard D. Krugman (eds.) (1999). *The Battered Child*. 5th ed. Chicago: University of Chicago Press.

Herrnstein, Richard J., and Charles Murray (1996). *The Bell Curve: Intelligence and Class Structure in American Life*. New York: Free Press.

Hiller, Susan, and Georgia M. Barrow (1999). *Aging, the Individual, and Society*. 7th ed. Belmont, CA: Wadsworth Publishing Company.

Hilts, Philip (1997). "Smoke Screen." In Jerome H. Skolnick and Elliott Currie (eds.), *Crisis in American Institutions*. New York: Longman, pp. 29–38.

Hirschi, Travis (2001). *Causes of Delinquency*. Somerset, NJ: Transaction.

Hochschild, Arlie R. (1997). *The Time Bind: When Work Becomes Home and Home Becomes Work*. New York: Henry Holt.

Hocker, Cliff (May 2004). "Worst Labor Market for Black Professionals in 25 Years." *Black Enterprise Online*. www.blackenterprise.com.

Hoebel, E. Adamson (1983). *The Law of Primitive Man*. New York: Atheneum.

Hoecker-Drysdale, Susan (1994). *Harriet Martineau*. Oxford: Berg Publishers.

Hoffman, Karen E. (November 9, 1998). "Internet as Gender-Equalizer?" *Internet World*.

Holt, John (1995). *How Children Fail*. New York: Dell.

Horrigan, John B. (2001). "Online Communities." Pew Internet and American Life Project. www.pewinternet.org.

Houseman, John (December 1948). "The Men from Mars." *Harper's Magazine 197*, 74–82.

Hoyt, Homer (1939). *The Structure and Growth of Residential Neighborhoods in American Cities*. Washington, DC: Federal Housing Authority.

Hull, N.E.H., William J. Hoffer, and Peter C. Hoffer (2004). *The Abortion Rights Controversy in America*. Chapel Hill, N.C.: University of North Carolina Press.

Hunt, Stephen, Malcolm Hamilton, and Tony Walter. (eds.) (1998). *Charismatic Christianity: Sociological Perspectives*. New York: St. Martin's Press.

Hurley, Jennifer A. (ed.) (1998). *Racism*. San Diego, CA: Greenhaven Press.

I

Ianzito, Christina (November 16, 2004). "Full House: When Kids Move Back Home." *The Washington Post*.

IDEA, International Institute for Democracy and Electoral Assistance (2005). "Turnout in the World—Country by Country Performance. www.idea.int.

Ikeda, Keiko (1998). *A Room Full of Mirrors*. Stanford, CA: Stanford University Press.

J

Jacoby, Sanford M. (1997). *Modern Manors: Welfare Capitalism Since the New Deal*. Princeton, NJ: Princeton University Press.

Janssen-Jurreit, Marie Louise (1982). *Sexism*. New York: Farrar Strauss Giroux.

Jencks, Christopher, and Meredith Phillips (September-October 1998). "America's Next Achievement Test: Closing the Black-White Test Score Gap." *The American Prospect 40*, 44–53.

Jensen, Arthur (Winter 1969). "How Much Can We Boost IQ and Scholastic Achievement?" *Harvard Educational Review 39*, 1–123.

Johnson, David W., and Frank P. Johnson (1994). *Joining Together*. 5th ed. Boston: Allyn and Bacon.

Johnstone, Ronald L. (2003). *Religion in Society*. 7th ed. Upper Saddle River, NJ: Prentice Hall.

Jones, James M. (1993). *Bad Blood* (expanded ed.). New York: Free Press.

K

Katz, James E., and Philip Aspden (December 1997). "A Nation of Strangers?" *Communications of the ACM*, 81–87.

Kelly, Delos H. (ed.) (2002). *Deviant Behavior.* 6th ed. New York: Worth.

Kephart, William M., and William Zellner (2000). *Extraordinary Groups.* 7th ed. New York: St. Martin's Press.

Kids Count Data Sheet (2005). Baltimore, MD: The Annie E. Casey Foundation, 2005.

Kitano, Harry H. (1993). *Japanese Americans.* New York: Chelsea House.

Klaus, Patsy A. (October 2004). "Crime and the Nation's Households, 2003." *Bureau of Justice Statistics Bulletin.*

Kleniewski, Nancy (2005). *Cities, Change, and Conflict.* 3rd ed. Belmont, CA: Wadsworth.

Kohn, Alfie (1992). *No Contest: The Case Against Competition.* Revised edition. Boston: Houghton Mifflin Company.

Konner, Melvin (July-August, 1999). "Darwin's Truth, Jefferson's Vision." *The American Prospect* 30–38.

Koprowski, Gene J. (February 25, 2005). "The Web: Online Privacy Under Attack." *UPI Perspectives.*

Kraybill, Donald B., and Marc A. Olshan (eds.) (1994). *The Amish Struggle with Modernity.* Hanover, NH: University Press of New England.

Kuhn, Thomas S. (1996). *The Structure of Scientific Revolutions.* 3rd ed. Chicago: University of Chicago Press.

L

Ladson-Billings, Gloria (1998). "From Soweto to the South Bronx: African Americans and Colonial Education in the United States." In Carlos Alberto Torres and Theodore R. Mitchell (eds.), *Sociology of Education.* Albany, NY: State University of New York Press, pp. 247–264.

Lamanna, Marianne, and Agnes Riedmann (1997). *Marriages and Families: Making Choices and Facing Change.* 6th ed. Belmont, CA: Wadsworth.

Lampert, Leslie (May 1993). "Fat Like Me." *Ladies Home Journal,* 154ff.

Lanier, Mark M., and Stuart Henry (2004). *Essential Criminology.* Boulder, CO: Westview Press.

Lapchick, Richard E. (2004). *2004 Racial and Gender Report Card.* The Institute for Diversity and Ethics in Sport, University of Central Florida.

Lapchick, Richard E., and Kevin J. Matthews (1999). *1998 Racial and Gender Report Card.* Center for the Study of Sport in Society: Northeastern University.

Lapchick, Richard E., and Kevin J. Matthews (2001). *2001 The Racial & Gender Report Card.* Center for the Study of Sport in Society: Northeastern University.

Laub, John H., and Janet L. Lauritsen (1998). "The Interdependence of School Violence with Neighborhood and Family Conditions." In Delbert S. Elliott, Beatrix A. Hamburg, and Kirk R. Williams (eds.), *Violence in American Schools.* New York: Cambridge University Press, pp. 127–155.

Leacock, Eleanor Burke (1969). *Teaching and Learning in City Schools.* New York: Basic Books.

Lebey, Barbara (2004). *Remarried with Children.* New York: Bantam.

Le Bon, Gustave (1960). *The Crowd.* New York: Viking.

Lee, Valerie E. (2002). *Inequality at the Starting Gate.* Economic Policy Institute.

"Left Out." (March 21, 1983). *Newsweek* 26–35.

Lemann, Nicholas (1992). *The Promised Land.* New York: Vintage.

Lemert, Charles, and Ann Branaman. (eds.) (1997). *The Goffman Reader.* Malden, MA: Blackwell Publishers.

Lemert, Edwin M. (1972). *Human Deviance, Social Problems, and Social Control.* 2nd ed. Englewood Cliffs, NJ: Prentice Hall.

Lester, David (1998). *The Death Penalty.* 2nd ed. Springfield, IL: Charles C Thomas.

Levin, Susanna (1996). "The Spoils of Victory: Who Gets Big Money from Sponsors, and Why." In D. Stanley Eitzen (ed.), *Sport in Contemporary Society.* 5th ed. New York: St. Martin's Press, pp. 367–372.

Levine, Daniel U., and Rayna F. Levine (1996). *Society and Education.* 9th ed. Boston: Allyn and Bacon.

Levine, Rhonda (1998). *Social Class and Stratification.* Blue Ridge Summit, PA: Rowman & Littlefield.

Liebow, Elliot (1967). *Talley's Corner.* Boston: Little, Brown.

Light, Ivan (1983). *Cities in World Perspective.* New York: Macmillan.

Linden, Eugene (March 22, 1993). "Can Animals Think?" *Time,* 55–61.

Linder, Eileen W. (ed.) (2002). *Yearbook of American and Canadian Churches.* Nashville, TN: Abingdon Press.

Lipman-Blumen, Jean, and Grace Gabe (2005). *Making Adult Stepfamilies Work.* New York: St. Martin's Press.

Little, Suzanne (February 1975). "Sex Roles in Faraway Places." *Ms.,* 77ff.

Lofland, John (1993). *Polite Protesters.* Syracuse, NY: Syracuse University Press.

Long, Dale J. (April–June 2005). "The Lazy Person's Guide to Internet Hoaxes, Myths and Legends." *CHIPS Magazine.* www.chips.navy.mil.

Longmire, Dennis R. (1996). "American Attitudes Among the Ultimate Weapon: Capital Punishment." In Timothy J. Flanagan and Dennis Longmire (eds.).

Americans View Crime and Justice. Thousand Oaks, CA: Sage, pp. 93–108.

Lopreato, Joseph (1990). "From Social Evolutionism to Biocultural Evolutionism." *Sociological Forum 5,* 187–212.

Lorber, Judith (2005). *Gender Inequality: Feminist Theories and Politics.* 3rd ed. Los Angeles, CA: Roxbury Publishing.

Ludwig, Jack (July 11, 2001). "Gallup Social Audit on Black/White Relations In The U.S." www.gallup.com.

M

Maccoby, Eleanor E. (1997). *The Two Sexes: Growing Up Apart, Coming Together.* Cambridge, MA: Belknap Press of Harvard University Press.

MacKenzie, Donald A., and Judy Wajcman (eds.) (1999). *The Social Shaping of Technology.* 2nd ed. Bristol, PA: Taylor & Francis, Inc.

Madon, S., L. Jussim, and J. Eccles (1997). "In Search of the Powerful Self-Fulfilling Prophecy." *Journal of Personality and Social Psychology 72,* 791–809.

Malthus, Thomas (1798). *An Essay on the Principle of Population.* London: Reeves and Turner.

Marriott, M. (August 11, 1991). "Afrocentrism: Balancing or Skewing History?" *New York Times* 1, 18.

Martin, Karin A. (August 1998). "Becoming a Gendered Body: Practices of Preschools." *American Sociological Review Association 63,* 494–511.

Martinez, Valerie J., R. Kenneth Godwin, Frank R. Kemerer, and Laura Perna (September 1995). "The Consequences of School Choice: Who Leaves and Who Stays in the Inner City." *Social Science Quarterly 76,* 485–501.

Mason, Philip (1970). *Patterns of Dominance.* New York: Oxford University Press.

Mathews, Tom (May 11, 1992). "The Siege of L.A." *Newsweek,* 30–38.

Mauer, Marc (1999). "The Crisis of the Young African American Male and the Criminal Justice System." www.sentencingproject.org/.

McCarthy, John D., and Mark Wolfson (December 1996). "Resource Mobilization by Local Social Movement Organizations: Agency, Strategy, and Organization in the Movement Against Drinking and Driving." *American Sociological Review 61,* 1070–1088.

McGinn, Daniel, and Joan Raymond (Winter 1997–98). "Workers of the World, Get Online." *Newsweek,* 32–33.

McLaren, Peter (1997). "Multiculturalism and the Postmodern Critique: Toward a Pedagogy of Resistance and Transformation." In A. H. Halsey, et al. (eds.), *Education.* New York: Oxford University Press, pp. 520–540.

McNamara, Justine M. (December 1, 2004). "The Welfare Myth." *Journal of Sociology and Social Welfare.*

McNamee, Mike, and Joann Muller (December 21, 1998). "A Tale of Two Job Markets." *Business Week 3609,* 38.

McPhail, Clark (1991). *Myth of the Madding Crowd.* Hawthorne, NY: Aldine de Gruyter.

Mead, George Herbert (1934). *Mind, Self and Society.* Chicago: University of Chicago Press.

Mead, Margaret (1950). *Sex and Temperament in Three Primitive Societies.* New York: Mentor Books.

Menaghan, E. G., and T. L. Parcel (1991). "Parental Employment and Family Life: Research in the 1980's." In A. Booth (ed.), *Contemporary Families.* Minneapolis: National Council on Family Relations, pp. 361–380.

Merton, Robert K. (1968). *Social Theory and Social Structure* (enlarged ed.). New York: Free Press.

____. (1996). *On Social Structure and Science.* Chicago: University of Chicago Press.

Michels, Robert (1949). *Political Parties.* New York: Free Press.

Micklin, Michael, and Dudley L. Poston, Jr. (ed.) (1998). *Continuities in Sociological Human Ecology.* New York: Plenum Press.

Milgram, Stanley (1963). "Behavioral Study of Obedience." *Journal of Abnormal and Social Psychology 67,* 371–378.

____. (1964). "Group Pressure and Action Against a Person." *Journal of Abnormal and Social Psychology 6,* 137–143.

____. (1965). "Some Conditions of Obedience and Disobedience to Authority." *Human Relations 18,* 57–76.

____. (1974). *Obedience to Authority.* New York: Harper & Row.

Miller, Greg, and Stuart Silverstein (February 5, 2000). "Even Corporate Perks Join the Dot.com Revolution. *The Los Angeles Times* A1.

Mills, C. Wright (2000). *The Sociological Imagination.* New York: Oxford University Press.

Mills, Kay. *Something Better for My Children: The History and People of Head Start.* New York: NAL/Dutton, 1998.

Mitchell, B., and E. Gee (October 1996). "Boomerang Kids and Midlife Parental Marital Satisfaction." *Family Relations,* 442–448.

Moen, Phyllis (1992). *Women's Two Roles.* New York: Auburn House.

Montagu, Ashley (1999). *The Natural Superiority of Women*. 5th ed. Thousand Oaks, CA: Altamira Press.

Moore, Joan, and Harry Pachon (1985). *Hispanics in the United States*. Englewood Cliffs, NJ: Prentice Hall.

Moorhead, Gregory, Richard Ference, and Chris P. Neck (1991). "Group Decision Fiascoes Continue: Space Shuttle Challenger and a Revised Groupthink Framework." *Human Relations 44*, 539–550.

Moorhead, Gregory, Christopher P. Neck, and Mindy S. West (February/March, 1998). "The Tendency toward Defective Decision Making within Self-Managing Teams: The Relevance of Groupthink for the 21st Century." *Organizational Behavior and Human Decision Processes*, 327–351.

Morganthau, Tom (October 24, 1994). "IQ: Is It Destiny?" *Newsweek*, 53–55.

Morris, Norval, and Michael Tonry (1990). *Between Prison and Probation*. New York: Oxford University Press.

Muldavin, Joshua (June 3, 1999). "Commentary: Market Reforms Breed Discontent." *Los Angeles Times* B9.

Murdock, George P. (1945). "The Common Denominator of Cultures." In Ralph Linton (ed.), *The Science of Man in the World Crisis*. New York: Columbia University Press, pp. 123–142.

Myers, David G. (2006). *Psychology*. 8th rev. ed. New York: Worth.

N

Nanda, Serena, and Richard L. Warms (2003). *Cultural Anthropology*. 8th ed. Belmont, CA: Wadsworth.

National Center on Elder Abuse (2005). "Elder Abuse Prevalence and Incidence." www.elderabusecenter.org.

National Jobs for All Coalition (2005). "September 2005 Unemployment Data", www.njfac.org.

National Marriage Project (July 2005). *The State of Our Unions: The Social Health of Marriage in America*. http://marriage.rutgers.edu.

"National Television Violence Study: Executive Summary." Studio City, CA: Mediascope, Inc., 1998.

Newborne, Burt. (2001). "Reclaiming Democracy." *The American Prospect* (March 12–26):18–24.

Newman, Katherine S. (1993). *Declining Fortunes*. New York: Basic Books.

____. (1999). *Falling from Grace*. Updated edition. Berkeley, CA: University of California Press.

Nie, Norman H., and Lutz Erbring (February 17, 2000). "Internet and Society: A Preliminary Report." Stanford Institute for the Quantitative Study of Society.

____ et al. (December 30, 2004). "What Do Americans Do on the Internet?" Stanford Institute for the Quantitative Study of Society.

Niebuhr, H. Richard (1968). *The Social Sources of Denominationalism*. New York: World.

Nisbet, Robert A. (2003). *The Present Age*. Indianapolis, IN: Liberty Fund.

Nolan, Patrick, and Gerhard E. Lenski (2005). *Human Societies*. 10th rev. ed. Boulder, CO: Paradigm Publishers.

Novak, Michael (1996). *The Unmeltable Ethnics*. 2nd ed. New Brunswick: Transaction.

O

Oakes, Jeannie, and Martin Lipton. In Laura I. Rendon and Richard O. Hope (eds.) (1996). *Educating a New Majority: Transforming America's Educational System for Diversity*. San Francisco: Jossey-Bass Publishers, pp. 168–200.

O'Brien, Joanne, and Martin Palmer (1993). *The State of Religion Atlas*. New York: Touchstone.

O'Donnell, Jayne (November 28, 2005). "Online Rumor Mill Dogs Companies." *USA Today*.

O'Dwyer, Thomas (October 27, 1999). "The Taliban's Gender Apartheid." *The Jerusalem Post 6*.

Office of Management and Budget. "A Citizen's Guide to the Federal Budget." *Budget of the United States Government Fiscal Year 2000*, 1999. www.access.gpo.gov/usbudget/fy2000/guide02.html.

Oliver, Christine, and Marjorie Smith (2000). *The Effectiveness of Early Interventions*. London: Institute of Education.

Ollman, Bertel (1998). *Market Socialism*. New York: Routledge.

Olzak, Susan, and Joane Nagel (eds.) (1986). *Competitive Ethnic Relations*. San Diego, CA: Academic Press.

Orfield, Gary A., et al. (1992). "Status of School Desegregation: The Next Generation." Report to the National School Board Association. Alexandria, VA: National School Board Association.

Ornstein, Robert, and Paul Ehrlich (2000). *New World New Mind*. Cambridge: MA: Malor.

O'Sullivan, Christine Y., Clyde M. Reese, and John Mazzeo (1997). *NAEP 1996 Science Report Card for the Nation and the States*. Washington, DC: National Center for Educational Statistics.

P

Palen, John J. (2004). *The Urban World*. 7th ed. New York: McGraw-Hill.

Passell, Peter (November 9, 1994). "'Bell Curve' Critics Say Early I.Q. Isn't Destiny." *New York Times* B10.

Patrick, Brian A. (2003). *The National Rifle Association and the Media*. New York: Peter Lang Publishing.

Patterson, James T. (1986). *America's Struggle Against Poverty: 1900–1985*. Cambridge, MA: Harvard University Press.

Patterson, Thomas E. (2004). *The American Democracy*. 7th ed. Boston: McGraw-Hill.

Pearson, Kent. "Subcultures and Sport." In John W. Loy, Jr., Gerald S. Kenyon, and Barry D. McPherson (eds.) (1981). *Sport, Culture, and Society*. 2nd ed. Philadelphia: Lee & Febiger, pp. 131–145.

Pearson, Patricia, and Michael Finley (1997). *When She Was Bad: Violent Women and the Myth of Innocence*. New York: Viking Penguin.

Peoples, James, and Garrick Bailey (2005). *Humanity: An Introduction to Cultural Anthropology*. 7th ed. Belmont, CA: Wadsworth.

Perry, Joellen, and Dan McGraw (September 6, 1999). "In Cleveland, It's a Back-to-School Daze." *U.S. News & World Review*.

Peterson, Kavan (2005). "School Vouchers Slow to Spread." *Stateline Online*. www.stateline.org.

Pfeffer, Jeffrey (1997). *New Directions for Organization Theory*. New York: Oxford University Press.

Phu, Vu Duy (December 14, 1998). "Vietnam—Anticipating IT." *Vietnam Economic News*.

Plog, Fred, and Daniel G. Bates. (1990). *Cultural Anthropology*. 3rd ed. New York: McGraw-Hill.

Pollard, Kelvin (1999). "U.S. Diversity is More than Black and White." Washington, DC: Population Reference Bureau.

Pontell, Henry N. (1984). *A Capacity to Punish*. Bloomington: Indiana University Press.

Popenoe, David (1999). *Life Without Father*. Cambridge, MA: Harvard University Press.

Pryor, Douglas W. (1999). *Unspeakable Acts: Why Men Sexually Abuse Children*. New York: New York University Press.

Q

Queen, Stuart A., Robert W. Habenstein, and Jill S. Quadagno (1985). *The Family in Various Cultures*. 5th ed. New York: Harper & Row.

Quintanilla, Michael (May 20, 1996). "Turning Off to Save the Family." *Los Angeles Times* E1–E2.

R

Redhead, Steve (1997). *Subcultures to Clubcultures*. Malden, MA: Blackwell.

Rendon, Laura J., and Richard O. Hope. (eds.) (1996). *Educating a New Majority*. San Francisco: Jossey-Bass Publishers.

Rennison, Callie Maroe (1999). "Criminal Victimization 1998, Changes 1997–98 with Trends 1993–98." U.S. Department of Justice, Bureau of Justice Statistics, Office of Justice Programs.

Reskin, Barbara (1993). "Sex Segregation in the Workplace." *Annual Review of Sociology 19*, 241–270.

Richmond, P. (January 19, 1986). "Weighing the Odds." *Colorado Springs Gazette Telegraph,* F1–F4.

Ridley, Matt (2003). *Nature Via Nurture*. New York: HarperCollins.

Riederer, Richard K. (March 1999). "Battered by the World Financial Crisis." *33 Metal Producing 37*, 42–45.

Riley, Nancy E. (1997). *Gender, Power, and Population Change*. Washington, DC: Population Reference Bureau.

Ritzer, George (1996). *McDonaldization of Society*. Revised edition. Thousand Oaks, CA: Pine Forge Press.

———. (1998). *The McDonaldization Thesis: Explorations and Extensions*. Newbury Park, CA: Sage Publications.

Rochon, Thomas R. (2000). *Culture Moves: Ideas, Activism, and Changing Values*. Princeton, NJ: Princeton University Press.

Roethlisberger, F. J., and William J. Dickson (1964). *Management and the Worker*. New York: Wiley.

Rosenthal, Robert, and Lenore Jacobson (1989). *Pygmalion and the Classroom*. New York: Irvington Publishers.

Rosenzweig, Jane (July-August 1999). "Can TV Improve Us?" *The American Prospect 45*, 58–63.

Ross, Alistair, et al. (2003). *Higher Education and Social Class*. New Westminster, Canada: Palmer Press.

Rubin, Lillian B. (1994). *Families on the Faultline*. New York: HarperCollins.

Rudolph, Frederick (1962). *The American College and University*. New York: Random House.

S

Sadker, Myra, and David Sadker (1995). *Failing at Fairness*. New York: Simon & Schuster.

Samuda, Ronald (1998). *The Psychological Testing of American Minorities.* 2nd ed. Thousand Oaks, CA: Sage Publications.

Samuelson, Paul A., and William D. Nordhaus (1995). *Microeconomics.* 15th ed. New York: McGraw-Hill.

Sandberg, Jared (July 19, 1999). "Spinning a Web of Hate." *Newsweek*, 28–29.

Sapir, Edward (1929). "The Status of Linguistics as a Science." *Language 5*, 207–214.

Sapolsky, Robert (October 1997). "A Gene for Nothing." *Discover*, 40–46.

Sarat, Austin. (ed.) (2001). *The Killing State: Capital Punishment in Law, Politics, and Culture.* New York: Oxford University Press.

Schaeffer, Richard T. (2005). *Racial and Ethnic Groups.* 7th ed. Englewood Cliffs, NJ: Prentice Hall.

Schaeffer, Robert K. (1997). *Understanding Globalization.* Lanham, MD: Rowman & Littlefield Publishers.

Scheper-Hughes, Nancy (1983). "Deposed Kings: The Demise of the Rural Irish Gerontocracy." In Jay Sokolorsky (ed.), *Growing Old in Different Societies.* Belmont, CA: Wadsworth, pp. 130–146.

Schmitt, John (August 2004). "The Rise in Job Displacement." Center for Economic and Policy Research.

____. (October 2005). "How Good is the Economy at Creating Good Jobs?" Center for Economic and Policy Research.

Schnitzer, Martin C. (2000). *Comparative Economic Systems.* 7th ed. Cincinnati, OH: South-Western College Publishing.

Schrag, Peter (1977). "The Forgotten American." In John Walton and Donald E. Carns (eds.), *Cities in Change.* 2nd ed. Boston: Allyn and Bacon, pp. 129–137.

Schwartz, Barry (1987). *The Battle for Human Nature.* New York: Norton.

Scott, Martin B. (1981). "The Man on the Horse." In John W. Loy, Jr., Gerald S. Kenyon, and Barry D. McPherson (eds.), *Sport, Culture, and Society.* 2nd ed. Philadelphia: Lee & Febiger, pp. 146–156.

Seligmann, Jean (July 26, 1999). "Husbands No, Babies, Yes." *Newsweek*, 53.

Sellin, Thorsten (1991). *The Penalty of Death.* Beverly Hills, CA: Sage.

Shapiro, Isaac, and Robert Greenstein (1999). *The Widening Income Gulf.* Washington, DC: Center on Budget and Policy Priorities.

Shapiro, Laura (May 28, 1990). "Guns and Dolls." *Newsweek*, 54–65.

Shattuck, John (August 14, 1997). "Ending Africa's Tragedy." *The Christian Science Publishing Society*, 19.

Sidel, Ruth (1998). *Keeping Women and Children Last.* rev. ed. New York: Penguin Putnam, Inc.

Simmel, Georg (1964). *Conflict and the Web of Group Affiliation.* Translated by Kurt H. Wolff. New York: Free Press.

Simmons, J. L. (1969). *Deviants.* Berkeley, CA: Glendessary Press.

Simmons, Sally Lynn, and Amelia E. El-Hindi (November 1998). "Six Transformations for Thinking about Integrative Curriculum." *Middle School Journal 30*, 32–36.

Singh, Sarban (September 16, 1998). "Shift in Focus." *Malaysian Business*, 54.

Sizer, Theodore (2004). *The Red Pencil: Convictions from Experience in Education.* New Haven, CT: Yale University Press.

Skolnick, Arlene S., and Jerome H. Skolnick (2004). *Family in Transition.* 13th ed. Boston, MA: Allyn & Bacon.

Skolnick, Jerome H. (July-August 1998). "The Color of Law." *The American Prospect 39*, 90–95.

Sloan, Allan (February 26, 1996). "The Hit Men." *Newsweek*, 44–48.

Smelser, Neil J. (1971). *Theory of Collective Behavior.* New York: Free Press.

____, and Richard Swedberg (eds.) (2005). *The Handbook of Economic Sociology.* 2nd ed. Princeton, NJ: Princeton University Press.

Smith, Michael D. (December 1979). "Hockey Violence: A Test of the Violent Subculture Hypothesis." *Social Problems 27*, 235–247.

Snipp, C. Matthew (1992). "Sociological Perspectives on American Indians." *Annual Review of Sociology 18*, 351–371.

____. (November 1996). "A Demographic Comeback for American Indians?" *Population Today 24*, 4–5.

Snyder, Howard N., and Melissa Sickmund (1999). *Juvenile Offenders and Victims: A National Report.* Rockville, MD: Juvenile Justice Clearinghouse.

Spitze, G. (1991). "Women's Employment and Family Relations: A Review." In A. Booth (ed.), *Contemporary Families.* Minneapolis: National Council on Family Relations, pp. 381–404.

Spitzer, Steven (1980). "Toward a Marxian Theory of Deviance." In Delos H. Kelly (ed.), *Criminal Behavior.* New York: St. Martin's Press, pp. 175–191.

Stacey, William, and Anson Shupe (December 1982). "Correlates of Support for the Electronic Church." *Journal for the Scientific Study of Religion 21*, 291–303.

Starr, Mark (February 7, 1994). "She Can Skate, But She Can't Hide." *Newsweek, 21.*

Stavans, Ilan (1996). *The Hispanic Condition.* New York: Harper Collins.

Stefancic, Jean, and Richard Delgardo (eds.) (1998). *The Latinola Condition.* New York: New York University Press.

Stockard, Jean, and Miriam M. Johnson (1992). *Sex and Gender in Society.* 2nd ed. Englewood Cliffs, NJ: Prentice Hall.

Stoll, Cliff (1995). *Silicon Snake Oil.* New York: Doubleday.

Straus, Murray A., David B. Sugarman, and Jean Giles-Sims (August 1997). "Spanking by Parents and Subsequent Antisocial Behavior of the Child." *Archives of Pediatrics and Adolescent Medicine,* 761–767.

Street-Level. www.street-level.org. 2005.

Sumner, William Graham (1906). *Folkways.* Boston: Ginn.

Sutherland, Edwin H. (1940). "White-Collar Criminality." *American Sociological Review 5,* 1–12.

____. (1983). *White-Collar Crime.* New Haven, CT: Yale University Press.

Symonds, William C. (February 7, 2000). "For-Profit Schools." *Business Week,* 64ff.

T

Taylor, Jonathan B., and Joseph P. Kalt (January 2005). *American Indians on Reservations: A Databook of Socioeconomic Change Between the 1990 and 2000 Censuses.* The Harvard Project on American Indian Economic Development.

Taylor, Shelley E., Letitia Ann Peplau, and David O. Sears (2005). *Social Psychology.* 12th ed. Englewood Cliffs: Prentice Hall.

Tellegen, Auke, D. T. Lykken, T. J. Bouchard, Jr., and M. McGue (August 1993). "Heritability of Interests: A Twin Study." *Journal of Applied Psychology* 649–661.

Thomas, Evan (April 7, 1997). "The Next Level." *Newsweek,* 28–36.

Thomas, Evan, and Lynette Clemetson (November 22, 1999). "A New War Over Vouchers." *Newsweek,* 46.

Thornton, Russell (1984). "Cherokee Population Losses During the Trail of Tears: A New Perspective and a New Estimate." *Ethnohistory 31,* 289–300.

Tilly, Charles (1978). *From Mobilization to Revolution.* Reading, MA: Addison-Wesley.

____. Social Processes (1997). Lantham, MD: Rowan and Littlefield, 1997.

Tilove, Jonathan (May-June 1999). "The New Map of American Politics." *The American Prospect.*

Toch, Thomas, and Warren Cohen (November 23, 1998). "Public Education: A Monopoly No Longer." *U.S. News & World Report,* 25.

Toland, John. *Adolph Hitler* (1976). Garden City, NY: Doubleday.

Tönnies, Ferdinand (1957). *Community and Society.* Translated and edited by Charles P. Loomis. East Lansing: Michigan State University Press.

Tremblay, Richard E. (2005). *Developmental Origins of Aggression.* New York: Guilford Press.

Trigaboff, Dan (June 8, 1998). "Drudge Begrudged." *Broadcasting & Cable 55.*

Trimble, J. E. (1988). "Stereotypical Images, American Indians, and Prejudice." In P. A. Katz and D. A. Taylor (eds.), *Eliminating Racism.* New York: Plenum Press, pp. 181–202.

Troeltsch, Ernst (1931). *The Social Teachings of the Christian Churches.* New York: Macmillan.

Turner, Jonathan H., Leonard Beeghley, and Charles H. Powers (1989). *The Emergence of Sociological Theory.* 2nd ed. Chicago: Dorsey Press.

Turner, Ralph H. (1964). "Collective Behavior." In Robert E. L. Faris (ed.), *Handbook of Modern Sociology.* Chicago: Rand McNally, pp. 382–425.

Turner, Ralph H., and Lewis M. Killian (1987). *Collective Behavior.* 3rd ed. Englewood Cliffs, NJ: Prentice Hall.

Turow, Joseph, and Andrea Kavanaugh (2003). *The Wired Homestead.* Cambridge, MA: The MIT Press.

U

U.S. Bureau of the Census (2005). *Current Population Survey, November 2004.* Washington, DC: U.S. Government Printing Office.

U.S. Bureau of the Census (2005). *Statistical Abstract of the United States, 2004–2005.* Washington, DC: U.S. Government Printing Office.

U.S. Bureau of the Census. (2000c). "Educational Attainment, by Race, and Hispanic Origin." Current Population Reports. www.census.gov/population/www/socdemo/education.html.

U.S. Bureau of the Census. "Educational Attainment— Total Money Earnings in 1999 of Persons 18 Years Old and Over, by Age, Race, Hispanic Origin, Sex, and Work Experience in 1999." Washington, DC: U.S. Government Printing Office, 2000e.

U.S. Bureau of the Census (2000a). "Money Income in the United States: 1999." Current Population Reports, P60–209. Washington, DC: U.S. Government Printing Office.

U.S. Bureau of the Census. *Money Income of Households, Families, and Persons in the United States: 1992.* Current

Population Reports. Series P-60. No. 184. Washington, DC: U.S. Government Printing Office, 1993a.

U.S. Bureau of the Census. (2000b). "Poverty in the United States, 1999." Current Population Reports, Series P60–210. Washington, DC: U.S. Government Printing Office.

____. (1993e). *1990 Census of Population, Social and Economic Characteristics, American Indian and Alaska Native Areas.* Section 1 of 2. CP-2–1A. Washington, DC: U.S. Government Printing Office.

U.S. Bureau of the Census. (2000d). *Statistical Abstract of the United States: 2000.* Washington, DC: U.S. Government Printing Office.

____. (1993i). *School Enrollment, Social and Economic Characteristics of Students: October 1992.* Current Population Reports. Series P-20. No. 474. Washington, DC: U.S. Government Printing Office.

____. (1998c). Current Population Reports Series, P23–194, *Population Profile of the United States: 1997.* Washington, DC: U.S. Government Printing Office.

____. (1999a). "Poverty 1997—Poverty Estimates by Selected Characteristics." *Current Population Survey, March, 1998.* http://www.census.gov/hhes/poverty/poverty97/pv97est1.html.

____. (1999b). "Income 1997—Table B." *Current Population Survey, March, 1998.* www.census.gov/hhes/income/income97/in97dis.html.

____. (1999e). "Asset Ownership of Households: 1993—Table F." www.census.gov/hhes/www/wealth/wlth93f.html.

____. (1999f) "Resident Population Estimates of the United States by Sex, Race, and Hispanic Origin: April 1, 1990 to April 1, 1999." *Population Estimates Program.* www.census.gov/population/estimates/nation/intfile3-1.txt.

____. (1993). U.S. Department of Labor, Bureau of Labor Statistics. *Employment in Perspective: Women in the Labor Force.* No. 865. Washington, DC: U.S. Government Printing Office.

____. (1997a). *Employment in Perspective: Women in the Labor Force.* Report 860. Washington, DC: U.S. Government Printing Office.

____. (1997b). *Employment and Earnings.* Washington, DC: U.S. Government Printing Office.

U.S. Department of Health and Human Services (2001). *Youth Violence: A Report of the Surgeon General.* www.surgeongeneral.gov.

U.S. Department of Labor, Bureau of Labor Statistics (2005). *Women in the Labor Force: A Databook.* www.bls.gov.

V

Valian, Virginia (1999). *Why So Slow? The Advancement of Women.* Cambridge, MA: MIT Press.

Virnoche, Mary E. (1998). "The Seamless Web and Communications Equity: The Shaping of a Community Network." *Science, Technology, & Human Values 23,* 199–220.

W

Walsh, Edward, and Roberto Suro (June 19, 1999). "NRA Achieves Its Goal: Nothing." *The Washington Post,* A1, A6.

Wallechinsky, David, and Irving Wallace (1981). *The People's Almanac #3.* New York: Bantam.

Weeks, John R. (2004). *Population.* 9th ed. Belmont, CA: Wadsworth.

Weingart, Peter, et al. (eds.) (1997). *Human by Nature: Between Biology and the Social Sciences.* Mahwah, NJ: Lawrence Erlbaum Associates.

Westoff, Leslie Aldridge, and Charles F. Westoff (1971). *From Now to Zero.* Boston: Little, Brown.

White, Lynn, and David B. Brinkerhoff (September 1981). "The Sexual Division of Labor: Evidence from Childhood." *Social Forces 60,* 170–181.

Who Owns Whom (2004). High Wycombe, UK: Dun and Bradstreet Ltd.

Whorf, Benjamin Lee (1956). *Language, Thought and Reality.* Edited by John B. Carroll. Cambridge, MA: MIT Press.

Whyte, William Foote (1993). *Street Corner Society.* 4th ed. Chicago: University of Chicago Press.

Wiesel, Elie (April 12, 1999). "The Question of Genocide." *Newsweek.*

Wildavsky, Ben (September 13, 1999). "Grading on a Curve: A New Controversy Erupts Over Race, Class, and SAT Scores." *U.S. News & World Report.*

Williams, Robin M., Jr. (1970). *American Society.* 3rd ed. New York: Knopf.

Wilson, Craig (February 25–27, 2000). "Why People Will Do Almost Anything to Get on TV." *USA Today* 1A, 2A.

Wilson, William Julius (1997). *When Work Disappears: The World of the New Urban Poor.* New York: Knopf.

Wingfield, Nick (June 15, 1998). "Family Planning: The Computer Server Promises to do to the Home What It Has Already Done for Business." *The Wall Street Journal* R18, R23.

Wirth, Louis (1945). "The Problem of Minority Groups." In Ralph Linton (ed.), *The Science of Man in the World Crisis*. New York: Columbia University Press, pp. 347–372.

Wolfe, Alan (1999). *One Nation, After All*. New York: Penguin.

World Health Organization (2002). *World Report on Violence and Health*. www.who.int.

World Population Data Sheet. (2005). Washington, D.C.; Population Reference Bureau.

Wright, Robert (1996). *The Moral Animal*. New York: Pantheon Books.

Wysocki, Diane Kholos (2003). *Readings in Social Research Methods*. 2nd ed. Belmont, CA: Wadsworth.

Y

Yamagata, Hisashi, et al. (November 1997). "Sex Segregation and Glass Ceilings: A Comparative Statics Model of Women's Career Opportunities in the Federal Government Over a Quarter Century." *American Journal of Sociology 103*, 566–632.

Yap, M. T. (1995). "Singapore's 'Three or More' Policy: The First Five Years." *Asia-Pacific Population Journal 10*, 39–52.

Young, T. R. (January 1986). "The Sociology of Sport: Structural Marxist and Cultural Marxist Approaches." *Sociological Perspectives 29*, 3–28.

Yuan, Lijun (2005). *Reconceiving Women's Equality in China*. Lanham, MD: Lexington Books.

Z

Zamble, Edward, and Vernon L. Quinsey (1997). *The Criminal Recidivism Process*. New York: Cambridge University Press.

Zborowski, Mark (1952). "Cultural Components in Response to Pain." *Journal of Social Issues 8*, 16–30.

____. (1969). *People in Pain*. San Francisco: Jossey-Bass.

Zellner, William W. (1999). *Countercultures: A Sociological Analysis*. 2nd ed. New York: St. Martin's Press.

Zigler, Edward, and Sally J. Styfco (eds.) (2004). *Head Start Debates*. Baltimore, MD: Brookes.

Zimbardo, Philip G., S. M. Anderson, and L. G. Kabat (June 26, 1981). "Induced Hearing Deficit Generates Experimental Paranoia." *Science*, 1529–1531.

Zweigenhaft, Richard L., and G. William Domhoff (1999). *Diversity in the Power Elite*. New Haven: Yale University Press.

Index

A

Aberle, David, 592–593
absolute poverty, 259
accommodation pattern of assimilation, 281
achieved status, 141–142
acting crowds, 586
Addams, Jane, 18, 19
adolescents
    athletes' chances of advancing to pros, 513
    crime of, 226–227
    definition of, 373
    developmental issues, 126–127
    deviance of, 204
    family issues, 373
    gang activity, 222–223
    popularity, 253
    population in U.S., 532
    and pregnancy, 215
    and school culture, 96–97
    and smoking, 213
    socialization of, 132
    sport behavior study, 510–511
    unemployment levels, 293
    and violence, 106–107
Afghanistan, gender roles in, 317
Africa, death rate of, 533
African Americans. *See also* minorities
    assimilation barriers, 291–292
    in central cities, 553
    civil rights movement, 596
    and crime, 218–219
    and education, 293, 300, 389, 402, 405, 420–421
    family structure, 373
    income of, 292, 300
    job opportunities, 292–293
    perceived economic situation, 275
    political advances, 293–294
    poverty rates, 260, 300
    in professional sports, 514–515
    profiling by police, 236–237
    unemployment of, 292–293
The Age of Spiritual Machines (Kurzweil), 408
age stratification, 330
ageism, 330–332. *See also* elderly persons
agricultural production trends, 161
agricultural societies
    and city development, 549
    elderly roles in, 330–331
    family structure in, 350

    industrialization of, 159–160
    mechanization of farming, 451
    social structure in, 156–157
AIDS, 564–565, 584–585
Allport, Gordon, 287
alternative movements, 593
altruistic suicide, 57
American Association for Retired Persons (AARP), 338
American Dream, 576–577
American Sociological Association, 60–61
Andersen, Margaret, 311
Anglo-conformity, 280
anomic suicide, 57
anomie, 210
anthropology, 7
anticipatory socialization, 129, 132
antiwar movement (American), 593–595
Aristotle, 183
Asch, Solomon, 184, 188–189
ascribed status, 141, 277
Asian Americans, 296, 300, 389, 402. *See also* minorities
assimilation, 280–281, 291–292
authoritarianism, 431
authority, 191–192, 425, 426–427
average (statistical definition), 46

B

baby boomers, 366, 554, 572
back-to-basics movement in education, 393
baseball, 508, 516
Bay of Pigs Invasion, 185
Beatles, 463
Becker, Howard, 214–215
behavior, 9–10, 73, 94. *See also* collective behavior
beliefs, 92, 479–480
Bell, Daniel, 162
The Bell Curve (Herrnstein and Murray), 405
Berger, Peter L., 35, 472
Bettelheim, Bruno, 120
bilateral family arrangement, 350
bilingual education, 397–398
biological determinism, 311, 312–314
birthrates, 531–532, 540
Black Like Me (Griffin), 42

blended families, 371–372
blue-collar workers, 450, 451, 452–453
Blumer, Herbert, 30–31, 586–587, 588
boomerang kids, 379
"born again" Christians, 486–487
bourgeoisie, 16, 243
brain activity, 312
Brunvand, Jan Harold, 582
Buddhism, 470
bullies, 200–201
bureaucracy, 190–195
bureaucratic model of education, 388–390
Burgess, Ernest, 556–557, 559
Byrd, James, Jr., 285

C

Calvin, John, 472
capital punishment (death penalty), 227, 229–230
capitalism, 440–442, 444, 472
capitalists, 16
Caplow, Theodore, 482–483
case studies
    American dream, 576–577
    definition of, 42
    deviance, 222–223
    on isolated children, 113–114
    pros and cons of, 45
    self-fulfilling prophecy in education, 414–415
    sport values, 510–511
casinos, 296
Casler, Lawrence, 113
caste systems, 266–267
casual crowds, 586
causation, 50–54, 125
census, 39, 41, 226, 536, 548
central-city dilemma, 553–554
Chagnon, Napoleon, 158
Challenger space shuttle disaster, 171
Chambliss, William, 222–223
change, 95–97, 129, 132
charismatic authority, 426–427
charter schools, 394
cheating in sports, 504, 506, 507
Cherokee Indians, 282
Cheyenne Indians, 208, 573
child development, 111, 113–114
children. *See also* adolescents
    abuse of, 367–368

parenting issues, 258, 317–318, 357, 358, 376–377
planning of, 542–544
and political affiliation, 434
in preindustrial societies, 154–155, 157
as primary group, 173
role conflict, 149–152, 372, 374–375
same sex domestic partners, 378
single persons, 378–379
social status transmittal, 359
and socialization, 121, 124, 357, 360
structural patterns of, 350–351
and telecommuting issues, 187
theoretical perspectives, 357–361
types of, 349–350, 371–374
violence in, 367–369
Family and Medical Leave Act (1993), 326
family of orientation, 349
family of procreation, 349
family planning, 542–544
fashions, 583, 592
fast food restaurant employment, 460–461
Feagin, Joe, 298–299
fecundity, 531
Federal Bureau of Investigation (FBI), 225–226
females. *See also* sexism
   abuse of, 367–369
   athletes' chances of playing professional sports, 513
   brain activity, 312
   dual-employment family issues, 374–375
   earnings vs. men, 323–324, 325
   educational inequality, 413
   elderly situation, 336
   homelessness, 274–275
   Internet-based job opportunities, 329
   in labor force, 318, 595
   political power of, 326–328
   poverty rates of, 261
   as single parents, 372–373
   sports activity, 495, 498, 524–525
   suicide rates, 331
feminism, 15, 360
feminization of poverty, 261
fertility, 531–532
fertility rates, 531–532, 540
field research, 42. *See also* case studies
Fine, Gary Alan, 508
folkways, 83. *See also* norms
football, 505, 514–515, 524–525
Ford Motor Company, 283
foreign competition, 455–456

formal organizations, 190
formal sanctions, 87–88
formal schooling, 390
for-profit schools, 395
freedom of the press, 445
friends. *See* peer groups
Fukuyama, Francis, 162–163, 572
functionalism
   ageism, 330–331
   definition and assumptions of, 25–27
   deviance, 209–212, 220
   education, 396–398, 411
   families, 357–359, 361
   gender roles, 316, 319
   hate crimes, 285
   Internet, 28–29
   political power, 436–439
   prejudice and discrimination, 286, 288
   religion, 467–470, 473
   social change, 578–579
   social interaction, 186
   social stratification, 250, 252
   social structure, 150
   socialization process, 115–116
   sport, 504–506, 509
   urbanization, 551
fundamentalism, 485–487, 488

G

Galileo, 54
Gallup Poll, 39
game stage of role taking, 118
gangs, 222–223, 558
gemeinschaft, 160
gender identity, 310–315, 342–343
gender inequality. *See* sexism
gender roles, 156, 160, 316–320, 321, 410, 524–525
gender socialization, 317–320
generalized other, 118
genocide, 281–282
gentrification, 554
Germany. *See* Nazi Germany
gesellschaft, 160
Givens, Beth, 228
Glock, Charles, 479
Goffman, Erving, 31, 216
golf, 518
"goth" counterculture, 98
Goulden, Joseph C., 445
graphs and tables, reading of, 48–49
Gray Panthers, 338
Greece (ancient), 516
Griffin, John Howard, 42
gross migration rate, 534

group behavior, 9–10
group pressure, 188–189
groups, 171–175, 177–179, 181–186, 190–196. *See also* collective behavior
groupthink, 171, 185

H

Hagedorn, James, 558
Harlow, Harry, 111, 113
Harris, Chauncy, 559, 560
Harris, Judith, 124
Harris Poll, 39
hate crimes, 285
hate groups, 287, 289
Head Start, 407
health insurance, 13
heredity and culture, 73
Herrnstein, Richard, 405
heterogamy, 355
hidden curriculum, 122–123, 409–411
hidden unemployment, 293
high school dropout rates, 412
high school graduation rates, 389
high school reunions, 130–131
Hilts, Philip, 213
Hinduism, 466, 470, 492–493
Hirschi, Travis, 211–212
history (study of), 7
Hitler, Adolf, 246, 426–427, 430
Hochschild, Arlie, 283, 374
hockey, 500, 505–506
Holmes, Lowell, 330–331
Holocaust, 281. *See also* Nazi Germany
Holt, John, 122
home schooling, 420–421
homelessness, 272–273
homogamy, 354–355
homosexuality, 378
Hopi Indians, 356
horizontal mobility, 265
horticultural societies, 155
Hoyt, Homer, 559
Hull-House, 19
human development index, 194
humanistic movement in education, 390
hunting and gathering societies, 154–155, 350, 427
Hurricane Katrina, 10, 174, 251, 578
hypothesis, 58
hypothesis of linguistic relativity, 78–79

forms of, 351–352
Hopi Indians, 356
marriage rates, 353, 364, 365
"Martian hysteria," 584
Martineau, Harriet, 15
Marx, Karl
background of, 16
on religion, 470
on social stratification, 242,
243–245, 250, 579
mass hysteria, 584–585
mass media. *See also* Internet
definition of, 124
electronic churches, 484
healthy skepticism of, 62
National Television Violence
Study, 136–137
and political socialization, 434
socialization influence, 117,
124–126
sports portrayal, 502
T.V. availability, 125
master status, 142–143
material culture, 92–93
matriarchy, 350
matrilineal family arrangement, 350
matrilocal family structure, 351
McDonaldization, 20–21
"me," 119
Mead, George Herbert, 30, 116,
117–119
Mead, Margaret, 313–314
mean (statistical definition), 46–47
mechanical solidarity, 17, 161
mechanization, 160
media. *See* mass media
median (statistical definition), 47
melting pot pattern of assimilation,
280–281
men. *See* males
meritocracy, 400–403
Merton, Robert, 26, 210–211
Mexican Americans, 294, 295. *See also*
Latinos
Michels, Robert, 196
Microsoft Corporation, 440–441
middle class, 255–256
migration, 534
Milgrim, Stanley, 188–189
Mills, C. Wright, 11, 439
minorities. *See also* discrimination;
prejudice; specific minority
group
and crime, 218–219
death penalty attitudes, 229
definition and characteristics of,
276–277
elderly situation, 333, 336

ethnic, 278
females as, 322
high school graduation rates, 389
Internet usage, 601
in Ireland, 279
political power of, 293–294, 295
population growth of, 530
poverty rates of, 260, 295, 296,
300
power of, 286
relationship with majority group,
280–282
and SAT results, 401–403
sport opportunities, 513–514
textbooks depiction, 410
in United States, 291–301
mobs, 587, 591
mode (statistical definition), 46
monkeys, social isolation experiment
of, 111, 113
monogamy, 351–352
monopolies, 440–441
morality, 84
mores, 84, 85, 87. *See also* norms
mortality, 533–534
multicultural education, 407
multinationals, 447, 449
multiple causation, 50
multiple nuclei theory of city growth,
557, 559, 560
Murray, Charles, 405
Muslims, 466, 470

N

A Nation at Risk, 393
National Commission on Excellence
in Education, 393
National Crime Victimization Survey
(NCVS), 226
National Television Violence Study,
136–137
Native Americans. *See also* minorities
crime and punishment traditions,
208
educational attainment, 296, 300
gender identity, 315
income of, 296, 300
marriage and courtship, 356
population transfer, 282
poverty rates, 300
on reservations, 296
SAT scores, 402
and social change, 567, 573
stereotypes, 286, 519
"nature versus nurture" debate, 73,
312–314, 405
Nazi Germany
crowd behavior of, 588

ethnocentrism of, 100
German army as primary group,
174
Hitler's power, 246, 426–427, 430
Holocaust impact, 281
prisoner-of-war camps, 120
negative correlation, 53
negative deviance, 205
neolocal family structure, 351
the Net. *See* Internet
net migration rate, 534
nettling, 93
New Guinea, 313–314
Newman, Katherine, 268, 460–461,
576–577
Nie, Norman, 112
Nisbet, Robert, 575
nonmaterial culture, 92, 93
norms. *See also* values
conformity to, 206–207, 210–212
and crowd behavior, 587–588
cultural etiquette, 82
definition of, 81, 83
enforcement of, 87–88
in Middle Ages, 249
sport as teacher of, 504–505
types of, 83–87
violation of, 204–205
Novak, Michael, 278
nuclear family, 349

O

obligations, 146–147
occupational sex segregation, 323
occupations, 247, 322–325, 435,
454–455. *See also* work and
workplace
Ogburn, William, 578
oligarchy, iron law of, 196
oligopolies, 440–441
Olympics, 506
open classrooms, 390–391
open-class system of mobility, 267
open-ended questions, 40, 41
organic solidarity, 17, 161–162
out-group, 178
overurbanization, 552

P

panic, 585
parenting. *See also* families
discipline, 376–377
and gender socialization, 316–318
grading of, 358
of single persons, 372–373
socialization of children, 357

Credits

Harvey/AP/Wide World Photos; **207** SW Production/Index Stock Imagery; **208** CORBIS; **209** AP/Wide World Photos; **210** Janine Wiedel Photolibrary/Alamy; **212** SW Production/Index Stock Imagery; **213** Lacy Atkins/AP/Wide World Photos; **215** (t)Tank McNamara © Miller/Hinds. Reprinted with permission of Universal Press Syndicate. All rights reserved; (b)William Plowman/AP/Wide World Photos; **216-217** Bettmann/CORBIS; **218** Cheryl A. Miller/AP/Wide World Photos; **219** (l)Pat Sullivan/AP/Wide World Photos; (r)Gregory Rice/AP/Wide World Photos; **221** DON EMMERT/AFP/Getty Images; **224** Andrew Brookes/CORBIS; **225** Jules Frazier/Getty Images; **228** Mauritius/Index Stock Imagery; **229** (t)Kimberly White/Reuters/CORBIS; (b)Damian Dovarganes/AP/Wide World Photos; **231** Billy E. Barnes/Photo Edit; **232** file photo; **234** The New Yorker/Cartoonbank.com; **238-239** Joel Stettenheim/CORBIS; **240-241** Janine Wiedel Photolibrary/Alamy; **242** AP/Wide World Photos; **244** © 1992, The New Yorker Magazine, Inc., W. Miller. (Reprinted with permission.); **246** (t)Brian Bohannon/AP/Wide World Photos; (bl)Rufus F. Folkks/CORBIS; (br)Ning Chiu/Entertainment Pictures/ZUMA/CORBIS; **248** Steven Begleiter/Index Stock Imagery; **249** Arte & Immagini SRL/CORBIS; **250** (l)John Maher/CORBIS; (r)Nancy Ney/CORBIS; **251** (t)Peter Griffith/Masterfile; (b)Funky Winkerbean © Tom Batiuk. Permission of King Features Syndicate.; **253** SW Production/Index Stock Imagery; **255** (t)Richard Drew/AP/Wide World Photos; (b)Frank Siteman/Getty Images; **257** Eric Draper/AP/Wide World Photos; **258** AP/Wide World Photos; **259** (l)David Longstreath/AP/World Wide Photos; (r)Mike Derer/AP/World Wide Photos; **262** Jeff Shesol (Reprinted with permission); **264** (t)Benelux Press/Index Stock Imagery; (b)Don Ryan/AP/World Wide Photos; **265** Lester Lefkowitz/CORBIS; **266** Steve Starr/Index Stock Imagery; **267** Stevan Morgain/AP/World Wide Photos; **268** Arni Katz/Index Stock Imagery; **270** www.cartoonstock.com; **274** John A. Giordano/CORBIS; **276** Gabe Palmer/CORBIS; **277** George Disario/CORBIS; **282** Woolaroc Museum, Bartlesville, OK; **283** file photo; **284** Bill Aron/PhotoEdit; **284** Uriel Sinai/Getty Images; **285** Dan Loh/AP/Wide World Photos; **286** Gary Conner/Index Stock Imagery; **287** file photo; **289** Gregory Kramer/Getty Images; **290** Peter Byron/Photo Edit; **292** Bebeto Matthews/AP/Wide World Photos; **293** Matt Campbell/EPA/CORBIS; **295** Eric Draper/AP/Wide World Photos; **296** Wilfredo Lee/AP/Wide World Photos; **297** CORBIS; **299** Phil Cantor/Index Stock Imagery; **301** Stephen Morton/AP/Wide World Photos; **303** Lee Lorenz/Cartoonbank.com; **307** ©1996 "The New Yorker Collection", Mick Stevens (Reprinted with permission.); **308** Holger Winkler/zefa/CORBIS; **310** (l)Jennie Woodcock/Reflections Photolibrary/CORBIS; (r)Hannah Gal/CORBIS; **312** BananaStock/SuperStock; Steve Niedorf Photography/Getty Images; **313** AP/Wide World Photos; **314** Daniel Hulshizer/AP/Wide World Photos; **315** CORBIS; **316** Mitch Diamond/Index Stock Imagery; **317** Zephyr Picture/Index Stock Imagery; **320** Wilfredo Lee/AP/Wide World Photos; **322** REUTERS/Lucian Read; **324** JLP/Sylvia Torres/CORBIS; **328** H.G. Rossi/zefa/CORBIS; **329** Lance Iversen/San Francisco Chronicle/CORBIS; **330** Getty Images; **331** Speed Bump © 2000 Tom Coverly; **332** Jose Luis Pelaez/Getty Images; **333** Omni Photo Communications/Index Stock Imagery; **335** (l)Ruth Fremson/AP/Wide World Photos; (r)Audrey Woods/AP/Wide World Photos; **336** Nancy P. Alexander; **340** Bernard Schoenbaum/Cartoonbank.com; **344-345** John and Lisa Merrill/CORBIS; **346** PureStock/SuperStock; **348** Image Source/Getty Images; **349** Tanya Breen/AP/Wide World Photos; **351** Tom Sanders/Imagestate; **355** Werner Bokelberg/Getty Images; **356** Phil Lauro/Index Stock Imagery; **357** Kindra Clineff/Index Stock Imagery; **359** Myrleen Cate/Index Stock Imagery; **360** Ranald Mackechine/Getty Images; **363** Jose Luis Pelaez, Inc./CORBIS; **367** Christel Gerstenberg/CORBIS; **369** Keith Brofsky/Getty Images; **370** Ron Fehling/Masterfile; **371** Bettmann/CORBIS; **374** Benelux Press/Index Stock Imagery; **375** © Chronicle Features, Gail Machlis. (Reprinted with permission.); **377, 378** CORBIS; **379** © 1989, "The New Yorker Collection", Henry Martin. (Reprinted with permission.); **380** Cuckoo's Nest/Hanna-Barbera/Wang Films/The Kobal Collection; **383** Mike Lester, The Rome News-Tribune; **386** Mark Peterson/CORBIS; **388** (l)AP/Wide World Photos; (r) Walter Hodges/Getty Images; **390** Gabe Palmer/CORBIS; **391** Tim Hynds/AP/Wide World Photos; **392** CORBIS; **393** Lynsey Addario/AP/Wide World Photos; **395** Calvin and Hobbes © 1992 Bill Watterson. Reprinted with permission of Universal Press Syndicate. All rights reserved.; **396** Tom & DeeAnn McCarthy/CORBIS; **400** Tami Chappell/REUTERS; **401** Mary Ann Chastain/AP/Wide World Photos; **402** © 1998, "The New Yorker Collection", Roz Chast. (Reprinted with permission.); **403** (l)Jim Scourletis/Index Stock Imagery; (r)Pablo Martinez Monsivais/AP/Wide World Photos; **405** Sony-Jeopardy/AP/Wide World Photos; **406** Lawrence Migdale Photography; **408** Janet Jarman/CORBIS; **409** Micheal Newman/PhotoEdit; **410** Richard T. Nowitz/CORBIS; **413** Nick Ut/AP/World Wide Photos; **414** Alan Levenson/Getty Images; **417** Daryl Cagle; **422** Richard T. Nowitz/CORBIS; **424** Tim Zielenbach/AFP/Getty Images; **425** Table Mesa Prod./Index Stock Imagery; **426** (tl)Alan Greth/AP/Wide World Photos; **426** (tr,b)AP/Wide World Photos; **427** Robert Nickelsberg/Time Life Pictures/Getty Images; **428** Michael Jung Pool/AP/Wide World Photos; **430** AP/Wide World Photos; **431** Jose Goitia/AP/Wide World Photos; **432** Greg Baker/AP/Wide World Photos; **433** Mario Tama/Getty Images; **434** (l)Itsu Inouye/AP/Wide World Photos; (tr)Maribeth Brown/AP/Wide World Photos; (br)Julie Malakie/AP/Wide World Photos; **441** (t)Jeff Christensen/AP/Wide World Photos; (b)Chris Polk/AP/Wide World Photos; **443** Tina Buckman/Index Stock Imagery; **444** Eugene Hoshiko/AP/Wide World Photos; **445** Matt Caulfield/AP/Wide World Photos; **446** The Cincinnati Enquirer/AP/Wide World Photos; **449** AP/Wide World Photos; **450** Susan Ragan/AP/Wide World Photos; **451** Roger Werth/AP/Wide World Photos; **453** Gary Tramontina/AP/Wide World Photos; **454** John Hayes/AP/

Wide World Photos; **455** © Toles, "The Buffalo News". (Reprinted with permission.); **456** Gail Oskin/AP/Wide World Photos; **458** Copyright 2005 J.D. Crowe/Cagle Cartoons; **461** Mark Richards/PhotoEdit; **464** Craig Brown/Index Stock Imagery; **465** (t)Image Port/Index Stock Imagery; (b)Rose Palmisano/AP/Wide World Photos; **466** AFP/Getty Images; **467** (t)Charles Becker/AP/Wide World Photos; (bl)Daniel Bailey/Index Stock Imagery; (br)Kadir Kir/Index Stock Imagery; **472** Archivo Iconografico, S.A./CORBIS; **474** Sanford/Agliolo/CORBIS; **475** Michael Long/Index Stock Imagery; **476** Bettmann/CORBIS; **477** Ted Streshinsky/CORBIS; **478** PhotosInternet/AP/Wide World; **479** (t)Calvin and Hobbes © 1992 Bill Watterson. Reprinted with permission of Universal Press Syndicate. All rights reserved.; (bl)Charles Dharapak/AP/Wide World Photos; (br) Bil Aron/Getty Images; **481** (tl)Joan Seidel/AP/Wide World Photos; (tr)Dave Martin/AP/Wide World Photos; (bl)Julie Vennitti/AP/Wide World Photos; (br)Dave Bartruff/Index Stock Imagery; **484** Union Rescue Mission Web/AP/Wide World Photos; **486** John Bazemore/AP/Wide World Photos; **488** AP/Wide World Photos; **490** David Spress/Cartoonbank.com; **493** John Moore/AP/Wide World Photos; **494** Jed Jacobsohn/Getty Images; **496** (l)ZEFA/Taste of Europe/Index Stock Imagery; (r)CORBIS; **497** (t)Paul Vathis/AP/Wide World Photos; (b)Patricia McDonnell/AP/Wide World Photos; **498** (t)Eric Risberg/AP/Wide World Photos; (c)Eric Risberg/AP/Wide World Photos; (b)Chris Gardner/AP/Wide World Photos; **498** Aaron Josefczyk/CORBIS; **499** AP/Wide World Photos; **500** Michael Brennan/CORBIS; **501** CORBIS; **502** Andrew Winning/Reuters/CORBIS; **503** (c) 1999, "The Green Bay Press Gazette," Joe Heller. (Reprinted with permission.); **505** Paul Spinelli/Getty Images; **507** Doug Pizac/AP/Wide World Photos; **508** Anne Griffith Belt/CORBIS; **510** Sidelines, (c) 1999, The Green Bay Press Gazette, Joe Heller. (Reprinted with permission.); **511** Mug Shots/CORBIS; **512** (c) 1991, Millar/Hinds, Universal Press Syndicate. (Reprinted with permission.); **513** Robin Nowacki/AP/Wide World Photos; **515** Brad Loper/Dallas Morning News/CORBIS; **517** (tl)Denise L. Oles/AP/Wide World Photos; (tr)Mark Lennihan/AP/Wide World Photos; (b)Duomo/CORBIS; **519** Paul Sakuma/AP/Wide World Photos; **521** Patrick Chappatte/The International Herald Tribune/Cagle Cartoons; **523** Bill Bachman/Index Stock Imagery; **525** Rhonda Simpson/AP/Wide World Photos; **526-527** Kim Kulish/CORBIS; **528** Keren Su/CORBIS; **530** Greg Baker/AP/Wide World Photos; **531** Susan Plageman/AP/Wide World Photos; **533** Dado Galdieri/AP/Wide World Photos; **536** © Toles, 1990, "The Buffalo News." (Reprinted with permission.); **539** Bettmann/CORBIS; **542** Bob Krist/CORBIS; **543** (t)John McConnico/AP/Wide World Photos; (b)Owen Franken/CORBIS; **545** Elizabeth Ellis/AP/Wide World Photos; **547** Chuck Savage/CORBIS; **548** (t)Cris Minerva/Index Stock Imagery; (b)Phil Lauro/Index Stock Imagery; **549** Powerstock/ZEFA/Index Stock Imagery; **552** Nick Ut/AP/Wide World Photos; **554** Eli Grothe/AP/Wide World Photos; **555** Erik Freeland/CORBIS; **559** John Connell/Index Stock Imagery; **562** Best of Latin America/Cagle Cartoons; **565** Mark Gibson/Index Stock Imagery; **566** Robert W. Kelly/Time & Life Pictures/Getty Images; **570** © King Features Syndicate, Jim Borgman. (Reprinted with permission.); **571** Dave Bartruff/Index Stock Imagery; **572** (t)Yellow Dog Productions/Getty Images; (b)Volodymyr Repik/AP/Wide World Photos; **573** Robert Holmes/CORBIS; **575** Jon Naso/Star Ledger/CORBIS; **577** Nell Redmond/AP/Wide World Photos; **578** Doglas C. Pizac/AP/Wide World Photos; **581** Gregg Newton/ZUMA/CORBIS; **582** Ted Soqui/CORBIS; **583** (tl)Darlene Hammond/Getty Images; **583** (tr,br)Bettmann/CORBIS; (bl)Mark Lennihan/AP/Wide World Photos; (bc)Frank Capri/SAGA/Getty Images; **584** Thomas E. Franklin/Bergen Record/Saba/CORBIS; **586** Irwin Thompson/Dallas Morning News/CORBIS; **587** Bob Galbraith/AP/Wide World Photos; **588** Paris Saris/AP/Wide World Photos; **589** Joe Raedle/CORBIS; **590** Eric Draper/AP/Wide World Photos; **591** "The Far Side," © Gary Larson. (Reproduced with permission.); **593** Kevin R. Morris/CORBIS; **594** John Filo/Getty Images; **596** Michael Mulvey/Dallas Morning News/CORBIS; **598** Pat Bagley/Salt Lake Tribune/Cagle Cartoons